A NEW HISTORY OF
SPANISH LITERATURE

A NEW HISTORY
OF
SPANISH LITERATURE

BY
JAMES FITZMAURICE-KELLY, F.B.A.

NEW YORK / RUSSELL & RUSSELL

HOUSTON PUBLIC LIBRARY

R0141062778
HUM

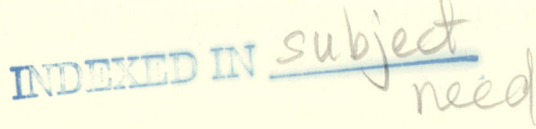

REPRODUCED FROM THE REVISED EDITION OF 1926
REISSUED, 1968, BY RUSSELL & RUSSELL
A DIVISION OF ATHENEUM PUBLISHERS, INC.
L. C. CATALOG CARD NO: 68-15120
PRINTED IN THE UNITED STATES OF AMERICA

TO

R. FOULCHÉ-DELBOSC
IN MEMORY OF A THIRTY YEARS'
UNCLOUDED FRIENDSHIP

PREFACE

SINCE the publication in 1898 of *A History of Spanish Literature* by James Fitzmaurice-Kelly, his book has passed through various transformations. It may be of interest to record them. A Spanish translation (which recently reached its eighth edition) by Señor Don Adolfo Bonilla y San Martín, with a preface by Marcelino Menéndez y Pelayo, was printed in Spain in 1901 ; a French translation by M. Davray appeared in Paris in 1904. In 1913 the author recast his work entirely, and writing it in French, issued it at Paris ; this version formed the basis of the new *Historia de la literatura española* (1914)—which is now reprinting for the fourth time—as well as of a German translation (1925) by Fräulein Elisabeth Vischer. It was the author's custom to have his copy of each new edition interleaved. The book accompanied him everywhere. He worked at it continually—revising, correcting and perfecting : he embodied in it the results, not only of his own research, but of the criticisms and suggestions which he noted on the blank pages. And he continued to do this until within three days of his death (November 30, 1923).

The present volume, *A New History of Spanish Literature*, is as distinct from its English forerunner published twenty-six years ago, as the *Historia de la literatura española* of 1914 is different from the first Spanish translation. But through all its successive changes, the work represents the unwavering effort of the author to approach each time more nearly his ideal of what was true. To the attainment of this end he devoted his whole life.

I should like to add that without the encouragement of M. Foulché-Delbosc and his constant help in reading the manuscripts of my husband, it would not have been possible for me to edit them. The only additions and modifications made in these relate mainly to dates and bibliographical references, or are such as were naturally involved by the passing of time from 1923 to 1924. I should also like to acknowledge the kindness of Mr. Aubrey F. G. Bell and Mr. J. B. Trend in correcting the proofs. I feel that M. Foulché-Delbosc would rather be thanked in my husband's own words, so I quote them:

' My warmest thanks are due now, as so often before, to my friend M. Foulché-Delbosc, who has not hesitated to suspend his own learned researches in order to aid me with an unfailing kindness and generosity for which I am profoundly grateful.'

JULIA FITZMAURICE-KELLY.

SYDENHAM, *November*, 1924.

CONTENTS

	PAGE
INTRODUCTION	xiii

CHAPTER

I. EARLY SPANISH VERSE — — — — — 1

Epics: *Poema del Cid, Cantar de gesta de los Infantes de Lara, Cantar de gesta de don Sancho II de Castilla, Roncesvalles*—Sacred Drama: *Auto de los Reyes Magos.* Poems of French or Provençal Origin—Gonzalo de Berceo—*Libro de Alexandre*—*Poema de Fernan Gonçalez.*

II. SPANISH PROSE BEFORE THE FOURTEENTH CENTURY — — — — — — 19

Didactic Compositions—Treatises of Arabic Origin—Alphonso X—Sancho IV—The *Libro de los Castigos e Documentos*—*Historia del Cauallero de Dios que auia por nombre Cifar.*

III. THE FOURTEENTH CENTURY — — — — 37

Poems in the *cuaderna via*—*Gran Conquista de Ultramar. Literatura aljamiada: Poema de José*—Don Juan Manuel—Juan Ruiz, *Arcipreste de Hita*—Didactic Compositions: Santob—*Poema de Alfonso Onceno*—Pero Lopez de Ayala.

IV. THE ROMANCERO — — — — — — 63

Cantar de Rodrigo—Origin of the *romances*—Different cycles.

V. ITALIAN INFLUENCE — — — — — 81

Didactic Compositions: *Libro de los quentos.* Clemente Sanchez de Vercial. *Danza de la Muerte*—*Cancionero de Baena*—Macias o Namorado—Rodriguez de la Cámara—Imperial—Paez de Ribera—Villena—Santillana—Mena—Don Pedro of Portugal—Travels:

ix

CONTENTS

Gonzalez de Clavijo. Tafur—Chronicles: Corral. Perez de Guzman. *Cronica del serenissimo rey don Juan el segundo deste nombre. Cronica de don Alvaro de Luna.* Diaz de Games. *Libro del Passo honroso*—Martinez de Toledo. Alfonso de la Torre.

VI. THE LATTER PART OF THE FIFTEENTH CENTURY   110

Spanish Poets at Naples—*Las Coplas del Provincial*—*Coplas de Mingo Revulgo*—Montoro—Cota—Alvarez Gato—Guillen de Segovia—Gomez Manrique's Pioneer Efforts in the Drama—Jorge Manrique—Lucena—Historians: Valera. Rodriguez de Almella. Palencia. Enriquez del Castillo. Hernando del Pulgar. Bernaldez—Introduction of Printing—Iñigo de Mendoza—Montesino—Padilla—Sanchez de Badajoz—Escrivá—*Amadis de Gaula*—Diego de San Pedro—*La Celestina.* Its Continuations—Pedro Manuel de Urrea.

VII. THE MIDDLE RENAISSANCE   150

Italian Scholars in Spain—*Question de amor*—The Drama: Enzina. Torres Naharro. Gil Vicente—Lebrixa—Leon Hebreo—The New School of Poetry: Boscan. Garci Lasso de la Vega. Sá de Miranda. Cetina. Acuña. Mendoza—Castillejo, representative of the Old School. Villegas—Ximenez de Urrea—Silvestre—Prose: Lopez de Villalobos. Perez de Oliva. Guevara—Continuations of *Amadis de Gaula*—The *Palmerin* Series—*Lazarillo de Tormes*—The Literature of Proverbs—Mysticism: Juan de Avila and Juan de Valdés—Historians: Ocampo. Mexia. Avila y Zuñiga. Hernandez de Oviedo. Las Casas. Lopez de Gómara. Diaz del Castillo.

VIII. THE LATE RENAISSANCE   209

The Salamancan School of Poetry: Fray Luis de Leon. Torre and Figueroa—The Sevillan School of Poetry: Herrera—Baltasar del Alcázar—Barahona de Soto—Zapata—Epics: Rufo Gutierrez. Ercilla. Continuations of *La Araucana*—The Pastoral Novel: Jorge de Montemayor. Sequels to *La Diana*—*Historia del Abencerraje y la hermosa Xarifa*—Mysticism: Santa Teresa. Luis de Granada. San Juan de la Cruz. Malon de Chaide. Juan de los Angeles. Estella—Arias Montano—Historians: Zurita. Morales. Mendoza—Scholars and Philosophers—The Drama: Rueda. Timoneda. Juan de la Cueva. Bermudez. Rey de Artieda. Virués. Lupercio Leonardo de Argensola. Miguel Sanchez.

CONTENTS

CHAPTER	PAGE
IX. THE GOLDEN AGE	265

Cervantes: His Earliest Compositions. His Captivity in Algiers. His Release. *La Galatea.* His Plays: *La Numancia. Don Quixote I.* The *Novelas Exemplares. Viage del Parnaso. Entremeses* and plays. *Don Quixote II. Persiles y Sigismvnda*—Lope de Vega. His Creative Faculty. His Early Life. He Joins the Armada. *La Dragontea. Arcadia. La Hermosvra de Angelica con otras diuersas rimas. El Peregrino en su patria. Jervsalen conqvistada. Los Pastores de Belen. La Dorotea.* His Achievement—*La Estrella de Sevilla*—Lope's Followers: Velez de Guevara. Guillen de Castro. Perez de Montalvan. Tirso de Molina. Mira de Amescua. Ruiz de Alarcon—The Picaresque Novel: Aleman. Lopez de Ubeda. Espinel—The Moorish Novel: Perez de Hita.—Góngora and his Followers—The *Romance artístico*.—Minor Poets—Religious Poetry—Epic Poetry: Villaviciosa. Hojeda. Azevedo — Balbuena. Mesa — Epistolary *genre*: Salazar. Antonio Perez—Historians: Mariana, Garci Lasso de la Vega, *el Inca*. Luis Cabrera de Córdoba—Religion and Polemics: Cipriano de Valera. Rivadeneyra. Marquez. Sigüenza — Scholarship. Aldrete. Cobarruuias. Lopez Pinciano.

| X. THE AGE OF CALDERON | 353 |

The Classical School of Poetry: The two Argensolas—Arguijo. Jauregui, Villegas. Rioja—Conceptism: Quevedo—The Picaresque Novel: Salas Barbadillo, Castillo Solórzano. Maria de Zayas. Liñan y Verdugo. Enriquez Gomez—Autobiographical Novels—Didactic Writers: Saavedra Faxardo. Gracian—The *Centon Epistolario* — Historians: Moncada. Mello — Mysticism: Nieremberg. Molinos — The Drama: Calderon. Rojas Zorrilla. Moreto. Coello. Solis, Dramatist and Historian. Diamante.

| XI. THE EIGHTEENTH CENTURY | 400 |

The Spanish Academy—Luzan and his Doctrines—Anti-nationalists: Nasarre and Montiano—The Gallicists: Nicolas Fernandez de Moratin. Cadalso. Samaniego, Iriarte. Feyjoo — The Novel: Isla — The Drama: Ramon de la Cruz. Gonzalez del Castillo. Leandro Fernandez de Moratin.—Jovellanos. Melendez Valdés—Scholarship and History: Mayans. Burriel. Masdeu. Muñoz.

CONTENTS

XII. THE REIGNS OF FERDINAND VII AND OF ISABEL II. (1808-1868) — 429

Quintana. Gallego—The Sevillan School. Romantic Drama: Martinez de la Rosa. The Duque de Rivas. Garcia Gutierrez. Hartzenbusch—Romantic Poets: Espronceda. Arolas. Pastor Diaz. Zorrilla. Garcia y Tassara—Drama: Breton de los Herreros. Ventura de la Vega. Gertrudis Gomez de Avellaneda. Tamayo y Baus. Lopez de Ayala. Eguilaz y Eguilaz — Poets: Campoamor. Bécquer — Historians: Conde. Lafuente — Essayists: Larra. Somoza. Mesonero Romanos.—The Novel: Fernan Caballero. Gil y Carrasco. Navarro Villoslada—Serious Prose: Cortés. Balmes. Quadrado.

XIII. SPANISH LITERATURE SINCE 1868 — 466

The Novel: Valera. Alarcon. Pereda. Pérez Galdos. Palacio Valdés. Pardo Bazán. Alas. Ganivet. Blasco Ibáñez. Valle-Inclán. Azorín. Pío Baroja. Trigo. Ricardo León. Pérez de Ayala. Miró. Répide. Gómez de la Serna.—Drama: Echegaray. Dicenta. Benavente. Linares Rivas. Marquina. Martínez Sierra — *Género chico*: Ricardo de la Vega. Joaquín and Serafín Alvarez Quintero—Poets: Núñez de Arce. Querol. Bartrina. Rosalía de Castro. Perés. Medina. Salvador Rueda—Darío. Silva. Delmira Agustini. Juan de Ibarbourou. Villaespesa. Jiménez — Politicians. Canóvas del Castillo. Castelar—Scholarship: Gayangos. Milá y Fontanals. Menéndez y Pelayo and his Disciples—Cuervo. Rodó.

INTRODUCTION

SPAIN is now more or less of a reality with a very genuine independent existence of its own. It was not always so. At an early period it is just a convenient geographical expression. The political unity of Spain, or, at least, a great step towards its achievement, took place in the reign of the Catholic Kings, that is towards the last third of the fifteenth century. The linguistic unity of Spain is not accomplished, any more than is the linguistic unity of Great Britain. But just as there is in Great Britain a generally accepted form of speech—standard English—there is a standard form of speech generally accepted in Spain. This is Spanish or, as the Spaniards themselves call it, Castilian. Castilian was in the first place the speech current in the province of Castile alone, then it was imposed as the legal form by the edicts of Alphonso X and other Spanish sovereigns in the thirteenth century.

To Rome, Spain owes her language and the entire fabric of her social life. Laws, arts—and later—religion, all the essentials of a stately and ordered civilization come to Spain from Italy. And Spain was not unworthy of the gifts bestowed on her by Rome. With the Roman Conquest begins the dawn of literature. With their laws, the Romans imposed their speech upon the broken tribes; and these in turn invaded the victorious capital of Latin politics and letters. On the downfall of the Roman Empire, Spain was held under for three centuries by the Goths. The student of literature has small cause to regret the loss of their rule in Spain. They left no trace behind them and Spain imposed upon her conquerors her local form of Latin speech. With the overthrow of Roderick in 711—the *annus mirabilis* of Islamism —all Spain was laid open to the Musulmans. The more indomitable Spaniards held out in the Pyrenean hills and there we must look for the cradle of the nation. The inhabitants of the south accepted their defeat. Those who embraced Islamism were despised as *muladíes*, and the vast majority, undergoing circumcision and adopting all but the religion of their latest masters, were known as *mozárabes*, just as during the Reconquest Moors similarly placed in the Christian provinces were styled *mudéjares*. So common was a knowledge of Arabic that the *mozárabes* read the Bible in that language. The balance altered with time. As the Reconquest spread—Leon was recovered in the ninth century, Toledo in 1085, Cordova in 1236, Granada not until 1492—the Moors found it necessary to speak the language of their conquerors, hence the *moros latinados*. Beyond some hundreds of words the greater number of which comprise technical terms, their own speech left no impress on the Spanish tongue.

Like all other Romance languages Spanish derives from vulgar Latin. The variety of romance which finally prevailed in the Peninsula was not that spoken by the free Christians of the north, but rather that used by the emancipated *mozárabes* of the southern and central provinces. What took place in France and Italy took place also in Spain: from political reasons as much as from superior culture and merit, the language of one centre, a province or it may be a city, crushed out its rivals. As France takes its speech from Paris and the Ile de France, as Italy takes its speech from Florence, so Castile dictates its language to Spain. In Asturias the country folk still talk *bable* and similar dialects flourish in the mountainous districts of Leon. The dialects of Andalusia derive from the Castilian spoken in New Castile. Galicia has a special dialect of its own and this may be regarded as a variety of Portuguese, whilst in Catalonia the popular speech is Catalan which is related to Provençal. Basque is talked in the Basque provinces: it has no concern with us as it is not even an Indo-European tongue. Nor need we consider whatever literary matter exists in Basque: such matter is small in amount and not specially valuable—not even very ancient and not very attractive. As to the extent in which Spanish is used, some variety of it is spoken in about twenty American Republics. Spanish is also spoken, in an archaic form much diluted with foreign elements, by the descendants of exiled Spanish Jews at Bucharest, Constantinople, Salonika and so forth.

Spain's intellectual debt to the Arabs has been grossly exaggerated. If Spanish thought owes anything to Arabic influence, if Spain derives from the Arabs the fables, the apologues, the moralities and the sententious maxims for which she is famous, she is much more indebted at the beginning of her written literature to France. The earliest specimens of Spanish literature which have come down to us are manifestly almost all written under French influence. In Castile and Leon the Northern French *trouvères* were the accepted models and, with the rest of Western Europe, Spain remained under the literary influence of France until the thirteenth century was well advanced. The appearance of Dante in the world of literature completely changed the situation, as only a man of genius can; the sceptre passed from France to Italy, which shortly attained the literary supremacy of Europe. Spain was not yet to feel this influence. She lay off the high-road of culture; engaged in battles against the Moors, she was 'lost in the world's debate.' It was not until towards the middle of the fifteenth century that Spaniards awoke to the fact that a new and vital literature had come into being in Italy. And this awakening was a prelude to Spain's Golden Age. Her period of real splendour is relatively short—about one hundred and fifty years. Spanish literature has its weak points. It is derivative; so are Latin, English, French and many other literatures. One cannot be sure in advance that it will appeal to the individual literary palate. It is, as a rule, an acquired taste. For Spanish literature, whilst possessing in a marked degree the three great qualities of humour, energy and originality, has a characteristic savour of its own.

A NEW HISTORY OF
SPANISH LITERATURE

I

EARLY SPANISH VERSE

IN Spain as elsewhere, primitive literature tends to be devotional or epical in character, but Spain has been exceptionally unlucky as regards the preservation of her early literary monuments. While there seems reason to think that there was once an abundant epical literature in Spain at a very early date, the oldest epic which survives is the *Poema del Cid*,[1] and this cannot be older than the middle of the twelfth century. It was published in 1779 by Tomas Antonio Sanchez (1725-1802) from the only manuscript copy which reaches us. This copy—a fourteenth century one—is defective. The beginning is missing : there are gaps

[1] Ed. A. M. Huntington, New York, 1897-1903. 3 vols. [with an English trans.] ; popular ed. A. M. Huntington, New York, 1909, 3 vols. ; ed. R. Menéndez Pidal [*Cantar de Mio Cid, texto, gramática, y vocabulario*] Madrid, 1908-1911 ; ed. R. Menéndez Pidal, Madrid, 1913 (Clásicos Castellanos, 24).— See : J. Ormsby, *The Poem of the Cid* [unfinished trans. with an interesting preface], London, 1879 (2nd ed., 1915) ; R. Menéndez Pidal, *El Poema del Cid y las crónicas generales de España*, in *Revue Hispanique*, V (1898), pp. 435-469 ; M. Menéndez y Pelayo, in *Tratado de los romances viejos* (*Antologia de poetas líricos*, etc. XI), Madrid, 1903, I, pp. 290-322 ; J. Cejador, *El Cantar de Mio Cid y la Epopeya Castellana*, in *Revue Hispanique*, XLIX (1920), pp. 1-310.

in the body of the poem, in two cases (after lines 2337 and 3507) of some fifty lines each. The assonances are badly handled : the copyist, a certain Per Abbat, evidently had no ear for metre. Yet with all its defects the *Poema del Cid* is a striking and effective piece of work in itself. It has a double theme—the warlike deeds of the Cid and the marriage of his two daughters to the cowardly Infantes de Carrion. It is in great part historical. Cervantes admirably sums up the question when he says : ' No doubt the Cid existed, but whether he did all the deeds ascribed to him is another matter.' In point of fact we know that the Cid's name was Ruy Diaz de Bivar (1040 ?-1099) and that he was the son of Diego Lainez. He made himself conspicuous for his valour in his youth and gained the name of *Campeador* after overthrowing a Navarrese knight in single combat. Later on he was called Sidi [=Lord] by the Arabs and became widely known by the hybrid epithet of *El Cid Campeador*. He supported Sancho II of Castile and when Sancho was murdered at Zamora in 1072, he rather reluctantly accepted Alphonso VI as King of Castile, and married his cousin Ximena Diaz. However, the Cid and Alphonso did not agree, and being exiled in 1081, the Cid entered the service of the Emir of Saragossa, fought successfully against the Conde de Barcelona, was reconciled with Alphonso VI, quarrelled with him again, set up on his own account, besieged Valencia in 1092, captured it in 1094, burned his chief enemies alive and occupied the city till his death—hence Valencia del Cid. A first-rate fighting man yet with the faults of his time—treachery and an implacable cruelty—he became in the popular imagination the heroic representative of victory, patriotism and religion.

The author of the *Poema del Cid* is unknown. He appears to have been a *juglar* from Medinaceli, perhaps from the Valle de Arbuyuelo. A good deal of colour is lent to this hypothesis by the topographical details. These are most abundant in the neighbourhood of Medinaceli and grow fewer and fewer as the Cid goes away from this point. Though convinced of the Cid's superiority to ordinary mortals, the poet endeavours to conform to historical fact, or, at least, not to be in open conflict with it. He may not have known, probably did not know, the Cid personally: but he lived too near the Cid's time to idealize him unreasonably and he may easily have known soldiers who served under the Cid. He takes the standpoint of a contemporary. He has an admirable sentiment of reality. At the utmost he is silent about the cruelties of the Cid, and this is a trait common to biographers. There are suggestions of French influence in his epic, particularly of *La Chanson de Roland*. The author has more than one string to his bow. The Cid is indeed in the foreground, either at the head of his legions or paternally thoughtful for the welfare of his wife and daughters—he has no romantic attachment; but the secondary characters are rendered faithfully with one or two strokes of the brush. He adds little personal touches as when he speaks of the Cid's horse: ' Des dia se preçio Bauieca en quant grant fue España ' or of his swords Colada and Tizon ' que mill marcos doro val.' His enthusiasm is high, and when he is at his best, the poem is full of martial spirit and the breath of battle. In spite of these qualities, the inspiration of the *Poema del Cid* flags at times. There are too many repetitions, too many dreary tracts full of nothing more interesting than proper names and topographical details. The irregularities of the assonanced versification are so baffling that it is thought no regular scheme was contemplated. The writer is hampered by an incomplete command of his instrument. This was almost inevitable, for the Castilian type had not yet attained its full development, for artistic purposes it was much less assured than Galician. The chronology of the *Poema* is confused : the particulars about the Cid and his family are often inaccurate. These are blemishes no doubt, but they are, after all, trifling matters. To have drawn a picture of the Cid which has been accepted by all posterity is an immense achievement. In subject and in spirit the *Poema del Cid* is emphatically Spanish. It has its importance as the earliest extant Spanish epic, but apart from that, its simplicity, its touches of realism, its local verisimilitude and its complete absence of rhetoric entitle it to rank as a highly original work.

The *Poema del Cid* was almost certainly not the first poem written on the exploits of the hero, but it is the oldest that reaches us. From certain assonanced prose passages in the chronicles we can infer the existence of previous compositions such as, for instance, a *Cantar del Rey Fernando*, with its sequel the *Cantar del Cerco de Zamora* shewing the Cid as a faithful vassal, just as in the *Poema* he is the unappreciated exile. A great many other personages, historical or legendary, were also the subject of epic compositions— figures like Bernardo del Carpio (who never existed in the flesh), men who really did exist like Roderick and Fernan Gonzalez. All these compositions have been lost. Possibly they may be reconstituted later by scholars in much the same way as Sr. Menéndez Pidal, acting upon the theory advanced in *De la Poesía heróico-popular castellana*, by Milá y Fontanals, has disinterred from the three recasts of the *Cronica General* the fragment of two *Cantares de gesta* on the Infantes de Lara and Sr. Puyol y Alonso from the *Cronica del Cid* a *Cantar de gesta de don Sancho II de Castilla*,[1] dating probably in its original form from the eleventh century. The *Cantar de gesta de los Infantes de Lara*[2] has perhaps a more poignant beauty than the *Poema del Cid*. Its theme is the slaying of the seven sons of Gonzalo Gustioz through the treachery of their uncle Ruy Velazquez. Their father, captive of the famous Almansor, Emir of Cordova, receives their heads in prison and he bids each a final farewell in terms of passionate feeling. He is visited in jail by Almansor's sister; she bears him a son called Mudarra Gonzalez —the subject of Lope de Vega's play *El Bastardo Mudarra*. In the fulness of time this son wreaks a terrible vengeance on the murderer of his brethren. Some three hundred lines of the poem have been reconstituted: they embody verse—and this is especially the case with the utterances of Gonzalo Gustioz—charged with the intense emotion of a far-off barbaric age in comparison with which the time of the Cid is relatively gentle and refined.

To the Carlovingian cycle belongs *Roncesvalles*,[3] a fragment of some hundred lines, discovered in a fourteenth century manuscript in the Archivo Pro-

[1] Ed. J. Puyol y Alonso, Madrid, 1911.
[2] See R. Menéndez Pidal, *La leyenda de los infantes de Lara*. Madrid, 1896.
[3] *Un nuevo cantar de gesta español del siglo xiii*. Ed. R. Menéndez Pidal, in *Revista de Filología Esp.*, IV (1917), pp. 105-204 [reprinted in *Poema de Mio Cid y otros monumentos de la primitiva poesía española*. Madrid, 1919, pp. 173-177].

vincial of Pamplona by Father Fernando de Mendoza. It is all that is left of the Spanish version of the legend of Roland as given in *La Chanson de Roland*, and was written probably very early in the thirteenth century. Like the *Poema del Cid* its versification is very irregular. It tells how Charlemagne found his dead warriors on the battle-field of Roncesvalles. The lament of the Emperor over Roland with its haunting note of desolate abandon is instinct with emotion in simplicity of appeal :

' que la vuestra alma bien sé que es en buen logare ;
mas atal viejo mezquino ¿ agora que faráde ? . . .
atal viejo meçquino, ¿ que lo conseyaráde ? ' [1]

Apparently the oldest dramatic composition in Spanish is the *Auto de los Reyes Magos*,[2] which was found about the end of the eighteenth century by Felipe Fernandez Vallejo, afterwards Archbishop of

[1] ' That your soul is in a happy place I know right well ; but I, unhappy and old, what would you have me do ? Who will advise me now, an old, unhappy man ? '

[2] Ed. R. Menéndez Pidal, in *Revista de Archivos*, etc., IV (1900), pp. 453-462 [reprinted in *Poema de Mio Cid*, etc., Madrid, 1919, pp. 183-191] ; ed. A. M. Espinosa, in *The Romanic Review*, VI (1915), pp. 378-385.—See : M. Cañete, in *Sobre el drama religioso antes y después de Lope de Vega*, in *Memorias de la Academia Esp.*, I (1870), pp. 368-412 ; A. Graf, in *Studii drammatici*. Torino, 1878, pp. 249-325 ; C. Lange, in *Die lateinischen Osterfeiern*. München, 1887 ; A. D'Ancona, in *Origini del teatro italiano*. 2nd ed., Torino, 1891, 2 vols. ; H. Anz, in *Die lateinischen Magierspiele*, Leipzig, 1905 ; A. M. Espinosa, *Notes on the versification of ' El misterio de los reyes magos,'* in *The Romanic Review*, VI (1915), pp. 378-401 [see H. R. Lang, *A Correction*, in *The Romanic Review*, VII (1916), pp. 345-349, and A. M. Espinosa, in *The Romanic Review*, VIII (1917), pp. 88-98] ; A. Bonilla y San Martín, in *Las Bacantes, o del origen del teatro*. Madrid, 1921.

EARLY SPANISH VERSE

Santiago de Compostela. He rightly assumed that it came from some Latin office. It appears to derive from the Gallo-Latin service used in Orleans at the Feast of the Epiphany. It is anonymous and its date is uncertain: it is in any case no older than the twelfth century. The *Auto* reaches us in a mutilated state as an unfinished fragment of one hundred and forty-seven lines. Its subject is indicated by the title. Led by the guiding star, the Magi appear one by one, then all three together. They discuss the meaning of the miraculous sign in the heavens and Baltasar makes clear the symbolic significance of the gifts which they have brought with them—the royal gold, the funereal myrrh and the divine incense:

'Si fure rei de terra, el oro quera;
si fure omne mortal, la mira tomara;
si rei celestrial, estos dos dexara,
tomara el encenso quel pertenecera.'[1]

The Magi rejoice over the birth of Christ: they meet Herod who asks them:

'Que decides, o ides? a quin ides buscar?
de qual terra uenides, o queredes andar?
Decid me uostros nombres, no m'los querades celar.'[2]

In much the same words Pallas asked Aeneas and his companions what brought them to Evander's realm:

'Iuvenes, quae causa subegit
ignotas temptare vias? quo tenditis? inquit.
Qui genus? unde domo? pacemne huc fertis an arma?'

---

[1] 'If he be an earthly King, he will choose the gold; if he be a mortal man, he will take the myrrh; if he be the King of Heaven, he will leave both gold and myrrh, his choice will be the incense which is his by right.'

[2] 'What say ye, or whither go ye? Whom go ye forth to seek? From what land are ye? Or to what land will ye hence? Tell me your names, nor seek to hide them from me.'

Alarmed at the Magi's story, Herod bids his Rabbis consult their sacred books to see if they can find any confirmation of its truth. The first Rabbi equivocates in reply; a second Rabbi appeals to the prophecies of Jeremiah and the piece breaks off as the two continue their recriminations.

A comparison with its French-Latin model shews that the *Auto de los Reyes Magos* has assimilated new elements. It has a greater dramatic spirit and a more vivid dialogue. Herod's perturbation is adroitly suggested. The Magi, whose names are given, are more critical than we should expect. Melchior and Gaspar wish to observe for another night the miraculous star. Balthasar wishes to observe it for three nights ' i mas de uero lo sabre.' This is a touch of critical realism a little surprising in a play written to be represented in the Cathedral of Toledo. Its author, probably some cleric, had the dramatic spectacular instinct. He had some literary artistic ambitions too, for he varies his metres rather skilfully, using lines of six, eight and twelve syllables. But the main interest of the *Auto de los Reyes Magos* is historical, its literary value is only relative. It survives as a unique specimen of what Shelley afterwards called the ' starry autos ' in their first phase. We find nothing more like it until we come to Gomez Manrique's simple dramatic essays in the fifteenth century.

Other poems in which French or Provençal influence is either proved or plausibly conjectured to exist are less natural, less forceful and less primitively simple than the poems belonging to the great epic cycles. Some, like the *Disputa del Alma y el Cuerpo* (published in 1856 by Pedro José Pidal (1809-1865), first Marqués de Pidal, who had previously edited (1841)

EARLY SPANISH VERSE

the *Vida de Santa Maria Egipciaqua*, the *Libro dels tres Reyes dorient* and the *Libro de Apolonio*), *Elena y Maria* and the *Vida de Maria Egipciaqua* are interesting only as illustrating the literary relations between Spain and France or from the point of view of versification. The *Disputa del Alma y el Cuerpo*[1] is a fragment of thirty-seven lines discovered by Tomás Muñoz y Romero (d. 1867) and belonging to the twelfth or early thirteenth century. Its origin is no doubt the Latin verses *Rixa animi et corporis* which were more or less generally treated in the Middle Ages, and appeared in France as the *Débat du corps et de l'âme* whose opening lines

> ' Un samedi par nuit
> Endormi dans mon lit '

are not inexactly reproduced in the Spanish version:

> ' un sabado esient, domingo amanezient,
> vi una grant vision en mio leio dormient.'[2]

Elena y Maria[3] is derived from a Latin poem—*Phillis et Flora*—of the twelfth century through its Picard adaptation *Le jugement d'Amour*. It is written in Leonese dialect, probably at the end of the thirteenth century. There are picaresque elements in it, and it

---

[1] Ed. R. Menéndez Pidal, in *Revista de Archivos*, etc., IV (1900), pp. 449-453 [reprinted in *Poema de Mio Cid*, etc. Madrid, 1919, pp. 209-210].—See: G. Kleinert, *Ueber den Streit zwischen Leib und Seele*. Halle a. S., 1880; M. Batchioukof, *Débat de l'âme et du corps*, in *Romania*, XX (1891), pp. 1-55, 513-576.

[2] ' It was on a Saturday as the Sabbath was dawning, I saw a great vision as I lay sleeping in bed.'

[3] Ed. R. Menéndez Pidal, in *Revista de Filología Esp.*, I (1914), pp. 52-96 [reprinted in *Poema de Mio Cid*, etc. Madrid, 1919, pp. 229-241].

SPANISH LITERATURE

differs considerably from the Latin original in the temper shewn by the two ladies as they discuss the relative merits of their lovers, the *caballero* and the *abad* who represent *las armas y las letras* of Don Quixote's discourse. The author has made an attempt at rhymed pairs of octosyllabic lines in imitation of his model, but the versification remains indefinite and irregular. This is the case again in the *Vida de Santa Maria Egipciaqua*,[1] a poem of fourteen hundred and fifty-one lines preserved in an Escorial manuscript and belonging to the same century. It is taken from *La Vie de Sainte Marie l'Egyptienne*, which is attributed to Robert Grosseteste (1175 ?-1253) and figures in his *Carmina Anglo-Normannica*.

Of greater interest as regards its subject is perhaps the *Libre dels tres Reyes dorient*,[2] another thirteenth century composition. Only fifty of its some two hundred and fifty lines deal with the Magi and the Star. The remaining two hundred tell of the flight of Mary— *La Gloriosa*—and of Joseph with their child. They fall in with thieves, one of whom has a small son ill with leprosy. This child is miraculously cured by being bathed in the same water as the holy Infant and grows up to be the repentant thief on the Cross. Probably of Provençal origin—as the presence of nine-syllabled couplets would seem to indicate—the fragment is handled with a simplicity which is missing in

[1] Ed. R. Foulché-Delbosc, Barcelona, 1907 (Textos cast. antiguos, 1).—See: A. Mussafia, *Ueber die Quelle der altspanischen Vida de S. Maria Egipciaca*, in *Sitzungsberichte der Kaiserlichen Akademie der Wissenschaften*, XLIII (1863), pp. 153-176.

[2] Facsimile of the Escorial MS. by A. M. Huntington, New York, 1904; ed. R. Menéndez Pidal, in *Poema de Mio Cid*, etc. Madrid, 1919, pp. 197-204.

EARLY SPANISH VERSE

compositions such as *Elena y Maria*, where the note of artificiality is immediately apparent. There is something arrestingly human in the figure of the sick child's mother bathing the infant Christ:

> ' Mientre lo banya al non faz
> sino caer lágrimas por su faz.' [1]

The *Libro de Apolonio*[2] is a much longer composition. It is probably by an Aragonese of some learning: the subject-matter, treated in Gower's (1325 ?-1408) *Confessio Amantis* and *Pericles, Prince of Tyre* (for some acts of which Shakespeare (1564-1616) is responsible), relates in six hundred and fifty-six stanzas the adventures of the Prince of Tyre. The *Libro de Apolonio* contains at least one clever piece of mediaeval portraiture in the character of Tarsiana, the princess turned gipsy, who is obviously the ancestress of Shakespeare's Marina, Cervantes's Preciosa, and Victor Hugo's Esmeralda. The moral reflexions inseparable from the time are a disqualification, but the use of monorhymed quatrains of fourteen syllables lends an interest to the poem. We are not justified, however, in assuming that this is an innovation of the author's merely because he invokes divine aid in composing his '*romançe de nueua maestria*.' The name of *cuaderna via* or *mester de clerecia*—the measure used by clerks as opposed to that of the unlettered strollers or

[1] 'As she bathes him, the tears flow unceasingly down her face.'

[2] Ed. C. Carroll Marden, Baltimore—Princeton, N.J.—Paris, 1917-1922. 2 vols. (Elliott Monographs in the Romance Languages and Literatures).—See: Comte de Puymaigre, in *Les vieux auteurs castillans*. Metz-Paris, 1861-1862; new ed. Paris, 1888. 1, pp. 229-250; S. Singer, *Apollonius aus Tyrus*. Halle a. S., 1895; F. Hanssen, *Sobre la conjugación del Libro de Apolonio* [*Anales de la Universidad de Chile*] 1896.

juglares, the *mester de jongleria*—was given to this monotonous form of versification (where every syllable is counted) destined to live for some time. The *Libro de Apolonio* derives originally from a Greek novel recast in the *Gesta Romanorum* and is not unaffected by Provençal influence. It is probably a thirteenth century work. To about the same period belongs the *Razon de Amor, con los Denuestos del Agua y el Vino*,[1] discovered by Hauréau (1813-1896) and published by A. Morel-Fatio (1850-1924) in 1887. These are really two separate poems, whether by two authors or one is as yet unknown. The Lope de Moros mentioned in the last line—'Lupus, me-feçit, de Moros'—is, no doubt, only an Aragonese copyist. The *Denuestos del Agua y el Vino* comes apparently from some unidentified French original like the *Disputoison du vin et de l'iaue*; and the *Razon de Amor* may possibly also be of French provenance, though in this case the theory of a Galician or Franco-Portuguese origin seems tenable. In the *Razon de Amor* there is something quite new: the note of personal appeal

'Qui triste tiene su coraçon
benga oyr esta razon'[2]

is at once struck and is never entirely lost. The simple lyrical treatment of the subject—the meeting and parting of two lovers—makes the poem stand out as a premature effort. The Castilian speech was too rigid, too inflexible still to lend itself to lyrical impulses:

[1] Ed. A. Morel-Fatio, in *Textes castillans inédits du xiii*ᵉ *siècle*, pp. 368-373 [*Romania*, XVI (1887)]; ed. R. Menéndez Pidal, in *Revue Hispanique*, XIII (1905), pp. 602-618 [reprinted in *Poema de Mio Cid*, etc. Madrid, 1919, pp. 215-223].

[2] 'Let him that is sad at heart come and hearken unto this argument.'

for some time Spanish taste and thought found readier expression in tediously pious compositions written in the *cuaderna via*. But the charm of the *Razon de Amor* is undeniable, and its historical interest is not less great, for it is the oldest Castilian lyric as yet discovered.

Hitherto we have been concerned with anonymous compositions. The earliest Spanish poet whose name reaches us is GONZALO DE BERCEO,[1] from his birthplace, Berceo. He was a secular priest attached to the Benedictine Monastery of San Millán de la Cogolla in the diocese of Calahorra. We know little of his life beyond the fact that he was a deacon in 1221, and that he figures in a legal document as being still alive in 1246. But in his compositions, which are mostly devotional and written in the *cuaderna via*, Berceo reveals himself: a credulous, simple-hearted peasant, he scolds himself for a 'miserable sinner'

[1] *Poesías*, ed. F. Janer, 1864, in Bib. de Autores Esp., LVII; *La Vida de Santo Domingo de Silos*, ed. J. D. Fitz-Gerald, Paris, 1904 (Bib. de l'École des Hautes Études, 149); *El Sacrificio de la Misa*, ed. A. G. Solalinde, Madrid, 1913; *Milagros de Nuestra Señora*, ed. A. G. Solalinde, Madrid, 1922 (Clásicos Cast., 44).—See: Comte de Puymaigre, in *Les vieux auteurs castillans*. Metz-Paris, 1861-1862; new ed. Paris, 1888, I, pp. 267-300; R. Lanchetas, *Gramática y vocabulario de las obras de Gonzalo de Berceo*, Madrid, 1900; J. D. Fitz-Gerald, *Versification of the Cuaderna via as found in Berceo's Vida de Santo Domingo de Silos*, New York, 1905; F. Hanssen, *Notas a la vida de Santo Domingo de Silos*, etc., in *Anales de la Universidad de Chile*, CXX (1907), pp. 715-763 [see also *Anales*, etc. 1894, 1895]; R. Becker, *Gonzalo de Berceos Milagros und ihre Grundlagen* ... Strassburg, 1910; J. D. Fitz-Gerald, *Gonzalo de Berceo in Spanish Literary Criticism before 1780*, in *The Romanic Review*, I (1910), pp. 290-301; H. Kling, *A propos de Berceo*, in *Revue Hispanique*, XXXV (1915), pp. 77-90; G. Cirot, *L'expression dans Gonzalo de Berceo*, in *Revista de Filología Esp.*, IX (1922), pp. 154-170.

(*pecador mezquino*) because he 'eats well, drinks well, dresses well and sleeps well.' He frankly says that he writes in the vernacular because he is not learned enough to write in Latin. He is proud to call himself the *juglar* of Santo Domingo de Silos—the Saint who founded the famous Benedictine Monastery of San Sebastian de Silos near Burgos—but he would resent being thought of as a mere *juglar*; his poems are *dictados* not *cantares*. Not even within his limitations can Berceo be called a great poet. He is very unequal, and his copiousness makes his inequality hard to bear at times. This is easily understood if we reflect that his subject-matter is never original—that its charm lies in its simplicity of treatment and its popular savour. All Berceo's works have a more or less definite origin. On Grimaldus's *Vita Beati Dominici Confessoris Christi et Abbatis* Berceo bases his *Vida del glorioso confessor Sancto Domingo de Silos*; St. Braulio's *Vita Aemiliani* furnishes him with the model of *La Estoria de Sennor Sant Millan tornada de latin en romance*, while St. Bernard's *Tractatus de planctu beatae Mariae* probably suggested *El Duelo que fizo la Virgen Maria el dia dela Passion de su fijo Jesu Christo*. Similarly from Prudentius and St. Jerome he borrows his *Martyrio de Sant Laurenço* and *Delos signos que aparesceran ante del juicio*. His very credulity is a source of artistic strength to him. He relates his pious legends and miraculous tales with an absolute good faith which is engaging. The *Vida de Sancta Oria, Virgen*, written in his old age, was perhaps the work that he valued most. Yet in his *Milagros de Nuestra Sennora* his simplicity is singularly attractive. He shews himself essentially of the people: he represents the Virgin belabouring the Evil One with blows

EARLY SPANISH VERSE

and menacing him in the rough speech of an angry peasant:

> 'Don falso alevoso : non vos escarmentades
> Mas io vos dare oi lo que vos demandades.'[1]

She is without dignity; her speech and at times her acts are those of the coarse and homely rustics among whom Berceo moves. Such is his simple faith, however, that his conception of *La Gloriosa*, the Wonder-Worker, is unaffected by the image that he evokes.

Of the twenty-five *Milagros* told by Berceo, eighteen are recounted by Berceo's contemporary, Gautier de Coincy, Prior of Vic-sur-Aisne (1177-1236). Both clerics drew on Latin sources. The particular text used by Berceo is to be found in a manuscript in the Royal Library of Copenhagen. Though Berceo had not inherited the great literary traditions of Gautier de Coincy, he survives comparison with his French rival. His power of selection is greater and he has the eminently Spanish gift of realistic vision. He has not always, perhaps, the finest tact and taste, one could hardly expect either from one placed as he was. But the quality of the appeal made by him is strong, and if there is lyrism perceptible in the *Introduccion* of the *Milagros de Nuestra Sennora*:

> 'Yo maestro Gonçalvo de Verçeo nomnado
> Iendo en romeria caeçi en un prado
> Verde e bien sençido, de flores bien poblado,
> Logar cobdiçiaduero pora omne cansado'[2]

---

[1] 'False and treacherous rascal: you do not amend your ways? but I will give you to-day what you are asking for...'

[2] 'I, Master Gonzalo de Berceo by name, when on a pilgrimage, did chance upon a meadow, green and sweet-smelling, full of flowers, a place to be desired by a weary man.'

it is even more marked in *El Duelo que fizo la Virgen Maria* ... which contains the song of the Jews who guard the Holy Sepulchre. This song is written in rhymed octosyllabic couplets : its heading *cantica* as well as the refrain *Eya velar* appear to imply that it was meant to be sung. Berceo's interest in popular songs and his desire to experiment in metres are alike refreshing. It is perhaps too wide a gap to bridge to suggest that Verlaine's beautiful lines : 'Voici mes pieds, frivoles voyageurs' may be dimly foreshadowed by Berceo's final invocation :

> ' Madre, a ti comendo mi vida, mis andadas,[1]
> Mi alma e mi cuerpo, las ordenes tomadas,
> Mis piedes, e mis manos, peroque consagradas,
> Mis oios que non vean cosas desordenadas.'

Yet it is not altogether astonishing that after an apparent neglect of some centuries, a strong reaction has set in, and Berceo in later years has found favour, not only with critics but, with poets.

Berceo is not greatly given to allegory ; he is more concerned with the stirring legend and the picturesque detail. This fact, together with alleged traces of the Leonese dialect, might seem to tell against the ascription to him of the *Libro de Alexandre*,[2] a heterogeneous

---

[1] 'Virgin Mother, to Thee I commend my life, my ways, my soul and my body, now held in Holy Orders, my feet and my hands henceforward consecrated, my eyes that they may not see things wrongful.'

[2] [Madrid MS.], ed. F. Janer, 1864, in Bib. de Autores Esp., LVII ; [MS. esp. 488 de la Bibliothèque Nationale, Paris], ed. A. Morel-Fatio, Dresden, 1906 [Gesellschaft für romanische Literatur, 10].—See : Comte de Puymaigre, in *Les vieux auteurs castillans*, Metz-Paris, 1861-1862 ; new ed. Paris, 1888, I, pp. 301-346 ; A. Morel-Fatio, *Recherches sur le texte et les sources du*

learned compilation of the early thirteenth century which deals with the exploits of the Macedonian conquerors. The poem exists in two manuscripts— one in Madrid and one, of more recent discovery, in Paris—whose final strophes differ. The Madrid manuscript speaks of a certain Juan Lorenzo Segura of Astorga as ' quien escrevió este ditado '; the Paris manuscript gives Berceo as the author. It is generally held that Juan Lorenzo, like Per Abbat, was a mere copyist: as regards Berceo, the authenticity of the last strophe in the Paris manuscript has been questioned. Since the evidence so far is not conclusive, the poem remains anonymous. It is the work of a writer well acquainted with the *Alexandreis*, the Latin epic of Gautier de Châtillon (*Galter el Bueno*, who is quoted textually), with the *Roman d'Alexandre* by Lambert le Tors and Alexandre de Bernai, the Latin *Ilias*, the *Roman de Troie* by Benoît de Sainte-More, the *Historia troiana* by Guido delle Colonne and other compositions of a similar kind. It has good passages—reminiscences of epics, picturesque descriptions and ingenious digressions. The writer, who was probably a cleric, shews dexterity in his use of the allegory and had cause to pride himself on his mastery of the *sillauas cuntadas* which go to make up the *mester de clerecia*.

The *Poema de Fernan Gonçalez*,[1] written between

Libro de Alexandre, in *Romania*, IV (1875), pp. 7-90; G. Baist, *Eine neue Handschrift des spanischen Alexandre*, in *Romanische Forschungen*, VI (1891), p. 272; M. Macías, *Juan Lorenzo Segura y el Poema de Alexandre*. Orense, 1913; R. Cillero, *Sobre el Libro de Alexandre*, in *Boletín de la R. Academia Esp.*, III (1916), pp. 308-314.

[1] Ed. C. Carroll Marden, Baltimore, 1904.—See: R. Menéndez Pidal, *Notas para el Romancero del Conde Fernán González*, in

1250 and 1271, shews the influence of the *Libro de Alexandre*. It is epic in character, but it is epic in its decline. The poem is not based on popular enthusiasm or spontaneous inspiration. The writer, probably a native of Santander and undoubtedly a cleric in the Monastery of S. Pedro de Arlanza (supposed to have been founded by Fernan Gonzalez (895?-970) who in point of popularity ran the Cid close), knew too much: he is careful to tell of the sources he collected and so forth. He borrows from Berceo, and from the *Libro de Alexandre*, consults the anonymous chronicle *Epitoma Imperatorum*, the chronicles of Lucas, bishop of Tuy, and of Turpin, possibly even the treatise *De laude Hispaniae*. These are more like the methods of the scholar than of the popular poet. But there are flashes of martial spirit now and then which redeem the dreariness of mere learning, and the *Poema de Fernan Gonçalez* would be worth mentioning, if only because one episode in it is said to have been worked up again in *Hernault de Beaulande*. There are so many instances of French influencing Spanish that one rejoices at the opportunity of quoting a case on the other side.

Homenaje á Menéndez y Pelayo. Madrid, 1899, I, pp. 429-507; C. Carroll Marden, *An Episode in the 'Poema de Fernan Gonçalez*,' in *Revue Hispanique*, VII (1900), pp. 22-27; F. Hanssen, *Sobre el metro del Poema de Fernan González* [*Anales de la Universidad de Chile*, CXV] 1904.

II

SPANISH PROSE BEFORE THE FOURTEENTH CENTURY

In all literatures verse seems to precede prose just as a child feels long before it can talk clearly. Prose comes into existence at a later stage and early prose is not apt to be very good. It is prone to be as dry as Bradshaw's railway-guide without Bradshaw's cold lucidity. And Spain is no exception to the general rule. Its first prose monuments date no earlier than the thirteenth century. The language lacks suppleness, the writers have an uncertain command of their instrument, the subjects treated are rarely original and not very interesting. They may be curious from a modern point of view as survivals of ancient literature or as forerunners of new developments, but that is all. They are mostly didactic works—the didactic element is the most marked characteristic of the thirteenth century—translations from the Arabic, treatises on jurisprudence, on the political education of princes or on the principles of government. The chronicles deal largely with events dating from the creation of the world: they are entirely uncritical and frequently apocryphal, and are therefore only partially valuable as historical monuments. But they faintly foreshadow the beginnings of historical research and in this respect they have importance as literary records. A great part of early prose is anonymous. It is almost inevitable that a period where the personal element is lacking should arouse less interest than an age where it is present. And the only literary figure in the thirteenth century is that of Alphonso X, who holds in the history of the development of Castilian prose and thought a considerably higher place than Berceo holds in that of its verse. Berceo only points the way, Alphonso X sets an approximate standard. He brings to bear in *Las Siete Partidas* a measure of comprehension in his considerations on matters of state that indicates a certain originality of mind, while his intellectual grasp of things and his widespread interests set him poles apart from Berceo. Their differences are all those that lie between an artless child and a man of the world. Their point of contact is the pioneer work that each did in the separate domains of prose and verse.

But before dealing in detail with the one important personage in this chapter, we must pass in review the earliest prose attempts of which we have any record. Nothing could be balder than the *Diez Mandamientos*,[1] a treatise of the early thirteenth century meant for the guidance of confessors; or than the two first parts of the *Anales Toledanos*[2] which are little more than a collection of historical facts and dates written between 1219 and 1250: the second part has perhaps the merit of being by a *moro latinado* who keeps the pre-

[1] Ed. A. Morel-Fatio, in *Textes castillans inédits du xiiie siècle*, pp. 379-382 [*Romania*, XVI (1887)].

[2] Ed. E. Florez, in *España Sagrada*. Madrid, 1799. XXIII, pp. 381-424.

PROSE BEFORE THE XIV CENTURY

judices of his race and registers the defects of the period with ill-concealed glee. There is progress in the prose of the *Fuero Juzgo*[1] (1241), a legal code translated from the *Forum Judicum* for the saintly King Ferdinand (1200-1252) who imposed it after the Reconquest on the Spaniards settled in Cordova, Seville and Murcia. But a code, however thrilling from a philological point of view, is not necessarily literature. The didactic tendency is manifest in the *Libro de los doze Sabios* or *El Libro de la Nobleza o Lealtat*,[2] one of the oldest treatises on the education of princes and the art of governing; in the *Flores de Filosofía*[3] whose thirty-eight chapters embody the wisdom of as many wise men, including Seneca; and in *El Libro de los buenos Proverbios*,[4] a combination of Greek philosophy and oriental wisdom translated from the Arabic of Hunain ibn Isḥâq al-ʿIbâdî (809-873). Perhaps the best specimens of Castilian prose at this stage are the two apocryphal letters added at the end of one of the manuscripts of the *Libro de Alexandre* by the copyist Juan Lorenzo de Astorga and ascribed to the Macedonian Conqueror. They are both of Arabic origin from compilations which have been

[1] Ed. R. Academia Española, Madrid, 1815.—See: M. Rodríguez y Rodríguez, *Fuero Juzgo, su lenguaje, gramática y vocabulario*. Santiago, 1905; R. de Ureña y Smenjaud, *La legislación gótico-hispana*. Madrid, 1905; R. de Ureña y Smenjaud, *Historia de la literatura jurídica española*. 2nd ed., Madrid. 1906 (2 vols. in one).

[2] Ed. A. M. Burriel, in *Memorias para la vida del santo Rey Fernando III*. Madrid, 1800. pp. 188-206.

[3] Ed. G. Knust, in *Dos obras didácticas y dos leyendas*. Madrid, 1878 (Soc. de Bibliófilos Esp., 17).

[4] Ed. H. Knust, in *Mittheilungen aus dem Eskurial*. Tübingen, 1879. pp. 1-65, 519-537 (Bib. des litt. Vereins in Stuttgart, CXLI),

done into Spanish under the titles of *Bocados de Oro* or *Bonium*[1] (the name of an imaginary King of Persia supposed to be the author) and *Poridat de las Poridades* (*secreta secretorum*). The *Bocados de Oro* is a pallid translation from the Arabic of Abû'l Wafâ Mubashshir ibn Fâtik. Speaking generally, where two versions of the same Arabic source are current in Europe, Spain, owing to its history, will be found to represent the oriental form, the western form spreads from France through a Latin translation of the original. This is a case in point. The first dated book ever printed in England was Caxton's *Dictes and Sayings of the Philosophers* (1477), the European version of the *Bocados de Oro*. Lord Rivers (1442 ?-1483), to whom it is due, had apparently never seen the Spanish book. He translated Guillaume de Tignonville's *Les ditz moraux des philosophes*, which was based in its turn on a Latin recast of the Arabic. To the inspiration of Ferdinand III of Castile we owe, as well as the *Fuero Juzgo*, the *Historia Gothica* or *De rebus Hispaniae* of Rodrigo Ximenez de Rada[2] (1170 ?-1247), Archbishop of Toledo. This deals with the period of the Gothic invasion down to 1243. By express command of the king it was at once translated into Spanish under the title of *Estoria de los Godos*.[3] Other Castilian versions followed and in 1266 a Catalan rendering appeared. The book in the vernacular attained a

[1] Ed. H. Knust, in *Mittheilungen aus dem Eskurial*. Tübingen, 1879, pp. 66-498, 538-601 (Bib. des litt. Vereins in Stuttgart, CXLI).

[2] See: R. Ballester y Castell, in *Las fuentes narrativas de la historia de España durante la edad media*. Palma de Mallorca, 1908. pp. 75 ff.

[3] Ed. A. Paz y Mélia, in *Colección de documentos inéditos para la historia de España*. 1887, LXXXVIII.

PROSE BEFORE THE XIV CENTURY

considerable popularity outside the learned class and was the first step towards founding a national school of historians. In this sense Ximenez de Rada prepared the way for the real founder of the Spanish historical school, ALPHONSO X of Castile[1] (1252-1284), whom all Spaniards know as *El Sabio*, the Learned.

If there be any truth in the saying that ' a historian is seen at his best when he does not appear,' then Alphonso X shews to extraordinary advantage. The *Cronica General* or the *Estoria d'Espanna* and the *Grande et general Estoria*, compiled under his directions

[1] *Las Siete Partidas*, ed. R. Academia de la Historia. Madrid, 1807. 3 vols.; *Opúsculos legales*, ed. R. Academia de la Historia. Madrid, 1836. 2 vols.; *Libros del Saber de Astronomía*, ed. M. Rico y Sinobas. Madrid, 1863-1867. 5 vols.; *Lapidario*, ed. J. Fernández Montaña. Madrid, 1881; *Das Spanische Schachzabelbuch des Königs Alfons des Weisen vom J.* 1283 *illustrierte Handschrift im Besitze der Königl. Bibliothek des Eskorial*. Leipzig, 1913; *Cantigas de Santa Maria*, I, II, ed. Marqués de Valmar (L. A. de Cueto). Madrid, 1889; *La Música de las Cantigas, estudio sobre su origen y naturaleza, con reproducciones fotográficas del texto y transcripción moderna*, III, ed. J. Ribera y Tarragó. Madrid, 1922. (R. Academia Esp.).—See: F. Martinez Marina, *Ensayo histórico-crítico sobre la legislación y principales cuerpos legales de los reinos de León y Castilla, especialmente sobre el código de Las Siete Partidas*, etc. Madrid, 1834; Comte de Puymaigre, in *Les vieux auteurs castillans*. Metz-Paris, 1861-1862, new ed. Paris, 1890. II, pp. 12-92; C. de Lollis, *Cantigas de amor e de maldizer di Alfonso el Sabio*, etc., in *Studj di filologia romanza*, II (1887), pp. 31-66; E. Cotarelo y Mori, in *Estudios de historia literaria de España*. Madrid, 1901. pp. 1-31; F. Hanssen, *Los versos de las Cantigas de Santa María*, etc., in *Anales de la Universidad de Chile*, CVIII (1901), pp. 337-373, 501-546; A. F. G. Bell, The 'Cantigas de Santa Maria' of Alfonso X [*The Modern Language Review*, X], Cambridge, 1915; R. Menéndez Pidal, *La Crónica General de Alfonso X*, 1916 [*Discurso*. R. Academia de la Historia]; J. B. Trend, in *The Music of Spanish History*. Oxford 1925. pp. 52-65 (Hispanic Notes and Monographs, X).

and personal supervision, are the work of a group of researchers such as Juan Gil de Zamora (who later wrote *De praeconiis Hispaniae* (1278-1282), Jofré de Loaysa, Martin de Córdoba, Bernardo de Brihuega, Garci Fernandez de Toledo and Suero Perez. The *Grande et general Estoria*—which is not yet in print—was begun while the *Cronica general* was still in preparation: it was finished probably in 1280 and contains details relating to Spanish history that are absent from the first work. But it is with the *Cronica general* that we are more immediately concerned. This chronicle gives a record of history from the creation of the world to the reign of Ferdinand III. It was begun perhaps in 1270: the third and fourth parts, written during the reign of Sancho IV (who is mentioned as the ruling king on p. 633), date from 1289 at the earliest. We do not know when it was finished. Its style is uneven, as we should expect it to be, since it is the work not only of several hands, but of men of different epochs. Internal evidence points conclusively to its joint authorship. Side by side with a mastery of the Arabic language and a knowledge of Arabic history exists such ignorance as is indicated by references to a purely imaginary crusade of Mahomet against Cordova. The first two parts of the *Cronica general*, which end with Roderick's overthrow, are based largely on Ximenez de Rada's preface in the *Historia Gothica* and on the chronicle of Bishop Lucas de Tuy, *el Tudense*, a less critical, more credulous writer than the Archbishop. For the rest every kind of source has been utilized: there are passages from the Bible and from Arabic historians—in ch. 909 the original Arabic is quoted at some length and in ch. 911 an Arab chronicler is mentioned by name: 'Et diz Abenalfarax en su arauigo, onde esta estoria fue sacada'—classical authors and popular legends have alike been put to contribution. To Alphonso X's artistic inspiration is perhaps due the insertion of whole prose portions of the *Cantares de gesta*. If this were so, our debt to him would be incalculably greater than it is, since indirectly he would have preserved not only the *Cantar de gesta de los Infantes de Lara*, but whatever *cantares de gesta* may in the fulness of time be disinterred from the *Cronica general*.

The story of the publication of Alphonso X's chronicle is not without interest. In 1541 Florian de Ocampo (1499 ?-1555) published in Zamora a *Cronica general* which was thought until 1896 to be the original *Cronica general* of Alphonso X. Critical interest is a late development in Spain. Otherwise certain facts which presently came to light might have aroused it. One was the discovery made by Gerónimo Zurita (1512-1580) that discrepancies—in some cases as vital as the omission of a whole reign—were to be noted in the various manuscripts of the chronicle. At much the same time Gonzalo Hernandez de Oviedo y Valdés (1478-1557), while collating the manuscripts, sent up his pitiful lament ' not one of them (at least of those which I have examined) is identical with any other, and in many respects they differ entirely.' Attempts were made in the reigns of Philip IV (1621-1665) and of Charles II (1665-1700) to procure a pure text, but the efforts of the official chroniclers, Tamayo de Vargas and Juan Lucas Cortés (d. 1701), came to nothing, unless indeed they stirred the Marqués de Mondéjar (1626-1708) to write his *Corrupcion de las cronicas impresas de nuestros reyes* with its indictment of Ocampo's bad faith in the first chapter. In 1794, fifty-six years after its foundation, the Academy of History suggested that the complete works of Alphonso X should be published. A beginning was made with his legal works in 1807, but owing to the disturbed state of the country a delay of twenty-nine years ensued. In 1836 the Academy was free to deal with the *Cronica general*. It acted with no undue haste, and it was left to foreign scholars to take the first step. This was done in 1860 by Wilhelm Holland who produced from the *Cronica general* a critical edition of the episode of the Infantes de Lara. In Spain itself the three members commissioned by the Academy in 1863 to prepare an edition of the *Cronica general* seem to have subsided into a fatalistic acquiescence and Florian de Ocampo's publication, though known to be imperfect, was accepted as the authentic text of Alphonso X. This was the position of things when Sr. Menéndez Pidal published in 1896 the *Cantar de gesta de los Infantes de Lara* and two years later the volume of the *Catálogo de la Real Biblioteca* entitled *Crónicas generales de España* (of which a third and much improved edition was issued in 1918). According to him, the *Cronica general* of Alphonso X and the *Cronica general* published in 1541 are two different works. In 1906 he issued what he holds to be the authentic text of Alphonso X's chronicle.[1] Its subsequent developments, Sr. Menéndez Pidal explains as follows : On Alphonso X's chronicle are based three other chronicles : the *Cronica abreviada* of Juan Manuel: a chronicle compiled in 1344 which embodies a recast of the chronicle of Abû Bakr Ahmad ibn Muhammad al Râzî of Cordova (d. 937),

[1] *Primera Crónica General.* Ed. R. Menéndez Pidal, 1906. I (Nueva Bib. de Autores Esp., 5).

PROSE BEFORE THE XIV CENTURY

and is called the *Cronica de 1344* or the *Segunda Cronica general*; a lost chronicle only known by its derivatives. From this last recast which embodied elements from the *Cronica de 1344* are derived four more chronicles : the chronicle of Florian de Ocampo now called the *Tercera Cronica general* : the *Cronica de veinte Reyes* ; and the *Cronica de Castilla* on which is based the *Cronica particular del Cid*. To these three we shall recur later, only adding that in the matter of chronicles it behoves us to move delicately. It is not improbable that further discoveries may result from the various readings of the manuscripts.

In 1251, the year before his accession to the throne, Alphonso X had *Kalila et Digna*[1] translated from the Arabic version of 'Abdallah ibn al-Muqaffa' (d. 757). The Sanscrit original of this work is lost : it is reproduced in great part in *Panchatantra*, published in 1848, but it is Barzûya's Pehlevī (Old Persian) rendering, now lost, that was used in the Arabic translation from which all versions of the work derive. *Kalila et Digna* is directly responsible for the beginning of Ramon de Béziers's Latin translation (1313), which did not, however, influence other European versions : these were based on a Latin recast of an Hebraic

---

[1] Ed. C. G. Allen, Mâcon, 1906 ; ed. J. Alemany Bolufer, Madrid, 1915 (Bib. selecta de Autores clásicos esp., 17).—See : I. G. N. Keith-Falconer, *Kalilah and Dimnah* [English trans. with preface and notes]. Cambridge, 1885 ; *The earliest English version of the Fables of Bidpai*, '*Morall Philosophie of Doni*,' translated by Sir Th. North [ed. J. Jacobs], London, 1888 ; H. L. D. Ward, in *Catalogue of Romances in the Department of Manuscripts in the British Museum*. London, 1893, II, pp. 149-181 ; L. Hervieux, *Les fabulistes latins depuis le siècle d'Auguste*. Paris, 1899, V ; G. Paris, in *Histoire littéraire de la France*, XXXVIII (1906), pp. 191-253.

rendering made by John of Capua (1263-1278). In Spain itself the book—a collection of tales very like *The Thousand and One Nights*—became the prototype of all works that sought to instruct ' por enxemplos de homes o de aves et de animalias.' To Alphonso's brother, Fadrique, whom he caused to be strangled in 1277, is due another translation from the Arabic text of *Sindibâd*. This is the *Libro de los engaños e los asayamientos de las mugeres*[1] (1253). The Castilian rendering preserves the oriental form of the book, unlike other western translations that are derived indirectly through a Greek medium. The story became known in Europe in the twelfth century under the alternative title of *The Book of Seven Sages* through the Latin translation of a native of Lorraine, Jean de la Haute-Seille, and through the *Dolopathos*, a French verse treatment of the same subject by Herbert, poet at the court of Philip-August (1180-1223). It is a collection of twenty-six stories told on seven separate nights to avert from the king's son the death with which he is threatened by a woman's wiles. Its scope is sufficiently indicated by the concluding words of the wise man : ' avnque se tornase la tierra papel, z la mar tinta, z los peçes della pendolas, que non podrian escreuir las maldades de las mugeres.'[2] A less drastic view of women is taken in a didactic fragment of much the same type—*El Capitulo que fabla de*

[1] Ed. D. Comparetti, in *Researches respecting the Book of Sindibâd*. London, 1882 (Publications of the Folk-Lore Society, IX) ; ed. A. Bonilla y San Martín, 1904 (Bibliotheca hispanica, XIV).

[2] ' Though the earth became paper, and the sea ink, and the fish thereof pens : it would not suffice to write down the evil that women do.'

PROSE BEFORE THE XIV CENTURY

los ejemplos e castigos de Teodor la donçella,[1] which is found attached to an Escorial manuscript of the *Bocados de Oro*. Its subject—the wisdom of a girl-slave at the Court of an Arab prince—evidently suited public taste, since it was dramatized, embellished with a love episode, four centuries later by Lope de Vega.

The Infante Don Juan Manuel tells us that his uncle had renderings made of the sacred and pseudo-sacred books of the Jews and Arabs.[2] Alphonso X's indefatigable interest in matters of literature may account for the ascription to him of works which he can never have written, such as the *Libro de las Querellas*,[3] whose very existence is mythical. It was inferred by two poems of which one—the romance beginning 'Yo salí de la mi tierra'—dates no further back than the fourteenth century as its rhythm and accentuation conclusively prove; the other, dedicated to Diego de Sarmiento and first published in 1663 was probably written by José Pellicer de Salas y Tovar (1602-1679). Here again the metre, a twelve-syllabled octave, called the *arte mayor*, did not come into use until some fifty years after Alphonso X's death. It remains to be seen whether in the process of further pruning *Las Cantigas de Santa Maria*, the work on which Alphonso X's reputation as a poet rests, may not be wrested from him. Doubts have been raised

[1] Ed. H. Knust, in *Mittheilungen aus dem Eskurial*. Tübingen, 1879. pp. 507-517, 613-630.—See M. Menéndez y Pelayo, *La Doncella Teodor*, in *Homenaje á D. Francisco Codera*. Zaragoza, 1904. pp. 483-511.

[2] A large part of the *Bible* is embodied in the *Grande et general Estoria*.

[3] See: E. Cotarelo y Mori, *El supuesto libro de las querellas del rey don Alfonso el Sabio*. Madrid, 1898.

on the point, notably by M. Groussac, but until definite proof is forthcoming against their attribution to Alphonso X, he may be considered the writer of some, at least, of these verses whose distinction lies in their singular charm and beauty. The manuscript, which is in Galician, includes some four hundred and twenty poems, devotional songs with the music to which they were meant to be sung, and canticles about the Virgin somewhat after the style of Berceo. Alphonso X had little more originality than Berceo, but he had much greater technical skill and was not infrequently inspired in his choice and treatment of a theme. He handles in no less than six variants with admirable skill the subject treated by Adelaide Procter (1825-1864) in *A Story of Provence* and by John Davidson (1856-1909) in *The Ballad of a Nun*. His version of the legend of the statue and the ring gives an impression of terror and poignant beauty as vivid as either Heinrich Heine (1797-1856) in *Die Götter im Exil* or Prosper Mérimée (1803-1870) in *La Vénus d'Ille*. Alphonso X's metrical dexterity is amazing. He varies his lines from four, five, eight, eleven, fifteen and even seventeen syllables; he introduces popular songs not unlike the simple *seguidillas* of to-day; he forms with the name *María* miraculous acrostical combinations in the taste of the age; at times by an insistent repetition of some slow refrain he produces the effect of a chanted litany. Withal the question arises: Why did Alphonso X write the *Cantigas* in Galician? Alphonso X had concentrated every energy on bringing Castilian into more general use: he had commanded that Castilian and not Latin should be the official language; he had drawn up rules for his secretaries and had been unwearying in his

PROSE BEFORE THE XIV CENTURY

efforts to obtain a greater uniformity in vocabulary and in orthography. We know that he wrote Castilian verse: one specimen ' Senhora por amor Dios ' is preserved in the *Canzoniere portoghese Colocci-Brancuti*[1] (n. 471). Whether he ever wrote in Provençal is unknown, for the lines in that language once thought to be by his hand are now shewn to be by At de Mons and by Giraldo Riquier. That Alphonso X knew something about Provençal versification is evident from the complicated system of rhymes in some of his songs to the Virgin. He knew quite enough to see that Castilian was still inapt as a vehicle of emotion, that it was inadequate to reveal shades of expression and that as yet only Galician had the delicate grace and flexibility of Provençal. If Alphonso X had not had the artistic perception to realize this, we might have to think of him as an author with the possibilities of poetic endowment rather than as a poet of rare accomplishment.

Alphonso X was a greater scholar than James I of England. He was placed in a more critical and dangerous position. If his deficiencies as a ruler were glaring, he paid dearly for them in his lifetime. In death, he was no more fortunate. The Jesuit Mariana, the greatest of all Spanish historians, sums him up in a famous passage : ' Dumque cœlum considerat observatque astra, terram amisit.' Yet from a literary standpoint, his achievement in the domain of history was great. His strength lay in the organization of learning, not in the issues of politics. His interests in this respect were as encyclopaedic as his aim was practical. We can pass over his purely technical works such as the *Libro de la Esfera* (1259), the *Libro*

[1] Ed. E. Molteni, Halle a. S. 1880.

de las Tablas Alphonsies, the *Libros del Saber de Astronomia* and the *Lapidario* (1278), as well as his works on chess and other compilations full of learning but of no literary merit. Alphonso X's claims to distinction are based, first and chiefly, on his histories, next on *Las Siete Partidas* and on the *Cantigas de Santa Maria*. *Las Siete Partidas* is a codex of laws drawn up by Alphonso X and his collaborators, of whom two were perhaps Fernan Martinez and Maestro Jácome *el de las leyes*. There is little doubt that Alphonso X personally revised, or attempted to revise, the language at least of most of the work that he initiated and to *Las Siete Partidas* as well as to the *Libro de la Esfera* we may hold that the words refer ' quant en el lenguage, enderezólo él por sí.' The idea of the book is adumbrated in the *Septenario*, an unfinished treatise (once thought to be identical with the *Especulo*) dealing with the seven subjects of learning: the *trivio*—grammar, logic and rhetoric—and the *quadrivio*—music, astrology, physics and metaphysics. Its title, given about a century after it was written (1256-1263) reflects the childishness of the age. Each division of the codex begins with one of the seven letters of Alphonso X's name, in the manner of an acrostic. This is the only weak point in a work remarkable of its kind. *Las Siete Partidas* had for object the unification of the Castilian legal system. This was not accomplished until 1348. But the fact that Spanish legislation derives wholly from Alphonso X's codex, and that until recently Florida and Louisiana were governed by laws drawn from it, gives some measure of its value as a monument of jurisprudence. *Las Siete Partidas* is important from other points of view. It contains not only passages of sober eloquence, but passages which throw light on contemporary manners: 'De como el rey deue guardar, que non diga palabras desconuenientes'; 'Como el rey ha de ser mesurado en comer o en beuer'; 'Que cosas deuen acostumbrar a los fijos de los reyes, para ser apuestos e limpios.'[1] It attains a high dignity of thought when it treats of the relations between king and people, Church and State and of the common welfare. Without it, many of the works of the period, including some by Juan Manuel, would be incomprehensible.

It was believed till recently that Alphonso X's literary mantle had descended on his son Sancho IV (1284-1295). To Sancho IV was ascribed the *Libro de los Castigos e Documentos*[2] written, so it was supposed, for his son the future Ferdinand IV (1295-1312). It has been irrefragably proved by M. Foulché-Delbosc and by M. Groussac that the *Libro de los Castigos e Documentos* is by a cleric who used extensively Juan Garcia de Castrogeriz's Castilian version of Aegidius Colonna's *De regimine principum* written about 1284 for Philip the Fair of France. Castrogeriz's version was made about 1345, some fifty years after Sancho's death. The ascription to Sancho IV of a share in the *Especulo* is entirely problematic. Still, if Sancho did not cast himself into literature, it may perhaps be assumed that he was friendly

[1] 'Why the king should abstain from unseemly language.' 'Why the king should eat and drink moderately.' 'Why the king's children should be taught to be cleanly.'

[2] Ed. P. de Gayangos, 1857, in Bib. de Autores Esp., LI.—See: P. Groussac, *Le livre des 'Castigos e Documentos' attribué au roi D. Sanche IV*, in Revue Hispanique, xv (1906), pp. 212-339; R. Foulché-Delbosc, *Les 'Castigos e Documentos' de Sanche IV*, in Revue Hispanique, xv (1906), pp. 340-371.

to it, for a certain number of compositions were put together in his reign and perhaps under his auspices. Among these must be mentioned the third and fourth parts of the *Cronica general*; the *Tesoro*, a translation of *Li Livres dou Tresor* by Brunetto Latini (1220-1295), made by the court physician Alonso de Paredes and Pero (or Pascual) Gomez, Sancho IV's secretary; and the *Lucidario*, a heterogeneous, encyclopaedic work based on the *Speculum Naturale* which has been wrongly attributed to Vincent de Beauvais (d. 1264). Sufficiently illustrative of its nature are the headings of its chapters: ' Donde estava Dios ante que fiziesse el cielo e la tierra '; ' Qual luz alumbra todo el mundo '; ' Porque non semeja un ome a otro '; ' Porque rraçon trae el cuervo la boca abierta quando non es cansado, et quando es cansado traela cerrada.'[1]

A more purely literary and more original work may be mentioned as belonging to the last part of Sancho's reign. This is the *Historia del Cauallero de Dios que auia por nombre Cifar*.[2] It relates the adventures of the knight Cifar, his wife Grima and of their two sons Garfin and Roboan. The knight goes forth from his land to seek fortune elsewhere. He is separated from his wife and sons and falls in with a *Ribaldo*, a squire in whom are perhaps adumbrations of Sancho Panza. But the *Ribaldo's* independence

---

[1] ' Where God was before he made heaven and earth.' ' What light gives light to all the world.' ' Why all men are not alike.' ' Why the crow opens his beak when he is not weary, and closes it when he is.'

[2] Ed. H. Michelant, Tübingen, 1872 (Bib. des litt. Vereins in Stuttgart, CXII).—See: C. P. Wagner, *The Sources of El Cavallero Cifar*, in *Revue Hispanique*, X (1903), pp. 5-104.

and sound practical sense are more suggestive of Cervantes's later conception of Sancho Panza, the Governor, than of the Sancho Panza in the earlier chapters of *Don Quijote*. When the knight finds the *Ribaldo* with a halter round his neck on the point of being hanged for theft and suggests consulting the justices, the squire shrewdly advises action first and deliberation next, since, as he says ' non vedes, que toda mi vida esta so el pie deste asno, e a un solo harre, sy lo mueven, e desides me que yredes a estar con los allcades a les demandar consejo. Cierto los omes buenos e de buen coraçon que tienen rason e derechon por sy, non deven dudar ni tardar el bien que han de faser; ça suelen desir que la tardança muchas veses enpece.'[1] He is a mine of proverbial sayings, a homely wit racy of the soil; and in one aspect of his character he foreshadows the picaroon. After many adventures the knight, who has married a princess and is now ruler over Menton, meets his wife Grima in a scene which is characteristically Spanish for its want of sentiment. The introduction of an enchanted lake whose mysteries are discovered by the *Caballero Atrevido*, and the adoption by the *Ribaldo* of the name *Caballero Amigo*, are among the elements which later figure so plentifully in the romances of chivalry. The book was printed in Seville in 1512, but its date of composition and its author are alike unknown. A Toledan cleric probably, he seems to have been well

[1] ' And do you not see that my life is wholly at the mercy of this ass's legs and of one shout if the ass is made to move, and you tell me that you will go and consult with the justices. Certes, good men and of good courage, who have right on their side, should not hesitate nor delay in doing good as it behoves them; for there is a saying that delay is often dangerous.'

acquainted with the works of Chrétien de Troyes and the *lais* of Marie de France. The *Caballero Cifar* is of great historical importance, for it not only presents a rough sketch of the romances of chivalry, but contains elements of the picaresque story. It is the first novel written in Spanish and it points in a rudimentary way to the creation of *Don Quijote*.

III

THE FOURTEENTH CENTURY

THE fourteenth century may be termed a period of distinct evolution in so far as the Castilian language is concerned. And coincident with its development as a medium for thought and for personal expression is the growth of individual talent. As the language assumes a greater independence, it tends to lose its primitive rigidity and becomes more ductile, more flowing, more clear, and more straightforward. In verse, though the monotonous *cuaderna via* still holds sway, we catch glimpses here and there of the lighter *arte mayor*, and the form of a new *genre*—the *romance*— is dimly outlined in the *Poema de Alfonso Onceno*. The note of individuality becomes increasingly apparent: in the Archpriest of Hita, Juan Ruiz, most markedly; in Juan Manuel, whose *El Conde Lucanor*, one of the earliest masterpieces of imaginative prose written in the Castilian language, broadcasts through Europe a rich fund of Arabic apologues and oriental tales; and in Pero Lopez de Ayala, the initiator of the picturesque in history and the remote precursor of the Italian School. Italy is first revealed to Spain through Boccaccio, not in his gay, licentious manner as narrator of *Il Decamerone*, but as the solemn and moralizing author of *De casibus virorum et feminarum illustrium*. This is not a Spanish freak of preference: the *De casibus* suggested *The Monk's Tale* to Chaucer, whose *Legend of Good Women* was likewise suggested by Boccaccio's *De claris mulieribus*. We cannot easily get into the frame of mind of those who honestly enjoyed the *De casibus*:

> ' Nature brings not back the mastodon,
> Nor we those times.'

But it was in the nature of things that the *De casibus* should be translated into Spanish by a contemporary of Chaucer, the famous Chancellor Pero Lopez de Ayala.

Early in the fourteenth century we find strayed vestiges of a remoter period in form and thought. Such is the anonymous *Vida de San Ildefonso*,[1] a poem in the manner of Berceo without Berceo's flashes of inspiration. Composed soon after the meeting held at Peñafiel in May 1302 to inaugurate the Feast of the Saint, it was probably the work of a beneficiary of Ubeda who had previously written a life of Mary Magdalene.

> ' E el de la Magdalena hobo en ante rimado
> Al tiempo que de Ubeda era benefiçiado.'

Another composition in the *cuaderna via*, the *Proverbios en rimo del sabio Salamon, rey de Isrrael*,[2] has been

[1] Ed. F. Janer, 1864, in Bib. de Autores Esp., LVII.—See: A. Restori, *Alcuni appunti su la Chiesa di Toledo nel secolo xiii*, in *Atti della R. Accademia delle Scienze di Torino*, XXVIII (1893), pp. 54-68.

[2] Ed. A. Paz y Mélia, in *Opúsculos literarios de los siglos xiv a xvi*. 1892. pp. 363-364 (Soc. de Bibliófilos Esp., 29); ed. P. Mazzei, in *Revue Hispanique*, LVII (1923), pp. 25-35.

THE FOURTEENTH CENTURY 39

ascribed to Pedro Gomez, son of Juan Ferrandes. There is little ground for the identification of this Gomez with Pero (or Pascual) Gomez, Alonso de Paredes's collaborator. The attribution to Pero Lopez de Ayala is equally baseless. The author, whoever he was, had a practical experience of men and affairs and his pessimistic view of both finds adequate expression in the metre of his choice. Of unknown authorship also is the *Gran Conquista de Ultramar*,[1] once believed to have been written by Sancho IV. It deals with the Crusades and was probably produced after 1312. The nucleus of the work seems to have been taken from the *Roman d'Eracle*, the French recast of the *Historia rerum in partibus transmarinis gestarum* by Guillaume de Tyr (d. 1184). Around this are gathered various popular traditions, elements from *Berte* and *Mainet*, the *Chevalier au Cygne* and passages from the *Chanson de Jérusalem* and from a recast of Gregorio Bechada's lost *Cansô d'Antiocha*. As a medium for the spread of French influence in Spain, the *Gran Conquista de Ultramar* has its importance, while it also connotes the first instance of a point of contact between Spanish and Provençal prose.

To about the same period belongs a well-known specimen of the *literatura aljamiada*, a curious form

[1] Ed. P. de Gayangos, 1858 (Bib. de Autores Esp., XLIV); *La leyenda del cauallero del çisne*, ed. E. Mazorriaga, Madrid, 1914. See: G. Paris, *La Chanson d'Antioche provençale et la Gran Conquista de Ultramar*, in *Romania*, XVII (1888), pp. 513-541; XIX (1890), pp. 562-591; XXII (1893), pp. 345-363; Comte de Puymaigre, in *Les vieux auteurs castillans*. Metz-Paris, 1861-1862; new ed. Paris, 1890, II, pp. 117-152; J. F. D. Blöte, *Mainz in der Sage vom Schwanritter*, in *Zeitschrift für romanische Philologie*, XXVII (1903), pp. 1-24; P. Groussac, in *Revue Hispanique*, XV (1906), pp. 265-289.

of literature where Spanish is written in the characters of the Arabic alphabet—that 'véritable agent de destruction' according to Renan. The term *aljamía* (*aljamí*=stranger) was originally applied to the particular form of corrupt Latin spoken by the *mozárabes*, in which sense the word occurs in the *Poema de Alfonso Onceno* :

> ' Dixieron los escuderos ;
> Sabedes bien la arauia,
> Sodes bien uerdaderos
> De tornarla en aljamía ? ' [1]

Its specialized meaning—as applied to a certain *genre*—is a later development. The specimen (which has been preserved in two very defective manuscripts) is the anonymous *Historia de Yúçuf* or *Poema de José*.[2] It is better known perhaps than it deserves to be on its intrinsic merits. It is written in the *cuaderna via* ; the internal evidence points to the author's being an Aragonese *morisco*. As it was intended to be read by Arabs—or, at any rate, by *mudéjares* or *mozárabes* impregnated with Arabic culture—the poem relates the story of Joseph in Egypt from an oriental point of view, being based in fact on the Koran's version of Joseph's experiences. Now one is often, or used to be often, told of the influence

---

[1] ' The squires said : Do you know Arabic well, are you really able to put it into *aljamía* ? '

[2] Ed. F. Janer, 1864, in Bib. de Autores Esp., LVII ; ed. H. Morf, Leipzig, 1883 ; ed. M. Schmitz, in *Romanische Forschungen*, XI (1901), pp. 315-411, 623-627 [all three ed. from the MS. of the Bib. Nacional at Madrid] ; ed. R. Menéndez Pidal, in *Revista de Archivos*, etc., VII (1902), pp. 91-129 [from the MS. of the Academia de la Historia at Madrid].—See : R. Menéndez Pidal, *Poema de Yúçuf* . . . in *Revista de Archivos*, etc., VII (1902), pp. 276-309, 347-362.

THE FOURTEENTH CENTURY

of Arabic literature on the form of Castilian literature. If there were any truth in that theory, one would expect to find some traces confirming it in the *Poema de José*. But nothing of the kind is discoverable. The author, whoever he was, is content to copy the Spanish models, and he works as well as he can in the *cuaderna via*. He is not very original and is not really very Arabic in his effects : now and then when he is off his guard, he indulges in an Arabic turn of the sentence. But he is not entitled to any higher praise than a recognition of his merits as an imitator of Castilian models.

A very considerable prose-writer is the Infante DON JUAN MANUEL[1] (1282-1348), the nephew of Alphonso X. Untroubled, apparently, by any modest doubts about the value of his work, he took measures to safeguard it. He was joint-regent of Spain during the minority of Alphonso XI, and was therefore well situated to look after his own interests. He had founded a monastery of Dominican monks at Peñafiel in 1318 and there about 1335 he deposited his manu-

[1] *Obras*, ed. P. de Gayangos, 1857, in Bib. de Autores Esp., LI ; *El Libro de las tres razones* and *El Libro de los estados, o del Infante*, ed. A. Benavides, in *Memorias de Don Fernando IV de Castilla*. Madrid, 1860. I, pp. 352-362 and pp. 444-599 ; *El Conde Lucanor*, ed. E. Krapf, revised ed. Vigo, 1902 ; ed. H. Knust [edited by A. Birch-Hirschfeld], Leipzig, 1900 ; *El libro de la caza*, ed. J. Gutierrez de la Vega, Madrid, 1879 (Bib. venatoria, 3) ; ed. G. Baist, Halle, 1880 ; *El libro del Cauallero y del Escudero*, ed. S. Gräfenberg, in *Romanische Forschungen*, VII (1893), pp. 427-550 ; *La Cronica complida*, ed. G. Baist, in *Romanische Forschungen*, VII (1893), pp. 551-556.—See : G. Baist, *Alter und Textueberlieferung der Schriften don Juan Manuels*. Halle, 1880 ; J. B. Trend, Introduction to *Count Lucanor, or The Fifty Pleasant Tales of Patronio* [Trans. by James York], London, 1924; A. Giménez Soler, *Don Juan Manuel* (in course of publication).

scripts, 'recelando yo, don Johan '—he says ' que los libros que yo he fechos non se ayan de trasladar muchas uezes y porque yo he visto que enel trasladar ... acaeçe muchas vezes ... que muda toda la entençion ... por guardar esto quanto yo pudiere, fizi fazer este uolumen en que estan escriptos todos los libros que yo fasta aqui he fechos ... et son doze.'[1] This sounds almost excessively cautious, but Juan Manuel's precautions really proved inadequate, for the manuscript has disappeared from Peñafiel and a certain number of Juan Manuel's writings are lost. It is not a little tiresome that among those missing should be the *Libro de los cantares* or *Libro de las cantigas*, a book of verses which was certainly in existence in 1575, since Gonzalo Argote de Molina (1549?-1597?) intended to print it after he had finished his edition (1575) of *El Conde Lucanor*. In the prologue of this book and of *El Libro del Caballero et del Escudero*, Juan Manuel gives us two separate—and different—lists of his works. From these lists it is evident that besides the *Libro de los cantares*, five, and perhaps six, other texts are now missing: the *Libro de la Caballeria* modelled probably between 1320 and 1322 on the *Libre del orde de Cauayleria* of Raymond Lull (1235-1315); a technical work, the *Libro de engeños*; a poetical treatise, *Reglas de como se debe trobar* and a *Libro de los Sabios*, all written before 1329; to these we may add the *Cronica complida*, unless

[1] 'And I, don John, fearing lest the books that I have made shall be transcribed many times and inasmuch as I have seen that in the transcription ... it often happens ... that the sense is entirely changed ... to guard against this as much as possible, I had this volume made in which are written all the books that I have composed up till now ... and they are twelve.'

indeed this exists in the *Chronicon domini Johannis Emmanuelis*.

Juan Manuel had a most varied career. He was a favourite of Sancho IV, who made him *adelantado mayor* of Murcia at the age of twelve. He was afterwards majordomo of Ferdinand IV *El Emplazado*, and later on he was one of the regents during the minority of Alphonso XI. Juan Manuel was by no means willing to surrender the regency and it is impossible to deny that he was a self-seeking intriguer. But he was far from being the atrocious rascal that Lope de Vega depicts him as being in *La Fortuna merecida* (1618). He loved power and was loth to abandon it. During his regency, and afterwards, he was constantly engaged in rebellions and civil wars. Finally he and Alphonso XI became reconciled, and he took part in the victory of Salado (1340), and in the crowning mercy of Algeciras (1344).

It might be thought that this long bout of fighting would leave Juan Manuel little time for literary composition. As a matter of fact, he wrote a great deal, and on very different subjects—chronicles, a treatise on falconry, encyclopaedic and allegorical imitations of Lull and verse. Finding that ' el cuydado ... mas faze al omne perder el dormir,'[1] he hit upon the plan of being read to at night, and during one vexed period in Seville he began to write a book in order to put from his mind agitating thoughts. This book was the *Libro del Caballero et del Escudero*: it is modelled upon Lull's *Libre del orde de Cauayleria* and may indeed be a recast of the lost *Libro de la Caballeria*. It treats of the perfect knight and is an encyclopaedia of all sciences, human and divine. A

[1] ' care is most active in banishing sleep.'

young knight on his way to court falls in with a holy hermit who teaches him the qualifications of a true knight—*el buen seso* and *la verguenza* as who should say practical commonsense and *le sentiment des choses*. Evidently Juan Manuel does not suffer fools gladly. The knight returns home from court full of honour, but wearying of his ignorance, he goes forth once more to seek the hermit that he may learn from him the nature of all things in heaven and on earth. It must be admitted that his desire for knowledge is at times embarrassing and that the hermit parries with some skill his questions touching the characteristics of angels. Juan Manuel is cautious in emitting opinions; he hedges and, except when he treads sure ground—as in the case of falconry, for instance—prefaces every answer with an apologetic remark. Here and there, however, a personal touch shews, and the man of action, forced to swift decisions in battle, is suddenly revealed in such words as ' enlas cosas que non an tiempo non puede omne tomar otro consejo, si non fazer lo mejor que entendiere, segund la priessa en que esta.'[1] The *Libro de la Caza* (1325-1326) is interesting for its technical vocabulary and for the fact that the names of two falcons are given as ' Lançarote ' and ' Galuan ': this indicates that stories from the Breton cycle were known in Spain at an earlier date than was imagined. There is, too, something almost infectious in the evident delight with which Juan Manuel recalls old hunting scenes : he betrays all a schoolboy's humour. As perhaps in early paintings the eye is caught by the exquisite little landscape in the background, rather than by the subject itself, so in the *Libro de la Caza*

[1] 'in a crisis, a man can take no other counsel but act as he thinks best according to the urgency of the case.'

THE FOURTEENTH CENTURY

the interest is arrested by the sudden quaint touches, the primitive simplicity of thought and the rich imagery of words. The *Libro de los Estados* or *Libro del Infante* is in two parts: the first division of one hundred chapters, finished on May 22nd, 1330, is a treatise on the education of the laity, the second, of fifty chapters, deals with the clergy. By the old device of a story, whose actors are the Pagan King Moravan, his son Johas and Johas's two mentors, the holy man Julio and the knight Turin, Juan Manuel expounds his views on every conceivable subject. From references made to it in his later works, it is easy to judge that the *Libro de los Estados* had a high place in his estimation. Based on Lull's *Blanquerna*, it embodies much wisdom from *Las Siete Partidas* and a great part of the story of Barlaam and Josaphat as told in the Hebrew work of Abraham Aben-Chasdai. This is the first appearance of the Buddhistic legend in Castilian literature; it was introduced again by Lope de Vega in his *Barlam y Josafá* (1618), and by Calderon in *La Vida es Sueño*. According to Gayangos, the personages in the *Libro de los Estados* are identifiable,—Johas and Moravan with Juan Manuel and his father, the knight with Lopez de Ayala, grandfather of the Chancellor, and Julio with St. Domingo. But as the saint died before Juan Manuel's father, the Infante Don Manuel, was born, the theory falls to the ground. The *Libro de los Castigos*, written for Ferrando, Juan Manuel's grandson, is a manual of sound advice containing frequent allusions to the *Libro de los Estados*. It is also called *Libro infenido*, because its author broke off at ch. xxvi, in order to write for Ferrando's friend, the monk Juan Alfonso, *Las maneras de amor*. This is the book of friendship, in which fifteen kinds of love are described: the eighth is the 'verdadero amor' —of friendship between man and man. Juan Manuel knows its value; he had one true friend ' non lo quiero nombrar por non me perder con los otros.'[1] Here speaks his habitual caution. The *Cronica abreviada* is simply a summary with dates of the facts given in the *Cronica general* of Alphonso X, for whom Juan Manuel had a deep veneration; while the *Libro de las Armas*, apart from the episode of Sancho IV's death, is an heraldic account of the writer's family. These works have little more importance than has the *Tratado en que se prueba por razon que Sancta Maria esta en cuerpo et alma en parayso*.

Juan Manuel's most famous work is the *Libro de los enxiemplos del conde Lucanor et de Patronio*, a book in four parts finished in 1335, whose best chapters are the first fifty-one. It transplants to Spain the oriental apologue, and in form is not unlike *The Thousand and One Nights*, Patronio taking the part of Scheherazade and the Conde Lucanor (that is to say Juan Manuel), the part of the Caliph. It has often been remarked, and cannot be denied, that there are resemblances between *Il Decamerone* and *El Conde Lucanor*, but this does not imply that the Castilian prince followed the Italian: *Il Decamerone* was written between 1348 and 1353, *El Conde Lucanor* between 1328 and 1335. The explanation of the similarities in the two books is to be found, no doubt, in the fact that both writers draw from common sources. It is certain that Juan Manuel had not the reckless genius, nor perhaps the exuberant temperament of his contemporary Juan Ruiz. Ruiz is a rowdy cleric,

[1] 'I prefer not to name him lest I lose the affection of the others.'

THE FOURTEENTH CENTURY 47

with no care for appearances, and an inimitable gusto for life and its enjoyments. Juan Manuel is more constantly on his dignity as becomes his high position. Burdened with responsibilities and sobered by harsh experiences, he is of more melancholy temper than the Archpriest. But though he has not Juan Ruiz's creative power, unrestrained humour and bubbling fancy, he does almost as much for Castilian prose as Ruiz does for Castilian verse. He had all Alphonso X's interest in things of the spirit; he had inherited as well his turn of the sentence,—a sentence which aimed at clearness and attained it, but which remained too long, too stiff, too heavy in texture. Juan Manuel does much to add to his inherited phrase the qualities of suppleness and ductility. In the case of Alphonso X, the nature of his subjects weighs him down. Not so with Juan Manuel. He too has his store of learning. He has read the *Disciplina clericalis* of Pedro Alfonso[1] (a Jew who became a Christian in 1106, and wrote the *Disciplina* after his conversion), and has *Kalila et Digna* at his finger tips, but he carries his knowledge lightly. He tells his story with point and taste, and his firm patrician simplicity sets off his sententious wisdom. Hence it is not surprising to meet with echoes of *El Conde Lucanor* in later literature both in and out of Spain: the tale of the Dean of Santiago and the Toledan wizard [Ex. xi], a little masterpiece in its kind, duly impressed Ruiz de Alarcon, who gave it a new spell of life in *La Prueba de las Promesas*. It would seem that Calderon came

---

[1] *Die Disciplina Clericalis des Petrus Alfonsi* ... ed. A. Hilka and W. Söderhjelm, Heidelberg, 1911 (Sammlung mittellateinischer Texte, 1).—See: V. Chauvin, in *Bibliographie des ouvrages arabes*, Liège-Leipzig. 1905, IV, pp. 1-44.

within the sphere of Juan Manuel's influence, since Calderon wrote a play called *El Conde Lucanor*, and the celebrated apologue in *La Vida es sueño* is a dramatic adaptation of *Exemplo x*. Though it is tolerably certain that Shakespeare took the idea of *The Taming of the Shrew* from another source, its original germ is in Juan Manuel [*Ex. xxxv*]. *Exemplo xxi* crops up again in *Gil Blas* and *Exemplo xxxii* is at the root of *The Emperor's New Clothes* by Hans Andersen (1805-1875). This is enough to shew how widely *El Conde Lucanor* has reacted on universal literature. As regards Juan Manuel's verse, all that remains of it are the quatrains which point the moral at the end of each chapter in *El Conde Lucanor*. These would seem to shew that the Infante was a master of the poetical form current in Galicia. But there is not enough material to judge by. It can only be conjectured that he wrote satires and must almost certainly have influenced the poets at court.

Hitherto in verse no work of undoubted genius has appeared. Berceo is not a writer of the highest rank, though he has merits of his own. There now comes in sight an author who can without hesitation be called a man of genius. This is JUAN RUIZ[1] (1283 ?-1350 ?), who was apparently for some considerable time Archpriest of Hita. Very little is definitely known about him. There is some reason

[1] Ed. paleográfica J. Ducamin, Toulouse, 1901 (Bib. méridionale, 7).—See: M. Menéndez y Pelayo, in *Antología de poetas líricos*, etc. Madrid, 1892. III, pp. LIII-CXIV; F. Hanssen, *Los metros de los cantares de Juan Ruiz* [*Anales de la Universidad de Chile*, CX] 1902; J. Puyol y Alonso, *El arcipreste de Hita*. Madrid, 1906; O. J. Tacke, *Die Fabeln des Erzpriesters von Hita im Rahmen der mittelalterlichen Fabelliteratur*, etc. Breslau, 1911.

THE FOURTEENTH CENTURY 49

to think that he was a native of Alcalá de Henares, and one would like to believe it, for that would make him a fellow-townsman of Cervantes. The date of his birth and of his death are equally unknown. It seems fairly certain that he had ceased to be Archpriest of Hita at the beginning of 1351, but it is not sure that he was dead before that date: it is always possible that he was deprived of his post, for *El Libro de buen amor* shews him as a signal sinner, the very reverse of an edifying ecclesiastic. He himself records that he was put in prison by order of the Archbishop of Toledo, Gil Alvarez Carrillo de Albornoz (1295?-1367), who was appointed to his see in 1339. Juan Ruiz may even have written his book while he lay in prison, since in its first three stanzas, he calls upon God to deliver him:

'libra Amj, dios mio, desta presion do yo yago.'

On the other hand, the testimony of the two existing manuscripts is conflicting. The Salamancan manuscript gives 1343 as the date of *El Libro de buen amor*, while the manuscript at Toledo fixes the year of its completion at 1330, nine years before Albornoz's preferment. But though there is a lack of biographical particulars concerning Juan Ruiz, he reveals his character clearly enough in his book which he calls *El Libro de buen amor*, a title not always kept by his editors.

It is plain that the Archpriest led a very unedifying life and he scarcely attempts to veil his misdeeds. Every now and then he lets drop a text which he utters with a professional unction, but this is not at all misleading: it does not cover the true scent, for such incidental flourishes are amply counteracted by the extreme frankness of the avowals in the body of the text. *El Libro de buen amor* may be regarded as an early example of a picaresque novel in rhyme. Its variety is extraordinary, and the author, besides possessing the gift of artistic candour, puts his miscellaneous learning to good purposes. He is always ready to parody a *cantar de gesta*, and, despite his cloth, to burlesque a hymn. His desultory reading is turned to profit; he borrows freely from Phaedrus, from Pedro Alfonso; he exploits the *Libro de Alexandre* and *El Libro de los engaños e los asayamientos de las mugeres*; he develops hints that he finds in the Latin *Pamphilus* and draws largely upon *La Bataille de Karesme et de Charnage* and other French *dits* or *fabliaux*. From all this it may be inferred that Juan Ruiz was not above imitation, and this is true; but his imitations have on them always the impress of original genius. He improves on what he takes from others and makes a living character of a wooden lay-figure. His personages survive: the personages that suggested them to him are long since dead. His touch imparts life to a mass of dry bones, and so his characters endure and pass on to succeeding generations. The two lovers, Melon de la Uerta and Endrina de Calatayud, annexed from *Pamphilus*, reappear as Calisto and Melibea in *La Celestina*, and perhaps take on a new incarnation as Romeo and Juliet. Don Furon steals into French literature as the famous 'valet de Gascogne' of Marot (1497-1544) and is the prototype of the rogue in all Spanish picaresque tales. Similarly Ruiz develops Trota-conventos from Ovid, stamps her with the seal of his genius and hands her on to Regnier (1573-1613) who re-baptizes her as Macette: but already she had become immortal

THE FOURTEENTH CENTURY 51

as Celestina in Castilian literature. And all this medley of material is enriched by a perpetual play of humorous irony and cynical, penetrating observation. Thanks to his indefatigable curiosity, posterity is endowed by Juan Ruiz with a panorama of the strange society of his tumultuous period. And he paints people as he saw them, in the true spirit of exact Spanish realism. He shrinks from no transcription—whether it be of Moorish dancers, of depraved priests or libidinous nuns, painted Jewesses, great ladies or the sunburnt daughters of the plough. Ruiz has no *penchant* for moral excellence in his characters, but he has a morality of his own, and this consists in rendering his vision of existence with convincing fidelity.

Ruiz is the first pre-eminent literary individuality in Castilian literature. Reared in Berceo's artistic traditions, he takes over the *cuaderna via* as he received it from his predecessors, but in his hands the metre becomes a new thing. He renders it more supple, more various, more speedy. And in this technical part of his art he was deeply absorbed. At the beginning of *El Libro de buen amor* there is a prose preface in which Ruiz avows with more or less truth that his main object was to supply models of rhythmical composition. He did this much—as he did more in other directions. He recast, as has been shewn, the *cuaderna via*: he went further afield, and transplanted from Galicia the *serranillas*, imparting to them a bitter-sweetness of his own; he was not above reproducing popular measures—*cantares cazurros*—which he picked up from wandering students, and in some of his metrical experiments (as in *De la Passion de Nuestro Señor Jhesu Christo*), he anticipates the *versos de arte mayor* which were to become, and to remain, the fashion for another two hundred years or so. As a metrist, as a dramatic creator, as a realistic force, as a guide and influence, Juan Ruiz has an unassailable claim to be the greatest figure in early Spanish literature. His countrymen have called him the Spanish Petronius. This will not do. He has not the polished perversity of the *arbiter elegantiarum*. Neither perhaps is Ticknor altogether right in calling Ruiz the Spanish Chaucer. Ruiz has not Chaucer's amiability and tenderness. His note is rather one of rasping irony. Possibly the nearest parallel to him would be found in La Fontaine (1621-1695): Ruiz is a harsher type of La Fontaine, more plebeian, more violent, more insolent, more daring.

If the fourteenth century is wanting in morality, it is for no lack of preachers, critics and admonishers. The counsels of the Archpriest may be suspect, but those of Lopez de Ayala have a note of deep gravity. Equally sincere are the *Proverbios morales* of the Rabbi Santob[1] or Semtob (=good name) or Santo. This writer, who introduced gnomic poetry into Spain, was a native, possibly, of Carrion de los Condes in Old Castile; at any rate, he lived there and dedicated his work to Peter the Cruel. The *Proverbios morales*, consisting of six hundred and eighty-six quatrains in lines of seven syllables, are redolent of Jewish and Arabic influence. And it is precisely this exotic note

---

[1] *Proverbios morales*, ed. F. Janer, 1864, in Bib. de Autores Esp., LVII.—See M. Menéndez y Pelayo, in *Antología de poetas líricos*, etc. Madrid, 1892. III, pp. cxxiv-cxxxvi; L. Stein, *Untersuchungen über die Proverbios morales von Santob de Carrion*. Berlin, 1900.

THE FOURTEENTH CENTURY

that makes Santob interesting. It is very easy to point out his defects: he is not a great poet, his notion of form is imperfect, his tendency to improve every occasion for sermonizing his readers is apt to be very wearisome, the burden is monotonous and the author's desire to be concise often makes him obscure. But he has compensating good qualities: he has the courage of his opinion, has a certain boldness of imagination and a gift of verbal invention which entitle this melancholy veteran to rank in the history of Spanish literature as the introducer of a new *genre*. Santob tells us that he was old when he wrote the dedication of the *Proverbios morales* in 1350 or thereabouts. He cannot, therefore, reasonably be credited with works written about half a century later—such as the *Revelacion de vn hermitanno*[1] (1382), a remodelling of the old theme already treated in *La Disputa del Alma y el Cuerpo* from the Latin *Rixa Animi et Corporis*. This is written in *versos de arte mayor* and shews signs of Italian influence. The *Doctrina de la Discriçion*[2] by Pedro de Veragüe was similarly ascribed to Santob. An anonymous poem of much the same date is the *Libro de miseria del homne*,[3] which is made up of five hundred and two stanzas written in the *cuaderna via*. It is a full paraphrase of *De contemptu mundi* attributed to Pope Innocent III. (1198-1216), and has a distinctly didactic aim.

Of Juan Manuel's nephew, Alphonso XI (1311-1350)

[1] Ed. F. Janer, 1864, in Bib. de Autores Esp., LVII.

[2] Ed. R. Foulché-Delbosc, in *Revue Hispanique*, XIV (1906), pp. 565-597.

[3] Ed. M. Artigas [*Bol. de la Bib. Menéndez y Pelayo*] Santander, 1920.

there exists only one poem preserved in the *Canzoniere portoghese della Biblioteca Vaticana*:

'En un tiempo cogi flores del muy nobre paraiso.'

It is a rather lackadaisical composition and not at all what one would expect from the hectoring conqueror of Salado, to whom with some superficial plausibility was long ascribed the *Poema de Alfonso Onceno*.[1] This poem is now known to have been written by Rodrigo Yanez or Yannes, perhaps a Galician or a Portuguese who adopted the Castilian form of his name Eannes.

'Yo Rodrigo Yannes la note
en lenguaje castellano,'

he says in stanza 1841. The manuscript was discovered by Diego Hurtado de Mendoza in Granada in 1573 and an extract from it was printed in Argote de Molina's *Nobleza del Andalvzia* (1588). It was perhaps translated from a Portuguese or Galician original, and is more in the nature of a chronicle than a poem. The author's chief concern is to give a faithful representation of the facts: he has more patriotic feeling than poetic inspiration and produces a sharper impression of the feeling against the *morisma* than is given by almost any other medieval work. The *Poema de Alfonso Onceno* denotes the approaching end of the epic; it is written by an authentic *juglar* who was an eye-witness of the deeds celebrated. It is a work of transition, and Yanez, when he substituted for the weightier Alexandrine two lines of eight syllables, unconsciously opened up the road for the introduction of the *romance*.

[1] Ed. F. Janer, 1864, in Bib. de Autores Esp., LVII.

THE FOURTEENTH CENTURY

Every literature has its points of weakness, and Spain is undeniably weak in history and in what is called the epistolary *genre*. So far as history is concerned, the result is not a little unexpected. One would have imagined that Spain would be at least as rich in historians as England : judging from the comparatively early date of Spain's primitive historical records, one might suppose that the Spanish endowment included a marked innate gift for historical studies. Under Alphonso X, the *Cronica general* was compiled and the same king gathered round him a group of researchers who worked under his directions. He had a high standard of what history should be, and perhaps he handed on this high tradition to his family. At any rate, Alphonso X's nephew, Don Juan Manuel, tried his hand at history and produced an abbreviation of his uncle's chronicle. History could not, however, be kept as a monopoly belonging to the royal family. It was taken up by the nobles who had an active part in the government and were generally acquainted with the main facts. One has a specimen of this in the chronicles of PERO LOPEZ DE AYALA[1] (1332-1407). Lopez de Ayala came of an influential stock, and

---

[1] *Rimado de Palacio*, ed. A. F. Kuersteiner, New York, 1920 (Bib. hispanica, XXI, XXII) ; *Cronicas de los reyes de Castilla Don Pedro, Don Enrique II, Don Juan I, Don Enrique III*, ed. E. de Llaguno Amírola, Madrid, 1779-1780. 2 vols.; *El libro de las aves de caça*, ed. P. de Gayangos, 1869 (Soc. de Bibliófilos Esp., 5).—See : R. de Floranes [y Encinas], *Vida de D. Pedro Lopez de Ayala*, in *Coleccion de documentos inéditos*, etc. 1851-1852, XIX and XX, pp. 5-49 ; M. Menéndez y Pelayo, in *Antología de poetas líricos*, etc. Madrid, 1893. IV, pp. ix-xxvii ; E. Fueter, *Ayala und die Chronik Peters des Grausamen*, in *Mittheilungen des Instituts für österreichische Geschichtsforschung*, XXVI (1905), pp. 225-246.

is one of the few Basques who have won a prominent place in Spanish literature. Beginning life as a page to Peter the Cruel in 1353, he remained in that King's service—except for a temporary defection to the Infante don Fernando de Aragon—until 1366, when he went over to the Pretender, Henry of Trastamara. In 1367 he was taken prisoner at Nájera by the Black Prince, but was speedily ransomed. Between 1379 and 1380, he seems to have been in Paris as Spanish Ambassador. Captured at Aljubarrota (August 14, 1385) by the Portuguese, he was prisoner at Oviedes for some eighteen months. During the minority of Henry III, Lopez de Ayala was one of the Regents. He was the bearer of a letter from Henry III to Charles VI of France in 1395 and seems to have been in Paris again the following year. His chancellorship dates from 1398. During his long life of seventy-five years, this most interesting person contrived always to be on the winning side and chronicled the chief events which occurred during the reigns of the kings whom he served, Peter the Cruel, Henry II, John II and Henry III. His account of Henry III is unfinished, for Lopez de Ayala died before Henry III, who survived till Christmas day of the same year (1407): it was continued later by Álvar Garcia de Santa Maria (1390-1460).

Others had worked on the same lines as Lopez de Ayala. The chronicles of the reigns of Alphonso X, Sancho IV, Ferdinand IV and Alphonso XI were written by an author who has been plausibly identified with Fernand Sanchez de Tovar, Lopez de Ayala's predecessor in the chancellorship. The difference between Sanchez de Tovar and Lopez de Ayala as writers was not one of method, but of temperament.

Lopez de Ayala was somewhat old-fashioned in his ideas. The notion of writing history came to him when he was re-translating Livy through the French version of Pierre Berçuire (d. 1362). Lopez de Ayala follows Livy by ascribing to his personages speeches which they never made : so far he deviates from fact. But this is a mere mannerism, a simple artifice of style. These speeches take the place of expository narratives and explain the motives by which the speakers were actuated. Of course, Lopez de Ayala may be mistaken in his explanations : so say the most modern of scientific historians. As to the facts, Lopez de Ayala is usually of meticulous accuracy. He had had a personal share in most of the events recorded by him, and was therefore well informed concerning them and, as a general rule, he is almost uncannily impartial. He seems to depart from his usual neutrality when he speaks of Peter the Cruel. It is not very easy, however, to paint a flattering portrait of Peter the Cruel, if one has any sort of regard for truth, and Lopez de Ayala had opportunities of studying his subject at close quarters since he was in Peter's service for about a dozen years. In 1366, Henry of Trastamara was proclaimed king at Calahorra ; and Lopez de Ayala thought that the moment had now come to go over to the other side. He records his own perfidy without attempting to disguise it. What he says is : ' Things now took such a turn, that those who had set out with Don Pedro left him, being agreed that they would not again go back to him.' There is something amazingly cool in this. Lopez de Ayala contrives by sheer indifference to mask the fact that he has committed treason. His unfairness to Peter the Cruel—if he was unfair to him—may consist in his acceptance of rumours hostile to the king and in his silence concerning the manœuvres of the opposition towards the king. But this may have been unconscious influence: Lopez de Ayala is never deliberately unfair. He does not travesty the facts. He had lived too long and too close to kings to be dazzled by them. Some of them had showered benefits on him, but one would never know who they were from Ayala's tone. He judges them all with a cool impartiality which is surprising. He is too haughty to have personal prejudices, or to shew them, at any rate. He talks of his benefactors as though they were enemies, of his enemies as though they had done him no harm. His allusions to his royal masters are usually couched in respectful terms; but he preserves his independence of judgement and passes sentence on them without hesitation. Respectful but never servile, Lopez de Ayala's neutrality tends to become caustic irony; he sees the essential trait of a situation, the main characteristic of a personage, and besides the gift of picturesque phrase he has the histrionic instinct, the knack of leading up to a dramatic scene. Lopez de Ayala at his best can easily be read in Prosper Mérimée's *Histoire de Don Pèdre Ier, roi de Castille* (1847-1848), which displays one master basing his work upon the notes of another who lived five hundred years before him. Both are kindred spirits, and both have the same disillusioned outlook upon the human comedy. Both were courtiers, but they are singularly free from the faults which are usually associated with the denizens of courts; perhaps the Spaniard is the freer of the two from such defects. Lopez de Ayala meant to write chronicles—plain chronicles—like those who went before him. Incidentally he transfigured dry records by adding picturesque detail. He made history live and set an example to those who followed him.

Lopez de Ayala's main interest lies undoubtedly in his chronicles, but there are some who consider the *Rimado de Palacio* his best work. The poem is a satire on all classes of men except the poor (*los pobres cuytados*). The manuscript of the Biblioteca Nacional de Madrid bears the words ' Este libro fizo el onrrado cauallero Pero Lopez de Ayala estando preso en Yngla terra e llama se el libro del Palaçio.'[1] This explanation was probably inserted by the copyist. It is not known that Lopez de Ayala ever was in England. His imprisonment by the Black Prince took place in the year 1367 and lasted but a short time. Internal evidence is against the ascription of the poem to that year. In stanza 215[2] there is mention of the schism under Pope Urbanus VI, in stanza 820 the schism is spoken of as having lasted twenty-five years: evidently stanza 215 cannot have been written before 1378 nor stanza 820 before 1403; in stanza 868 there is a reference to a convent of nuns built by Lopez de Ayala's father in 1372. This is not perhaps definite proof, but taken in conjunction with the absence of evidence that Lopez de Ayala ever went to England, it is cumulative and weighs against the statement in the manuscript. The current theory is that Lopez de Ayala wrote much of the

[1] 'This book was written by the noble knight Pero Lopez de Ayala when he was a prisoner in England and it is called the book of the Court.'

[2] Ed. A. F. Kuersteiner, 1 (Bib. hispanica, xxi).

Rimado de Palacio when he was in captivity at Oviedes:

> 'Yo estaua ençerrado en vna casa escura
> Trauado de vna cadena asaz grande z dura.'[1]

The latter part which reveals the tolerance of age was probably written at the end of the Chancellor's career. The want of method in the book inevitably recalls Juan Ruiz. Like Ruiz, Lopez de Ayala witnesses audibly against his generation. He exposes the loose morals of the day, the universal corruption, the love of luxury: all classes of society from pope to soldier who feed on the 'sangre de los pobres cuytados' pass under the lash of his merciless satire. But where Juan Ruiz, the gay picaroon, only laughs at the human race, Lopez de Ayala illustrates with relentless inexorability its cruelty and evil. He is less vehement, perhaps, than his French successor Agrippa d'Aubigné (1552-1630), but if he does not inveigh, he never strikes the softer note. D'Aubigné may say:

> 'Cachez-vous sous ma robe en mes noires forêts...'

for Lopez de Ayala, the world has no refuge, no pity for the downtrodden:

> 'Sy el cuytado es muy pobre z non tiene cabal,
> Non le valdran parientes nin avn el decretal:
> "Muera, muera," dizen todos por este cuytado tal
> Ca es ladron manifiesto e meresçe mucho mal.'[2]

---

[1] 'I was shut up in a dark house fastened to a long and hard chain.'

[2] 'If a man be very poor, weighed down with cares and without means, neither laws nor papal decrees will avail him: "Crucify him, crucify him," is the universal cry, "for he is a thief most manifest and deserves much ill."'

THE FOURTEENTH CENTURY

He states with the cold impartiality of the historian; the grim relentlessness of his outlook on life is summed up in the verse:

> 'Asy pasa, mal pecado, pasó z pasara.'

He possesses besides a gift of brilliant characterization, of which his description of the merchants is a case in point:

> 'Fazen escuras sus tiendas e poca lunbre les dan;
> Por Broselas muestran Ypre e por Melinas Rroan.
> Los paños violetes bermejos les parescera[n];
> Al contar de los dineros las finiestras alçaran.'[1]

Stanza 706 brings to an end Lopez de Ayala's sermon or satire, which is written in the *cuaderna via*, the metre which he uses for his personal confessions where he laments having wasted his time reading about 'Amadis' and 'Lançarote'; elsewhere he makes metrical experiments, uses *versos de arte mayor* in the stanzas which deal with the schism but returns again to the *cuaderna via* in the epilogue to the poem—a paraphrase of St. Gregory's *Job*.

The *Libro de la caza de las aves, et de sus plumages et dolencias et melecinamientos* known also as the *Libro de la cetreria*, a treatise on falconry, was probably written while the author was still a prisoner at Oviedes; it is dedicated to Gonzalo de Mena (d. 1401), bishop of Burgos and an ardent huntsman. The great chancellor was not unlike Alphonso X as regards intellectual curiosity. Nothing came amiss to him. He tried his hand at the new metrics and was not

---

[1] 'They darken their shops and give them little light; for lace from Bruges and Mechlin they shew lace from Rouen. Purple cloth and scarlet look alike to them; when they count their money, they open the windows.'

unsuccessful with the *versos de arte mayor*; to his numerous translations Spain owes her first interest in things Italian. His versions of Livy, of St. Isidore's *De summo bono sive De sententiis*, of St. Gregory's commentary on *Job*, of Boethius's *De Consolatione philosophiae* reveal his humanistic tendencies, while his translation of Boccaccio's *De casibus virorum et feminarum illustrium* (which was finished in 1422 by Alonso de Cartagena and Juan Alfonso de Zamora) marks an epoch by fixing the dawn of Italian influence between the years 1356 and 1364. Lopez de Ayala's rendering of *Le Roman de Troie*, of which a recast had been made by a cleric in Alphonso XI's reign, was based not on Benoît de Sainte-More's original text, but on the Latin version by Guido delle Colonne. This is significative of Lopez de Ayala's inclinations. The instinct which served him so profitably in politics accompanied him into literature. Once again he was on the winning side. He died before he could finish his translation of Boccaccio: death claimed him when he had translated eight books out of ten. But he lived long enough to see the Italian influence carrying all before it.

IV

THE ROMANCERO

THE *Romancero*[1] is the general collection of the eminently Spanish verse compositions known as *romances* (ballads). In its present restricted meaning the *romance* is a popular epical-lyric poem of sixteen-syllabled lines with a uniform assonance from beginning to end. This definition applies to old *romances* only, and by old is meant a *romance* not later than the fifteenth century.

The oldest ballads are in a sense fragments of long popular epics. The earliest Spanish epic which survives is the *Poema del Cid*, and in point of time this stands about half-way between *La Chanson de*

[1] *Cancionero de Romances*. Facsimile of the Antwerp ed. n.d. by R. Menéndez Pidal, Madrid, 1914; *Romancero general*. Facsimile of the 1600 ed. by A. M. Huntington, New York, 1903. 2 vols.; *Romancero general* ... ed. A. Duran, 1849-1851. 2 vols. (Bib. de Autores Esp., X, XVI); *Primavera y Flor de Romances* ... ed. F. J. Wolf and C. Hofmann, Berlin, 1856. 2 vols. [reprinted with additions by M. Menéndez y Pelayo, in *Antología de poetas líricos*, etc. Madrid, 1898-1900. VII-X]; *Romancero de Barcelona*, ed. R. Foulché-Delbosc, in *Revue Hispanique*, XXIX (1913), pp. 121-194; *Les romancerillos de la Bibliothèque Ambrosienne*, ed. R. Foulché-Delbosc, in *Revue Hispanique*, XLV (1919), pp. 510-624; *Spanish Ballads*, ed. G. le Strange, Cambridge, 1920; *Romancero judeo-*

Roland and *Das Nibelungenlied*—about the middle of the twelfth century. There are epical touches in the *Poema de Fernan Gonçalez* composed in the latter half of the thirteenth century. Then there is a break until the *Poema de Alfonso Onceno*. Here the long Alexandrine divides into two lines of eight syllables each and the versification of the *romance* is well in sight. This revolutionary change was not made at a single stride. It had been gradually coming on. The most popular hero of the Middle Ages, the man most frequently celebrated in song, was the Cid, and it is not surprising to find some premonitions of the approaching revolution in compositions where he figures as the protagonist. He had been sung in the *Poema del Cid* as the misunderstood patriot ill-used by a king who was really a Leonese, though he ruled over Castile. This was obviously a great success with the multitude, and it then became necessary to exhibit the Cid at all stages of his career, as a precociously gallant youth, as a rebellious feudal baron and so forth.

español, ed. R. Gil, Madrid, 1911 ; *Romancero nuevomejicano*, ed. A. M. Espinosa, in *Revue Hispanique*, XXXIII (1915), pp. 446-560.—See : M. Milá y Fontanals, in *De la poesía heróico-popular castellana*. Barcelona, 1874 ; C. Michaëlis de Vasconcellos, *Romanzenstudien*, in *Zeitschrift für romanische Philologie*, XVI (1902), pp. 40-89 ; M. Menéndez y Pelayo, *Tratado de los romances viejos* (*Antología de poetas líricos*, etc. XI, XII). Madrid, 1903-1906 ; R. Menéndez Pidal, in *L'Epopée castillane à travers la littérature espagnole* [French trans. by H. Mérimée]. Paris, 1910 ; R. Foulché-Delbosc, *Essai sur les origines du Romancero. Prélude*. Paris, 1912 ; P. Rajna, *Osservazioni e dubbi concernenti la storia delle romanze spagnuole*, in *The Romanic Review*, VI (1915), pp. 1-41 ; S. G. Morley, *Are the Spanish 'Romances' written in quatrains?* in *The Romanic Review*, VII (1916), pp. 42-82 ; G. Cirot, *Le mouvement quaternaire dans les romances* in *Bulletin hispanique*, XXI (1919), pp. 103-142.

THE ROMANCERO

The *Cronica general de 1344* contains many of the most popular stories about the Cid, incorporated from epic poems which now appear to have passed out of existence. There is, however, a recast of the chief of these poems in a fifteenth century manuscript: its real title is long and clumsy: *Cronica rimada de las cosas de España desde la muerte del rey don Pelayo hasta don Fernando el Magno, y mas particularmente de las aventuras del Cid*.[1] It is not convenient to use a title of nearly thirty words, and it is easier to speak of this strange composition by some shorter name: *Cantar de Rodrigo* or *Las mocedades de Rodrigo*. It is twelve hundred and twenty-five lines in length and begins with a piece of prose slightly assonanced. The Cid only appears on the scene at l. 280—as a boy of twelve. He challenges and kills the Conde de Gormaz, who has ill-treated and wounded some shepherds of Diego Lainez, the Cid's father. The Conde de Gormaz had a daughter called Ximena. She appears before the king and consents to pardon the Cid if he will marry her. It is a curious request, and the Cid vaguely feels the impropriety of marrying the daughter of the man whom he has slain. However, King Ferdinand begs him to accede to the lady's prayer, and he does so in an insolent mood, insulting both her and the king. Then he goes on a pilgrimage to Compostela, has a miraculous experience which urges him on to further deeds of prowess. He overcomes

[1] Facsimile of the MS. in the Bibliothèque Nationale by A. M. Huntington, New York, 1904; ed. B. P. Bourland, in *Revue Hispanique*, XXIV (1911), pp. 310-357; ed. R. Menéndez Pidal, in *Poema de Mio Cid*, etc., Madrid, 1919. pp. 247-297.— See: M. Menéndez y Pelayo, in *Tratado de los romances viejos* (*Antología de poetas líricos*, etc. XI), Madrid, 1903. I, pp. 337-345.

the Count of Savoy and heads an expedition to Paris, where he challenges the King of France and all the Knights of the Round Table. Finally he grants the King of France a truce of one year, and just as he seems likely to extend it to twelve the poem breaks off. The real Cid was never in Paris in his life: the Knights of the Round Table never existed. The *juglar* whose work was used in the *Cronica de 1344* cared little enough about facts and history: the recaster cared less. The aim of both was to make the Cid seem important and picturesque, to exhibit him bullying kings, popes and magnates. It is plain that the old epic had received its death-blow. If it was ever an aristocratic form of intellectual entertainment it had long since ceased to be so. The *Cantar de Rodrigo* is essentially popular in its inspiration. It represents the Cid in the romantic aspect in which Guillen de Castro presented him before Corneille drew on Castro, and to it in some indirect way may be traced the symbolic exhibition of the Cid in *La Légende des Siècles* of Victor Hugo (1802-1885), the terrible vision of him offered in the *Poèmes Tragiques* of Leconte de Lisle (1820-1894), and the glittering medallions of the famous chief, against the background of the later *conquistadores*, as he appears in the splendid *Trophées* of José Maria de Heredia (1842-1906).

The genuine old epic is moribund. What was true in it was annexed to the domain of history. What was imagination was remoulded in another form. A profound structural modification has occurred in the *Cantar de Rodrigo*. Some passages are merely prose, but that might be due to a defective copy. Here and there the *cuaderna via* peeps out. The assonances are simplified. The normal type of the versification

THE ROMANCERO

is a sixteen-syllabled line, each hemistich forming a verse of what became later the artistic *romance*. A new kind of poetry is about to come into existence. This is the typical *romance*, concerning whose origin Sr. Menéndez Pidal holds the following theory:—Aristocratic in the beginning, the Spanish epic came down in the world, and fell into the hands of wandering minstrels who recited or sang in public squares or market-places, adding new elements, love-stories or picturesque episodes calculated to hit the taste of a popular audience. In this way the multitude inherited a body of poetry originally composed for the nobles. Fragments of the recited verses remained in the memory of their hearers, and on this basis they created spontaneously the old *romances*.—It is very difficult to believe in this spontaneous and collective authorship of a whole series of poems. Poetry is an individual expression of a personal emotion. There is less difficulty in supposing that among the comparatively uneducated class there may have been some man with a genuine feeling for poetry and with some instinct for versification. Such a man might take a hint from a *cantar de gesta*, and with this as his starting point might launch forth into an independent composition of his own. In that sense a certain number of old *romances* may be fragments of *cantares de gesta*. But such composition is not spontaneous and is not collective. It is derivative and personal.

There is an impassioned dispute as to the age of the oldest *romances*, and it is a dispute of long standing. It used to be held that some *romances* dated from the time when the Spanish language attained an independent existence of its own. This position was found to be untenable and had to be abandoned. Then there came into vogue the theory of an Arabic origin for the *romances*, a theory set afoot, as it appears, by the French prelate Huet, Bishop of Avranches. This necessitated the sacrifice of some four or five hundred years, and the *romances* were then declared to have been composed, not in the eighth or ninth, but in the twelfth or thirteenth centuries. The deeper investigations go, the more the claims to antiquity of the *romances* have to be reduced. Further reduction is inevitable, and though the fact that the bulk of the oldest *romances* are anonymous makes it difficult to settle their chronology, it would be rash to assume that they came into being before the fifteenth century.

The first unmistakable reference to the *romances* is made by the Marqués de Santillana, a shifty politician but a charming poet, a man of alert curiosity in all that concerned literature. Some few years before 1450, Santillana drew up for the benefit of Don Pedro, the Constable of Portugal, himself a poet of some accomplishment in the fantastic manner of Juan de Mena, a conspectus of literary achievements in Spain. Santillana's opinion of the makers of *romances* is couched in unflattering terms : ' Contemptible are those poets,' he writes, ' who, neglecting order, rule and rhythm, compose these chants and *romances* in which base folk take delight.' It is a curious coincidence that to the very period when Santillana was pouring forth his disdain, belong the oldest *romances* that bear any author's name. Three (*El Conde Arnaldos*, *Rosa Florida* and the ballad of the *Infantina*), belonging to about 1440, are under the name of Juan Rodriguez de la Cámara and are preserved in a *Cancionero* of the British Museum ; however, it seems very possible that these are not original compositions but artistic recasts of

THE ROMANCERO

romances already in existence. To much the same date belong two other *romances* (*Terrible duelo fasia* and *Retrayda esta la reyna*) bearing the name of a certain Carvajal or Carvajales, a Spanish poet in the train of Alphonso V, the Aragonese king who entered Naples in triumph in 1443. That *romances* were at first regarded as non-literary compositions is a legitimate inference from Santillana's remark. The chances are that, if printing had not been introduced into Spain in the same year (1474) as the Catholic kings, Ferdinand and Isabella, came to the throne, the older *romances* would be unknown, for nobody thought them deserving of being written down on illuminated parchments. But a change was nearer at hand than Santillana could possibly foresee. Probably before his death occurred the attraction of the new form was felt by persons of a literary turn like Rodriguez de la Cámara and Carvajal. The fact remains, however, that the number of *romances* to which a positive date can be assigned is relatively small. Now and then the existence of a *romance* before a certain date can be inferred by the fact that it happens to be quoted in some work as, for instance, the *Romance de Lanzarote* in the *Gramatica . . . sobre la lengua castellana* (1492) of Antonio de Lebrixa.

The oldest *romances* derived, no doubt, from detached fragments of *cantares de gesta*, but they possessed a lyrical quality of their own, were more easily remembered because of their relative brevity, and became as popular as the extinct *cantares de gesta* had been before them. The *romances* were capable of assimilating a much greater variety of matter than the *cantares de gesta*, which had dealt mainly with the martial exploits, real or imaginary, of heroes like

Charlemagne, King Roderick and the Cid or of the legendary Knights of the Round Table.

The vogue of the *romances* was extraordinary. Despite the protests of fastidious judges like Santillana, they carried all before them. They formed the poor man's library, constituted his education, filled his ears with music, stirred his imagination, stimulated his patriotism, and taught him nearly all the history that he was ever to know. Fabulous figures like Bernardo del Carpio became as real as historical personages like the Cid, and the long struggle with the Moors supplied the ballad-makers with an inexhaustible fund of matter, dramatic, romantic, full of dazzling colour and rich in picturesque contrasts. Gradually there came into existence a special type of ballad, the *romance fronterizo* or border-ballad, written in the first instance by some gifted man-at-arms or perhaps done into Castilian by a *moro latinado*, who conformed to Castilian models of ballad-making. In the early period these border-ballads are apt to be among the best ballads in the *romancero* : historical narratives told with infinite spirit by a witness stirred to the depths. An admirable specimen of the most authentic is the early *Abenamar, Abenamar | moro de la moreria*, of which a very pallid rendering is given by Chateaubriand (1768-1848), in *Les Aventures du dernier Abencérage* (1808). The *Romance de Abenamar*, which cannot be earlier than the month of July 1431, just about the time of the famous battle of la Higueruela, embodies a conversation between John II and his ally Abenamar. It is a particularly interesting example : it is forcible and direct in diction, yet it is *morisco* not only in historical sentiment—the courted city rejects the advances of the Castilian King—but

THE ROMANCERO

also in its artistic inspiration; the conception of the beleaguered city regarded as a possible bride is thoroughly oriental with no parallel in medieval literature out of Spain. The *romance: Moricos, los mis moricos,* | *los que ganais mi soldada* is probably an earlier example of the border ballad dealing with the siege of Baeza in 1407; to much the same date belongs the picturesque fragment of *Reduan, bien se te acuerda* | *que me diste la palabra* with its vivid characterization of Reduan, Muhammad VII's captain.

' Reduan le respondia | sin demudarse la cara :
 Si lo dije no me acuerdo, | mas cumplire mi palabra.' [1]

The siege of Antequera (1410) is sung in *De Antequera partio el moro* | *tres horas antes del dia*; the ballad *Alora, la bien cercada,* | *tu que estas en par del rio* on the death of Diego de Ribera (1434), which took place at Alora, has the interest of being mentioned in Juan de Mena's *El Laberinto* (1444 ?). *Alla en Granada la rica* | *instrumentos oi tocar* deals with the battle of Los Alporchones (1452), while *Jugando estaba el rey moro* | *y aun al ajedrez un dia*, assigned to some time after 1460, throws light on the relations which existed between the Governor Faxardo and the reigning Mussulman king of Granada. More interesting and better known is the ballad on the loss of Alhama (1482), *Paseabase el rey moro* | *por la ciudad de Granada*. Perez de Hita remarks that this *romance* had an Arabic original which the inhabitants of Granada were not allowed to sing: its effective refrain ¡ *Ay de mi Alhama !* gives colour to this statement. Shortly after the capture of Alhama, the town of Loja was besieged,

[1] ' Reduan replied without a change in his face, "I do not remember having said so, but I will keep my word." '

and here Rodrigo Giron, Grand Master of the Order of Calatrava at the early age of twelve, met his death and was sung in such ballads as *Por la vega de Granada | un caballero pasea* and *¡ Ay Dios, que buen caballero | el Maestre de Calatrava!* A Christian knight who also figures in the *romances fronterizos* is Alonso de Aguilar, killed in 1501 on the banks of the Rio verde— whence *¡ Rio Verde, Rio Verde ! | ¡ cuanto cuerpo en ti se baña !* which was rendered into English by Thomas Percy (1729-1811), Bishop of Dromore. Another ballad on the same subject begins *Estando el rey don Fernando | en conquista de Granada*.

Apart from the *romances fronterizos*, there are, according to Menéndez y Pelayo's classification, eleven cycles or groups of the *romances* proper. In the first group, relating to Roderick and his overthrow, two ballads have a certain celebrity due perhaps to Cervantes, who in *Don Quijote* (II, ch. xxxiii) refers to the legend on the death of Roderick told in *Despues que el rey don Rodrigo | a España perdido habia* and (II, ch. xxvi) quotes from *Las huestes de don Rodrigo | desmayaban y huian*. This ballad contains the memorable passage given in Lockhart's rendering :

' Last night I was the King of Spain—to-day no King am I ;
Last night fair castles held my train—to-night where shall I lie ?
Last night a hundred pages did serve me on the knee,—
To-night not one I call mine own : not one pertains to me ' ;

and in Victor Hugo's *Les Orientales* (xvi)

' Hier j'avais des châteaux : j'avais de belles villes.'

The same theme is used by Landor in *Count Julian* (Act IV). None of the Röderick *romances* are old : Wolf admitted six as being early, but these have since

THE ROMANCERO 73

been found to derive from the *Coronica Sarrazyna* written about 1443 by Pedro de Corral.

In the second group dealing with the legendary hero Bernardo del Carpio, there are forty-six ballads in all, of which one only is old. This is *Con cartas y mensajeros | el rey al Carpio envio*: it contains the almost proverbial line

' Mensajero eres, amigo, | no mereces culpa, no '

quoted by Sancho Panza (*Don Quijote*, II, ch. x). Three others, *Andados treinta y seis años | del rey Alfonso el Casto ; En corte del casto Alfonso | Bernaldo a placer vivia; En gran pesar y tristeza | era el valiente Bernaldo*, which were once believed to be old, are based on metrical recasts of the *Cronica general*. Similarly *Por las riberas de Arlanza | Bernardo del Carpio cabalga* is first met with in Timoneda's *Rosa española* (1573).

The third group—of Fernan Gonzalez—fares nearly as ill in the matter of old *romances*: only one, the well-known *Castellanos y leoneses | tienen grandes divisiones*, is entire; there exists, however, the fine old fragment *Buen conde Fernan Gonzalez | el rey envia por vos*. The story of the Conde de Castilla imprisoned in Leon and rescued by his wife is preserved in a passage of twelve lines—*Por los palacios del Rey | pelegrina va una tarde*—embodied in *La peregrina*, a traditional Asturian ballad beginning *En la ciudad de Leon | (Dios me asista y non me falte)*.

The group of the Infantes de Lara contains a fair number of old ballads. The legend gave rise to two —perhaps three—*cantares de gesta*: it is on the second *cantar*, written probably between 1268 and 1344, that are based the *romances*. One of these, *A cazar va don Rodrigo | y aun don Rodrigo de Lara*, has been splendidly encrusted by Victor Hugo in *Les Orientales* (xxx). Another, *A Calatrava la vieja | la combaten castellanos*, with its recast *Ay Dios que buen caballero | fue don Rodrigo de Lara*, shews Rodrigo de Lara swearing to avenge the insult offered his wife by the youngest Infante; *Partese el moro Alicante | vispera de sant Cébrian* contains the poignant scene where Gonzalo Gustioz recognizes the heads of his murdered sons: the barbarity of presentation is justified by the intense emotion that culminates in his words to the youngest:

'¡ Hijo Gonzalo Gonzalez! | Los ojos de Doña Sancha !
¡ Que nuevas iran a ella | que a vos mas que a todos ama !'

The two ballads, *Quien es aquel caballero | que tan gran traicion hacia* and *Cansados de pelear | los seis hermanos yacian*, counted as old by Wolf, are thought by some to be by the Caballero Cesáreo, an Imperial knight who withholds his name on the ground that he was 'reserved for greater things.'

The fifth group embraces the various episodes of the Cid's history: its ballads are based mainly on three old *cantares de gesta*—fragments of two are found in the *Cronica de* 1344 and of the third in the *Cronica general*—and on the *Cantar de Rodrigo*. It is noticeable that the few ballads which derive directly from the *Poema del Cid* have little artistic interest or merit. Some of the best known ballads on the Cid are later productions such as: *Afuera, afuera, Rodrigo | el soberbio castellano*; *Ese buen Diego Lainez | despues que hubo yantado*; *En las almenas de Toro | allí estaba una doncella*, the subject of which is treated in Lope de Vega's *Las Almenas de Toro*. Only about a dozen of the group of two hundred and fifty Cid *romances* belong to the fifteenth century. Among these are: *Riberas del*

Duero arriba | cabalgan dos Zamoranos; Por aquel postigo viejo | que nunca fuera cerrado; Doliente estaba, doliente | ese buen rey Fernando and *Ya cabalga Diego Ordoñez | del real se habia salido*: in none of these, however, does the Cid figure personally. Perhaps the oldest of the cycle is *Helo, helo por do viene | el moro por la calzada* of which Gibson's translation gives an excellent idea. Three other ballads are worth noting as deriving from a lost *cantar de gesta* closely connected with the *Cantar de Rodrigo*: these are *Dia era de los reyes | dia era señalado; En Burgos esta el buen rey | asentado a su yantar* and *Cada dia que amanece | veo quien mato a mi padre*. From *Dia era de los reyes* Leconte de Lisle has taken for his *Ximena*—based on *Sentado esta el señor Rey* in Juan de Escobar's *Romancero del Cid* (1612)—the passage beginning *Con mancilla vivo, rey*, not the happiest lines in the poem into which they were imported by contamination from *A Calatrava la vieja*. The French poet was better inspired when he took from *Cabalga Diego Lainez* his *L'Accident de don Iñigo*, and *La Tête du Comte* from *Llorando Diego Lainez* (also in Escobar's collection). This is a comparatively late ballad and so is *En Sant Pedro de Cardeña* by Sepúlveda, but nobody reads Sepúlveda while everybody reads Théophile Gautier (1811-1872), who from this poem derives *Le Cid et le Juif*, so that Sepúlveda has a sort of second-hand celebrity.

The sixth group which includes ballads on historical or fictitious events before the accession of Peter the Cruel is less interesting. To it belongs *Yo sali de la mi tierra | para ir a Dios servir*, once attributed to Alphonso X, and *Valasme, nuestra señora | cual dicen de la Ribera*, where the Carvajales, doomed to die by Ferdinand *El Emplazado*, foretell his death within thirty days. Both these are old *romances*. Of later date is *Dia era de San Anton | ese santo señalado* with its derivative *Ya se salen de Jaen | los trescientos hijosdalgo* which was first printed in Timoneda's *Rosa Española*.

Of the historical ballads which deal with Castilian history from 1350 onwards, none (with the exception, perhaps, of *Entre la gente se dice | y no por cosa sabida*) for obvious reasons, as Milá y Fontanals shrewdly observes, can have been composed during Peter the Cruel's lifetime. Two artistic later *romances*: *Doña Maria de Padilla, | no os mostredes triste, no* and *Yo me estaba allá en Coimbra | que yo me la hube ganado* have been used with much effect by Leconte de Lisle. The ballad *Villanueva, Villanueva*, on the death (1497) of the Infante don Juan, son of the Catholic kings, is an instance of popular inspiration. And in this context may be mentioned two ballads which were thought at one period to be considerably earlier in point of time : *En Arjona estaba el duque* and Alonso Hurtado de Velarde's (d. 1638) *Si el caballo vos han muerto*.

There is little to be said about the eighth group of ballads dealing with historical events outside Castile. *Miraba de Campo-Viejo | el rey de Aragon un dia* has been attributed to a soldier in Alphonso V's train at Naples and must have been written at much the same date as Carvajal's *Retrayda esta la reina*. There is an admirable English version of it by John Hookham Frere, a great expert and enthusiast for *cosas de España*.

The romances connected with the Carlovingian cycle are numerous, and some are particularly well known because they have been quoted copiously by Cervantes. Among these are *Mala la vistes, franceses | la caza de Roncesvalles*, frequently used in the form given in *Don Quijote* (II, ch. ix) *Mala la hubistes, franceses | en esa de Roncesvalles; Por la matanza va el viejo | por la matanza adelante* related, according to Menéndez y Pelayo, with the Hague fragment in *Monumenta Germaniae historica*: *Scriptores* (v. III, pp. 708-710, n.); *Domingo era de Ramos | la Pasion quieren decir* and *En Paris esta doña Alda | la esposa de don Roldan* inspired by *La Chanson de Roland* (ll. 3705-3722). These all deal with episodes from Roncesvalles. On Gaiferos there are such old ballads as the penetrating fragment *¡ Arriba, canes, arriba! | ¡ que rabia mala os mate!*; *Media noche era por filo | los gallos querian cantar*; *Estabase la condesa | en su estrado asentada*; *Vamonos, dijo, mio tio | a Paris esa ciudad* which has points of resemblance with Southey's *Garci Ferrandez* and *Asentado esta Gaiferos | en el palacio real* which is recalled by Maese Pedro's puppet-show (*Don Quijote* II, ch. xxvi). Valdovinos figures in *Nuño Vero, Nuño Vero—buen caballero probado* and in *Tan clara hacia la luna | como el sol a mediodia* reminiscent of the *Chanson de Saisnes* by Jean Bodel d'Arras (d. 1210). The ballads *Helo, helo por do viene | el infante vengador*; *De Merida sale el palmero, | de Merida esa ciudad* and *Por las sierras de Moncayo | vi venir un renegado* have a distinct quality of passion and fire. However, not more than half a dozen of these *romances* are really old and they have not spread beyond the Pyrenees nor, apart from *Don Quijote*, had much influence in Spanish literature except, perhaps, *¡ Oh Belerma! ¡ Oh Belerma! | por mi mal fuiste engendrada!* which has been delightfully parodied by Góngora, whose views on the merits of this cycle one is, on the whole, nearer sharing than Cervantes's.

The *Romance de Lanzarote* is only old as *romances* go. It is parodied in *Don Quijote* (I, ch. ii), and is believed to have some relation with the *Roman de la Charette*. But neither Lancelot nor any other knight of the Round Table appears in ancient Spanish literature : apart from one reference in an illegible chronicle, no allusion to the Arthurian legends is found in Spanish previous to the fourteenth century, when Juan Manuel mentions two hawks of his which he called Lancelot and Gawain, and about twenty years afterwards the Archpriest of Hita refers casually to Tristan. But the Arthurian legends were not generally known in Spain till much later, hence it is not surprising that, besides *Nunca fuera caballero | de damas tan bien servido*, the only old *romances* in this group are *Ferido esta don Tristan | de una mala lanzada* and *Tres hijuelos habia el rey | tres hijuelos, que no mas* which derives from *Lancelot et le cerf au pied blanc*, a vanished French version now represented by a Dutch *Lancelot*. Calderon has introduced this ballad rather clumsily and inopportunely in his burlesque *Céfalo y Procris*. All three *romances* are most beautiful, but they have not attracted any attention out of Spain and not much attention in Spain.

To the eleventh and last group belong the fantastic and chivalresque *romances*, one of which *Mis arreos son las armas | mi descanso es pelear* is very widely known because it is used by the innkeeper in *Don Quijote* (1 ch. ii) ; one line of it *Mi cama son duras peñas | mi dormir siempre es velar* is quoted by Camões in *Filodemo*. Equally well known, perhaps, are *Rosa fresca, rosa fresca | tan garrida y con amor ; Fonte-frida, Fonte-frida, | fonte-frida y con amor ; Yo me era mora Moraima | morilla de un bel catar*, supposed to be based on an Arabic original ; *A cazar va el caballero | a cazar como solia* ; *La bella mal maridada | de las lindas*

THE ROMANCERO

que yo vi, glossed by Gil Vicente, Castillejo and Montemayor; *Blanca sois, señora mia | mas que el rayo del sol* and *¡Ay cuan linda eres, Alba | mas linda que no la flor!* But for some inexplicable reason none of these charming poems seem to have travelled much outside Spain. Better luck attaches to *El Conde Arnaldos*, which is familiar to everybody in Longfellow's recast and of which Flecker has also given a version. Of the dainty little piece, *Por el mes era de mayo | cuando hace la calor* there is only a fragment of which an English rendering [1] has been attempted in the following lines:

'It was the budding month of May when the sun mounts up the sky,
When the bunting chants its clear note and the nightingales reply,
When, on their faithful service bent, all lovers hasten by—
Save one—the broken-hearted—who must in dungeon lie.
I know not when the day begins, or twilight draweth nigh,
But for a little singing-bird, commencing dawn on high,
An archer slew that little bird. God! may that archer die!'

What purports to be a fuller version may be found in the *Silva de Romances*: but it is difficult to believe that these thirteen lines—would-be artistic, pretentious and sentimental—are from the same hand as the first inimitable fragment.

The oldest *romances* with a few exceptions are either found in the *Cancionero de Hernando del Castillo* [2] (1511) or in early sixteenth century broadsides. No special collection of *romances* was made till the middle of the

[1] By James Fitzmaurice-Kelly.

[2] Ed. [1511] J. A. de Balenchana, 1882. 2 vols. (Soc. de Bibliófilos Esp., 21); facsimile of the 1520 ed. by A. M. Huntington, New York, 1904.

century when the *Cancionero de Romances* was published at Antwerp by Martin Nucio and the *Silua de varios romances* at Saragossa by Esteban de Nágera. The vogue of the *romances* reached its highest point in the sixteenth century. They were known to everyone. Lope de Vega and all his school worked bits of *romances* into their plays. Philip II, gloomy as he often was, could quote with delight from the *Romancero*. Now in Spain itself scholars and artists scour the countryside to pick up vestiges of *romances* from old simple folk who know scarcely anything else. And now the whole world admits the merits of those untaught singers whom Théophile Gautier has described as ' ces poètes inconnus qui écrivent mieux que personne.'

V

ITALIAN INFLUENCE

THE fifteenth century gave birth to the *Romancero*, but this was not its only glory. In its appreciation of Italian genius it foreshadows the age of splendour in Castilian literature. When Lopez de Ayala translated Boccaccio, he could not know that he was setting an example which would be eagerly followed nor that Italian models would be increasingly translated and imitated, any more than his successors—men like Villena, Imperial, Santillana and Mena (to whom is due the perfection of the *versos de arte mayor*)—could know that they were preparing the way for a literary revolution. It is, perhaps, not unsymbolical of the spread of ideas that the fifteenth century should witness the appearance in Spain of the first book of travel by the hand of one 'who made the Golden Journey to Samarcand,' nor that the immense success of the *Coronica Sarrazyna* as an indication of popular taste should anticipate the advent of *Amadis de Gaula* (in Montalvo's recast), and the chivalresque novel. Belonging to this period, in point of time alone, are two didactic compositions in the taste of the thirteenth century. One is the *Libro de los quentos*[1] formerly

[1] Ed. P. de Gayangos, 1857, in Bib. de Autores Esp., LI; ed. G. T. Northup [*Modern Philology*, v], Chicago, 1908.—See:

called, from a misreading of the manuscript, *Libro de los gatos*. It is a collection of short stories and fables written in a slightly diffuse style some time between 1400 and 1420, and taken from the *Fabulae* or *Narrationes* of the English Cistercian monk Odo of Cheriton (d. 1247). *El libro de enxemplos por a. b. c.* (or *Suma*), composed between 1400 and 1421 by Clemente Sanchez de Vercial[1] (1370 ?-1426 ?), consists of stories alphabetically arranged and drawn from such sources as *Barlaam and Josaphat*, St. Isidore of Seville and Pedro Alfonso. The manuscript, as originally found, was defective and began at the letter *c*. In 1878, however, Morel-Fatio discovered the missing fragment and thus brought up the total of three hundred and ninety-five *ejemplos* to four hundred and sixty-seven. According to him, Sanchez de Vercial, who between 1421 and 1425 wrote a *Sacramental en romance*, merely translated one of the numerous *Alphabeta exemplorum* popular in the Middle Ages. The Spanish version contains no evidence of local colour. That is true. It is also true that Morel-Fatio's theory is based mainly on the existence of a Catalan book of much the same type, *Recull de exemplis e miracles, gestes e faules e altres ligendes, ordenades per a. b. c*, which has been proved to be a translation of the *Alphabetum narrationum* by Etienne

H. Knust, *Das Libro de los Gatos*, in *Jahrbuch für romanische und englische Literatur*, VI (1865), pp. 1-42, 119-141; G. C. Keidel, *Notes on Æsopic Literature in Spain and Portugal during the Middle Ages*, in *Zeitschrift für romanische Philologie*, XXV (1901), pp. 720-730.

[1] *El libro de exemplos* . . . ed. A. Morel-Fatio, in *Romania*, VII (1878), pp. 481-526.—See: T. F. Crane, in Introduction to *The Exempla . . . of Jacques de Vitry*. 1890 (Folk-Lore Society Publications, 26).

ITALIAN INFLUENCE

de Besançon (d. 1294). The legend of Buddha as found in *Barlaam and Josaphat* made its way into Europe through a Greek translation of an Arabic recast from the Sanscrit original *Lalita-Vistara*. Translated into Latin towards the twelfth century, it became generally known through Vincent de Beauvais's summary, *Speculum historiale*, written about 1250, and was frequently utilized in Spain after its introduction by Juan Manuel in his *Libro de los Estados*.

The *Danza de la Muerte*,[1] written probably in the first half of the fifteenth century and too hastily ascribed to Santob, seems likely to be a recast of some unknown French original. But this is a matter for conjecture. It evidently bears a relationship to the *Totentanz* (1463) of Lübeck and the *Danse Macabre* of the Saints Innocents of Paris. The *Danza de la Muerte*, after a few prose lines, is written in *versos de arte mayor*, which were not known till Santob was dead. The substance of the *Danza* is satirical and allegorical: Death invites thirty-three victims to a sinister festival: a cleric and a layman always alternate. Thus there is a Pope, then an Emperor, next a Cardinal and a King; these are followed by a patriarch and a duke and so forth. Nothing could be more unlike Santob's concise, gnomic manner. The *Danza* is not, except superficially, dramatic, but it gave rise to productions such as *Las cortes de la Muerte*, a drama begun by Micael de Carvajal and finished by Luis Hurtado, to which reference is made later in *Don Quijote* (II, ch. xi).

[1] Ed. R. Foulché-Delbosc, Barcelona, 1907 (Textos castellanos antiguos, 2).—See: W. Seelmann, in *Die Totentänze des Mittelalters*. Norden-Leipzig, 1893; H. R. Lang, *A passage in the 'Danza de la Muerte,'* in *The Romanic Review*, III (1912), pp. 415-421.

If, however, the *Danza de la Muerte* is little more than an arrangement of a French original, the chief merit of its unknown author would lie in his improvement on the octaves of the *versos de arte mayor*, which are still only faintly adumbrated in Lopez de Ayala and the Archpriest of Hita.

From the time of Alphonso X there had existed in Portugal and in Galicia a school of lyrical poets whose delicate compositions are reproduced in the *Canzoniere portoghese della Biblioteca Vaticana*,[1] the *Canzoniere portoghese Colocci-Brancuti* and the *Cancioneiro da Ajuda*.[2] Towards 1445, Juan Alfonso de Baena made a Spanish song-book of the same kind, the *Cancionero de Baena*,[3] and included in it somewhat at random contributions from contemporary and from earlier poets. His anthology thus represents the last Castilian writers of the Galician school and the Castilian Italianates. Baena figures in it as the author of some poor performances: the one good poem to his credit, dedicated in 1443 to John II, he omits to put in. The Galician school has such representatives as Alfonso Alvarez de Villasandino (or de Illescas), an importunate beggar and dexterous versifier whom Pero Niño, the flaunting Conde de Buelna, employed to write his love-songs; Gonzalo Rodriguez, the merry-humoured Archdeacon of Toro, who was one of the witnesses of the Treaty between Castile and Portugal in 1383 on the occasion of John I's marriage with the daughter of King Ferdinand of Portugal,

[1] Ed. E. Monaci, Halle a. S. 1875.
[2] Ed. C. Michaëlis de Vasconcellos, Halle, 1904, 2 vols.
[3] *Cancionero de Baena*, ed. E. de Ochoa, Madrid, 1851.—See: M. Menéndez y Pelayo, in *Antología de poetas líricos*, etc. Madrid, 1893. IV, pp. xxxviii-xcvi.

ITALIAN INFLUENCE

and whose verses are as redolent of the joy of living as any by the Archpriest of Hita; Juan Rodriguez de la Cámara and Macias *o Namorado*. To these two, always closely linked in association, a legend attaches. Nothing definite is known about Macias,[1] the eternal lover, though he is wrongly supposed to have been a page to Henry III or to Villena. Of his merits as a poet it is difficult to judge, since there are only five compositions of his in the *Cancionero de Baena*: other poems, said to be by him, are fragmentary and more or less authentic. Macias survives by virtue of his legend. As the *grande e virtuoso martir de Cupido* he has passed into history and is celebrated by Santillana in *El Infierno de los Enamorados*; by Lope de Vega in *Porfiar hasta morir*; by Larra in *El doncel de don Enrique el Doliente* (1834) and in *Macias* (1834): he reappears in *La Celestina* and in *El Español mas amante y desgraciado Macias* (1704). According to Don Pedro, the Constable of Portugal, Macias, summoned by a jealous husband to stand aside, cried out that until death ended his troubles and his life, he would not stir from the place where his lady had once stood, whereupon he was instantly slain. This is one version of the story: another runs that as he lay in the dungeon of Arjonilla, he was overheard singing his platonic love and was shot by an arrow flung from the husband's bow. It is worth noting that his myth seems to be based on his own song, *Ai sennora, en quen fiança*. Macias's friend and admirer

---

[1] *Poesías*, ed. H. A. Rennert, in *Macias, o Namorado, a Galician trobador*, Philadelphia, 1900; ed. H. R. Lang, in *Cancioneiro gallego-castelhano*. New York, 1902.—See: M. Menéndez y Pelayo, in *Antología de poetas líricos*, etc. Madrid, 1893. IV, pp. lvii-lxii.

Juan Rodriguez de la Cámara [1]—also called from his birthplace del Padron—was probably born about the end of the fourteenth century and died towards the middle of the fifteenth century. An unfortunate love-passage with some court-lady, through which he seems temporarily to have lost his reason, gave rise to the wildest tales about him. Rumour said that he was loved by a queen, and tradition would make him the lover of Isabel, the Portuguese wife of John II whose marriage with the Castilian king took place in 1447; of Juana, who married Henry IV in 1455; of an unnamed Queen of France. The little that is known about Rodriguez de la Cámara tells against these conjectures. His exile followed probably on the affair at Court; he went on a pilgrimage to Jerusalem; he entered the service of Cardinal Juan de Cervantes (d. 1453), who was Bishop of Tuy from 1430 to 1438 and later Archbishop of Seville; in 1445 he became a Franciscan friar. It would be surprising if Rodriguez de la Cámara were really the author of the three famous *romances*—*El Conde Arnaldos*, *Rosa Florida*, the *Infantina* —which bear his name: his only contribution to the *Cancionero de Baena* shews little poetical accomplishment. Apart from his admiration for Macias and his own legend, he is remembered as the writer of *El sieruo libre de Amor* (1439-1440), which he composed while he was in the train of Juan de Cervantes. The book—a novel of sentiment purporting to relate

---

[1] *Obras*, ed. A. Paz y Mélia, 1884 (Soc. de Bibliófilos Esp., 22). —See: P. J. Pidal, *Vida del trovador Juan Rodríguez del Padrón*, in *Estudios literarios*, 1890. II, pp. 7-37 (Col. de Escritores Cast., 83); P. Atanasio Lopez, *La literatura crítico-histórica y el trovador Juan Rodríguez de la Cámara o del Padrón*. Santiago, 1918.

his amorous adventures—is based on Boccaccio's *Fiammetta*, and contains the allegorical *Estoria de dos amadores, Ardanlier e Liesa*. The translation into French of his *Triunfo de las donas* argues a certain vogue, but nothing more. Rodriguez de la Cámara's interest lies elsewhere; in his preference for Castilian he announces the approaching supremacy of that language.

With the exception of the Chancellor Lopez de Ayala, who figures once in the *Cancionero de Baena*, Pero Ferrus (or Ferrandes) is the oldest representative of the Castilian school. He forms a link between the two schools and is interesting chiefly for his passing reference (found in the *Dezyr, Los que tanto profasades*, addressed to Lopez de Ayala) to *Amadis de Gaula— Amadys el muy fermoso*. A truer poet is Ferrant Sanchez Talavera, Knight of the Order of Calatrava, who died probably a little before 1443. His *dezir, Por Dios, señores, quitemos el velo*, on the death of the Admiral Ruy Diaz de Mendoza, anticipates in some measure the *Coplas* of Jorge Manrique and entitles the writer to a place considerably above other contributors to the *Cancionero de Baena*. On the Italian side the most potent force was undoubtedly Francisco Imperial,[1] a Genoese by descent, son of an Italian father who settled as a jeweller at Seville. It would be futile to pretend that Imperial was a great poet, but he had all the gifts that were needed for his object—a thorough knowledge of Italian, a happy faculty of versifying in Spanish and a boundless admiration for Dante. In his *Dezir a las syete virtudes* he records the vision splendid which he perceived as

[1] See: M. Chaves, *Micer Francisco Imperial: apuntes bio-bibliográficos*. Sevilla, 1899.

he lay asleep in an enchanted garden enclosed by battlements of emerald. A venerable sage approaches holding a book written all in characters of gold and beginning *En medio del camino*. Imperial follows his guide to where the seven cardinal virtues stand, with their attendant virtues, all symbolized by female figures of extraordinary beauty. It is not till the close of the poem that Imperial recognizes his illustrious companion, and perhaps this is not surprising, for the guide is presented as a man of sweet and gentle aspect, wearing an immensely long beard. In the last verse Imperial wakens with a bound and, the vision being ended, finds in his hand a copy of Dante ' open at the chapter which salutes the Virgin,' the last canto of *Il Paradiso*. But the intelligent reader has long before anticipated the revelation. The atmosphere is Dante's; the ideas are Dante's; and, as though to dissipate every shadow of doubt, several passages reproduce the very words of Dante. This is not plagiarism or anything approaching it; it is frank and undisguised transplantation of Dante from Italy to Spain. This is the work that Imperial was born to do, and he did it with complete success. He stimulated curiosity concerning the great Florentine poet and communicated his enthusiasm to others more influential than himself. Among his disciples were Ferrant Manuel de Lando (d. 1417 ?), who was continually engaged in polemics with the coarse-fibred Villasandino; and Gonzalo Martinez de Medina (d. 1403 ?), in whose harsh yet fine stanzas there is mention of Guelphs and Ghibellines. Another contemporary, Ruy Paez de Ribera, whose period of literary activity extends from 1397 to 1424, escapes the direct influence of Dante and gives evidence of a distinct and original talent.

ITALIAN INFLUENCE

Descended from a noble family, he seems to have fallen upon evil times and in his *dezires* he illustrates poignantly the sadness of poverty and age : certain passages have a finality which recalls Lopez de Ayala's stanzas on the *pobres cuytados*

> ' El pobre non tiene parientes ni amigo
> Donayre nin seso, esfuerço e sentido.' [1]

One of the oddest and most enigmatic figures in the history of Spanish literature is Enrique de Villena [2] (1384-1434), upon whom posterity has insisted on conferring a marquisate. Villena was the grandson of a king, but though he humiliated himself in the most shameful way, allowing his wife, Maria de Castilla, to be the mistress of Henry III, he failed to obtain a marquisate in his life-time. He appears, however, in all the usual books of reference as the Marqués de Villena, and posterity, which has raised him to this rank, has also chosen to regard him as a wizard or necromancer. His library was burnt by the public executioner after his death, because it was supposed to contain books on magic. Villena lent a certain colour to the fable by writing a treatise on the

[1] ' The poor man has no relations nor friend : he is without charm, without brains, without courage, without feeling.'

[2] *Arte de trobar*, ed. M. Menéndez y Pelayo, in *Antología de poetas líricos*, etc. Madrid, 1894. v, pp. 3-17; *Arte cisoria*, ed. F.-B. Navarro, Madrid-Barcelona [1879]; *Libro del Aojamiento o Fascinología*, in *Revista contemporánea*, iv (1876), pp. 405-422 ; *El Libro de la Guerra*, ed. L. de Torre, in *Revue Hispanique*, xxxviii (1916), pp. 497-531 ; *Tres Tratados*, ed. J. Soler, in *Revue Hispanique*, xli (1917), pp. 110-214.—See : E. Cotarelo y Mori, *Don Enrique de Villena ; su vida y obras*. Madrid, 1896 ; M. Schiff, *La première traduction espagnole de la Divine Comédie*, in *Homenaje á Menendez y Pelayo*. Madrid, 1899. i, pp. 269-307.

evil eye, *Libro del Aojamiento o Fascinologia*, which is remarkable only as a monument of credulity. His first work, the allegorical *Libro de los Trabajos de Hercules*, written in Catalan in 1417, was shortly afterwards translated into Castilian and was first printed in 1482; it is as likely to interest modern readers as his treatises on leprosy and consolation. The *Arte cisoria* or *Tractado del arte del cortar del cuchillo* (1423), a prose epic on the pleasures of eating, reveals Villena as the glutton that his contemporary, Perez de Guzman, believed him to be; 'comia mucho,' he says of him. He adds that Villena was 'muy sotil en la Poesia, gran historiador, e muy copioso y mezclado en diversas sciencias. Sabia hablar muchos lenguages...'[1] Villena's verse has disappeared; his prose is about as bad as it can be. But he has picturesqueness and his fame as a necromancer finds echoes in Quevedo's *Visita de los chistes*; in Ruiz de Alarcon's *La Cueva de Salamanca*; in Rojas Zorrilla's *Lo que queria ver el marqués de Villena* and in Hartzenbusch's *La redoma encantada*. Though not an author of distinction, Villena was a patron of literature, a man of versatile talent and of great intellectual curiosity. Contemptible as his character was, he must be regarded as one of the pioneers of the Renaissance in Spain. Though the value of his translation is not great intrinsically, the fact remains that he was the first man to translate the whole of *La Divina Commedia* into Spanish; Dante translated into prose necessarily loses in the process, but perhaps he loses less than any other poet of his rank. Villena's translation brought Dante into

[1] 'Very skilful in poetry, a great historian, a copious writer versed in various sciences. He could speak many languages.'

ITALIAN INFLUENCE

vogue, made him the fashion and thus imparted a fresh impulse to the Italian movement in Spain.

The result was speedily seen in the work of Villena's friend, Iñigo Lopez de Mendoza[1] (1398-1458), who, after the battle of Olmedo (May 19, 1445), became Marqués de Santillana and Conde del Real de Manzanares. According to his own account of the matter, Santillana was no great scholar, and one would scarcely expect him to be anything of the sort, considering the prominent part that he played in politics and on many a field of battle. But he was what Villena could never have been—an authentic lyric poet. His father, Diego Hurtado de Mendoza (d. 1404), wrote the charming *cossante*, *A aquel arbol, que mueve la foxa*; and the son inherited the father's gift. Santillana's friendship with Villena had an intellectual basis; they first met at the *jochs florals* presided over by Villena in 1414 at Saragossa. To Villena Santillana dedicated his *Pregunta de Nobles* while, at Santillana's prayer,

---

[1] *Obras*, ed. J. Amador de los Rios, Madrid, 1852; *Cancionero*, ed. R. Foulché-Delbosc, in *Cancionero castellano del siglo xv*. 1912. I, pp. 449-575 (Nueva Bib. de Autores Esp., 19); *Bıas contra fortuna*. Facsimile of the Seville ed. [1502] by A. M. Huntington, New York, 1902; *Il proemio del marchese di Santillana*, ed. L. Sorrento, in *Revue Hispanique*, LV (1922), pp. 1-49.—See: M. Menéndez y Pelayo, in *Antología de poetas líricos*, etc., Madrid, 1894. V, pp. lxxviii-cxliv; B. Sanvisenti, in *I primi influssi di Dante, del Petrarca e del Boccaccio sulla letteratura spagnuola*. Milano, 1902. pp. 127-186; M. Schiff, *La bibliothèque du marquis de Santillane*. 1905 (Bib. de l'École des Hautes Études, 153); A. Vegue y Goldoni, *Los sonetos 'al itálico modo' de don Iñigo Lopez de Mendoza, marqués de Santillana*. Madrid, 1911; C. R. Post, in *Mediaeval Spanish Allegory*. Cambridge, Mass., 1915. pp. 202-233; J. Seronde, *Dante and the French influence on the Marqués de Santillana*, in *The Romanic Review*, VII (1916), pp. 194-210.

Villena wrote his *Arte de trobar* (1415-1417) and translated Virgil and Dante, and on Villena's death Santillana wrote the *Defunssion de don Enrique de Villena, señor dotto e de exçellente ingenio*, a very indifferent piece of work. Like Lopez de Ayala before him, Santillana was not troubled by any unnecessary scruples of loyalty, and though John II conferred on him a marquisate, when the time seemed opportune he abandoned his royal master. His adaptable temperament served him well in literature: neither verse nor prose came amiss to him. His conspectus of poetry, the famous *Carta* to Don Pedro, Constable of Portugal, is written in a pleasant, ductile prose-style. But it is as a poet that Santillana excels. In him are combined the graces of both France and Italy. He is seen to most advantage when he reproduces the *aubades*—the morning songs—of the Provençal troubadours—in his mountain lays or *serranillas*, in his *dezires* and *vaqueiras*. These are replenished with an exquisite and abiding charm, a natural simplicity and elegance which defy the attacks of Time. Highly as Santillana thought of the Provençal singers and of Northern *trouvères* like Alain Chartier (1394?-1440?), he never made the mistake of placing them on the same level as Dante. Dante is for him the greatest of modern poets. He gives a high place, however, to Petrarch. On the immortal episode of Francesca da Rimini is based *El Infierno de los enamorados*, in which Santillana tells of Macias and his unhappy love; *La Comedieta de Ponça* (1444), a poem in dialogue dealing with the victory of the Genoese in 1435 over the fleets of Castile and Aragon, is penetrated with reminiscences from Petrarch, the Petrarch of *Il Trionfo della Morte*, who, together with Dante and Boccaccio, is invoked

ITALIAN INFLUENCE

in the opening lines. Petrarch again is responsible for the form of *El Triumphete de Amor*. Nor must it be supposed that Santillana's knowledge of Dante was limited to *La Divina Commedia*. There exists a fairly complete catalogue of Santillana's library which shews that it contained manuscripts of *La Vita Nuova*, *Il Canzoniere* and *Il Convivio*, as well as the available literature on the Florentine poet and his work: Villena's translation, a Spanish version of Benvenuto da Imola's commentary on *L'Inferno* and *Il Purgatorio*, a Spanish translation of a Latin commentary on the entire *Divina Commedia* and Boccaccio's life of Dante.

Yet Italianism was not Santillana's only inspiration nor, perhaps, was it always his best. In the *Bias contra Fortuna* (1448), he seeks to console his cousin, the Conde de Alba, for his imprisonment by Don Alvaro de Luna (1385?-1453), against whom he wrote the bitter diatribe *Dotrinal de Privados* (1454). Every line of this poem is charged with an intense hatred: the depth of feeling which characterizes it endows it with enduring qualities. Santillana himself most esteemed a group of forty-two sonnets which, as he proudly says, are *fechos al italico modo*. He might well pique himself on his achievement, for he was the first Spaniard who ever attempted the sonnet form. He deserves all praise for his courage, but the experiment was premature. It was repeated no more successfully some few years later by Johan de Villalpando, an Aragonese whose four hybrid sonnets written in *versos de arte mayor* may be found in the *Cancionero*[1] of Herberay. Santillana's sonnets betoken the most

[1] See: B. J. Gallardo, in *Ensayo*, etc. Madrid, 1863. I, col. 451-567.

assiduous study of Petrarch, but industry is not the one thing needful for a poet. Santillana is hampered on the sonnet's narrow plot of ground. His real charm lies elsewhere : he survives through the youthful freshness and delicacy of his graceful songs, which have been surpassed by none, not even Lope de Vega.

The leading poet of the period and an inspired master of the *versos de arte mayor* was JUAN DE MENA[1] (1411-1456). A Cordovan, he had all the brilliancy as well as the defects of his fellow-countrymen, Seneca, Lucan, Herrera and Góngora. But deeper than the influence of his native soil on Mena was that of Italy. When he was still at an impressionable age, he studied the Italian writers in their own land. He returned to Spain full of ambition to latinize his own language and to imitate Dante, a wish always fraught with unhappy results. Mena's productions are not numerous and all shew an exceptional regard in respect to form. The best known is *El Laberinto de Fortuna* (1444 ?), which was once baptized *Las Trezientas*. The poem originally consisted of two hundred and ninety-seven stanzas, three were added, in order to conform, so it was thought, with the popular title. Tradition adds that Mena, at the request of John II,

---

[1] *Cancionero*, ed. R. Foulché-Delbosc, in *Cancionero Castellano del siglo xv*. 1912. I, pp. 120-221 (Nueva Bib. de Autores Esp., 19); *El Laberinto de Fortuna* [ed. R. Foulché-Delbosc], Mâcon, 1904. See: M. Menéndez y Pelayo, in *Antología de poetas líricos*, etc. Madrid, 1894. v, pp. cxlviii-ccvi ; R. Foulché-Delbosc, *Étude sur le 'Laberinto' de Juan de Mena*, in *Revue Hispanique*, IX (1902), pp. 75-138 [Spanish trans. by A. Bonilla y San Martín, Madrid, 1903] ; B. Sanvisenti, in *I primi influssi di Dante, del Petrarca e del Boccaccio sulla letteratura spagnuola*. Milano, 1902. pp. 81-125 ; C. R. Post, *The Sources of Juan de Mena*, in *The Romanic Review*, III (1912), pp. 223-279.

ITALIAN INFLUENCE

sought to add sixty-five more stanzas to his poem to make one for each day of the year. But death cut him off before he had reached the twenty-fifth. Tradition is nearly always wrong, and never more so than in this case. The additional stanzas are not at all in the manner of Mena : moreover they contain severe criticism on John II, which would tend to make their ascription to Mena impossible. These twenty-four stanzas with the first three which were added are evidently by the hand of an independent poet and, as M. Foulché-Delbosc has shewn, Mena's share in the work is limited to the original two hundred and ninety-seven stanzas. *El Laberinto de Fortuna* is an allegorical vision after Dante : it unfolds the drama of history as seen by the seer in his miraculous journey through the past, the present and the future. In spite of the frequent obscurities, the cumbersome erudition and the fatiguing lack of simplicity, some of the episodes—those on the death of Davalos and the *sacrificio del conde de Niebla*—are very beautiful. The quiet courage of the count and his unswerving patriotism are admirably revealed in the sombre dignity of the last stanzas.

The merit of *El Laberinto de Fortuna* consists partly, perhaps, in its having reached a higher plane than had hitherto been attained in Castilian art. Its lofty ideals, its fire, the heroic actions so eloquently described in it, stirred the multitude to emulation. Mena's skill in his chosen metrical form, his stately stanzas, achieving at times a genuine beauty, and his imaginative vision gained for him a prestige which his misplaced erudition and intentional obscurity should not completely dim for us. Now impressive, now merely pompous, his verse is unequal, but it is nearly always excellent as regards technique. The same cannot be said of Mena's prose. His *Coronacion* (1438) or *Calamicleos* (as he wished it to be called), a poem on the crowning of Santillana at Parnassus with reminiscences from Dante and Jean de Meung, contains a prose commentary. This is a truly appalling performance, as bad as anything by Villena, and it is not the only incriminating evidence against Mena as a prose-writer. To him have been assigned the *Coplas de ¡Ay, Panadera!*[1] (1445), but their sprightliness of tone renders the ascription improbable. Mena's influence may be seen in some of the Neapolitan Spaniards: Carvajal, for instance, who handled with dexterity the *versos de arte mayor*, and in Don Pedro[2] (1429-1466), Constable of Portugal, and from 1464 to 1466 King of Aragon. Driven to Spain in 1449 by political events, Don Pedro spent seven years in Castile and wrote in Castilian. He was, perhaps, the first Portuguese to use that language as a literary medium; we must not lose sight of the theory according to which the author of the *Poema de Alfonso Onceno* was a Portuguese. In all Don Pedro's works a distinctly personal note is visible: though one may be called a satire and another

[1] Ed. B. J. Gallardo, in *Ensayo*, etc., Madrid, 1863. I, col. 613-617.

[2] *Coplas*, in *Cancioneiro de Reesende*, facsimile of the 1516 ed. by A. M. Huntington, New York, 1904, ed. E. H. von Kausler [*Cancioneiro Geral de Garcia de Resende*], 1846-1852. 3 vols. (Bib. des lit. Vereins in Stuttgart, 15, 17, 26); *Sátira de felice é infelice vida*, ed. A. Paz y Mélia, in *Opúsculos literarios de los siglos xiv. á xvi.* 1892. pp. 47-101 (Soc. de Bibliófilos Esp., 29); *Tragedia de la insigne Reyna Doña Ysabel*, ed. C. Michaëlis de Vasconcellos, in *Homenaje á Menéndez y Pelayo*, Madrid, 1899. I, pp. 637-732.—See: M. Menéndez y Pelayo, in *Antología de poetas líricos*, etc. Madrid, 1898. VII, pp. cx-cxxxii.

ITALIAN INFLUENCE

a tragedy, they are nothing of the kind. They are lyrical compositions in which the exile's feelings find relief. In the *Coplas del contempto del mundo* he sings with chastened melancholy life's disillusions: he recurs to the same theme in the *Tragedia de la insigne Reyna Doña Isabel*, a dialogue of alternating prose and verse shewing influences of *The Book of Job*, of Boethius and of Boccaccio. The *Satyra de felice e infelice vida* is an imitation of Rodriguez de la Cámara's *Sieruo libre de Amor*. Don Pedro's prose has all the defects of Mena's: his verse is relatively pure and has many of Mena's qualities.

To the region of travels belongs the *Historia del gran Tamorlan, e Itinerario y enarracion del viaje, y relacion de la embaxada* by Ruy Gonzalez de Clavijo[1] (d. 1412). It is the account of a journey from Puerto de Santa Maria to Samarcand, undertaken on March 22, 1403, by the author, the friar Alfonso Paez de Santa Maria and Gomez de Salazar as envoys from Henry III to Tîmûr. Salazar died on the way in July 1404, but his companions reached the Mongolian capital in September of the same year, and left it most unwillingly in the middle of November. Gonzalez de Clavijo draws a striking picture of the terrible conqueror in his old age and of the state of things in Central Asia: the appalling punishments inflicted on profiteers in boots or in meat: the joviality of Tîmûr's wife who felt it a stain on her hospitality if any guests were sober enough to stand up on their feet: tales of

[1] *Historia del gran Tamorlan.* Madrid, 1782; *Narrative of the Embassy of Ruy Gonzalez de Clavijo to the Court of Tîmûr at Samarcand, A.D. 1403-6.* Translated... by Sir Clements R. Markham. London, 1860 (Hakluyt Society).

strange animals seen for the first time—ostriches, elephants and giraffes. All these experiences are related with agreeable frankness by Gonzalez, who set a fashion. Mariana writes that the *Historia del gran Tamorlan* contains, besides a relation of the embassy, ' muchas otras cosas asaz maravillosas, si verdaderas ': many will agree with him, but this need not interfere with the enjoyment of the book whose clear style makes its reading comparatively easy. About thirty years after his death, Gonzalez de Clavijo had a successor in Pero Tafur[1] (1410?-1484 ?), later *regidor* of Cordova, who describes his travels in *Andanças e viajes, por diuersas partes del mundo auidos*. These were published in 1874 from a manuscript of the eighteenth century. Tafur seems to have left Spain in the autumn of 1435 and was away some three and a half years. He had not the violent shocks of Gonzalez de Clavijo in the way of barbaric sights ; he has neither such marvels to record nor such a capacity for astonishment : he pushed as far as the Valley of Hebron where, as he engagingly relates, are the tombs of Adam and Eve. Tafur is more interested in persons than in things, and he is perhaps too obviously anxious to speak of the great people—Niccolò Conti (1419-1444), for instance—whom he met. But it would be unfair to say that he was a snob writing for snobs. He wrote from the exuberance of his spirit, putting down what he thought would best amuse and interest his readers ; and nobody can deny that he tells his story with humour, with good humour and with a disarming

[1] *Andanças é viajes*, ed. M. Jimenez de la Espada, 1874 (Col. de libros esp. raros ó curiosos, 8).—See : R. Ramírez de Arellano, in *Boletín de la R. Academia de la Historia*, XLI (1902), pp. 273-292.

simplicity. He was not, however, like Gutierre Diaz de Games, a born writer.

Perhaps some ambition to vie with the interest of Lopez de Ayala's work was responsible for the *Coronica Sarrazyna* of Pedro de Corral,[1] who was afterwards described by Perez de Guzman as a lewd and presumptuous fellow, the author of a book which he qualifies as a 'mentira y trufa paladina.' Corral appears to have begun in perfect good faith by following the *Cronica general*, the *Cronica Troyana* and the chronicle of the Moor al-Razî, recast in the *Cronica de 1344*. This involved much checking and comparing, work not congenial to Corral's temperament. The alternative title of his *Coronica Sarrazyna* was the *Cronica del rey don Rodrigo con la destruycion de España*, and as there were few extant chronicles concerning the last Gothic king, Corral proceeded to invent his authorities: a certain Eleastras, a certain Alanzuri and a certain Carestas. These persons had no existence out of Corral's ingenious fantasy: they therefore cannot have written the chronicles on which the *Coronica Sarrazyna* professed to be based. Perez de Guzman was undoubtedly right: the *Coronica Sarrazyna* was almost wholly an invention. But nothing could correct its vogue. The great Catalan poet, Ausias March, refers solemnly to it as though it were genuine history. As a matter of fact it was much more in the nature of a chivalresque novel. Its interest lies in the fact that the oldest *romances* concerning King Roderick are derived from it, and as the *Coronica Sarrazyna* was compiled about the year 1443, it

[1] See: J. Menéndez Pidal, in *Leyendas del último rey godo*. Madrid, 1906.

follows that the oldest Roderick ballads must be of later date than 1443. This is a purely incidental interest. As history, Corral's work is worth nothing. Nobody acquainted with the circumstances of its production would ever dream of making a definite statement on its authority. But it was not so in the fifteenth century. Textual criticism was then in its infancy and Corral's statements were then and for long afterwards accepted as Gospel.

Sounder historical and critical sense than Corral's was possessed by Lopez de Ayala's nephew FERNAN PEREZ DE GUZMAN[1] (1376 ?-1460 ?), who has already been quoted as a severe judge of Corral's performance. He was supposed, on insufficient grounds, to have had a hand in preparing the *Cronica del serenissimo rey don Juan el segundo deste nombre* and, if he really had taken part in this compilation, he would deserve to be credited with an excellent piece of unadorned prose-composition. He began as a poet and is thus represented in the *Cancionero de Baena*. He was an indefatigable versifier; thirteen thousand verses—among which may be mentioned the *Coplas de vicios e virtudes*, the lament on the death of Alonso de Cartagena (d. 1456), and the *Loores de los claros varones de España*—remain to

[1] *Las Generaciones, Semblanças y Obras*, etc., ed. R. Foulché-Delbosc, Mâcon, 1907; *Mar de istorias*, reprint of the 1512 ed. by R. Foulché-Delbosc, in *Revue Hispanique*, XXVIII (1913), pp. 442-622; *Cancionero*, ed. R. Foulché-Delbosc, in *Cancionero castellano del siglo xv.* 1912. I, pp. 575-759 (Nueva Bib. de Aut. Esp., 19); *Some unpublished poems of Fernan Perez de Guzman*, ed. H. A. Rennert, Baltimore, 1897.—See: M. Menéndez y Pelayo, in *Antología de poetas líricos*, etc. Madrid, 1894. V, pp. l-lxxviii; R. Foulché-Delbosc, *Étude bibliographique sur Fernan Perez de Guzman*, in *Revue Hispanique*, XVI (1907), pp. 26-55.

testify to his zeal. His *Coplas* went into seven or eight editions when the age of printing came; but it is not as a poet that Perez de Guzman survives. His reputation is based on the last part of a book whose title, *Mar de istorias*, may have been drawn from the *Mare historiarum* of the Dominican Giovanni Colonna (b. 1298). The work falls into three parts, of which the first deals with kings and emperors like Alexander and Charlemagne; the second part refers to saints and sages and one is a little surprised to find Merlin and Godefroi de Bouillon in such choice company. To these sections Perez de Guzman contributes very little, except, of course, the style and an occasional dry remark of his own, as when he mentions the legend of the Holy Grail and observes that it is a strange story full of wonderful details, which make agreeable reading, but are not to be accepted wholesale because of their strangeness. It is different with the third part which has the long title: *Las Generaciones, Semblanças y Obras de los ecelentes reyes de España don Enrique el tercero y don Juan el segundo, y de los venerables perlados y notables caualleros que en los tiempos destos reyes fueron*. Perez de Guzman alleges that this work was originally suggested by the *Historia Troiana* of Guido delle Colonne. Something like what Perez de Guzman did had been done before in Spain by Juan Gil de Zamora: but it had been done in Latin, not in Castilian. *Las Generaciones, Semblanças y Obras* is not exactly history. The book, however, is rich in historical portraits and this has caused Perez de Guzman to be compared with Tacitus and with Saint-Simon: he has neither the laconic concentration of the one nor the malignant curiosity of the other. He is more like Plutarch, though perhaps he lacks Plutarch's gossiping geniality. He describes all, or nearly all, the principal persons who were prominent in the reigns of Henry III and John II, and he acquits himself admirably of his task. His judgements are personal and do not err on the side of indulgence. Nothing is more striking than his impartiality. This is all the more remarkable, because he was partly mixed up in the politics of his time and must have had very pronounced personal dislikes and preferences. But he rarely allows them to interfere with his verdicts. He is always ready to blame a friend or a relative: he is equally ready to do justice to an enemy. He has no touch of sentimentality, he is naturally rather hard, he is an austere magistrate who shews very little consideration for those who come before him. Most of those on whom he passes sentence are men. There is one woman whose portrait is in his gallery. This happens to be Catherine of Aragon, John of Gaunt's daughter. He dismisses her curtly as: 'mucho gruesa, ... y en el talle y meneo del cuerpo, tanto parecia hombre como muger ... honesta .. no bien regida en su persona';[1] Henry III he describes as being 'muy grave de ver e de muy aspera conversacion, ansi que la mayor parte del tiempo estaba solo e malenconioso'[2]; the Constable Ruy Lopez de Avalos appears as 'hijo de un hombre de baxo estado ... hombre de buen cuerpo y de buen gesto ... muy alegre e gracioso ... muy sofrido e sin sospecha; pero como en el mundo no hay hombre sin tacha, no fue franco, y

[1] 'Very stout ... in stature and gait as like a man as a woman—honest—not careful of her person.'

[2] 'Grave in face and harsh in speech, lonely and melancholy for the most part.'

aplaciale mucho oir astrologos.'[1] Perez de Guzman has nobody quite so flamboyant or criminally interesting among his sitters as Peter the Cruel and he works on a smaller scale than Lopez de Ayala; but he has the same clear vision, equal penetration in analyzing motives and a greater surety of verbal art. It may be said that he is a trifle censorious, but then his portraits of Fernando de Aragon and of Pablo de Santa Maria shew that he could appreciate virtue when he saw it. He has the prejudices of his class : that is all that can be alleged against him except, perhaps, that his standard of virtue is impossibly high in the world of politics. His severity is unfailing; he is a just judge, but a hanging judge, and his summings-up are little masterpieces of picturesque and concise expression.

It is possible that the ascription to Mena of the *Cronica del serenissimo rey don Juan el segundo deste nombre*,[2] was due to the fact that he held the office of chronicler to John II. It is not very unnatural that the official chronicle of John II's reign should be assumed to be written by that king's official chronicler. But the thing is not acceptable in the present case. The prose-style—not distinguished but natural and clear—is much too good for Mena. If the chronicle is a composite work written in collaboration by some such authors as Pedro Carrillo de Albornoz, Diego de Valera or Lope de Barrientos, it is conceivable that

[1] 'Son of a man of lowly estate . . . well built with a handsome bearing . . . merry and amiable . . . patient and unsuspicious; but as no man is faultless, not straightforward and overfond of hearing astrologers.'

[2] Ed. Marqués de la Fuensanta del Valle, J. Sancho Rayón and F. de Zabálburu in *Coleccion de documentos inéditos*, etc. Madrid, 1891. xcix, pp. 81-464, and c, pp. 3-411.

Mena was one of them, so far as supplying materials went. So far as the style went, he must have been kept carefully in the background. According to Lorenzo Galindez de Carvajal (1472-1527?) the original sketch of the chronicle is due to the brother of Pablo de Santa Maria (1350-1432)—the Jew convert Alvar Garcia de Santa Maria who finished Lopez de Ayala's chronicle. With much less reason Alvar Garcia de Santa Maria is regarded as being the author of the *Coronica de don Alvaro de Luna, condestable de los reynos de Castilla y Leon*.[1] This remarkable chronicle was not printed till 1546, about a century after Alvaro de Luna was put to death. It was then brought out at Milan by another Alvaro de Luna, great-grandson of the statesman. Nobody supposes, however, that the younger Alvaro wrote this chronicle. Don Alvaro de Luna 'lived in his enemies' day'; he was in advance of his time. But he had his faults. For the author of the chronicle these faults are invisible: to him don Alvaro is the 'mejor caballero que en todas las Españas ovo en su tiempo.' It rarely happens that anybody appears impeccable to those of his own household. The halo is placed round one's head later, and if this holds good in the case of don Alvaro de Luna, it may, perhaps, be assumed that his *Cronica* was compiled about half a century after his ignominious death. There was much activity shewn in the compilation of private chronicles about this date, and to this time may be provisionally assigned the *Cronica particular del Cid*,[2] which was published in 1512 by Juan Lopez de Velorado, abbot of San

[1] Madrid, 1784.

[2] Facsimile of the 1512 ed. by A. M. Huntington, New York, 1903; ed. V. A. Huber, Stuttgart, 1853.

Pedro de Cardeña. It derives from Alphonso X's *Cronica general*, through a lost recast made after 1344. This recast yielded three chronicles, one of which, the *Cronica de Castilla*, gave the *Cronica particular del Cid*, on which were based many of the Cid *romances*.

The chronicle *El Victorial*, which was probably begun in 1431, was published by E. de Llaguno Amirola in 1782 with the title of *Cronica de don Pero Niño, conde de Buelna*:[1] it was done into French in 1867 by the Comte de Circourt and the Comte de Puymaigre, who included in their translation passages omitted in the Spanish edition. Pero Niño was by his own account a remarkable man : but nothing about him was more remarkable than his happiness in choosing a proxy and his precautions against oblivion. When he was a young man and wanted love-songs for his mistress, he employed Alvarez de Villasandino to write them (*Cancionero de Baena* 10, 32, 33, 42); he himself composed his epitaph in which he modestly records that he was ' ever the victor, never the vanquished by sea and land.' It is in this key that his chronicle is written by his squire, GUTIERRE DIAZ DE GAMES (1379 ?-1450), who discharged his task with astonishing skill. He always exhibits his master as first in battle, first in peace, first in love-affairs. There was never a more dreadful wild-fowl among the ladies. He led every charge to victory. The whole thing would be intolerable if Diaz de Games were a trifle less skilful. But, as it happens, he knew how to diversify the interest of his story : he sprinkles his

---

[1] Ed. E. de Llaguno Amirola, Madrid, 1782; ed. L. Lemcke, *Bruchstücke aus den noch ungedruckten Theilen des Vitorial*, Marburg, 1865; French trans. by Comte A. de Circourt and Comte de Puymaigre, Paris, 1867.

pages with apt literary quotations (some from the *Libro de Alexandre*), places his scene as often as he can abroad and diverts the reader with his enthusiasm for the ballads and roundelays that he heard at the Castle of Renaud de Troie, near Rouen. He is thoroughly aware of the fact that one may easily grow weary of continual recitals of extravagances; he counterbalances these by an occasional serious reflexion and by a flight of genuine eloquence. He has an eye for the striking detail, is always vigilant and at times rises to a high level, as in ch. 22, which may well bear comparison with Cervantes's famous discourse on arms and letters.

Many of Diaz de Games's pages are concerned with accounts of tournaments, notably in the Place de la Petite-Bretagne, or in the Cousture Sainte-Catherine near Paris, in which naturally Pero Niño distinguished himself supremely. Apart from historical evidence, there are other signs that the craze for tourneys spread greatly in John II's reign. The *Libro del Passo honroso defendido por el excelente cauallero Suero de Quiñones*[1] (written by Pero Rodriguez de Lena and abridged in 1588 by Juan de Pineda) gives a record of how Suero de Quiñones, a young knight of twenty-five, held the bridge of San Marcos at Orbigo near León against all challengers for a month in the summer of 1434. It was not a very formidable affair: one of the engaged was killed and eight or nine others were wounded. This is typical of what was rampant everywhere in Spain, and this extravagance was bound to be reflected in literature. It is mirrored in the *Coronica Sarrazyna*, an unavowed book of chivalry

[1] Facsimile of the 1588 Salamanca ed. by A. M. Huntington, New York, 1902; ed. R. Academia de la Historia, 1783.

ITALIAN INFLUENCE

whose success might have enabled any shrewd person to prophesy that when a confessed novel of chivalry was laid before the public, it would carry all before it. It is more likely than not that a large part of the greatest of chivalresque novels, *Amadis de Gaula*, was already in existence. But printing was not yet introduced into Spain, and the manuscript of *Amadis de Gaula* was only read in courts and palaces.

There are points of resemblance between Corral's *Coronica Sarrazyna* and the *Chronica intitulada Atalaya de las Coronicas* (1443) of Alfonso Martinez de Toledo[1] (1398 ?-1470 ?), afterwards Archpriest of Talavera. He is said to have been born in Toledo, but little is known of his life beyond the bare facts that in 1438 he was chaplain to John II and that ten years later he occupied a high post at the Cathedral of Toledo as well as an exceedingly remunerative chaplaincy. It is not by his *Atalaya de las Coronicas* that this clever cleric is remembered, but by a previous work generally known as *El Corbacho* (1438), which the writer had expressly desired should be entitled *Arcipreste de Talauera*, as though he wished to commemorate his sacred office. Six or seven editions of this work were printed between 1495 and 1547; some of these are entitled *El Corbacho*, others *Tratado contra las mugeres* or *Reprobacion de loco amor*. It was not until 1901 that the book received its correct name, *El Arcipreste de Talauera*. The title *El Corbacho*, which prevailed for so long, gave rise to the theory that Martinez de Toledo had undergone the influence of Boccaccio, but the similarities between *Il Corbaccio* and the Spanish book are purely superficial.

[1] *Arcipreste de Talavera*, ed. C. Pérez Pastor, 1901 (Soc. de Bibliófilos Esp., 35).— See M. Menéndez y Pelayo, in *Orígenes de la Novela*. 1905. I, pp. xc-cxx (Nueva Bib. de Autores Esp., 1).

Martinez de Toledo was evidently acquainted with the *Libre de les Dones* of Francesch Eximeniç (d. 1409) which had a great vogue in the Archpriest of Talavera's young days at Barcelona : his copy of it is still preserved. But though the subject matter of both writers is alike, their method of treatment differs. *El Arcipreste de Talauera* is an amorphous compilation written in an involved style, and though often obscure it is not lacking in force. Martinez de Toledo has a poor opinion of the human race; he finds fault with men and vituperates them with a hearty candour : but he bethinks himself that he is a man and proceeds to launch a furious diatribe against women. This attack would be more specious, if it were more moderate ; the length and monotony of his censure end by fatiguing all but the most cynical readers. Martinez de Toledo has nothing very new to say ; but he indicts half the human race with undeniable vigour ; he had his reward in the enthusiasm which his tirades elicited. *La Celestina* owes to him the inspiration of one passage at least. As a piece of polemics *El Arcipreste de Talauera* has outlived its day. But there is literary quality in the writer's invective ; he is another prose Ruiz, abounds in envenomed insults and democratizes his prose by enamelling it with a copious supply of homely proverbs, and his flouts and scoffs and jeers may still be read with interest by anybody sufficiently versed in Spanish to read him at all. He has not made that task easier by the choice of his vocabulary, which is perplexing to the best experts.

At the opposite extreme is Alfonso de la Torre,[1]

---

[1] *Vision delectable* . . . ed. A. de Castro, 1855, in Bib. de Autores Esp., xxxvi.—See : J. P. W. Crawford, *The Seven Liberal*

who about 1440 wrote the *Vision deletable de la philosophia e de las otras sçiençias* at the request of Juan de Beamonte, prior of the order of St. Jerusalem and tutor to the hapless Carlos de Viana (1421-1461), the prince whom Lope de Vega pillories in *El piadoso aragonés*. The vision is an unoriginal encyclopaedia which owes a great deal to St. Isidore of Seville's *Etymologiae*, the *Anticlaudianus* and a treatise on logic by Al-Ghazālī (1058-1111). Torre's intrinsic merits are therefore not remarkable. But he writes with dignified serenity and is a master of rather old-fashioned prose. Perhaps this archaism of manner told against him. At any rate he does not seem to have been widely read. His book was done into Italian in 1556 by Domenico Delphini, who, either through his own fault or owing to a misunderstanding, came to be regarded as its real author. In 1663, the son of the Spanish Jew publisher settled at Amsterdam, Francisco de Cáceres, chanced upon Delphini's book and resolved to translate it into Spanish. He was under the impression that he was introducing a foreign novelty into Spain, whereas he was only re-translating a work which had been compiled in Spain more than two hundred years before his time.

Arts in the 'Vision delectable' of Alfonso de la Torre, in *The Romanic Review*, IV (1913), pp. 58-75; J. P. W. Crawford, *The 'Vision delectable' of Alfonso de la Torre and Maimonides' 'Guide of the Perplexed,'* in *Publications of the Modern Language Association of America*, XXI (1913), n.s., pp. 188-212.

VI

THE LATTER PART OF THE FIFTEENTH CENTURY

THE early half of the century saw the definite establishment in Spain of Italian influence : after 1474 a vast field was opened to intellectual curiosity by the introduction of the art of printing. Not everybody, it is true, welcomed the discovery. One aristocratic poet, Manuel de Urrea, lamented the hard fate which condemned him to be read in kitchens by scullions and wenches, whereas, had he lived one hundred years sooner, his poems would have been inscribed on illuminated parchments over which the fairest ladies in the land might have pored. He was no doubt an exception and felt too deeply the degradation of being born in a late unromantic age. A fresh impetus was lent to the development of both the hieratic and the secular drama by the knightly troubadour, Gomez Manrique, an admirable example of the great feudal baron. He combines the sacred and the profane and thus has a double title to a conspicuous place in the annals of the Spanish stage. By one of the whimsies of fortune, he is not nearly so well known as his nephew, Jorge Manrique, the author of *Coplas* which Lope de Vega maintained should be printed in letters of gold. Besides the *Coplas* the fifteenth century produced one other masterpiece, *La Celestina*; and in *Amadis de Gaula* it opened the way to the long series of chivalresque novels whose extravagances were to suggest to Cervantes the idea of *Don Quijote*. To *La Celestina* and *Amadis de Gaula* belongs the honour of being the two earliest Spanish works to go the round of the world.

While the *versos de arte mayor* were being written by Mena at the court of John II, a corresponding poetical activity was afoot among the Spanish poets in the suite of Alphonso V of Aragon (1416-1458) at Naples. A good many of these were Catalans, but when they found themselves in an Italian atmosphere, some of them left off writing in Catalan and took to Castilian instead. They are represented principally in the *Cancionero de Stúñiga*,[1] whose two first poems—*A cabo de mis dolores* and *Oh triste partida mia*—are by Lope de Stúñiga, one of the knights who with his cousin, Suero de Quiñones, shared the honours of the chivalrous deeds celebrated in the *Passo honroso*. These writers were naturally not untouched by Italian influence. Johan de Andújar,[2] for instance, had

[1] Ed. Marqués de la Fuensanta del Valle and J. Sancho Rayon. Madrid, 1872 (Col. de libros esp. raros ó curiosos, 4).—See: B. Croce, in *Primi contatti fra Spagna e Italia* [*Atti dell' Accademia Pontaniana*, XXIII] Napoli, 1893; B. Croce, in *La lingua spagnuola in Italia*. Roma, 1895; G. Mazzatinti, in *La biblioteca dei rè d'Aragona in Napoli*. Rocca S. Casciano, 1897; A. Farinelli, in *Rassegna bibliografica della letteratura italiana*, VII (1899), pp. 261-292; B. Croce, in *La Spagna nella vita italiana durante la Rinascenza*. Bari, 1917; A. Farinelli, in *Giornale stor. della lett. ital.*, LXXI (1918), pp. 243-302.

[2] *Loores*, etc., ed. R. Foulché-Delbosc in *Cancionero castellano del siglo xv*. 1915. II, pp. 210-215 (Nueva Bib. de Autores Esp., 22).

evidently read Dante before he wrote his *Loores al señor Rey don Alfonso*, which was first printed in the *Rimas inéditas del siglo xv* of Eugenio de Ochoa (1815-1872). A more outstanding figure was Carvajal[1] (or Carvajales), who has already been mentioned in connexion with the *romances*. He reproduces with happy effect the martial note of Mena's music, which is heard also in the allegorical *Nao de Amor* of Johan de Dueñas.[2] But the stream of inspiration of these poets soon ran dry. We pay them a passing tribute and return to Spain where the deplorable Henry IV was on the throne.

His turbulent reign was marked by the production of political satires, some of them of a very virulent kind, marked by the grossest personalities. A satire of this bad type is found in *Las Coplas del Provincial*. It is too coarse for quotation and would be negligible if it had not caused so much pain to private persons that frequent attempts were made to suppress it. It has some ability: but it is the ability of a malignant criminal who has not been identified as yet. *Las Coplas del Provincial*[3] were written between 1465 and 1473. They have been ascribed variously to Rodrigo Cota, to Anton de Montoro, to Hernando del Pulgar and

[1] *Canciones*, etc., ed. R. Foulché-Delbosc, in *Cancionero castellano del siglo xv.* 1915. II, pp. 601-619 (Nueva Bib. de Autores Esp., 22).

[2] *La Nao de Amor* [and other poems], ed. R. Foulché-Delbosc, in *Cancionero castellano del siglo xv.* 1915. II, pp. 195-204 (Nueva Bib. de Autores Esp., 22).

[3] Ed. R. Foulché-Delbosc, in *Revue Hispanique*, v (1898), pp. 255-266.—See M. Menéndez y Pelayo, in *Antología de poetas líricos*, etc. Madrid, 1896. VI, pp. iv-xiii; R. Foulché-Delbosc, *Notes sur 'Las coplas del Provincial,'* in *Revue Hispanique*, VI (1899), pp. 417-446.

to Diego de Acuña, but they are more likely to be the work of a group of obscene libellers. More readable are the anonymous *Coplas de Mingo Revulgo*[1] (1456), a satire in thirty-two octosyllabic stanzas in which the shepherds, Mingo Revulgo and Gil Arribato, speak respectively on behalf of the lower and the upper classes. They both recognize that Esperilla (Spain) is going to ruin; Mingo Revulgo puts all the blame for this on the wretched king Candaulo (Henry IV), on the Portuguese shepherdess (Guiomar de Castro, the King's mistress) and on the wolf who ravens in the fold (Beltran de la Cueva, the king's favourite). Gil Arribato argues that the Spanish people have brought their evil fate on themselves and that things must be worse before they can be better. It is doubtful whether the *Coplas de Mingo Revulgo* are really a popular composition; they seem to be so in certain passages, but those lines may be merely an imitation of popular forms of speech by a clever literary person who used this trick to lend dramatic colour to an undramatic work.

The *Coplas de Mingo Revulgo* are much less violent, and are therefore more telling, than *Las Coplas del Provincial*. Violence is the characteristic of many compositions of this period. It is a trait found in abundance in the verse of *el Ropero de Córdoba*, Anton de Montoro[2] (1404?-1480?), who, when he was not in his shop—he was a second-hand clothes-dealer—

[1] Ed. B. J. Gallardo, in *Ensayo*, etc. Madrid, 1863. I, col. 823-854.

[2] *Cancionero*, ed. E. Cotarelo y Mori, Madrid, 1900.—See: M. Menéndez y Pelayo, in *Antología de poetas líricos*, etc. Madrid, 1896. VI, pp. xx-xxxviii; R. Ramírez de Arellano, *Ilustraciones á la biografía de Antón de Montoro*, in *Revista de Archivos*, etc.

enjoyed himself hurling insults at all and sundry. Allowances should, perhaps, be made for Montoro. Fate was not kind to him. His position was humble, his means were small, he was a convert Jew not welcomed by Christians and detested as an apostate by his former brethren: he had a thick skin, was steeped in a bad social condition, and did not realize how wounding his vituperation was to others, even though those others, in self-defence, retorted on him in his own vein. He had no delicacy of taste, no gift of lofty inspiration : on the massacres instigated by Fernando Alonso de Córdoba, an episode which Lope de Vega has immortalized in *Los Comendadores de Córdoba* (1587 ?), he only succeeded in producing a dull, prosaic poem. The ascription to him of two most scandalous pieces in the *Cancionero de obras de burlas provocantes a risa* (1519)—the *Pleyto del Manto* and an obscene parody of *Las Trezientas*—as well as of *Las Coplas del Provincial* is suggestive of the reputation that he made for himself. But Montoro, though a low and paltry creature, had wit, as he shews in his onslaughts against that wretched rhymester, Juan Poeta (or Juan de Valladolid), son of the public town-crier. And besides wit, Montoro had character of a kind. Though he had abandoned the Jewish religion, he made no attempt to sever himself from his race, and he rises to real dignity of expression in his protests against the persecutions and massacres to which the Jews of his time were beginning to be subjected some twenty or thirty years before they were expelled *en masse* from Spain.

IV (1900), pp. 723-735 ; E. Buceta, *Antón de Montoro y el 'Cancionero de obras de burlas,'* etc., in *Modern Philology*, XVII (1919), pp. 651-658.

Montoro spent a good deal of his very real talent in futile controversies and insolent attacks. He was perhaps justified as regards the Toledan RODRIGO COTA[1] (d. before 1495), a baptized jew like Montoro himself, but ashamed of his descent. This brought down upon him the wrath of Montoro, who brands him unmercifully in *Gentilhombre de quien so* for exciting the populace against his brethren. On very slender grounds Cota has had ascribed to him all manner of compositions from the *Coplas de ¡ Ay Panadera!* to the opening scenes of the *Celestina*. More authentic and of significant interest is the burlesque Epithalamium, discovered by M. Foulché-Delbosc, and written by Cota about 1472 to revenge himself on the King's Treasurer who had omitted to invite him to his wedding. But this antisemite Hebrew's title to fame rests on the *Dialogo entre el amor y un viejo*. Though there is no ground for thinking that this piece was ever intended for the stage, it is full of dramatic vivacity and its action is clear, arresting and swift. It was imitated by Juan del Enzina in *Del amor* and in *Cristino y Febea* and more textually reproduced in a recast made apparently in Naples. The versification is admirable,

[1] *Obras*, ed. R. Foulché-Delbosc, in *Cancionero Castellano del siglo xv*. 1915. II, pp. 580-591 (Nueva Bib. de Autores Esp., 22); *Diálogo entrel Amor y vn Viejo* [and an *esparsa*], ed. J. A. de Balenchana, in *Cancionero general de Hernando del Castillo*. Madrid, 1882. I, pp. 297-308 (Soc. de Bibliófilos Esp., 21); [ed. R. Foulché-Delbosc and A. Bonilla y San Martín] Madrid, 1907 (Bib. Oropesa, IV); *Une poésie inédite de Rodrigo Cota*, ed. R. Foulché-Delbosc, in *Revue Hispanique*, 1 (1894), pp. 69-72.—See: A. Miola, *Un testo drammatico spagnuolo del xv secolo*, etc., in *In memoria di Napoleone Caix e Ugo Angelo Canello. Miscellanea di filologia e linguistica*. Firenze, 1886. pp. 175-189; M. Menéndez y Pelayo, in *Antología de poetas líricos*, etc. Madrid, 1896. VI, pp. ccclxxvi-ccclxxxiii.

the tone of the dialogue in harmony with the subject. Love essays his wiles against an old man who, pleading age and reason, bids the god leave '. . . el pobre coraçon —retraydo en su rincon': he is persuaded to listen, submits and is mischievously derided for his submission. The delicate restraint of the satire, its humour and its dainty execution make of the *Dialogo entre el amor y un viejo* a veritable little masterpiece.

Apart from his loyal constancy to racial traditions, Montoro had little to recommend him but his scurrilous wit, and it is rather astonishing to find that he was esteemed by Juan Alvarez Gato[1] (1430 ?-1496 ?), a knightly poet on whom great praise is showered by a strong opponent of Montoro, Gomez Manrique. Alvarez Gato's poems and *villancicos*, delicate in sentiment and dainty in form, make him no unworthy predecessor of Juan del Enzina. His name instinctively recalls that of his *Muy grande amigo*, Hernan Mexia,[2] one of the *veinticuatro* of Jaen, known for the satire *Los defectos de las condiciones de las mugeres*. This was based on Pedro Torrellas's *Coplas de las calidades de las donas*, a feeble work which gave rise, however, to innumerable replies and counter-replies. In untrammelled fancy, vigour and mischievous grace Mexia leaves his model far behind.

[1] *Cancionero*, ed. R. Foulché-Delbosc, in *Cancionero castellano del siglo xv*. 1912. I, pp. 222-269 (Nueva Bib. de Autores Esp., 19).—See: M. Menéndez y Pelayo, in *Antología de poetas líricos*, etc. Madrid, 1896. VI, pp. xxxix-liv; C. Michaëlis de Vasconcellos, in *Revista Lusitana*, VIII (1902), pp. 241-244.

[2] *Cancionero*, ed. R. Foulché-Delbosc, in *Cancionero castellano del siglo xv*. 1912. I, pp. 269-287 (Nueva Bib. de Autores Esp., 19); ed. H. A. Rennert, in *Der spanische Cancionero des Brit. Mus.* Erlangen, 1895.

Pero Guillen de Segovia (1413-1474 ?),[1] a native of Seville, deserves mention for his verse-translation of the Seven Penitential Psalms, *Los salmos penitenciales*, which are to be found in the *Cancionero general de Hernando del Castillo* (1511), an anthology in which are represented most of the fifteenth century poets. The *Salmos* have a dignity of expression and a note of personal inspiration that is lacking in the earlier prose version of the Scriptures by the Rabbi Mosé Arragel de Guadalajara. Guillen de Segovia's few poems, as well as his rhymed dictionary, *La Gaya de Segovia o Silva copiosissima de consonantes para alivio de trobadores* modelled on Jaime March's *Libre de concordances* (1371 ?), are still unpublished. Guillen de Segovia was unfortunate in his life. A follower of Alvaro de Luna, he fell into poverty after his patron's death on the scaffold and was only saved from despair by the offices of a kindly friar who introduced him into the household of the Archbishop Carrillo.

With GOMEZ MANRIQUE[2] (1415 ?-1490 ?) the drama seems to come into new life again. Spanish literature practically begins with a play, the *Auto de los Reyes Magos*. There is nothing else to compare with

[1] *Los siete salmos penitenciales*, ed. J. A. de Balenchana, in *Cancionero general de Hernando del Castillo*. Madrid, 1882 (Soc. de Bibliófilos Esp., 21).—See : O. J. Tallgren, *Estudios sobre la Gaya de Segovia. Capítulos de introducción á una edición crítica.* Helsinki, 1907 ; H. R. Lang, *The so-called 'Cancionero de Pero Guillen de Segovia,'* in *Revue Hispanique*, XIX (1908), pp. 51-81.

[2] *Cancionero*, ed. R. Foulché-Delbosc, in *Cancionero castellano del siglo xv.* 1915. II, pp. 1-154 (Nueva Bib. de Autores Esp., 22). —See : M. Menéndez y Pelayo, in *Antología de poetas líricos*, etc. Madrid, 1896. pp. lv-ciii.

it for over two centuries. Innocent III issued in
1210 an edict prohibiting religious plays on account
of the secular elements which disfigured them, causing
more amusement than edification. These half-sacred
and half-lay plays were then given outside in some
public square capable of holding large crowds. The
restraints of the sanctuary being removed, further
licence was indulged in. Short sketches, personal
caricatures of local men, were written. These were
the *juegos de escarnio* which were finally forbidden
by statute. The suppression of such plays would
appear to have been complete: at any rate none of
them survive. But the passion for scenic presentation
is irrepressible. We have evidence that plays continued to be given in the Eastern provinces of Spain.
At Elche to this day there is performed on the fourteenth and fifteenth of August each year a play on the
Assumption of Our Lady—the *Misterio de Elche*[1]—
based on the fourteenth century *Representació de la
Asumpció de madona Santa Maria*. All through the
reigns of John II and Henry IV we read of *momos*,
spectacular plays at court. Evidently the drama was
beginning to raise its head again, and if somebody of
position would only support it, it was likely to have a
chance of success. Gomez Manrique was the man
destined to do this. A great noble, who took an active

[1] *Auto lírico-religioso en dos actos, representados todos los años
en la iglesia parroquial de Santa María de Elche los días 14 y 15
agosto.* Madrid, 1896. (*Boletín de la Sociedad esp. de excursiones.*)
See: M. Milá y Fontanals, in *Obras completas.* Barcelona,
1895. VI, pp. 221 and 324-347; F. Pedrell, *La Festa d'Elche
ou le drame lyrique liturgique espagnol.* Paris, 1906; H.
Mérimée, in *L'Art dramatique à Valencia.* Toulouse, 1913.
pp. 45 ff; J. B. Trend, in *A Picture of Modern Spain.* London,
1921. pp. 213-231.

part in the rebellions against John II and Henry IV, he had no literary ambitions. In a dedicatory letter to the copy of his *Cancionero* which was coaxed out of him by the Conde de Benavente, he asks that ' Muy magnifico e virtuoso señor' to keep the work hidden under lock and key, so that—he adds with a flash of attractive humour—he may continue to enjoy the good opinion of those to whom his works are unknown. Frankly, it is not as a poet that Gomez Manrique appeals to us chiefly,—though he has some good pieces. His reply to Torrellas : *Coplas que fizo Mosen Pero Torrellas contra las damas, contradichas por Gomez Manrique* is characteristically chivalrous, and there is genuine emotion in the *Defunzion del noble caballero Garci-Lasso de la Vega* as well as in the stanzas to his wife on the death of his two sons. He is historically interesting also because he writes occasionally in Galician and is the last of the Castilian poets to use the Galician tongue.

Gomez Manrique played his rôle in the development of the drama, not by means of patronage, but by direct and personal intervention. Among his works is a play on the Nativity : *La representacion del Nacimiento de Nuestro Señor*, the oldest *auto del nacimiento* in Spanish. St. Joseph, the Virgin, an angel, three shepherds, a choir of angels and the angels Gabriel, Michael and Raphael appear in the piece, which is one hundred and eighty lines long. Naturally the dramatic action is slight; yet the scene is set and illustrated with a fitting simplicity, and the play ends with a touching cradle-song to the Divine Infant who has grown rather restless when the instruments of His future Passion—the lance and the nails and so forth—are shewn to Him one by one. Reminiscences of this song have, perhaps, found their way into Lope de Vega's *Pastores de Belen*. The *Representacion* was performed in the convent at Calabazanos where the author's sister, Da. Maria Manrique, was Mother-Vicar at the time, A simpler piece still is the [*Lamentaciones*] *fechas para Semana Santa* with the refrain ¡*Ay dolor!* which would imply that it was chanted in the open air. Gomez Manrique's *Cancionero* contains one or two things of similar character, but these do not seem to have been acted. He was luckier with two little allegorical pieces. One is a *momo* to commemorate the birth of a nephew: it is a trifle in which Justice, Prudence, Temperance, Fortitude, Faith, Hope, and Charity, each recited a stanza. The other is a trifle too but is not without interest, for it was written at the command of the Infanta Isabel to celebrate the birthday of her brother Alfonso, and was produced at Arévalo on Nov. 14, 1467. Gomez Manrique's brothers had been prominent in the notorious scene at Avila nearly two and a half years earlier, when Henry IV was dethroned in effigy and the child Alfonso was proclaimed king; the writer himself was a strong partisan on the same side. He acquitted himself not ungracefully in the difficult business of writing words to be recited by courtly amateurs with no experience of the stage. He introduces the nine Muses, one of whom appears in dumb show, while each of the others declaims a stanza. The names of the seven court-ladies who had speaking parts are given; the climax is reached when the Infanta recites her congratulatory *décima*. This piece does not call for criticism, but many would remember it simply because the Infanta acted it and spoke her stanza with the rest. We do not usually associate

Isabel the Catholic with frivolities: perhaps her first and last appearance on any stage was at Arévalo in Gomez Manrique's dramatic allegory. It is only a graceful trifle, but this and his Calabazanos piece have won him a place in the history of the Spanish stage. In both departments of the drama—sacred and lay—Gomez Manrique has the enviable title of a precursor. Nothing of his is popular, but the glory of being a pioneer is his.

His nephew JORGE MANRIQUE[1] (1440?-1479), on the other hand, is known wherever Spanish is spoken. A partisan of Queen Isabel's, he was killed in an encounter at the castle of Garci-Muñoz. He has written about fifty poems altogether, ingenious and clever enough, but little more than respectable in their various kinds. Anything else he wrote is completely overshadowed by the *Coplas por la muerte de su padre* (c. 1476). These have been excellently translated by Longfellow; imitated by Camões in the *Carta terceira* (published by Juromenha); glossed by Silvestre once and by Montemayor twice. Towards the middle of the sixteenth century they were translated into Latin and also set to music by Alonso de Mudarra (1546) and by Venegas de Henestrosa (1557). There is no originality in the substance of the *Coplas*. Death is one of the great commonplaces of the world, and

[1] *Cancionero*, ed. R. Foulché-Delbosc, in *Cancionero castellano del siglo xv*. 1915. II, pp. 228-256 (Nueva Bib. de Autores Esp., 22); *Coplas por la muerte de su padre*, new critical ed. by R. Foulché-Delbosc, Madrid, 1912.—See: L. de Salazar y Castro, in *Historia de la casa de Lara*. Madrid, 1697. II, pp. 407-411; M. Menéndez y Pelayo, in *Antología de poetas líricos*, etc. Madrid, 1896. VI, pp. civ-cli; J. Nieto, *Estudio biográfico de Jorge Manrique e influencia de sus obras en la literatura española*. Madrid, 1902; *La traduction latine des 'Coplas' de Jorge Manrique*, ed. R. Foulché-Delbosc, in *Revue Hispanique*, XIV (1906), pp. 9-21.

there is nothing new to be said about it. It is Jorge Manrique's manner which gains him immortal fame: he intones the great commonplaces with a noble solemnity and sets his dirge to unforgettable music.

> ' y aunque la vida murio,
> nos dexó harto consuelo
> su memoria.'

His magnificent melody expresses what the humblest of us feels. Nothing in Spanish has come home more closely to the universal heart. By some miracle of genius, the otherwise frivolous Jorge Manrique is for one splendid instant the spokesman of the human race, and this gay trifler takes rank amongst the great immortals.

Prose is represented by Juan de Lucena[1] (d. 1506), author of the *Vida beata* (1483), written probably in 1463 and notable for its excellent style. Its originality is practically null, for Lucena follows, as close as may be, the *Dialogus de felicitate vitae* (1445) by Bartolommeo Fazio who, with Enea Silvio Piccolómini, later Pius II (1458-1464) and author of the *Historia de duobus amantibus* (1444)—a work excellently translated into Spanish and printed in 1496—was among the numerous Italian scholars whom Alphonso V gathered round him at Naples. Lucena calls his work a 'moral dialogue.' In the high Ciceronian manner, he introduces the Marqués de Santillana, Mena and Alfonso de Cartagena (1384-1456), *decus praelatorum*, Bishop of Burgos. In the second and third parts, he appears himself as an embarrassed phantom flitting uneasily

[1] *Libro de vida beata* and *Carta . . . exhortatoria á las letras*, ed. A. Paz y Mélia, in *Opúsculos literarios de los siglos xiv á xvi*. 1892. pp. 105-217 (Soc. de Bibliófilos Esp., 29).

about and only speaking when he is distinctly addressed. The subject of the discussion is the eternal question of what is happiness : it is resolved by the doubtful conclusion that happiness is not attainable in this world, which is but a preparation for the boundless felicity of the next. Lucena handles this commonplace with a certain ease of style which carries off its tedious familiarity. That is his single merit, for he really contributes nothing to the argumentative side of the case. To invest well-worn ideas with an air of novelty by sheer force of pleasing manner is to do a good deal and that is the sum of Lucena's accomplishment. His *Epistola exhortatoria a las letras*, an extravagant panegyric of Queen Isabel, survives by its form alone.

The more ambitious work of Diego de Valera [1] (1412-1487 ?), though it purports to be history, is in great part fiction. He wrote—at the request, he says, of Queen Isabel—a *Coronica de España* (1482), best known as the *Valeriana*. If Queen Isabel did ask him to write a history, she shewed a good deal less than her usual sound judgement and shrewd insight. Valera had no gift of criticism. He would have made an excellent third with Amadis and Don Quixote. He was a knight-errant *doublé* with a political missionary. At first he is content to follow with docility the record of events given in the *Cronica general* : as he draws on, he comes to his own time and allots

[1] *Memorial de diversas hazañas*, ed. C. Rosell, 1878, in Bib. de Autores Esp., LXX ; *Epístolas . . . con otros cinco tratados del mismo autor*, ed. J. A. de Balenchana, 1878 (Soc. de Bibliófilos Esp., 16).—See : M. Menéndez y Pelayo, in *Antología de poetas líricos*, etc. 1894. v, pp. ccxxxvi-cclvi ; G. Cirot, in *Bulletin hispanique*, XI (1909), pp. 425-442 ; L. de Torre y Franco-Romero, *Mosén Diego de Valera* [*Bol. de la R. Academia de la Historia*, LXIV]. Madrid, 1914.

himself an important rôle in contemporary developments. His anxiety to be in the limelight is so patent, his vanity is so obvious, his *parti-pris* is so conspicuous and so undissimulated that nobody could be misled. It is difficult to believe that he was taken quite seriously by his contemporaries. It may be that he benefited by the absence of other good chronicles. It may be that people were delighted with his unintentional and unedifying self-revelations. There is no denying, too, that Valera has a pretty pen. This is very evident in his *Epistolas enviadas en diversos tiempos a diversas personas*. A better historian than Valera is Diego Rodriguez de Almella[1] (1426 ?-1492 ?), Archpriest of Santibañez, chaplain to Queen Isabel and afterwards canon of Carthagena, who wrote the *Tractado que se llama Valerio de las estorias escolasticas de España* (1487). He took for his model the *De dictis factisque venerabilibus* of Valerius Maximus. Rodriguez de Almella's defect is that he will be always pointing a moral to adorn the tale. His medley of moralizing and chronicling was greatly to the taste of his age, went into several editions and attained a popularity which tempted the author to compose another historical work entitled *Batallas campales* (1487). But this fell rather flat at the time and has not been much appreciated since.

The work of the Latin scholar and historian Alfonso de Palencia[2] (1423-1492) offers an appalling picture

[1] See: G. Cirot, in *Les histoires générales d'Espagne entre Alphonse X et Philippe II* (1284-1556). Bordeaux, 1905. pp. 16-18, 53-54.

[2] *Dos tratados*, ed. A. M. Fabié, Madrid, 1873 (Libros de antaño, 5); *Cronica de Enrique IV*, Spanish trans. by A. Paz y Mélia, 1904-1908. 4 vols. (Col. de Escritores Cast., 126, 127, 130, 134); *Guerra de Granada*, Spanish trans. by A. Paz y Mélia, 1909 (Col. de Escritores Cast., 138).—See: G. Cirot, *Les Décades*

of Henry IV's reign. Brought up in the household of Alfonso de Cartagena, Palencia removed to Italy and spent several years in the service of the Cardinal Bessarion (1403-1472), where he came to know Jorge de Trebisonda (1396-1484). In 1456, he succeeded Juan de Mena as official chronicler to Henry IV. In the same year and before his appointment to that post he wrote, first in Latin and then in Castilian, *La guerra y batalla campal de los perros contra los lobos*, whose date he gives as 1457, no doubt in error, as he records in the last chapter his desire to be named chronicler. It is an allegorical description of a pitched battle between wolves and dogs symbolizing political strife and written in a terse and forcible style. The same quality attracts in the *Tratado de la perfeçion del Triunfo militar* (1459), another allegorical work interspersed with tales of travel. Palencia's estimate of the Spaniard as a fighting-man shews critical sense as well as strong patriotic feeling. The tendency to latinize his prose is a considerable blemish, though not an unnatural one in a writer to whom Latin probably came more easily than Castilian. His dictionary, *Vniuersal vocabulario en latin y en romance* (1490), was eclipsed by Lebrixa's work which appeared two years later. Only part of the *Gesta hispaniensia ex annalibus suorum dierum* has been published: the description of the state of things between 1440 and 1474 recalls in its vigorous denunciation of all classes the *Coplas del Provincial*. At the date when he wrote

d'Alfonso de Palencia, la Chronique castillane de Henri IV attribuée à Palencia, etc., in *Bulletin hispanique*, XI (1909), pp. 425-442; A. Paz y Mélia, *El cronista Alonso de Palencia. Su vida y sus obras; sus 'Décadas' y las 'Crónicas' contemporáneas; ilustraciones de las 'Décadas' y Notas varias*, Madrid, 1914.

it, Palencia had left the service of Henry IV and he applies the branding-iron so untiringly that his work loses its historical character and becomes a tale of wrongs borne by an angry witness. Apart from this, his relation is interesting. It reveals Palencia as a prolific narrator who unites a gift of mordant irony with powers of penetration. A chronicle of this period, once believed to be by him, deals with much the same events viewed from a similar standpoint, but the ignorance of Latin shewn in it precludes the ascription, and it has now been proved by Sr. Paz y Mélia to be a poor translation of Palencia's chronicle. To the same scholar are due an abridged translation of the *Gesta* and the discovery of a work on the war which led to the conquest of Granada : this treats of the occurrences between 1480 and 1489, but it was interrupted in 1492 by Palencia's death.

A less unfavourable picture of Henry IV is given by his chaplain and counsellor Diego Enriquez del Castillo[1] (1433-1504 ?) in the *Cronica del rey don Enrique IV*. To this a strange story attaches. Enriquez del Castillo was by way of compiling his chronicle from day to day. Some forty days after the battle of Olmedo (Aug. 20, 1467), in which Henry IV's troops were victorious, Enriquez fell into the hands of the enemy at Segovia. His account of the battle was found on him. It was so unflattering that the chronicler was threatened with death. A full version of the story is found in the *Gesta* of Palencia, to whom the manuscript was entrusted for the purpose

[1] *Cronica del rey don Enrique el quarto*, ed. C. Rosell, 1878, in Bib. de Autores Esp., LXX.—See : J. B. Sitges, *Enrique IV y la excelente señora llamada vulgarmente Doña Juana la Beltraneja. 1425-1530*. Madrid, 1912.

of remoulding it. Palencia asserts that he sent it to the Archbishop Carrillo (1422-1482), one of the characters most roughly handled in it. At any rate Enriquez del Castillo lost the sketch of his chronicle as well as his notes and had to rely upon his memory for a relation of the first thirteen years of Henry IV's reign, whence, perhaps, the paucity of dates and a certain incoherence in the second redaction. This was written in the time of the Catholic Kings; the author's anxiety to please both sides, his disconcerting neutrality where Henry IV is concerned and his pompous, declamatory style make the work less interesting than it may have been in its original form. Enriquez del Castillo's strong point is personal description. He has a picturesque vision of individuals; but that is not enough to make an historian, even when the author has a sounder judgement, a finer sense of values and a better style than Enriquez del Castillo. A personal chronicle of this period, *Relacion de fechos del condestable Miguel Lucas de Iranzo*, attributed to Juan de Olid, gives an interesting picture of Spanish life at the time and contains some striking passages.

Enriquez del Castillo shewed some skill as a portrait painter, his description, for instance, of Henry IV in the *Cronica*—' that royal colossus with a crushed nose, a head and mane like a lion's, a cowardly debauchee who found his sole innocent pleasure in listening to melancholy music.' The same gift is possessed in a much higher degree by Hernando del Pulgar[1] (1436-1493?), author of the *Libro de los*

[1] Hernando del Pulgar has occasionally been confused with another celebrated person of a rather similar name, Hernando Perez del Pulgar (1451-1531?) who performed great feats of

claros varones de Castilla[1] (1486). It may be that Pulgar is not above borrowing at times, and he has not the sententious weight of his predecessor, Perez de Guzman. But he is a worthy second to that very great master. The *Libro de los claros varones* is excellent in fidelity and style and far superior to Pulgar's *Chronica de los muy altos y esclarecidos reyes catholicos don Fernando y doña Isabel de gloriosa memoria.* This was brought out in 1565 by the grandson of the great humanist Lebrixa and the grandson then ascribed the book to Lebrixa himself. The mistake, a very natural one, was corrected in 1567. It seems that Pulgar had lent his manuscript to Lebrixa to translate it into Latin and that Lebrixa had forgotten to return the manuscript to Pulgar's heirs. The *Chronica* is nothing more than a fulsome and insipid panegyric. Pulgar's reputation rests on his *Libro de claros varones* and on his *Cartas* (1485 ?).

Within this period falls the discovery of the New World, and this was accomplished, or perhaps re-accomplished, by Christopher Columbus, who is known in Spain as Cristobal Colon. Much interesting and illuminating information concerning him is given in the *Historia de los reyes catolicos don Fernando y doña*

arms at the siege of Granada and won for himself the sobriquet of *El de las hazañas.* He also wrote a history—*Breve parte de las hazañas del excelente nombrado Gran Capitan* (1527)—but did not wield the pen as skilfully as the sword.

[1] *Claros Varones de Castilla*, ed. E. de Llaguno y Amírola, Madrid, 1775 ; ed. J. Domínguez Bordona, 1923 (Clásicos cast., 49) ; *Crónica de los señores Reyes Católicos*, ed. C. Rosell, 1878, in Bib. de Autores Esp., LXX ; *Cartas*, ed. E. de Ochoa, 1850, in Bib. de Autores Esp., XIII.—See : P. Mazzei, *Un manoscritto della ' Cronica de los reyes católicos di Hernando del Pulgar,'* in *Revue Hispanique*, LVI (1922), pp. 345-349.

LATTER PART OF THE XV CENTURY 129

Isabel written by Andrés Bernaldez[1] (d. 1513). Bernaldez was chaplain to Diego Deza (1444-1523), Archbishop of Seville, and *cura* of Los Palacios from 1488 to 1513. He is always reverential, almost idolatrous, in his attitude to Columbus, to whom he assigns fourteen of his chapters. It is not great writing, but the man is simple and sincere and that is not so common an experience as it might be.

With the introduction of printing coincident with the accession to the throne of the Catholic kings in 1474, the sphere of literature was widened. The first book to be printed in the Peninsula was apparently *Les Obres o trobes dauall scrites les quals tracten de lahors dela sacratissima verge Maria* (1474), a book of sacred verse, from the Press of Lamberto Palmart in Valencia. Most of its forty-four contributors were Catalan; however, Francisco de Castellvi, Francisco Barceló, Pedro de Civillar and an anonymous versifier —*Hum Castellá sens nom*—wrote in Castilian. Printing, probably, has preserved for Spain her *romancero*. The Marqués de Santillana, it will be remembered, makes a contemptuous reference to the *romances* as compositions which formed the delight of lewd fellows of the baser sort. That no doubt was true at the time when the remark was made. But as the epics had come down in the world, so the *romances* went up. While the Marqués de Santillana was still alive, one or two poets of higher social condition than those whom he had dismissed with so patronizing an air, had put their names to *romances*, though their effrontery was,

[1] *Historia de los Reyes Católicos*, etc., ed. F. de Gabriel Ruiz de Apodaca, 1869-1870. 2 vols. (Soc. de Bibliófilos Andaluces); ed. C. Rosell, 1878, in Bib. de Autores Esp., LXX.

perhaps, not made known to the literary marquis. Nor was this all. It is conceivable that he would have looked down on Rodriguez de la Cámara and Carvajal, and it is only too likely that these poets would have endured his airs of superiority without any deep resentment. But even the Marqués de Santillana would have professed, if he did not feel, a deep respect for the clergy and he would have been aghast to know that men in that sacred profession were yielding to the vulgar literary taste. Yet so it was. Fray Iñigo de Mendoza [1] found room in his *Cancionero* for *romances* of an edifying type. His *Vita Christi por coplas* (1482), a poem in double *quintillas* in a mordant satirical vein, embodies dramatic elements which foreshadowed Enzina's nativity plays. But the main interest of the *Vita Christi* lies in the fact that its author introduced into it *romances*. And the development continued. Scandal invented disagreeable stories about Mendoza, but even slander left untouched the name of the Franciscan Ambrosio Montesino,[2] who was under the patronage of Queen Isabel and is reported to have been Bishop of Sardinia. Montesino was a venerable person. His *Vita Christi cartuxano* (1502-1503) found favour with Santa Teresa, who recommends it to her nuns in the *Libro de las Constituciones*. In the *Cancionero de diuersas obras de nuevo trobadas* (1508), a work mostly pietistic in character, he attacks with a certain verve the predominant social views of the day. It conveys to Spain a touch of Italian realism from Jacopone da Todi (1230 ?-1306):

[1] *Cancionero*, ed. R. Foulché-Delbosc, in *Cancionero castellano del siglo xv.* 1912. pp. 1-120 (Nueva Bib. de Autores Esp., 19.)

[2] *Cancionero de diversas obras de nuevo trovadas*, ed. J. de Sancha, 1855, in Bib. de Autores Esp., xxxv.

LATTER PART OF THE XV CENTURY

it also contains *romances*. Many of these, like Mendoza's, are devout in savour, ballads on St. Francis of Assisi, St. John the Baptist and so forth. But there is among the works ascribed to Montesino a *romance* on the death (1491) of Isabel's son-in-law, Alphonso of Portugal—*Hablando estaua la reyna*, a fragmentary anonymous copy of which Gaston Paris found in a contemporary French manuscript. This *romance* is not in the nature of a masterpiece. In fact, it is, perhaps, a little doubtful whether Montesino wrote it. As may be seen from Asenjo Barbieri's *Cancionero musical de los siglos xv y xvi*, Montesino was too much given to adaptations of popular songs, too good-natured in acceding to the requests which were made to him. For instance, he wrote three separate recasts of *Por las sierras de Madrid*, a *villancico* set to music for six voices by Francisco Peñalosa (1470 ?-1538), and the earliest example of an *ensalada*. In the case of the *romance* on Alphonso of Portugal, Montesino may very well have adapted an already existing poem. But that he wrote other ballads is beyond cavil. And when respectable bishops took to writing *romances*, the fortune of the *genre* was assured.

Everybody was not, of course, converted at once. The influence of Mena was strong and continued to be strong for a considerable time. Under that influence came the Carthusian Juan de Padilla[1] (1468-1522 ?), whose first work seems to have been *El Laberinto del duque de Cadiz con Rodrigo Ponce*

[1] *Los doze Triumphos de los doze Apostoles* and *Retablo de la vida de Cristo*, ed. R. Foulché-Delbosc, in *Cancionero castellano del siglo xv*. 1912. I, pp. 288-449 (Nueva Bib. de Autores Esp., 19).—See: M. Menéndez y Pelayo, in *Antología de poetas líricos*, etc. Madrid, 1896. VI, pp. ccxxxix-cclxiii.

de Leon (1493). In the *Retablo del cartuxo sobre la vida de nuestro redenptor Jesu Christo* (1516), a copy of which figured in Santa Teresa's library, Padilla somewhat drily versifies the life of the Saviour. There is no great attraction in the heavy allegory of his *Doze triunphos de los doze Apostoles* (1521) written in *versos de arte mayor*. Even the taste of contemporaries revolted against the pompous pretence of Padilla. But he has good lines, especially when he imitates a good original like Dante. He was reprinted in great part in 1841-42 by Miguel del Riego (d. 1844), who made himself ridiculous by comparing Padilla with Homer. He is not the least like Homer, and the best that can be said of him is that he successfully imitated Mena.

Another imitator of Mena was Garci Sanchez de Badajoz[1] (1460?-1526?), who is said to have gone out of his mind as the result of an unhappy love-affair. He reproduces the metre of Jorge Manrique's *Coplas* in the *Lamentaciones de Amor*; follows Dante in the *Infierno de Amor*; Mena and the Marqués de Santillana in his poem *Claro Escuro* and betrays reminiscences in *Las Liciones de Job*, a daring parody verging on blasphemy. But he can strike a personal note and he reaches now and then a high level of excellence as in the *romance*: *Caminando por mis males* and in *Vn sueño que soñó* or in *esparsas* such as *El graue dolor estraño* and in the *villancico*: *Lo que queda es lo seguro*, while his skill in handling the popular form of the *redondillas* stirred the enthusiasm of Lope de Vega.

---

[1] *Recopilacion en metro*, ed. V. Barrantes, 1882-1886. 2 vols. (Libros de antaño, 11, 12).—See: J. López-Prudencio, *Diego Sánchez de Badajoz*. Madrid, 1915.

Joan Escrivá,[1] ambassador of the Catholic Kings at Rome in 1497, is the author of the most celebrated poem *Ven, muerte, tan escondida*. Lope de Vega delighted in it and glossed it in the *Rimas sacras*; Calderon quoted it in one of the most moving scenes of *El mayor monstruo, los celos* (Act. III, xi); it is mentioned in *Don Quijote* (II, ch. 38), and has been excellently translated by the late Archdeacon Churton. Escrivá was a Valencian, and it is all the more remarkable that he should have produced a little gem in Castilian which was not his native tongue.

Poets are the fine flower of humanity. We always salute them as though they were of different clay from the rest of mankind.

'I salute thee, Mantovano, I that loved thee since my day began,
Wielder of the stateliest measure ever moulded by the lips of man.'

But everybody does not share that view. A writer who was himself a brilliant versifier once said: 'I have found the lover's crown of laurel better than the poet's wreath of bays.' The quotation of that line brings to mind the first model lover of the modern imaginative world: Amadis of Gaul, the type of invincible prowess and unconquerable fidelity. *Amadis*

[1] *Canciones*, ed. J. A. de Balenchana, in *Cancionero General de Hernando del Castillo*. 1882. I, pp. 517-518, 592, 606; II, pp. 421-444 (Soc. de Bibliófilos Esp., 21).—See: M. Menéndez y Pelayo, in *Antología de poetas líricos*, etc. Madrid, 1896. VI, pp. cccxxxi-cccxxxv; C. Michaëlis de Vasconcellos, *Historia de uma canção peninsular*, in *Scritti varii di erudizione e di critica in onore di Rodolfo Renier*. Torino, 1912. pp. 627-649.

de Gaula[1] seems to have been printed in the last years of the fifteenth century (the oldest edition we have is that of 1508, represented by the unique copy, now in the British Museum). Its full title is *Los quatro libros del virtuoso cauallero Amadis de Gaula.* The person responsible for this text was Garci Rodriguez de Montalvo, who declared that he had only written the fourth book and that, as regards the other three, he had merely arranged them from old originals which he had modernized and improved. In the 1519 edition published at Rome, the author is called Garci Ordoñez de Montalvo; in the edition of *Las Sergas de Esplandian* (1525), he appears as García Gutierrez de Montalvo. But that is a trifle. What are the originals of which Rodriguez de Montalvo speaks? One hears of *Amadis de Gaula* long before 1508. It is mentioned in Juan Garcia de Castrogeriz's translation of *De regimine principum* in 1350; Pero Ferrus (or Ferrandes) speaks of it in the *Cancionero de Baena*, to which he was the oldest contributor; in his time *Amadis* consisted of three books; *Amadis* is mentioned also by Lopez de Ayala in the *Rimado de Palacio*, where he bitterly accuses himself of frivolity

[1] Ed. P. de Gayangos, 1857, in Bib. de Autores Esp., XL.—See: E. Baret, *De l'Amadis de Gaule et de son influence sur les mœurs et la littérature au xviᵉ et au xviiᵉ siècle.* 2ᵉ ed. Paris, 1873; Th. Braga, *Historia das novellas portuguezas de cavalleria (Formação do Amadis de Gaula).* Porto, 1873; M. Menéndez y Pelayo, in *Orígenes de la Novela.* 1905. I, pp. CXCIX-CCXLVIII (Nueva Bib. de Autores Esp., I); R. Foulché-Delbosc, *La plus ancienne mention d'Amadis*, in *Revue Hispanique*, XV (1906), p. 815; G. S. Williams, *The "Amadis" Question*, in *Revue Hispanique*, XXI (1909), pp. 1-167; H. Thomas, *The Romance of Amadis of Gaul.* London, 1912 [reprinted in *Spanish and Portuguese romances of chivalry.* Cambridge, 1920).

for being fascinated by it. Later, towards the middle of the fifteenth century we hear of *Amadis* in Portugal, where it is ascribed to a certain Vasco de Lobeira. Who was this Vasco de Lobeira? First of all he was identified with a namesake who was dubbed knight in 1385. Let us assume that he was knighted at about the usual age of twenty-one. Then he was born in 1364. But *Amadis* is mentioned as being in existence in 1350. Everybody has given up the theory that Vasco de Lobeira wrote *Amadis*. Nevertheless the notion that *Amadis* was of Portuguese origin throve in the 'inviolate' shade. Miguel Leite Ferreira declared that he had seen the Portuguese originals in the archives of Aveiro in 1598: he was uncommonly lucky—these originals were not seen before Leite Ferreira's arrival at the castle of Aveiro and they have not been perceived since his departure. As a general rule, if a Portuguese document is not forthcoming, you are met with the statement that it was lost in the Lisbon earthquake. The assertion is not permissible in the present case, for the much-sought-for Portuguese original had vanished nearly thirty years (1726) before the earthquake occurred.

Nicolas de Herberay, who translated *Amadis* (1540-1543) into French and made it fashionable, anticipated Leite Ferreira's story. Herberay also alleged that he had seen part of the manuscript originals, but—the variant is worth noticing—these originals were in French, *en langage Picard*: his view was that the Spanish book was the recast of a French work. Recently the Portuguese theory derived some colour from the fact that the *villancico*: *Leonoreta, fin roseta* at the end of bk. II, ch. xi, of *Amadis* was found in the *Canzoniere portoghese Colocci-Brancuti* (Nos. 230, 232A), and this little poem is there signed by a certain Joan de Lobeira (1258-1285). So far as it goes, this is a point in favour of the Portuguese contention. But how far does it go? Is it not possible that the *villancico* may have been inserted in the text of *Amadis* rather late? The question cannot be answered lightly in the negative. The substance of the book gives some support to Herberay's theory. *Amadis* contains many reminiscences of the Breton lays, of Tristan, Lancelot du Lac, Maugis, Renaud and other works of French provenance. Was the original book in the Peninsula written in Portuguese or Spanish? We cannot be quite sure, though, as the Arthurian legend was much less tardy and much less widespread in Spain than in Portugal, there is perhaps a slight presumption in favour of Portugal. This Peninsular *Amadis*, was it an original composition? Surely not. So many points of resemblance to the French legends of the Round Table cannot be the result of simple chance. The probability is that the Portuguese—or it may be Spanish—*Amadis* came from the French. Did it come from a single book or was it a sort of patch-work of various texts? On the whole, perhaps the balance of evidence inclines in favour of the latter supposition. The closer we look at the text, the more our difficulties multiply. Neither its chronology nor its topography is helpful, not to say illuminating. The nomenclature of the characters sheds no light on these baffling problems. Amadis does not appear to be a Spaniard. He is Amadis de Gaula. Very good: but what is meant by Gaula? Is it Wales or is it France? Sometimes it is one, sometimes it is the other. Vindilisora and Bristoya are Windsor and Bristol, but Gravisanda is not Gravesend nor is Bangil Bangor.

It would be idle to pretend that the countless readers of *Amadis de Gaula* are absorbed in seeking solutions to the questions that have been adumbrated. What interested its earliest readers was, on the one hand, the immutable love of Amadis, son of King Perion, for the lovely Oriana, daughter of Lisuarte, King of Britain. Amadis is the perfect knight, the *preux chevalier*; Oriana is the irresistible *charmeresse*: and both are types of eternal fidelity. Lest the monotony of an unchanging passion pall, the interest of *Amadis de Gaula* is diversified by adventures innumerable in which commingle giants, dwarfs and dragons. Amadis is brave beyond the dreams of Achilles, and especially in the latter sections, *Amadis de Gaula* is the standard hand-book of Knight-errantry. In that respect it has a didactic value inasmuch as it throws light upon the social institutions of a bygone epoch. Secondly, it is to be remarked that love constitutes the supreme, and perhaps the unique, inspiration of all Amadis's acts. This love is relatively pure, faithful, delicate and poetic. It is a reflexion of the spotless exaltation of Percival and Galahad, or at any rate of the absorbing passion of Lancelot and Tristan. The love-scenes are eminently human and no less eminently Spanish. What could be more Spanish than the *coup de foudre* when Amadis first sees Oriana? Or than the interview of the two lovers at the palace-window, which reads like a vague anticipation of the deathless balcony-scene in *Romeo and Juliet*? All this is superbly human: all this has the power to enlist our sympathy and to stir our deeper emotions. Lastly, and this is—or at least was—a characteristically Spanish trait, a trait of the Spain of the Renaissance, personal loyalty is one of Amadis's most typical and most engaging qualities. His fealty to king Lisuarte is complete. Oriana comes first of all, no doubt, and this is as it should be : but after that most gracious lady, it is on behalf of his King that Amadis breaks so many lances and lays low so vast a multitude of giants.

It often has been said that there is nothing Spanish in *Amadis de Gaula*. It is true that Amadis is not Spanish; that the traditions, the element of the marvellous and even the landscape lead us to think of a very different civilization. That is true as regards non-essentials. But there is something to be said also for the view of the rather *grincheux* Brunetière : ' Il n'y a jamais eu de roman, ni plus romanesque, ni plus chevaleresque, ni par conséquent plus espagnol.' No imaginative work has corresponded more closely to the ideals of a whole epoch. It satisfied to some extent the thirst for adventures awakened by the discovery of the New World, by the commerce with strange races under strange stars, by the marvellous feats of the *conquistadores* long before Cortés saw the peak of Darien, or gazed in wonderment upon the golden cupolas of Mexico. Of the style we can claim for its numerous prose no other merit than that of continuous fluency and, at times, of pleasing adequacy. But *Amadis de Gaula* was not read by many as a model of technique. It was read because it opened a window on the infinite, the unknown, the marvellous, and for its adroit compound of earthly love and mystic passion. Not all who pored over its pages were as simple-hearted as the ladies of whom D. Francisco de Portugal tells us : ' Amadis is dead,' they replied when asked why they were in tears. *Amadis de Gaula* charmed the tedious hours of men and women more

LATTER PART OF THE XV CENTURY 139

exigent. After the defeat at Pavia, Francis I read *Amadis* to lighten the melancholy of his prison-cell in Madrid; St. Ignatius delighted in it; Santa Teresa wrote an imitation of it while still a young girl; Italy went into transports of delight over the book, Bernardo Tasso put it into verse; Cervantes, while he caricatured its faults, admitted that it was 'the best of all books of its kind'; Du Bellay had already anticipated this judgment in his quaint Renaissance French:

> 'Tant que le monde demourra
> Le lai d'Amadis ne mourra.'

A few chivalrous novels have earlier dates on their title-pages: the Catalan *Libre de valeros e strenu cavaller Tirant lo blanch*,[1] exists in an edition issued at Valencia in 1490; *El Baladro del sabio Merlin con sus profecias*[2] appeared in Castilian in 1498; the *Historia de los nobles caualleros Oliueros de Castilla y Artus dalgarve*[3] in 1499 and *Tristan de Leonis*[4] in 1501—these two are from French originals. All these

[1] Facsimile of the 1490 Valencia ed. by A. M. Huntington, New York, 1904.—See: J. A. Vaeth, *Tirant lo Blanch*. New York, 1918.

[2] Ed. A. Bonilla y San Martín, in *Libros de Caballerías*, 1907. I, pp. 1-162 (Nueva Bib. de Autores Esp., 6).

[3] Facsimile of the 1499 Burgos ed. by A. M. Huntington, New York, 1902; ed. A. Bonilla y San Martín, in *Libros de Caballerías*. 1908. II, pp. 443-523 (Nueva Bib. de Autores Esp., 11).—See: R. Foulché-Delbosc, in *Revue Hispanique*, IX (1902), pp. 587-595.

[4] Reprint of the 1501 ed. by A. Bonilla y San Martín, 1912 (Soc. de Bibliófilos Madrileños, 6); reprint of the 1528 ed. by A. Bonilla y San Martín, in *Libros de Caballerías*. 1907. I, pp. 339-457 (Nueva Bib. de Autores Esp., 6).—See: G. T. Northup, *The Spanish prose Tristram source question*, in *Modern Philology*, XI (1913), pp. 259-265.

romances of chivalry are certainly older than the most ancient edition of *Amadis de Gaula* which comes down to us. But *Amadis de Gaula* begot a whole generation of successors—'todos los demas han tomado principio y origen deste.' That is fundamentally true and that alone would suffice to give *Amadis de Gaula* a prominent place in literary history.

Contemporary with Montalvo was Diego de San Pedro,[1] a Jew who administered the town of Peñafiel and other places in Castile on behalf of D. Pedro Giron, the Grand Master of the Order of Calatrava. San Pedro is apt to be a little underrated, perhaps because of his Israelite descent which would rouse a prejudice against him in Spain. He was not a great writer, it is true, but he was an accomplished man of letters. He is the author of graceful poems, a little artificial and alembicated, yet redolent of natural charm, which may be read in the *Cancionero General*. His *Tractado de amores de Arnalte y Lucenda* (1491) was translated into French (1546) by Herberay and had an enormous success. But what keeps his memory green is the *Carcel de Amor* (1492) written some time after 1465 and deriving from an earlier form of *Amadis de Gaula*. The book is well put together, and is veined throughout with a penetrating sentimentalism in which Leriano and Laureola figure. There is no lack of alarming adventures: these are set off by the personal confessions of the author, by Dantesque allegorical passages and by cloying love-letters. The

[1] *Carcel de amor*, reprint of the 1492 Seville ed. by R. Foulché-Delbosc, 1904 (Bib. hispanica, xv); *Arnalte y Lucenda*, ed. R. Foulché-Delbosc, in *Revue Hispanique*, xxv (1911), pp. 220-282.—See A. Giannini, *La " Carcel de Amor," y el " Cortegiano " de B. Castiglione*, in *Revue Hispanique*, xlvi (1919), pp. 547-568.

Carcel de Amor closes with the suicide of Leriano. The Church was not slow to fulminate against it, but the Churchmen thundered in vain. The book was translated into Italian in 1513, into French in 1526 : from the French version derives the English translation made about 1540 by Lord Berners (1467-1533). In Spain the *Carcel de Amor* went into some thirty editions, so that the suicide scene became familiar to innumerable readers.

Among those who were impressed by it was the author of a very celebrated work in sixteen acts, originally entitled *Comedia de Calisto y Melibea*.[1] Later the title was changed to *Tragicomedia de Calisto y Melibea* and the number of acts was brought up to twenty-one. The name *Tragicomedia* is an improvement on *Comedia*, but neither title is good, for each

[1] Facsimile of the first known ed. (1499) by The Hispanic Society, New York, 1909 ; reprint of the 1499 ed. by R. Foulché-Delbosc, 1902 (Bib hispanica, xii) ; reprint of the 1501 ed. by R. Foulché-Delbosc, 1900 (Bib. hispanica, i).—See : James Fitzmaurice-Kelly, Introduction to *Celestina or the Tragicke-Comedy of Calisto and Melibea Englished . . . by James Mabbe, anno 1631*. London, 1894 (The Tudor Translations, vi) ; R. Foulché-Delbosc, *Observations sur la Célestine* i, ii., in *Revue Hispanique*, vii (1900), pp. 28-80, 510 ; ix (1902), pp. 171-199 ; A. Bonilla y San Martín, *Antecedentes del tipo celestinesco en la literatura latina*, in *Revue Hispanique*, xv (1906), pp. 372-386 ; H. Warner Allen, Introduction to *Celestina, or the Tragi-Comedy of Calisto and Melibea translated by James Mabbe anno 1631* . . . London [1908], 2nd. ed. London, 1923 ; M. Menéndez y Pelayo, in *Orígenes de la Novela*. 1910. iii, pp. i-clxx (Nueva Bib. de Autores Esp., 14) ; E. Martinenche, Introduction to *La Célestine*. Paris, n.d. (Les cent chefs d'œuvre étrangers, 33) ; R. E. House, *The Present Status of the Problem of Authorship of the Celestina*, in *Philological Quarterly*, ii (1923), pp. 38-47 ; R. E. House, M. Mulroney and I. G. Probst, *Notes on the Authorship of the Celestina*, in *Philological Quarterly*, iii (1924), pp. 81-91.

gives the idea of a dramatic work, intended for representation on the stage. It is true that the *Comedia* is divided up into scenes, but it was clearly never intended for the stage: its mere length forbids that notion, and the slow movement of the action is anything but dramatic in character. Gradually the book came to be known as *La Celestina* from one of its characters. This title was used in Italy as early as 1519 and it has now been adopted universally even in Spain itself. The date of *La Celestina* is not known. There is an obscure reference in it to the surrender of Granada, but this may bear different interpretations. Some think that it implies the town's impending surrender in 1492; others think that this passage was written nine years before the surrender; others, again, argue that the passage refers to the past and must have been composed some six or seven years after Boabdil's overthrow. It is not easy to say when the book was first printed. The redaction in sixteen acts survives in two editions—each unique: one printed at Burgos in 1499 and one at Seville in 1501. It seems likely that there was an edition earlier than 1499, though it has not yet come to light. All later editions print twenty-one acts; while three, the earliest of which appeared in 1526, add a twenty-second act, the *Auto de Traso*. The *Auto de Traso* is unanimously rejected as an apocryphal interpolation. But here unanimity comes to an end. Who wrote the rest of the book? The 1501 edition contains a vague attribution of the first act, which is much the longest, to an 'old author.' This statement occurs in a preliminary letter: in later editions, the letter becomes more precise and the 'old author' is identified with Juan de Mena or Rodrigo Cota. This is quite unplausible. Neither

Mena nor Cota could be called an 'old author' with propriety. Mena died in 1456 and Cota died between 1472 and 1495. Moreover Mena could not have written the fine prose of the first act: we unhappily know what his prose was like. Cota was a poet and did not, so far as we are aware, seek distinction in prose. Nobody can take these ascriptions seriously. The 1501 edition contains at the end an acrostic (probably introduced by the proof-corrector, Alonso de Proaza): *El bachiller Fernando de Rojas acabo la comedia de Calysto y Melybea y fve nascido en la pvebla de Montalvan.* There is also a reference to Rojas in a legal deposition made in 1525-1526 by the Jew Alvaro de Montalvan, who in his sworn statement calls himself the father-in-law of the 'Bachiller Rojas, que compuso a *Melibea*.' He appears to have been a Jew: according to tradition he became *alcalde* of Talavera de la Reina and was still alive on March 21, 1538. The problem of composition and authorship remains unresolved. Some scholars, among whom was M. Menéndez y Pelayo, hold that the twenty-one acts are by the hand of Rojas; M. Foulché-Delbosc thinks (1) that the sixteen original acts are the work of one man, (2) that this author is unknown, and (3) that he had no share in the later additions. Opinion is now almost unanimous in favour of his first conclusion. If Rojas be accepted provisionally as the author of *La Celestina*, there remains his assertion that he did not write the first act. This is an awkward circumstance, for nobody has found stylistic differences between that and the rest. Perhaps the explanation is that he found the first act in existence, and rehandled it so freely that the unity of style becomes explicable. But the fact that Rojas would have been about twenty years of age when he wrote the work—a fact revealed by the discovery of fresh documents—is against its attribution to him. The psychological insight shewn is too great, so is the profound pessimism of the tone. These are characteristics rather of a man who has lived long enough to be disillusioned. And there is no doubt that the additions are not in the happy manner of the original.

However, these literary puzzles, though interesting, do not affect the intrinsic merit of the book. This merit consists not in poetic imaginative invention, but in accurate observation, in the creation of characters, in the psychological insight into emotion, in the sympathetic picture of human passions and in the amplitude and dignity of form. The author takes a very simple theme: the growing passion of Calisto for Melibea, the opposition of her parents, the means taken to overcome this opposition, the tragic ending of Calisto who is killed by accident, and the final suicide of Melibea. And all these episodes give the author the opportunity of calling up a whole crowd of personages of the lower orders, bullies, shameless servants and other figures tragic, charming, or repulsive. Among these picturesque creations stands foremost the diabolical Celestina who has become one of the great protagonists of literature leading up to the repulsive figure of the nurse in *Romeo and Juliet*. The author lacks taste and measure; but he has a pitiless eye for human weakness. One feels in the very crudity of his presentations that he has the living model always before him. He supplies us with a counterpart to *Amadis de Gaula*. In *Amadis* are portrayed the lofty aspirations of a section of society under the influence of the chivalresque ideals. The *Celestina* makes us acquainted with the lower passions and vices of this same society. It is not an optimistic picture of humanity : the *Celestina* stresses rather our weaknesses, blemishes and objections. The author is not under the spell of a poetic vision. But he is profoundly conscious of the *entraînement* of passion ; he understands the basis of poetry which underlies the irresistible infatuation of what Shakespeare calls the ' star-crossed lovers ', and nobody exceeds him in the force with which he depicts the irrefragable fatality that impels the most beautiful of created beings to ruin, which takes refuge at last in the desperate remedy of death and nothingness. *Amadis de Gaula* portrays society as it might be in conditions much less inconceivable. The *Celestina* unfolds the panorama of existence as it actually is. Most readers can check some, at least, of its portraiture for themselves. And it is to the exactitude of its psychological insight and the embracing universality of its truth that the *Celestina* owes its imperishable renown. *Amadis de Gaula* has withered from its sheer extravagance and has grown wan under the scathing irony of Cervantes. The *Celestina* does not take us to enchanted islands where Beltenebros perishes under Oriana's proud disdain. It is essentially human and introduces us to real men and women : creatures of the same flesh and blood as ourselves. It is not amusing : the author had neither wit nor humour. It may be that he has not even good humour. But he feels the innate tragedy of things and has the gift of communicating his emotions. He borrows freely : not least from Juan Ruiz. His Celestina herself is developed from the Archpriest's Trotaconventos ; his two lovers, Calisto and Melibea, are derived from the Archpriest's Don Melon de la Uerta and D[a.] Endrina de Calatayud ; he imitates Martinez de Toledo and others whom he mentions with an unaffected candour. He can afford to do it, for whatever he borrows he makes his own, and his individual originality remains intact. In the matter of style, he may be at times a little heavy. But he has the sentiment of beauty and makes the most of an instrument still imperfect. He has all the verve and *brío* of Juan Ruiz, free from the shackles of metre. He has all the ironic eloquence of Martinez de Toledo with an added force and splendour of his own. Hence one can easily understand how his work carried everything before it. It was continued, commentated, imitated, rendered into several European tongues and may, perhaps, have been in Shakespeare's mind when he wrote *Romeo and Juliet*. The fashion of *Amadis de Gaula* has passed away. The *Celestina* endures for ever, is responsible indirectly for the picaresque novel, and lies at the root of all realistic presentation. Whoever wrote it endowed European literature with a masterpiece. That is a great thing to say, for masterpieces do not greatly abound. But in this case it can be maintained.

Perhaps the first of the *Celestina's* many imitators was Pedro Manuel de Urrea[1] (1486 ?-1535 ?) who brought out his *Cancionero* in 1513. This contains a certain amount of imitative rubbish, but it also contains some pleasing and ingenuous love-poems. Urrea

[1] *Penitencia de Amor*, reprint of the 1514 Burgos ed. by R. Foulché-Delbosc, 1902 (Bib. hispanica, x) ; *Cancionero*, 1878 (Bib. de Escritores Aragoneses, II, 2).—See : M. Menéndez y Pelayo, in *Antología de poetas líricos* etc. Madrid, 1898. VII, pp. ccliv-cclxxx ; R. Foulché-Delbosc, *La ' Penitencia de Amor' de Pedro Manuel de Urrea*, in *Revue Hispanique*, IX (1902), pp. 200-215 ; M. Menéndez y Pelayo, in *Orígenes de la Novela*. 1910. III, pp. clx-clxvii (Nueva Bib. de Autores Esp., 14).

seems to have had literary instincts, but little literary ambition. What he lacked in this way, his mother, the Condesa de Aranda, possessed in abundance. She appears to have been responsible for the publication of his *Cancionero*. So we may infer from a passage preliminary to the *Cancionero* where Urrea expresses his disgust for the democratization of literature through the art of printing. All this is very ungrateful, if very human, on Urrea's part. He would have been forgotten long ago but for his *Cancionero*, in which the best thing no doubt is an *Egloga*, a dramatic arrangement of the first act of the *Celestina*. This has a real interest of its own, for it foreshadows the coming of the future Spanish drama. The *Celestina* would appear to have had an irresistible attraction for Urrea: he wrote in 1514 a prose imitation of it called *Penitencia de amor*. In the *Egloga* the employment of verse causes one to forget the source for the moment. The use of prose in the *Penitencia de amor* as a vehicle of expression is a mistake, though it denotes intrepidity: for one is constantly reminded of the original, and this is unlucky for Urrea, who is not of a stature to bear so heavy a burden. But nothing can deprive him of the credit of inaugurating a long literary imaginative series which went on pretty steadily till 1632 at least, when Lope de Vega published his *Dorotea*. As almost everything of Lope is famous, the *Dorotea* has rather eclipsed the earlier imitations of the *Celestina*. This is natural, but it involves some injustice: amongst others to Feliciano de Silva,[1] who is known to everybody because a crack-brained sentence of his—*la razon de la sinrazon*—is quoted in *Don Quijote*. But in spite

[1] See: H. Thomas, in *Dos romances anónimos del siglo xvi*. Madrid, 1917.

of Cervantes, Feliciano de Silva had merits : he had a gift of invention and an amazing facility which has caused people to compare him with Dumas *père*. We shall meet Feliciano de Silva later in connexion with the books of chivalry which his generation devoured as eagerly as a preceding generation devoured *Les Trois Mousquetaires* and its continuations. But Feliciano de Silva, though best known for his romances of chivalry, never wrote anything better than *La segunda comedia de Celestina* (1534 ?). Another imitation not lacking in interest or literary quality is the anonymous *Tragicomedia de Lisandro y Roselia* (1542).[1] An adaptation of the *Celestina*—*A new commodye in English in manner of an enterlude ryght elygant and full of craft and rethoryk* (to quote only the opening words of its interminable title)—was brought out over a century before Corneille's *Cid*, itself of Spanish origin, and was done into English. This work, published by John Rastell (d. 1536), brother-in-law to Sir Thomas More, is much too long for the stage ; it has the further disadvantage of ending with a tedious 'morall conclusion and exhortacyon to vertew,' which the adaptor has tacked on in the clumsiest fashion. Maladroit as is this *New commodye*, it has the merit of novelty inasmuch as it wrenches itself away from the mediaeval allegorical tradition, gives us human beings tossed by human emotions instead of wan abstractions, prefaces the way for the drawing of character and, in its presentation of Calisto and Melibea, may well have counted for something in the treatment of that other immortal couple Romeo and Juliet. For it is very possible, and perhaps rather more than possible, that Shake-

[1] Madrid, 1872 (Col. de libros españoles raros ó curiosos, 3).

speare knew the *New commodye* fairly well. We have evidence that there was a revival of interest in the *Celestina* towards the end of the sixteenth century: according to an entry in the *Stationers' Register* under February 24, 1591, it was proposed to print a Spanish edition in London. And it was in 1591 that Shakespeare wrote *Romeo and Juliet*.

VII

THE MIDDLE RENAISSANCE

A NEW WORLD had been discovered by an Italian adventurer, and it had fallen into the lap of Spain, at last a solid unit in the political system. The prestige of the new Spanish Monarchy was multiplied a thousandfold in a night. There was a universal scramble to be attached in some way to Spain. Spaniards—even of the most infamous character like Alexander VI (1492-1503)—were elected to the Papacy; an English king married Catherine of Aragon ; Philip the Fair of Austria wedded another daughter of Ferdinand and Isabella : the offspring of this marriage was the predestined Emperor Charles V., the Spanish Caesar. Italians poured into Spain and their superior training swiftly brought them to the front. Two Italians, the brothers Antonio and Alessandro Geraldino, were appointed tutors to the children of Ferdinand and Isabel ; the Lombard Pietro Martir d'Anghiera (1459 ?-1526) spread the light of the Renaissance on every side, and says with a touch of justifiable pride that all the grandees of Castile have sat as pupils at his feet ; the Sicilian Lucio Marineo Siculo (1460 ?-d. after 1533) was elected to the Chair of Latin at the University of Salamanca and with Antonio de

Lebrixa placed classical scholarship in Spain on a solid foundation. The results were soon seen in editions of classical texts, and in the issue of numerous translations. Spaniards eager to drink the waters of learning at their source, migrated to Italy, and by degrees it became common for men of letters to make what would now be called an Italian tour.

Occasionally a Spanish book was printed in Italy, as for instance the *Question de amor de dos enamorados* [1] (1513?), which has a literary dependence on the *Carcel de amor*. A great part of its interest lies in the fact that it is a *roman à clef*, especially now that the key has been found by the Italian philosopher Sig^r. Benedetto Croce. Sig^r. Croce's key will not open all locks. We do not yet know who the author of the book is. He is identified with Vasquiran, one of the characters in the novel. Is this Vasquiran identical with the Vazquez who contributed two poems to the *Cancionero general*, one of which, the *Dechado de amor*, reads like a first sketch of the *Question* ? In these matters it is safer to take refuge in a resigned agnosticism. It is something to know that Belisena is Bona Sforza, later Queen of Poland, that Persiana is Pescara, Fabricano Fabrizio Colonna, and to have portraits of these personalities limned from the life. All this is valuable and the presentation of the curious medley of two civilizations, Italian and Spanish, in the atmosphere of Naples is a precious contribution to the reconstruction of a brilliant period of social history. There are good verses in the *Question de amor*, but its interest lies

[1] Ed. M. Menéndez y Pelayo, in *Orígenes de la Novela*. 1907. II, pp. 41-98 (Nueva Bib. de Autores Esp., 7).—See: B. Croce, *Di un antico romanzo spagnuolo relativo alla storia di Napoli*, 'La Cuestion de Amor,' Napoli, 1894.

in its vitality and vigorous rendering of picturesque figures in iridescent surroundings.

The Italians had had more than enough of Gonzalo de Córdoba, whose campaigns had desolated Southern Italy; they might have been spared the *Historia Parthenopea* (1516), a tedious epic in which the great captain's exploits are sung by Alonso Hernandez. But the epic is worth mentioning as a Spanish book published at Rome: it is evidence that a Spanish-speaking public existed in Italy. Corroborative testimony is not wanting. JUAN DEL ENZINA [1] (1469 ?-1529 ?) who has been called the 'patriarch of the Spanish theatre,' himself mentions his frequent journeys to Rome; a contemporary letter written by Stazio Gadio describes the performance of Enzina's *Egloga . . . en la qual se introducen dos enamorados, llamada ella*

[1] *Teatro completo*, ed. M. Cañete and F. A. Barbieri, Madrid, 1893 (Bib. selecta de Autores clásicos Esp., 9); *Egloga interlocutoria*, ed. U. Cronan, in *Revue Hispanique*, XXXVI (1916), pp. 475-488; *Poesías*, ed. F. A. Barbieri, in *Cancionero musical de los siglos xv y xvi*. Madrid, 1890; ed. R. Mitjana, in *Cancionero de Uppsala*, 1909; *Arte de poesía castellana*, reprinted by M. Menéndez y Pelayo, in *Antología de poetas líricos*, etc. Madrid, 1894. V, pp. 30-47.—See: R. Mitjana, *Sobre Juan del Encina, músico y poeta* (*Nuevos datos para su biografía*). Málaga [1895]; M. Menéndez y Pelayo, in *Antología de poetas líricos*, etc. Madrid, 1898. VII, pp. i-c; E. Cotarelo y Mori, in *Estudios de historia literaria de España*. Madrid, 1901. pp. 103-181; R. Mitjana, *Nuevos documentos relativos a Juan del Encina*, in *Revista de Filología Esp.*, I (1914), pp. 275-288; J. P. W. Crawford, *The source of Juan del Encina's Égloga de Fileno y Zambardo*, in *Revue Hispanique*, XXXVIII (1916), pp. 218-231; R. E. House, *A Study of Encina and the "Égloga Interlocutoria,"* in *The Romanic Review*, VII (1916), pp. 458-469; R. Mitjana, *Estudios sobre algunos músicos españoles del siglo xvi*. Madrid, 1918, pp. 1-51; R. Espinosa Maeso, *Nuevos datos biográficos de Juan del Encina*, in *Boletín de la R. Academia Esp.*, VIII (1921), pp. 640-656.

THE MIDDLE RENAISSANCE

Placida y el Vitoriano in the palace of Jacopo Serra, Archbishop of Arborea (d. 1517), at Rome on August 10, 1513. Enzina seems to have been born at La Encina, to have studied in Salamanca with Antonio de Lebrixa and to have witnessed the surrender of Granada as one of the train of some great noble. In 1492 he entered the service of the second Duke of Alba and began writing for the stage while he was still a member of his household. But six years of gilded servitude were enough for Enzina. A skilful musician, he seems to have applied for a musical post in the cathedral of Salamanca and failing to obtain this he made his way privately to Italy in 1502. He obtained from Alexander VI a benefice in Salamanca and on his return to Spain in 1509 was given speedy and, apparently, unmerited preferment. His frequent absences, while he held the appointments of Archdeacon and Canon at Málaga, added to the fact that he was only a deacon at the time, led to endless differences with the Chapter. He was in Rome in 1512, from 1514 until the spring of 1516, and again in 1519, when he was appointed Prior of Leon. In the same year he made a pilgrimage to Jerusalem, was ordained priest and celebrated his first Mass in the Holy City. He related his journey in the *Tribagia o sacra via de Hierusalem* (1521 ?), a commonplace, uninspired poem and his last work. He died shortly before January 10, 1530.

Enzina's earlier pieces, written while he was still in the Duke of Alba's suite, appear in his *Cancionero* (1496); sixty-eight additional songs set to Enzina's own music are to be found in Asenjo Barbieri's *Cancionero musical de los siglos xv y xvi*. The prologue to his *Cancionero—Arte de poesia castellana—*contains little that is original: Enzina merely repeats the doctrines exposed in Guilhem Molinier's *Leys d'amors* (1324), which was much in vogue among Provençal writers; here and there he inserts some theory of Antonio de Lebrixa. But if Enzina could not express his ideas theoretically, he embodied them in his dramatic compositions. His Christmas and Easter plays are full of realistic touches and contain many allusions to contemporary events. This realistic tendency is most pronounced in two little eclogues, the seventh—*representada en requesta de vnos amores*—and the eighth, given in 1494 and 1495. These, like the *Jeu de Robin et de Marion* by Adam de la Halle (1240?-1288?), clearly indicate the merging of lyric poetry into dramatic poetry. The *débat amoureux* is in some sort an aristocratic convention, but it is treated in a more popular and naturalistic spirit by the Archpriest of Hita and to the treatment of Juan Ruiz we return with Enzina. His knight wins Pascuala from the simple shepherd Mingo: but the knight, to achieve success, has to become a shepherd for the time being, and with this metamorphosis the aristocratic tradition goes overboard. The majority of Enzina's dramatic productions end with a *villancico* or a *cantarcillo* which is either sung by dancers or is accompanied by a dance. This is an extremely interesting feature from the historical point of view: in most cases we have the text of what was sung, and in three cases the musical notation. At the end of the *Auto* (or *Coplas*) *del Repelon*, where the *sayagués* dialect is conspicuous, a fourth shepherd is introduced in order that the actors may sing in four-part harmony. This combination of music and recitation leads onwards to the modern *zarzuela*, and makes Enzina the founder of the lyric stage in Spain.

THE MIDDLE RENAISSANCE

Enzina's work is essentially Spanish. Rome may or may not have improved his morals—Alexander VI was on the papal throne when Enzina arrived there—but it certainly did not improve his art. It may have supplied him with themes, for instance the *Egloga de Fileno, Zambardo e Cardonio*, in which are described a shepherd's love and suicide, derives from the second eclogue of Antonio Tebaldeo (1463-1537). Enzina went through his various phases like the rest of the world, but he went through them in his native land. He is at his crudest in the *Auto del Repelon*, which deals with the adventures of two shepherds in a market and which Menéndez y Pelayo regarded as the first genuine Castilian *entremés*. Its primitive humour, its coarseness, its simplicity of structure are thoroughly popular. But Enzina did not confine himself to these exercises in realism. He was a scholar in his way; he calls his pieces eclogues; he follows Virgil in idealizing country-life, while he keeps in touch with fact by making his shepherds talk a language of their own—*sayagués*—a language which hardened into a convention later but which is dramatically effective in Enzina's hands. He courageously enlarges the scope of the play, introduces more personages on the stage and varies his dialogue to suit each person's social condition. This is seen particularly in the *Egloga de Cristino y Febea*, imitated from Cota's *Dialogo entre el amor y un viejo*, and in *Placida y Vitoriano*, the best, perhaps, of Enzina's productions in spite of its crude scene of suicide at the end. Some reserves must be made in speaking of Enzina's art. It has all the hesitations, the uncertainties, the awkward angularity of inexperience. The movement of his pieces is slow and Enzina's taste is defective;

to raise a sensation or a laugh, he will go out of his way to burlesque the prayers for the dead as in *Placida y Vitoriano*. But for these defects, his intrepidity, his intellectual curiosity, his steady vision, his naïf candour do more than atone. He experimented in all directions, borrowed few hints only, and in the drama improved all that he touched. He purged the *juegos de escarnios* of their grossness and brutality ; he lifted the profane drama out of the gutter, provided it with a higher standard, ensured it a career in the future. That is a great thing for any one man to do ; and Enzina did it. We have to wait long before we find a worthy successor to him in the secular drama. He had given such an impulse to the stage that those who tried to repeat his triumphs were innumerable.

An immediate follower, Lucas Fernandez [1] (1474 ?-1542), does indeed show a decided dramatic instinct in his *Auto de la Passion* (1514). He has all his predecessor's tastes and inclinations ; he has less originality and talent. His *Auto* may be more poetic in conception and execution than anything of the same kind by Enzina ; in other respects Fernandez makes no perceptible advance on what Enzina had done. As for Vasco Diaz Tanco de Frexenal (author of *Jardin del alma cristiana*, 1551) and a dozen others who wrote or are reported to have written with an appalling copiousness for the Spanish stage ; who professes to have read them ?

[1] *Farsas y églogas al modo y estilo pastoril y castellano*, ed. M. Cañete, Madrid, 1867 (Bib. selecta de Autores clásicos Esp., 3).—See : A. Morel-Fatio, *Notes sur la langue des Farsas y églogas de Lucas Fernandez*, in *Romania*, x (1881), pp. 239-244 ; R. Espinosa Maeso, *Ensayo biográfico del Maestro Lucas Fernandez* (¿ 1474 ?-1542), in *Boletín de la R. Academia Esp.*, x (1923), pp. 567-603.

THE MIDDLE RENAISSANCE 157

A more original and various ability is shewn by BARTOLOMÉ DE TORRES NAHARRO[1] (d. 1531?) who was born at Torre de Miguel Sexmero in the province of Estremadura. He seems to have been a soldier and to have been captured by piratical Moors who imprisoned him in Algiers. On his release, he made his way to Rome and there took orders, being apparently attached to the household of that Spanish cardinal, Bernardo Carvajal (1456?-1522), who was reported to have his eye on the popedom. He later passed into the service of Fabrizio Colonna in Naples in 1516, and in the following year published in that city his *Propaladia* (Praises of Minerva). These facts are contained in a Latin letter written to Josse Badde (1462-1535) by 'Mesinerius I. Barberius Aurelianensis' —Messinier Barbier d'Orléans—Torres Naharro's friend, and printed, as an introductory preface to his works. Torres Naharro's verse, with the exception of four *romances* and the *Retracto*, an elegy on the death of the first duke of Nájera (d. 1515), has little literary interest. As regards his plays he indirectly insinuates that he had never heard of Enzina: according to Barbier he sets up to be 'the first to write plays in the [Spanish] vernacular.' We must assume Barbier to have misunderstood some phrase incautiously dropped

---

[1] *La Propaladia*, ed. M. Cañete y M. Menéndez y Pelayo, 1880-1900. 2 vols. (Libros de antaño, 9, 10).—See: A. L. Stiefel, *Zur Bibliographie des Torres Naharro*, in *Archiv für das Studium der neueren Sprachen und Literaturen*, CXIX (1907), pp. 195-196; J. E. Gillet, *Une édition inconnue de la 'Propalladia' de Bartolomé de Torres Naharro*, in *The Romanic Review*, XI (1920), pp. 26-36; M. Romera-Navarro, *Estudio de la " Comedia Himenea " de Torres Naharro*, in *The Romanic Review*, XII (1921), pp. 50-72; A. Lenz, *Torres Naharro et Plaute*, in *Revue Hispanique*, LVII (1923), pp. 99-107.

by Torres Naharro. He had manifestly studied Enzina very carefully, so carefully, in fact, that he imitates him in his *Dialogo del Nascimiento*, written about 1512. But it was not on these lines that Torres Naharro was destined to evolve. He had much larger ideas of scenic possibilities than had his predecessor. His dramaturgical theories are propounded in the *Prohemio*, a preface to his *Propaladia*, the fantastic title of the volume in which his plays are included. He divides each of these into five acts and he separates them into two main classes: the *comedia a noticia* or realistic drama, in which all the material is a literal transcription of episodes which have really happened; and the *comedia a fantasía* or romantic drama, into which are introduced episodes that are pure invention, incidents which might be true and which actually seem true but are not so. The acts he calls *jornadas* (resting-places), an expression which may have been suggested to him by the French *journées* of the *mystères*. At the beginning of each piece he has a prologue or *introito*. He has an interest in the study of character: he makes his plots more complicated: he greatly increases the number of personages as compared with writers who went before him. Torres Naharro is most distinguished as a practitioner in the romantic drama. In this branch his *Comedia Imenea* calls for special attention. The central theme is simple; the plain love-story of Imeneo for Febea. But a new *motif* is to be noted in the development of the piece. Febea's brother is presented as intervening in the interest of social decorum or public opinion. We have here for the first time, perhaps, in Spanish literature, the appearance of the 'point of honour,' the *pundonor* which was to be so much emphasized by Lope de Vega,

THE MIDDLE RENAISSANCE

and which was to form the capital feature of the cloak and sword plays—*comedias de capa y espada*—that make up the bulk of Calderon's secular theatre. Other *comedias a fantasía* are the *Comedia Seraphina*, and the *Comedia Áquilana*, while among the *comedias a noticia* may be mentioned the *Comedia Soldadesca* and the *Comedia Tinellaria* which, so Torres Naharro affirms, was acted before Leon X (1513-1521) and the future Pope Clement VII (1523-1534). It is less easy to classify the allegorical *Comedia Trofea* which is all about the triumphs of the Portuguese under Dom Manuel of Portugal, and the *Comedia Jacinta* which really belongs to both classes and may be called a play of an intermediate type.

In all these plays we are in the presence of a new departure. Shepherds and shepherdesses continued to be presented with more and more realism on the Spanish stage for many years to come; yet in Torres Naharro we can discern a definite break with the established pastoral tradition. His example was followed, but not instantly, in Spain. Torres Naharro was before his time. He was read, we may be sure, for his *Propaladia* was reprinted several times in Spain itself—five times between 1520 and 1545. He was read by budding dramatists and amateurs of the theatre such as Jaime de Güete, Bartolomé Palau, Castillejo or Micael de Carvajal; but it is not nearly so sure that his plays were acted. The evidence is rather against this notion; his theatre required material elaboration which, though it was obtainable in Italy, was beyond the modest resources of strolling companies in Spain. There is a difference of opinion as to his diction. It is the fashion to frown on him for introducing Italianisms into his Spanish; very likely there is a basis for this charge. Torres Naharro lived in Rome and Naples and spoke Italian habitually so that it had become almost his natural tongue. Little incorrections of speech, intrusions of Italian idioms are to be found in all his plays. It is true that there were not many Italian plays in existence for him to imitate, and, if there had been, Torres Naharro was not content to be a mere copyist or adapter. There are points of contact between his *Comedia Seraphina* and the *Mandragola* and between his *Comedia Calamita* and the *Suppositi* which are assuredly not the result of accident. Torres Naharro borrows hints from Machiavelli (1469-1527) and Ariosto, but he uses what he takes with independence, and he borrows very little. He has not the idyllic fancy of Enzina, he is far below Gil Vicente in depth of imagination and poetic charm : for acting purposes he is a sounder craftsman than either of them. Spain was destined to produce a race of dramaturges whose ingenuity in contriving intricate plots and startling coincidences was invaluable to playwrights in other countries. Torres Naharro is the first of this long line. His is not the highest form of art ; but it is a new point of departure, and whatever may be the absolute merits of his plays, their historical importance is undeniable.

The first sign of his influence at work is perceptible not in Spain but in Portugal. In the sixteenth century and the beginning of the seventeenth century, Portuguese writers used the Spanish language as skilfully and about as perfectly as they used their own. And Spain at this period produced no dramatist as gifted as the Portuguese GIL VICENTE,[1] who was a most

[1] *Obras*, ed. J. Mendes dos Remedios, Coimbra, 1907-1914. 3 vol. ; *Auto da Alma*, ed. A. F. G. Bell [*The Modern Language*

charming poet as well as a successful playwright and musician. He is generally supposed to have been born about 1465 and to have died about 1536. Of his forty-three extant plays, eleven are in Spanish, twelve in Portuguese and the remainder in a mixture of Spanish and Portuguese, a literary convention comparable with the use of the *sayagues* dialect by Enzina. An interesting feature in Gil Vicente's work is that, though he wrote for the Court to which he was attached in some capacity, his subjects are frequently popular and their inspiration is nearly always so. Vicente in his earlier pieces, such as the *Monologo da Visitação* or *Monologo do Vaqueiro* (1502), the *Auto pastoril castelhano* (1503) and the *Auto dos Reis Magos* (1503), is a frank imitator of Enzina, whose influence is also visible in the *Auto da Sibilla Cassandra* (1513 ?). This is a fantastic medley in which the personages are Solomon disguised as a shepherd paying his addresses to the coy Cassandra disguised as a shepherdess : Cassandra is provided with three uncles who prove to be Abraham, Moses and Isaiah, and with three aunts who are the Persian, Cimmerian and Erythræan sibyls. In this bewildering extravaganza the oddities of presentation

Review, XIII] 1918; *Four Plays* [*Auto da Alma, Exhortação da guerra, Farsa dos Almocreves, Tragicomedia pastoril da Serra da Estrella*] text with English trans. by A. F. G. Bell, Cambridge, 1920 ; *Auto de la Sibila Casandra*, ed. A. Giráldez, Madrid, 1921.
—See: E. Prestage, *The Portuguese Drama in the sixteenth century: Gil Vicente*, in *The Manchester Quarterly*, XVI (1897), pp. 235-264 ; M. Menéndez y Pelayo, in *Antología de poetas líricos*, etc. Madrid, 1898. VII, pp. clxiii-ccxxv ; J. I. de Brito Rebello, *Gil Vicente*. Lisboa, 1912 ; C. Michaëlis de Vasconcellos, *Notas Vicentinas* [*Revista da Universidade de Coimbra*] 1912-1922. 4 vols.; A. Braamcamp Freire, *Vida e Obras de Gil Vicente*. Pôrto, 1919; A. F. G. Bell, *Gil Vicente*. Oxford, 1921 (Hispanic Notes and Monographs. Portuguese Series, 1).

are lost sight of owing to the author's infinite wealth of allegory, his power of poetic evocation and the delightful lyrical mosaics with which he tesselates the fabric of his flashing, restless fantasy.

All this is far above and far beyond Enzina's work, and the same ennobling faculty is present to an even greater degree in the trilogy, *Auto da Barca do Inferno* (1517), *Auto da Barca do Purgatorio* (1518), and *Auto da Barca da Gloria* (1519), which was present in Lope's mind when he wrote *El Viaje del Alma*. In his secular plays Gil Vicente displays a disconcerting variety. He passes swiftly from the urbane high comedy of the *Comedia do Viuvo* (1514) to the hard amalgam of magical and realistic elements in the powerful but repulsive *Comedia de Rubena* (1521), in which is traceable the influence of the *Celestina* and upon which Calderon based *El lirio y la azucena*; he exploits the books of chivalry and shews a fine discretion in selecting the episodes which he poetizes in *Dom Duardos* (1525?) and in *Amadis de Gaula* (1533). Gil Vicente has not Torres Naharro's dramatic instinct, nor has he the Spaniard's creative force. His characters have a certain mistiness and uncertainty of outline. The conception is often fine, but the lyric poet in Gil Vicente is irrepressible. There is nothing in Torres Naharro as charming as the famous song: 'Muy graciosa es la doncella,' which occurs in the *Auto da Sibilla Cassandra*. This song is something to be thankful for. Gil Vicente is occasionally maladroit in the preparation of scenic effects, but he has the sense of beauty, a magical charm of utterance, a honeyed accent; and any weakness in the matter of stagecraft is redeemed by the exaltation and rapture of his lyrical passages. These remain unmatched till we come to

THE MIDDLE RENAISSANCE 163

Lope de Vega and Calderon, both of whom evidently studied Gil Vicente to their profit. To have influenced these two great glories of the peninsular stage is a remarkable exploit.

Meanwhile the cultivation of Italian went steadily forward in Spain. Benedetto Gareth [1] (1450 ?-1514), who issued his Italian *Rime* in 1506, dropped his Catalan name of Gareth and assumed that of Chariteo. Even more striking was the case of the Valencian poet, Berthomeu Gentil, who became so profoundly Italianized that one of his eighteen Italian sonnets—*Soneto en diálogo, de Dio*—has imposed upon successive generations of astute Italian scholars, and was regularly included among the poems of Luigi Tansillo (1510-1568) till a few years ago, when it was restored after over three centuries to its rightful owner. Among the numerous translations of the classics made at this period in Spain, modern Italian writers came in for a very fair share of attention, Boccaccio, Petrarch and Dante being all three represented in various Spanish versions issued between 1496 and 1515. Boccaccio had already reacted on Juan de Flores, whose *Breue tractado . . . de Grimalte y Gradissa* (1495 ?) is a sequel to *Fiammetta*, while his *Tractado . . . donde se contiene el triste fin de los amores de Grisel y Mirabella* is imitated from *Filocolo*. The anonymous French version of *Grisel y Mirabella* was reprinted twenty times in a century; the original was used as a text-book for the study of Spanish and thus found its way into foreign literatures. Reminiscences of it are to be seen in Ariosto's *Orlando furioso*, in Lope de Vega's *Ley executada* (1633), in *Women*

[1] *Le Rime di Benedetto Gareth detto Il Chariteo*, ed. E. Pèrcopo, Napoli, 1892. 2 vols.

pleas'd by Fletcher (1579-1625), and in *Le prince déguisé* (1636) by Georges de Scudéry (1601-1667).

But in the general revival of learning no name stands out so prominently as that of the great scholar, ANTONIO DE LEBRIXA [1] (1442 ?-1522), who returned to Spain in 1470 after ten years spent in Italy. Professor of Grammar at Salamanca, he resigned his Chair as the result of some academic difference and went over to the University of Alcalá de Henares, recently founded (1508) by the Cardinal Francisco Ximenez de Cisneros (1436-1517). There his scholarship proved invaluable in the preparation of the Polyglot Bible; he was personally responsible with the Cretan Demetrio Ducas, Hernan Nuñez de Toledo and Juan de Vergara for the Greek text. His pronunciation of Greek was in accordance with the theories of Erasmus, as Ingram Bywater (1840-1914) has shewn. The *Introductiones latinae* (1481), the *Gramatica . . . sobre la lengua castellana* (1492), the *Interpretatio dictionum ex sermone latino in hispaniensem* (1492) and the *Interpretacion de las palabras castellanas en lengua latina* (1495 ?) bear eloquent testimony to his learning.

Among Spanish writers of Italian must be included Judas Abrabanel or, as he is more generally known, Leon Hebreo [2] (1460?-1520). His case is an excep-

---

[1] *Gramática castellana*, phototype reproduction of the princeps (1492) by E. Walberg, Halle a. S. 1909.—See: I. Bywater, in *The Erasmian Pronunciation of Greek and its precursors*, etc. Oxford-London, 1908; P. Lemus y Rubio, *El Maestro Elio Antonio de Lebrixa 1441 ?-1522*, in *Revue Hispanique*, XXII (1910), pp. 459-508; XXIX (1913), pp. 13-120.

[2] *La tradvzion del Indio de los tres Dialogos de Amor de Leon Hebreo . . . por Garcilasso Inga de la Vega*, ed. A. Bonilla y San Martín, in *Orígenes de la Novela*. 1915. IV, pp. 278-459 (Nueva Bib. de Autores Esp., 21).—See: M. Menéndez y Pelayo, in

tional one. Driven from Spain by the edict of March 31, 1492, he fled to Italy and there wrote his *Dialoghi di Amore*, which appeared posthumously in 1535. Reminiscences in *Gli Asolani* and *Il Cortegiano* seem to shew that Bembo and Castiglione may have read the work in manuscript. Leon Hebreo had spent the first thirty years of his life in Spain; his choice of Italian as a vehicle was undoubtedly the result of circumstances, and indeed the Italian text is disfigured by innumerable Spanish idioms. The *Dialoghi* with their medley of neoplatonic and Spanish mysticism were translated three times into Castilian, and the French version by Pontus de Thyard (1521-1605) became the fashion among the poets of the Pléiade and may have counted for something in Du Bellay's *Si nostre vie est moins qu'une journée*, and in *Comme on souloit, si plus on ne me blasme* of Ronsard (1524-1585). Montaigne (1533-1592), who possessed a copy, tells us: "Mon page faict l'amour et l'entend : lisez luy Leon Hebreu et Ficin" (*Essais*, III, ch. v.). The Spanish version left some traces on Herrera and Camões as well as on the prose of Luis de Leon and of Malon de Chaide; Cristóbal de Fonseca (d. 1621) and Nieremberg praised it and a faint echo of its doctrine is heard in Bernardino de Rebolledo's *Discurso de la hermosura y el amor* (1652).

A vast influence was exercised in every part of Western Europe by *Il Cortegiano* (1528) of Baldassare

Historia de las ideas estéticas en España. 1884. II, Pt. i., pp. 11-66 (Col. de Escritores Cast., 19); B. Zimmels, *Leo Hebraeus, ein jüdischer Philosoph der Renaissance: sein Leben, seine Werke und seine Lehren.* Breslau, 1886; B. Zimmels, *Leone Hebreo, Neue Studien.* Wien, 1892; E. Solmi, *Benedetto Spinoza e Leone Ebreo.* Modena, 1903; J. de Carvalho, *Leão Hebreu, Filosofo.* Coimbra, 1918.

Castiglione (1478-1529). It was destined to mould the character of that starry paladin, Sir Philip Sidney. But over twenty years before Sidney was born, *Il Cortegiano* came into the hands of a young Spaniard serving in Italy. This was Garci Lasso de la Vega, who sent the book to his friend, Juan Boscan, with an earnest request that he would translate it, and this Boscan did.[1] We have come to a decisive moment in the literary relations of Spain and Italy. The two men who have just been mentioned were to bring about a literary revolution. Italian methods had long been in the air; Santillana tried to transplant the sonnet but without success and Villalpando fared no better. But that was nearly a century earlier, and the steady infiltration of Italian influences had now done its work. The hour was ready and the men were ready. JUAN BOSCAN[2] (d. 1542), whose name in Catalan was Boscá, studied under Lucio Marineo Siculo and then became tutor to Don Fernando Alvarez de Toledo (1507-1582), a young man destined to obtain, as the Duke of Alba, a terrible reputation for severity as the military chief of the reaction represented by Spain. Boscan was anything but a great poet, and if he had written verses, they were in the nature of exercises on the accepted Spanish metres, the sort of thing that any gallant and

[1] Boscan's translation led Luis Milan to write his *Libro intitulado El Cortesano* . . . (1561).—See: J. B. Trend, *Luis Milan and the Vihuelistas*. Oxford, 1925 (Hispanic Notes and Monographs. Spanish Series, XI).

[2] *Obras*, ed. W. I. Knapp, Madrid, 1875; *Las Treinta*, ed. H. Keniston, New York, 1911 (Hispanic Society of America, 84); *El Cortesano*, ed. A. M. Fabié, Madrid, 1873 (Libros de antaño, 3).—See: M. Menéndez y Pelayo, in *Antología de poetas líricos*, etc. Madrid, 1908. XIII; E. Pèrcopo, *Giovanni Boscàn e Luigi Tansillo*. Arpino, 1913.

THE MIDDLE RENAISSANCE

accomplished gentleman might write. Then in the summer of 1526 Boscan had a chance encounter which affected his own methods and led to a poetic revolution in Spain. He himself in a letter to the Duchess of Soma tells us what happened. At Granada he fell in with the Venetian ambassador Andrea Navagero. Navagero pressed Boscan to experiment in the Italian measures, more complicated and more artistic than those already used in Spain. Boscan appears to have given no decided answer at the moment. But Navagero's suggestion had not fallen on stony ground. Boscan began experimenting cautiously, recognizing that his self-imposed task was a difficult one. He saw the imperfections of his early attempts, he had all the proverbial pertinacity of the Catalan, persisted in the new paths and became an enthusiast for the Italian system of metrics. His verse was published posthumously by his widow in 1543—*Las obras de Boscan y algunas de Garcilasso de la Vega repartidas en quatro libros*, and in this volume it is easy to trace his poetic evolution. The first book contains poems written in the old Spanish manner; the Italianizing efforts of Boscan begin in the second book, which is preceded by an epistle to the Duchess of Soma, a sort of literary manifesto of the new school: it contains eleven *canciones* in the Italian manner, and ninety-two sonnets. The third book contains a rather tedious poem: the *Historia de Leandro y Hero* derived from Musaeus and eked out with Bernardo Tasso's (1493-1569) version of Musaeus, whom Boscan imitates, so far as the measure the *versi sciolti* (blank verse) is concerned; the *Octava Rima* imitated from Bembo (1470-1547), certain elegiac verses and two epistles of real interest.

Boscan was not a great genius: he was a man of

literary aspirations open to new ideas and he slowly acquired a fair amount of mastery of the new materials which had fascinated him. He did not succeed with the *versos sueltos*, which are not specially adapted to assimilation in Spanish, and he had all the weaknesses of the pioneer. But he gave poetic taste a definitive direction ; he revolutionized the metrics of a nation ; he fixed the type of the hendecasyllabic ; he succeeded in naturalizing the sonnet, tercets and the *cancion* of Tuscany. And it is all the more extraordinary that this should have been done by a man who was not a Castilian at all. Something of the Catalan clung to him inseparably. This is what Herrera meant long afterwards when he reproached Boscan for remaining ' a foreigner though decked out in the precious garb of Petrarch.' Boscan lives in literary history as the triumphant leader of a forlorn hope. He triumphed where a man of much greater natural gifts, like Santillana, had failed. He might not have succeeded, had he stood alone. A kindly fate provided him with a favourable opportunity and, what was still more important, an invaluable ally.

This was GARCI LASSO DE LA VEGA [1] (1503-1536), of whom we have already spoken. No name is more glorious in the annals of Spanish chronicle and poetry.

---

[1] *Obras*. Facsimile of the 1626 Lisbon edition by A. M. Huntington, New York, 1903 ; *Poesías*, ed. T. Navarro Tomás, 1911 (Clásicos Castellanos, 3) ; *Églogas*, ed. James Fitzmaurice-Kelly, Oxford, 1918 ; *Poesías varias*, ed. James Fitzmaurice-Kelly, Oxford, 1918.—See : E. Fernandez de Navarrete, *Vida del célebre poeta Garcilaso de la Vega*, in *Coleccion de documentos inéditos*, etc. Madrid, 1850. XVI, pp. 9-287 ; B. J. Gallardo, in *Ensayo*, etc. Madrid, 1888-1889. III, col. 317-333, IV, col. 1271-1325 ; Marqués de Laurencín, *Documentos inéditos referentes al poeta Garcilaso de la Vega*. Madrid, 1915 [see A. B. in *Revista*

His illustrious descent, his magnificent presence, his irresistible personal charm, his romantic valour and his heroic death have combined to make him the idol of a nation. At the age of seventeen he entered the Emperor's service. On the occasion of the rising of the *Comuneros* (1520-1521), he had to choose between his personal attachment to his brother, Pedro Lasso de la Vega (d. 1554), who was one of the leaders of the rebellion, and his sense of public duty and gratitude to the Emperor. The choice was difficult, but Garci Lasso resolved to stand by the dynasty. He served against the *Comuneros* and was wounded in the face at the battle of Olías. His engaging loyalty delighted Charles V, and henceforward his record was one of prolonged campaigning. In 1526 he married Elena de Stúñiga, one of the Empress's ladies-in-waiting; in 1529 he went to Bologna to see Charles V formally crowned by the Pope, whose capital he had recently sacked. Then Garci Lasso was sent on a special mission to France, but he was speedily recalled because of an old indiscretion that was raked up against him. He was accused of encouraging the marriage between his nephew and Isabel de la Cueva, maid of honour to the Empress and niece of the Duke of Alburquerque. To anybody reading the evidence nowadays it seems that Garci Lasso really hurried on the wedding before the imperial decree forbidding it could arrive. He was certainly present at the ceremony. The Empress

crítica hispano-americana, I (1915), pp. 173-177]; H. Keniston, *Garcilaso de la Vega. A critical Study of his Life and Works.* New York, 1922 (Hispanic Notes and Monographs. Peninsular Series); E. Mele, *Las poesías latinas de Garcilaso de la Vega y su permanencia en Italia*, in *Bulletin hispanique*, xxv (1923), pp. 108-148, 362-370; xxvi (1924), pp. 35-51.

was furious and Garci Lasso was exiled in 1532 to the Grosse Schütt-Insel, on the Danube: here he wrote *Danubio, rio divino*, one of his best poems. Through the intervention of the Duke of Alba he was released three months later and sent to Naples, where he attached himself to the service of Don Pedro de Toledo, Marqués de Villafranca and uncle of the Duke of Alba. There he became the intimate friend of Bembo, who calls him 'the best loved Spaniard who ever came to Italy': he was no less the friend of Tansillo. After serving with distinction on the field of battle and in diplomacy, Garci Lasso took part in the campaign of Provence in 1536. Everything went well for the Spaniards till they came to Muy, near Fréjus. Here the Imperial troops were held at bay for a moment by a handful of French archers. The Spanish artillery was brought to bear, a breach was made in the fort, and Charles V seems to have lost patience because the place was not instantly carried by storm. The Emperor's impatience appears to have stung Garci Lasso to the quick. He at once put himself at the head of the storming-party. He laid aside his glittering helmet so that he might be the more easily recognizable by his troops. In order that he might have freer movement and be among the foremost in the advance, he put off his cuirass. He was the second man to enter the breach and on that morning of September 23 he was mortally wounded. He was picked up by Gerónimo Ximenez de Urrea, a bad translator upon whom Cervantes has used his branding-iron with no compassionate hand. It is easy to forget Ximenez de Urrea's translation of *Orlando furioso* (1549): it is not easy to forget that he rescued Garci Lasso under fire. His gallantry was

THE MIDDLE RENAISSANCE

useless. Garci Lasso was removed to Nice, and there he lingered until October 13, when he expired in the arms of the future St. Francis Borgia (1510-1572), a soldier like himself at that period of his career. Garci Lasso reminds one vaguely of Sir Philip Sidney, a Sidney more romantic, more exquisite and not less heroic. He was a '*spirto gentil*' as Tansillo said.

We count him a Spanish poet, of course. But it would require very little ingenuity to argue that he was in a sense an Italian poet, a Neapolitan poet. His many-sidedness was extraordinary. He wrote with about equal ease verses in Spanish, in Italian and in Latin. And all through his verses the Italian influence is noticeable. Here you catch an echo of Sannazaro, there an echo of Bernardo Tasso, and a savour of Petrarch. Some of the finest touches in his first eclogue are inspired by Tansillo's *I due pellegrini*: he calls into contribution Dante, Martial and Horace. And everywhere, and constantly, we are conscious of the eternal presence of the divine Virgil, so well called by Sainte-Beuve the ' poet of the Latin races.' Garci Lasso wrote comparatively little : three eclogues, five *canciones*, an epistle, besides thirty-eight sonnets. But all his work is of a most lovely and refined quality. It is true that his essays in the *versos sueltos* are not good. He failed also in his second eclogue when he strove to lend variety to his tercets by introducing the *rima percossa*, the rhyme in the middle of the hendecasyllabic. He is derivative, of course. The *rima percossa* is an idea borrowed from Sannazaro ; the *lira*, which takes its name from the only noun in the first line of the *Cancion a la Flor de Gnido*, is a copy of Bernardo Tasso's favourite measure. The point is that Garci Lasso contrives to acclimatize his material ;

his transplantation has been so successful that the elder Tasso's claim to priority has been overlooked in Italy itself. Literature is full of surprises. Few surprises are greater than to find the measure in which the sensuous, half-pagan *Flor de Gnido* is written adapted to the lofty purposes of Luis de Leon and the exultant ecstasy of St. John of the Cross. Boscan, who was a gentleman, recognized his friend's superiority as an artist. He avows that but for Garci Lasso's encouragement, he would have lost heart and abandoned his own tentative essays. It is to Boscan's credit that he makes so manful an avowal. Garci Lasso does with perfection and with ease all that Boscan does with effort and incomplete ambition. It may be that we are not now as susceptible to Garci Lasso's charm as were his contemporaries. This is mainly due to the fact that the pastoral convention adopted by him is no longer in vogue. Garci Lasso aims at being sweet, and if we admit the legitimacy of that aim we shall soon feel the dreamy enchantment of his melodious numbers. Not Virgil himself has a keener sense of beauty: '*O dulces prendas, por mi mal halladas*' and the *Cancion a la Flor de Gnido* are likely to subsist as long as anything in the Spanish language. It would not have troubled Garci Lasso to be told that his poems were artificial. He meant them to be. For him, poetry, being an art, was necessarily artificial; he merely asks us to accept the conditions of his convention, to accompany him into an enchanted Arcady of amaranths and asphodels where we can enjoy at least for a moment the illusion of reality. What Garci Lasso gives us is not a transcription of life: the workaday, commonplace existence that we know. He wields the keys of a happy, golden land

THE MIDDLE RENAISSANCE 173

where beauty is the chief element and where the vulgarities of life are unknown. Every note from his lute echoes with an elfin melody. His golden voice still rings in our ears and among contemporaries his charm was limitless.

Boscan and Garci Lasso had been friends in life and in death they were not divided. Garci Lasso's poems fill the fourth book of Boscan's *Obras*. No doubt the appearance of Garci Lasso's poems in print helped to spread his reputation. He became so much the vogue that it was perhaps thought necessary to counteract his humanistic, indifferent spirit by bringing out a sort of Christian parody of his verses and Boscan's: *Las obras de Boscan y Garcilasso trasladadas en materias Christianas y religiosas* (1575) by Sebastian de Cordova Sazedo. Garci Lasso was probably orthodox enough, and he must have conformed readily in externals: otherwise he could not have held for a day his position as Charles V's favourite at the later period of the Emperor's reign. But we can easily see that Garci Lasso is not touched by religious zeal: all his interests were centred on the imaginative world of his own creation, a world where paganism holds its own and where he dwells like a beautiful sylvan being, listening to the chants of golden-throated shepherds and fleeing hamadryads.

Meanwhile a similar movement was evident in the work of the well-known Portuguese poet, Francisco de Sá de Miranda[1] (1485?-1558). But Sá de Miranda worked independently; he had been a pioneer

[1] *Poesías*, ed. C. Michaëlis de Vasconcellos, Halle, 1885. See: C. Castello Branco, *Sa de Miranda*. Porto, 1886; Th. Braga, *Sá de Miranda e a Eschola italiana*. Porto, 1896; C. Michaëlis de Vasconcellos, *Novos estudos sobre Sâ de Miranda*,

of the Italianizing movement in Portugal some years before he saw a copy of Garci Lasso's manuscript, which was given him about 1534-1535 by his friend Antonio Pereira Marramaque. He began by writing *cantigas* and *esparsas*, which may be found in Resende's *Cancioneiro geral*. A visit to Italy (1521-1526) proved the determining factor in his art. About two years after his return, Sá de Miranda attempted the pastoral genre : his Italian tendencies are more marked in *Aleixo*, an eclogue in hendecasyllabics composed between 1528 and 1532. Of his hundred and ninety poems collected by Sra. Michaëlis de Vasconcellos, seventy-five are in Spanish. A good poet in Portuguese, Sá de Miranda is a good poet also in Spanish. Some of his five eclogues written in Spanish, particularly the one on the death of Garci Lasso—*Nemoroso* —deserve high praise, although an exigent critic might find in them lusitanisms which blemish sound work.

Another convert to the new school was Gutierre de Cetina[1] (1518 ?-1554 ?), a Sevillan soldier who served in Italy and Germany in 1542-1547. There he won favour with Diego Hurtado de Mendoza and addressed to him a verse epistle noteworthy for more than the magnificent audacity with which its writer asks his patron for a painting by Titian. In 1547 he went to

in *Boletim da Segunda Classe* (Academia das Sciencias de Lisboa), v (1912), pp. 9-230; A. F. G. Bell, in *Studies in Portuguese Literature*. Oxford, 1913. pp. 81-113.

[1] *Obras*, ed. J. Hazañas y la Rua, Sevilla, 1895. 2 vols.—See : P. Savj-López, *Un petrarchista spagnuolo*. Trani, 1896 ; J. Cejador, *El Madrigal de Cetina*, in *Revue Hispanique*, LVII (1923), pp. 108-114; F. Rodríguez Marín, in *Nuevos datos para las biografías de cien escritores de los siglos xvi y xvii*. Madrid, 1923. pp. 105-182; A. F. G. Bell, in *The Modern Language Review*, xx (1925), pp. 179-183.

Mexico and though he returned to Spain, where he seems to have written copiously, Mexico claimed him as her own. He happened to be in a street of Los Angeles when a midnight brawl took place, and he was killed by mistake for someone else. Cetina is apt to be a little underrated because he is so imitative. Many of his poems are merely free translations from Petrarch, Ariosto and Ausias March. But he can sing about himself if so minded, and one grows rather weary of hearing Vandalio's—that is Cetina's—unlucky love-affair with Amarillida. This may be unjust, for the incessant re-appearance of Amarillida implies remarkable constancy on the poet's part. However, we do not insist on constancy in a poet. We ask him to stir us, interest us, and charm us; and that is what Cetina does in *Ojos claros, serenos*, one of the most celebrated poems in Spanish. As this delightful madrigal is a snatch of song only ten lines long, it lodges in every memory, however unretentive, and ensures Cetina as absolute immortality as anybody can dare to hope for. Apart from this one song, Cetina's dexterity in metrics should claim some recognition, for he was as skilled a craftsman in the sonnet-form as Garci Lasso de la Vega.

Another Italianate, Hernando de Acuña [1] (1522?-1586?), served in Piedmont under the soldier-poet, Don Alonso de Avalos, Marqués del Vasto. Acuña says a good deal about Vasto and the marchioness

---

[1] *Contienda de Ayax*, etc., ed. J. J. Lopez de Sedano, in *Parnaso español*. Madrid, 1770. II, pp. 21-51; *Varias poesías*. Madrid, 1804.—See: N. Alonso Cortés, *Don Hernando de Acuña. Noticias biográficas*. Valladolid, 1913; J. P. W. Crawford, *Notes on the Poetry of Hernando de Acuña*, in *The Romanic Review*, VII (1916), pp. 314-327.

whom he celebrates under the names of Silvia and Galatea. He had a considerable success with his *El Caballero determinado* (1553), a translation of Olivier de la Marche's (1425-1502) *Le Chevalier délibéré*, which was a favourite with the Emperor. Charles V, who was not a man of letters, had no taste in poetry, and perhaps liked the poem chiefly because it celebrated his great-grandfather, Charles le Téméraire (1433-1477), killed at the siege of Dijon. There is a story that Charles V translated *Le Chevalier délibéré* into prose, suggesting that his prose-version should be rhymed, and he appears further to have suggested that the rhymed version might be published at the expense of his secretary, Van Male (d. 1560 ?). However this may be, *El Caballero determinado* came out in 1553. Whether Charles V had anything to do with it is very doubtful. Acuña went over body and soul to the Italian methods, but does not seem to have published anything else in his lifetime. His *Varias poesias* (1591) appeared posthumously. They contain some ambitious attempts like the *Contienda de Ayax Zelamonio y de Vlisses sobre las armas de Achiles*, but this is less ambitious than it seems, for on examination it proves to be a version in blank verse of part of the twelfth book of Ovid's *Metamorphoses*. Acuña was not an original talent: he draws freely on Ovid and has left renderings of the *Orlando innamorato* by Boiardo (1434-1494), and of minor poets like Muzzarelli (1490 ?-1516) and Castellani. But he had a ready pen, excelled as a writer of occasional society verse, and on rare occasions touches a graver note: for instance, in the celebrated sonnet which contains the famous line:

'Vn Monarca, vn Imperio y vna Espada.'

He has a vein of humour, as he makes plain in his parody of Garci Lasso's *lira*. Gerónimo de Urrea (who had re-translated in 1555 *Le Chevalier délibéré*), or Luis Zapata, must have smiled at the lines on the 'good knight and bad poet' at whose expense Acuña made merry.

In Acuña's works is printed a *Carta de Dido a Eneas* from Ovid. But this free rendering in tercets is also ascribed to DIEGO HURTADO DE MENDOZA[1] (1503-1575), one of the most interesting figures in the history of Spanish humanism. A soldier, a cleric in minor orders, a diplomatist, a scholar and a historian, Mendoza was likewise a poet. The fifth son of the second count of Tendilla and first Marqués de Mondéjar he was brought up in Granada, and in Salamanca. He is said to have fought in the battle of Pavia (1525) and at Tunis (1535), where he gave proof of high valour. In 1537-1538 Mendoza was in England as Envoy Extraordinary to arrange two marriages: one between

---

[1] *Obras poéticas*, ed. W. I. Knapp, 1877 (Col. de libros esp. raros ó curiosos, 11); *Poesías*, ed. A. de Castro, 1854, in Bib. de Autores Esp., XXXII; *Poésies burlesques et satiriques inédites*, ed. A. Morel-Fatio, in *Jahrbuch für romanische und englische Sprache und Literatur*, II (1875), pp. 63-80, 186-209; *Mechanica de Aristotiles*, ed. R. Foulché-Delbosc, in *Revue Hispanique*, v (1898), pp. 367-405.—See: C. Graux, *Essai sur les origines du fonds grec de L'Escurial*. 1880 (Bib. de l'École des Hautes Études, 46); J. Fesenmair, *D. Diego Hurtado de Mendoza, ein spanischer Humanist des xvi. Jahrhunderts*. München, 1882-1884; E. Señán y Alonso, *D. Diego Hurtado de Mendoza*. Jerez, 1886: R. Foulché-Delbosc, *Un point contesté de la vie de Don Diego Hurtado de Mendoza*, in *Revue Hispanique*, II (1895), pp. 208-303; R. Foulché-Delbosc, *Le portrait de Mendoza*, in *Revue Hispanique*, XXIII (1910), pp. 310-313; R. Foulché-Delbosc, *Les œuvres attribuées à Mendoza*, in *Revue Hispanique*, XXXII (1914), pp. 1-86.

Henry VIII and the Duchess of Milan, niece of Charles V, and the other between Mary Tudor and Don Luis of Portugal. Upon the failure of this mission, Mendoza went to the Netherlands and in 1539 to Venice, where he remained as ambassador until about 1547. In 1542 he represented Charles V at the Council of Trent, and seems to have harassed the other deputies by his incessant activities. In 1554 he was recalled from Rome to Spain, and with the accession to the throne of Philip II his diplomatic career came to an end. The phrase ascribed to him at Trent by the historiographer Juan Paez de Castro (d. 1570), 'Estudiemos, señor Juan Paez,' is characteristic of the man. An untiring worker himself, he was indefatigable in his efforts to encourage learning and to promote other men's labours. In Venice, he was the patron of the Aldine Press; a Greek and Arabic scholar he collected manuscripts with ardour; from Suliman II, the Magnificent (1520-1566), from Greece and Turkey through the medium of Nicolas Sofiano he secured all the Greek MSS. that he could obtain, and he had transcribed for his own library—now in the Escorial—most of Bessarion's Greek collection. The first edition of Josephus printed in Bâle in 1544 was made from three of Mendoza's manuscripts. He commentated Aristotle and translated his *Mechanica*.

Mendoza had excelled in the old measures to an extent that drew admiration from Lope de Vega long afterwards. But his sojourn in Italy and his own instincts as a Renaissance scholar led him to try the new metres: perhaps his best attempt is the *Fabula de Adonis, Hipomenes y Atalanta*. His talent had a picaresque bent; he deals wittily with all manner of

THE MIDDLE RENAISSANCE

unpoetical themes: his success in handling these commonplace subjects was undoubted. They reveal to us a Mendoza very different from the solemn ambassador and historian of the Alpujarra campaign. Though Mendoza joined the band of innovators, he never quite mastered the technique of the new school, but the fact that he abandoned metres in which he excelled for novelties that he failed to master is eloquent testimony to the completeness of the victory won by Boscan and Garci Lasso de la Vega.

We can well imagine that, though in the narration of the Italianizing poetic movement events are presented with an air of peaceful continuity, such a revolution in long-established practice could not be brought about without conflict and protests from the partisans of the old measures. It is undeniable that some reforming measure was needed, for the Spanish lyrical verse seemed to be on the point of perishing from exhaustion when the innovators appeared on the scene. The form and the metre alike of the old lyrical poetry clamoured for reform. It is quite an arguable point, however, that it might have been better had this rejuvenescence of the lyrical verse been brought about in another way. Lyrical verse might take on a new form or a new set of forms. There was always the risk of its losing in this process something of its native savour, of its essential individuality and of substituting instead ideas and forms of art not readily to be assimilated by the Spanish genius. Now the greatest of the Italianates, Garci Lasso de la Vega, might be regarded as a Neapolitan poet: what is true of Garci Lasso is still truer of the lesser poets of this group. There is excellent work among their productions, no doubt; but their lyrical verse is devoid of the characteristic flavour of the authentic Spanish lyric. It is ingenious, delicate, charming, but it is not specially racy of the soil. It lacks the saving virtue of independent originality: the trail of imitation is over it all. No doubt the *versos de arte mayor* were insufficiently ductile, and subject to considerable irregularities. That is true. But they had in themselves great potentialities, and in the hands of an accomplished craftsman like Juan de Mena they were capable of producing effects more sonorous and not less artistic than those of the Italian hendecasyllabic. We must not lose sight of the fact that all the popular forms of old Spanish verse were profoundly rooted in the soil whence they drew the very sap of their existence. At that moment the metrical forms of lyrical poetry were so intimately associated with the subjects of lyrical verse that the adoption of the new methods seemed certain to effect a radical change in the themes which constituted the essence of lyrical poetry. The opponents of the Italian innovations had, therefore, a good deal to say for their view. They were beaten, not on the question of pure merit, but because the innovators had the advantage of possessing in Garci Lasso de la Vega a man of indubitable genius. The Italianates won in the main issue—the naturalization of the Italian measures. Some of the old measures, the *quintilla*, the *décima* and, above all, the *romance* survived out of the general ruin. The Spanish conservatives did not produce anybody of transcendent gifts.

Among the partisans of the old methods there was, however, a man of brilliant talent, a cleric called Cristóbal de Castillejo [1] (1490 ?-1550), who had once

[1] *Obras*, ed. R. Fernandez, Madrid, 1792. 2 vols. (Col. de Ramon Fernandez, 12, 13); *Poesías*, ed. A. de Castro, 1854,

been secretary to Mendoza. Born in Ciudad Rodrigo, he took service under Charles V's brother, Ferdinand, who became successively King of Bohemia (1526), of the Romans (1531), and of Hungary (1540). Castillejo's official duties compelled him to live for the most part out of Spain. He was at the Diet of Augsburg and followed Ferdinand to Austria and Bohemia. He was assigned a pension from the funds belonging to the bishopric of Avila and became in consequence involved in a lawsuit with the Bishop. His family was ennobled in 1532 ; Castillejo himself refused a titulary bishopric in 1535, and in 1536 he was given a benefice in Ardegge in the diocese of Passau. This he resigned in 1539, possibly to go to Venice in the suite of Mendoza. There used to be a legend current that Castillejo returned to Spain in his extreme old age, and that he died, almost a centenarian, in the odour of sanctity at the Carthusian monastery of Valdeiglesias near Toledo in 1596. This is a pious but baseless invention. Castillejo entered a Carthusian monastery, that is true. But he entered it when quite young before he attached himself to King Ferdinand. He died at Vienna, on June 12, 1550, according to his tombstone in Wiener-Neustadt cemetery.

in Bib. de Autores Esp., XXXII ; *Sermon de Amores*, ed. R. Foulché-Delbosc, in *Revue Hispanique*, XXXVI (1916), pp. 509-595 ; *Dialogo de Mugeres*, ed. L. Pfandl, in *Revue Hispanique*, LII (1921), pp. 361-429.—See : C. L. Nicolay, *The life and works of Cristóbal de Castillejo*. Philadelphia, 1910 ; J. Menéndez Pidal, *Datos para la biografía de Cristóbal de Castillejo*, in *Boletín de la R. Academia Esp.*, II (1915), pp. 3-20 ; R. Foulché-Delbosc, *Deux Œuvres de Cristóbal de Castillejo*, in *Revue Hispanique*, XXXVI (1916), pp. 489-508 ; L. Pfandl, *Der ' Diálogo de Mugeres' von 1544, und seine Bedeutung für die Castillejo-Forschung* [*Archiv für das Studium der neueren Sprachen und Literaturen*, CXL] Braunschweig-Hamburg, 1920.

There is something very attractive about Castillejo: nothing saintly at all. His saintliness is not very apparent in the charming pagan verses which he was fond of writing to Ana (Anna von Schaumburg). There is something mundane in Castillejo's talent: something mischievous, impertinent and gay. It is all the more strange if we bear in mind that he was an invalid for a long while and that his health was never strong. He saw the ludicrous side of everything, enjoyed life thoroughly, and, though condemned to move in the suffocating air of courts, was never happier than in describing popular customs in witty metres. He does every now and then write in the Italian metres as if to shew that he could excel in them if he chose. As a rule, however, he has nothing but scorn for the innovators, especially for Boscan. He imitates Ovid with success, and his adaptations of Catullus—*Vuestros lindos ojos, Ana* (car. li) and *Dame, amor, besos sin cuento* (car. v)—are really models in the way of combined charm and fidelity. He was not above imitating moderns, if they were dead like Petrarch, as in the *Torre del Viento*, or if they wrote in Latin like Boscan's friend Navagero, from whose *De Cupidine et Hyella* Castillejo takes *Al amor preso*. But he appears to have been sincerely convinced that the introduction of the new forms was a device to hide a fundamental poverty of thought. This is the general drift of, not his best but, his best known poem, *Contra los que dejan los metros castellanos y siguen los italianos*. Castillejo's prolonged absence from Spain probably explains why he did not exercise a more decisive influence in the struggle against Italian forms. He seems also to have been indifferent about literary renown. Some of his work struggled into print, perhaps without his

THE MIDDLE RENAISSANCE

knowledge in 1543-1544. His poems as a whole were not available till 1573. They consist of three books, very diverse in the inspiration of their contents: charming love-songs, witty essays in badinage, moral treatises in some of which, the *Sermon de amores*, for instance, the moral element is singularly absent, parodies or adaptations of old *romances* such as *La bella malmaridada* ; *Tiempo es ya, Castillejo* ; *Por la dolencia va el viejo* ; glosses of Jorge Manrique's verses, translations and literary problems or satires. These last attracted most attention, but they were not published till long after Boscan, Garci Lasso and Castillejo himself were dead. In 1573 the result was no longer in doubt. The Italianizers had carried all before them. Castillejo was not without imitators in Spain and in France, where Chapelain (1595-1674 ?), Voiture (1598-1648), and Sarrasin (1604 ?-1655) undoubtedly underwent his influence.

Antonio de Villegas (d. about 1551) is the author of the *Inventario* printed posthumously in 1565. This contains a very feeble paraphrase on the eternal subject of Pyramus and Thisbe, eighteen compositions written in *décimas* and an epistle which displays an elegant facility. The *Inventario* contains, however, something of much more interest than any of these things : the *Historia del Abencerrage y la hermosa Xarifa*. But it is only too probable that Villegas never wrote a line of this delightful work. Castillejo shakes his head disapprovingly over a certain captain Luis de Haro,[1] whom he reports as having gone over to the Italianates. Castillejo is likely enough to be well

[1] *Coplas*, in *Cancionero general de 1554*, ed. A. Morel-Fatio, in *L'Espagne au xvi° et au xvii° siècle*. Heilbronn, 1878. pp. 525-528.

informed on a point of this kind; but Haro's Italianizing efforts would appear to be lost. He is represented to us only by four poems in Nágera's *Cancionero*; these are commonplace futilities in quite the old manner. Two other poets perhaps should be mentioned here. Gerónimo Ximenez de Urrea [1] (1513-1574 ?), the Aragonese Captain who picked up Garci Lasso de la Vega when mortally wounded at Muy. He fails in his translation (1549) of *Orlando furioso* and fails equally in another of *Le Chevalier délibéré*, but he was not altogether unsuccessful in the *Libro del invencible caballero Don Clarisel de las Flores y de Austrasia*, a chivalresque novel whose first part was not published until 1879. The organist at Granada, Gregorio Silvestre [2] (1520-1569), son of João Rodrigues, doctor to John III of Portugal, began by writing verse in the old manner and then went over to the other side, because it was becoming fashionable. He is not a great poet, but he attains success in both the old style and the new.

Rather prominent in his own way as a writer of didactic prose was Francisco [Lopez] de

---

[1] *Don Clarisel de las Flores y de Austrasia*, ed. J. M. Asensio. 1879 (Soc. de Bibliófilos Andaluces).—See: G. Borao, *Gerónimo Urrea y su novela inédita Don Clarisel de las Flores*. Zaragoza, 1867.

[2] *Poesías*, ed. A. de Castro, 1854, in Bib. de Autores Esp., XXXII and ed. J. de Sancha, 1855, in Bib. de Autores Esp., XXXV; *Algunas poesías atribuídas a Gregorio Silvestre*, ed. M. L. Guzmán, in *Revue Hispanique*, XXXV (1915), pp. 439-475.—See: D. García Peres, in *Catálogo razonado ... de los autores portugueses que escribieron en castellano*. Madrid, 1890. pp. 518-532; H. A. Rennert, in *Modern Language Notes*, XIV (1899), col. 457-465; F. Rodríguez Marín, in *Luis Barahona de Soto*, etc. Madrid, 1903. pp. 32-35.

Villalobos [1] (1473 ?-1549 ?), court physician in the time of Ferdinand and Charles V. His *Sumario de la medicina* ... (1498), a juvenile professional work in *versos de arte mayor*, is less well known than its derivative, *Los Secretos de philosophia y medicina* (1539) by Alonso Lopez de Corella. This is a dull performance of no literary merit reprinted in 1546 under the title *Trezientas preguntas de cosas naturales* ... The *Sumario* could not have saved Villalobos from oblivion, but a prose-work, *Libro intitulado Los problemas* (1543), which deals with astronomy as well as with practical morals in a picturesque and flexible style, includes the interesting and ingenious *El tractado de las tres grandes* ('la gran parlería, la gran porfía' and 'la gran risa'—talkativeness, stubbornness and laughter), and to this Villalobos owes his not inconsiderable renown. In addition to his fluent and vivid style, Villalobos was the possessor of a pretty wit, shimmering and mordant. He had in him the making of a real man of letters, but the exercise of his profession absorbed his powers in another direction, his Jewish ancestry was held against him and he had the unenviable gift of making enemies. The variety of his accomplishments and interests led him to translate Plautus's *Amphytrion* in 1515, and to gloss (1524) two books of Pliny's *Natural History*. In an unlucky moment of politeness, Villalobos sent his two glosses to the famous humanist, Hernan Nuñez de Toledo. That atrabiliar

---

[1] *Libro intitulado Los Problemas*...; *Tractado de las tres grandes*...; *Cancion*...; *Anfitrion*, ed. A. de Castro, 1855, in Bib. de Autores Esp., XXXVI; *Algunas obras*, ed. A. M. Fabié, 1886 (Soc. de Bibliófilos Esp., 24); *Diálogo*, ed. A. Paz y Mélia, in *Sales Españolas*. 1902, II, pp. 3-33 (Col. de Escritores Cast., 121).

personage, forgetful of the proverbial warning against looking a gift-horse in the mouth, devoted much time to a critical examination of the glosses, and, full of self-satisfaction, belaboured Villalobos's effort unmercifully. But Villalobos was not the man to take an attack lying down, and he replied in an outburst of splenetic wit, which must have come as a surprise to Nuñez de Toledo, who was not so accustomed to receive insults as to offer them.

More learned and perhaps a trifle pedagogical is the manner of HERNAN PEREZ DE OLIVA [1] (1494 ?-1531), professor of moral theology and rector of Salamanca, who studied successively in Salamanca, Alcalá de Henares, Paris, and Rome. He was one of the first learned Spaniards who saw the possibility and even advisability of using Spanish instead of Latin for the discussion of serious questions. His theories are set forth in stately and dignified Castilian in the *Dialogo de la dignidad del hombre*, which was continued in 1546 by Francisco Cervantes de Salazar [2] (1514 ?-1575), professor of rhetoric at Osuna. In 1553 Salazar went to Mexico, where he was ordained in 1555; he rose to be canon and finally rector of the University of Mexico, occupying as well the post of official chronicler from 1560 onwards. His *Cronica de la Nueva España* was not published till 1914. A clear

[1] *Diálogo de la dignidad del hombre*, ed. A. de Castro, 1873, in Bib. de Autores Esp., LXV.—See: M. Menéndez y Pelayo, *Páginas de un libro inédito*, in *La Ilustración española y americana*, XIX (1875), pp. 154-155, 174-175.

[2] *Obras que Francisco Ceruantes de Salazar ha hecho, glossado i tradvcido*. Madrid, 1772; *Crónica de la Nueva España*, ed. M. Magallón, Madrid, 1914 (The Hispanic Society of America). See: J. García Icazbalceta, in *Obras*. México, 1897. IV, pp. 17-52.

THE MIDDLE RENAISSANCE 187

prose style distinguishes Alexo Venegas del Busto (1493 ?-d. after 1543), who wrote on death and other cheerful topics of the same kind. He is the author of *Agonia del Transito de la Muerte* (1537 ?) and *Primera parte de las differencias de libros que ay en el universo* (1540). The efforts of these three men were without result at the time, but the unique position of Latin had nevertheless received a shock.

A writer of the didactic type who won universal fame was the Bishop of Mondoñedo, ANTONIO DE GUEVARA[1] (1480 ?-1545). A native of Santander, he joined the Franciscan order, was appointed Commissioner of the Inquisition at Valencia, where he converted, according to his boast, twenty-seven thousand *morisco* families; he continued this work at Granada, and was made bishop of Guadix (1528) before he received the see of Mondoñedo (1537). Guevara was the official historiographer of Charles V and wrote the *Libro aureo de Marco Aurelio, emperador y eloquentissimo orador*. This appeared in 1528 without the author's permission, and within a year the work was

---

[1] *Libro del emperador Marco aurelio cõ relox de principes* . . . Valladolid, 1529; *Menosprecio dela Corte y Alabanza dela Aldea*, ed. J. de San Pelayo Ladrón de García, Bilbao, 1893; ed. M. Martínez de Burgos, 1915 (Clásicos Castellanos, 29); *Arte de marear*, ed. J. de San Pelayo Ladrón de García, Bilbao, 1895; *Epistolas familiares*, ed. E. de Ochoa, 1850, in Bib. de Autores Esp., XIII.—See: M. Menéndez y Pelayo, in *Orígenes de la Novela*. Madrid, 1905. I, pp. ccclxv-ccclxxv; J. M. Gálvez, *Guevara in England (Kapitel I und II)*. Berlin, 1910; R. Foulché-Delbosc, *Bibliographie espagnole de Fray Antonio de Guevara* [*Revue Hispanique*, XXXIII] 1915; H. Vaganay, *Antonio de Guevara et son œuvre dans la littérature italienne. Essai de bibliographie* [*La Bibliofilia*] Firenze, 1916; *The Diall of Princes* [select passages from Sir Thomas North's translation], ed. K. N. Colvile, London, 1919.

re-printed four times. In 1529, Guevara intervened and published an amplified edition under the title: *Libro llamado Relox de Principes, en el qual va encorporado el muy famoso libro de Marco Aurelio*; another edition was published the same year with the heading: *Libro del emperador Marco Aurelio con Relox de Principes*. Guevara has really written a fantastic work founded on an imaginary life of Marcus Aurelius. He alleged that he was writing history based on a manuscript supposed to be in Florence. No such manuscript ever existed, and the assertion is obviously one of the ingenious devices to which novelists resort in order to enhance the interest of their imaginative flights. The *Relox de Principes* is the ideal of the perfect ruler. It need scarcely be said that the ideal prince ought to be a sound Christian, a feat rather difficult on the part of Marcus Aurelius, the protagonist of the book. Book III has a special interest, for in chapters ii.-v. we meet with the long episode of the Danubian peasant, familiar to readers of La Fontaine (*Fables*, xi. 7). Guevara's book was translated into Italian (1543), into German (1599), into Latin (1606), into Dutch (1612), and into Armenian (1738). The first edition was translated into French by René Bertaut de la Grise, *Le Livre dore de Marc Aurèle* (1531), while *Lorloge des princes* (1540) would seem to be by the same author in collaboration with Antoine du Moulin. In England Lord Berners's version was published posthumously in 1534, and according to one theory, this version would have been responsible for the introduction of euphuism.

Guevara was a prolific writer. In the *Decada de Cesares* (1539), he follows his authorities but does not hesitate to intercalate anything that he imagines will add to the interest of the work. His *Epistolas familiares* (1539-1542) were so much admired that they were frequently styled the *Golden Epistles* and became as popular in France as *Marco Aurelio*. Now there was at Soria just then a lecturer called Pedro Rhua who had been greatly impressed by the fact that he had noted some mistakes in Guevara. He was naïf enough to point them out in a letter to Guevara, who gave a rather snubbing answer to the effect that he wrote to amuse himself, and that save in religious matters, he claimed the most absolute liberty to say and think what he liked. Rhua returned to the attack in a third *Carta* (1549); this time he levelled his charges against Guevara's *Libro del Menosprecio dela corte y alabança dela aldea* as well. There is something very annoying, it must be admitted, in Guevara's self-sufficiency. There was hardly any subject on which he did not feel qualified to express an opinion. In the *Epistolas familiares* there is a total absence of the free abandon which characterizes all good private letters. They are simply a medium in which Guevara's mania for moralizing, advising and counselling everybody about everything finds free vent. You may be a doctor, or a soldier or a Jew; Guevara embarrasses you at once by thrusting on you his opinion as to how you ought to behave. He will be pointing a moral; talks about Lamia the courtesan à propos of the sibyl and is always airing his learning. A niece of his loses a little dog and Guevara means to be sympathetic. But in his endeavour to cheer up the girl, he can think of nothing more consoling to tell her than that things might have been worse, and that it was a more serious matter for Eve when Abel was killed. Can there be anything more futile, more unbecoming a bishop? Guevara also wrote a book to teach sailors their business: *Libro delos inuentores del marear y de sesenta trabajos que ay en las galeras* (1539); he harps on the dangers of life at court in the *Libro de Auiso de priuados y doctrina de cortesanos* (1539), and in the *Libro de Menosprecio dela corte y alabança dela aldea* (1539) contrasts court life and life in the country. Needless to say that Guevara did not fail to produce devout professional works such as the *Oratorio de religiosos y exercicio de virtuosos* (1542) and the *Monte Caluario* (1545-1549).

It is rather difficult to deny all merit to anybody who has enjoyed so widespread and so lasting a reputation as Guevara. He had merits distinctly: he has vigour and at times he writes quite well. He was, as Spaniards are apt to be, deliberately eloquent and he drops with astonishing facility into the declamatory style. But he is not always eloquent and not always moralizing. He has many notes: is sarcastic, ironical, dignified, confiding. He sometimes has a flight of stately phrasing. He has, it is true, a tiresome trick of talking as if he were in the pulpit, and his oleaginous eloquence is not attractive. But he excels in wit, in ingenuity and in rhetorical effects. He is redundant and verbose: but he is not indifferent in the matter of style; on the contrary, he is one of the earliest Spanish writers who is visibly concerned with stylistic problems. Guevara had read rather more than he could assimilate. Like Seneca, he resorts to violent antitheses and three-piled metaphors. Like Cicero, he indulges in mere verbiage, in incessant repetitions. It is perhaps an exaggeration or worse to ascribe to Guevara any responsibility for the Euphuism introduced into England by Lyly. But it is quite certain that his

THE MIDDLE RENAISSANCE 191

Menosprecio dela corte and the *Auiso de priuados* exercised a real influence on French satire through *Le Courtisan retiré* (1574) of Jean de la Taille (1540-1611). A man who has interested Sir Thomas North (1535 ?-1601 ?), Montaigne, Brantôme (1540-1614), and Henry Vaughan (1622-1695) cannot be dismissed as negligible. Guevara occupied a great place in the literature of his own time, and his historical importance is almost beyond one's power to exaggerate.

The chivalresque novels which were available to everybody in Charles V's reign are now no longer accessible. Their popularity was immense and extended to all classes. Mendoza travelled about with a movable library of those novels: Charles V himself was an impassioned admirer of them. Many persons took these fantastic tales for the gospel truth. Simon de Silveira, a Portuguese poet, swore on the Bible that he believed every word in *Amadis de Gaula* to be true: the chronicler Juan del Castillo writing in 1587 solemnly records that when Philip II married Mary Tudor at Winchester, he undertook to abdicate if King Arthur returned to claim the throne of England. These books were for the most part continuations of *Amadis de Gaula*, but there was another family in fiction hardly less famous, the family of *Palmerin*. In a general way the *Amadis* series is usually said to consist of twelve different parts, inclusive of the four parts which make up the first printed *Amadis de Gaula*. Montalvo, the publisher of these first four books, wrote as a continuation a fifth book which he called *Las Sergas del muy virtuoso cauallero Esplandian*[1] ... whose first known edition bears the date 1510. The sixth book, *Florisando, principe de Cantaria* (1510),

[1] Ed. P. de Gayangos, 1857, in Bib. de Autores Esp., XL.

the nephew of Amadis, was written by Paez de Ribera, an Andalusian of whom we know nothing. The seventh book, *Los grandes fechos en armas de Lisuarte de Grecia fijo de Esplandian, y assi mesmo de los de Perion de Gaula* (1514), was, as Dr. Henry Thomas has clearly demonstrated, by Feliciano de Silva, Cervantes's favourite butt. At this point there intervened a certain bachelor, Juan Diaz, who published an eighth book, *Lisuarte de Grecia* (1526), in which he killed off Amadis, for good and all as he thought. This was not at all to the liking of Silva, who brought Amadis to life again in the ninth book, *Chronica del muy valiente y esforçado principe y Cauallero de la Ardiente Espada, Amadis de Grecia, hijo de Lisuarte de Grecia* (1530), and followed up this feat with the first two parts (1532) of *Don Florisel de Niquea*, the tenth book. Two more parts (1535-1551) of *Don Florisel* constitute the eleventh book and the twelfth is *Don Silves de la Selva* (1546), ascribed to Pedro de Luxan, an attribution which seems questionable.

The opposition series begins with *El libro del famoso y muy esforçado cauallero Palmerin de Oliua*[1] (1511), said to be the work of a rather mysterious woman, to whom is also ascribed the second book in the series: *Primaleon* (1512). Claims are also put in for a certain Francisco Vazquez of Ciudad-Rodrigo, but he is just as elusive as the lady. The third book, the anonymous *Cronica del muy valiente y esforçado caballero Platir, hijo del emperador Primaleon* (1530), is not a work of great interest or entertainment. The last of the

[1] See: H. Vaganay, in *Les Romans de chevalerie italiens d'inspiration espagnole: Essai de bibliographie*, in *La Bibliofilia*, IX (1908), pp. 121-131.

Palmerin series, *Palmeirim de Inglaterra*,[1] is now admitted to have been written in Portuguese in 1544 by Francisco de Moraes Cabral (1500 ?-1572), *o Palmeirim*, so nicknamed after his hero. A curious thing about this work is that a Spanish translation of it appeared in 1547-1548, while the earliest known Portuguese edition dates from 1567. The Spanish translator is called Luis Hurtado (1530 ?-1579), and perhaps some will see a dramatic propriety in the name. Cervantes makes the priest in *Don Quijote* describe *Palmeirim de Inglaterra* as 'a thing unique' and suggest that it be 'shut up in a box like that which Alexander found among the spoils of Darius, meant to hold the works of Homer.' Moraes was not a Homer, but he wrote a very good book of its kind and the last that need detain us here. About the middle of the century, the chivalresque *genre* began to shew signs of exhaustion. Writers took to interlarding their prose with verse, and drew nearer to the pastoral convention. Some adumbration of pastoralism is already noticeable in Silva's *Amadis de Grecia*. Another variant of the chivalresque novel is the *caballeria a lo divino*, where romantic knightly adventures were presented in the form of an allegory as a cover for pious teaching and edifying doctrine. A shocking example of this sort was given by Hieronymo de Sempere in his *Libro de cavalleria celestial del pie de*

[1] Ed. A. Bonilla y San Martín, in *Libros de Caballerías*. 1908. II, pp. 1-374 (Nueva Bib. de Autores Esp., 11).—See: C. Michaëlis de Vasconcellos, *Versuch über den Ritterroman Palmeirim de Inglaterra* [*Zeitschrift für romanische Philologie*], Halle, 1883; W. E. Purser, *Palmerin of England*. London, 1904 [See James Fitzmaurice-Kelly, in *Revue Hispanique*, x (1903), pp. 614-635]; H. Thomas, *The Palmerin Romances* [*Transactions of the Bibliographical Society*, XIII], London, 1916.

la Rosa Fragante (1554), and in the *Segunda Parte de la caualleria de las hojas de la Rosa Fragante* (1554). This pious, perverse parodist exhibits Christ as the Knight of the Lion, Satan and St. John the Baptist as the Knight of the Serpent and the Knight of the Desert respectively, and the twelve apostles as the Knights of the Round Table.

At about this period was inaugurated the picaresque novel, an autobiographical novel of low life and the exact counterpart of the books of chivalry. The picaresque *genre* is intimately associated with the historical and economic development of Spain. The wars of Ferdinand and Charles V were an expensive luxury. Commerce and agriculture were destroyed. The middle or trading-class had no chance of prosperity. Everybody who wanted to get on went to court to obtain a sinecure if possible. The capital became the camping-ground of adventurers of all sorts, from shady politicians to recognized criminals. The full effect of this economic situation did not begin to be universally visible till about the end of the sixteenth century, when Mateo Aleman wrote *Guzman de Alfarache*. But to a keen observer the social change was already manifest and such an observer was the author of *La Vida de Lazarillo de Tormes*.[1] This little book, published

[1] Ed. H. Butler Clarke, Oxford, 1897 ; ed. R. Foulché-Delbosc, 1900 (Bib. hispanica, III) ; ed. J. Cejador y Frauca, 1914 (Clásicos castellanos, 25) ; ed. A. Bonilla y San Martín, Madrid, 1915 (Clásicos de la Literatura esp., I).—See : A. Morel-Fatio, *Recherches sur Lazarille de Tormes*, in *Études sur l'Espagne.* 2nd ed. Paris, 1895. I, pp. 109-166 ; F. W. Chandler, *Romances of Roguery*. I. New York, 1899 ; R. Foulché-Delbosc, *Remarques sur 'Lazarille de Tormes,'* in *Revue Hispanique*, VII (1900), pp. 81-97 ; F. De Haan, *An Outline of the History of the Novela*

anonymously, attained a vast and well-deserved celebrity when it appeared and that celebrity still continues. The three oldest editions known came out in 1554 at Alcalá de Henares, Burgos and Antwerp. But it is quite possible that the book was printed earlier. It used to be generally ascribed to Mendoza, but Mayans, and, after him, Morel-Fatio have made the attribution difficult. Whoever was the author, he was a man of genius so far as observation goes. He was not always original and was not above adapting to his purpose old-fashioned tales such as were floating about in the underworld of literature. There is nothing strange in this, Cervantes did the same thing later. The story purports to be the autobiography of a certain Lázaro who serves seven masters in succession and paints them all with audacious truth, a blind man, a miserly priest, a squire, a mendicant monk, a vendor of papal bulls and indulgences, a chaplain and a policeman. This gives Lázaro an opportunity of describing many classes of society, and he acquits himself, not indeed with elegance of style but, with an unadorned simplicity and directness which bespeak the hand of a master. He is realistic with incomparable brevity and vigour; he wastes no word yet he omits no essential. He has produced a masterpiece, an echo of which comes down to us in a passage of *David Copperfield*. The book ends with something like a vague promise of a continuation, and in fact a so-called second part appeared

Picaresca in Spain. The Hague-New York, 1903; F. W. Chandler, *The Literature of Roguery*. Boston, 1907. 2 vols.; J. D. M. Ford, *Possible foreign sources of the Spanish novel of roguery*, in *Kittredge Volume*, 1913; *The Life of Lazarillo de Tormes* [English trans. by L. How with an introduction by C. P. Wagner]. New York, 1917.

at Antwerp in 1555, but this is evidently conceived by a feebler brain and executed by a far less adroit hand. It is not very likely that *Lazarillo de Tormes* introduced the word *lazarillo* (a blind man's guide) into the Spanish language, for *lazarillo* is used almost in that sense by Sebastian de Horozco in his dramatization of St. John's ninth chapter. Unluckily we do not know the date of Horozco's work, so we cannot tell who was first in the field. The word is found in the same sense in Francisco Delicado's coarse novel, *La loçana Andaluza* (1528). *Lazarillo de Tormes* made its way in Spain. It seems also to have been accepted out of Spain. It was translated into English by David Rowland in 1568, and the Rowland version was printed in 1576.[1] Now there is a copy of *Til Howleglas* in the Bodleian which contains the following note in Gabriel Harvey's handwriting : ' This *Howleglas*, with Skoggin, Shelton and *Lazarillo* given me at London of Mr. Spenser xx December [15]78, on condition ... by reading of them over before the first of January immediately entering ; otherwise to forfeit unto him my Lucian in fower volumes.' We do not know whether Gabriel Harvey had to part with his Lucian or not. But it is interesting to find that *Lazarillo* was clearly known to the author of *The Faerie Queene*.

In *La Philosophia Vulgar* of Juan de Mal Lara[2] (1525 ?-1571), we have an instance of the literature of proverbs[3] in which Spain so greatly abounds.

[1] Reprinted Oxford, 1924.

[2] See : J. Gestoso y Perez, in *Nuevos datos para ilustrar las biografías del Maestro Juan de Malara y de Mateo Aleman*. Sevilla, 1896.

[3] *Vocabulario de refranes y frases proverbiales y otras fórmulas comunes de la lengua castellana en que van todos los impresos antes y otra gran copia que juntó el maestro Gonzalo Correas,*

THE MIDDLE RENAISSANCE

Mal Lara's numerous plays are mostly lost and he is remembered as a humanist and a scholar. *La Philosophia Vulgar*, whose first part only appeared in 1568, consists of proverbs taken from Hernan Nuñez de Toledo's collection with a commentary by Mal Lara. It had been preceded by the *Refranes que dizen las viejas tras el huego*, the oldest collection of this kind ; by Blasco de Garay's *Dos cartas en que se contiene, como sabiendo una señora que un su servidor se querria confesar : le escribe por muchos refranes* (1541), a literary curiosity which was imitated by Quevedo in a *Cuento de Cuentos* ; by Pedro Vallés's *Libro de Refranes* (1549), containing four thousand three hundred proverbs,

ed. M. Mir, Madrid, 1906 (R. Academia Esp.) [See : E. Alarcos, *Datos para una biografía de Gonzalo Correas*, in *Boletín de la R. Academia Esp.*, VI (1919), pp. 524-551 ; VII (1920), pp. 47-81, 198-233] ; *Libro de refranes copilado por el orden del A. B. C. [por Mosén Pedro Vallés]*. Facsimile of the 1549 Saragossa ed. by M. García Moreno, Madrid, 1917 ; *El Refranero general español*, ed. J. M. Sbarbi, Madrid, 1874-1878. 10 vols. [See J. M. Sbarbi, *Monografía sobre los refranes, adagios y proverbios castellanos*. Madrid, 1891] ; *Altspanische Sprichwörter*, etc. ed. J. Haller, Regensburg, 1883, 2 vols. in one ; *Zweihundert altspanische Sprichwörter*, ed. J. Cornu, in *Festschrift zum viii Allgemeinen deutschen Neuphilologentage in Wien Pfingsten*, 1898, pp. 195-207 ; *Refranes que dizen las viejas tras el fuego*, ed. U. Cronan, in *Revue Hispanique*, XXV (1911), pp. 134-219 ; *Proverbes judéo-espagnols*, ed. R. Foulché-Delbosc, in *Revue Hispanique*, II (1895), pp. 312-352 ; ed. M. Kayserling, in *Revue Hispanique*, IV (1897), p. 82 ; ed. A. Galante, in *Revue Hispanique*, IX (1902), pp. 440-454 ; *Proverbes judéo-espagnols de Turquie*, ed. A. Danon, in *Zeitschrift für romanische Philologie*, XXVII (1903), pp. 72-96 ; *Libro de Proverbios. Comunmente llamados refranes o vulgares ... copilados y glosados por el licenciado Sebastian de Horozco*, ed. E. Cotarelo y Mori, in *Boletín de la R. Academia Esp.*, II (1915), pp. 646-706 ; III (1916), pp. 98-132, 399-428, 591-604, 710-721 ; IV (1917), pp. 383-396 [unfinished.]

and by the collection of six thousand maxims in the *Refranes, o proverbios en romance* of Hernan Nuñez de Toledo which were edited in 1555 by Leon de Castro. The *Recopilacion de refranes y adagios comunes y vulgares de España* by Sebastian de Horozco is still unpublished: it comprises over eight thousand proverbs. His *Teatro universal. De los Proverbios, Adagios, o comúnmente llamados Refranes Vulgares que más ordinariamente se usan en nra. España* is so far only published in part. But the best collection of this kind is that of the Greek and Hebrew scholar Gonzalo Correas (d. 1631) which was published in 1906.

An example of distinguished prose is afforded in the work of the mystic Juan de Ávila [1] (1500-1569), the apostle of Andalusia frequently invoked by the romantics of 1830, who figures in *Hernani* (1830) as 'Saint-Jean d'Avila,' though he was not beatified until 1894. His *Epistolario espiritual para todos estados* (1578) reveals a kindly spirit, shrewd wisdom and practical commonsense. Juan de Avila was an ardent missioner and an enthusiastic preacher. Like many of his contemporaries, he came under the ban of the Inquisition and suffered in 1532 a short term of imprisonment. Perhaps his best work—a favourite with St. Ignatius of Loyola—is the *Audi, filia, et vide*, a paraphrase in a hundred and thirteen chapters of Psalm xliv, which he wrote in 1530 for a young nun. It was published without his knowledge in 1556; and only received the sanction of the Church in 1574 when

[1] *Las obras del Beato Juan de Avila*, ed. J. Fernández Montaña, 2nd. ed. Madrid, 1901. 4 vols.; *Epistolario espiritual*, ed. V. García de Diego, Madrid, 1912 (Clásicos Cast., 11).—See: A. Catalán Latorre, *El beato Juan de Avila: su tiempo, su vida y sus escritos, y la literatura mística en España.* Zaragoza, 1894.

THE MIDDLE RENAISSANCE 199

it was issued under the title *Libro espiritual que trata de los malos lenguages del mundo, carne y demonio*.

A great writer of didactic prose is the heterodox JUAN DE VALDÉS[1] (d. 1541) who removed to Rome in 1531, having incurred suspicion in Spain. He became chamberlain to Clement VII, and at the latter's death he entered the service of the Cardinal Ercole Gonzaga at Naples. Here he taught his ascetic doctrines to a select circle of listeners among whom were the monk Bernardino Ochino (1487-1564), the bishop Pier Paolo Vergerio (1495 ?-1565), Vittoria Colonna and Giulia Gonzaga (d. 1566). More richly

[1] *Diálogo de Mercurio y Carón*, ed. E. Boehmer, in *Romanische Studien*, VI (1881), Heft XIX; *Diálogo de la lengua*, ed. E. Boehmer, in *Romanische Studien*, VI (1895), Heft XXII; *Trataditos*, ed. E. Boehmer, Bonn, 1880; *Ziento i diez consideraziones*, ed. L. de Usóz y Rio, Londres, 1863; *Le cento e dieci divine considerazioni di Giovanni Valdesso*, ed. E. Boehmer, Halle a. S. 1860; *Commentary upon I Cor.*, English trans. by J. T. Betts, London, 1883.—See: B. B. Wiffen, *Life and Writings of Juan Valdes otherwise Valdessio*. London, 1865; E. Boehmer, in *Spanish Reformers*. Strassburg-London, 1874. I, pp. 63-130 (Bibliotheca Wiffeniana); Fermin Caballero, *Conquenses ilustres*. Madrid, 1875. IV; M. Carrasco, *Alfonso et Juan de Valdés, leur vie et leurs écrits religieux*. Ginebra, 1880; M. Menéndez y Pelayo, in *Historia de los Heterodoxos Españoles*. Madrid, 1880. II, pp. 149-206; 1882, III, pp. 844-848; E. Boehmer, in *Revista Cristiana*. Madrid, 1885-1887; P. J. Pidal, in *Estudios literarios*. 1890. II, pp. 113-142 (Col. de Escritores Cast., 83); B. Croce, *Una data importante nella vita di Juan de Valdés*, in *Archivio storico per le provincie napolitane*, 1903, fasc. I; W. Webster, in *Gleanings in Church History*. London, 1903. pp. 136-157; J. Heep, *Juan de Valdés in seinem Verhältnis zu Erasmus und dem Humanismus*. Leipzig, 1909; L. Miguélez, *Sobre el verdadero autor del 'Diálogo de la lengua,' según el códice escurialense*. Madrid, 1918 [See E. Cotarelo y Mori, in *Boletín de la R. Academia Esp.* V (1918), pp. 121-150; VI (1919), pp. 473-523, 671-698; VII (1920), pp. 10-46, 158-197, 269-289].

endowed than his brother, Alfonso de Valdés (d. 1532), who was secretary to Charles V and author of the *Dialogo en que particularmente se tratan las cosas acaecidas en Roma el año MDXXVII*—a colloquy between the knight Lactancio and an Archdeacon published anonymously in 1528 with the object of proving that the Sack of Rome (1527) was a punishment from the Almighty and of urging the Emperor to walk in the steps of the Reformation—Juan shared the same Erasmic sympathies and, like Alfonso too, he had a pretty Attic wit. This he uses to great effect in the *Dialogo de Mercurio y Caron* (1528), an anonymous satire in the manner of Lucian with reminiscences from some *danse macabre*, which deals with the Church and its abuses and the attempts of Henry VIII to divorce Catherine of Aragon. Strikingly fearless, written with simplicity and in flawless Spanish, it is one of the most beautiful prose-works produced in Spain in the sixteenth century. Evidently it was present in Cervantes's mind when he wrote ch. xlii of the second part of *Don Quijote* : for the resemblance between Don Quixote's advice to Sancho Panza and the King's counsels to his son is marked. It is the only work which Valdés published. His other writings, composed during his sojourn in Naples, were issued posthumously. They include commentaries on the Epistle of St. Paul to the Romans (1556) and on the First Epistle to the Corinthians (1557); two translations, *El Salterio traduzido* and *El Evangelio segun San Mateo*, published in 1880. His doctrinal compositions have gone astray with the exception of forty of the *Ciento y diez Consideraciones Divinas*, whose Spanish version was not printed until 1880.

More didactic than the *Dialogo de Mercurio* is the

Dialogo de la lengua, an important literary document written probably between 1534 and October 1536, and published in 1737 without any author's name attached to it. The work is generally ascribed to Valdés, but a recent theory has raised the question of its attribution to Juan Lopez de Velasco, who died in 1598. The *Dialogo de la lengua* is cast in the form of a conversation which is suppposed to take place in Naples. Four persons take part in it: two Italians named Marcio and Coriolano and two Spaniards whose names are Torres (or Pacheco) and Valdés. The subject treated is the Spanish language with special reference to its grammar and its correct usage from the point of view of aesthetics and of literary history. It is so rich in ideas—regard being had to the date of its composition—in suggestiveness, in literary charm that it is justly considered one of the best things in literature. The philological explanations are, of course, long since superseded, but the criticism of writers remains as intelligent and pointed as ever, the arrangement of the matter is excellent and the style is so admirable that we need not hesitate to compare it with the style of Cervantes. Naturally Valdés has not Cervantes's variety, genius nor smiling grace. But he has Cervantes's naturalness, his ease, and a correction which is not always found in the writings of the greater man.

With a few illustrious exceptions which include the names of Mendoza and Mariana, Spanish historians lack the sentiment of art. There is the case of Florian de Ocampo[1] (1499 ?-1555), canon of Zamora, for instance, who was the first to publish in 1541 a chronicle

[1] *Coronica general de España*. Madrid, 1791. 2 vols.—See: G. Cirot, *Les Histoires générales d'Espagne entre Alphonse X et Philippe II* (1284-1556). Bordeaux-Paris, 1905. pp. 97-147 ;

which, until the end of the nineteenth century, was thought to be the *Cronica general*. Ocampo wrote on his own account *Los quatro libros primeros de la Cronica general de España* (1543), adding a fifth book in the reprint of 1553. He planned so huge a scale that he was unable to bring his work lower down than the Roman period. He writes so dully, however, that one cannot but rejoice that the remaining chapters of this unreadable masterpiece have disappeared. Ocampo's credulity is limitless, he cannot weigh evidence and he has no critical sense. His contemporary Pero Mexia [1] (1499 ?-1551) is identified conjecturally with the 'Caballero Cesareo,' author of certain spirited *romances* to be found in Sepúlveda's collection: Mexia wrote the *Silua de varia lecion* (1540), one of the many derivatives of the *Apophthegmata* of Erasmus, and the *Dialogos eruditos*. The *Silua* is at the base of *Tamburlaine* (1590) and of Lope de Vega's *La inocente sangre*. But as Mexia died before either Marlowe (1564-1593) or Lope de Vega was born, he had not the satisfaction of this vicarious immortality. And doubtless he would have set more value on his *Historia imperial y cesarea* (1545) or the unfinished *Historia de*

A. Morel-Fatio, *Historiographie de Charles-Quint*. Paris, 1913. pp. 79-86; M. Bataillon, *Sur Florian Docampo*, in *Bulletin hispanique*, XXV (1923), pp. 33-58.

[1] *Relacion de las comunidades de Castilla*, ed. C. Rosell, 1852, in Bib. de Autores Esp., XXI; *Historia de Carlos Quinto*, ed. J. Deloffre [*Revue Hispanique*, XLIV]. New York-Paris, 1918. See: M. Menéndez y Pelayo, *El Magnífico Caballero Pero Mexia*, in *La Ilustración española y americana*, 1876, pp. 75, 78, 123, 126; A. Morel-Fatio, *Historiographie de Charles-Quint*. Paris, 1913. pp. 73-79; R. Costes, *Pedro Mexia, chroniste de Charles-Quint*, in *Bulletin hispanique*, XXII (1920), pp. 1-36, 256-268; XXIII (1921), pp. 95-110.

Carlos Quinto, which was edited in 1918 only. These are quite painstaking compilations. One might be worse employed than in reading them, as Cervantes once said on a similar occasion.

That, after all, is but moderate praise, however. A better writer than Ocampo or Mexia was LUIS DE AVILA Y ZÚÑIGA[1] (d. after 1572), whose *Comentario . . ., de la guerra de Alemaña hecha de Carlo. V. Maximo Emperador Romano Rey de España. En el año de M.D.XLVII* (1548) has considerable interest from two points of view. The style is clear and comparatively concise; the matter, no doubt, was received from Charles V himself in whose suite Avila was. Avila was the son of the Conde de Risco and the brother of the Marqués de las Navas; appointed ambassador at Rome—a burlesque *romance* in the *Cancionero de Yxar* on the Cortes de Monzón is attributed to him— he remained always a great favourite of Charles V, whom he accompanied to Yuste after the Emperor's abdication. Avila is not precisely critical; he relates with an elegant simplicity what Charles V told him or wished to have generally believed. He would have thought it treason to criticize his master whom he puts upon the level of the greatest commanders. And Charles V returned this appreciation in his own rough and clumsy way. Somebody was once talking of Avila's work before Charles V, who cut short the conversation with the remark: 'Yes, my exploits are not as great as those of Alexander but . . . then Alexander had not the luck to have such a historian as I have.' Although Charles V did not greatly abound with witty remarks, this story is easier to believe than

[1] *Comentario de la guerra de Alemania*, ed. C. Rosell, 1852, in Bib. de Autores Esp., XXI.

the legend that the second book of the *Comentario* is not by Avila at all: according to Prudencio de Sandoval, Bishop of Pamplona, it was stolen by Avila from the narrative of some ordinary soldier. We have irrefragable contemporary evidence against the tradition from the Emperor's Flemish secretary, Willem Van Male, who tells us that he made his Latin translation (1550) of the *Comentario* from Avila's original text, which was kept in Charles V's room.

So far we have spoken of historians who wrote on Spain or on events connected with the development of Spain in Europe. But the New World had been discovered in 1492 and that continent was the subject of copious dissertations. There was nothing copious about Hernando Cortés[1] (1485-1547), who was not by vocation a man of letters at all. He was a man of deeds, and he had on his side the glorious gift of youth. As Disraeli said, Cortés was not thirty-seven when he brought down a mighty Empire as though it were a house of cards. Cortés does not attempt fine writing, but all his official reports are to the point and have in them something of his laconic vigour. His terse concentration is in marked contrast with the vapid diffuseness of Gonzalo Hernandez de Oviedo y Valdés[2]

[1] *Cartas y relaciones al emperador Carlos V*, ed. P. de Gayangos, Paris, 1866; *Escritos sueltos*, in *Biblioteca histórica de la Iberia*, México, 1871, XII.—See: F. A. MacNutt, *Letters of Cortés*, etc. New York-London, 1908; F. A. MacNutt, *Fernando Cortés and the Conquest of Mexico* (1485-1547), New York-London, 1909.

[2] *Historia general y natural de las Indias*, ed. J. Amador de los Rios, Madrid, 1851-1855. 4 vols. (R. Academia de la Historia); *Las Quincuagenas de la nobleza de España*, ed. V. de la Fuente. Madrid, 1880 [unfinished] (R. Academia de la Historia).—See: A. Morel-Fatio, in *Revue historique*, XXI (1883), pp. 179-190.

THE MIDDLE RENAISSANCE 205

(1478-1557), who was present at the surrender of Granada and fought in Italy under Gonzalo de Córdoba. He knew Columbus and had occasion to meet him before and after his journey to America, whither he himself went in 1514 in some official capacity. Most of his productions, including the chivalresque novel *Don Claribalte* (1519); the *Reglas de la vida espiritual y secreta theologia* (1549), a translation from an Italian work of mysticism; and the compilation published in part in 1880 under the abbreviated title *Las Quinquagenas de la nobleza de España* are forgotten. The *Batallas y Quinquagenas* is a better piece of work than *Las Quinquagenas*, but has not been published yet. There remain Oviedo's *Sumario de la natural y general istoria de las Indias* (1526) and the two parts of the *Historia natural y general de las Indias, Islas e Tierra Firme del mar oceano* (1535-1557). These have no literary quality, but they contain observations of some scientific value. Oviedo's impressions had the merit of novelty. He had journeyed at least six times (1514-20-26-32-36-49) to the New World, and had looked at it with fresh and curious eyes, so that his careless manner was easily forgiven him by most contemporaries.

Hernandez de Oviedo is often inaccurate and shelters himself behind official authority. This method was particularly detestable in the eyes of Bartolomé de las Casas [1] (1474-1566) who, as Bishop of Chiapa (1542-1550) in Mexico, had a closer acquain-

---

[1] *Colección de obras*, ed. J. A. Llorente, Paris, 1822; *Historia de las Indias*, ed. Marqués de la Fuensanta del Valle y J. Sancho Rayon, Madrid, 1875-1876. 5 vols. (*Col. de documentos inéditos*, etc. LXII-LXVI); *Apologética Historia sumaria*, etc., ed. M. Serrano y Sanz, 1909 (Nueva Bib. de Autores Esp., 13).—See:

tance with the facts and in his capacity of champion of the oppressed Indians contrives to point out also Oviedo's countless errors. It is likely enough that Las Casas himself was guilty of exaggerations amounting to errors in his *Breuissima relacion de la destruycion de las Indias* (1552), in which he protests vehemently against the ill-treatment by his own countrymen of the native Indians on the American Continent. The *Breuissima relacion*, which was translated into seven languages, is rather a speech for the prosecution than anything else. Las Casas was called to the bar, not to the bench of history. Still he produced a formal *Historia de las Indias*, an unfinished work which remained unpublished till 1875-1876. It is a good book, and the passages relating to Columbus have a special value. The *Historia* was begun in 1527 and completed in 1550 when the writer resigned his bishopric. This first draft was somehow lost during the author's lifetime. Las Casas, undaunted by misfortune, set to work on a second draft. He was then over seventy years of age and had lost something of his pristine fire. That affected his work, and he only wrote three decades instead of the six which he had originally contemplated. He made a will forbidding the publication of the *Historia* till forty years after his death. His wishes were only nominally respected, for his manuscripts were used by Antonio de Herrera (1559-1625), who also levied contribution on Cervantes de Salazar's *Cronica*, in his *Historia de los hechos de los Castellanos en las Islas i Tierra firme del mar oceano*

A. M. Fabié, *Vida y escritos del Padre Fray Bartolomé de las Casas. Obispo de Chiapa.* Madrid, 1879 (*Col. de documentos inéditos*, etc. LXX); F. A. MacNutt, *Bartholomew de las Casas*, etc. New York-London, 1909.

(1601). Las Casas is not a great writer. We know from his chief opponent, Juan Ginés de Sepúlveda[1] (1490 ?-1573), that he was a most eloquent speaker. Perhaps he needed the stimulus of debate and general opposition. At any rate, his stormy eloquence does not succeed in communicating itself through the soporific medium of pen and ink. The soul of loyalty, this noble figure is greater as a practical philanthropist than as an author.

Considerable narrative powers were possessed by Francisco Lopez de Gómara[2] (1511-1557 ?) who likewise wrote a *Primera y Segunda Parte de la historia general de las Indias con todo el descubrimiento y cosas notables que han acaescido dende que se ganaron hasta el año de 1551. Con la conquista de Mexico, y de la nueua España* (1552). This is mainly a panegyric on Cortés, whose chaplain Lopez de Gómara was. He has left two other works: the *Choronica de los muy nombrados Omiche y Haradin Barbarrojas*, published in 1853, and the *Anales del Emperador Carlos Quinto*, a chronicle of events which occurred between 1500 and 1556, first published in 1912 by Mr. Roger Merriman. Lopez de Gómara is a Froude of the sixteenth century: he writes admirably and had the honour of being quoted by Montaigne. His work went into some twenty editions in various languages

[1] See: A. F. G. Bell, *Juan Ginés de Sepúlveda*. Oxford, 1924 (Hispanic Notes and Monographs. Spanish Series, ix).

[2] *Primera y segunda parte de la Historia General de las Indias*, ed. E. de Vedia, 1852, in Bib. de Autores Esp., xxii; *Choronica de los muy nombrados Omiche y Haradin Barbarrojas*, in *Memorial histórico español*. Madrid, 1853. vi, pp. 327-439; *Annals of the Emperor Charles V*, text with English trans. by R. B. Merriman, Oxford, 1912.—See: C. Pérez Pastor, *Bibliografía madrileña*. Madrid, 1907. Pt. iii, p. 416.

before its course was suddenly arrested by the history of Bernal Diaz del Castillo [1] (1492-1581 ?), deliberately entitled *Historia verdadera de la Conquista de la Nueva España* and issued in a defective edition in 1632. Diaz del Castillo, who had served under Cortés, wrote in extreme old age at Guatemala, but he wrote about what he knew at first hand. He was most interested in horses : he stops very often to say that ' so and so rode a chestnut horse, another a grey.' But he abounds in interesting details : he tells about the first dances in the New World and describes how the soldiers of Cortés capped their chief's quotations from the *romances*. And then he will break off suddenly to say that Lopez de Gómara says such and such things, ' which,' adds the indignant old soldier, ' are all lies— *mas todo es mentiras*.' As against Lopez de Gómara, Diaz del Castillo's authority holds good. He has not indeed the qualities of the philosophic historian ; but he writes with ease and fluency. The everyday details that he gives, though perhaps beneath the dignity of the muse of history, add to the savour of his work. The *Historia verdadera* was admirably translated into French (1877-1887) by José-Maria de Heredia, author of *Les Trophées*.

[1] *Historia verdadera de la conquista de la Nueva España*, ed. G. García, México, 1904. 2 vols.—See : J.-M. de Heredia's French trans. Paris, 1877-1887. 4 vols.; A. P. Maudslay's English trans. London, 1908-1912. 4 vols. (Hakluyt Society, 23-25, 30) ; R. B. Cunninghame Graham, *Bernal Diaz del Castillo*, etc., London, 1915.

VIII

THE LATE RENAISSANCE

THE new school of poetry founded by Boscan and Garci Lasso de la Vega separated into two groups of poets with Seville and Salamanca for their respective centres. The greatest name in the Salamancan school is that of FRAY LUIS DE LEON [1] (1528 ?-1591). Born at Belmonte in the province of Cuenca, he doubtless owed to his father, a lawyer of some distinction, his clear vision of facts and his gift of direct analysis,

---

[1] *Obras*, ed. A. Merino, Madrid, 1804-1816. 6 vols. [reprinted with a preface by C. Muiños Sáenz, Madrid, 1885. 6 vols.]; ed. G. Mayans y Siscar, 1855, in Bib. de Autores Esp., XXXVII [See also Bib. de Autores Esp., XXXV, LIII, LXI and LXII]; *Poesías originales*, ed. F. de Onís, San José de Costa Rica, 1920; *La Perfecta Casada*, ed. E. Wallace, Chicago, 1903; ed. A. Bonilla y San Martín, Madrid, 1917 (Clásicos de la Literatura Esp., 7); *De los nombres de Cristo*, ed. F. de Onís, 1914-1917. 3 vols. (Clásicos Castellanos, 28, 33, 41); *El perfecto predicador*, ed. C. Muiños Sáenz, Madrid, 1886-1887; *Exposicion del Miserere*, facsimile of the 1632 Barcelona ed. by A. M. Huntington, New York, 1903.—See: A. Coster, *Luis de León* (1528-1591), in *Revue Hispanique*, LIII (1921), pp. 1-468; LIV (1922), pp. 1-346; James Fitzmaurice-Kelly, *Fray Luis de Leon. A biographical fragment*. Oxford, 1921 (Hispanic Notes and Monographs, I); A. Coster, *Bibliographie de Luis de León*, in *Revue Hispanique*, LIX (1923), pp. 1-104; A. F. G. Bell, *Fray Luis de Leon: a Study of the Spanish Renaissance*. Oxford, 1925.

while his Jewish descent on his mother's side may, as M. Adolphe Coster suggests, account for his stubbornness of character, power of abstraction, and love of music. As the eldest son, he was destined to follow his father's profession, and in 1542 was sent to Salamanca to study law. He preferred a religious vocation, entered an Augustinian convent early in 1543 and professed the following year. In 1560, he took his degree of licentiate of theology in Salamanca. He was unsuccessful then in his application for a professorship, but in 1561 he was given the Chair of St. Thomas as professor of Theology. In 1565 he was transferred to the Durand Chair of Scholastic Theology and Biblical Criticism. Brilliant as he was, Luis de Leon failed to win popularity. Though a knot of personal admirers existed among his own students, the University as a whole rather admired than loved him. He was humble enough in all essentials, but he set a proper value on himself and his attainments. He had a caustic tongue and rarely measured his words from fear of consequences: moreover his inherited trait of anticipating attack possibly created for him enemies who, before his violent denunciations, existed in his imagination only. As early as 1562 he had the misfortune to quarrel with the Professor of Greek, Leon de Castro, a venomous reactionary who had commented Isaiah; four years later he made another powerful enemy in Bartolomé de Medina, whose election to the Chair of Theology he strongly opposed. Castro and Medina did not fail to note the fearless independence of his speeches on the Vulgate at the public debates held in honour of the Provincial Chapter's meetings (1565-1566), summoned at Salamanca by the Archbishop of Com-

THE LATE RENAISSANCE

postela. A course of critical lectures on the same subject in the University year 1567-1568 swelled the list of accusations which were being hoarded against him until the hour should be ripe. Unfortunately, proof more directly prejudicial to him was not wanting. In a moment of grave imprudence Luis de Leon had translated (1561) into the vernacular the Song of Solomon for the benefit of a nun, Isabel de Osorio, and had carelessly left his manuscript in an open drawer. There it was found by a young lay brother, who made copies of it for his friends. When Luis de Leon awoke to the danger, the mischief was beyond recall. Meanwhile the attention of the Inquisition had been drawn to errors of faith among the Salamancan professors: an official was sent down early in 1572 to make inquiries and to invite further disclosures. On March 1, the Professor of Hebrew, Gaspar de Grajar, was arrested on the charge of carrying on a Jewish propaganda. Luis de Leon, who was on friendly terms with Grajar, and whose relations with Castro had become increasingly strained since he had served with him on the Committee for revising Vatable's version of the Bible, realized that danger threatened him personally. He sought to avert the blow by informing against himself. On March 5, he visited Diego Gonzalez, the Inquisition official, told him about the vernacular translation of the *Cantar de los Cantares* and explained that his *De Fide* lectures might be open to misrepresentation. The following day he handed in to him a written confession. At the same time he sought to obtain official approval in high places. But it was too late. The accusations brought against Grajar and another professor of Hebrew, Martin Martinez de Cantalapiedra, implicated Luis de

Leon also, and on March 24, 1572, he was arrested. The proceedings dragged out for four years, during which Luis de Leon was plied with questions in the hope that from sheer weariness he might make some admission damaging either to himself or to his friend, the great scholar and divine, Benito Arias Montano who, like Luis de Leon, was supposed in his Polyglot Bible to have unduly favoured rabbinical interpretations of the sacred text. The inquiry failed. In September 1576 the Committee made a recommendation that the torture test should be applied to Luis de Leon, adding the charitable corollary that in view of his poor health ' a moderate amount of agony ' would perhaps suffice. The recommendation of the local committee was set aside; Luis de Leon was formally reprimanded for past imprudences, warned to be more careful in future and was set free on December 11, 1576.

The tide had turned in his favour and he returned to Salamanca with something like an aureole of triumph round him. His chair had been occupied since 1573; a provisional one was immediately created for him. But Luis de Leon never won the complete confidence of the Holy Office. Some years later he was admonished for his views on predestination. Still Salamanca, as a whole, was proud of him, and his versatility was shewn by his election to the Chair of Moral Philosophy in 1578 and to that of Biblical Criticism in 1579. The very number of his interests was used as a weapon against him. He was appointed to serve as a member of the commission to report on the project of reforming the Calendar in 1582. This, together with his duties (1588) as confessor and adviser to the Carmelite nuns, caused him to intermit some of his lectures. His old enemy Castro had died

THE LATE RENAISSANCE

(shortly before October 17, 1585); but Castro's tradition survived him. An attempt was made to deprive Luis de Leon of his chair. It failed egregiously. Meanwhile his brethren of the Augustinian Order stood by him and honoured themselves in 1591 by electing him Provincial of the Order of Castile. He was at the end of his career; on August 23, 1591, he died, nine days after his election.

Luis de Leon's prose is strong, impressive, sonorous, but not ductile. He has a trick of beginning his sentences with the copulative *y*, and this lends an air of archaic stiffness and displeasing monotony to his pages. We are, perhaps, not sufficiently in accord with the matter to do complete justice to the style of *La Perfecta Casada* (1583), written for Maria Varela Osorio. This is a brilliant paraphrase of ch. xxxi. of the *Book of Proverbs* and gives rules of conduct for the ideal wife. But Luis de Leon must not be taken too seriously about wives. He knew nothing, could know nothing about them. And in the case of *La Perfecta Casada* one seems to see the streak of the oriental in him. He dogmatizes at third and fourth hand: Vives's *De institutione feminae Christianae* may very well have been one of his sources of inspiration. Setting aside his unfinished posthumous treatise, the *Exposicion del libro de Job* (1779), we turn with more satisfaction and more sympathy to his great masterpiece of mysticism, *De los nombres de Christo* (1583-1585) in which, especially in the second part, his prose takes on a greater suppleness and more animated colour than in *La Perfecta Casada*.

Luis de Leon's poems appeared precisely forty years after his death and were instantly recognized by good judges as of extraordinary merit. They were issued (1631) by Quevedo to stem the current of gongorism which was then at the flood. Quevedo's edition, which was sadly incomplete and disfigured by innumerable blunders, was reprinted later on in the same year 1631 at Milan. Then all interest in Luis de Leon apparently died out. This indifference continued well beyond the first half of the eighteenth century, a most disastrous period in the history of Spanish literature. Luis de Leon tells us that his poems were mere playthings of his youth, toys which he collected to entertain the leisure of his friend Pedro Portocarrero (d. 1600) who was at the time bishop of Calahorra. The tone of gentle disillusion, of philosophic resignation, characteristic of Luis de Leon's greatest poems, would prevent our taking literally the assertion that these compositions date from the poet's youth. It is obvious that the *décima*

> 'Aqui la envidia y mentira
> me tuvieron encerrado....'

cannot have been written before December 1576, when Luis de Leon was nearly fifty years of age. The third ode, dedicated to Portocarrero, refers to Don John of Austria's campaign in 1569, while *Del mundo y su vanidad* deals with the defeat of King Sebastian of Portugal in 1578. The whole collection of poems consists of three books, of which only the first contains Luis de Leon's original compositions; the second includes translations from Greek, Latin and Italian authors and the third renderings from the Bible. It is sometimes alleged against Luis de Leon that he is monotonous in tone and, no doubt, his sacred profession was something of a limitation to him in his choice of subjects. Still he could burst his chains asunder

THE LATE RENAISSANCE

when the mood was on him, and few would guess that the *Profecia del Tajo* was the handiwork of an Augustinian monk, remote from human temptations and breathing most readily on the chill heights of mysticism. In the sphere of pure devotion he nowhere rises to a purer height than in the lines *Y dexas, Pastor santo* and in his *Noche serena*. Luis de Leon is always competent and adequate, but artistry is not his supreme virtue as a poet. He is ever prone to be a little rugged, to outstrip all rivalry by simple excellence and intellectual force rather than by any refinement of technique. He strikes an absolutely new note in Spanish literature —a note rarely repeated till we catch its heavenly strain once more in the *Intimations of Immortality* of Wordsworth (1770-1850). There is the same aspiring intuition, the same splendid simplicity, the same lofty expression of sublime reflexion in both poets. Luis de Leon is often indifferent to beauty of form and is sometimes, if rarely, culpably careless of it. But what he has to say, he says with a pregnant simplicity more telling than all the verbal ingenuity of the world.

In the same year (1631) that he published Luis de Leon's poems, Quevedo, still with the aim of arresting the gongoristic movement, issued a small book of verse by Francisco de la Torre,[1] the real or fictitious name of a poet belonging to the Salamancan group. The manuscript bore the official licence of Alonso de Ercilla (d. 1594). By the time that Quevedo chanced upon it, Torre's identity was forgotten. Quevedo

---

[1] *Obras*. Facsimile of the 1631 Madrid ed. by A. M. Huntington, New York, 1903.—See: J. P. W. Crawford, *The Source of an Eclogue of Francisco de la Torre*, in *Modern Language Notes*, xxx (1915), pp. 214-215.

ascribed the book to the Bachiller Francisco de la Torre, whom he identified with the Bachiller de la Torre praised by Boscan in his *Octava Rima*. Manoel de Faria e Sousa in his commentary (1639) to *Os Lusiadas* rectified this mistake, pointing out that Lope de Vega had been on friendly terms with the writer of the verses, who lived considerably after his homonym. The idea that the poems might be apocryphal was not broached until 1753 when they were reprinted by Luis Josef Velazquez who attributed them to Quevedo: he was supported by Luzan and Montiano. But this theory is untenable. The melancholy simplicity of this elusive poet is poles apart from the harsh brilliancy of Quevedo.

Many of Torre's poems are translations from the Italian. Book I, Sonnet 23, for instance, is taken from Torquato Tasso (1544-1597), from whom Spenser (1553 ?-1599) borrowed for the eighty-first sonnet of his *Amoretti* ; sonnets four to twelve and sonnet fourteen in Book II are versions from Benedetto Varchi (1502-1565) ; and the fifteenth and twenty-third sonnets of the same book are from Giambattista Amalteo (1505-1573). Where Varchi writes *Filli, deh non fuggir, deh Filli, aspetta,* Torre has *Ay, no te alexes, Fili, ay Fili, espera* ; for Tasso's *Bella è la Donna mia, se del bel crine,* Torre gives *Bella es mi Ninfa, si los laços de oro* ; Amalteo's *Notte che nel tuo dolce e alto oblio* is echoed by the Spaniard as *Noche, que en tu amoroso y dulce olvido*. Examples of this kind could be multiplied. In his more original poems, Torre recalls Garci Lasso de la Vega. He is less charming, less seductive, less inspired, but his graceful, amorous verses, particularly *La Cierva*, have a personal note.

The work of Torre bears a striking resemblance to

that of another Salamancan, Francisco de Figueroa [1] (1536-1617 ?). Fernandez-Guerra y Orbe held that it was practically impossible to distinguish between the compositions of the two poets. " Barajad las poesías del ... bachiller [de la Torre] con las de su camarada Figueroa y os costará ímprobo trabajo distinguirlas y conocer su dueño." [2] Figueroa has a title to distinction as the first poet who succeeded in acclimatizing the *versos sueltos* in Spain : this he does in the *Egloga pastoral* (*Thirsi, pastor del mas famoso rio*). He seems to have served in the Italian campaigns, where he became known as a graceful versifier ; he was married in 1575 at Alcalá de Henares; travelled in the Netherlands in 1597 and on returning to Alcalá, abandoned his art to dedicate himself, he says, to

[1] *Obras.* Facsimile of the 1626 ed. by A. M. Huntington, New York, 1903 ; *Poesías,* ed. A. de Castro, 1857, in Bib. de Autores Esp., XLII ; *Poésies inédites de Francisco de Figueroa,* ed. R. Foulché-Delbosc, in *Revue Hispanique,* XXV (1911), pp. 317-344 ; *Sonetos de Francisco de Figueroa,* ' el Divino,' ed. A. U., in *Revista crítica hispano-americana,* I (1915), pp. 169-171 ; *Varias composiciones inéditas* ... ed. A. Lacalle Fernández, in *Revista crítica hispano-americana,* v (1919), pp. 148-168.—See : J. P. W. Crawford, *Notes on three sonnets attributed to Francisco de Figueroa,* in *The Modern Language Review,* II (1907), pp. 223-227 ; R. Menéndez Pidal, *Observaciones sobre las poesías de Francisco de Figueroa* (*con varias composiciones inéditas*), in *Boletín de la R. Academia Esp.,* II (1915), pp. 302-340, 458-496 ; U. A., *A propos de quatre sonnets attribués à Francisco de Figueroa,* I, II, in *Revue Hispanique,* XL (1917), pp. 260-263 ; XLIII (1918), pp. 563-565 ; A. Lacalle Fernández, *Varias composiciones* ... *precedidas de un estudio bio-bibliográfico,* in *Revista crítica hispano-americana,* v (1919), pp. 122-147.

[2] ' Confuse the poems of ... the *bachiller* [de la Torre] with those of his comrade Figueroa and you will find it extremely hard to distinguish them and recognize their respective authors.'

matters more suited to his ripe years. His poems were not published until 1625, when the historian Luis Tribaldos de Toledo (d. 1634) issued over sixty in Lisbon. They were probably written before 1573, and must have been known before their publication, since Cervantes quotes one in *La Galatea*, where he presents Figueroa as Tirsi. Figueroa, mindful perhaps of Virgil's example, had given instructions on his deathbed that all his works should be burnt. His wishes were apparently disregarded, for besides the verses published in 1625 some fifteen poems have been discovered by M. Foulché-Delbosc and another fifty by Sr. Menéndez Pidal. According to Juan Verzosa (1523-1574) who knew him in Italy, Figueroa versified with equal facility in Italian and in Spanish : in some of his elegies (I, III, V) he introduces a medley of Spanish and Italian lines. He inclines to the pastoral tradition and shews himself an excellent imitator of Garci Lasso de la Vega in *Entre doradas flores*, for which he adapts the *lira* form. In blank verse, which after him becomes an accomplished fact in Spanish metrics, he avoids the peril of the assonant and skilfully alternates the caesura.

The Sevillan school of poetry included such prominent men as Juan de Mal Lara, Francisco Pacheco (1535-1599), Diego Giron (d. 1590), an Italianate who succeeded Mal Lara as professor, and Francisco de Medina (1544 ?-1615). Its recognized leader was FERNANDO DE HERRERA[1] (1534 ?-1597), an authentic

[1] *Algunas obras*, critical ed. by A. Coster, Paris, 1908 ; *Poesías*, ed. V. García de Diego, 1914 (Clásicos Castellanos, 26) ; *Versos*, ed. A. Coster, 1919 (Bib. romanica) ; *L'hymne sur Lépante*, ed. A. Morel-Fatio, Paris, 1893 ; *Fernando de Herrera. Controversia sobre sus Anotaciones á las obras de Garcilaso de la Vega*.

THE LATE RENAISSANCE

poet whose modest stipend as a cleric in minor orders at Seville left him free to pursue his bent unhindered. Much of his verse is addressed to Eliodora who figures in it as the *sol*, *estrella* and *luz* of Herrera. This lady was Leonor de Milá (1537?-1581?), wife of Columbus's grandson, Alvaro Colon de Portugal, second Conde de Gelves (d. 1581). In these petrarchist compositions (*Algunas obras*, 1582; *Versos* 1619) it is difficult to judge whether Herrera's ecstatic admiration for the Countess was only platonic : but he can at times strike a note of real emotion as in the line

'Ya pasó mi dolor, ya sé qué es vida.'

Antoine de Latour defined the nature of Herrera's attachment as the poet's ' innocent immorality,' perhaps that is as near the true state of things as any discussion of the problem will bring us. Many of Herrera's works are lost ; for instance, the *Gigantomachia*, an epic on Amadis, several lyrical pieces, the *Istoria general del mundo hasta la edad de Carlos Quinto* and some translations. But, besides his poetical works, we have his *Relacion de la guerra de Cipre, y sucesso de la batalla naual de Lepanto* (1572); the *Obras de Garci Lasso de la Vega con anotaciones* (1580), and *Tomas Moro* (1592), a biographical sketch of Sir Thomas More.

Poesías inéditas, ed. J. M. Asensio, 1870 (Soc. de Bibliófilos Andaluces) ; *Poésies inédites*, ed. A. Coster, in *Revue Hispanique*, XLII (1918), pp. 557-563 ; *Relacion de la Guerra de Cipre y suceso de la batalla naval de Lepanto*, ed. M. Salvá y P. Sainz de Baranda, in *Coleccion de documentos inéditos*, etc. Madrid, 1852. XXI, pp. 242-382.—See: R. M. Beach, *Was Fernando de Herrera a Greek scholar?* Philadelphia, 1908 ; A. Coster, *Fernando de Herrera (El Divino) 1534-1597*. Paris, 1908 ; F. Rodríguez Marín, *El " divino " Herrera y la Condesa de Gelves*. Madrid, 1911.

Herrera's glory as a poet rests on his patriotic compositions : in these he is original and stirring. His ode (1571) to Don John of Austria on the occasion of the Moorish rising in the Alpujarras ; the song (1572) celebrating the victory of Lepanto and the elegy on the death and defeat (August 8, 1578) of King Sebastian of Portugal at Alcázar-Kebir have an inspired passion and fire, a dignity of style, and a biblical phrasing which invest them with a veritable grandeur. Herrera makes a bold use of neologisms and is prodigal of metaphors. His interest in stylistic problems may account for a certain chilliness, a savour of artificiality in some of his poems. But he enriched the themes of Garci Lasso de la Vega's verse tradition and perfected its form. His principles are embodied in the commentary (1580) to Garci Lasso de la Vega which gave rise to an angry controversy. Six years previously, in 1574, the humanist and the friend of Luis de Leon, Francisco Sanchez [1] (1523-1600) *el Brocense* (so-called from his birthplace, Las Brozas, in Extremadura) had issued the *Obras del excelente poeta Garci Lasso de la Vega*; this edition roused some feeling among the Castilians who accused Sanchez of over-emphasizing the poet's lack of originality. When Herrera's edition appeared, they were no better pleased that an Andalusian should commentate a Castilian poet : Sanchez's partisans took offence because Herrera omitted to mention his edition and an undignified polemic ensued. The first shots were fired by a certain 'Damasio'; Juan Fernandez de Velasco, Conde de Haro (d. 1613), came in a good second with his *Observaciones* published under the pseudonym of

[1] See : A. F. G. Bell, *Francisco Sanchez el Brocense*. Oxford, 1924 (Hispanic Notes and Monographs, Spanish Series, VIII).

THE LATE RENAISSANCE 221

the 'Licenciado Prete Jacopin, vecino de Burgos.' Herrera, called 'an ass in a lion's skin,' showed little of the quality which had gained him the title of *El divino*, and retaliated in the same urbane tone as his critic. The pamphlets of both were issued in 1870: Herrera's commentary, which provoked the warfare, remains unpublished. There are good things in it beside much that is bad, and on the whole Herrera shews himself a critic somewhat in advance of his time. We have fragments of his prose in the dedication of Part I of *Don Quijote* to the seventh Duque de Béjar (1577?-1619), where Cervantes gives us a mosaic of phrases taken from Medina's preface and from Herrera's epistle to the Marqués de Ayamonte, so that Herrera survives in a circuitous fashion as a prose-writer. As a lyric he deserves to be more read than he is.

A Sevillan unaffiliated to any school was the poet Baltasar del Alcázar [1] (1530-1606), whose ingenious sonnet on a sonnet found numerous imitators. He served under the Marqués de Santa Cruz and afterwards entered the households of the Duque de Alcalá, and of the Conde de Gelves. Alcázar's merry humour is well illustrated in *La Cena jocosa*. He displays in his epigrams a mordant wit which has earned him the sobriquet of the Andalusian Martial. He has the grace and something of the cynicism of Martial, but he lacks Martial's vigour.

Luis Barahona de Soto [2] (1548-1595), whose *Primera parte de la Angelica* (1586) was inspired by Ariosto,

[1] *Poesías*, ed. F. Rodríguez Marín, Madrid, 1910 (Bib. selecta de Autores clásicos esp., 12).

[2] *Primera parte de la Angelica*, facsimile of the princeps (Granada, 1586) by A. M. Huntington, New York, 1904;

was born at Lucena in the province of Cordova. The *Angélica* professes to be a sequel to the *Orlando furioso*. Cervantes, often weak and over-indulgent in criticism, thought highly of it; the priest in *Don Quijote* calls it by its popular title, *Las Lágrimas de Angélica*, and adds : ' I should shed tears myself were such a book burned, for its author is one of the best poets, not merely in Spain, but in all the world.' Lope de Vega and Mendoza were of much the same mind, while in the eighteenth century Luzan maintained that Barahona de Soto's work would be more esteemed than Ariosto's, had it chanced to appear first. However that may be, the *Angélica* has not stood the test of time : beside its model it is a wan and pallid adaptation. Its second part survives in fragments incorporated in the *Diálogos de la Montería*, a work written some time after 1586 and ascribed to Soto by Sr. Rodríguez Marín. A failure in epic poetry, Soto shews in his versions of Ovid as well as in some of his minor poems that he can be both graceful and melodious as a lyrist. Luis Zapata[1] (1526-1595), who also tried the epic, has little to recommend him except his industry and Cervantes's praise. He spent thirteen years over the fifty cantos of *Carlo famoso* (1566) and, undaunted by its failure, lived to maltreat (1592) Horace. As a

Poesías [*villancico*], ed. J. de Sancha, 1855, in Bib. de Autores Esp., XXXV ; [*soneto, tercetos*], ed. A. de Castro, 1857, in Bib. de Autores Esp., XLII ; ed. B. J. Gallardo, in *Ensayo*, etc., Madrid, 1866. II, col. 25-33 ; *Diálogos de la Montería*, ed. F. R. Uhagón, 1890 (Soc. de Bibliófilos Esp., 27).—See : F. Rodríguez Marín, *Luis Barahona de Soto : estudio bibliográfico y crítico*. Madrid, 1903.

[1] *Miscelánea*, ed. P. de Gayangos, in *Memorial histórico español*, XI (1859).—See : J. Menéndez Pidal, *Vida y obras de Don Luis de Zapata*, 1915 [*Discurso*. R. Academia Esp.].

THE LATE RENAISSANCE 223

prose-writer, Zapata has good points—his *Misceldnea* is an interesting and agreeable collection; as an epic poet he has none. And in justice to Cervantes it must be added that the *Carlo famoso* (which, by the way, Cervantes assigns to Luis de Avila) was consigned unread to the flames. A similar fate, with perhaps less justice, befell the *Primera y segvnda parte de el Leon de España* (1586) by Pedro de la Vezilla Castellanos : this contains some pleasant verses and was utilized by Lope de Vega in *La amistad pagada* and *Las famosas asturianas*.

Three epic poems of this period are praised by Cervantes as 'the best that have been written in Castilian in heroic verse,' able to compare with 'the most famous of Italy.' One is *La Austriada* (1584) whose hero is Don John of Austria. Here, as with Zapata, we have a case of mistaken vocation. Juan Rufo Gutierrez[1] (1547 ?-d. after 1620), the author, shews in his *Seyscientas apotegmas ... y otras obras en verso* (1596) a witty perception and a natural gift of narration. In *La Austriada*, however, he merely produces a tedious composition in twenty-four cantos. The first eighteen of these are, as M. Foulché-Delbosc has pointed out, only a rhymed version of Mendoza's *Guerra de Granada*, which Rufo must have seen in manuscript. He reveals, it is true, some power in

[1] *La Austriada*, ed. C. Rosell, 1854, in Bib. de Autores Esp., XXIX ; *Las Apotegmas ...*, ed. A. G. de Amezúa y Mayo, 1923 (Soc. de Bibliófilos Esp., Nueva Serie, 1).—See : R. Foulché-Delbosc, *Étude sur la 'Guerra de Granada' de Don Diego Hurtado de Mendoza*, in *Revue Hispanique*, 1 (1894), pp. 101-165 and 338 ; R. Ramírez de Arellano, *Juan Rufo, jurado de Córdoba*. Madrid, 1912 ; R. Foulché-Delbosc, *L'authenticité de la 'Guerra de Granada,'* in *Revue Hispanique*, XXXV (1915), pp. 476-538.

his descriptive passages, but he has spoilt by versification what might have proved a useful chronicle, and his epic is far from being one of ' the richest treasures of poetry that Spain possesses.'

A more artistic effort was *La Araucana* by Alonso de Ercilla y Zúñiga [1] (1533-1594), who fought against the Araucanos in 1555. He had before him a distinguished career as a soldier when a quarrel with a brother-officer, Juan de Pineda, cut it short. Both young men were condemned to death, but the sentence was commuted at the eleventh hour. Pineda became an Augustinian monk: Ercilla was sent to prison as having given greater provocation. He was released before 1558, when he took part in the battle of Quiapo (Dec. 14), and in 1562, he returned to Europe with the first fifteen cantos of his song which he had composed by camp-fires on stray bits of leather or skin or on scraps of paper that he had managed to collect. Ercilla did not forgive his commanding officer, Garcia Hurtado de Mendoza, for the part that he had played in his disgrace, and assigns him an insignificant part in *La Araucana*. Ercilla was made a knight of Santiago in 1571 and appointed literary censor, but he failed to obtain the post of Secretary to the State which he greatly coveted.

It would seem that the first book to be printed

[1] *La Aravcana*, facsimile of Part I (princeps Madrid, 1569) and Part II (Çaragoça, 1578) by A. M. Huntington, New York, 1902-1903. 2 vols; ed. J. T. Medina [Centenary ed. with documents, notes, biography, etc.] Santiago de Chile, 1910-1918. 5 vols.—See: A. Bello, in *Obras completas*. Santiago de Chile, 1883. VI; A. Royer, *Étude littéraire sur l'Araucana*. Dijon 1879; J. L. Perrier, *Don García de Mendoza in Ercilla's 'Araucana,'* in *The Romanic Review*, IX (1918), pp. 430-440.

THE LATE RENAISSANCE

in America was Juan de la Magdalena's[1] (d. 1579) translation (1535 ?) of the *Escala espiritual* (1505) by San Juan Clímaco. The first Spanish poem written in America was the *Conquista de la Nueva Castilla*, an anonymous work of no literary merit which was not published till 1848. Ercilla's poem is the first work of literary merit produced on the American continent. *La Araucana* was published in 1569: its continuations, which brought up the number of cantos to thirty-five, were printed in 1578, 1589-1590, and in 1597 the three parts were issued at Madrid in a revised edition of thirty-seven cantos, the thirty-fifth original canto becoming the thirty-seventh. Whether the two additional cantos are authentic is not known. The subject-matter is the rebellion of the Araucanos. Voltaire praised the speech of the old chief, Colocolo; the speeches of Lautaro and Caupolican are even more remarkable in their high oratorical effect. And this is precisely where the poem as an epic fails. It is epic neither in form nor effect. Ercilla had great powers of declamatory eloquence, a gift of vivid description and skill as a narrator: he had not the poet's temperament. Though lines of isolated beauty may stand out in the memory, the work as a whole leaves no general impression; passages of distinction are suddenly marred by some trivial detail. At his best Ercilla is a most eloquent orator: as a poet he is not completely successful. Perhaps he had an intuition of something lacking when he introduced such mechanical devices as visions of Bellona, supernatural prophecies and so forth. Withal *La Araucana* remains the best artistic epic yet written in Spanish: its early

[1] See: J. T. Medina, in *La Imprenta en México*. Santiago de Chile, 1909. I, p. 374.

part is full of martial fire and has a refreshing spontaneity which reveals something of Ercilla's engaging personality.

Ill-pleased with the part allotted to him in *La Araucana*, Garcia Hurtado de Mendoza hired a staff of salaried flatterers to redress the balance in his favour. One of these was a young Chilean poet, Pedro de Oña [1] (1570-after 1643 ?), who did his best in the *Primera parte de Arauco domado* (1596) without success, apparently, since this part was put on the Index by the Lima Inquisition and no second part appeared. A second poem of Oña's, *El Ignacio de Cantabria* (1639), is even more tedious than the *Arauco domado*. Meanwhile *La Araucana* led to a series of imitations and continuations. In 1597 Diego de Santistevan Osorio,[2] who had a boy's hero-worship for Ercilla, attributed to him all kinds of imaginary adventures in the *Quarta y Quinta Parte de la Araucana*. Another sequel appears to have been written by the Andalusian Fernando Alvarez de Toledo,[3] but its loss will be regretted by no one who has read the same author's *Puren indomito*, a wretched imitation of the *Arauco domado*, unpublished for some two and a half centuries. An avowed disciple of Ercilla was Juan de

[1] *Arauco domado*, critical ed. by J. T. Medina, Santiago de Chile, 1917.—See: M. Menéndez y Pelayo, in *Antología de poetas hispano-americanos*. Madrid, 1895. IV, pp. xvii-xxix; J. T. Medina, in *Biblioteca hispano-chilena*. Santiago de Chile, 1897. I, pp. 42-79; J. A. Ray, in *Drake dans la poésie espagnole (1530-1572)*. Paris, 1906. pp. 153-157.

[2] *Quarta y quinta parte en que se prosigue y acaba la historia de D. Alonso de Ercilla*. Madrid, 1735.—See: C. Pérez Pastor, in *Bibliografía madrileña*. Madrid, 1907. III, pp. 478-479.

[3] *Puren indomito*, ed. D. Barros Arana, Paris, 1862 (Bib. americana, I).

THE LATE RENAISSANCE

Castellanos[1] (1522-1607?), a native of Alanis in the province of Seville. As a young soldier he served in America, took orders and obtained a benefice at Tunja in 1556 or thereabouts. His *Elegías de varones ilustres de Indias* was composed between 1570 and 1590: it was issued in four parts, the first in 1589, the second and third in 1847 and the last in 1886. Castellanos shews a praiseworthy attention to historical fact, but he has no poetical inspiration.

The introduction of the pastoral novel is another of Spain's debts to Italy. Jacopo Sannazaro (1458-1530) was an Italian of Spanish descent and one is tempted to think that there must have been something subtly Spanish in his talent. At least, it appealed with peculiar force to the Spanish temperament, and his *Arcadia* (1502) was indirectly responsible for the Spanish pastoral novel, whose influence through the *Diana* of Montemayor was felt on European literature for half a century. This convention appealed strongly to Cervantes: it appealed also to Shakespeare, who borrows from the *Diana* in *Two Gentlemen of Verona*, and to John Keats (1795-1821) as may be seen in *Endymion*. Sannazaro's first imitator in the Peninsula was the Portuguese Bernardim Ribeiro (1482?-1552) whose *Menina e moça* takes its name from the

[1] *Elegías de varones ilustres de Indias*, Parts I-III, ed. B. C. Aribau, 1847 (Bib. de Autores Esp., IV); Pt. IV [*Historia del nuevo reino de Granada*], ed. A. Paz y Mélia, 1887. 2 vols. (Col. de Escritores Cast., 44, 49).—See: M. A. Caro, *Joan de Castellanos*. I. *Noticias sobre su vida y escritos*. II. *Castellanos como cronista: paralelo con Oviedo*, in *Repertorio Colombiano* (Bogotá), III (1879), pp. 356-368, 435-456; M. Menéndez y Pelayo, in *Antología de poetas hispano-americanos*. Madrid, 1894. III, pp. viii-xviii.

first three words of the novel. *Menina e moça* was not printed until 1554, but it certainly served as a model to JORGE DE MONTEMÔR[1] (1520 ?-1561), who was born in Montemôr-o Velho and whose castilianized name is Montemayor. A musician by profession, he was attached to the household of the Infanta Maria, elder sister of the future King Philip II., and during this period he published the *Exposicion moral sobre el Psalmo lxxxvi del real propheta David* (1548). In 1551 he entered the service of the Infanta Juana, and upon her marriage with Juan III of Portugal's eldest son, the Infante Juan, accompanied the royal pair to Lisbon as *apousentador* (courier). According to Professor Rennert, there are good reasons to think that Montemayor was in the suite of the future Philip II when he came to England. It has also been said that Montemayor was a soldier and that he fought at the Battle of St. Quentin (1557). He lived for some time in Valencia, where he appears to have written, at any rate in part, the *Diana*. He was killed in Piedmont as a result of some affair of gallantry.

Montemayor began by writing *villancicos* and a beautiful gloss on Jorge Manrique's *Coplas*, but he trimmed his sails to the breeze and composed in the new style an epistle, two eclogues, and thirty-two

[1] *Los siete libros de la Diana*, ed. M. Menéndez y Pelayo, in *Orígenes de la Novela*. 1907. II, pp. 251-336 (Nueva Bib. de Autores Esp., 7).—See: G. Schönherr, *Jorge de Montemayor: sein Leben und sein Schäferroman*, etc. Halle, 1886; James Fitzmaurice-Kelly, *The Bibliography of the " Diana enamorada,"* in *Revue Hispanique*, II (1895), pp. 304-311; M. Menéndez y Pelayo, in *Orígenes de la Novela*. 1905. I. pp. cdxlviii-cdlxxviii (Nueva Bib. de Autores Esp., 1); H. A. Rennert, in *The Spanish Pastoral Romances*, 2nd ed. Philadelphia, 1912. pp. 18-58 (Publications of the University of Pennsylvania).

THE LATE RENAISSANCE

sonnets. These appeared in his *Obras*, dedicated to the Infante Juan of Portugal and his wife and published at Antwerp in 1554. Placed on the Index, the *Obras* were not reissued again until 1558 in a revised edition whose first volume was called *Segundo Cancionero* and the second *Segundo Cancionero spiritual*. Montemayor also translated (1560) the Catalan poems of Ausias March, and though Lope thought ill of the effort, there is no good reason why one should agree with him, unless, of course, one believes that literal exactitude is the supreme merit of a translation. A fuller idea of Montemayor's position as a lyrical poet may be gleaned from the miscellaneous verses scattered up and down in the *Diana*. Some of these, mostly in the old style, are models of grace and eloquence. But his reputation depends really on *Los siete libros de la Diana* (1559 ?), the forerunner of Sir Philip Sidney's *Arcadia* (1590) and of the *Astrée* (1607-1627) by Honoré d'Urfé (1568-1625). The *donnée* is simple enough—the love-affairs of a young shepherdess Diana with the shepherd Sireno who seems intended to represent Montemayor himself. Lope de Vega sought to see in Diana a lady from Valencia de Don Juan near León; according to Faria e Sousa the lady's name was Ana and she was still something of a beauty when Philip III met her in 1603. The love-affairs of Diana and Sireno are not very happy from the romantic reader's point of view, for Diana ends by wedding the shepherd Delio. There are subsidiary episodes, such as that of Felix and Felismena borrowed from Bandello's (1480 ?-1560 ?) *Novelle* (36. Pt. 2a). The *Diana* had a very great vogue in its own time, and it no doubt deserved it. But it is difficult to get up any genuine enthusiasm about the book now. The truth of the matter is that the form pastoral is essentially artificial; the falsity of the *genre* was to the taste of the time and lent itself easily enough to Montemayor's alembicated talent which was alien from realism. It is often said that Garci Lasso de la Vega is artificial, and so he is, but his artificiality has a charm that is all its own and accords well with his elfin, melancholy Virgilian music. The effect is different when the vehicle is pedestrian prose. The contact with reality is missed: in its place there is a pleasing sweetness, a gracious gallantry, a delicate fancy, a fineness the only defect of which is that it is superfine. Still, Montemayor won the admiration of Sir Philip Sidney and of Shakespeare. His verses, despised by Cervantes, have been admirably translated by Frere, and his numerous imitators include Desportes (1546-1606) and Sarrazin (1605-1654).

Among Montemayor's Spanish imitators was a Salamancan doctor, Alonso Perez, who wrote *La segunda parte de la Diana* (1564). He boasts that he is Montemayor's friend and that his books contain little that is 'not stolen or imitated from the best Latins and Italians.' Neither of these qualifications overwhelms one with awe, and one is inclined to feel rather grateful that Alonso Perez was snatched up to Heaven before he had time to issue the third part with which he threatened mankind. A continuation of much greater merit is *La primera parte de Diana enamorada* (1564) by Gaspar Gil Polo [1] (d. 1591?). Cervantes, prone to like many things and particularly

[1] *La Diana Enamorada*, ed. M. Menéndez y Pelayo, in *Orígenes de la Novela*. 1907. II, pp. 337-398 (Nueva Bib. de Autores Esp., 7).—See: H. A. Rennert, in *The Spanish Pastoral Romances*. 2nd ed. Philadelphia, 1912. pp. 72-85.

THE LATE RENAISSANCE

apt to overpraise them, had the highest opinion of the *Diana enamorada*, which he said should be preserved ' as if it came from Apollo himself.' Perhaps the cause of this enthusiasm is no more recondite than that it gave Cervantes an opportunity of making a pun. Gil Polo, more merciful than Montemayor, brings Diana and Sireno together again. He has a clear prose-style, and his verse, written in all kinds of metres known at that period, has distinct literary quality, particularly in the *Cancion de Nerea* in the third book of the *Diana Enamorada*. Gil Polo was shamelessly imitated, as Professor Rennert has pointed out, by Hieronymo de Texeda, a Spanish professor in Paris, whose *Diana de Montemayor nuevamente compuesta* (1627) contains also reminiscences from Alonso Perez's *Diana*. *Los diez Libros de Fortvna d'Amor* (1573) by the soldier Antonio de lo Frasso and *Los nueue Libros de las Hauidas* (1566) by Hierónimo Arbolanche stirred even Cervantes to exasperation. His irony was lost upon Pedro Pineda, a Spanish Jew refugee in London, who reprinted Lo Frasso's absurd book. Artificiality reached its culminating point in *El Pastor de Fílida* (1582) of Luis Galvez de Montalvo [1] (1549 ?-1591 ?). 'No Pastor that, but a highly polished courtier,' as Cervantes ingenuously says. His own *Galatea* (1585), itself anything but a masterpiece, was followed by the *Desengaño de Celos* (1586) of Bartolomé Lopez de Enciso who is possibly the author of *La Montañesa*, a play acted in Seville in 1618; the *Primera Parte de las Nimphas y Pastores de Henares* (1587), an immature work by a Salamancan student called Bernardo Gonzalez de Bovadilla; and

[1] *El Pastor de Fílida*, ed. M. Menéndez y Pelayo, in *Orígenes de la Novela*. 1907. II, pp. 399-484 (Nueva Bib. de Autores Esp., 7).

El Pastor de Iberia (1591) by the Andalusian Bernardo de la Vega who went to South America, obtained a canonry in Tucumán and was apparently still alive in 1623. The passion for pastoralism continued for over a quarter of a century after *Don Quijote* and *Guzman de Alfarache* had given a new direction to the novel, as one may see from *La Cintia de Aranivez* (1629) by Gabriel de Corral[1] (1588-1640), and *Los Pastores del Betis* (1633) by Gonzalo de Saavedra (1568?-1632); but these are authors outside the literary movement and their works are without importance. Meanwhile in much the same way as Sebastian de Cordova Sacedo had tried to check the influence of Boscan and Garci Lasso de la Vega, so Bartolomé Ponce in his religious parody, *Primera Parte de la Clara Diana a lo diuino* (1582?), attempted to stem the flood of pastoralism. He did not lack precedents in his own country, quite apart from the Italian *spiritualizzamenti* such as *Il Petrarca spirituale* (1536), where Girolamo Malipiero presents Laura as the Christ and Love as the Eternal Father. But this sort of parody, though it apparently shocked none, was powerless to arrest the fashion.

Montemayor's unexpected death in 1561 had put an end to all hopes of his promised sequel to *Diana*. In the posthumous editions, the publishers increased the bulk of the book by inserting a tale called the *Historia del Abencerraje y la hermosa Xarifa*.[2] It did

[1] See: N. Alonso Cortés, in *Miscelánea vallisoletana*. Valladolid, 1912. I, pp. 147-180; H. A. Rennert, in *The Spanish Pastoral Romances*. 2nd ed. Philadelphia, 1912. pp. 192-198.

[2] Ed. G. le Strange, Cambridge, 1924.—See: M. Menéndez y Pelayo, in *Orígenes de la Novela*, I, pp. ccclxxv-ccclxxx (Nueva Bib. de Autores Esp., I); H. Mérimée, in *Bulletin hispanique*, XXI (1919), pp. 143-166.

not happen to be by Montemayor, but that did not trouble the thrifty publishers. They got a few excellent pages for nothing and that for them was the main point. This very short story is found first of all in Antonio de Villegas's *Inventario*, which was licensed for printing in 1551 but was not published until 1565. It is extremely unlikely that Villegas was the author: he may have touched it up a little but that is all. It is a charming anonymous sketch in what was afterwards to become a separate *genre*—the Mauresque novel.

In the domain of mysticism where Nicolas Antonio records some three thousand works, the chief name is that of SANTA TERESA DE JESUS [1] (1515-1582), in the world Teresa de Cepeda y Ahumada. To her has been ascribed the beautiful anonymous sonnet: *No me mueve, mi Dios, para quererte*, but equally with that of St. Ignatius of Loyola, of St. Francis Xavier, of Pedro de los Reyes and of Miguel de Guevara, to all of whom it has been attributed, her claim must be rejected. Santa Teresa was a poet, but she was a poet in prose—in the *Castillo Interior*, for example.

[1] *Obras*, ed. V. de la Fuente, Madrid, 1881, 6 vols; *Escritos*, ed. V. de la Fuente, 1861-1862, 2 vols. (Bib. de Autores Esp., LIII, LV); *Las Moradas*, ed. T. Navarro Tomás, 1910; 2nd ed. 1916 (Clásicos cast., 1).—See: G. Cunninghame Graham, *Santa Teresa: her life and times*. London, 1894. 2 vols.; H. de Curzon, *Bibliographie térésienne*. Paris, 1902; A. Morel-Fatio, *Les lectures de Sainte Thérèse*, in *Bulletin hispanique*, X (1908), pp. 17-67; M. Mir, *Santa Teresa de Jesús: su vida, su espíritu y sus fundaciones*. Madrid, 1912; *La vida de la madre Teresa de Jesús escrita de su misma mano*, etc. [with an introduction by G. Cirot] (Bib. romanica); E. Juliá Martínez, *La cultura de Santa Teresa y su obra literaria*. Castellón, 1922; *The Letters of Santa Teresa* [trans. and notes by the Benedictines of Stanbrook], London, 1922. 4 vols.

Her songs have the charm of simplicity, have a kind of infantile grace which lacks art. And unfortunately art is an indispensable factor in verse. Her taste lay in the popular forms as in her carol: *Hoy nos viene a redimir*. She delighted in Escrivá's *Ven, muerte, tan escondida*, some echo of which has strayed into her poem beginning: *Vivo sin vivir en mí*, generally known as Santa Teresa's gloss. It is as a practical reformer and a mystic that Santa Teresa is pre-eminent. With St. Ignatius of Loyola she heads the Catholic reaction, but where St. Ignatius is only a great party leader, Santa Teresa makes her appeal to all denominations, not least to Protestant England, where she is quoted by Jeremy Taylor (1613-1667), praised by Richard Crashaw (1613?-1649), and William Law (1686-1761), and where in more recent days the agnostic Anthony Froude (1818-1894) ranks her literary gifts with those of Cervantes, while in Catholic Spain her manuscript of the *Libro de las Misericordias de Dios* rests in the Escorial not far from a page of St. Augustine. Santa Teresa reveals herself to us in her letters, in the *Libro de su vida* and in the *Libro de las Fundaciones*: a whole literature has gathered around her name, and in modern days her biography envisaged from quite another point of view has been re-written by Gabriela Cunninghame Graham (d. 1906). Here only the salient points of the saint's life can be indicated. Born at Avila, at the age of seven she set out to seek martyrdom; her first literary venture was a chivalresque novel written in 1529 in collaboration with her brother Rodrigo de Cepeda. Two years later she ran away from home to become a nun, and in 1534 (Nov. 3) she professed in the Carmelite Convent of Avila. Her feverish energy, her spiritual ecstasy and ill-health all

THE LATE RENAISSANCE

combined to age her prematurely but, undaunted by poverty and persecution, she continued indomitable to the end, a marvel of devotion and self-sacrifice, and in spite of her saintliness a singularly human figure whose mystical sense was never incompatible with a great gift of organization and a striking directness of vision.

Santa Teresa's natural pride of race—she was *de sangre limpia* in character and in descent—remained with her all her life. She stated it as an unalterable fact. Indifferent to the applause of the multitude, she was not interested in literature as literature and wrote only when outside pressure compelled her. Yet her style has a noble simplicity, a sober clarity, and an archaic savour that give a peculiar distinction to her prose. She may be diffuse: she is never obscure. Her manuscripts, which were entrusted by Sor Ana de Jesús to Fray Luis de Leon, were edited by him in 1588 with the most scrupulous care; he tells us that he followed the originals closely ' sin mudarlos, ni en palabras, ni en cosas de que se habian apartado mucho los traslados que andaban.'[1] Santa Teresa discloses in her works every aspect of her varied temperament: she rises to an ecstatic sublimity in the *Camino de perfeccion*; in the *Libro de las Fundaciones* she is intellectual and austere; confidential in the *Libro de su vida*; maternal, admonishing, encouraging and personal, shrewd and even a little hard in her letters. She was born to command and to organize; she is clearly contemptuous of feminine weakness: ' Es muy de mugeres, y no querria yo, hijas mias, lo fuéssedes en

---

[1] ' without changing them, either as regards the words or the meaning where there were wide differences among the current copies.

nada, ni lo pareciéssedes, sino varones fuertes,'[1] she writes in the *Camino de perfeccion*. A practical reformer, she has little patience with visionaries, nor is she blind to the evils of relaxed monastic discipline, ' monasterio de mugeres con libertad ... mas me parece es passo para caminar al infierno las que quisieren ser ruines, que remedio para sus flaquezas.'[2] Santa Teresa belonged to the race of those

> 'Whose sinewy wings by choice do fly
> In the fine mountain-air of public obloquy.'

And while she dealt in a spirit of sound commonsense with the details of every-day life, she embraced—in the words of Luis de Leon—' the highest and most generous philosophy that was ever dreamed.'

More akin to Santa Teresa than her friend San Juan de la Cruz as regards practical austerity, the Dominican LUIS DE GRANADA[3] (1504?-1588), whose family name was Sarria, was the son of a laundress at a convent in Granada, his native city. He owed his education to the patronage of the second Conde de

[1] 'That is very like a woman, and I would not have my daughters be, or seem to be, women in anything, but brave men.'

[2] ' a women's convent without discipline ... seems to me to be rather a short-cut to Hell for those who are inclined to go wrong, than a remedy for their weakness.'

[3] *Obras*, ed. J. J. de Mora, 1848-1849. 3 vols. (Bib. de Autores Esp., VI, VIII, XI); ed. Fr. J. Cuervo, Madrid, 1906-1908. 14 vols.—See: Fr. J. Cuervo, *Biografía de Fray Luis de Granada*. Madrid, 1895; Fr. J. Cuervo, *Fr. Luis de Granada y la Inquisición*, in *Homenaje á Menéndez y Pelayo*. Madrid, 1899. I, pp. 733-743; Fr. J. Cuervo, *Fray Luis de Granada, verdadero y único autor del libro de la Oracion*. Madrid, 1919; 'Azorín,' in *Los dos Luises y otros ensayos*. Madrid, 1921. pp. 19-97; 'Azorín,' in *De Granada a Castelar*. Madrid, 1922. pp. 23-50.

THE LATE RENAISSANCE

Tendilla (1436-1516); he professed in 1525 and almost immediately became famous as a preacher and confessor. Towards the year 1555 Luis de Granada went to Portugal, where he was made Provincial of his Order and confessor to Queen Catalina (d. 1578). His version (1538) of the *Imitation of Christ* was his first published work : it was followed in 1554 by the *Libro de la oracion y meditacion*. In 1556-1557 appeared the first redaction of the *Guia de Pecadores*, which was issued in 1567, and is a distinct and independent composition. The first redaction of the *Guia* and the *Libro de la oracion y meditacion* were put on the Index (1559), where they figured beside works by Juan de Avila and Francisco de Borja. Luis de Granada came to Spain prepared to defend his cause, but on finding that the friend upon whom he had relied, the Archbishop of Toledo, Bartolomé Carranza (1503-1576), was in prison, he hastened to alter the offending passages of his book and returned to Portugal. He was not, however, to escape further suspicion : charges of *iluminismo* were unjustly brought up against him for his credulity in testifying to the false stigmata of the Portuguese nun, Sor Maria de la Visitacion (who was condemned on Dec. 7, 1588). This was shortly after the publication of the *Introduccion del simbolo de la Fe* (1582-1585). His books had a vast success, particularly the *Guia de Pecadores*. Regnier quotes it as Macette's favourite work, Gorgibus in *Sganarelle* recommends it to Célie ; it was praised by St. François de Sales (1568-1622) and by Fénelon (1651-1715), and read by José Marchena as he lay under sentence of death by Robespierre. Luis de Granada's forty years in the confessional gave him a deep insight into the frailties of human nature : his absolute sincerity, his learning and his fervour are admirable. His defects are those of the public speaker: antithesis, an abuse of rhetoric, a certain mechanical turn of the phrase. But at his best, he is moving, eloquent, persuasive, and the suavity of his style, indicative of his gentle nature, has won him a reputation which seems likely to increase.

More mystic than ascetic is SAN JUAN DE LA CRUZ[1] (1542-1591), whose work for the monasteries of the Carmelite Order followed the same lines as Santa Teresa's for the convents. A student at the University of Salamanca, his family name was Juan de Yepes y Alvarez; on entering the Carmelite order in 1564 he took the name of Fray Juan de San Matias. He became a discalced monk in 1567, the year that he first knew Santa Teresa, and in 1568 he adopted the name by which he is generally known. Like Santa Teresa, but in a greater degree, he suffered hardships and persecutions and died in sad circumstances before he was fifty years of age. San Juan de la Cruz lacks Santa Teresa's practical gifts, but in the domain of mystic verse he has no rival in Spanish literature: his influence outside Spain is visible in Coventry Patmore's (1823-1896) *The Unknown Eros*. In the *Obras espirituales* (1618) Spanish mysticism finds its highest expression. San Juan de la Cruz moves on a plane inaccessible to most mortals; he abides ' on the

---

[1] *Obras*, critical ed. by G. de San Juan de la Cruz, Toledo, 1912-1914. 3 vols —See: M Menéndez y Pelayo, *De la poesía mística*, in *Estudios de crítica literaria*, 2nd ed. 1893. 1st series. pp. 1-27 (Col. de Escritores Cast., 15); M. Domínguez Berrueta, *El misticismo de San Juan de la Cruz en sus poesías*. Madrid, 1894; R. Encinas y López de Espinosa, *La poesía de San Juan de la Cruz*. Valencia, 1905.

THE LATE RENAISSANCE

phantom verge of things.' But his ecstatic raptures are full of movement and colour ; his mystical abstractions are expressed in concrete terms of great beauty and their emotional appeal cannot be gainsaid. His prose-style can be clear and forcible ; where it seems extremely obscure, as in the commentary to his poems, the difficulty will be found in the subject. The obscurity is in the thought, not in the expression which, once the thought is familiar, is often wonderfully happy. Still, it is not as a prose-writer that San Juan de la Cruz concerns us : he makes his appeal through the music of his verse, in the *Noche obscura del Alma*, in the *Canciones entre el Alma y el Esposo*, in the *Llama de amor viva*.

Pedro Malon de Chaide [1] (1530?-1596), an Augustinian monk who composed for Beatriz Cerdan the *Libro de la conversion de la Magdalena* (1588), is a much less attractive character than Juan de Avila or Luis de Granada. His book betrays the influence of the very models that he condemns most harshly—Boscan, Garci Lasso de la Vega, chivalresque romances and 'frivolous love-books.' While his intolerance must alienate sympathy, his austere doctrine and gorgeous colouring explain his popularity. A purer mystic is the Franciscan Juan de los Angeles [2] (1536 ?-1609), a native of Avila, whose *Trivmphos del amor de Dios* (1590), a compendium of which was issued in 1600 under the title of *Lvcha espiritual y amorosa entre Dios y el alma*, is a psychological work influenced by

[1] *La conversion de la Madalena*, ed. B. C. Aribau, 1853, in Bib. de Autores Esp., XXVII.—See : P. J. Pidal, in *Estudios literarios*. 1890. II, pp. 143-175 (Col. de Escritores Cast., 83).

[2] *Obras Místicas*, ed. Fr. J. Sala, 1912. Pt. I (Nueva Bib. de Autores Esp., 20).

Ruysbroeck (1293-1381). It is distinguished by a singular beauty of expression and depth of intuition, qualities which mark the two parts of the *Dialogos de la conquista del espiritual y secreto Reyno de Dios* (1595-1608). Juan de los Angeles is superior to Diego de Estella [1] (1524-1578), a friar in his own order, whose *Meditaciones devotissimas del amor de Dios* (1578) are nevertheless remarkable for fervour and eloquence, as St. François de Sales discovered for himself and proclaimed to the world. A touch of mysticism is perceptible in the few extant verses of the famous theologian and scholar, BENITO ARIAS MONTANO [2] (1526?-1598). A friend of Luis de Leon, he may possibly be responsible for the lines *A la hermosura exterior de Nuestra Señora* ascribed to the latter. Arias Montano had a shrewd and kindly nature and a veritable passion for books. It was largely owing to his acquisitions in Flanders that Philip II's library at the Escorial became a marvel of its kind. He loved beauty intrinsically and shewed this in the scholarly form and clear type of his Polyglot Bible. Recalled from Italy owing to the machinations of Leon de Castro, he was cleared through Mariana's intrepid verdict of the charges levelled at him by the Inquisition, but the experience disillusioned him and he retired into private life.

[1] *De la vanidad del mundo*, in *Tesoro de escritores místicos españoles*, III, 1847 (Col de los mejores Autores Esp., 44).

[2] *Paráfrasis sobre el Cantar de Cantares de Salomon*, ed. J. N. Böhl de Faber, in *Floresta de rimas antiguas castellanas*. Hamburgo, 1825. III, pp. 41-64; *Correspondencia*, ed. Marqueses de Pidal y de Miraflores and M. Salvá, 1862, in *Coleccion de documentos inéditos*, etc. XLI, pp. 127-418.—See: A. F. G. Bell, *Benito Arias Montano*, Oxford, 1922 (Hispanic Notes and Monographs. Spanish Series, v).

THE LATE RENAISSANCE

The prose-writers of distinction in this period are to be found among the philosophers or historians. GERÓNIMO ZURITA[1] (1512-1580), a disciple of Hernan Nuñez de Toledo, is an excellent example of an exact writer. His literary merit may be open to question, but in the *Anales de la Corond de Aragon* (1562-1579) he gives a careful and well-planned outline of history based on scientific research. Zurita was the first Spanish historian to obtain his materials direct from original documents, to collate these with documents from foreign archives and to realize that travelling is a necessary adjunct to the historian's resources. In power of selection he excels his predecessors and avoids the pitfall of beginning with Noah. He lacks, it is true, the gift of picturesque narration, of sympathetic intuition, but his solid qualities of accuracy and method give him a unique position in the development of Spanish scientific history. His friend, AMBROSIO DE MORALES[2] (1513-1591) followed Zurita's accurate methods in *La Coronica general de España* (1574-1586), a continuation of Ocampo's work. It is a trifle disappointing to find Morales so arid in style, one is inclined to expect more literary feeling from a relation of Perez de Oliva (whose works Morales published in 1586), yet his exactness in the *Coronica* and in *Las antigvedades de las civdades de España* (1575) is a definite asset.

[1] See: D. J. Dormer, *Progressos de la historia en el reyno de Aragón, y elogios de Gerónimo Zvrita, sv primer coronista*. Zaragoza, 1680; C. Pérez Pastor, in *Bibliografía madrileña*. Madrid, 1907. Pt. III, p. 523.

[2] *Corónica general de España que continuaba Ambrosio de Morales*. Madrid, 1791-1792. 6 vols.—See: C. Pérez Pastor, in *Bibliografía madrileña*. Madrid, 1907. Pt. III, p. 432; E. Redel, *Ambrosio de Morales*. Córdoba, 1909.

One of the greatest names on the bede-roll of Spanish literature, DIEGO HURTADO DE MENDOZA,[1] is another of Spain's really good historians. A man versed in public affairs and an excellent writer of sound critical instinct, he proved worthy of the confidence which Charles V reposed in him. Philip II was more difficult to please and—ostensibly because of riots at Siena where Mendoza was Governor—recalled him to Spain. This gave Mendoza his opportunity. We have already referred to him as a partisan of Garci Lasso de la Vega and Boscan. In Italy, he had distinguished himself by his ardour for scholarship, especially for Greek. Altogether he was a typical son of the Renaissance : not a great poet, his true vehicle was prose. Philip II helped him to find it. One

[1] *Guerra de Granada*, ed. C. Rosell, 1852, in Bib. de Autores Esp., XXI ; ed. R. Foulché-Delbosc [in course of publication] ; *Cartas*, ed. R. Foulché-Delbosc, in *Archivo de investigaciones históricas*, II (1911), pp. 155-195, 270-275, 463-475, 537-600.— See : *Calendar of Letters, Despatches and State Papers, relating to the negotiations between England and Spain* [ed. P. de Gayangos], V, Pt. II (1888); VI, Pt. I. (1890); *Letters and Papers, foreign and domestic, of the reign of Henry VIII* [ed. J. Gairdner], XII, Pts. I, II (1890-1891) ; XIII, Pts. I, II (1892-1893) ; R. Foulché-Delbosc, *Étude sur la "Guerra de Granada,"* in *Revue Hispanique*, I (1894), pp. 101-165, 338 ; R. Foulché-Delbosc, *Notes sur la bibliographie de la "Guerra de Granada,"* in *Revue Hispanique*, VII (1900), pp. 247-248 ; R. Foulché-Delbosc, *Le portrait de Mendoza*, in *Revue Hispanique*, XXIII (1910), pp. 310-313 ; *Documents relatifs à la Guerre de Grenade*, ed. R. Foulché-Delbosc, in *Revue Hispanique*, XXXI (1914), pp. 486-523 ; R. Foulché-Delbosc, *Les œuvres attribuées à Mendoza*, in *Revue Hispanique*, XXXII (1914), pp. 1-86; A. Morel-Fatio, *Quelques remarques sur la Guerre de Grenade de Don Diego Hurtado de Mendoza*, in *Annuaire*, Paris, 1914. pp. 5-50 (École Pratique des Hautes Études); R. Foulché-Delbosc, *L'Authenticité de la "Guerra de Granada,"* in *Revue Hispanique*, XXXV (1915), pp. 476-538.

day in June 1568, an altercation arose between Mendoza and a young courtier called Diego de Leiva. This took place in the Royal Palace. The pair came to blows. Leiva drew a dagger, which Mendoza seized and hurled out of the window. Both men had committed *lèse-majesté* by brawling in the precincts of the Court. What happened to Leiva is not known. He may have been a paltry courtier whose fate interested nobody but his friends. Mendoza was a very different personage. He purged his fault by going into exile at Granada, and became the historian of the rising of the Moors in the Alpujarras. The moment was favourable. Mendoza's offence took place in 1568. The rising lasted from 1568 to 1571, when it was put down by Don John of Austria. Mendoza was well placed, therefore, for writing his *Guerra de Granada*, which was not published until 1627 by Luis Tribaldos de Toledo in Lisbon. Mendoza speaks so frankly of what occurred that the late publication of the manuscript is very comprehensible. Truth and exactness are but two qualities of a great historian. Such a man must also have dramatic vision, a power of analysis and a knack of adequate narration. Mendoza has these gifts in an extraordinary degree, and as he has knowledge also, his equipment is fairly complete. He knows instinctively what is of importance and his artistic sense enabled him to place an event of that order in its appropriate setting. In this section of his work he was aided by his study of classical writers. Just as Lopez de Ayala had followed the lead of Livy, so Mendoza takes Sallust and Tacitus for his models. One can see the influence of Sallust in the general rhetorical phrase of Mendoza; his appreciation of Tacitus appears rather in determinate episodes. The famous description of the Duque de Arcos pent up with his command in Calaluy is obviously based upon the celebrated passage in which Tacitus records the discovery by Germanicus of Varus's dead legions. Mendoza tries to reproduce in Spanish Sallust's majestic rhetoric and Tacitus's intense vividness and concentration of phrase. It may be that he was not equal to either of his high exemplars : it must, however, be admitted that he comes near the splendid fluency of the one and the tense sombreness of the other. He had not much time to revise his work, for he died only four years after the war. This may account for traces of Latin constructions which have been noted in the *Guerra de Granada*; but these criticisms on Mendoza's supposed defects are mostly from Capmany, a carping Catalan who distinguished himself by his malignity towards Quintana. Mendoza's manner was not impeccable, but on the whole it is above criticism. Its blemishes, such as they may be, are outbalanced by its positive qualities of lucidity and force.

The Erasmian CRISTÓBAL DE VILLALON[1] (1501 ?-1560 ?), is the author of the *Tragedia de Mirrha* (1536) imitated from Ovid, and of *El Crotalon*, a stinging satire in the manner of Lucian, written about 1557, but not

[1] *El Crotalon de Christophoro Gnosopho*, ed. Marqués de la Fuensanta del Valle, 1871 (Soc. de Bibliófilos Esp., 9) ; ed. M. Menéndez y Pelayo, in *Orígenes de la Novela*. 1907. II, pp. 119-250 (Nueva Bib. de Autores Esp., 7) ; *Ingeniosa comparación entre lo antiguo y lo presente*, ed. M. Serrano y Sanz, 1898 (Soc. de Bibliófilos Esp., 33) ; *Dialogo que trata de las trasformacyones de Pitágoras*, ed. M. Menéndez y Pelayo, in *Orígenes de la Novela*. 1907. II, pp. 98-118 (Nueva Bib. de Autores Esp., 7) ; *Viaje de Turquía*, ed. M. Serrano y Sanz, in *Autobiografías y memorias*. 1905. pp. 1-149 (Nueva Bib. de

published until 1871. Villalon has a suave and flowing style: in this he differs from most philosophers, who, from Plato to Schopenhauer, are, with a few signal exceptions, more concerned with matter than form. He stands apart also in that he uses Castilian as a vehicle in contrast to thinkers like Juan Luis Vives [1] (1492-1540), Gomez Pereira [2] (1500-1569 ?), Sebastian Fox Morcillo [3] (1526 ?-1559 ?), and Francisco Sanchez (1550-1623) who wrote in Latin. Another Spanish humanist and doctor who followed Villalon's example in this respect was Juan Huarte de Sant Juan [4] (1530 ?-1591 ?), whose *Examen de ingenios*

Autores Esp., 2); *El Scholastico* [1 only], ed. M. Menéndez y Pelayo, 1911 (Soc. de Bibliófilos Madrileños, 5); *Tragedia de Mirrha*, ed. R. Foulché-Delbosc, in *Revue Hispanique*, XIX (1908), pp. 159-183.—See: F. A. de Icaza, *Miguel de Cervantes Saavedra y los Orígenes de "El Crotalón,"* in *Boletín de la R. Academia Esp.*, IV (1917), pp. 32-46.

[1] See: A. Bonilla y San Martín, *Luis Vives y la filosofía del Renacimiento*. Madrid, 1903; G. Desdevises du Dezert, *Luis Vives*, etc., in *Revue Hispanique*, XII (1905), pp. 373-412; *The Dialogues*, trans. by F. Watson, London, 1908; *On education*, trans. of *De tradendis disciplinis* by F. Watson, Cambridge, 1915; F. Watson, *Luis Vives. El gran Valenciano* (1492-1540.) Oxford, 1922 (Hispanic Notes and Monographs. Spanish Series, IV).

[2] See: M. Menéndez y Pelayo, in *La Ciencia Española*, 1887. II, pp. 165-282 (Col. de Escritores Cast., 57); N. Alonso Cortés, in *Revue Hispanique*, XXXI (1914), pp. 1-29.

[3] See: U. González de la Calle, *Sebastián Fox Morcillo*. Madrid, 1903.

[4] *Examen de Ingenios*, ed. A. de Castro, 1873, in Bib. de Autores Esp., LXV.—See: J.-M. Guardia, *Essai sur l'ouvrage de J. Huarte: Examen des aptitudes diverses pour les sciences*, Paris, 1855; J.-M. Guardia, *Philosophes espagnols: J. Huarte*, in *Revue philosophique*, XXX (1890), pp. 248-294; R. Salillas, *Un gran inspirador de Cervantes. El doctor Juan Huarte y su Examen de ingenios*. Madrid, 1905.

para las sciencias (1575) illustrates the theory, then new, of the interdependence of the mind and the body, and shews that the author anticipated Bacon by taking observation and experience as the basis of philosophy : in another direction, perhaps less to his credit, he anticipated Lavater. José de Acosta[1] (1539-1600), who had spent sixteen years in the New World, transcribed his experiences in the *Historia natural y moral de las Indias* . . . (1590), a storehouse of informing facts marked with independence of spirit and abounding in philosophic generalizations which drew warm praise from so competent a judge as Humboldt. Pedro Simon Abril[2] (1530?-1595 ?), professor of humanities at Saragossa, shews himself a master of direct, expository prose in his *Apvntamientos de como se deuen reformar las dotrinas* (1589), which are replenished with sound doctrine and intellectual subtlety. Miguel Sabuco y Alvarez is now thought to be the author of the *Nueva filosofía de la naturaleza del hombre* . . . (1587) once attributed to his daughter Oliva Sabuco[3] (1562-1622 ?), whose name figures on the title-page. It reveals a delicate penetration and a

[1] *Historia natural y moral de las Indias.* Madrid, 1894. 2 vols. —See : J. R. Carracido, *El P. José de Acosta y su importancia en la literatura científica española.* Madrid, 1899.

[2] See : J. Mario e Hidalgo, *Cultura intelectual y artística* (*Estudios para la historia de la ciudad de Alcaraz*) in *Revista de Archivos*, etc., XVIII (1908), pp. 384-415 ; M. Marfil, *Pedro Simon Abril : sus ideas políticas y sociales*, in *Nuestro tiempo*, VIII (1908), pp. 195-205.

[3] *Obras*, ed. O. Cuartero, Madrid, 1888 ; *Coloquios* (2), ed. A. de Castro, 1873, in Bib. de Autores Esp., LXV.—See : J.-M. Guardia, in *Revue philosophique*, XII (1886), pp. 42-60, 272-292 ; J. M. Hidalgo, *Doña Oliva de Sabuco no fué escritora*, in *Revista de Archivos*, etc., VII (1903), pp. 1-13.

certain gift of irony and would be a remarkable instance of philosophical promise if it were indeed the work of so young a woman.

With the acceptance of the Italian measures in Spain, the old school of Spanish verse had withered and died ; and from that day to this most Spanish poets of distinction have written in Italian metres. But in the drama no decisive stage had yet been reached. The Spanish public was slowly becoming acquainted with the masterpieces of antiquity ; in 1517 had appeared Lopez de Villalobos's translation of Plautus's *Amphytrion*, some eight years later Perez de Oliva brought out an adaptation of the same play, followed this up in 1528 with *La Vengança de Agamenon* (perhaps the first rendering of Sophocles into any modern language), and with an adaptation of Euripides, *Hecuba Triste*, which he finished shortly before his death in 1533. No doubt these versions were carefully read by rival scholars—Hernan Nuñez de Toledo's denunciation of Villalobos's fragmentary commentary on Pliny points this way—but the renderings and criticisms left the general public cool. They may have encouraged men like Juan Maldonado and Juan Perez to write their Latin plays in the third or fourth decade of the sixteenth century, and they may have been responsible for such productions as *Ate relegata et Minerva restituta* at Alcalá and other universities. But it is safe to say that they had next to no influence on the more popular dramatists of the day till much later in the century. Yet a drama of some kind lived on in Spain ; Cañete furnishes a list of thirty-eight playwrights whose works were actually printed before 1540. Few or none of these survive to-day. The caustic, witty Tory, Cristóbal de Castillejo, wrote one play, the *Comedia de la Costanza* : we can only judge of this by the mutilated fragments reproduced in Cañete's *Teatro Español del siglo xvi*, and these testify convincingly to Castillejo's licentious wit and command of dialogue. Castillejo, we feel sure, did better work than Agustin Ortiz, the author of a poorly versified play in five acts, the *Comedia Radiana*[1] (1534?), in which is audible an early echo of Gil Vicente ; or than Jaime de Güete,[2] author of a *Comedia llamada Vidriana*, commonplace and vulgar enough, but unobjectionable in comparison with the same writer's *Comedia intitulada Tesorina* which fully deserved to be placed upon the Index, as it finally was, after everybody had been reading it for thirty years. Bartolomé Palau[3] (b. 1525?), a native of Burbáguena, owes something to Torres as well as to Güete in his *Farsa llamada Salamantina* (1552), but then Palau owes something to Gil Vicente whose *Breve Summario da Historia de Deos* (1527) he

[1] Ed. R. E. House [*Modern Philology*, VII], Chicago, 1910.

[2] *Comedia intitulada Tesorina* and *Comedia llamada Vidriana*, ed. U. Cronan, in *Teatro español del siglo xvi*. 1913. I, pp. 81-265 (Soc. de Bibliófilos Madrileños, 10).

[3] *Historia de la gloriosa Santa Orosia*, ed. A. Fernandez-Guerra y Orbe, Madrid, 1883 ; *Victoria de Christo*, ed. L. Rouanet, in *Colección de Autos, Farsas y Coloquios del siglo xvi*. 1901. IV, pp. 375-394 (Bib. hispanica, VIII); *Farsa llamada Salamantina*, ed. A. Morel-Fatio, in *Bulletin hispanique*, II (1900), pp. 237-304 ; *Farsa llamada Custodia del hombre*, ed. L. Rouanet, in *Archivo de investigaciones históricas*, I (1911), pp. 356-390, 536-564 ; II (1911), pp. 93-154.—See : L. Rouanet, *Bartolomé Palau y sus obras*, in *Archivo de investigaciones históricas*, I (1911), pp. 267-274 ; R. E. House, *The Sources of Bartolomé Palau's " Farsa Salamantina,"* in *The Romanic Review*, IV (1913), pp. 311-322 ; M. S. y S., *Bartolomé Palau y su historia de Santa Librada*, in *Boletín de la R. Academia Esp.*, IX (1922), pp. 301-310.

has disfigured with many additions in a huge mystery play entitled *Victoria de Cristo*. If Palau deserves to be remembered at all, it is because he was the first writer to attempt the historical drama in his *Historia de la Gloriosa Santa Orosia* (between 1550 and 1570). His contemporary Micael de Carvajal,[1] in his *Tragedia llamada Josephina* (1535?) displays a command of verse and of dialogue. His unfinished *Auto de las Cortes de la Muerte* (1557) was completed by Luis Hurtado, the daw in peacock's feathers, who was long passed off on us as the author of the original *Palmeirim de Inglaterra* and who provided the two hundred and fifty lines needful to finish Perálvarez de Ayllon's *Comedia Tibalda*[2] (1553), a dreary exercise in pastoralism. Francisco de Avendaño has secured a place in history from the fact that in the *Comedia Florisea*[3] (1551), he reduces the number of acts from five to three. This little piece of mechanics might seem hardly worth mentioning. But great importance was attached to it in Spain: so much so that Cervantes, Rey de Artieda and Virués each thought that he individually had invented it, each claimed credit in the most perfect good faith for a change which had apparently originated long before in the *Auto de Clarindo* (1535?). A word of mention is due to

[1] *Las Cortes de la Muerte*, ed. J. de Sancha, 1855, in Bib. de Autores Esp., xxxv; *Tragedia llamada Josefina*, ed. M. Cañete, 1870 (Soc. de Bibliófilos Esp., 6).

[2] Ed. A Bonilla y San Martín, 1903 (Bib. hispanica, XIII).

[3] Facsimile of the 1553 ed. [with a preface by A. Bonilla y San Martín] Madrid, 1914 (*Obras dramáticas del siglo xvi*. 1st series); ed. A. Bonilla y San Martín, in *Revue Hispanique*, XXVII (1912), pp. 390-498.—See: L. Pfandl, *Die Comedia Florisea von 1551*, in *Zeitschrift für rom. Philologie*, XXXIX (1919), pp. 182-199.

Hernan Lopez de Yanguas,[1] the first writer, perhaps, to produce in his *Farsa sacramental en coplas* (1520) a genuine *auto sacramental*; to Diego Sanchez de Badajoz;[2] a most copious playwright who had clearly read Gil Vicente, as well as Enzina and who, though a priest, included one of the most objectionable pieces ever printed in Spain in his *Recopilacion en metro* (1554?); to Juan de Pedraza, the Segovian sheep-shearer who skilfully adapted a worn theme in the *Farsa llamada Dança de la Muerte*[3] (1551) and to Francisco de las Natas, author of the *Comedia llamada Tidea*[4] which was published by Mr. Urban Cronan in 1913. Though there may be some individual merit in all these works, we need delay with no single author but pass to the man who indubitably made the Spanish theatre a genuinely popular institution.

[1] *Farsa del mundo y moral*, ed. L. Rouanet, in *Colección de Autos, Farsas*, etc. 1901. IV, pp. 397-433 (Bib. hispanica, VIII); *Egloga ... en loor de la Natividad de nuestro Señor*, ed. E. Kohler, in *Sieben spanische dramatische Eklogen*. Dresden, 1911. pp. 192-209 (Gesellschaft für romanische Literatur, 27). See: E. Cotarelo, *El primer auto sacramental del teatro español y noticia de su autor el bachiller Hernan López de Yanguas*, in *Revista de Archivos*, etc., VII (1902), pp. 251-272; A. Bonilla y San Martín, *Fernan Lopez de Yanguas y el Bachiller de la Pradilla*, in *Revista crítica hispano-americana*, I (1915), pp. 44-51.

[2] *Recopilacion en metro*, ed. V. Barrantes, 1882-1886. 2 vols. (Libros de antaño, 11, 12).—See: J. López Prudencio, *Diego Sánchez de Badajoz*. Madrid, 1915.

[3] Ed. F. Wolf, in *Sitzungsberichte der Kaiserlichen Akademie der Wissenschaften*, VIII (1852), pp. 114-150 [Spanish trans. by J. Sanz del Rio in *Coleccion de documentos inéditos*, etc., 1853. XXII, pp. 509-562]—See: J. Mariscal de Gante, in *Los autos sacramentales*, etc. Madrid, 1911. pp. 60-63.

[4] Ed. U. Cronan, in *Teatro español del siglo xvi*. 1913. Pp.1-80 (Soc. de Bibliófilos Madrileños, 10).

THE LATE RENAISSANCE 251

This was LOPE DE RUEDA [1] (1510 ?-1565), a goldbeater of Seville, who wearied of his humdrum business and joined a strolling company of actors. In course of time he rose to be what was called an *autor de comedias*, that is a managing director or impresario who wrote plays and acted in them. When and how did Rueda begin his connexion with the stage ? It is conjectured that he found an opening in the company of Muzio, an Italian who was performing in Seville in 1538. One cannot be sure if this is so, but if it was so, it would help to explain Rueda's uncommon familiarity with the Italian drama. He is first heard of in 1551, when his company acted before the future Philip II in Valladolid with some success, apparently, since the Town Council of that city allotted him in 1552 a yearly income. In 1554 he again acted before the prince, this time in Benavente ; he and his strolling players were at Segovia in 1558, at Seville in 1559, in 1561 at

[1] *Obras*, ed. Marqués de la Fuensanta del Valle, Madrid, 1895-1896. 2 vols. (Col. de libros esp. raros ó curiosos, 23, 24) ; ed. E. Cotarelo y Mori, Madrid, 1908, 2 vols. (Bib. selecta de Autores clásicos Esp., 10, 11) [See Alonso de San Martín [A. Bonilla y San Martín and J. Puyol y Alonso], *Silba de varia lección*, etc. Madrid, 1909 ; E. Cotarelo y Mori, *Satisfacción a la R. Academia Esp.*, etc. Madrid, 1909 ; Alonso de San Martín, *Sepan cuantos ... Coroza crítica*, etc. Madrid, 1910] ; *Entremes del mundo y no nadie*, ed. R. Foulché-Delbosc, in *Revue Hispanique*, VII (1900), pp. 251-255 ; *Comedia llamada Discordia y questión de amor*, ed. F. R. de Uhagón, in *Revista de Archivos*, etc., VI (1902), pp. 341-354 ; *Registro de representantes*, ed. A. Bonilla y San Martín, Madrid, 1917 (Clásicos de la Literatura esp., 9).—See : A. L. Stiefel, *Lope de Rueda und das italienische Lustspiel*, in *Zeitschrift für romanische Philologie*, XV (1891), pp. 183-216, 318-343 ; L. Rouanet, in *Intermèdes espagnols du xviie siècle* ... Paris, 1897 ; N. Alonso Cortés, *Un pleito de Lope de Rueda ; nuevas noticias para su biografía.* Madrid-Valladolid, 1903 ; S. Salazar, *Lope de Rueda y su teatro.* Habana, 1911.

Toledo and Madrid whence they moved on to Valencia. We find him at Seville in 1564 and in 1565 at Cordova where he made his will on March 21 of that year; he died shortly afterwards, and, according to Cervantes, was buried in the Cathedral. In 1552 or thereabouts, Rueda married a certain Mariana, a dancer and singer attached from 1545 to 1551 to the household of the third Duque de Medinaceli, who died without paying Mariana her salary. Rueda was consequently involved in a lawsuit which he would seem ultimately to have won. Upon the death of Mariana, Rueda married in 1561 a widow, Rafaela Angela (or Angela Rafaela) Trilles, a native of Valencia. And in this city the bookseller Juan Timoneda published *Las quatro comedias y dos colloquios pastorales del excellente poeta y gracioso representante Lope de Rueda* (1567); a second edition was issued in 1576.

Rueda was a better educated man than strolling actors are now apt to be. He has left us formal plays in which the different strata of his inspiration are visible. It is evident that he has read Plautus, for his captains—his *matamoros*—are so many variants on the Plautine *miles gloriosus*. The Italian influence is everywhere visible: the *Comedia de los Engañados*, for instance, is adapted from *Gl' Ingannati*, a play based on one of Bandello's novels and composed in 1531 by a literary society—the *Intronati*—at Siena. It was reproduced in the collection of Barnabe Rich (1540?-1620?) where Shakespeare probably read it before writing *Twelfth Night*. The *Comedia llamada Armelina* appears to be an amalgam of Anton Francesco Raineri's *Altilia* (1550) and Giovan Maria Cecchi's *Servigiale* (1561); the *Comedia Eufemia*, like *Cymbeline*, deals with an episode taken from *Il Decamerone* (II, 9),

THE LATE RENAISSANCE

but was probably adapted from some intermediary Italian play, and the *Comedia llamada Medora* is in many scenes nothing but a literal translation of Gigio Artemio Giancarli's *Zingana* (1545).

However, it is not in these elaborate and pretentious pieces that one gets to know the more authentic and characteristic Rueda. The popularisation of the theatre is to be discovered in his *pasos* or short interludes in which he caricatures some well-known personage, as perhaps the now forgotten playwright, Palau, who is deplorably ill-treated under the name of Xáquima. The ebullient humour of these farcical little pieces is not always to modern taste : it verges on horse-play, but it hit the popular fancy of the day, and even now the immitigable merriment and joyous vivacity of these dramatic trifles will draw a discreet smile from more fastidious and sophisticated readers. Rueda survives the test of reading. He is in no wise dependent on the stage-carpenter or on the executant skill of the trained declaimer. His dialogue bubbles with energy and movement; his characters impress themselves on the mind and he is the master of a vigorous prose-style, varied, flexible, and strong. There is nothing pompous or mincing in his manner ; he writes the language of the multitude (as he was bound to do, since most of the personages in his *pasos* are of a comparatively humble position in life), but he raises this language to a high power which enchanted contemporaries and had its effect on those who came after him. It is more than likely that Cervantes himself is Rueda's debtor : that he learned from Rueda something of the value of simplicity and verisimilitude. And that he admired Rueda as an actor and dramatist (and even poet) we know from a very celebrated passage which would suffice to immortalize Rueda's name, even if Rueda's works had completely perished. But when all is said and done, we may come back to our original point: that Rueda's great achievement consisted in popularizing the theatre.

His appeal did not fall on deaf ears. Within a short time after Rueda's death, the country was overrun with strolling companies, beginning with the *bululú* of only one actor, the *ñaque* where we have two actors who present *entremeses*, the *gangarilla* of three or four men with a boy to act a woman's part—though actresses existed already in 1534 or even before, they were not generally recognized until 1587—the *cambaleo* consisted of five men and a singer; the *garnacha* of five to six men, a woman and a boy; the *boxiganga* of two women, six or seven men and a boy; and finally the full-blown *farándula* and the still more prosperous *compañía* made up of sixteen experienced actors, fourteen minor actors and a repertory of fifty plays, any of which could be represented at half an hour's notice. The feverish desire for dramatic entertainments spread all over the land, and native talent did not suffice to becalm that fever. Celebrated actors from abroad were warmly welcomed at Madrid; there, for instance, in 1574, Alberto Nazeri de Ganassa and his troup carried all before them. Soon after his visit, permanent theatres were opened in Madrid —the Teatro de la Cruz in 1579 and the Teatro del Príncipe in 1582. The court and the populace showed the same irrepressible enthusiasm; but the verdict of the populace decided the future of a piece. Kings and courtiers might strive to set a fashion in these matters: they succeeded later on, unfortunately.

THE LATE RENAISSANCE 255

But at this stage of dramatic development they were powerless for good or evil. If this were so at the official centre, much more was it the case in the remote flourishing cities—places like Valencia and Seville. To supply the immense demand for theatrical novelties a vast crowd of dramatists came into being. Most of them are negligible, and among many the Italian influence is clearly visible. The plays of Rueda's brother manager, Alonso de la Vega [1] (d. 1565?), are derived from Italian models, either indirectly, as in the *Comedia llamada Tholomea* and the *Tragedia llamada Seraphina* which are influenced by Rueda's *Armelina*, or directly, as in the *Comedia de la Duquesa de la Rosa* which is from Bandello's *Novelle* (II, 44). Other imitators of Rueda were Diego de Negueruela in the *Farsa llamada Ardamisa* [2] and Andrés de Prado in the *Farsa llamada Cornelia* [3]; Sebastian de Horozco [4] (1510?-1580?), whose *Cancionero* contains, besides three dramas on religious subjects—such as dramatized episodes from St. Matthew—two extremely outspoken *entremeses*, one of which has been described as the twin-brother of Enzina's *Auto del Repelon*. His

[1] *Tres comedias*, ed. M. Menéndez y Pelayo, 1905 (Gesellschaft für romanische Literatur, 6); *Amor vengado (paso)* ed. E. de Ochoa, in *Tesoro del teatro español*. 1838. I, pp. 200-201 (Col. de los mejores Autores esp., 10).—See: J. Sánchez-Arjona, in *Noticias referentes á los anales del teatro en Sevilla desde Lope de Rueda hasta fines del siglo xvii*. Sevilla, 1898, p. 18.

[2] Ed. L. Rouanet, 1900 (Bib. hispanica, IV.)

[3] Ed. C. Pérez Pastor, in *La Imprenta en Medina del Campo*. Madrid, 1895. pp. 330-337.

[4] *Noticias y obras inéditas de este autor dramático desconocido*, ed. J. M. Asensio y Toledo, Sevilla, 1867 (Soc. de Bibliófilos Andaluces); *Cancionero*, ed. A. M. Gamero, Sevilla, 1874 (Soc. de Bibliófilos Andaluces).

Representacion de la historia evangélica del capitulo nono de Sanct Joan, whose date is unknown, includes among its characters a boy Lazarillo, an interesting parallel with the protagonist of *Lazarillo de Tormes*. The attribution to Lorenzo de Sepúlveda the *romancista* of the anonymous *Comedia llamada de Sepúlveda*, based on Ariosto's *Il Negromante* and on Niccolò Secchi's *Gl' Inganni* (1547), rests only on the similarity of names. Luis de Miranda is the author of the *Comedia Prodiga*[1] (1554), which bears a fortuitous resemblance with Cecchi's *Il figliuol prodigo* (c. 1570), but the chronology precludes imitation on the Spaniard's part. Of Pedro Navarro (or Naharro) there is extant one only of the six plays familiar to Lope de Vega : this is *La Marquesa de Saluzia, llamada Griselda*,[2] a verse-comedy in four acts, preserved in a late edition (1603). Juan de Mal Lara, the humanist, is responsible according to Cueva for some thousand tragedies, but of these only the titles of two have come down to us, the *Tragedia de Absalon* and the *Comedia Locusta* which was acted by the Salamancan undergraduates in 1548. Under these circumstances, Mal Lara has less importance than the scholar Jaime Ferruz (1517-1594), canon of Valencia and author of the *Auto de Cain y Abel*.[3]

Rueda's friend and publisher, Juan Timoneda[4]

[1] Ed. J. M. de Alava, 1868 (Soc. de Bibliófilos Andaluces).

[2] Ed. C. B. Bourland, in *Revue Hispanique*, IX (1902), pp. 331-354.

[3] Ed. L. Rouanet, in *Colección de Autos, Farsas*, etc. II, pp. 150-166 (Bib. hispanica, VI).—See : M. Cañete, in *Teatro español del siglo xvi*. Madrid, 1885. pp. 251-294 (Col. de Escritores Cast., 28).

[4] *Obras completas*, ed. M. Menéndez y Pelayo, 1911, 1 vol. published [*Teatro profano*] (Soc. de Bibliófilos Valencianos, 1);

(d. 1583), was a versatile man : a tanner, a bookseller, and a playwright. He states, indeed, that he was the first to write *pasos* in prose. One cannot accept his statement as decisive. At any rate he shows no originality in any other respect. His surviving works are mostly re-arrangements of material pillaged from everybody; from Boccaccio, whose *Filocolo* inspires the prologue of two comedies (*La Comedia de Amphitrion* and *Los Menemnos*); from Plautus (through Lopez de Villalobos's translation) in *La Comedia de Amphitrion* and in *Los Menemnos*, which is also influenced by Ariosto's *Nigromante*, source of the *Comedia llamada Cornelia*; from Torres Naharro in the *Comedia llamada Aurelia*, printed in the collection entitled *Turiana* (1565). The success of his *Auto de la Oveja perdida*, a morality play on the parable of the lost sheep, was not due to any originality on Timoneda's part, but to the subject-matter itself. *El sobremesa y alivio de caminantes* (1563) is but a wan and pallid collection of traditional anecdotes and legends, more agreeably read in Melchior

Comedia de los Menemnos and *Los Ciegos y el Mozo*, [ed. N. y L. Fernandez de Moratin], 1846, in Bib. de Autores Esp., II; *Autos* [*Aucto de la Fuente de los Siete Sacramentos, Aucto de la Fée; Aucto de la oveja perdida*], ed. E. Gonzalez Pedroso, 1865, in Bib. de Autores Esp., LVIII; *El Sobremesa y Aliuio de caminantes*, facsimile of the 1569 ed. by M. Garcia [Moreno], Madrid, n.d.; *El buen aviso y portacuentos*, ed. R. Schevill, in *Revue Hispanique*, XXIV (1911), pp. 171-254.—See: M. Menéndez y Pelayo, in *Orígenes de la Novela*. 1907. II, pp. xli-lviii (Nueva Bib. de Autores Esp., 7); J. Mariscal de Gante, in *Los autos sacramentales*, etc. Madrid. 1911. pp. 63-77; R. Schevill, in *Some forms of the Riddle Question*, etc. [University of California Publications, 2). Berkeley, 1911; J. P. W. Crawford, *Notes on the 'Amphitrion' and 'Los Menemnos' of Juan de Timoneda*, in *The Modern Language Review*, IX (1914), pp. 248-251.

de Santa Cruz de Dueñas's *Floresta Española* (1574); *El buen Aviso y Portacuentos* (1564) is little more than a medley of jesting stories, good, bad, and indifferent, while *El Patrañuelo* (1576), which contains twenty-two tales unrelieved by any personal touch, is considerably below Johannes Pauli's *Schimpf vnd Ernst* (1522) in narrative power. It is too much the custom to take Timoneda seriously. He was intelligent and alert, no doubt, but he had the very useful talent of the successful business man rather than the keen vision and the expressive neutrality of the literary dramatist.

To find a dramatist of real importance we must visit Seville instead of Valencia. This was JUAN DE LA CUEVA[1] (1550?-1610?), of whose personal history next to nothing is known. He appears to have studied under Mal Lara: from 1574 to 1577 he was in New Spain, whither he was accompanied by his younger and only brother Claudio, who was an official of the Inquisition. In 1607 he seems to have left Seville and to have removed to Cuenca. He was still alive in 1609 as his signature in a copy of the *Exemplar poetico* testifies. It is generally admitted that he remained poor always. Cueva is said to have had a deep attachment to Felipa de la Paz, whom he celebrated

---

[1] *Comedias y Tragedias*, ed. F. de Icaza, Madrid, 1917. 2 vols. (Soc. de Bibliófilos Esp., 40); 'Egemplar poético,' ed. J. J. Lopez de Sedano, in *Parnaso español*. Madrid, 1774. VIII, pp. 1-68.—See: B. J. Gallardo, in *Ensayo*, etc. Madrid, 1866. II, col. 637-736; F. Wulff, *De las rimas de Juan de la Cueva: primera parte*, in *Homenaje á Menéndez y Pelayo*. Madrid, 1899. II, pp. 143-148; E. Walberg, *Juan de la Cueva et son "Exemplar poético,"* in *Acta Universitatis Lundensis*, XXXIX (1904); Adalbert Hämel, *Juan de la Cueva und die Erstausgabe seiner Comedias y Tragedias*, in *Zeitschrift für romanische Philologie*, XLIII (1923), pp. 134-153.

under the name of Felicia; allusions have also been made to some affair of gallantry between him and Brigida Lucia de Belmonte, whom he met at the house of Argote de Molina. But this is probably an entirely gratuitous invention. Cueva tempted fortune in many fields of literature and was a man of wide ambitions. He has good moments as a poet, for instance in *El Llanto de Venus en la muerte de Adonis* (1582), but these moments are extremely rare. We need not linger over the *Viaje de Sannio* and the *Coro Febeo de romances historiales* (1588), a most devitalized work. The multiplication-table is more full of surprises, Bradshaw is richer in romantic excitement than the *Coro Febeo*. In the drama Cueva is another man altogether. The *Primera parte de las comedias y tragedias de Juan de la Cueva* was published in 1583; no second part followed though the first had sufficient readers to warrant its being reprinted in 1588. Cueva has explained his dramaturgical theories in a rhymed treatise entitled the *Exemplar poetico*, written some twenty-three years after the publication of his plays. He begins by saying that he found all plays of older date very tiresome, whether they dealt with native or with classical themes; he declares himself decidedly against the famous dramatic unities which had been made almost into an article of faith by the pseudo-Aristotelian theorists of the Renaissance; and he advocates the dramatization of picturesque episodes in the popular history of Spain. This last involved a striking innovation. It is possible, no doubt, that unknown to Cueva, he may have been anticipated in this respect. But even so, if we have a genuine national theme of earlier date in Bartolomé Palau's *Historia de la gloriosa Santa Orosia*, it must be regarded as an isolated effort in which chance counted for a good deal. With Cueva the introduction of autochthonous episodes is all part of a deliberate theory just as is his insistence on the introduction of a variety, even of a wealth of metrical forms; he meant to put the Spanish drama on a new basis, to strengthen it, to vitalize it anew and to beautify a more solid structure than had heretofore existed. And it must be admitted that this adventurer succeeded in a measure. He gave the Spanish theatre a new impulse and direction. Lope de Vega and Calderon surpass him later: the one in luxuriant invention, the other in artistic technique; but they work along the line of advance traced by Cueva and they share his liking for modernity.

In *La Comedia del saco de Roma, y mverte de Borbon* ... which deals with the pillaging of the Eternal City by the armies of Charles V, Cueva set an example which Lope de Vega often followed; in *La Comedia de la muerte del Rey don Sancho*, *La Tragedia de los siete Infantes de Lara* and *La Comedia de la Libertad de España, por Bernardo del Carpio* he treats episodes of legendary or national history; in *La Comedia del Infamador*, where the voluptuary Leucino is a prominent personage, Cueva gives us an anticipation of the cloak and sword play and it must be said that in creating the character of Leucino he may well have suggested to Tirso de Molina the character of the famous Don Juan. In his declining years he found himself outshone by Lope de Vega's inspired improvisations and—especially as regards Lope de Vega—Cueva would seem to have taken his defeat badly, to have sulked over his rival's triumph and to have abandoned working for the stage. He produced in 1603 a tiresome epic poem—*Conquista de la Betica*—

which is, perhaps, better forgotten. The fact remains that Cueva was the first to adumbrate the methods which were to be developed more perfectly by Lope de Vega and others. There were some of the Old Guard who refused to surrender, among them the great Cervantes. But Cervantes's plays did not affect the evolution of the Spanish stage.

The Galician Gerónimo Bermudez [1] (1530 ?-1599 ?) published, under the pseudonym of Antonio de Sylva, the *Primeras tragedias españolas, Nise lastimosa y Nise laureada, doña Inés de Castro y Valladares, princesa de Portugal* (1577). The *Nise lastimosa* is practically a translation of the Portuguese Antonio Ferreira's *Inés de Castro* (written between 1553 and 1567); this contains fine passages by the side of which Bermudez's original contribution falls very flat. Andrés Rey de Artieda [2] (1549-1613), a Valencian known as 'Centinela' in the *Academia de los Nocturnos*, was first a poet, then a soldier who fought and was wounded at Lepanto, and later a playwright. He has been credited with the authorship of pieces entitled *Amadis de Gaula, Los Encantos de Merlin* and *El Principe vicioso*, but his only extant play is *Los Amantes* (1581), the first scenic adaptation of a theme which was

[1] *Nise lastimosa* and *Nise laureada*, ed. J. J. Lopez de Sedano, in *Parnaso español*. Madrid, 1772. VI; ed. E. de Ochoa, in *Tesoro del teatro español*. Paris, 1840. I, pp. 309-348 (Col. de los mejores autores esp., 10).—See: J. P. W. Crawford, *The influence of Seneca's tragedies upon Ferreira's Castro and Gerónimo Bermudez's Nise lastimosa and Nise laureada*, in *Modern Philology*, XII (1914), pp. 171-186.

[2] *Los Amantes*, ed. F. Carreres y Vallo [with a biographical and bibliographical notice by F. Martí Grajales], Valencia, 1908.—See: E. Cotarelo y Mori, in *Sobre el origen y desarrollo de la leyenda de los Amantes de Teruel*. 2nd ed., Madrid, 1907.

utilized later by Tirso de Molina, Perez de Montalvan and Hartzenbusch. Rey de Artieda has dramatic instinct, but his technique is uncertain and he was completely eclipsed by the advent of Lope de Vega, whom he covertly criticizes in his *Discursos, Epistolas y Epigramas* (1605), published under the name of Artemidoro.

Cristóbal de Virués,[1] a Valencian captain like his friend Rey de Artieda, was wounded at Lepanto and served in the Italian campaigns. He earned a measure of fame by his poem *El Monserrate* (1588) which he recast in 1602, but the five plays included in his *Obras tragicas y liricas* (1609) are perhaps less alien to modern taste as regards subject-matter. *La infelice Marcela* reveals one of those mechanical contrivances on which authors of the period prided themselves—a division into three parts; *La gran Semiramis* is an amalgam of horrors and pedantry; the *Átila Furioso* is remarkable for its deaths and scenes of slaughter. With all their defects these plays have at least the merit of being innovations. In *Elisa Dido* Virués returns to the old manner, which was also cultivated by that mediocre versifier, Joaquin Romero de Cepeda,[2] a native of Extremadura, whose *Obras* (1582) include a *Comedia Salvaje*, imitated from *La Celestina*, and a *Comedia llamada Metamorfosea*, a pastoral play.

[1] *La gran Semiramis*. London, 1858; *Historia del Monserrate*, ed. C. Rosell, 1851, in Bib. de Autores Esp., XVII.—See: E. von Münch-Bellinghausen, *Virues' Leben und Werke*, in *Jahrbuch für romanische und englische Literatur*, II (1860), pp. 139-163.

[2] *Comedia Salvaje* and *Comedia llamada Metamorfosea*, ed. E. de Ochoa, in *Tesoro del teatro español*. I, pp. 286-308 (Col. de los mejores Autores Esp., 10).—See: B. J. Gallardo, in *Ensayo*, etc. Madrid, 1889. IV, col. 254-259.

Lupercio Leonardo de Argensola [1] (1559-1613) has a much finer talent than any of these writers. His poems are distinguished for their studied elegance and perfect polish, but he mistook his vocation when he became a dramatist. Cervantes says of his three plays that all who heard them were charmed, astounded, and interested. It was a rare stroke of luck for Argensola to be praised and accepted in this fashion; it was much too good to last. *Filis* has disappeared; but the other two tragedies were discovered and duly printed (1772) in the *Parnaso español* by Lopez de Sedano (1730-1801 ?). Never was there a greater disappointment. Perhaps Cervantes wrote with a twinkle in his eye; most likely all that he remembered about Argensola's three plays was that (as he frankly says) they made a great deal of money. If Cervantes and his friends were indeed charmed with Argensola's tragedies, they were easily pleased: that they were astounded, one can readily believe. In the *Alejandra*, imitated from the *Marianna* (1565) of Ludovico Dolce (1508-1568), we hear of two murders committed before the play opens, seven more murders and one suicide follow. The *Isabela* shows more consideration for our nerves: there are only six murders in the play, but then there are two suicides. You feel as though you are being dragged through a shambles by a demented butcher. Perhaps the most interesting passage in Argensola's tragedies occurs in the prologue.

[1] *Poesías*, ed. A. de Castro, 1857, in Bib. de Autores Esp., XLII; ed. R. Foulché-Delbosc, in *Revue Hispanique*, XLVIII (1920), pp. 372-391; *Obras sueltas*, ed. Conde de la Viñaza, Madrid, 1889, 1 (Col. de Escritores Cast., 69) [contains *Isabela* and *Alejandra*].—See: J. P. W. Crawford, *Notes on the Tragedies of Lupercio Leonardo de Argensola*, in *The Romanic Review*, v (1914), pp. 31-44.

Speaking by the mouth of Fame, Argensola virtuously announces that he intends to have no dealings with

> comedias amorosas,
> Nocturnas asechanzas de mancebos,
> Y libres liviandades de mozuelas
> Cosas que son acetas en el vulgo.

Evidently this refers to some recent intruder who had committed the unpardonable crime of pleasing the public and ousting the old-fashioned playwrights off the boards. There can be no doubt as to the culprit's name. In 1598, Argensola went further, he begged for the suppression of the *comedia nueva* as represented by Lope de Vega.

With Cueva one other dramatist of this period may be regarded as having anticipated Lope de Vega's methods. This is Miguel Sanchez,[1] secretary to the bishop of Cuenca, and celebrated as the author of the *Cancion a Christo crucificado*, whose mystical beauty led to its attribution to Luis de Leon; and of the *romance*: *Oyd, señor don Gayferos | lo que como amigo os hablo*. Only two of his plays have reached us: *La Guarda cuidadosa* and *La Isla barbara*, both published by Professor Rennert. These are neatly planned and neatly worked out, but that is the most that can be said of them, and Sanchez does not appear to have exercised any powerful influence on dramatic development.

[1] *La Isla barbara* and *La Guarda cuidadosa*, ed. H. A. Rennert, Boston, 1896; *Poesías*, ed. A. Duran, 1849, in Bib. de Autores Esp., x; ed. J. de Sancha, 1855, in Bib. de Autores Esp., xxxv; ed. A. de Castro, 1857, in Bib. de Autores Esp., xlii.— See: A. L. Stiefel, in *Literaturblatt für germanische und romanische Philologie*, 1897, pp. 95-98; J. D. Fitzgerald, in *Modern Language Notes*, xiii (1898), pp. 100-108.

IX

THE GOLDEN AGE

It has often been remarked that the year 1564 is a turning-point in the intellectual history of mankind. In 1564 Michael Angelo died; in 1564 Shakespeare was born; and henceforward in the intellectual sphere the northern countries steadily gain at the expense of the south and more particularly at the expense of Italy. She lost most, because she had most to lose. In 1564 the Council of Trent issued its decrees, and while the Church enlisted the services of many men of rare ability, there was a lack of towering literary genius in Italy after the death of Tasso in 1595 till comparatively recent times. Spain, also, was declining in importance, though the fact was not yet visible to ordinary observers. Francis Bacon, indeed, noted it, but he stood alone. Seven years before Tasso's death, the defeat of the Armada (1588) had shaken Spain; but the period immediately ensuing this disaster is the most glorious in Spain's literary history. She produced men of genius like Cervantes and Quevedo whose romances and satirical tales were read all over Europe; and as she produced other men of genius like Lope de Vega and Calderon, whose plays supplied the dramatists of Italy, France, England, Holland, and Germany with the material for an endless succession of comedies, Spain may be said to have had for a long while a monopoly of the literature of entertainment. Her great writers were undoubtedly men of singular independence and originality; their work adds point to the saying that Spain is not quite in the European current of thought.

MIGUEL DE CERVANTES SAAVEDRA [1] (1547-1616) is

[1] *Obras completas*, ed. R. Academia Esp. [Facsimile of the first editions I-VI. Madrid, 1917; VII, *Obras sueltas* (ed. F. Rodríguez Marín), Madrid, 1923]; ed. R. Schevill and A. Bonilla y San Martín, Madrid, 1914-1923. 12 vols. published.— *Primera Parte de la Galatea.* Facsimile of the 1585 ed. by A. M. Huntington. New York, n.d. 2 vols.—*Don Quixote.* Facsimile of the two 1605 Madrid editions and of the 1615 Madrid ed. by The Hispanic Society. New York. n. d. 3 vols.; ed. James Fitzmaurice-Kelly and J. Ormsby, London, 1898-1899. 2 vols.; ed. F. Rodríguez Marín, Madrid, 1911-1913. 8 vols. (Clásicos Castellanos); critical ed. by F. Rodríguez Marín, Madrid, 1916-1917. 6 vols.—*Novelas ejemplares* [*La Gitanilla, Rinconete y Cortadillo, La Ilustre Fregona, El Licenciado Vidriera, El Celoso extremeño, El Casamiento engañoso* and *Novela y Coloquio que pasó entre Cipion y Berganza*], ed. F. Rodríguez Marín, Madrid, 1914-1917. - 2 vols. (Clásicos Cast., 27, 36); *Cinco Novelas ejemplares* [*La Gitanilla, Rinconete y Cortadillo, El Celoso Estremeño, El Casamiento engañoso* and *Novela y Coloquio que pasó entre Cipion y Berganza*] [ed. R. J. Cuervo], 1908. (Bib. romanica); *Rinconete y Cortadillo,* critical ed. by F. Rodríguez Marín, Sevilla, 1905, 2nd ed. Madrid, 1920; *El casamiento engañoso* and *Coloquio de los perros,* critical ed. by A. G. de Amezúa y Mayo, Madrid, 1912; annotated ed. by F. Rodríguez Marín, Madrid, 1918; *El licenciado Vidriera,* ed. N. Alonso Cortés, Valladolid, 1916; *La ilustre fregona,* critical ed. by F. Rodríguez Marín, Madrid, 1917—*La tía fingida,* ed. A. Bonilla y San Martín, Madrid, 1911; ed. J. T. Medina, Santiago de Chile, 1919—*Entremeses* (9) [including the anonymous *Entremés de los Habladores*] ed. E. Cotarelo y Mori, in *Colección de Entremeses,* etc. Madrid, 1911. 1, pp. 1-51 (Nueva Bib. de Autores Esp., 17); ed. A. Bonilla y San Martín, Madrid, 1916; *Los rufianes de Cervantes*: *El rufián dichoso* and *El*

THE GOLDEN AGE

famous through a single book whose first part was published when he was fifty-eight years of age, and the second part ten years later. It is therefore not surprising that he was obscure while he lived. Early biographers have supplied him with a handsome genealogical tree dating back to the tenth century. This is pure fantasy. The remotest ancestor of Cervantes who can be traced is his great-grandfather,

rufián viudo, ed. J. Hazañas y La Rúa, Sevilla, 1906—*Varias obras inéditas*, etc., ed. A. de Castro, Madrid, 1874; *Epístola á Mateo Vázquez* [ed. E. Cotarelo y Mori], Madrid, 1905; *Una joyita de Cervantes* [" Voto a Dios que me espanta esta braveza"], ed. F. Rodríguez Marín, Madrid, 1914.—See: M. Fernandez de Navarrete, *Vida de Miguel de Cervantes Saavedra*. Madrid, 1819; *Le voyage au Parnasse*, French trans. by J. M. Guardia, Paris, 1864; A. Morel-Fatio, *Le " Don Quichotte" envisagé comme peinture et critique de la société espagnole du xvie et du xviie siècle*, in *Études sur l'Espagne*. Paris, 1895. 1st series, pp. 297-382; L. Rius, *Bibliografía crítica de las obras de Miguel de Cervantes Saavedra*. Madrid, 1895-1905. 3 vols.; James Fitzmaurice-Kelly, Introductions to *The History of Don Quixote of the Mancha* [Shelton's trans. 1612, 1620], London, 1896. 4 vols. (The Tudor Translations, xiii-xvi); C. Pérez Pastor, *Documentos cervantinos hasta ahora inéditos*. Madrid, 1897-1902. 2 vols.; R. Foulché-Delbosc, *Étude sur 'La Tía Fingida,'* in *Revue Hispanique*, vi (1899), pp. 256-306; R. Foulché-Delbosc, *Puesto ya el pie en el estribo*, in *Revue Hispanique*, vi (1899), pp. 319-321; R. Foulché-Delbosc, *La plus amcienne œuvre connue de Cervantes*, in *Revue Hispanique*, vi (1899), pp. 508-509; J. Apraiz, *Estudio histórico-crítico sobre las Novelas ejemplares de Cervantes*. Vitoria, 1901; James Fitzmaurice-Kelly, Introductions to *The Complete Works of Miguel de Cervantes Saavedra* [Trans. by J. Ormsby, H. Oelsner, A. B. Welford and N. MacColl], Glasgow, 1901-1903. 7 vols.; F. A. de Icaza, *Las 'Novelas ejemplares' de Cervantes*. Madrid, 1901, 2nd ed. 1915; F. Rodríguez Marín, *El Loaysa de 'El celoso extremeño.'* Sevilla, 1901; J. Cejador y Frauca, *La lengua de Cervantes*. Madrid, 1905-1906. 2 vols.; James Fitzmaurice-Kelly, *Cervantes in England*. London, 1905; J. Brimeur,

Rodrigo de Cervantes, husband of Catalina de la Vera, sometimes called Catalina de Cabrera. Their son, Juan, an obscure country lawyer, had three children, of whom one, Rodrigo, became the father of the great

Supplément français à la Bibliographie de Rius, in *Revue Hispanique*, xv (1906), pp. 819-842; R. Schevill, *Studies in Cervantes: Persiles y Sigismunda*, in *Modern Philology*, IV (1906), pp. 1-24, 677-704, and in *Publications of Yale University*, XIII (1908), pp. 475-548; M. A. Buchanan, *Cervantes as a Dramatist*. 1. *The Interludes* [*Modern Language Notes*, XXIII], Baltimore, 1908; James Fitzmaurice-Kelly, in *Chapters on Spanish Literature*. London, 1908. pp. 120-162; B. Croce, in *Saggi nella letteratura del Seicento*. Bari, 1911. pp. 125-159; R. Foulché-Delbosc, *Cervantica*, II, in *Revue Hispanique*, xxv (1911), pp. 481-483; James Fitzmaurice-Kelly, *Miguel de Cervantes Saavedra : A Memoir*. Oxford, 1913 [Spanish trans. by B. Sanín Cano, revised and augmented, Oxford, 1917]; F. Rodríguez Marín, *Nuevos documentos cervantinos hasta ahora inéditos*. Madrid, 1914; F. Rodríguez Marín, *El andalucismo y el cordobesismo de Miguel de Cervantes*, Madrid, 1915; A. Bonilla y San Martín, *Cervantes y su obra*. Madrid [1916]; James Fitzmaurice-Kelly, *Cervantes and Shakespeare* [*Proceedings of the British Academy*, VII], 1916; F. A. de Icaza, *De cómo y por qué ' La Tía Fingida ' no es de Cervantes y otros nuevos estudios cervantinos* [reprinted from *Boletín de la R. Academia Esp*. I, II], Madrid, 1916; F. Rodríguez Marín, *El doctor Juan Blanco de Paz*. Madrid, 1916; A. Bonilla y San Martín, *De crítica cervantina*. Madrid [1917]; R. Schevill, *Cervantes*. New York, 1919; James Fitzmaurice-Kelly, *Cervantes*, in *The Year Book of Modern Languages*. Cambridge, 1920. pp. 139-150.—N. Sentenach, *Le portrait de Cervantes*, in *Revue Hispanique*, xxv (1911), pp. 13-18; R. Foulché-Delbosc, *Le ' Iauregui' de l'Académie Espagnole*, in *Revue Hispanique*, xxv (1911), pp. 476-482; J. Puyol, *El supuesto retrato de Cervantes*. Madrid, 1915; J. Puyol, *El supuesto retrato de Cervantes. Réplica a una contestación inverosímil*. Madrid, 1915; A. Báig Baños, *Historia del retrato auténtico de Cervantes*. Madrid, 1916; J. Puyol, *El supuesto retrato de Cervantes. Resumen y conclusiones*. Madrid, 1917; F. Rodríguez Marín, *El retrato de Miguel de Cervantes. Estudio sobre la autenticidad de la tabla de Jáuregui* . . . Madrid, 1917.

writer. Rodrigo de Cervantes was a mediocre practitioner of a lowly type, who wandered from town to town cupping and blistering the few patients unfortunate enough to consult him. In or after March 1543 he married Leonor de Cortinas. The future author of *Don Quijote* was the fourth of their seven children; he was born at Alcalá de Henares and was baptized in Santa Maria la Mayor on Sunday, October 9, 1547. Little is known about Cervantes's youth. It is plain that he can never have had much formal schooling, that he picked up his smattering of education at hazard, and that he studied only in the university of practical experience. But it is also plain that he was an omnivorous desultory reader. He must have read innumerable romances of chivalry, the fashionable pastorals, picaresque stories, the chief poets of the day and the countless popular ballads which he quotes or burlesques at every turn. All that he learned from books he learned in his boyhood, accompanying his father on his dreary pilgrimages, staying in wayside taverns, rubbing shoulders in the marketplaces with men of all conditions, watching strolling actors like Lope de Rueda, of whom he speaks so eulogistically fifty years later. No doubt, there was then born in him the ambition, which he never abandoned, to make a reputation as a dramatist. This was not to be: he was destined to win immortality in another province of literature and, in the meanwhile, he had to earn his daily bread.

The earliest known literary attempt of Cervantes is a sonnet—discovered by M. Foulché-Delbosc: it is dedicated to Isabel de Valois, the third wife of Philip II, and was probably composed between 1560 and 1568. A *copla*, four *redondillas*, an elegy, perhaps also a sonnet, figure in the *Hystoria y relacion verdadera de la enfermedad, felicissimo transito, y sumptuosas exequias funebres de la Serenissima Reyna de España doña Isabel de Valoys nuestra Señora* (1569), published on the occasion of Isabel de Valois's death (October 3, 1568). This volume was edited by a Madrid schoolmaster named Juan Lopez de Hoyos who twice calls Cervantes his 'amado discípulo.' The elegy, dedicated to Cardinal Diego de Espinosa, professes to be written 'en nombre de todo el estudio.' Some have inferred from these phrases that Cervantes was an usher at Madrid under Lopez de Hoyos. It may have been so. In December 1569, Cervantes was in Rome, and it was no doubt at this time that he became chamberlain to Giulio Acquaviva (d. 1574), who had been sent to Madrid as pontifical legate in 1568. He probably joined the army in the autumn of 1570, and was placed in Diego de Urbina's company of Miguel de Moncada's infantry then serving under Marco Antonio Colonna, to whose son Ascanio Cervantes dedicated *La Galatea*. On October 7, 1571, Cervantes took part in the historic battle of Lepanto and received three gunshot wounds, one of which crippled his left hand. He was evidently as proud of having fought at Lepanto as of writing *Don Quijote*, perhaps prouder. He took part in the operations before Navarino (1572) and at Tunis (1573); in 1574 he was garrisoned at Palermo as a *soldado aventajado*. As such, he must give ten years of service before he could hope for promotion. He made up his mind to seek it in Spain, procured letters of recommendation from Don John of Austria and from the Duke of Sessa, Viceroy of Naples; and in September 1575 set sail with his brother Rodrigo on the *Sol*.

THE GOLDEN AGE

He had no suspicion that his military career was over; but so it was. The *Sol* was attacked off Les Saintes Maries by Moorish corsairs, and after a fierce engagement many of those on board, including Cervantes, were carried off as slaves to Algiers. The letters from Don John of Austria and the Viceroy led the Moors to assume that Cervantes was a prisoner of exceptional importance; it was determined to ask a huge ransom for him. He made five desperate attempts to escape, and, on two occasions, would have got safe away, had it not been for the treachery of a comrade. With great effort and by means of dubious expedients, his family had scraped together a small sum of money which was entrusted to two Trinitarian monks, Fray Juan Gil and Fray Anton de la Bella, who regularly negotiated for the ransom of Christian slaves in Algiers. But the amount was wholly insufficient, and the monks were more anxious to secure the release of an Aragonese prisoner, named Jerónimo Palafox, than to secure the release of Cervantes. Fortunately for the world, Hassan the Dey fixed Palafox's ransom at an impossible price, and, as this amount could not be raised, the available money was devoted to rescuing Cervantes. He had a very narrow escape. It was Hassan's last day of office; his slaves were already shipped on galleys, bound for Constantinople; and the news of his release was brought to Cervantes as he sat in chains on board.

After five years of slavery he returned to Spain in December 1580. His outlook was not a bright one; Don John was dead; and at the age of thirty-three Cervantes had to begin life again. From an *Informacion* which Cervantes signed in 1590, it has been thought that he served at the Azores and in Portugal;

but the wording is loosely expressed and the services of Rodrigo are mentioned in a confused and confusing way with those of Miguel. Cervantes was a captive until after the campaign in Portugal was over, and it is at least doubtful if he can have served at the Azores. He seems to have been in Portugal after his return from Algiers and to have carried despatches from Thomar to Orab and Mostaganem. This mission soon came to an end; Cervantes failed to obtain permanent employment, and, in default of anything better, took to literature. The plays which he wrote to amuse his fellow-prisoners have disappeared and all that remains of his work during captivity are two laudatory sonnets (1577) addressed to Bartolomeo Ruffino, his fellow captive at Argel, who was engaged on writing an account of the taking of Tunis; twelve octaves (1579) to Antonio Veneziano (1543-1593); and a verse epistle to Mateo Vazquez, Philip II's Secretary of State, some seventy lines of which Cervantes later incorporated in *El trato de Argel*. Meanwhile he seems to have made his way among the rather mediocre literary men at the capital. He wrote a eulogistic sonnet for the *Romancero* (1583) of Pedro de Padilla (b. 1550), and another similar sonnet in 1584 for Rufo Gutierrez's *La Avstriada*. Luis Galvez de Montalvo wrote a like sonnet for the *Primera Parte de la Galatea dividida en seys libros* (1585), a pastoral romance which Cervantes had probably finished by the end of 1583. *La Galatea* really has as little to do with pastoral life as the *Notes on the construction of Sheepfolds* by Ruskin. It has all the faults that Hazlitt (1778-1830) condemns in Sir Philip Sidney's *Arcadia*: 'the original sin of alliteration, antithesis and metaphysical conceit . . . the

THE GOLDEN AGE

systematic interpolation of the wit, learning, ingenuity, wisdom, and everlasting impertinence of the writer.' Cervantes borrows from Sannazaro the original idea and arrangement; from Leon Hebreo he takes a digression on beauty; the *Canto de Caliope* with its strings of praises on contemporary poets is based on the *Canto de Turia* in Gil Polo's *Diana enamorada*. In spite of these imitations there is a measure of originality in *La Galatea* and a certain distinction in its prose. But academic correctness alone never saved any book from oblivion. *La Galatea* is based on an unreal convention and it is significant that though Cervantes continued to promise a second part for over thirty years, this sequel never appeared. He sold this first effort outright to his townsman, Blas de Robles, for 1336 *reales*. On December 12, 1584, Cervantes married Catalina de Palacios Salazar y Vozmediano (d. 1626), a fatherless girl of Esquivias, who was eighteen years younger than himself, and set up housekeeping at Madrid. Owing to Cervantes's roving existence, the pair saw little of one another till the last ten years of their married life. It may have been at about this period that Isabel de Saavedra, Cervantes's natural daughter was born; her mother was Ana Franca de Rojas.

Meanwhile Cervantes was becoming known as a copious and fluent versifier. Whenever one of his friends brought out a book, Cervantes was always ready with a sonnet to introduce it. Any occasion served as an excuse, and some of these occasions were extremely odd. An acquaintance of his, Francisco Diaz, published in 1588 a medical treatise on kidney diseases and Cervantes burst into song on this uninspiring theme. There are verses by his hand in

Padilla's *Jardin espiritval* (1585) and *Grandezas y Excelencias de la Virgen Señora nuestra* (1587); in Gabriel Lopez Maldonado's *Cancionero* (1586), and in the *Philosophia cortesana moralizada* (1587) of Alonso de Barros (1522 ?-1604 ?)., But the question of ways and means began to press heavily on Cervantes. *La Galatea* was not an inexhaustible gold mine, and it was probably at about this period that Cervantes wrote the twenty or thirty plays—his arithmetic is always delightfully vague—which he produced, so he says, in about five years. We have the titles of some of these plays: *El trato de Constantinopla y muerte de Selin*, *La Gran Turquesca*, *La Jerusalen*, *La Batalla Naval*, *La Amaranta*, *El Bosque amoroso*, *Arsinda* and *La Confusa*; obviously this last was a special favourite with the author, who describes it as *buena entre los mejores*, but he may have exaggerated its merits in the retrospect. The Conde-Duque de Olivares (1587-1645) appears to have possessed a copy of *La Batalla Naval*, and the *Arsinda* was still extant in 1673 when Matos Fragoso mentions it in *La Corsaria catalana*. But only two of the plays written at this period have reached us: these are *El trato de Argel* and *La Numancia*, both published in 1784. *El trato de Argel* depicts the life led by the Christian slaves at Argel and the passion of the Moorish girl Zara for the Spaniard Aurelio, the lover of Sylvia, a subject which Cervantes treated some thirty years later in *El Amante liberal*. Among the captives is a certain Saavedra, evidently Cervantes, and the account of the toils endured by him and his fellow-prisoners offers interest, but the introduction of the allegorical figures, Opportunity and Necessity, the appearance of a lion and of the Devil are futile expedients; the situations are improbable,

THE GOLDEN AGE

the versification poor and the play completely lacks dramatic merit.

The same defects—the introduction of abstractions and the want of dramatic unity—are evident in *La Numancia* which remains, however, Cervantes's finest play. He had a noble canvas: the fourteen years' siege and final conquest of Numantia by the eighty thousand Romans under Scipio Africanus and their entry into what was a city of the dead. Cervantes, like Milton, saw his race as 'an old and haughty nation, proud in arms.' Scipio's speech when Viriato, the last survivor, flings himself from the tower is stirring and impressive; there are the same high qualities of impassioned eloquence in the scene between Marquino and the corpse. These episodes are dramatic in their appeal, but they gain nothing from the context. There are isolated passages of beauty in *La Numancia*; the love of Morandro for Lyra is charmingly treated, and the versification has merit, if not so much as Shelley's generous praise would imply: 'There is little, I allow, to be called *poetry* in this play; but the command of language and the harmony of versification is so great as to deceive one into an idea that it is poetry.' The play found great favour with the German romantics; at one period it charmed Goethe (1747-1832). As a dramatic piece it fails; it survives only as a manifestation of deep patriotic feeling. And one would fain put faith in the legend of its revival at the siege of Saragossa (1809); Cervantes would have wished for no higher tribute.

The year after Cervantes's marriage, his father died. His mother and sisters were now dependent on him, and, while his responsibilities increased, his income diminished. He found formidable competitors among the playwrights ; he was beginning to be voted old-fashioned, and it became necessary for him to seek employment outside of literature. The Invincible Armada was being equipped at this time, and Cervantes was appointed to the post of commissary through the influence of Diego de Valdivia in August 1587. This appointment was officially confirmed in January 1588. The task of requisitioning wheat and oil was not congenial to Cervantes, but the work enabled him to live without the fear of starvation before his eyes. The new post had its drawbacks, as he soon found ; he was excommunicated for requisitioning wheat belonging to the clergy at Ecija and had to offer a humble apology for his inopportune zeal. The year was not very favourable to Spain or to Cervantes personally. Spain's Invincible Armada came to grief. Cervantes wrote two odes on the Armada, one prophetic of victory, the other condolatory of disaster. After the defeat he went to Seville where he lived with Tomas Gutierrez, an actor who shewed him constant kindness. But Cervantes found his occupation of commissary to the galleys sordid and repugnant, and in 1590 he tried to get an appointment in Central America, failed and went back to his tax-collecting. The *Flor de varios y nuevos romances* (1591) of Andrés de Villalta includes a ballad by Cervantes, and in 1592 he undertook to write for Rodrigo Osorio six plays for fifty ducats each ; no payment was to be made for any one play unless it was considered one of the best ever put on the Spanish stage. This ambitious plan came to nothing. In 1595 he wrote a sonnet to the Marqués de Santa Cruz (1526-1588), which was published in the *Comentario en breve compendio de disciplina militar* (1596) of Cristóbal Mosquera de

THE GOLDEN AGE

Figueroa (1544 ?-1610), and a satirical sonnet on the Duque de Medina Sidonia (1550-1615); he also won a prize of three silver spoons at a poetical joust in Saragossa. The same year the Sevillan banker, Simon Freire de Lima, with whom Cervantes had deposited public moneys, absconded. Cervantes, unable to refund the amount, had to appeal to the Treasury to make a first claim on the bankrupt's estate. For some time now he had been in trouble with his superiors. A blunder had led to his being imprisoned for a fortnight in 1592. His bookkeeping scandalized the official mind. The irregularities in his accounts threw no reflexion on Cervantes's personal honour, but they undoubtedly went to prove that he was unfitted for routine work and as a result of this last episode he was cashiered.

From 1595 to 1603 Cervantes lived in great misery at Seville, in and out of jail, apparently on the ground that he had failed to appear before the Exchequer Court with his vouchers and accounts. The plain truth is that he did not respond to the Treasury summonses, because he had not the money to pay for the journey from Seville. Imprisoned in 1597, he was released at the end of that year, during which he would seem to have written nothing except perhaps a sonnet—of dubious authenticity—on the death of Herrera. Towards the end of 1598 he composed two sonnets and some *quintillas* on the death of Philip II, and in 1602 a laudatory sonnet for the second edition of Lope de Vega's *La Dragontea*. In 1603-1604 he was at Valladolid, the new temporary capital, whither he had been summoned to discharge his debts. On September 26, 1604, the privilege of *El Ingenioso Hidalgo Don Quixote de la Mancha* was granted, and in

January 1605 the book was published at Madrid by Francisco de Robles, bookseller to the king. The date and place of its composition are alike unknown; it was begun after 1591, as early in the work there is an allusion to Bernardo de la Vega's *El Pastor de Iberia* (1591). It used to be said that *Don Quijote* was written partly in the prison-cells of Argamasilla de Alba: it is probable that Cervantes lived at Argamasilla, but if he ever began the book in prison, then Seville has the likelier claim. *Don Quijote* was evidently known and discussed in literary circles before its publication; Lopez de Ubeda mentions it in *La Picara Justina* (1605; privilege of 1604), and Lope de Vega in a letter dated August 14, 1604, says that there is no new poet 'tan malo como Cervantes, ni tan necio que alabe a don Quijote.'[1] In spite of Lope de Vega and his clique *Don Quijote* carried all before it. In Spain it had four editions in 1605, it was twice pirated in Portugal the same year and in 1607 was published at Brussels. In Paris the episode of *El Curioso impertinente* was incorporated by César Oudin (d. 1625) in the second edition (1608) of Julian de Medrano's *Silva curiosa*; Nicolas Baudouin published the text of the same story with a French translation in 1608, and the following year an anonymous French recast of Marcela's story with the discourse on arms and letters appeared under the title: *Homicidio de la fidelidad, y la defensa del honor*. But nowhere, perhaps, has *Don Quijote* been more welcome than in England. It was first translated here by Thomas Shelton in 1612; here, also, the first critical edition of the text was published. Here another great

[1] 'as bad as Cervantes, or foolish enough to praise *Don Quijote*.'

THE GOLDEN AGE

novelist arose who put forth a new conception of the book's manifold significance : its intellectual variety, its artistic vigour, its pregnant philosophy of life. This was Fielding (1707-1754) who proudly says that his *Joseph Andrews* was 'written in the manner of Cervantes, author of *Don Quixote*.' Sterne (1713-1768), and Smollett (1721-1771), Dickens (1812-1870) and Thackeray (1811-1863), all followed the same great model. And among dramatists, George Wilkins, Middleton (1570-1627), Ben Jonson (1573-1637), Cyril Tourneur (1575-1625), Nathaniel Field (1587-1633), and Fletcher shew reminiscences of *Don Quijote*.

Cervantes himself says that the principal object of his work was to destroy the romances of chivalry, and no doubt that was his original intention. But the day of these was already passing, and *Don Quijote* only hastened their end. Unconsciously he began to modify that intention ; the possibilities of the subject slowly revealed themselves. Before he was aware of it, he found himself committed to a far larger enterprise than he had thought of—the prose-epic of Spain. Not content with the elaborate portraiture of the two imposing central figures, he furnishes his rich gallery with likenesses of secondary figures, all revealing the dexterous touch of the consummate craftsman. The fussy, friendly priest and the pleasant, officious barber ; the book-hating niece, and the book-burning housekeeper; the spluttering Biscayan and the brusque goatherd Pedro ; the left-handed landlord, and the kindly, one-eyed wench Maritornes ; the charming, mercurial Dorothea, and the provident, conjugal Teresa—each figure in this gallant procession has become part of the visible world. To those of more fastidious literary taste, Cervantes offers the sedulous imitation of stately rhetoric in the sonorous passage on the Golden Age, the concise summary of a typical romance of chivalry, and, best of all, the incomparable burlesque description of the mighty hosts advancing in order of battle to the blare of trumpet and the tuck of drum under the command of the Lord of the Silver Bridge, the dread Duke Micocolembo and the undaunted giant who ruled the three Arabias. And to vary the interest of these resounding mock-heroics, we have the episodes of Marcela, of Luscinda, of Fernando; the tale of those most tragic comedians, Lothario and Anselmo, developed from the *Orlando Furioso*; the narrative of the Captive's breathless escapes in Algiers; essays in the pastoral and sentimental kinds, digressions in psychological analysis and in poignant autobiography. All the national life of Spain is poured into *Don Quijote*; apart from its merit as a romance, it is a document of the first importance as a contribution to the history of the Later Renaissance in the Peninsula. It stands, like Moses, between the living and the dead: it marks the end of mediaevalism and signalizes the victory of modernity with its spirit of scientific observation. We need pay no attention to those who would persuade us to regard it as a well of esoteric symbolism. First and last, *Don Quijote* is a masterpiece of entertainment. Its humour remains undimmed; something of its magic is conveyed even in the least faithful of translations; its mature and benignant wisdom has captivated thinkers so far apart in time, temperament, doctrine, and race as Locke, Kant and Schopenhauer.

But luck continued to run against its author. In June 1605 he was arrested on a charge of being

THE GOLDEN AGE

concerned in the murder of a certain Gaspar de Ezpeleta who was wounded in the street of Valladolid where Cervantes lodged. This was a most unpleasant experience for Cervantes. It has prejudiced him unspeakably. Biographers thought that they were doing him a service in concealing the charges brought up by a witness against Isabel de Saavedra. This conspiracy of silence proved unfortunate, for Cervantes was suspected of conniving at his daughter's irregularity with the Portuguese Simon Mendez. The years 1605-1608 are more or less of a blank. In 1609 Cervantes joined the pious confraternity of the *Esclavos del Santísimo Sacramento*, and in the following year published a sonnet to the memory of Diego Hurtado de Mendoza. He also made the acquaintance of the Conde de Lemos (1576-1622), who proved a kindly patron. But his disappointments were not at an end. Lemos became Viceroy of Naples in 1610, and took several literary men with him in his suite. Cervantes was not chosen as he expected to be, and smarted under what he took for a slight. His mortification drove him back to literature. He joined the *Academia Selvaje* founded by Francisco de Silva (d. 1618 ?), and is heard of as being present at a disorderly meeting of it in 1612, the date of the privilege for the *Novelas exemplares* (1613).

The *Novelas ejemplares*, for which Cervantes received sixteen hundred *reales*, and twenty-four free copies, are twelve short stories composed, probably, at long intervals of time. They are of unequal merit; two of them, *Rinconete y Cortadillo* and the *Novela y Coloquio que passò entre Cipion y Berganza, perros del Hospital de la Resurreccion, que està en la ciudad de Valladolid, fuera de la puerta del Campo, a quien comunmente llaman los perros de Mahudes* are little masterpieces, six are excellent, the rest are relatively poor ; though anybody else might be proud enough to write them. But they all express the author's individuality, and none of them lacks charm. Had Cervantes published nothing else, he would hold an eminent position in the history of Spanish literature. In 1814 Agustin Garcia Arrieta printed *La Tia fingida* as one of Cervantes's *Novelas*: it now figures in many editions. The discovery of the manuscript was only made in 1788, and the ascription of it to Cervantes was arrived at mainly by a process of elimination. The *Novelas Ejemplares* had a wide success with contemporaries, and many of the subjects were dramatized by the leading playwrights of the day. Outside Spain they found numerous imitators. *La Gitanilla* proceeds originally, it is true, from the character of Tarsiana in the *Libro de Apolonio*, but it is Cervantes's conception which is reproduced by Weber (1786-1826) and Wolff (1782-1828) in Preciosa, by Victor Hugo in Esmeralda, by Middleton and Rowley (1585 ?-1642 ?) in *The Spanish Gipsie*, where we find also reminiscences from *La Fuerza de la sangre* upon which Fletcher bases his *Queen of Corinth*. His *Love's Pilgrimage* derives from *Las dos doncellas*, *Rule a Wife and have a Wife* from *El casamiento engañoso*, and *Chances* from *El celoso extremeño*. From this last story Bickerstaffe (1735-1812) took *The Padlock*. The titles of *Cornélie*, *La Force du Sang* and *La Belle Egyptienne* by Alexandre Hardy (d. 1631 ?), of *Les deux Pucelles* by Rotrou (1609-1650), of *L'Amant libéral*[1] by Georges de Scudéry and of *Le Docteur de verre*

[1] *La Belle Provençale* of Regnard (1655-1709) is also based on *El Amante liberal*.

by Quinault (1635-1688), are sufficiently indicative of their sources. It is even possible that *El licenciado Vidriera* suggested to Molière (1622-1673) the sonnet-scene in *Le Misanthrope*. Sir Walter Scott (1771-1832) confesses that the *Novelas* had first inspired him ' with the ambition of excelling in fiction,' and doubtless he derived more than encouragement from Cervantes since a passage from *Rinconete y Cortadillo* would seem to have suggested the famous description of Alsatia in *The Fortunes of Nigel*.

In 1614 Cervantes published the *Viage del Parnaso*, a mock heroic poem on the versifiers of the day imitated from the *Viaggio in Parnaso* (1582) of Cesare Caporali (1530-1601). Cervantes's delicate irony found no expression in verse ; his critical instinct was not his strongest point and the *Viaje del Parnaso* is little more than a panegyric. It is otherwise with Apollo's supplementary prose-letter, which was an after-thought added on July 22, 1614, and inspired by Sancho Panza's letter to his wife Teresa.

> Dans les nobles desseins dont l'âme est occupée,
> Les vers sont le clairon, mais la prose est l'épée.

It was now nine years since the First Part of *Don Quijote* had been published and the promised Second Part had not appeared. If Cervantes had feared to stake his all upon a doubtful issue, the reception given to his *Novelas Ejemplares* shewed that he still retained his hold upon the public, and this may have given him courage to go forward with the Second Part. Yet, even so, he dallied a good deal. He wrote more eulogistic verses : a sonnet for Diego de Rosel y Fuenllana's *Parte primera de varias aplicaçiones y transformaciones* . . . (1613), some quatrains for Gabriel

Perez del Barrio Angulo (1558 ?-1652) and some stanzas (1615) in honour of Santa Teresa who had just been canonized.

What Cervantes most desired was recognition as a dramatist: he would have given *Don Quijote* ten times over for one of the successes which Lope de Vega obtained on the stage almost every week in the year. Cervantes had been brought up in the school of the Senecan drama and the three unities were matters of faith with him ; he was born too late, the three unities were slain before his eyes and his plays went out of fashion. Late in life he tried to assimilate the new principles of the romantic drama introduced by Lope de Vega, as, for instance, in *La casa de los zelos, y selvas de Ardenia* ; he was too old to change and did not succeed greatly, except in a few interludes, especially those written in prose. He brought out his *Ocho comedias y ocho entremeses nvevos* in 1615. His skill in portraiture is realized in *El viejo zeloso*, imitated in *The Fatal Dowry* by Massinger (1583-1640), who based *The Renegado* on Cervantes's *Baños de Argel*. Similarly *La cueua de Salamanca* suggested the German farce *Der Bettelstudent* as well as Calderon's *Dragoncillo*. Three *entremeses*, *Los habladores*, *La carcel de Sevilla*, and *El hospital de los podridos* are printed in the 'Séptima Parte' (1617) of Lope de Vega's plays, but Lope strenuously declares that they are not by him ; if their ascription to Cervantes were correct they would go to prove that he could rivalize with Luis Quiñones de Benavente in his own domain. *Los habladores*, in particular, has a rare spice of humour and reminiscences of it are visible in *Gert Westphaler* by Holberg (1684-1754). *Pedro de Urdemalas*, which contains a hit at Lope de Vega, is perhaps Cervantes's best example in this *genre*. In his more formal plays Cervantes was always hampered by the convention which required that such plays should be written in verse. This recalls another of his high ambitions. He had always longed to be a poet, but (he adds ruefully) nature had denied him the gift of poetry. Not altogether; he does himself injustice; he had imagination, fancy, feeling, ideas, an embellishing vision—everything except the glamour of verbal magic. Nature had not denied him the gift of poetry: she had denied him the gift of song: he was a poet lacking the accomplishment of verse. This is not to say that he has no occasional felicities; no harmonious numbers in his verses: but the inspiration is intermittent and fugitive. Cervantes never reveals to us the vision splendid of a world invisible: his real genius lay in the field of humanistic observation.

He had reached the fifty-ninth chapter of his continuation when he learned that a spurious sequel to *Don Quijote* had been issued (1614) at Tarragona with the name of Alonso Fernandez de Avellaneda on the title-page. Who was Fernandez de Avellaneda? Cervantes thought that the name was a pseudonym and the world has followed Cervantes's lead on this point. But it has not been possible to unmask Avellaneda. He has been identified with a whole list of names, such as Luis de Aliaga (1565-1626), Philip III's confessor; Bartolomé Leonardo de Argensola, Lopez de Ubeda, author of *La Picara Justina*; Lope de Vega, Tirso de Molina, Ruiz de Alarcon, Gaspar Schöppe (1576-1649), who was thought—without much foundation—to be the original of *El licenciado Vidriera*; the Dominican Alonso Fernandez (1569?-1633), author of the *Historia y anales de la Civdad y Obispado de Plasencia* (1627); Alfonso Lamberto, an insignificant scribbler; Juan Martí, to whom was once ascribed the spurious sequel of the *Primera Parte de Guzman de Alfarache*; Juan Blanco de Paz (1537 ?-1594 ?), Cervantes's fellow-prisoner in Argel, and Fray Luis de Granada, who had died twenty-six years previously, and finally—and most absurdly—with Cervantes himself. For once Cervantes lost his equanimity; stung out of patience by this shabby trick, and still more by the personal insults contained in Avellaneda's preface, he finished the true sequel and brought it out in 1615. The closing chapters shew some signs of haste and many signs of anger and resentment. These defects are due to Avellaneda's intervention, but perhaps without Avellaneda's insolent intrusion, Cervantes would have left *Don Quijote* unfinished. In the nature of things, Second Parts are apt to lack the element of novelty which is found in First Parts; but in the sequel to *Don Quijote*, Cervantes decisively refuted his own theory that Second Parts are never good. Opinions will vary on the respective merits of the two parts of *Don Quijote*. The First Part is undoubtedly the popular favourite. But one cannot apply the methods of universal suffrage to literary criticism. Votes in these matters must be weighed as well as counted, and some weighty votes support the popular verdict. So great a critic as Goethe preferred the First Part, and Charles Lamb and Hallam are on the same side. It is true that the Second Part, as compared with the First, is less fresh, less rich in farcical episode, in burlesque force and in the more obvious effects of humour. It is vastly superior in construction, in poetic conception, in style, in verisimilitude, and, above

THE GOLDEN AGE

all, in character-drawing. The *dueña* is a creation which may take rank with Sancho Panza, and the portrait of the ill-omened physician on the island of Barataria is painted by the hand of a consummate master. Don Quixote and Sancho Panza are both more mature, more logical, more humorously lifelike. Cervantes had learned to love Don Quixote for his very weaknesses, and the geniality which was the basis of his own delightful temperament led him to humanize the quaintness and ennoble the ambitions of Sancho Panza. The enjoyment of existence was strong in him till his last gasp, and he communicated to his creations his own irrepressible vitality and sunny gaiety and humour. As George Meredith put it, Cervantes's book is 'a well-spring of characters which are saturated with the Shakespearean comic spirit ; with more of what we will call blood-life in them than is to be found anywhere out of Shakespeare ; and they are of this world, but they are of the world enlarged to our embrace by imagination and by great poetic inspiration.' *Don Quijote* survives as a marvel of evocation, as a splendid synthesis in which the factors of romance and realism are blended to perfection, as a gorgeous pageant of society in Spain, and as a masterly representation of life as life has been everywhere at all periods of historical time.

It will be seen that Cervantes's mind and pen were busier than they had ever been. In addition to the four volumes which he produced in three years, he kept up his supply of fugitive verses ; he mentions the titles of five other works which he had in hand : *El Engaño a los ojos*, *Las Semanas del Jardin*, *El famoso Bernardo*, the sequel to *La Galatea*, and *Los Trabaios de Persiles y Sigismvnda, Historia setentrional* (1617), the only one of them destined to see the light and it appeared posthumously: all the rest, if they ever got beyond the stage of projects, have perished. Cervantes had worked at *Persiles y Sigismvnda* for some three years and felt sure of its success. At first his previsions seemed likely to be right; six or seven editions appeared in Spain in 1617; two French versions were issued in 1618, an English version was published in 1619. But this popularity was ephemeral. *Persiles y Sigismvnda* ceased to attract after 1630; it was not reprinted between 1629 and 1719. Cervantes was now well known in Spain, but no one was sufficiently interested in him to preserve his manuscripts. Strangers from abroad could learn nothing very definite about him. The suite of the French ambassador contained enthusiastic admirers, full of curiosity concerning him. All they could learn was that he was 'old, a soldier, a gentleman and poor.' Meanwhile his health was failing fast, and by the end of 1615 he was a doomed man. On April 19, 1616, he wrote the famous and pathetic dedication of *Persiles y Sigismvnda* to his absent patron, the Conde de Lemos. There he quotes the lines from the *romance*: '*Puesto ya el pie en el estribo*,' but he was still full of hope and courage and plans. Yet his course was run. He died on April 23, 1616; he was buried 'with his face uncovered,' as we read in the official record. His remains are in the Trinitarian convent at Madrid, but the precise spot is not known. No gorgeous sepulchre commemorates him: and none is needed. For he has himself provided a more imperishable monument than any carved in brass or marble. Three centuries have come and gone and his supremacy is unshaken. He ranks among those few mighty masters, whom you can count on the fingers

THE GOLDEN AGE

of one hand, who speak to all the world down all the length of all the ages. If glory be a distinction, then, as Sir William Napier said, for such a man Death is not a leveller.

Perhaps no author, except Victor Hugo, has had a career at once so glorious and so long as LOPE FELIX DE VEGA CARPIO[1] (1562-1635). His miscellaneous

[1] *Obras*, ed. R. Academia Esp., Madrid, 1890-1913. 15 vols. published [II-XIII with prefaces by M. Menéndez y Pelayo]; ed. E. Cotarelo y Mori, Madrid, 1916-1920, 5 vols. (in course of publication), [R. Academia Esp. New Ed.]; *Comedias escogidas* (109), ed. J. E. Hartzenbusch, 1853-1860, 4 vols. (Bib. de Autores Esp., XXIV, XXXIV, XLI, LII); *Comedias inéditas* [*Amor, pleito y desafío, Amor con vista, La prueba de los amigos, Un pastoral albergue*], ed. Marqués de la Fuensanta del Valle and J. Sancho Rayon, 1873 (Col. de libros esp. raros o curiosos 6); *Sin secreto no ay amor*, ed. H. A. Rennert, Baltimore, 1894; *Los Guzmanes de Toral*, ed. A Restori, 1899 (Romanische Bib., 16); *Las Bvrlas veras*, ed. S. L. Millard Rosenberg, 1912 (Publications of the University of Pennsylvania, 2); *La Moza de Cántaro*, ed. M. Stathers, 1913 (New Spanish Series, 11); *Peribañez y el Comendador de Ocaña*, ed. A. Bonilla y San Martín, 1916 (Clásicos de la Literatura esp., 3); *Comedias*, I [*El remedio en la desdicha, El mejor alcalde, el rey*], ed. J. Gómez Ocerín y R. M. Tenreiro, 1920 (Clásicos Cast., 39); *Amar sin saber a quien*, ed. M. A. Buchanan and B. Franzen-Swedelius, New York, 1920 [See R. Foulché-Delbosc, in *Revue Hispanique*, L (1920), pp. 269-295]; *El Cuerdo loco*, ed. J. F. Montesinos, 1922 (Teatro Antiguo Esp., 4); *Entremés de los Sordos*. Facsimile by A. M. Huntington, New York, 1903; *Los achaques de Leonor*, ed. L. Pfandl, in *Revue Hispanique*, LIV (1922), pp. 347-416.—*Autos*, ed. E. Gonzalez Pedroso, 1865, in Bib. de Autores Esp., LVIII—*Degli 'Autos' di Lope de Vega Carpio* [*Auto de la Vuelta de Egipto, Auto de la Concepción* and *Comedia del Negro del Mejor Amo*], ed. A Restori, Parma, 1898.—*Colección de las obras sueltas, asi en prosa como en verso*. Madrid, 1776-1779. 21 vols; *La Dorotea*, ed. A. Castro, Madrid, 1913 (Bib. Renacimiento)—*Obras no dramáticas*, ed. C. Rosell, 1853 (Bib. de Autores Esp., XXXVIII.)—*Rimas ... con el nvevo arte de hazer Comedias deste tiempo*.

works, ranging from light macaronic rhymes to tender elegiacs and pompous epics, fill twenty-one huge

Facsimile of the 1609 ed. by A. M. Huntington, New York, 1903. 2 vols. ; *Arte nuevo de hazer comedias en este tiempo*, ed. A. Morel-Fatio, in *Bulletin hispanique*, III (1901), pp. 365-405 ; *Romancero Espiritval, para recrearse el alma con Dios* ... Facsimile of the 1624 ed. by A. M. Huntington, New York, 1903.—*Poesías*, ed. A. Duran, 1851, in Bib. de Autores Esp., XVI, ed. J. de Sancha, 1855, in Bib. de Autores Esp., XXXV, and ed. A. de Castro, 1855-1857, in Bib. de Autores Esp., XXXVI and XLII ; *Poésies de Lope de Vega, en partie inédites*, ed. E. Mele, in *Bulletin hispanique*, III (1901), pp. 348-364 ; *Some unpublished verses of Lope de Vega*, ed. J. P. W. Crawford, in *Revue Hispanique*, XIX (1908), pp. 455-465.—*Novelas a la señora Marcia Leonarda*, reprint of the 1621 and 1624 editions by J. D. Fitz-Gerald and L. A. Fitz-Gerald, Erlangen, 1913.—See : C. A. de la Barrera, *Biografía*, in *Obras de Lope de Vega*. 1890. 1 (R. Academia Esp.) ; M. Menéndez y Pelayo, *Estudios sobre el teatro de Lope de Vega*, reprinted from the introductions to the *Obras de Lope de Vega* II-XIII (R. Academia Esp.) by A. Bonilla y San Martín, Madrid, 1919-1923, 4 vols. published [*Obras completas*, X-XIII] ; F. Grillparzer, *Studium zum spanischen Theater*, in *Sämtliche Werke*, ed. A. Sauer, Stuttgart, n.d. XVII ; [J. Ormsby], *Lope de Vega*, in *The Quarterly Review*, CLXXIX (1894), pp. 486-511 ; C. Pérez Pastor, *Datos desconocidos para la vida de Lope de Vega* in *Homenaje á Menéndez y Pelayo*. Madrid, 1899, I, pp. 589-599 ; James Fitzmaurice-Kelly, *Lope de Vega and the Spanish drama*. Glasgow-London, 1902 ; H. A. Rennert, *The Life of Lope de Vega*, Glasgow, 1904 [Spanish ed. by H. A. Rennert and A. Castro, Madrid, 1919] ; *The New Art of writing plays*, trans. by W. T. Brewster with introduction by B. Matthews, New York, 1914 ; H. A. Rennert, *Bibliography of the Dramatic Works of Lope de Vega Carpio based upon the Catalogue of John Rutter Chorley*, in *Revue Hispanique*, XXXIII (1915), pp. 1-284 ; E. Gigas, *Études sur quelques " Comedias " de Lope de Vega*, in *Revue Hispanique*, XXXIX (1917), pp. 83-111 ; LIII (1921), pp. 557-604 ; M. A. Buchanan, *The Chronology of Lope de Vega's Plays*, 1922 (University of Toronto Studies. Philological Series, 6) ; J. Millé y Giménez, *Lope de Vega en la ' Armada Invencible,'* in *Revue Hispanique*, LVI (1922), pp. 356-395 ; L. Pfandl, *El Desposorio del Alma con Christo*, in *Revue Hispanique*, LVI (1922), pp. 396-402.

THE GOLDEN AGE

quartos. Though they include much which would suffice to make the reputation of any ordinary man, it is possible to neglect them when dealing with Lope. Considered as a dramatist only, his title is well-established if copiousness is a qualification. Juan Perez de Montalvan says that Lope wrote eighteen hundred plays not to speak of some four hundred autos. Lope himself tells us that he had written fifteen hundred plays up to 1632. Most of these have disappeared, though possibly many which are thought to be lost are hidden in the collections with the names of other writers attached to them. There still remain some four hundred and sixty-nine authentic plays and about fifty authentic *autos sacramentales*. But if Lope were merely a playwright of unparalleled copiousness, his position in the history of literature would be far less conspicuous than it actually is. What makes him such a glorious figure is his creative power. He might have written quite as much, and been no more important than Hardy is in the history of French literature. Lope was the inventor of a new *genre*, and this invention, on such a scale as his, is a title to immortality. The development of the Spanish theatre up to the time of his appearance has already been traced. It begins with arrangements or amplifications of the strictly liturgical drama; it takes on a more secular character in the hands of Enzina and Lucas Fernandez, but the association with ecclesiastical models is still close; it reaches a new phase in the work of Torres Naharro, produced out of Spain in the noonday of the Italian Renaissance; it has a savour of homely, national wit in the unpretentious, popular, rollicking *pasos* or interludes of Lope de Rueda, in whose more elaborate plays the Italian influence predominates. This Italian influence affects Rueda's contemporary Alonso de la Vega to about the same degree, and in a modified shape it affected Virués and Argensola, Juan de la Cueva and Cervantes. Yet Cueva and Miguel Sanchez are the only two dramatists who may be regarded as having to some extent anticipated Lope's methods. Cueva made a distinct step forward by choosing national themes, by utilizing old *romances* and by attempting the *capa y espada* play. He had talent, ideas, and ambition; but he had neither perseverance nor creative force and his innovations are timid. To bring about a literary revolution a man of exceptional genius was required, and it was a necessity of the situation that genius should be combined with fertility. In Lope the combination was attained.

The son of Felices de Vega (d. 1578) and of Francisca Fernandez Flores (d. 1589), both natives of the Valley of Vega in Carriedo hard by the Asturian chines, Lope was born at Madrid on November 25, 1562. He was a marvellous child: he dictated verses before he could write, was an expert fencer, and a good dancer. Still, though he carried all before him at the Theatine school, he was perhaps not very happy there, for he ran away with a schoolfellow. The adventurous pair got as far as Segovia: there they were arrested and sent home rather crestfallen. At the age of ten, Lope translated into verse Claudian's *De raptu Proserpinae*, and two years later composed *El verdadero amante*, which was acted by the prominent impresario and actor, Nicolas de los Rios (d. 1610). The play (which Lope describes as his first) may be found in the Fourteenth Part (1620) of his theatre; it consists of three acts, a division which he adopted later instead of the usual four or five. But as the first act is evidently a recast of two, one need not be bound to the theory that *Los Hechos de Garcilasso de la Vega, y Moro Tarfe* must be Lope's earliest piece, because it is written in four acts. On leaving school, Lope seems to have been page to Jerónimo Manrique de Lara (d. 1595), bishop of Cartagena, and later of Alcalá. The bishop, struck with the boy's talent, sent him to the University of Alcalá de Henares, where he remained possibly from 1577 to 1581. It was there, perhaps, that he acquired that taste for out-of-place learning on which Cervantes dwells with malicious humour in the preface to the First Part of *Don Quijote*. In Madrid, Lope made the acquaintance of Jerónimo Velazquez (d. 1613), an enterprising stage-manager whom he supplied gratis with plays. He also fell in love with Velazquez's daughter, Elena Osorio (d. 1637), wife of the actor Cristóbal Calderon (d. 1595), and the *Filis* of Lope's verses. In 1583 he took part in an expedition to the Azores under the Marqués de Santa Cruz, and is mentioned as a writer of established reputation in *La Galatea* (1585). Towards the middle of 1587, Lope, angered with Elena Osorio who had transferred her affections to Francisco Perrenot de Granvela, nephew of the famous Cardinal, revenged himself by publishing defamatory reports against the Velazquez family. He was arrested on a charge of criminal libel, and when brought to trial in February 1588 was found guilty. He was sentenced to banishment from Madrid for eight years and from the whole of Castile for two years; if he infringed the decree of the court he was to be executed. Lope appeared to comply and withdrew to Valencia. He seems to have returned to Madrid in a month or two and eloped with Isabel, daughter of Diego de Ampuero y Urbina (d. 1623), King at Arms. On May 10, 1588, he married Isabel by proxy and within three weeks he was out of range on board the *San Juan*, a ship that formed part of the Invincible Armada. Lope took part in the expedition, converted, so he says, the paper on which he had written verses to Elena Osorio into gun-wads, saw his brother killed beside him during the fighting in the Channel and came back with the wreck of the defeated fleet. He brought his sheaves with him : the manuscript of *La Hermosvra de Angelica*.

After his return to Spain, Lope first settled in Valencia, and either then, or more probably during a later visit (1599), came to know some of the dramatists in that city: Francisco Agustin Tárrega[1] (1554?-1602), author of *La enemiga favorable*, praised by the canon in *Don Quijote* (I, ch. xlviii.), and of *La Fundacion de la orden de Nuestra Señora de la Merced* which suggested to Lope *La Vida de San Pedro Nolasco* ; Gaspar Honorat de Aguilar[2] (1561-1623), author of *El mercader amante*, also praised by the canon ; Carlos Boyl Vives de Canesmas[3] (1577 ?-1617), author of

[1] *Comedias* (4), ed. R. de Mesonero Romanos, 1857, in Bib. de Autores Esp., XLIII ; *Los moriscos de Hornachos*, ed. C. B. Bourland [*Modern Philology*, I, II], Chicago, 1904.

[2] *Comedias* [*El mercader amante, La gitana melancólica, La venganza honrosa*], ed. R. de Mesonero Romanos, 1857, in Bib. de Autores Esp., XLIII ; *Poesías* (6), ed. E. Mele, in *Bulletin hispanique*, III (1901), pp. 330-335.—See : F. Martí Grajales, *Gaspar Aguilar, noticia biográfica*, in *Cancionero de la Academia de los Nocturnos de Valencia*. Valencia, 1906. II, pp. 167-206 ; H. Mérimée, *Sur la biographie de Gaspar Aguilar*, in *Bulletin hispanique*, VIII (1906), pp. 393-396.

[3] *El marido asegurado* and *Loa*, ed. R. de Mesonero Romanos, 1857, in Bib. de Autores Esp., XLIII.—See : H. Mérimée, *Un*

El marido asegurado and of a sonnet dedicated to Lope which Lope reprinted in the *Fiestas de Denia* (1599), and Guillen de Castro, of whom we shall have occasion to speak later. Between 1589 and 1590, Lope removed to Toledo and thence to Alba de Tormes, where he entered the household of the fifth Duque de Alba. He was soon at work again writing for the stage, not a very austere school of morality in those days. A fragmentary copy of *El favor agradecido* is dated Alba de Tormes, October 29, 1593. After the death of his wife in 1595, Lope went from bad to worse and was concerned in all sorts of scandalous adventures. He was prosecuted for his relations with Antonia Trillo de Armenta in 1596, and in 1597 he began an intrigue with the wife of the actor Diego Diaz (d. 1603), Micaela de Lujan, whom he celebrates as Camila Lucinda. But though foolish and dissipated, Lope was no idler. In 1598 his first considerable works were printed : *La Dragontea*, a violently patriotic epic in which the Dragon, easily recognizable as Sir Francis Drake (1540 ?-1596), is severely handled, and which, in spite of its inspiration, fails through its long allegorical episodes ; and the *Arcadia, prosa y versos*, a pastoral novel in a rich poetic prose where Lope figures as Belardo and the Duque de Alba as Anfriso. The *Arcadia* is now hard to read, but it is worth looking at for the graceful verses which it contains. In 1598 also, Lope found time to marry again : his second wife was Juana de Guardo, daughter of an avaricious man who had made a small fortune in pork-packing. His

romance de Carlos Boyl, in *Bulletin hispanique*, VIII (1906), pp. 163-171 ; H. Mérimée, in *L'Art dramatique à Valencia*, etc. Toulouse, 1913. pp. 448-452, 636-640 (Bibliothèque méridionale, 16).

enemies accused Lope of being a mere fortune-hunter and rained epigrams on him. But this is absurd. Lope lived quite happily with Juana, for whom he had a very real affection.

Meanwhile Lope had passed into the household of the Marqués de Malpica, whom he left in order to attach himself to the Marqués de Sarria, Cervantes's patron, and Conde de Lemos. He wrote *Isidro* (1599), a devout poem in *quintillas* in honour of Madrid's patron-saint, and published *La Hermosvra de Angelica con otras diuersas rimas* (1602); in this volume are to be found two hundred sonnets which include some of Lope's most spontaneous lyrical work. *La Hermosvra de Angélica*, written in great part during the expedition of the Armada, was continually re-touched and polished by Lope but it suffers from comparison with its model *Orlando furioso*: it has fine passages, but it is marred by lengthy digressions. Lope sought to win ground with other productions such as *El Peregrino en su patria* (1604), which, according to George Borrow (1803-1881), contains 'the best ghost-story in the world.' In 1604, too, Lope republished a collection of his *Rimas* and struck up a friendship with the Duke of Sessa (1582-1642), who was not an edifying companion. In 1609 appeared his *Iervsalen conqvistada*, a historico-narrative poem in which he tries to vie with Tasso: on the title-page Lope figures as a Familiar of the Inquisition. At about this time Lope took to devotion and later (1614) entered holy orders. This was a grave error of judgement. In spite of his *Qvatro soliloquios* ... (1612), it is obvious from his private correspondence that Lope had no genuine religious vocation. In 1611 he joined the Third Order of Saint Francis, and the following year

THE GOLDEN AGE

wrote for the death of his little son, Carlos Felix, *Los Pastores de Belen, prosas y versos divinos* (1612), which contains the exquisite cradle-song with the refrain:

> que se duerme mi Niño,
> tened los ramos !

In 1613 his wife died, her last years embittered by Lope's liaison with Micaela de Luján, two of whose children, Lope Felix del Carpio y Luján (1607-1634 ?) and Marcela (1605 ?-1688), inherited some of their father's brilliant gifts. There are lines reminiscent of Lope in Marcela's poems composed after she had professed (1622) in the Discalced Trinitarians. This period of Lope's life is marked by great sins and follies. His name was associated with Marta de Nevares Santoyo (1591-1632), wife of Roque Hernandez de Ayala, and again his enemies took care not to spare him. Even the good-natured Cervantes referred with savage irony in the Second Part of *Don Quijote* to Lope's ' virtuous occupation.' Lope survived this thrust and many others of the same kind. His faults of character and conduct are partially redeemed by his literary achievement. The very persistence and violence of the attacks on Lope are tributes to his eminence. The most envenomed and personal of these was the *Spongia* (1617) of Pedro de Torres Rámila who adopted the pseudonym of Trepus Ruitanus Lemira. Lope alludes to this work in the prologue of his *Trivnfo de la Fee, en los Reynos del Japon. Por los años de 1614 y 1615* (1618), a prose-composition dedicated to Mariana. The *Spongia* has disappeared, but something of its contents may be learnt from the *Expostulatio Spongiae* (1618), an answer published by Julius Columbarius (the pseudonym adopted by Lope's friend Francisco Lopez de Aguilar Coutiño) in collaboration with Alonso Sanchez de la Ballesta ; and from Lope's reply, *La Filomena con otras diuersas Rimas, Prosas y Versos* (1621), where the thrush (Torres Rámila) is confronted with the nightingale (Lope). Besides this piece of polemics, *La Filomena* contains a tale, *Las Fortunas de Diana*, dedicated to Marcia Leonardo (Marta de Nevares Santoyo) ; but neither in this nor in the three stories, *La Desdicha por la Honra, La prudente venganza, Guzman el bravo,* inserted in the poem *La Circe, con otras Rimas y Prosas* (1624), does Lope excel as a narrator. Little more interest is offered by the *Trivnfos divinos con otras rimas sacras* (1625), a tedious imitation of Petrarch ; or the religious epic, *La Corona tragica* (1627), which gives an ideal presentation of Mary Stuart ; or the *Lavrel de Apolo con otras Rimas* (1630), a panegyric on some three hundred versifiers remarkable for its omissions as well as for the cheap and florid compliment in which Lope frequently indulged.

Of very different merit is *La Dorotea* (1632), a prose-drama approximating to autobiography, in which there are reminiscences of *La Celestina* as well as much admirable verse and a style rich and archaic. Lope had presided at the poetical jousts held at Seville in 1620 and 1622, there he had witnessed his son Lope Felix's youthful triumphs, had encouraged Calderon's early attempts, and, as *El Maestro Burguillos*, had recited some occasional verse which delighted the audience. He now issued the *Rimas hvmanas y divinas del Licenciado Tomé de Burgvillos* (1634), which contains the heroi-comic poem, *La Gatomachia*, a brilliant parody on the Italian epics. But time began to tell upon him. In his last years he met with one or two professional checks: the star of Calderon was beginning to rise and menaced Lope's long supremacy. In his last years also, Lope underwent grievous domestic trials. Marta de Nevares Santoyo lost her sight and reason, and died in 1632; Lope's son, Lope Felix del Carpio y Lujan, who might have made a considerable name in literature, was drowned off the coast of Venezuela in 1634; his daughter, Antonia Clara de Vega y Nevares (1617-1664), ran off with some court-gallant. Lope took these trials to be punishments for his sins and sank into a deep despair. He did penance, beating himself with his scourge till the walls of his little room in the Calle de Francos were flecked with blood. Still he went on working, prepared two volumes of plays for publication, and on August 23, 1635, wrote a sonnet and the *Silva* called *El siglo de oro*. He fell ill and died four days later. Immense crowds followed his funeral procession, which went out of the direct route in order to pass by the convent of the Trinitarian nuns, where Lope's daughter, Marcela, had taken the vows. Lope was buried under the high altar of St. Sebastian's Church in the Calle de Atocha, but his coffin was removed in the seventeenth century and his exact resting-place is now unknown. Tribute was paid to his memory in the *Fama posthvma* . . . (1636), published by Perez de Montalvan in which one hundred and fifty-three authors, of whom six only were dramatists, collaborated; and in the same year Fabio Franchi edited the *Essequie poetiche*, a similar collection of poems from Lope's Italian admirers. This volume was dedicated to the Conde de la Roca, who is suspect of having forged *El Centon Epistolario*.

Lope has been mentioned as a poet. He was a great poet at moments, but he is very unequal—as much so as Wordsworth. There are splendid lines in his worst pieces and feeble lines in his best. Had he written nothing but his lyrics, he would rank as a charming poet. But his lyrics are, of course, mere by-products of his versatile genius. His fame depends on his plays, on which he set at first so little value. It cannot be denied that such blemishes as anachronisms, geographical blunders, the travesty of historical facts, liberties taken with hagiology by transferring one saint's miracles to the account of another saint, the accumulation of improbable incidents and so forth are frequent in Lope's theatre. Considering the speed at which he wrote, such mistakes were inevitable and, as he set the pace to other dramatists (as well as the fashion), similar oversights are still more numerous in the works of his imitators. But the most damaging charge against the new school of playwrights was evidently thought by contemporaries to be their neglect of the dramatic unities. The chief culprit did not deny his offences against what everybody was agreed to call the canons of art. Lope knew the canons of art as well as the best of them, and paid those rules the compliment of accepting them—in theory. In the *Arte nuevo de hazer comedias en este tiempo* (1609 ?) Lope's doctrines are almost identical with those of Cervantes in *Don Quijote*: he affects to follow the pseudo-Aristotelian rules of the Renaissance doctrinaires; but as he ends by admitting that down to 1609 he had observed those rules in only six plays out of four hundred and eighty-three written at that date, he need not be taken too seriously as a theoretical exponent of art. His achievement lay on the practical side. He gave to the Spanish theatre the stamp that characterizes it. Before his time plays were written in five acts or in four : some of Lope's own earliest pieces are in four. He imposed the convention of three acts—introduced by Avendaño. And this was not his sole contribution to the mechanics of dramaturgy. He drew up a code of rules on versification : laments should, he thinks, be written in *décimas* ; sonnets are to be preferred in moments of suspense, or to mark time ; the *romance* form is adapted to narrative, but the octave is even still more suitable for such passages ; matters of gravity are best set forth in tercets, and when lovers are on the scene, the dialogue should be given in *redondillas*. This was not an empty counsel of perfection, for Lope carried his precepts into effect, and the richness of his metrical resource is bewildering. Such wealth of ornamentation has no parallel, and does as much credit to the audiences who could appreciate it as the poet who could contrive it. There are later Spanish dramatists who may excel in other qualities, but in the matter of rhythmical diversity and elaboration of decorative device Lope is unapproached.

Lope created an entire literature. He wrote as much as all the Elizabethan and Jacobean dramatists put together. He had to satisfy an insatiable and critical audience and he did this successfully for over fifty years. No one acquainted with his works can deny his versatility. He is eminent in every kind. One does not naturally associate his careless elegance and sunny nature with tragedy, and in truth his tragedies are not oppressively numerous. Still he has produced sombre masterpieces such as *Las Paces de los Reyes* and *El Caballero de Olmedo*. Lope is always great when he attempts tragedy, and if he does not attempt it oftener, it is because the public insisted on something in his lighter vein. In this lighter vein, in pieces like *Las bizarrias de Belisa*, *La dama melindrosa*, *El anzuelo de Fenisa*, we have gaiety, wit, movement, realism, and realization of character. His lack of purely literary pre-occupation is a drawback. He allowed the first eight volumes of his plays to be issued by anybody who chose to print them; between 1617 and 1625 he revised twelve volumes, then ceased to take any further interest until 1635, when he began to prepare another volume which was issued posthumously. And the consequence is a series of pirated editions in which, as Lope himself says, one line from his pen is lost among a hundred others interpolated by some gagging actor or by some not too scrupulous manager. Even so, enough remains to give some idea of the heights which he could attain in this respect. Verbal beauty is not his chief aim. It is often there, but it is there by a happy accident. Lope cannot, or at least does not, maintain an even level of excellence. It is plain that he is being pressed by managers, and that he is too anxious to respond to all the calls made upon him. Perhaps this is at the root of a common criticism: that Lope's last acts are apt to be weak. This cannot be denied: in *La batalla de honor*, to give only one instance, a magnificent effect is spoilt by a feeble close. But this is not a defect peculiar to Lope; the same blemish is to be observed in *Julius Caesar*. Lope has faults of his own. He is a Spaniard all over: he has the defects of his race as well as its good qualities. He is too complacent; he has the Spanish desire to please, to be conspicuous; he borders on insincerity at times; his note is too em-

THE GOLDEN AGE

phatic; his colouring is too crude; he is so determined to attract that he will stoop to almost any means to achieve his end. Further, he is so excessively clever that his cleverness is apt to be fatiguing. He never spares for an effect, and his very *graciosos* are at times too entertaining. This is quite true and, so far as it goes, it diminishes Lope's charm. But it is fair to show the obverse side of the medal. Lope has an artistic conscience of his own, defies the gongorists, pours scorn on the elaborate scenery which came very rapidly into vogue. He almost says that 'when the stage-carpenter comes in, the dramatist goes out.' He needed no artificial stimulus of the mechanical kind. His dramatic conception is so puissant, his gifts of presentation are so alert and poignant that he makes visible the whole panorama of existence. All his work for the stage is informed by a healthy realism. The coincidences may be too startling, the plot may not be plausible, but the characters themselves are alive from head to foot. No one's heroes are more seductive, no one's heroines are more delightful, no one's *graciosos* are more slyly humorous and roguish, and quick in apt retort. His scope takes in all conditions of human beings. He portrays kings and serving-men with an impartial brush, he paints the average middle-class to which he belonged in all its picturesque outbursts of nonsensical extravagance, alternating with shrewd poetical instinct; he utilizes for dramatic purposes all the rich store of his nation's history, drawing on chronicles, on old *romances*, on popular traditions. All the notes are touched on his lyre. He flits from ' grave to gay, from lively to severe '; he is now sombre, now pathetic, now diverting, now steeped in humour. He has the secret of communicating a contagious emotion, of inventing appropriate dialogue gemmed over with a polite and debonair wit. And he has the unique power of creating the most charming heroines — appealing, tender, courageous, and devoted.

In his own lifetime Lope's reputation was universal. As early as 1603, one of his plays, *La fuerza lastimosa* was given in the Sultan's seraglio at Constantinople. Others—*El animal profeta*, *San Julian* and *La madre de la mejor*—were done into Nahuatl by Bartolomé de Alba in 1641 and performed at Mexico. In France Lope was laid under contribution by Sainte-Beuve's favourite, Rotrou. Rotrou's *L'heureuse Constance* is from *El poder vencido*, his *Bague d'oubli* is from *La sortija del olvido*, his *Laure persécutée* from *Laura perseguida*, his *Heureux naufrage* from *El naufragio prodigioso*, his *Saint Genest* from *Lo fingido verdadero*, while his *Cosroès* is based in part on *Las mudanzas de la fortuna y sucesos de don Beltran de Aragon*, and in part also on *Chosroës* of Louis Cellot (1588-1658). We may pass by mediocrities like Boisrobert (1592-1662) who from *El mayor impossible* takes *La folle gageure*. Cyrano de Bergerac (1619-1655) derives *Le Pédant Joué* from *El robo de Elena*; Corneille in *La suite du Menteur* draws on *Amar sin saber a quien* and his *D. Sanche d'Aragon* owes something to *El palacio confuso*. And as to Molière, Lope's possibilities did not escape him. *Les Femmes Savantes* is influenced by *La dama melindrosa*; *L'École des maris* combines *La discreta enamorada* and *El mayor impossible*; similarly *L'École des femmes* is an amalgam of *La dama boba* and *El acero de Madrid*, and this last play suggested a happy touch in *Le Médecin malgré lui*, while a trace of *El perro del hortelano* may perhaps be detected in *Tartufe*. Nor was Lope's vogue in France ephemeral. As late as 1700, Lesage (1668-1747) thought it well to translate *Guardar y guardarse* under the title of *Dom Félix de Mendoce*. In England signs of Lope's influence are less manifest. Still *The Young Admiral* of Shirley (1596-1666) is based on *Don Lope de Cardona* and as Lope is mentioned by Butler (1612-1680) in *Hudibras*, research may reveal borrowings from him in the Restoration dramatists. It would take one too far to trace Lope into Italy and Germany; for information on these matters reference may be made to the works of Signor Farinelli and Schneider.

Lope no doubt lacks Shakespeare's ample and embracing note. He does not portray universal human nature, but human nature as it manifested itself at a given time in given conditions. He is not the dramatist of humanity all the world over. He is the typical dramatist of his own race; his scope is restricted, but the power of his appeal is intense. This constitutes his greatest claim to glory. Nearly every Spanish dramatist derives from him. Almost everybody owes him much; he owes hardly anything to anybody. He took over the old morality plays of the Middle Ages and vitalized them anew amid the quickening breath of his devout imagination; he took over the pompous tragedies in which mouthing kings and ranting queens strutted a noisy hour, and humanized them by his varied knowledge of Spanish nature, by his sense of the irrevocable, by his comprehending and therefore sympathetic attitude to human weakness; he took over the strident farce and purged it of its boisterous humours, substituting in their stead his more graceful and urbane inventions, his sparkling merriment, his delicate fantasy. Subtract Lope from the panorama of Spanish literature and it loses one of its most splendid and picturesque figures. At the same time, the world is deprived of a new and enchanting form of art. Nobody is so manifold as Lope in sources of entertainment. Nobody renders more facilely the intensity of emotion which smoulders beneath the cold, courteous exterior of the Spaniard. Nobody has contributed more lavishly to the general store of dramatic creation. Before Lope's time, the Spanish theatre was incoherent and disorganized. He found it a ramshackle building, disproportionate in dimensions and disparate in materials. He left it— not a perfectly solid temple of art but—a steadfast structure, gorgeously embellished and fit to withstand the assaults of that incorrigible traitor, Time.

Ascribed to Lope de Vega until 1920, when M. Foulché-Delbosc in the introduction to his critical edition of the text made this ascription no longer possible, *La Estrella de Sevilla*[1] remains of unknown authorship. Its *donnée* is closely akin to that of Guillen de Castro's *Las Mocedades del Cid*, if we substitute monarchical sentiment for honour: in both plays the hero's hesitation and self-torment are revealed in a monologue. It is not, however, in the subject-matter that the strength of *La Estrella de Sevilla* lies, but in the lofty simplicity of its presentation. The dialogue is swift, forcible, and

[1] Ed. R. Foulché-Delbosc, in *Revue Hispanique*, XLVIII (1920), pp. 533-678; ed. H. Thomas, Oxford, 1923; *La Stella di Siviglia*, Italian trans. with text by A. Giannini, Firenze, 1924.—See: R. Foulché-Delbosc, *La Estrella de Sevilla*, in *Revue Hispanique*, XLVIII (1920), pp. 497-533; A. Lenz, *Eine Neuausgabe der 'Estrella de Sevilla,'* in *Zeitschrift für romanische Philologie*, XLIII (1923), pp. 92-108; A. F. G. Bell, *The Author of the 'Estrella de Sevilla,'* in *Revue Hispanique*, LIX (1923), pp. 296-300.

THE GOLDEN AGE

arresting; the action remains consistently dignified and restrained though the most vital passions are brought into conflict; the strangely noble conception of the principal characters is sustained throughout. In structure and technique alike *La Estrella de Sevilla* is the masterpiece of the *comedia heroica*.

Lope de Vega had outlived most of his immediate contemporaries and had trained a race of dramatists, who, if they fell short of him in fertility and creative power, were almost his equals in technical dexterity and ingenious invention. Luis Velez de Guevara [1] (1578 ?-1644) was in his day a sort of rival to Lope. But he had not Lope's gift of poetry, nor Lope's miraculous skill in extracting all the possibilities of a dramatic situation. He added nothing very individual except an occasional touch of the cynical cleverness which informs *El Diablo cojuelo* (1641), and keeps the tale alive. Of his eighty existing plays, the two most attractive are *Mas pesa el rey que la sangre*, which illustrates the monarchical tradition, and *Reinar despues*

[1] *El Diablo Cojuelo*, ed. A. Bonilla y San Martín, 1910 (Soc. de Bibliófilos Madrileños, 2); ed. F. Rodríguez Marín, 1918 (Clásicos Cast., 38).—*Comedias* (6), ed. R. de Mesonero Romanos, 1858, in Bib. de Autores Esp., XLV; *El águila del agua y batalla naval de Lepanto*, ed. A. Paz y Mélia, in *Revista de Archivos*, etc., X (1904), pp. 182-200, 307-325; XI (1904), pp. 50-67; *La Serrana de la Vera*, ed. R. Menéndez Pidal and Mª. Goyri de Menéndez Pidal, Madrid, 1916 (Teatro antiguo esp., 1); *El rey en su imaginación*, ed. J. Gómez Ocerín, Madrid, 1922 (Teatro antiguo esp., 3); *Algunas poesías inéditas*, ed. A. Bonilla y San Martín [*Revista de Aragón*], 1902; *Cinco poesías autobiográficas*, ed. F. Rodríguez Marín [*Revista de Archivos*, XIX], 1908.—See: F. Pérez y González, *El diablo cojuelo*. Madrid, 1903; C. Pérez Pastor in *Bibliografía madrileña*. Madrid, 1907. III, pp. 499-515; E. Cotarelo, *Luis Vélez de Guevara y sus obras dramáticas*, in *Boletín de la R. Academia Esp.*, III (1916), pp. 621-652; IV. (1917), pp. 137-171, 269-308, 414-444.

de morir, whose final scenes particularly strike a note rarely heard in the annals of the Spanish theatre. In spite of his limitations, Velez de Guevara was no contemptible dramatist, and in *El Diablo cojuelo* he wrote a very successful story in the picaresque vein. This tale attracted the attention of Lesage, whose recast of it in *Le Diable boiteux* (1707) made the Spanish original famous the world overlong and gave Velez de Guevara an assured position quite apart from any reputation that he may have attained on the boards. The fact remains that the book owes its popularity to Lesage. His humane spirit suffuses the rude Spanish taste with a refinement and delicacy truly French. *El Diablo cojuelo* is a purely Spanish book of realistic observation : *Le Diable boiteux* has the good taste and measure of the classics.

GUILLEN DE CASTRO Y BELLVIS[1] (1569-1631), a coastguard captain from Valencia, attained a wide reputation through Corneille's imitation of his plays on the Cid. Castro seems to have been already known in 1599 : on his return from the kingdom of Naples where, in 1603, he had been governor of Scigliano, he settled at Madrid and through the influence of his

[1] *Comedias* (7), ed. R. de Mesonero Romanos, 1857, in Bib. de Autores Esp., XLIII ; *Las Mocedades del Cid* and *Las Hazañas del Cid*, ed. W. Fœrster, Bonn, 1878 ; ed. A. Sánchez Moguel, Madrid, 1885 ; ed. W. von Wurzbach, n.d. (Bib. romanica) ; ed. V. Said Armesto, Madrid, 1913 (Clásicos Cast., 15) ; *Las Mocedades del Cid*, ed. E. Mérimée, Toulouse, 1890 (Bib. méridionale, 1st series, 2) ; *El tao de San Anton* and *El renegado arrepentido*, ed. A. Schaeffer, in *Ocho Comedias desconocidas*. Leipzig, 1887. I, pp. 83-145 ; II, pp. 1-74 (Col. de Autores Esp., 47, 48) ; *Ingratitud por amor*, ed. H. A. Rennert, Philadelphia, 1899 ; *Comedia del pobre honrrado*, ed. M. Serrano y Sanz, in *Bulletin hispanique*, IV (1902), pp. 219-246, 305-341 ; *El ayo de su hijo*, ed. H. Mérimée [*Bulletin hispanique* VIII, IX, XI],

THE GOLDEN AGE

old friend and admirer, Lope, found an opening for his dramatic work. *Las Mocedades del Cid* and *Las Hazañas del Cid*, printed in 1618 (or possibly earlier) in the First Part of his *Comedias* (whose Second Part bears the date 1625) are a dramatic adaptation of the national legend. Corneille drew freely on both plays in his masterpiece, and in every respect but one he far outrivals his model. The weak point of *Le Cid* as compared with *Las Mocedades del Cid* is Corneille's adherence to the unities. The time which Castro allows to elapse between Ximena's grief and the beginning of her love for the Cid increases the probabilities of the plot. But if beside Corneille's play Castro's piece reads as a primitive sketch, it has a compensating quality in its charm of simplicity. *El Prodigio de los Montes*—the source of Calderon's *El mágico prodigioso*—has been attributed to Castro, but it may be the same play as Lope de Vega's *La Bárbara del Cielo* under a secondary title. With more probability Stiefel has suggested that Fletcher's piece, *Love's Cure*, is based on Castro's *La fuerza de la costumbre*.

A dramatist who died before he could fulfil the promise shewn in *Sufrir mas por querer mas* and *A gran*

Bordeaux [1906-1909]; *Quien malas mañas ha tarde ó nunca las perderá*, ed. E. Juliá Martínez [*Revista de Archivos*, etc., XXXIII], Madrid, 1916.—See: A. Fée, in *Études sur l'ancien théâtre espagnol*: *Les trois Cid* [G. de Castro, Corneille, Diamante], Paris, 1873; F. Martí Grajales, in *Cancionero de la Academia de los Nocturnos de Valencia*. Valencia, 1906. III, pp. 119-188; H. Mérimée, *Pour la biographie de don Guillén de Castro* [*Revue des langues romanes*, L], Montpellier, 1907; C. Pérez Pastor, in *Bibliografía madrileña*. Madrid, 1907. III, pp. 344-362; H. Mérimée, in *L'Art dramatique à Valencia*, etc. Toulouse, 1913. pp. 538-632 (Bib. méridionale, 2nd series, 16) *daño, gran remedio* was Geronimo de Villayzan [1] (1604-1633), with whom may be mentioned Cristóbal de Monroy y Silva (1612-1649), who shews a pleasing talent in *El ofensor de sí mismo* and gives a recast of Lope's *Fuente Ovejuna* in a play of the same title. But Lope's most ardent disciple was his young friend, Juan Perez de Montalvan [2] (1602-1638), son of Alonso Perez, the king's bookseller, who in 1626 pirated Quevedo's *El Buscon*. Perez was condemned the following year by the courts, and a literary quarrel ensued between Quevedo and Montalvan, who took his father's part. Quevedo nourished a grievance on his side and delighted in pricking the bubble of Montalvan's airs and graces. He wrote the celebrated epigram in which he bantered Montalvan for tricking out with embellishments his father's name of Perez. Montalvan published *Para Todos* in 1632, which Quevedo ridiculed in *La Perinola* (1633), prophesying that Montalvan would die mad. He lived to see his prophecy fulfilled. It is not impossible that Montalvan

[1] See: J. Monreal, in *Cuadros viejos*. Madrid, 1878. p. 151.

[2] *Comedias* (7), ed. R. de Mesonero Romanos, 1858, in Bib. de Autores Esp., XLV; *La Monja Alferez*, reprinted by James Fitzmaurice-Kelly, in *The Nun Ensign*. London, 1908. pp. 145-287.—*Poesías*, ed. A. Duran, 1851, in Bib. de Autores Esp., XVI, ed. A. de Castro, 1857, in Bib. de Autores Esp., XLII and ed. J. E. Hartzenbusch, 1860, in Bib. de Autores Esp., LII; *Some Poems of Dr. Juan Pérez de Montalvan*, ed. G. W. Bacon, in *Revue Hispanique*, XXV (1911), pp. 458-467.—*Fama póstuma á la vida y muerte del Dr. Frey Lope Félix de Vega Carpio*, ed. J. E. Hartzenbusch, 1853, in Bib. de Autores Esp., XXIV; *Sucesos y prodigios de amor*, ed. E. Fernandez de Navarrete, 1854, in Bib. de Autores Esp., XXXIII.—See: *The Nun Ensign*, trans. by James Fitzmaurice-Kelly, London, 1908; G. W. Bacon, *The life and dramatic works of Dr. Juan Pérez de Montalván* (1602-1638) [*Revue Hispanique*, XXVI] New York-Paris, 1912.

had some share in the concoction of a gross libel on Quevedo, published under the pseudonym of Arnaldo Franco-Furt and entitled *El Tribunal de la Iusta Venganza* (1635).

Montalvan is said to be the author of a poem, *Orfeo en lengua castellana* (1624), written in competition with Jauregui: this poem is also alleged to have been improvised by Lope in order to introduce his friend to the public. But Montalvan was already known in 1619 by his comedy *Morir y disimular*, while the points of similarity between the style of the *Orfeo* and that of Lope are no greater than those to be noted between Lope and Marcelo Diaz Callecerrada in his *Endimion* (1627). In any case, the *Orfeo* attracted the notice of a rich Peruvian who left Montalvan a pension. Montalvan had a certain dramatic instinct, but he completely lacked originality and wrote at too great a speed. His prose, for instance, the *Sucessos y Prodigios de amor, en Ocho novelas exemplares* (1624), met with considerable success in its day: of all his works, however, only one play, *Los Amantes de Teruel*, still offers a measure of interest.

A much more powerful personality is that of the Mercenarian monk, Gabriel Tellez (1571?-1648), universally known under the pseudonym of TIRSO DE MOLINA.[1] He was born in Madrid, studied apparently

[1] *Comedias* (53), ed. E. Cotarelo y Mori, 1906-1907, 2 vols. (Nueva Bib. de Autores Esp., 4, 9); *Teatro escogido* (36 plays and fragments of 11 more), ed. J. E. Hartzenbusch, Madrid, 1839-1842. 12 vols.; *Comedias escogidas* (37), ed. J. E. Hartzenbusch, 1848 (Bib. de Autores Esp., v); *Obras* I [*El Vergonzoso en palacio* and *El burlador de Sevilla*], ed. A. Castro, 1910, 2nd ed. 1922 (Clásicos Cast., 2); *Don Gil de las calzas verdes*, ed. B. P. Bourland, New York, 1901 (New Spanish Series, 1); *La villana de Vallecas*, ed. A. Bonilla y San Martín,

in Alcalá de Henares, professed in 1601, and is first heard of as a dramatic author in 1610. In 1615 he went as a missioner to Santo Domingo and received the title of *definidor general* of that island, a title which he bore in Guadalajara, where we find him in 1618. In 1620, while he was at Madrid, Lope dedicated to

1916 (Clásicos de la Literatura Esp., 5). *Autos sacramentales* [*No le arriendo la ganancia* and *El colmenero divino*], ed. E. Gonzalez Pedroso, 1865, in Bib. de Autores Esp., LVIII.— *Cigarrales de Toledo*, ed. V. Said Armesto, Madrid, 1913 (Bib. Renacimiento) ; *Los tres maridos burlados*, ed. C. Rosell, 1851, in Bib. de Autores Esp., XVIII ; *Vida de la Santa Madre Dª Maria de Çervellon*, etc., ed. M. Menéndez y Pelayo, in *Revista de Archivos*, etc., XVIII (1908), pp. 1-17, 243-256 ; XIX (1908), pp. 262-273 ; XXI (1909), pp. 139-157, 567-570.—*Entremeses del siglo xvii atribuidos al Maestro Tirso de Molina*, ed. El Bachiller Mantuano [A. Bonilla y San Martín], Madrid, 1909 Col. ' Oro Viejo,' 1).—See : P. Muñoz Peña, *El teatro del maestro Tirso de Molina* : *Estudio crítico-literario*. Valladolid, 1889 ; James Fitzmaurice- Kelly, *Don Juan* [*The New Review*], London, 1895 ; M. Menéndez y Pelayo, in *Estudios de crítica literaria*, 1895, 2nd series, pp. 131-198 (Col. de Escritores Cast., 106) ; A. Farinelli, *Don Giovanni, note critiche*. Torino-Roma, 1896 ; A. Farinelli, *Cuatro palabras sobre Don Juan y la literatura donjuanesca del porvenir*, in *Homenaje á Menéndez y Pelayo*. Madrid, 1899. I, pp. 205-222 ; R. Menéndez Pidal, *El condenado por desconfiado*. 1902 [*Discurso*. R. Academia Esp.] ; A. Morel-Fatio, ' *La Prudence chez la femme*,' *drame historique de Tirso de Molina*, in *Études sur l'Espagne*. Paris, 1904. III, pp. 27-72 ; E. Cotarelo y Mori, in *Comedias de Tirso de Molina*. 1906. I, pp. iii-lxxx (Nueva Bib. de Autores Esp., 4) ; B. de los Ríos de Lampérez, in *Del siglo de oro*. Madrid, 1910. pp. 1-112, 229-275 ; B. de los Ríos de Lampérez, *El* '*Don Juan* ' *de Tirso de Molina*, in *Archivo de investigaciones históricas*, I (1911), pp. 7-30 ; Th. Schröder, *Die dramatischen Bearbeitungen der don Juan-Sage*, etc. Halle, 1912 [Beihefte zur *Zeitschrift für rom. Philologie*, 36] ; S. G. Morley, *Color Symbolism in Tirso de Molina*, in *The Romanic Review*, VIII (1917), pp. 77-81 ; J. Cejador, ' *El Condenado por desconfiado*,' in *Revue Hispanique*, LVII (1923), pp. 127-159.

him *Lo fingido verdadero* : and he dedicated to Lope *La Villana de Vallecas*. In spite of these courtesies, the two authors would not seem to have been on friendly terms. Tirso de Molina competed at the feasts of St. Isidore in 1622 without success : four years later (1626) he was named superior of the monastery of Trujillo, a post which he occupied for three years. In 1632 he became chronicler of his order, and *definidor* of the province of Castile ; in 1645 he was appointed superior of Soria, where he died on March 12, 1648.

His history of the Mercenarian Order is still unpublished as a whole : his genealogical table of the house of the Conde de Sástago (1640) and the *Vida de la Santa Madre Dª Maria de Cerbellon* have no concern with literature. Tirso de Molina's first work of importance is the *Cigarrales de Toledo* (1621 ?), a collection of tales in prose and verse told during five days of festivities following upon a wedding. The title is taken from a Toledan word used to describe the country-houses set among fruit-trees and fountains in which the neighbourhood of Toledo abounds. Tirso announced a series of verses and stories for twenty days, but he stops at the fifth day with the promise of a second part, which was never fulfilled. Throughout there is evidence of Italian influence : one of the tales, *Los tres maridos burlados*, is closely allied to a versified story in the *Mambriano* of the ' Ciego de Ferrara ' (Francesco Bello). The real interest of the book lies in its three plays : *Como han de ser los amigos*, *El celoso prudente* and *El vergonzoso en Palacio*. Another collection entitled *Deleitar aprovechando* (1635) includes three devout tales of little value and some *autos*, one of which, *El Colmenero divino*, is Tirso's best attempt in the *genre*. But Tirso's fame rests principally on his creation of a universal type Don Juan, who appears in *El Burlador de Sevilla y Combidado de piedra*, a piece published in 1630 in a provincial collection of plays called *Doze comedias nvevas de Lope de Vega Carpio, y otros autores*. In this volume the play bears Tirso's name, but it is not included in the authorized edition of his works. This fact has inclined critics, notably Signor Farinelli, to think the ascription suspect, and the discovery in 1878 of a new version of the play under Calderon's name has confirmed their doubts. However, up to the present, Tirso is credited with the invention of a type which Mozart (1756-1791) has made popular all the world over, and whose re-incarnations in the works of Dorimon (1628-1693), Villiers, Molière, Byron and Zorrilla have failed to render the haughty and aristocratic pride of the original. The ascription to Tirso of *El Condenado por desconfiado* is also a matter of dispute: this justly celebrated play gives a powerful presentation of the conflict between free-will and predestination. But if these titles to fame were removed, it would still remain beyond question that in *La prudencia en la muger* Tirso has produced the best historical drama of the Spanish language. His dignified presentment of Dª Maria de Molina is drawn with a sympathy and restraint well in harmony with the character of that tragic personality.

Tirso is also a master of light comedy in such plays as *Marta la piadosa*, where he draws a picture of oily hypocrisy as forcible as anything in the best scenes of *Tartufe*, in *Don Gil de las calzas verdes* and *La Villana de Vallecas*. His plays were published in five parts the first part in 1627, the second and fourth in 1635, the third in 1634, and the fifth in 1636. The sixth part promised by the author never appeared; the fifth part contains eleven plays only, eight in the second part do not seem to belong to Tirso or, at least, not wholly. Already in 1635, his popularity was on the wane, and by 1638 he ceased writing for the stage. Even now he is not greatly read abroad; but that Shirley's *The Opportunity* (1634) should be founded on *El castigo del penseque* (1613) proves that Tirso's reputation had crossed the Channel during his own lifetime. In France, Montfleury (1640-1685) based *La Dame Médecin* on *El Amor médico*, and Scarron (1610?-1660) used scenes from the same play for his *Jodelet duelliste*. In Spain, Tirso's reputation, like Lope's, is likely to increase. He is not as copious as Lope, and, like Lope, he is represented by a mere fraction of his work: but he almost equals the master in his portrayal of feminine characters and outshines him in power of malicious observation and roguish gaiety.

Only brief mention can be made of such practitioners of the *nueva comedia* as Diego Ximenez de Enciso [1] (1585-1633?), whose *El principe Don Carlos* suggested to Calderon some traits in *La vida es sueño*; Felipe Godinez (1588-1637?) of Jewish descent and a

[1] *Los Médicis de Florencia*, ed. R. de Mesonero Romanos, 1858, in Bib. de Autores Esp., XLV.—See: R. Schevill, *The Comedias of Diego Ximenez de Enciso*, in *Publications of the Modern Language Association of America*, XVIII (1903), pp. 194-210; J. P. W. Crawford, *El Príncipe Don Carlos of Ximénez de Enciso*, in *Modern Language Notes*, XXII (1907), pp. 238-241; E. Cotarelo, *Don Diego Jiménez de Enciso y su teatro*, in *Boletín de la R. Academia Esp.*, I (1914), pp. 209-248, 385-415, 510-550; E. Levi, *Storia poetica di Don Carlos*. Pavia, 1914. 2nd ed. Roma [1924].

victim of the Inquisition as well as Quevedo's butt in *La Perinola*, who wrote *Aun de noche alumbra el sol*; Antonio Hurtado de Mendoza[1] (1586-1644), the suave courtier-poet, upon whose *El marido hace muger, y el trato muda costumbre* Molière based *L'École des Maris* and whose *Empeños del mentir* seems to have given hints to Lesage in *Gil Blas*; Luis de Belmonte Bermudez[2] (1587?-1650?), author of the recently published poem *La Hispalica*, perhaps too of the play *El Diablo predicador* derived from Lope's *Fray Diablo*, and, according to tradition, intrepid planner of a sequel to the *Coloquio de los perros*; and Luis Quiñones de Benavente[3] (1589?-1651), whose *Jocoseria* (1645) contains *entremeses* such as *El Borracho* and *El Guardainfante* unsurpassed later by Ramon de la Cruz. Quiñones de Benavente may have influenced Beaumarchais, if, as is thought, *Le Barbier de Séville* contains reminiscences of *El Borracho*.

[1] *El Marido hace mujer, y el trato muda costumbre, Los empeños del mentir* and *Cada loco con su tema, ó el montañés indiano*, ed. R. de Mesonero Romanos, 1858, in Bib. de Autores Esp., XLV; *Entremeses* [*El examinador Miser Palomo* and *Getafe*], ed. E. Cotarelo y Mori, in *Colección de Entremeses*, etc. 1911. I, pp. 322-335 (Nueva Bib. de Autores Esp., 17); *Poesías*, ed. A. Duran, 1851, in Bib. de Autores Esp., XVI and ed. A. de Castro, 1857, in Bib. de Autores Esp., XLII.

[2] *El diablo predicador, y mayor contrario amigo*, and *La renegada de Valladolid*, ed. R. de Mesonero Romanos, 1858, in Bib. de Autores Esp., XLV; *Hispalica*, ed. S. Montoto, Sevilla, 1921.—See: B. J. Gallardo, in *Ensayo*, etc. Madrid, 1866. II, col. 59-69; L. Rouanet, *Le diable prédicateur, comédie.... traduite en français*. Paris-Toulouse, 1901 (Bibliothèque espagnole, 2).

[3] *Entremeses*, ed. C. Rosell, Madrid, 1872-1874. 2 vols. (Libros de antaño, 1, 2).—See: L. Rouanet, in *Intermèdes espagnols* (*Entremeses*) *du xviie siècle* ... Paris, 1897.

Antonio Mira de Amescua[1] (1577 ?-1644), to whom Gracian attributed the *Cancion real a vna mudanza* six years before it was published anonymously in Josef Alfay's *Poesias varias de grandes ingenios españoles* (1654), shews talent as a writer of *autos* and of secular plays. He has the creative instinct; he is eloquent, impressive, and forcible. But apart from the *Cancion real a vna mudanza*, which has also been ascribed to Góngora and Bartolomé Leonardo de Argensola, Mira de Amescua's reputation is based less on the intrinsic merit of his plays than on the fact that the themes of these were extensively borrowed by contemporary dramatists. From *El Esclavo del Demonio* Calderon drew *La Devocion de la Cruz* and Moreto *Caer para levantar. La Rueda de la Fortuna* may have influenced both Corneille and Calderon: and two of Mira de Amescua's plays, *La adversa fortuna de Don Bernardo de Cabrera* and *El exemplo mayor de la desdicha, y capitan Belisario* suggested respectively to Rotrou *Don Bernardo de Cabrera* and *Bélisaire*.

The Mexican hunchback, JUAN RUIZ DE ALARCON[2] (1580 ?-1639), whose quarrels with Lope, Góngora,

[1] *Comedias* (5), ed. R. de Mesonero Romanos, 1858, in Bib. de Autores Esp., XLV; *Comedia famosa del esclavo del demonio*, ed. M. A. Buchanan, Baltimore, 1905; *Poesías*, ed. A. de Castro, 1857, in Bib. de Autores Esp., XLII.—See: C. Pérez Pastor, in *Bibliografía madrileña*. Madrid, 1907, III, pp. 427-431; N. Díaz de Escobar, *Siluetas escénicas del pasado: Autores dramáticos del siglo xvii: El Doctor Mira de Amescua*, in *Revista del Centro de estudios históricos de Granada y su reino*, I (1911), pp. 122-143; F. Sanz, *El doctor don Antonio Mira de Amescua*, in *Boletín de la R. Academia Esp.*, I (1914), pp. 551-572.

[2] *Comedias* (26 and a fragment), ed. J. E. Hartzenbusch, 1852 (Bib. de Autores Esp., XX) [See also XLII and LII]; *No hay mal que por bien no venga* (*Don Domingo de Don Blas*), ed. A. Bonilla

Quevedo and others fill far too much space in literary history, studied in Salamanca between 1600 and 1605, returned to America in 1608 and once more—in 1613 —visited Spain, where he was appointed a member of the Council of the Indies in 1626. His first play, *El semejante a si mismo*, based on Cervantes's *El Curioso impertinente*, raised enemies against him at once. Cristóbal Suarez de Figueroa[1] (1571 ?-1645 ?), author of *La Constante Amarilis* (1609), of the encyclopaedic *Plaza vniversal de todas ciencias y artes* (1615)— an adaptation of *La Piazza Vniversale de tvtte le professioni del mondo* (1585), by Tommaso Garzoni

y San Martín, 1916 (Clásicos de la Literatura esp , 2) ; *Teatro* [*La verdad sospechosa, Las paredes oyen*], ed. A. Reyes, 1918 (2nd ed. 1923) (Clásicos Cast., 37).—See : L. Schmidt, in *Ueber die vier bedeutendsten Dramatiker der Spanier*. Bonn, 1858 ; L. Fernandez-Guerra y Orbe, *D. Juan Ruiz de Alarcon y Mendoza*. Madrid, 1871 ; F. Rodríguez Marín, *Nuevos datos para la biografía del insigne dramaturgo D. Juan Ruiz de Alarcon*. Madrid, 1912 ; P. Henríquez Ureña, *Don Juan Ruiz de Alarcon* [*Nosotros*], México, 1914 ; N. Rangel, *Noticias biográficas del dramaturgo mexicano D. Juan Ruiz de Alarcón y Mendoza* [*Boletín de la Bib. Nacional de Mexico*], 1915 ; A. Reyes, *Ruiz de Alarcon y las Fiestas de Baltasar Carlos*, in *Revue Hispanique*, XXXVI (1916), pp. 170-176 ; S. G. Morley, *Studies in Spanish Dramatic Versification of the Siglo de Oro. Alarcon and Moreto* [*University of California Publications in Modern Philology*, 7], 1918.

[1] *El Pasagero*, ed. F. Rodríguez Marín, 1913 (Bib. Renacimiento, 4) ; ed. R. Selden Rose, 1914 (Soc. de Bibliófilos Esp., 38).—See : H. A. Rennert, *Some documents in the life of Christoval Suarez de Figueroa*, in *Modern Language Notes*, VII (1892), col. 398-410 ; J. P. W. Crawford, *The Life and works of Christóbal Suárez de Figueroa* [Publications of the University of Pennsylvania], Philadelphia, 1907 [Spanish trans. by N. Alonso Cortés, Valladolid, 1911] ; J. P. W. Crawford, *Suarez de Figueroa's 'España defendida' and Tasso's 'Gerusalemme liberata,'* in *The Romanic Review*, IV (1913), pp. 207-220.

THE GOLDEN AGE

(1549-1589)—and of the epic poem *España defendida* (1612), a crotchety fellow, but a good writer, cruelly alludes to Alarcon in *El Passagero* (1617) as ' el gimio en figura de hombre, el corcovado imprudente, el contrahecho ridículo.' Whatever were Alarcon's faults of temper, and it is fair to remember that he received much provocation from enemies who taunted him with his deformity, his intellectual probity is beyond reproach. The number of his plays (collections of which appeared in 1628 and 1634), is comparatively small, but they are carefully planned and finished in every detail. He has a high reputation as a moralist, especially among those who have not read *El desdichado en fingir*; but it is true that he lends to the drama a moral significance which it had not possessed before, while at the same time he avoids preaching at his audience. The moral of *La verdad sospechosa* is that lying, though an elegant accomplishment, does not pay in the long run. Corneille said that he would have given his two finest works to have written it: as it is, he constructed on it *Le Menteur*, and so supplied the French stage with its first genuine high comedy. Alarcon had a share of popularity in his own day, especially among the women who patronized the theatre; but Montalvan records that there was a certain *extrañeza*—not so much oddity as exotic savour—in his work, and perhaps on this account he appeals more strongly to foreigners than do most of his contemporaries. His *Ganar amigos* is an admirable example of national drama. Alarcon carries weight because he conveys the impression of a grave sincerity: the tirades in *Los pechos privilegiados* are not a glittering display of rhetorical fireworks, but a real criticism of life. And he breaks new ground in *Mudarse por mejorarse* and in *El Examen de Maridos*, both excellent illustrations of character-drawing, and profoundly interesting as records of social manners.

Forty years had elapsed since the publication of *Lazarillo de Tormes* when in 1599 the Sevillan MATEO ALEMAN[1] (1547-1614 ?) produced his *Primera Parte de Gvzman de Alfarache*. Aleman was the first person who had the courage to put his name on the title-page of a picaresque story. Little is known of his life. The son of a medical man, he seems to have begun a university career in Seville where he studied medicine and to have continued at Salamanca and Alcalá de Henares. He is said by Luis de Valdés, one of his friends, to have fought in Italy, but, though *Guzman de Alfarache* abounds in details concerning Italian towns and military life, there is no confirmation of the fact. Aleman married rather against his will in 1571 and in 1580 was arrested for debt. He appears to have intended to go to America in 1582, but gave up the notion on being appointed Chief

---

[1] *Guzman de Alfarache*, ed. B. C. Aribau, 1846, in Bib. de Autores Esp., III; ed. F. Holle, 1913-1914 (Bib. Romanica); *Odas de Horacio, traducidas por Mateo Aleman*, ed. M. Pérez de Guzmán y Boza, Cádiz, 1893; *Sucesos de D. Frai Garcia Gera, Arçobispo de Méjico*, ed. A. H. Bushee, in *Revue Hispanique*, xxv (1911), pp. 359-457.—See: F. de Haan, in *An Outline of the History of the Novela Picaresca in Spain*. The Hague-New York, 1903; F. W. Chandler, in *The Literature of Roguery*. London-Boston-NewYork, 1907; F. Rodríguez Marín, *Vida de Mateo Alemán*, 1907 [*Discurso*. R. Academia Esp.] (2nd ed. Sevilla, 1907); U. Cronan, *Mateo Aleman and Miguel de Cervantes Saavedra*, in *Revue Hispanique*, xxv (1911), pp. 468-475; R. Foulché-Delbosc, *Bibliographie de Mateo Aleman (1598-1615)*, in *Revue Hispanique*, XLII (1918), pp. 481-556; James Fitzmaurice-Kelly, Introduction to *The Rogue* . . [trans. by James Mabbe], London, 1924, 4 vols. (The Tudor Translations. Second Series, ii-v).

THE GOLDEN AGE

Accountant in Madrid. Imprisoned again in 1594, he left Madrid for Seville in 1601 and in the following year was once more in jail, having got into the hands of Madrid money-lenders. In the Spring of 1604, Aleman went to Lisbon to press the sale of his *San Antonio de Padva* (1604); he published there the *princeps* of the *Segunda Parte de la Vida de Gvzman de Alfarache, Atalaya de la vida umana* (1604). He complains that though his book is entitled *Watch-Tower of the Human Life*, people insisted on calling it the *Pícaro*. His memory was at fault: only the second part has the full title. In 1608 he went to America. A passage in the *Ortografía castellana* (1609), published at Mexico, might make one suppose that Aleman was a printer, but this is conjecture. It is certain that he published there the short sketch, *Svcesos de D. Frai Garcia Gera (Guerra) arçobispo de Mejico* (1613). The date of his death is unknown.

In *Guzman de Alfarache*, which consists of two parts, each divided into three books, Aleman draws a striking picture of a rogue's precarious existence. At first Guzman gets the worst of it, but he learns from experience and grows hardened in iniquity. He robs his masters and sets up as a man of fashion. Tricked out of his money, he enlists at Almagro, and we get a curious glimpse of military discipline, for Guzman plays every sort of prank including highway robbery. The First Part ends as he passes into the household of the French Ambassador, who intends to use him as an instrument to manage his *amours*. Aleman announced a Second Part in his last chapter and, as in the case of Cervantes, he was anticipated by a spurious sequel, published under the name of Matheo Luxan de Sayauedra whose identification with Juan José Martí

(d. 1604) lacks the evidence of proof. Aleman's reply to this provocation is contained in the Prologue to the second part where he speaks of Sayauedra's 'great learning, his nimble wit, his deepe judgement, his pleasant conceits, and his generall knowledge in all humane and divine letters.' But in the body of his text, he borrows from Sayauedra and introduces him into the story as a friend of Guzman. On the way home from Genoa, a storm springs up, Sayauedra goes mad, calls himself Guzman and jumps overboard to meet with death in the seas. Having thus disposed of his opponent, Aleman goes on to promise a third part, which seems never to have been written. In both parts there are intercalations: the story of Ozmin and Daraja, and the tale of Don Luis de Castro taken from Masuccio's *Il Novellino* (XLI), which also formed the basis of Beaumont and Fletcher's *The Little French Lawyer* and of Scarron's *La Précaution Inutile*. But these stories, although out of tune with Guzman's sordid rascality, are not as great blots on the book as are the tedious moralizing digressions, which were so much to the taste of the seventeenth century. And this defect is even more apparent in the second part, which gives more importance also to the picaroon than to his masters. The popularity of the book was immense: in less than five years, twenty-nine editions were issued. In England, *Guzman de Alfarache* translated in 1622 by James Mabbe (1572-1642 ?), reached a fourth edition by 1656. Aleman has a vigorous and supple prose-style completely in harmony with the matter of his book, which Hazlitt considered 'extraordinary.' Still it must be admitted that as a picaroon tale *Guzman de Alfarache* takes rank below its predecessor.

THE GOLDEN AGE

Lazarillo de Tormes, Guzman de Alfarache, and the *Libro de Entretenimiento de la Picara Ivstina* (1605), are all novels of the primitive type of picaresque invention. The least interesting of the three is the last. The fact that *Don Quijote* is mentioned in the text of *La Pícara Justina*, which contains an example of the *versos de cabo roto*, would point to the conclusion that the writer knew Cervantes. It seems likely from the *Viage del Parnaso* that Cervantes knew the author and had no very high opinion of him. *Versos de cabo roto* were used by Alonso Alvarez de Soria [1] (1573-1607), who died by the hangman's hand at Seville. The title-page of *La Pícara Justina* bears the name of Francisco Lopez de Ubeda,[2] which was alleged to be the pseudonym of a Dominican monk, Fray Andrés Perez, author of a *Vida de San Raymundo de Peñaforte* (1601), and of two volumes of sermons. This is an ancient literary tradition, but as there really existed a Lopez de Ubeda, there seems no reason to doubt that he wrote the book as he claims to have done. *La Pícara Justina* is full of prolix moralizing evidently modelled on *Guzman de Alfarache*. It professes also to be an *Ars Poetica*, about fifty different measures appear in the versified glosses that precede each chapter. Lopez de Ubeda scarcely pretends to any originality: his alembicated, affected, and complex style makes one grateful that the sequel promised in the text never

---

[1] See: F. Rodríguez Marín, *El Loaysa de 'El celoso extremeño.'* Sevilla, 1901; H. R. Lang, *Versos de cabo roto*, in *Revue Hispanique*, xv (1906), pp. 92-97.

[2] *La Pícara Justina*, ed. J. Puyol y Alonso, 1912. 3 vols. (Soc. de Bibliófilos Madrileños, 7-9).—See: R. Foulché-Delbosc, *L'auteur de la 'Pícara Justina,'* in *Revue Hispanique*, x (1903), pp. 236-241.

appeared. But it is not true that *La Pícara Justina* is honeycombed with lubricity. The book contains coarse passages which were in the taste of the time. There is nothing in it, however, that deserves the name of lubricity, a vice more characteristic of the French *conteurs* than of the emphatic Spaniard and the thrasonical Englishman of the seventeenth century.

In 1618 appeared the *Relaciones de la vida del Escudero Marcos de Obregon*, by VICENTE ESPINEL[1] (1551-1624), a clerical picaroon, who dedicated his work to the Archbishop of Toledo, Bernardo de Sandoval y Rojas, who had befriended Cervantes when he was in extremities. Espinel seems to have been a rogue all his life long. In his youth he studied at the University of Salamanca, whence he was rusticated; from Salamanca he went to Seville, where he startled the inhabitants by his irregular habits. Having set sail for Italy, he fell into the clutches of Barbary pirates and was kept as a slave at Algiers till he was ransomed. On his release, he went to Italy, entered the army and is alleged to have served also in the Netherlands. Thence he returned to Spain, where shortly before May 1587 he was ordained. He contrived to get appointed chaplain at Ronda and calmly resided in Madrid until the people of Ronda insisted on his presence, but when in Ronda he led such a disorderly life that a formal complaint was made by the chief magistrate and the most prominent citizens. The Bishop was obliged to deprive Espinel of his

---

[1] *Vida del escudero Marcos de Obregon*, ed. J. Pérez de Guzmán, Barcelona, 1881 (Bib. Arte y Letras, I); ed. S. Gili Gaya, Madrid, 1922-1923, 2 vols. (Clásicos cast., 43, 51).—See: B. J. Gallardo, in *Ensayo*, etc., Madrid, 1866. II, cols. 951-953; L. Claretie, in *Lesage romancier*. Paris, 1890. pp. 203-261.

living and of another living which the ardent pluralist held. Espinel went to Alcalá, took the degree of Master of Arts and ingratiated himself with the Bishop of Plasencia, who in 1599 appointed him Chaplain and—as he was a good musician—choirmaster. This enabled him to live at Madrid.

Espinel had originality and intelligence. He shewed this in his *Diversas Rimas* (1591), which contain good versions of Horace. His translation of the *Ars poetica* gave rise in the eighteenth century to a bitter controversy between Tomas de Iriarte and Lopez de Sedano. But though his poems thus chanced to come into notice again, and the form of the *décima* known as the *espinela* is due to him, it is as a picaresque writer that Espinel survives. He had only to write his own life as material to make a picaresque tale. *Marcos de Obregon* owes something of its actual vogue to the fact that episodes from it have been utilized by Lesage in *Gil Blas*. Its introduction of classical stories and fanciful inventions is not in tune with the realism which is the essence of the picaroon convention, yet apart from this there remains a large residue of excellence, a purity of style, a unity of subject and a relative tolerableness on the part of the prototype.

Already in the sixteenth century a new literary form was adumbrated in the *Historia del Abencerraje y la hermosa Xarifa*. This was the Moorish novel which GINES PEREZ DE HITA (1544 ?-1619 ?)[1] developed in

[1] *Guerras civiles de Granada*, ed. B. C. Aribau, 1846, in Bib. de Autores Esp., III; ed. P. Blanchard-Demouge, Madrid, 1913-1915. 2 vols.; *Poesías*, ed. A. Duran, 1851, in Bib. de Autores Esp., XVI.—See: N. Acero y Abad, *Ginés Pérez de Hita*. Madrid, 1888; C. Pérez Pastor, in *Bibliografía madrileña*. Madrid, 1907. III, p. 450.

the *Historia de los vandos de los Zegries y Abencerrages* ... (1595), continued under the name *Segunda Parte de las Guerras civiles de Granada* ... (1604?), a title which ultimately prevailed. Perez de Hita appears to have been born in Mula in 1544 or 1546 and to have settled in Murcia after his marriage in 1597. He describes his work as a translation from a Moor called Ibn Hamin; this statement carries no weight since he cites as his authority the chronicler Esteban de Garibay y Zamálloa (d. 1599). The First Part is vastly superior to its sequel, which describes the revolt of the Moors in the Alpujarras. Here Perez de Hita, who took an active part in the incidents depicted, is hampered by his knowledge of the facts. But in the early part his imagination has free rein, and his vivid and fantastic pictures of Moorish life in the beleaguered city of Granada are set down in a graceful, glowing style which enhances the value of their presentation. The *Guerras Civiles* was a special favourite with Voiture and the *précieuses*; its influence is visible in the series of Hispano-Mauresque novels beginning with the *Almaide* of Mlle. de Scudéry (1607-1701) and the *Zaïde* of Mme. de Lafayette (1634-1693). Perez de Hita was a delightful prose-writer but a poor poet, and while the First Part of the *Guerras Civiles* is tesselated with beautiful border-ballads and some of the best *romances moriscos*, borrowed probably from the first parts of the *Romancero general*, the Second Part contains vastly inferior compositions, frequently by Perez de Hita's own hand.

Besides the drama and the novel a third—and less beneficent—literary manifestation occurred in Spain during the seventeenth century. This was the pest of extravagant preciosity and verbal gymnastics which is known as gongorism. It used to be contended that this plague was imported into Spain from Italy by Luis Carrillo y Sotomayor (1583-1610), a poet who died too young and who wrote too little to produce much effect. Carrillo had served as a soldier in Italy and had come under the influence of Marino (1569-1625), who was then at the height of his fame, though his *Adone* (1623) was not yet published. LUIS DE GONGORA [1] (1561-1627) was the hierophant of the new poetic sect, the *cultos* (hence *culteranismo*, at first called *la nueva poesía*)—the learned, the exquisite—to whom Góngora made his esoteric appeal. There are obvious points of resemblance between Góngora in his second phase and Marino. But there is one decisive argument against the theory of the Italian poet's direct

[1] *Obras poéticas* [and *Epistolario*], ed. R. Foulché-Delbosc. 1921. 3 vols. (Bib. hispanica XVI, XVII, XX); *Vingt-six lettres de Gongora*, ed. R. Foulché-Delbosc, in *Revue Hispanique*, X (1903), pp. 184-225.—See: J. Pellicer de Salas y Touar, *Vida de Don Luis de Gongora*, ed. R. Foulché-Delbosc, in *Revue Hispanique*, XXXIV (1915), pp. 577-588; M. Cañete, *Observaciones acerca de Góngora y del culteranismo en España*, reprinted in *Revue Hispanique*, XLVI (1919), pp. 281-311; E. Churton, *Gongora*, London, 1862. 2 vols.; C. G. Child, *John Lyly and Euphuism*. Erlangen-Leipzig, 1894 (Munchener Beiträge zur roman. und engl. Philologie, 7); M. González y Francés, *Góngora racionero*. . . . Córdoba, 1896; M. González y Francés, *Don Luis de Góngora vindicando su fama ante el propio obispo*. Córdoba, 1899; R. Foulché-Delbosc, *Note sur trois manuscrits des œuvres poétiques de Gongora*, in *Revue Hispanique*, VII (1900), pp. 454-504; R. Foulché-Delbosc, *Bibliographie de Gongora*, in *Revue Hispanique*, XVIII (1908), pp. 73-161; L.-P. Thomas, *Le lyrisme et la préciosité cultistes en Espagne*. Halle a. S.-Paris, 1909; L.-P. Thomas, *Gongora et le gongorisme considérés dans leurs rapports avec le marinisme*. Paris, 1911; A. Farinelli, *Marinismus und Gongorismus*, in *Deutsche Literaturzeitung*, 1912, col. 11-13-14-22; A. Reyes, *Góngora y 'La Gloria de Niquea,'* in *Revista de Filología Esp.*, II (1915), pp. 274-282; E. Díez

responsibility for the phenomenon of gongorism. The most exaggerated of Góngora's poems, *El Polifemo*, was written over a dozen years before Marino's *Adone* was printed. Nor can the blame be laid on Carrillo's *Obras* (1611) published two years after the radical change in Góngora's methods took place. The new phase was first apparent in the *Panegyrico al duque de Lerma*, written in the early part of 1609. The date is important: it removes at once all possibility of Góngora's connexion with the parallel movement of euphuism which began in 1578 or 1580. Carrillo, however, is not wholly blameless. As Lucien-Paul Thomas points out, there is at the end of his *Obras* a prose document, *Libro de la Erudicion poetica*, which circulated in manuscript and gave rise to considerable discussion in literary circles. In this treatise Carrillo enlarges on his theory that obscurity in a poet is a merit rather than a defect; this is the view that Góngora adopts and puts into practice in such poems as the *Fabvla de Polifemo y Galatea* and *Soledades*.

Luis de Góngora was born at Cordova on July 11, 1561. His father was Francisco de Argote, a *juez de bienes*, official of the Inquisition at Cordova and, it is

Canedo, M. L. Guzmán and A. Reyes, *Contribuciones a la bibliografía de Góngora*, in *Revista de Filología Esp.*, III (1916), pp. 171-182; IV (1917), pp. 54-64; James Fitzmaurice-Kelly, *Góngora* [*Transactions of the Royal Society of Literature*, XXXV]. London, 1917; A. Reyes, *Cuestiones gongorinas sobre el texto de las 'Lecciones solemnes' de Pellicer*, in *Revue Hispanique*, XLIII (1918), pp. 505-519; A. Reyes, *Reseña de estudios gongorinos* in *Revista de Filología Esp.*, V (1918), pp. 315-336; A. Reyes, *Cuestiones gongorinas. Pellicer en las cartas de sus contemporáneos*, in *Revista de Filología Esp.*, VI (1919), pp. 268-282; H. Thomas, *Three translators of Góngora and other Spanish poets* [*Revue Hispanique*, XLVIII], 1920; M. Artigas, *Don Luis de Góngora y Argote. Biografía y estudio crítico*. Madrid, 1925.

also alleged, *corregidor* of that city. The poet bore his mother's name; this was uncommon, but by no means without precedent. At the age of fifteen years Góngora was sent to study law at Salamanca. He appears to have amused himself a good deal there and to have got into debt, though he already held the benefices of Cañete de las Torres, Guadalmazán and Santaella to which, doubtless, he was appointed by the influence of his maternal uncle who came to the student's aid on this and other occasions. Gongora was back in Cordova in 1582, and in 1584 he was clearly a poet of some prominence, for he is praised by Cervantes in the *Canto de Caliope*. In 1585 he received a Cathedral stall, and by August 14 of that year he must have been at least in minor orders, for he was present at a Chapter-meeting. The date of his ordination is not known, but from 1599 Góngora figures in the capitular lists as a deacon. Meanwhile everybody was not satisfied with the conduct of the young ecclesiastic. Complaints concerning him were made in 1589 to the Bishop, who ordered an inquiry to be held into the truth of the charges. This official indictment was not very grave. Góngora was accused of insufficient zeal in attending the Cathedral services ; he was said to have talked during the Divine Office, to have formed part of a gossipy circle, to have frequented bull-fights (an amusement nominally forbidden to clerics), and to have written verses of a profane kind. Góngora admitted some of the charges : he is much more guarded in his answers as to the remaining accusations and becomes almost impatient when he says that ' at the offices, I have always been as silent as anybody else : for I have nobody to answer me if I wanted to talk, as my neighbour on one side of me is a deaf man, on the other an indefatigable singer.' He adds that most of the poems ascribed to him are not his, that his own verses do not deserve the reproaches levelled against them, that some of them may be light but nothing more. It will be seen that Góngora's answer is by no means categorical in its denials and that he virtually admits no small part of the accusations against him. He seems to have satisfied his superiors, however, for he was constantly entrusted with special missions in different parts of Spain. Many of his poems reflect this aspect of his life and reveal an observation of nature which places Góngora somewhat apart from his generation. No small number of his compositions appeared in the *Romancero General* and in Espinosa's *Flores de Poetas ilvstres de España* published at Valladolid, where Góngora happened to be at the time (1605). In 1609, business took him to Burgos, Vitoria and Pontevedra. This voyage seems to have greatly bored Góngora : possibly his health was beginning to fail ; he suffered from violent headaches and his bodily activities became impaired. It has been suggested that Góngora may have been out of his mind at this period. This seems unlikely, for in 1610 he was put in charge of the capitular revenues. Priests do not deliberately put their financial affairs in the hands of persons menaced with insanity. Towards 1612 Góngora moved to Madrid ; he may at this time have been appointed chaplain to the king, a post which he was holding on December 23, 1617. With the fall of the Duque de Lerma he lost a powerful protector, and a few years later he returned in poverty to Cordova. His feeble health grew worse, he lost his memory and died from an apoplectic seizure on May 23, 1627.

Góngora's talent was entirely lyrical. Such plays as exist of his : *Las Firmezas de Isabela* (1613), the two fragments, *Comedia Venatoria* and *El Doctor Carlino*, recast by Antonio de Solis (and possibly an *entremes*, *Destruycion de Troya*, of doubtful authenticity)—shew a lack of dramatic instinct which the author's sparkling wit does not redeem. He was curiously indifferent as regards his manuscripts; these circulated freely and were frequently altered and retouched. Collected by Juan Lopez de Vicuña, they were published in 1627 with the title *Obras en verso del Homero español*. The privilege of this edition bears the date 1620, at which period Vicuña would seem to have quarrelled with Góngora. No compositions of a later date figure in his book, which was attacked on its publication by Góngora's friends—not without grounds—as being defective, incorrect and unauthoritative. Much the same charges can be brought against Gonzalo de Hozes y Córdoua's edition which was issued in 1633. And this is not astonishing; since Hozes merely reproduces Vicuña's text with the addition of a few poems inedited and otherwise. It is only since 1921 that there exists an authorized edition of Góngora's writings prepared and arranged in chronological order by M. Foulché-Delbosc, who based his text on the manuscript of Antonio Chacon in the Biblioteca Nacional of Madrid. Chacon's copies of the poems had been revised by Góngora himself, who supplied dates to each piece : the calligraphic manuscript was dedicated to the Conde-Duque de Olivares. Thus after nearly three hundred years Góngora can be read in an authentic text which must prove indispensable for a careful study of the poet.

Góngora began by imitating Herrera : his ode to

the Armada is an excellent instance of his powers in this respect. But Góngora had gifts which Herrera lacked : a fine simplicity, a merry wit and a delicate, penetrating irony. These qualities are admirably revealed in his youthful *letrillas* and *romances*. He possessed besides a craftsman's love of his art : in whatever manner he writes Góngora's preoccupation with the form and finish of his work is evident. He has all Herrera's sonority and—apart from the occasional incidence of unnecessary hyperbaton, of recondite metaphors—little or nothing that indicates his second manner. And he has many strings to his lyre : he is dignified in the *Oda al armamento de Felipe II contra Inglaterra*, fantastic and charming in *Angelica y Medoro*, naive and delightful in his carols or *romances* like *Hermana Marica, Que se nos va la Pascua*. Góngora was not unaware of his great talents. The failure of Espinosa's anthology must have been a disappointment to him : he was ambitious for literary distinction and had before him the examples of Cervantes and Lope de Vega, who, starting from humble beginnings, had won fame at Madrid. His move to the capital may well have had another end in view than social promotion.

However that may be, it was in 1609 that Góngora inaugurated his second phase with the *Panegyrico al duque de Lerma* and in the *Cancion* on the taking of Larache. In these compositions he makes a direct appeal to the *cultos*; he deliberately puts aside the simple charm and incisiveness of diction which are among his greatest attractions and substitutes for these qualities intentional extravagance and enigmatical allusiveness well summed up by Fabrice's remark in *Gil Blas* : ' C'est l'obscurité qui en fait tout le mérite.'

THE GOLDEN AGE

Perhaps the most typical examples of gongorism are to be seen in the *Fabvla de Polifemo* and in the *Soledades*. It would seem that Góngora had occasional doubts about the issue of the struggle in which he was on the point of engaging, for in the summer of 1613 he sent the manuscript of the *Soledades* to his friend Pedro de Valencia (1555-1620), one of the most distinguished humanists of the time. Valencia's verdict was not reassuring: courteously but unmistakably he condemned the innovation, criticized what he called the *cacosyntheton* and *cacozelia* of the new verses and pointed out other defects. This disapproval was a mild foreshadowing of the controversy which soon raged round Góngora. He took no open part in the battle. Now and then he would compose a few caustic verses which generally raised a laugh at their victim's expense. Jauregui perhaps showed himself the most heated of Góngora's opponents in his letter entitled: *Antidoto contra las Soledades*; in the preface to his *Rimas* (1618) he protests against the poems 'which only contain an adornment or a garment of words, being phantoms without soul or body,' and once again, but more mildly, he returns to the charge in the *Discurso poetico contra el hablar culto y obscuro* (1624). A more formidable critic was Lope de Vega. And though he went out of his way to conciliate Góngora, for whom he seems to have had a real personal affection, though he dedicated to the poet his *Amor secreto hasta celos* (1623) and frequently made friendly overtures, Góngora was adamantine. Lope's name carried weight; he was the chief obstacle to the success upon which Góngora had set his heart; it was not his friendship that Góngora desired but his authority on the right side of the balance. And this Lope could not give: rather, he says: 'You can make a *culto* poet in twenty-four hours; a few inversions, four formulas, six Latin words, or emphatic phrases—and the trick is done.' But Lope was easily open to attack. His snobbery and his disorderly life offered so many assailable points to Góngora's scathing irony. Though not nearly so irregular in his habits as Lope, Góngora was not in his youth an ascetic. This might have made him more lenient in passing judgement on Lope's frailties. It is, however, to be observed that he was naturally severe.

Góngora exercised more influence after his death than during his lifetime. He lived long enough to foresee the triumph of *culteranismo*. He was undoubtedly a man of genius. He considered himself an innovator. There may be a difference of opinion as to the worth of his innovations. He introduced no new poetic form, no fresh metrical combination: he enriched and enlarged the existing moulds by his gorgeous colouring and his sparkling humour. As regards his later phase, his intentions were wholly praiseworthy, his practice was much less laudable. There is a measure of truth in d'Alembert's words: "Malheur aux productions de l'art dont toute la beauté n'est que pour les artistes." As against this, it must be admitted that Góngora set a new ideal of artistic execution and that his concern for impeccable workmanship is reflected in the work of every succeeding Spanish poet for whom beauty of form has any meaning.

Nothing could arrest the tide of gongorism; it swept all before it and made converts of its most zealous opponents. Jauregui succumbed to the new fashion. Even Lope became infected by it: asked

THE GOLDEN AGE

by Camus, bishop of Belley (1608-1628), what one of his sonnets meant, Lope is said to have answered that he did not know himself. Tirso de Molina, Calderon and all the younger dramatists came under its influence; Quevedo, who was himself to become victim to false principles equally disastrous, might make merry at the expense of the *cultos* in his prologue (1631) to Luis de Leon's *Obras*; Francisco Cascales [1] might rail in his *Cartas philologicas* (1634), Faria e Sousa proclaim in the commentary (1639) to *Os Lusiadas* that beside Camões, Góngora was as a fly to an eagle. Nothing availed: a whole school declared in favour of gongorism. José Pellicer de Salas y Tovar in his *Lecciones solemnes*...(1630) hailed Góngora as the Andalusian Pindar; Martin de Angulo y Pulgar issued his *Epistolas satisfactorias* (1635) in reply to Cascales's *Cartas*; Cristóbal de Salazar Mardones in his *Ilvstracion y Defensa de la Fabvla de Piramo y Tisbe* (1636) and Garcia de Salcedo Coronel (d. 1651) in the commentary to his edition (1636-1644-1648) of Góngora's works, displayed much patience, ingenuity and misplaced skill in trying to solve the riddle of Góngora's obscurities. A distant echo of the battle was borne over from Peru where Juan de Espinosa Medrano (1632-1688) in his *Apologetico en favor de don Luis de Gongora*..(1694) threw ridicule on Faria e Sousa. It was a full hundred years before Spain shook off the influence of Góngora. When the reaction came, it blotted out gongorism. For a time the word became

---

[1] *Tablas poéticas*, 2nd. ed. Madrid, 1779; *Cartas filológicas*, ed. E. de Ochoa, 1870, in Bib. de Autores Esp., LXII; *Juicio acerca de Góngora*, ed. A. de Castro, 1854, in Bib. de Autores Esp., XXXII.

synonymous with all that was bad in literature. And the censure falls with justice upon Góngora's followers who, lacking his genius, could only ape his later mannerisms. As the grave, quick-witted Gracian remarked, these followers were like the courtiers at Naples who sought to imitate their king, but could only mimic the contortion of his lips.

Perhaps the most famous of Góngora's direct imitators is Juan de Tarsis, second Conde de Villamediana[1] (1580-1622). Banished from Madrid for gambling excesses in 1608, he served in Italy, where he met Marino. He returned to the capital in 1617, and made so many enemies in high places by his satires that he was once more banished in 1621. He returned in the same year to be Chamberlain to Queen Isabel, for whom he is said to have shown an avowed and unbridled passion. On May 15, 1622, a performance was given of his play, *La gloria de Niqvea, y descripcion de Aranivez*, in which the queen had a role; this was followed by Lope de Vega's *El Vellocino de oro*. A fire broke out on the stage: Villamediana carried the queen out from the flames. Scandal reported that he had deliberately started the fire. Though warned that his life was in danger, he refused to take precautions. His indifference was to cost him dear. In August of that same year 1622, as he stepped out from his coach, he was dealt a murderous thrust by an unknown hand, and crying out: '¡ Jesús ! ¡ Esto es hecho ! ' he fell back dead. His *Poesías*

[1] *Poesías.* ed. A. de Castro, 1857, in Bib. de Autores Esp., XLII.—See: E. Cotarelo y Mori, *El conde de Villamediana.* Madrid, 1886; C. Pérez Pastor, in *Bibliografía madrileña.* Madrid, 1907. III, pp. 482-487; A. Reyes, *Góngora y 'La Gloria de Niquea,'* in *Revista de Filología Esp.*, II (1915), pp. 274-282.

were published in 1629. In the two pieces *Fabvla de Faeton* and *Fabvla de la Fenix* he shews himself more gongoristic than Góngora. But when he chooses, he has some of Góngora's direct simplicity as in the often quoted lines:

> ¡ Qué galan que entró Vergel
> con cintillo de diamantes !
> Diamantes que fueron antes
> de amantes de su muger

In this vein of mordant satire and cruel, stinging sarcasm Villamediana has no rival. Another aspect of his talent—his delicate craftsmanship and dainty finish—was copied by Voiture in his *rondeau Pour vos beaux yeux*, a charming adaptation from Villamediana.

Contemporaneous with Villamediana was Hortensio Felix Paravicino y Arteaga[1] (1580-1633), whose social position as court preacher made him a powerful ally in the cause of gongorism. He set the fashion in his sermons, which were issued in 1641 under the title *Oraciones evangelicas y Panegiricos funerales*. His verses, *Obras posthumas divinas y humanas* (1641), published under the name of Felix de Arteaga, shew the pernicious influence that he wielded. Under this influence came writers such as Agustin de Salazar y Torres[2] (1642-1675), whose *Las estaciones del dia*

---

[1] *Poesías*, ed. A. Duran, 1851, in Bib. de Autores Esp., XVI and ed. J. de Sancha, 1855, in Bib. de Autores Esp., XXXV.—See: A. Reyes, *Las dolencias de Paravicino*, in *Revista de Filología Esp.*, V (1918), pp. 293-297.

[2] *Poesías*, ed. A. Duran, 1851, in Bib. de Autores Esp., XVI and ed. A. de Castro, 1857, in Bib. de Autores Esp., XLII; *Comedias* [*El encanto es la hermosura* ... and *Elegir al enemigo*], ed. R. de Mesonero Romanos, 1859, in Bib. de Autores Esp., XLIX.

included in the *Cythara de Apolo* (1681) shew that in happier circumstances he might have produced good work.

The *romance artístico* which conserves the metre (eight syllables with the assonance in alternating lines) of the popular ballad but with a strophical form—quatrains—came into being in the last twenty years of the sixteenth century, won favour and ended by being generally adopted. A very great number of *romances artísticos* were published in the *Romancero General*,[1] an anthology whose different parts, printed separately since 1588, appeared together in the successive editions of 1600 and 1604 and in a more complete form in 1614. They were written for the most part by Lope de Vega, Góngora and Liñan de Riaza. The *romances artísticos* have in many cases surpassing merits: finish of form, wit, grace and fluidity. And if they lack the simple charm, the fresh ingenuous fancy, the inspiring vitality of the more primitive compositions of this *genre*, they gain in artistry by the intervention of individual genius.

An important collection of verse published by Pedro Espinosa[2] (1578-1650) and entitled *Primera Parte de las Flores de Poetas ilustres de España* (1605) reproduces examples from past and present authors, so that we have poems from Camões and Luis de Leon

[1] Facsimile by A. M. Huntington, New York, 1904. 2 vols.; ed. A. Duran, 1849-1851. 2 vols. (Bib. de Autores Esp., x, xvi).

[2] *Obras*, ed. F. Rodríguez Marín, Madrid, 1909; *Flores de poetas ilustres de España*, ed. J. Quirós de los Rios and F. Rodríguez Marín, Sevilla, 1896. 2 vols.—See: F. Rodríguez Marín, *Pedro Espinosa: Estudio biográfico, bibliográfico y crítico*. Madrid, 1907.

as well as from Pedro Liñan de Riaza[1] (d. 1607), author of the charming ballad, *Assi Riselo cantaba*, so frequently ascribed to Góngora ; and Luis Martin de la Plaza (1577-1625 ?), who modelled his dainty madrigal *Iba cogiendo flores* on a sonnet of Tasso. Espinosa, whose verse also figures in the *Flores*, seems to have been unhappy in his love-affairs with Cristobalina Fernandez de Alarcon (1576-1646), the lady whom he calls Sibila de Antequera ; he was not more fortunate with his anthology, whose merit and representativeness—it contained such leading names as Lope, Góngora and Quevedo besides those of many minor poets—should have ensured its success. This was not so, apparently, since the *Segunda Parte* prepared by Juan Antonio Calderon was published only in 1896. Other versifiers should perhaps find room here: Gabriel Lopez Maldonado,[2] nicknamed *El Sincero* in the *Academia de los Nocturnos* at Valencia, who issued in 1586 his *Cancionero* ; and Gabriel Lobo Lasso[3] de la Vega (1559 ?-1615 ?), author of *Romancero y Trajedias* (1587), the *Primera parte de Cortes valeroso, y Mexicana* (1588) recast in 1594 with the addition of thirteen new stanzas under the shorter title of *Mexicana* ; and *Elogios en loor de los tres famosos varones Don Jayme, Rey de Aragon, Don Fernando Cortes,*

[1] *Rimas* . . . Zaragoza, 1876 (Bib. de Escritores Aragoneses, II. Sección literaria, 1).—See : C. Pérez Pastor, in *Bibliografía madrileña*. Madrid, 1907. III, pp. 412-413.

[2] See : C. Pérez Pastor, in *Bibliografía madrileña*. Madrid, 1907. III, pp. 418-420.

[3] See : C. Pérez Pastor, in *Bibliografía madrileña*. Madrid, 1907. III, pp. 403-404 ; A. Restori, *Il 'Manojuelo de Romances,'* in *Revue Hispanique*, x (1908), pp. 117-148 ; M. Artigas, *Lobo Lasso de la Vega*, in *Revista crítica hispano-americana*, III (1917), pp. 157-166.

Marques del Valle, y Don Aluaro de Baçan, Marques de Santa Cruz (1601), a kind of anthology more remarkable for the illustrious names that it contains than for its intrinsic interest.

Among the ecclesiastics of this period many wrote in verse on subjects devout or otherwise. Juan Lopez de Ubeda,[1] who published the *Vergel de flores diuinas* (1582) and the *Cancionero general de la Doctrina Cristiana* (1596), and Francisco de Ocaña,[2] author of the *Cancionero para cantar la noche de Navidad y las fiestas de Pascua* (1603), are inferior in talent to José de Valdivielso[3] (1560?-1638), whose lyrical gift is evident in the *Primera parte del Romancero Espiritual...* (1612). The simple fervour and spontaneous lyrism of this verse-collection recall the *Noble Numbers* of Herrick (1591-1674). Valdivielso does not attain the same level either in his *Doze Actos Sacramentales y dos Comedias Divinas* (1622) or in the *Vida, excelencias y muerte del gloriosissimo Patriarca y Esposo de Nuestra Señora San Joseph* (1604?), a tedious sacred epic which had several editions. Luis de Ribera,[4] who emigrated to Mexico towards 1589, shews in his

[1] *Poesías*, ed J. de Sancha, 1855, in Bib. de Autores Esp., xxxv.
[2] *Poesías*, ed. J. de Sancha, 1855, in Bib. de Autores Esp., xxxv.
[3] *Romancero espiritual*, ed. M. Mir, 1880 (Col. de Escritores Cast., I); *Vida, excelencias, y muerte del gloriosísimo Patriarca San Josef*, ed. C. Rosell, 1854, in Bib. de Autores Esp., xxix; *Poesías*, ed. J. de Sancha, 1855, in Bib. de Autores Esp., xxxv and ed. A. de Castro, 1857, in Bib. de Autores Esp., xlii; *Autos sacramentales* (5), ed. E. Gonzalez Pedroso, 1865, in Bib. de Autores Esp., lviii,—See: J. Mariscal de Gante, in *Autos sacramentales*. Madrid, 1911. pp. 123-143.
[4] *Poesías*, ed. J. de Sancha, 1855, in Bib. de Autores Esp., xxxv.

Sagradas Poesias (1612) a genuine feeling for beauty and devotion.

José de Villaviciosa[1] (1589-1658), author of *La Moschea* . . . (1615), studied law, obtained a post under the Inquisition, and became Canon of Cuenca and later Archdeacon of Moya. His burlesque epic on the battle of the ants and flies is a close imitation of the *Moschaea* by Teofilo Folengo (1496 ?-1544), which is based on the *Batrachomyomachia* and satirizes the *Aeneid*, *Orlando Innamorato* and the *Mambriano*. Villaviciosa was a skilful versifier and a dexterous parodist: he displays as well a merry wit in *La Moschea*, which was, however, eclipsed by Lope's *Gatomachia*. Notwithstanding these clever burlesques, the epic continued to appeal to Spanish poets. Juan de Arjona[2] (d. circ. 1603), *cura* of Puente de Pinos, anticipated Pope (1688-1744) and Gray (1716-1771) with a version of the *Thebaid*, which remained unprinted until 1855. Arjona had spent six years upon his rendering when death surprised him, and the translation was finished with the addition of three cantos by Gregorio Morillo (d. after 1618), chaplain to the Archbishop of Granada. It is unfortunate that Arjona's powers were wasted on Statius's unwieldy poem, but, as it is, his exercise suffices to display his rare mastery of versification and the persistent attraction of the epic form.

The sacred epic was attempted with success by

[1] *La Mosquea*, ed. C. Rosell, 1851, in Bib. de Autores Esp., XVII.—See: J. P. W. Crawford, *Teofilo Folengo's Moschaea and José de Villaviciosa's La Mosquea* [*Publications of the Modern Language Association of America*, XXVII], 1912.

[2] *La Tebaida, de Estacio*, ed. A. de Castro, 1855, in Bib. de Autores Esp., XXXVI.—See: B. J. Gallardo, in *Ensayo*, etc. Madrid, 1863. I, col. 300-302.

Diego de Hojeda[1] (1570?-1615), a Sevillan who, in order to escape his family's opposition, went to Lima to become a Dominican, was made prior of Lima Monastery, and was eventually dismissed and sent as a simple friar to Cuzco, whose prior he had once been. In the twelve books of *La Christiada* (1611), which relate the events beginning with the Last Supper to the laying of Christ in the sepulchre, Hojeda follows the biblical account with commendable fidelity. His narrative is managed with unusual skill; his embellishments are always appropriate, and *La Christiada* easily takes rank with the *Messias* (1751-1773) of Klopstock (1724-1803). Gifted with imagination, dignity of conception and a fine sense of melody, Hojeda only lacks the power of dramatic presentation to give him a high place among his kind. An analogous talent is that of Alonso de Azevedo,[2] a canon of Plasencia. His *Creacion del Mundo* (1615), which he published at Rome, is derived in part from Du Bartas's *La Sepmaine* and from Tasso's *Il mondo creato* (1600-1607), but the Spanish Catholic has avoided the verbal extravagances of the Gascon Huguenot, has improved the framework and added many descriptive passages of considerable beauty which entitle him to no small share of the praise bestowed on his French predecessor by the appreciative Goethe.

Something of his contemporary Góngora's influence, which Azevedo escaped possibly owing to his absence from Spain, is noticeable in the poems of Bernardo de

[1] *La Cristiada*, ed. C. Rosell, 1851, in Bib. de Autores Esp., XVII.—See Fr. Justo Cuervo, *El maestro Fr. Diego de Ojeda y La Cristiada.* Madrid, 1898.

[2] *Creacion del mundo*, ed. C. Rosell, 1854, in Bib. de Autores Esp., XXIX.

Balbuena[1] (1568-1625?), Bishop of Puerto Rico (1620), who is alleged to have written a *Divino Christiados*, which was destroyed by the Dutch in the war of 1625 together with a treatise on poetry and a pastoral novel. The earliest of his surviving works is the *Grandeza mexicana* (1604), but he is best known by the *Siglo de oro, en las selvas de Erifile* (1608), and *El Bernardo, o Victoria de Roncesvalles* (1624). The *Siglo de oro*, an imitation of Sannazaro's *Arcadia* with an accentuated note of artificiality, is remarkable for the melody of its eclogues while *El Bernardo* might compete with the *Orlando Furioso* were it not that the author falls somewhat short of Ariosto's patrician irony. Even so *El Bernardo* is amazingly rich in passages of scenic description, in intense local colour, and in a copious pomp of diction. Balbuena's exuberance will be found excessive by modern readers, and the very force of his emphasis, the clangour of his tone, become monotonous at last. Yet at his best, his resounding music, his brilliant hues and gorgeous eloquence defy the effect of time and the capriciousness of popular taste.

Cristobal de Mesa (1558?-1633), chaplain to the Conde del Castellar and a friend of Tasso and Ercilla, is the author of *Las Navas de Tolosa* (1594), *Valle de lagrimas y diuersas Rimas* (1607) and *El Patron de España* (1612). In these somewhat tedious versified exercises he shows to less advantage than in the *Restavracion de España* (1607), which teems with

[1] *Siglo de oro en las selvas de Erifile y Grandeza mejicana*, ed. R. Academia Esp., Madrid, 1821; *El Bernardo, ó Victoria de Roncesvalles*, ed. C. Rosell, 1851, in Bib. de Autores Esp., XVII.—See: M. Fernandez Juncos, *D. Bernardo de Balbuena, obispo de Puerto-Rico: estudio biográfico y crítico*. Puerto-Rico, 1884.

reminiscences from Virgil and Tasso. Mesa also made a Spanish rendering of the *Iliad* which has not been published.

A predecessor of Balbuena in scenic description was Eugenio de Salazar[1] (1530 ?-after 1601), whose *Silva de varia poesía* is in greater part unpublished. He was Governor of the Canary Islands, then *oidor* in Santo Domingo and later in Mexico. A facile versifier, his real merit rests on his *Cartas*, published in 1866 ; in these his gay light-heartedness and shrewd wit secure him an honourable place among letter-writers. In the epistolary *genre* ANTONIO PEREZ[2] (1540 ?-1611), Philip II's secretary, is a conspicuous

[1] *Cartas*, ed. P. de Gayangos, 1866 (Soc. de Bibliófilos Esp., 1); E. de Ochoa, 1870, in Bib. de Autores Esp., LXII; *Cartas inéditas*, ed. A. Paz y Mélia, in *Sales españolas*. 1902. II, pp. 211-276 (Col. de Escritores Cast., 121); *Silva de Poesía* [extract], ed. B. J. Gallardo, in *Ensayo*, etc. Madrid, 1889. IV, col. 326-395.—See : A. Mussafia, *Ueber eine spanische Handschrift der Wiener Hofbibliothek*, in *Sitzungsberichte der Kaiserlichen Akademie der Wissenschaften*, LVI (1867), pp. 83-124 ; C. Pérez Pastor, in *Bibliografía madrileña*. Madrid, 1907. III, pp. 469-470.

[2] *Las obras y relaciones*. Geneva, 1631 ; *Cartas*, ed. E. de Ochoa, 1850, in Bib. de Autores Esp., XIII ; *Lettres d'Antonio Perez écrites pendant son séjour en Angleterre et en France*, ed. A. Morel-Fatio, in *L'Espagne au xvi*[e] *et au xvii*[e] *siècle*. Heilbronn, 1878. pp. 269-314.—See : *Coleccion de documentos inéditos*, etc., I, 1842, pp. 95-96, ed. M. Fernandez Navarrete, M. Salvá and P. Sainz de Baranda ; XII, 1848 ; XIII, 1848, pp. 365-393 and XV, 1849, pp. 397-553, ed. M. Salvá and P. Sainz de Baranda ; LVI, 1870, ed. Marqués de Miraflores and M. Salvá ; Mignet, *Antonio Perez et Philippe II*. Paris, 1845 ; G. Muro, in *Vida de la Princesa de Eboli*. Madrid, 1877 ; A. Morel-Fatio, in *L'Espagne au xvi*[e] *et au xvii*[e] *siècle*. Heilbronn, 1878. pp. 257-268 ; C. Fernández Duro, in *Estudios históricos del reinado de Felipe II*. 1890 (Col. de Escritores Cast., 88) ; M. Hume, *El enigma de Antonio Pérez*, in *Españoles e Ingleses en el siglo xvi*. Madrid-

figure. His *Cartas*, written mainly after his flight from Spain, are models of ingenious phrasing. Perez rarely strikes a natural note ; from his circumstances he must be always begging or intriguing or acknowledging benefits, but he acquits himself in a singularly happy vein. His *Relaciones* (1598) are more remarkable for their manner than for their clear presentation of facts : Perez is too closely concerned in his tale of wrongs, too intent on stylistic problems, to give a simple and impartial account. He fails to enlist the sympathies that he sets out to win : both the *Cartas* and the *Relaciones* leave the uncomfortable impression of some ulterior view, and this lack of sincerity is prejudicial to Perez's real qualities : his courage, his great endurance, his powers of organisation and his gift of speech—' de una muy cortesana eloquencia,' as Gracian tells us.

Great historians are rare everywhere. The combination of learning, critical judgement and literary accomplishment which goes to make up their equipment is very infrequent. But it is found in JUAN DE MARIANA[1] (1535 ?-1624), the greatest of Spanish historians. A natural son of the Dean of Talavera, Mariana joined the Jesuits in 1554, passing his

Londres, 1903. pp. 167-203 ; A. Lang, *The murder of Escovedo*, in *Historical Mysteries*. London, 1904. pp. 35-54 ; A. González Palencia, *Fragmentos del Archivo particular de Antonio Perez* . . . in *Revista de Archivos*, etc., XXXVIII (1918), pp. 252-262, 411-420 ; XXXIX (1918), pp. 354-364 ; XL (1919), pp. 316-325 ; XLI (1920), pp. 136-144 ; XLII (1921), pp. 111-135, 293-312 ; Julia Fitzmaurice-Kelly, *Antonio Perez*. Oxford, 1922 (Hispanic Notes and Monographs. Spanish Series, VI).

[1] *Obras*, ed. F. Pí y Margall, 1854, 2 vols. (Bib. de Autores Esp., XXX, XXXI) ; *Historia general de España*, Madrid, 1780-1804. 3 vols. ; ed. V. Blasco and V. Noguera y Ramon, Valencia,

noviciate under Francisco de Borja at Simancas. He studied in the University of Alcalá de Henares, was ordained in 1561 and was then appointed professor of Theology at Rome. He spent nearly all his youth in teaching abroad ; he was professor at Loreto till 1565, in Sicily till 1569, in Paris next and—report says—in the Netherlands. It was not till 1574 that he returned to Spain. He settled down at Toledo and seemed to have before him a prospect of learned leisure. But this was not to be. The case of Luis de Leon was still in suspense. Leon de Castro had thrown out at Valladolid a cloud of suspicions against Arias Montano on the ground that his Polyglot Bible tended to interpret certain controverted passages in a Rabbinical sense. Mariana was appointed to report upon these charges. After an examination which lasted over two years Mariana reported cautiously in favour of Arias Montano's innocence. It is likely that the leading Jesuits looked askance at Mariana : none the less, his reputation for fearlessness was established from thence onwards.

Mariana had still to prove that he could write as well as he could sift evidence, and this he demonstrated in his *Historia de España*. His original idea was to supply a foreign public with information about Spain's

1783-1796. 9 vols. ; ed. J. Sabau y Blanco, Madrid, 1817-1822. 20 vols.—See : G. Cirot, *Mariana historien*. Bordeaux-Paris, 1905 ; G. Cirot, *A propos du 'De rege' des 'Septem Tractatus' de Mariana et de son ou de ses procès*, in *Bulletin hispanique*, x (1908), pp. 95-99 ; P. U. Gonzalez de la Calle, *Ideas político-morales del P. Juan de Mariana*, in *Revista de Archivos*, etc., XXIX (1913), pp. 388-406 ; XXX (1914), pp. 46-60, 201-228 ; XXXI (1914), pp. 242-262 ; XXXII (1915), pp. 400-419 [See also XXXIX (1918), pp. 267-287 ; XL (1919), pp. 130-140, 231-247, 418-430, 536-551].

past, and with this end in view he brought out his work in 1592 in Latin, which he chose as a sort of international language. This was a successful venture, so much so in fact that he acted as his own translator and published a Castilian version (1601-1608-1617-1623). He was thus enabled to enlarge and correct his history. Naturally he made some mistakes, and one of these was pointed out by Lupercio Leonardo de Argensola. Mariana did not accept the rebuke in silence, and his reply is interesting inasmuch as it reveals his aims and something of his methods. 'I never pretended to write a history of Spain in which every detail should be exact. That would be an endless task. What I strove to do was to put into readable Latin the materials which others had collected.' This is a candid avowal. It did not suffice for some critics who were bent on finding fault. Among these was a certain Pedro Mantuano (1585?-1656) who attacked Mariana in a series of *Advertencias* ... (1611). Mantuano had the impudence to say that when he was twenty-six he could have extemporized a history as good as Mariana's. Nobody took Mantuano at his own valuation. No doubt he succeeded in scoring some points against Mariana, whose work covered too much ground to be free from error : but we know that Mariana had not aimed at meticulous exactitude. Mariana's real strength lies in his co-ordinating power, his sense of proportion and, above all, in his admirable prose-style—a prose a little archaic in manner but full of pith and marrow. He is on a level with his theme, varies his writing with the events which he records and, as Ticknor justly says, has contrived 'the most remarkable union of picturesque chronicling with sober history that the world has ever seen.'

Mariana will be read in spite of his weaknesses in matters of secondary detail. These are unimportant in essence. They are blemishes no doubt. But whatever his weaknesses as a writer, Mariana was a potent personality as a man. This he had shown in the case of Arias Montano. He had other opportunities of displaying his fortitude. Ravaillac assassinated Henry IV of France in 1610. An attempt was made to prove that Mariana had taught the doctrine of tyrannicide in *De Rege et Regis Institutione*, which had been officially sanctioned and appeared in print in 1599. The Gallicans were at once up in arms, and caused the book to be burned at the Sorbonne in ignominious circumstances. The Jesuits took alarm, their General lost his head and disowned Mariana. Again Mariana got into trouble over his *Tractatus vii* (1609); three of these treatises, one on immortality, one on the supposed visit to Spain of St. James and one on the currency, led to their author's imprisonment at a later date. Mariana's views were doubtless orthodox. But he had not the knack of making friends; intrepid people seldom have. Yet, after all, these personal qualities are relatively important only in so far as they are reflected in his literary work. That work stamps Mariana as the first of Spanish historians, without a rival in his own time and without a successor fit to unloose the thong of his sandal.

But it is not to be supposed that the historical art perished with him, though the apostolic succession underwent some interruption. Garci Lasso de la Vega, *el Inca*[1] (1539?-1615), had an extremely picturesque descent. His father was said to be a

[1] *La tradvzion del Indio de los tres Dialogos de Amor de Leon Hebreo* ... ed. A. Bonilla y San Martín, in *Orígenes de la Novela*.

THE GOLDEN AGE

cousin of the great poet and his mother was a cousin of Atahualpa. The Inca is the first native American to play a part in Spanish literature. He was civilized enough to disbelieve in the striking legends of the native races; he was not well enough trained to analyze the Spanish version of the invaders' exploits. This was perhaps comprehensible and accounts for the uncritical tendency of the Inca's talent. He began by translating (1590) Leon Hebreo's neo-platonic treatise: his version was placed on the Index. He turned to historical themes in *La Florida del Ynca* (1605), where he describes Hernando de Soto's expedition, and wrote about his own ancestors in the *Comentarios reales que tratan de el origen de los Incas . . .* (1609-1617). The Inca failed to write satisfactory history, but we are indebted to him for a glowing rhetorical account of picturesque events, and for the record of what he took to be facts but are really rather contributions to Indian folklore—a matter of which one would know next to nothing were it not for his expansive confidences.

In contrast to the Inca's compositions is the work of Luis Cabrera de Córdoba [1] (1559-1623)—*Relaciones de las cosas sucedidas en la Corte de España, desde 1599*

1915. IV, pp. 278-459 (Nueva Bib. de Autores Esp., 21); *Los Comentarios reales de los incas*, ed. H. H. Urteaga [Introduction by J. de la Riva Agüero], Lima, 1918. 2 vols.—See: J. de la Riva Agüero, in *La Historia en el Perú*. Lima, 1910; J. de la Riva Agüero, *Elogio del inca Garcilaso*, in *Revista Universitaria* (Lima), I (1916), pp. 335-412; Julia Fitzmaurice-Kelly, *El Inca Garcilaso de la Vega*. Oxford, 1921 (Hispanic Notes and Monographs. Spanish Series, II).

[1] *Felipe segundo, rey de España*. Madrid, 1876-1877. 4 vols.; *Relaciones*, etc. Madrid, 1857.—See: C. Pérez Pastor, in *Bibliografía madrileña*. Madrid, 1906. II, pp. 193, 445 and 474-477.

hasta 1614, a bald but useful account which ends on July 6, 1614. This was not printed until 1857, and can therefore not have exercised much contemporary influence. But Cabrera de Córdoba had theoretical views which he advanced in his *De Historia, para entenderla y escrivirla* (1611) and he gave a practical example in his *Filipe Segvndo Rey de España* (1619), which stops abruptly at the year 1583. Cabrera de Córdoba perhaps might have written a scholarly monograph. He was too near the subject of his theme to write history in the true sense. But he is mostly exceedingly accurate and recognizes that exactitude, in the measure of the possible, is a supreme virtue in the historian. And he writes with a dry precision which has every merit except that of being readable.

A typical Spanish heterodox of this period was Cipriano de Valera[1] (1532?-1625), a monk of San Isidro del Campo. He was a fellow-student of Arias Montano at Seville, and after adopting the reformed doctrines fled in 1557 to Geneva where he was received into the Italian Church. Thence he went to England, took a degree at Cambridge, was elected Fellow of Magdalene sometime between 1560 and 1563 and married an Englishwoman. He published in London a Castilian version of the New Testament in 1596 and of the whole Bible at Amsterdam in 1602. This rendering is based on the translation (1569) made by Casiodoro de Reyna (d. 1582 ?), but Valera's recast has the distinction of style. In the opposite camp are to be found the Jesuit Pedro de Rivadeneyra[2]

[1] See: M. Menéndez y Pelayo, in *Historia de los Heterodoxos españoles*. Madrid, 1880. II, pp. 491-497.

[2] *Obras escogidas*, ed. V. de la Fuente, 1868 (Bib. de Autores Esp., LX).

THE GOLDEN AGE

(1527-1611), a competent prose-writer and a formidable polemist in his *Tratado de la Religion y Virtudes que deue tener el Principe Christiano* ... (1595) directed at Machiavelli, Bodin and others; the Augustinian Juan Marquez (1564-1621), who follows much the same lines in *El Governador Christiano* ... (1612) written in eloquent and flowing Castilian; the Jeronimian friar José de Sigüenza[1] (1544?-1606), whose *Historia de la Orden de San Geronimo* (1595-1600-1605) is an admirable specimen of artistic prose, and the Jesuit Martin de Roa (1555-1637?), author of *El Estado de las almas de purgatorio* (1619), which reveals the same excellent qualities of style.

Among the humanists may be mentioned the ecclesiast Bernardo Aldrete (1560?-1641), canon of Córdoba, who wrote *Del origen, y principio de la lengva Castellana ò Romance que oi se usa en España* (1606) and *Varias antigvedades de España, Africa y otras provincias* (1614). Aldrete has not a great gift of critical perception, but he combines intellectual curiosity with a clear prose-style. To Sebastian de Cobarruuias Orozco[2] (d. 1613), canon of Cuenca, is due the *Tesoro de la lengva castellana, o española* (1611), the only

---

[1] *Historia de la Orden de San Jerónimo*, 2nd ed. J. Catalina García, 1907-1909. 2 vols. (Nueva Bib. de Autores Esp., 8, 12); *La historia del rey de los reyes y señor de los señores*, ed. L. Villalba Muñoz, El Escorial [1917], 3 vols.

[2] See: C. Pérez Pastor, in *Bibliografía madrileña*. Madrid, 1906, II, pp. 197-200; J. M. Hill, *Index verborum de Covarruvias Orozco: Tesoro de la Lengva castellana, o Española*. Madrid, 1674-1675. 1921 (Indiana University Studies, VIII); A. González Palencia, *Datos biográficos del licenciado Sebastián de Covarrubias y Horozco*, in *Boletín de la R. Academia Esp.*, XII (1925), pp. 39-72, 217-245 (to be continued).

good Spanish dictionary published since the time of Lebrixa. Lastly it should be said that a certain originality of thought characterizes the work of Alonso Lopez[1] (called *Pinciano* from the Latin name, *Pincia*, of his birthplace Valladolid), physician to Maria, widow of Maximilian II. He composed a juvenile epic, *El Pelayo*, published in 1605, and the *Philosophia antigva poetica* (1596). This is really a commentary on Aristotle's *Poetica* and at the same time a protest in favour of the classical tradition and against the romantic movement headed by Lope. It is marked by a singular independence of spirit, a fairly catholic taste, acute observation, wide learning, a style archaic and somewhat colourless but exact and adequate to didactic purpose.

[1] *Filosofía antigua poética*, ed. P. Muñoz Peña, Valladolid, 1894.—See: C. Pérez Pastor, in *Bibliografía madrileña*. Madrid, 1907. III, p. 421.

X

THE AGE OF CALDERON

AMONG the conservatives who sought to re-act against gongorism, the most delicate talent was that of BARTOLOMÉ LEONARDO DE ARGENSOLA [1] (1562-1631), rector of Villahermosa. His *Conqvista de las islas Molvcas* (1609) is uncritical but attractive: its polished style adds charm to the primitive and sentimental legends which form the main matter of the book. It was written at the request of the Conde de Lemos, who invited its author to accompany him to Naples. The invitation gave some offence to Cervantes, who had hoped that it might be extended to him. Bartolomé, who was appointed chronicler of Aragon in 1613 in

[1] *Poesías*, ed. A. de Castro, 1857, in Bib. de Autores Esp., XLII; ed. R. Foulché-Delbosc, in *Pour une édition des Argensolas*, pp. 76-180 [*Revue Hispanique*, XLVIII] 1920; *Unveröffentliche Gedichte der Brüder Argensola*, ed. L. Pfandl, in *Revue Hispanique*, LV (1922), pp. 175-188; *Algunas obras satíricas*, ed. Conde de la Viñaza, Zaragoza, 1887; *Obras sueltas*, ed. Conde de la Viñaza, 1889, II (Col. de Escritores Castellanos, 75); *Conquista de las Islas Molucas*, ed. M. Mir, 1891 (Bib. de Escritores Aragoneses, Sección literaria, VI).—See: A. Paz y Mélia, in *Sales españolas*, 1890. 1ª serie, pp. 379-383 (Col. de Escritores Castellanos, 80); R. Foulché-Delbosc, in *Pour une édition des Argensolas*, pp. 1-55 [*Revue Hispanique*, XLVIII], 1920; L. Pfandl, *Unveröffentliche Gedichte der Brüder Argensola*, in *Revue Hispanique*, LV (1922), pp. 161-173.

succession to his brother Lupercio, published in this official capacity the *Primera Parte de los Anales de Aragón* (1630), an account of the events from 1516 to 1520 in continuation of Zurita's work; but in spite of his unfailing grace of manner, Bartolomé's chronicle is too minutely detailed to be readable.

The two brothers were destined to survive by their verse: Lupercio failed in the drama, Bartolomé's historical ventures could not have saved his name from oblivion. When their *Rimas* were published posthumously in 1634, Lope de Vega gave them the seal of his approval, declaring that it seemed as if the brothers 'had come from Aragon to reform among our poets the Castilian language, which is suffering from new horrible phrases, more puzzling than enlightening.' Their model is Horace and their renderings of the ode *Beatus ille* and the satire *Ibam forte via sacra* count among the happiest. Their original work is characteristically pure in idiom and perfect in form, revealing a quality of delicate ingenuity which deserves recognition. Lupercio's manifold preoccupations left him less free to devote himself to poetry than Bartolomé, who unites with his brother's gifts a greater solidity of thought and a more rigid doctrine. A follower of Terence, dogmatic and intensely conservative, he sought for no applause but limited himself to his own circle: consequently he exercised little influence on his generation in spite of his sound theories and the standard of excellence that he frequently attains.

The Sevillan Juan de Arguijo[1] (1564?-1623), another of the Old Guard, continued the tradition of

[1] *Sonetos*, ed. J. Colon y Colon, Sevilla, 1841; *Poesías*, ed. A. de Castro, 1854, in Bib. de Autores Esp., XXXII; *Cuentos recogidos* ... ed. A. Paz y Mélia, in *Sales españolas*. 1902.

Herrera: but his admirable sonnets left no mark. Juan de Jauregui [1] (1583-1641), whose version (1607) of Tasso's *Aminta* as well as his *Rimas* (1618) and *Antídoto* are characterized by a sober purity of diction, in the *Orfeo* (1624) shews visible traces of gongorism. This tendency is exaggerated to excess in his rendering of Lucan's *Farsalia*, published in 1684, but begun in 1614. In this case, however, Jauregui may have merely reproduced the defects of his model, a gongorist in anticipation. Esteban Manuel de Villegas [2] (1589-1669), a native of Matute, gave proof of genuine poetic feeling in *Las Eroticas o Amatorias* (1617-1618), whose title-page bore the image of a rising sun and the arrogant device: *Me surgente, quid istae?* Villegas speaks of his 'dulces cantinelas' written at the age of fourteen, but Sr. Alonso Cortés is probably right in assuming that this remark applies only to the first twenty-two compositions in the third book of the *Eróticas*. Even so, this would reveal an amazing precocity, which is borne out by Villegas's adaptations from Anacreon. The young poet was not to

2ª serie, pp. 91-209 (Col. de Escritores Castellanos, 71).—See: B. J. Gallardo, in *Ensayo*, etc. Madrid, 1863. I, col. 284-289.

[1] *Poesías*, ed. A. de Castro, 1857, in Bib. de Autores Esp., XLII; *Aminta* [trans. from Tasso], Barcelona, 1906.—See: J. Jordán de Urríes y Azara, *Bibliografía y estudio crítico de Jáuregui*. Madrid, 1899; C. Pérez Pastor, in *Bibliografía madrileña*. Madrid, 1907. Parte III, pp. 204-224; M. Guillemot, '*L'Apocalypse*' *de Jauregui*, in *Revue Hispanique*, XLII (1918), pp. 564-581 [with 24 reproductions].

[2] *Las Eróticas, y traduccion de Boecio*. Madrid, 1797. 2 vols.; *Eróticas ó Amatorias*, ed. N. Alonso Cortés, 1913 (Clásicos Cast., 21)—See: A. Cánovas del Castillo, *Noticias y Documentos*, etc, in M. Menéndez y Pelayo, *Historia de los heterodoxos españoles*. Madrid. 1882. III, pp. 859-875.

fulfil the promise shown in *De un paxarillo* and similar pieces. Married towards 1626, Villegas took to the practice of law, fell into the net of the Inquisition, and was exiled in 1659 to Santa María de Ribarredonda because of light conversation concerning matters of faith. Nothing very grave was proved against him. A manuscript of satirical verses was confiscated by the Holy Office, and the last days of the poor embittered attorney were spent on a rendering (1665) of Boethius, an occupation which soothed the vanity that has led some to think Villegas a madman.

Francisco de Rioja[1] (1583-?1659), a canon of Seville, shone in his day with a borrowed lustre as the author of *A las ruinas de Itálica*, which appears to have been written in 1595 by Rodrigo Caro[2] (1573-1647); and of the *Epístola moral a Fabio*, now ascribed to Andrés Fernandez de Andrada, one of whose relatives was responsible for *El Arte de la Gineta*. Rioja published nothing in his life-time, but his *Poesías inéditas* (1797), his sonnets and his charming *silvas* to the flowers entitle him to a place in literature. Two minor poets who might have ranked among the saner influences of the period had they lived in Spain,

[1] *Poesías*, ed. C. A. de la Barrera, 1867 (Soc. de Bibliófilos Esp., 2); *Adiciones á las Poesías de D. Francisco de Rioja*, ed. C. A. de la Barrera, 1872 (Soc. de Bibliófilos Andaluces).—See: A. Fernandez-Guerra y Orbe, *La Cancion ' A las ruinas de Itálica,' ya original, ya refundida, no es de Francisco de Rioja*, in *Memorias de la Academia Esp.*, I (1870), pp. 175-217; A. de Castro, *La ' Epístola moral' no es de Rioja*. Cádiz, 1875.

[2] *Obras*, ed. M. Menéndez y Pelayo, 1883-1884. 2 vols. (Soc. de Bibliófilos Andaluces).—See: A. Sánchez and S. Castañer, *Rodrigo Caro: Estudio biográfico y crítico: trabajo de investigación sobre documentos inéditos*. Sevilla, 1914.

THE AGE OF CALDERON 357

are Francisco de Borja, Prince of Esquilache[1] (1581-1658), and the Conde Bernardino de Rebolledo[2] (1597-1676), who served in Italy before he was appointed Spanish Ambassador at Copenhagen (1648-1662). There he wrote the *Selva militar y política* (1652) and his *Ocios*, whose style is free from the extravagances of contemporary poets, but lacks lyrical spontaneity.

The founder of the Conceptist School is generally considered to be the Segovian Alonso de Ledesma[3] (1552-1633), whose *Conceptos espirituales y morales* (1600-1612) and *Juegos de Noche Buena . . . con vnas Enigmas hechas para honesta recreacion* (1611) were followed by the *Peregrinos pensamientos, de mysterios diuinos* (1614) of Alonso de Bonilla,[4] a native of Baeza. Neither poet was of the stuff to carry through an innovation and it fell to a man of genius, FRANCISCO DE QUEVEDO Y VILLEGAS[5] (1580-1645), who had

[1] *Poesías*, ed. A. Duran, 1851, in Bib. de Autores Esp., XVI, ed. C. Rosell, 1854, in Bib. de Autores Esp., XXIX, ed. A. de Castro, 1857, in Bib. de Autores Esp., XLII and ed. L. A. de Cueto (Marqués de Valmar), 1869, in Bib. de Autores Esp., LXI.

[2] *Poesías*, ed. A. de Castro, 1857, in Bib. de Autores Esp., XLII.—See: E. Gigas, *Grev Bernardino de Rebolledo: Spansk Gesandt i Kjøbenhavn 1648-1659*. Kjøbenhavn, 1883.

[3] *Poesías*, ed. J. de Sancha, 1855, in Bib. de Autores Esp., XXXV.—See: Marqués de Laurencín, *Un libro muy raro de Alonso de Ledesma, en edición no conocida ni descripta*, in *Revista crítica hispano-americana*, 1 (1915), pp. 147-149.

[4] *Sonetos, Villancicos, Coloquios pastoriles, Glosas*, ed. J. de Sancha, 1855, in Bib. de Autores Esp., XXXV.

[5] *Obras* [prose], ed. A. Fernandez-Guerra y Orbe, 1852-1859, in Bib. de Autores Esp., XXIII, XLVIII; [*Poesías*], ed. F. Janer, 1877, in Bib. de Autores Esp., LXIX; *La Vida del Buscon*, ed. R. Foulché-Delbosc, 1917 (The Hispanic Society of America);

ridiculed the bad taste of *culteranismo*, to be the leader of the *conceptismo* movement, the new literary plague. The *conceptistas* purposely eschewed the obvious, strained after ambiguous phrases and " points," toyed with ideas, playing with them as the gongorists played with words, subtilized them and laid upon words a greater burden of meaning than they could well bear. Praised by Justus Lipsius as one of Spain's glories, Quevedo had a distinguished university career at Alcalá de Henares and Valladolid. In spite of a club-foot, he was an admirable fencer and indomitably courageous. No sooner did he arrive in Madrid than he set the gossips agog by killing a panther which had somehow escaped into the street. At a later date he surprised everybody by disarming Luis Pacheco de Narvaez, the celebrated fencing-master, who became his enemy for life. A flash of illuminative wit and a self-consciousness of physical limitations appear in Quevedo's famous remark to Valerio Vicencio in *Su Espada por Santiago* (1628) : " He says that I am limp and am blind ; if I denied it—in view of my sight and gait—I should be lying from head to foot." Quevedo's readiness with his sword affected the course of his life. In 1611 he chanced to be in the Church of

Los Sueños, ed. J. Cejador, 1916-1917, 2 vols. (Clásicos Cast. 31, 34) ; *Epistola al Conde Duque de Olivares* [Ed. R. Foulché-Delbosc and A. Bonilla y San Martín], 1909 (Bib. Oropesa, 5)— See : A. Fernandez-Guerra y Orbe, *Vida de Don Francisco de Quevedo Villegas*, 1852, in Bib. de Autores Esp., XXIII, pp. xxxix-cxviii ; E. Mérimée, *Essai sur la vie et les œuvres de Francisco de Quevedo (1580-1645)*. Paris, 1886 ; R. Foulché-Delbosc, Notes sur le ' *Buscon*,' in *Revue Hispanique*, XLI (1917), pp. 265-291 ; James Fitzmaurice-Kelly, R. D. Perés, N. Alonso Cortés, V. García Calderón and H. Peseux-Richard, in *Revue Hispanique*, XLIII (1918), pp. 1-78.

THE AGE OF CALDERON 359

St. Martin and there saw a man behaving badly to a lady near him. Quevedo rebuked the offender, who resented this interference. A duel took place and Quevedo, having severely wounded his opponent, fled to Sicily. Shortly afterwards he became Chancellor of the Exchequer at Naples, where the third Duke of Osuna (1574-1624) was viceroy. This was a decisive step; henceforward Quevedo was immersed in politics and to some extent became involved in the Venetian conspiracy: disguised as a beggar he escaped from two sbirri who were told off to assassinate him. Osuna fell from power in 1620; Quevedo fell with him and was exiled to his estate at Torre de Juan Abad. When his period of banishment was over, Quevedo was made secretary to the king. This was a purely titular office. In 1630 he was exiled again, apparently because he opposed the appointment of Santa Teresa as patron-saint of Spain with St. James. This does not argue any pietistic preferences, and perhaps may be explained by the fact that Quevedo was a Knight of the Order of Santiago. Olivares, who knew that the satirist was hostile to him, manoeuvred to get him out of the way by offering Quevedo the embassy at Genoa. But Quevedo's silence was not to be bought, and to the Minister's annoyance the offer was rejected by him. Olivares's turn came at the end of 1639. Under the King's napkin there was found a copy of verses in which the sovereign was urged to get rid of his incompetent ministers. It was suspected, no doubt rightly, that the verses were written by Quevedo, who was seized at midnight and whirled off to the monastery of St. Mark in Leon, where he was detained in an underground cell for four years. Olivares fell from favour in 1643. Quevedo was released at once.

But it was too late. His spirits and health were completely broken, and though he lingered for two years more, he had ceased to be dangerous to his enemies. The old volcano was extinct, or at least only gave out intermittent flashes as in the remark on his deathbed about the music which his confessor urged should be played at his funeral : ' Let those pay, who hear the music.'

Quevedo began his public literary career in 1620 with a life of St. Thomas of Villanueva : twenty-four years later he wrote a life of St. Paul (1643-1644). These edifying efforts, like the moral works of the author, are practically dead. So are a great many of his political tracts, as for instance, the *Política de Dios* . . (1626), the *Memorial por el patronato de Santiago* (1628) and the *Primera Parte de la vida de Marco Bruto* (1644), which have lost their interest with the circumstances in which they were written. They are, moreover, curiously difficult to read because of their subtle and alembicated style. This defect, very obvious in Quevedo's serious prose-works, is much less discernible in his picaresque novel *Historia de la vida del Buscon* . . . (1626), which was written about 1608 and is often called *El Gran Tacaño*. A picaresque novel is not the place for literary posing or attitudinising : a tale of realistic incidents does not lend itself to fantastic freaks of preciosity. The narrative style need not be bald : almost inevitably it must be direct. And the *Buscon*'s style is very direct indeed. It gives the impression of one of the cruellest books in the world. The outlook is brutally sinister, there is an almost revolting love of cruelty for its own sake, a determination to force the facts and to spare no disgusting detail. The book is coarse, no doubt, but in acrid

THE AGE OF CALDERON

brilliancy of execution it has no parallel. Many of Quevedo's burlesque writings apart from his verse-compositions are picaresque in their inspiration; not only the *Cartas del Caballero de la Tenaza* (1627), but the *Libro de todas las cosas y otras muchas más* as well as the *Premáticas contra las cotorreras*. An attempt was made by Quevedo to infuse the drama with the picaresque element. The ground was prepared for some transplantation of the kind. The *graciosos* swarmed upon the boards, and in each *gracioso* there were at least the potentialities of a picaroon. Lope de Vega writes that he first introduced the *gracioso* into *La Francesilla* about the year 1602 when Quevedo would be about twenty-two years old. Possibly it was at this impressionable age that Quevedo wrote *Pedro Vazquez de Escamilla*, a dramatic effort which was never finished. He also produced a number of light and diverting *entremeses*. His best-known and most characteristic work is the *Sueños* (1627). These are really five in number, though most editions publish seven or eight; the last of the five authentic *Sueños*, according to Quevedo himself, is the *Sueño de la muerte*. *La Fortuna con seso* was written after 1635 and published posthumously; the *Discurso de todos los diablos, o Infierno emendado* (1628) is a continuation of the *Política de Dios* . . . not a vision; the *Casa de los locos de amor* is not by Quevedo : it was first ascribed to Lorenzo Van der Hammen, but is now thought to be by Antonio Ortiz Melgarejo. The *Sueños* belong to a more elaborate type of satire than the *Cartas del Caballero de la Tenaza*, and utilized the machinery of the vision (which had hitherto been used for edifying purposes) for criticizing the crimes and absurdities of the writer's own time : satirizing corrupt administration of so-called justice in *El alguacil alguacilado*, and ridiculing the swindlers of all classes in *El juicio final*. They attained an immense vogue, both in Spain and out of it. They were skilfully imitated by the Murcian cleric Salvador Jacinto Polo de Medina[1] in his *Hospital de incurables y viage de este mundo y el otro* (1636) and by Francisco Santos in *Dia y Noche de Madrid* (1663)[2] : they were done into French in 1627, into German in 1639, into Dutch in 1641, into Latin in 1642, into English in 1667 and into Italian in 1704. Strange to say, the *Sueños* were an immense success in Wales : Ellis Wynne published them in 1703 under an adapted form as *Visions of the Sleeping Bard*. This is a protestantized version of the *Sueños* of which at least twenty-three editions have been published.

Quevedo is too immitigably Spanish, too representative of the seventeenth century to please generally, and though his literary renown is high, his vogue has declined in consequence both in Spain and abroad. He has a reputation for extreme impropriety, and it is impossible to deny that he is extremely outspoken even for the age in which he lived. His more serious verse is marred by conceptisms : in a lighter vein he is always ingenious, daring even, full of force and grace. He attempted too much. He might have been great as a poet, as a novelist, as a philosophic writer, as a statesman or as a satirist. In any one department he would have excelled. Undoubtedly he sought to be all things at once. He never meets with direct disaster,

[1] *Poesías*, ed. A. Duran, 1851, in Bib. de Autores Esp., XVI ; ed. A. de Castro, 1857, in Bib. de Autores Esp., XLII.

[2] *Dia y Noche de Madrid*, ed. E. Fernandez de Navarrete, 1854, in Bib. de Autores Esp., XXXIII.

THE AGE OF CALDERON

but he seldom achieves an unquestionable success. Versatile ambition, like everything else in this world, has to be paid for; Quevedo paid a high price, but perhaps not too high. It must be admitted that he made a new departure in fiction and that, in the *Sueños* especially, he enlarged the scope and framework of the novel. Excelling in caricature, he fell short of Cervantes in impartiality of vision and in broadness of sympathy. Cervantes's version of the truth is exact and disinterested. The exactitude of Quevedo's portraiture is less obvious, less convincing. He is not, perhaps, so concerned with fidelity as with exhibiting his own wit.

There were not wanting genuine Spanish efforts in the work of Alonso Gerónimo de Salas Barbadillo [1] (1581-1635), who led off before *Marcos de Obregon* with *La Hyia de Celestina* (1612), which continues the episodes of *La Celestina* and was adapted by Scarron in *Les Hypocrites* and recast in a scene of *Tartufe*. Perhaps Salas Barbadillo's best work is *El curioso y sabio Alexandro, fiscal y juez de vidas agenas* (1634), a model of sparkling wit which is little known, however, out of Spain. There seems to have been an increase of professional interest and a decrease of general interest about this time in the picaresque novel. In 1619 *La desordenada codicia de los bienes agenos* by a certain " Doctor Carlos Garcia," apparently a Spanish refugee, was published in Paris with a French translation by

[1] *Obras*, ed. E. Cotarelo y Mori, 1907-1909. 2 vols. (Col. de Escritores cast., 128, 139); *La hija de Celestina*, ed. J. López Barbadillo, 1907 (Col. clásica de obras picarescas, 1); *Entremeses* (14), ed. E. Cotarelo y Mori, in *Colección de Entremeses*, etc. 1911. I, pp. 243-302 (Nueva Bib. de Autores Esp., 17).—See: C. Pérez Pastor, in *Bibliografía madrileña*. Madrid, 1907. III, pp. 466-469.

the unfailing Sieur Davdigvier. Alonso de Castillo Solórzano[1] (1584 ?-1647 ?), the superior of Salas Barbadillo in the picaresque field, is the author of two novels, *La niña de los embustes, Teresa de Manzanares* (1632) and *Las Aventuras del Bachiller Trapaza* (1637), which were utilized by Lesage in *Gil Blas*. *La Garduña de Sevilla y anzuelo de las bolsas* (1642), translated in 1661 by Boisrobert, is one of the most diverting of Castillo Solórzano's picaresque stories. It shews an assured progress in technique, a greater faculty of arrangement and avoids most of the digressions in which contemporary novels abounded. Castillo Solórzano is also the author of the plays, *El Marques del Cigarral* and *El Mayorazgo figura*, upon which Scarron based *Dom Japhet d'Arménie* and *L'Héritier ridicule ou La Dame intéressée*; from *Los Alivios de Casandra* (1640) Scarron drew three out of the four stories in *Le Roman Comique*; the fourth he took from *El juez de su causa* by Maria de Zayas y Sotomayor (1590-1661),[2] whose entertaining *Novelas amorosas y*

[1] *La Garduña de Sevilla, y anzuelo de las bolsas*, ed. F. Ruiz Morcuende, 1922 (Clásicos Cast., 42); *La niña de los embustes, Teresa de Manzanares* and *Noches de placer*, ed. E. Cotarelo y Mori, Madrid, 1906 (Col. selecta de antiguas novelas esp., 3, 5); *Las harpías en Madrid y tiempo de regocijo*, ed. E. Cotarelo y Mori, Madrid, 1907 (Col. selecta de antiguas novelas esp., 7); *Tardes entretenidas*, ed. E. Cotarelo y Mori, Madrid, 1908 (Col. selecta de antiguas novelas esp, 9); *Jornadas alegres*, ed. E. Cotarelo y Mori, Madrid, 1909 (Col. selecta de antiguas novelas esp., 11); *Comedias* [*El Mayorazgo figura* and *El Marqués del Cigarral*], ed. R. de Mesonero Romanos, 1858, en Bib. de Autores Esp., XLV; *Entremeses* (5), ed. E. Cotarelo y Mori, in *Colección de Entremeses*, etc. Madrid, 1911. I, pp. 303-321 (Nueva Bib. de Autores Esp., 17).

[2] *Novelas* [*El Castigo de la Miseria, La fuerza del Amor, El Juez de su causa* and *Tarde llega el desengaño*], ed. E. Fernandez

exemplares (1637-1647) give a faithful picture of the manners and customs of the day. They may be, and doubtless are, coarse : Ticknor condemns *El prevenido engañado* for its ' shameless indecency ' ; on the other hand its wit and verisimilitude have caused this very tale to be imitated in *La précaution inutile* of Scarron, while it has furnished traits to Molière in *L'École des Femmes* and to Sedaine (1719-1797) in *La gageure imprévue*. Picaresque experiments were made by Antonio Liñan y Verdugo[1] in his *Gvia y Aviso de Forasteros* . . .(1620), a collection of tales revealing shrewd observation and written in a good prose-style ; and by Francisco de Lugo y Davila (d. 1660 ?) whose *Teatro popular* (1622) contains eight *novelas morales*, one of these, *De las dos hermanas*, was recast by Nicolas Lancelot in *Les Novvelles Tirées Des plus celebres Auteurs Espagnols* (1628) under the title of *La Dévote Hypocrite*.

Though the romance of the picaroon was wider in scope than the pastorals and the chivalresque novels, inasmuch as it gave greater amplitude to observation and was more closely allied to the facts of life, it had its limitations. There was no guarantee that the public would not tire of the non-heroic as it had tired of the excessively heroic. Obviously a literature of scamps,

de Navarrete, 1854, in Bib. de Autores Esp., XXXIII.—See : L. E. V. Sylvania, *Doña María de Zayas y Sotomayor*: *a contribution to the study of her works*, in *The Romanic Review*, XIII (1922), pp. 197-213 ; XIV (1923), pp. 199-232.

[1] *Guia y avisos de forasteros que vienen a la Corte* . . . , Barcelona, 1885 (Bib. clásica esp., 14) ; ed. [from the princeps 1620] M. de Sandoval. Madrid, 1923 (Bib. selecta de Clásicos Esp.).— See : J. Sarrailh, *Algunos datos acerca de D. Antonio Liñan y Verdugo* . . . , in *Revista de Filología Esp.*, VI (1919), pp. 346-363 ; VIII (1921), pp. 150-160.

however merry, could only have a transient vogue. A recurrence to idealism was certain. Even when the picaresque element was not cast aside, it was often used fantastically as in *El Diablo Cojuelo*; sometimes the rogue was suppressed as in *Dia y noche de Madrid* by Francisco Santos, a study in low life written in a style so infected by *conceptismo* as to be almost unintelligible. A return to romance is observable in the *Varia Fortuna del soldado Pindaro* (1626) by Gonzalo de Céspedes y Meneses [1] (1585?-1638), who had already shewn romantic inclinations in the *Poema tragico del español Gerardo y Desengaño del amor lascivo* (1615-1617), on which Fletcher drew for *The Spanish Curate* and *The Maid of the Mill*. Céspedes, whose first novel, the *Historias peregrinas y exemplares* (1623), had met with some success abroad, wrote an uncritical and conceptist history, *Primera parte de la historia de D. Felipe el IIII* (1631), published in Lisbon. He sought to attain an artistic unity and to eclipse the incoherence of the picaresque stories. It is, perhaps, not too much to say that he knew how to mingle the picaresque with the romantic.

A writer of versatile talent was the Jew Antonio Enriquez Gomez [2] (1602-1662?), also called Enrique Enriquez de Paz, who won some repute by his play *A lo que obliga el honor*. He is best remembered for

[1] *Discursos trágicos ejemplares del Español Gerardo...*, *Fortuna varia del soldado Pindaro*, ed. C. Rosell, 1851, in Bib. de Autores Esp., XVIII; *Historias peregrinas y ejemplares*, ed. E. Cotarelo y Mori, Madrid, 1906 (Col. selecta de antiguas novelas esp., 2).

[2] *Vida de Don Gregorio Guadaña*, ed. E. Fernandez de Navarrete, 1854, in Bib. de Autores Esp., XXXIII; *Comedias* [*Celos no ofenden al sol* and *A lo que obliga el honor*], ed. R. de Mesonero

the picaresque novel *El Siglo Pitagórico y Vida de Don Gregorio Guadaña* (1644), dedicated to the Marshal of Bassompierre (1579-1646). The book is coarse and ill-constructed, but the style, though not very good, is fairly direct. While gongorism invaded verse and conceptism raged in prose, the picaresque novels were generally free from these manifestations of a literary plague. This is the case with the novel in dialogue by Gerónimo de Alcalá Yañez y Ribera [1] (1563-1632), *Alonso, Mozo de mvchos Amos* (1624-1626) as well as with the more or less true autobiographies of Alonso de Contreras [2] (to whom Lope de Vega dedicated in 1625 *El Rey sin reino*); of Diego Duque de Estrada [3] (1589-1647), *Comentarios de el desengañado de sí mismo*; of the Cordoban Juan Valladares de Valdelomar [4] (1553-1618 ?), whose *Cavallero Venturoso*, finished in 1617, was not printed until 1902; and of the anonymous author of the *Vida y hechos de Estebanillo Gonzalez*,

Romanos, 1858, in Bib. de Autores Esp., XLVII; *Poesías*, ed. A. de Castro, 1857, in Bib. de Autores Esp., XLII.—See: J. Amador de los Rios, in *Estudios históricos, políticos y literarios sobre los judíos de España*. Madrid, 1848, pp. 569-607.

[1] *El donado hablador Alonso, mozo de muchos amos*, ed. C. Rosell, 1851, in Bib. de Autores Esp., XVIII.—See: T. Baeza y Gonzalez, in *Apuntes biográficos de escritores segovianos*. Segovia, 1877. pp. 185-188; G. M. Vergara y Martín, in *Ensayo de una colección bibliográfico-biográfica de noticias referentes a la provincia de Segovia*. Guadalajara, 1903. pp. 429-430.

[2] *Vida del capitan Alonso de Contreras*, ed. M. Serrano y Sanz, Madrid, 1900.

[3] *Comentarios de el desengañado de sí mismo* ... ed. P. de Gayangos, 1860 (*Memorial histórico español*, XII).

[4] *Cavallero venturoso*, ed. A. Bonilla y San Martín and M. Serrano y Sanz, 1902. 2 vols. (Col. de libros picarescos, 5, 6).

hombre de buen humor[1] (1646), which professes to be the autobiography of Piccolomini's page and buffoon. The descriptive passages in it are numerous, for Estebanillo Gonzalez covers more ground than any other picaresque hero. He is a coward and a drunkard throughout; he has been compared with Falstaff, but he has none of Falstaff's humane qualities.

Among didactic writers DIEGO SAAVEDRA FAXARDO[2] (1584-1648), author of the *Idea de vn principe politico christiano* ... (1640), is distinguished by a clear prose-style, free from conceptism. His purity of diction has been attributed to his frequent absences from Spain, but as the evil was widespread, Saavedra may be credited with resisting qualities of a personal nature. His *Republica literaria* is more interesting than his earlier work: it was first published under the title *Juicio de Artes y Sciencias* (1655) as the work of one Claudio Antonio de Cabrera: a recent discovery has established Saavedra's rights to its authorship. It is curious and not a little strange that no mention is made in this work of either *La Celestina* or *Don Quijote*. A greater name than Saavedra's is that of the Jesuit philosopher BALTASAR GRACIAN Y MORALES (1601-1658),[3] who professed in 1619, became professor and

[1] *Vida y hechos de Estebanillo Gonzalez.* Ed. E. Fernandez de Navarrete, 1854, in Bib. de Autores Esp., XXXIII.—See: E. Gossart, in *Les Espagnols en Flandre* ... Bruxelles, 1914. pp. 243-296.

[2] *Obras*, 1853, in Bib. de Autores Esp., XXV; *El texto primitivo de la 'República Literaria,'* ed. M. Serrano y Sanz, Madrid, 1907; *República literaria*, ed. V. García de Diego, 1922 (Clásicos Cast., 46).—See: Conde de Roche y J. P. Tejera, *Saavedra Fajardo*. Madrid, 1884; 'Azorín,' in *De Granada a Castelar*. Madrid, 1922. pp. 79-136.

[3] *El Discreto, Oráculo manual y arte de prudencia* and *El Héroe*, ed. A. de Castro, 1873, in Bib. de Autores Esp., LXV; *El Héroe*

THE AGE OF CALDERON

later rector in the College of Jesuits at Tarragona. His sermons, popular in their day, have not survived; nor probably have all his lay-writings. Many of these were published by his friend, the archæologist Vincencio Juan de Lastanosa (1607-1684?), and all, with the exception of *El Comvlgatorio* (1655) and *El Criticon* I, appeared under the pseudonym of Lorenzo Gracian Infanzon. Gracian's first work was *El Heroe* (1637), for which he drew freely on the *Detti memorabili di personaggi illustri* (1608) of Giovanni Botero (1540-1617) and on *L'Honneste-homme* (1630) of Nicolas Faret (1600?-1646). In this, as in *El Politico Don Fernando el Catholico* (1640), Gracian, like his predecessors Guevara, Rivadeneyra and Marquez, seeks to initiate princes in the art of governing. Two books said to have been dedicated to the prince Baltasar Carlos (1629-1646) are the *Arte de Ingenio, Tratado de la Agvdeza* (1642), recast as *Agvdeza y Arte de Ingenio* (1648), and *El Discreto* (1646), whose preliminary acrostic discovers the author's name. The latter work is the ideal of the perfect ' caballero ' : it is less ambitious and simpler in style than the ultra-conceptist *Agvdeza y Arte de Ingenio*, which reveals a wide range of reading, but its exaggerated subtlety of thought is only occasionally redeemed by flashes of good taste. Gracian's most famous book is perhaps *El Criticon* (1651-1653-1657): it was issued in three parts (the first of which came out under the anagram

and *El Discreto*, ed. A. Farinelli, Madrid, 1900; *El Héroe*, reprint of the 1639 ed. by A. Coster, Chartres, 1911 ; *El Criticón*, ed. J. Cejador, Madrid, 1913-1914. 2 vols. (Bib. Renacimiento, 3, ⁊).—See: A. Coster, *Baltasar Gracian*, 1601-1658, in *Revue Hispanique*, XXIX (1913), pp. 347-752 ; A. F. G. Bell, *Baltasar Gracián*. Oxford, 1921 (Hispanic Notes and Monographs. Spanish Series, III).

Garcia de Marlones=Gracian de Morales), and has been called the Spanish *Pilgrim's Progress*. Written twenty-one years before its English counterpart, its three parts correspond to the stages of man's life—the spring and summer of youth, the autumn of manhood and the winter of old age—and tell the story of Critilo's and Andrenio's travels through Spain, France, Germany and Italy. The satirical touches in which it abounds, but principally the fact that it was published without their official licence, caused Gracian's superiors to deprive him of his chair and to banish him to Tarazona.

Gracian's philosophy of life is best resumed in his *Oraculo manual, y Arte de Prudencia* (1647). It is doubtful whether any copy of the first edition is extant. There is a German translation (1862) by Schopenhauer (1788-1860), whose admiration for Gracian originated, perhaps, in a common bond of thought. If Gracian's pointed aphorisms seem to anticipate La Rochefoucauld (1613-1680), it is because both writers probably drew from the same sources: the Spanish philosopher lacks, however, the concise perfection and lightness of touch of the French moralist. Though Gracian may, to quote his own words, 'flaunt his unhappiness as a trophy,' he remains always dignified; his pessimism is not at all a pose, it is as personal as it is profound. A fine and delicate observer, he could when he chose express himself simply and clearly: his close relationship with conceptism led him astray. Gracian held that " Most men esteem that which they do not understand and admire that which passes their comprehension." This maxim he applied to his style and consciously compressed his meaning to the point of obscurity. Results have proved the falsity of his calculations. Gracian's

THE AGE OF CALDERON

conceptist style has not only undermined his authority as a critic but has alienated readers from him and to-day his books are read by a limited minority alone.

The *Centon Epistolario* [1] is a collection of one hundred and five letters whose subject-matter is largely drawn from the chronicle of John II. It purports to be the work of the bachelor Fernan Gomez de Cibdareal, physician to that king. The first edition is dated Burgos 1499. In reality the book is a literary forgery and was printed in Italy, a discovery which is due in great part to the researches of the philologist Cuervo. It is most probable that the *Centon Epistolario* was put together about 1630 by the Conde de la Roca, Juan Antonio de Vera y Figueroa (1583?-1658), who was at one time ambassador in Venice and whose family pride took the eccentric form of circulating a mass of forgeries to exalt the historic importance of the house of Vera. He shews ignorance of old Castilian and has disfigured his text by the introduction of Italian idioms and forms of speech. Nevertheless he has talent and a certain historic gift, and has produced an undeniably clever piece of work.

In 1623 there appeared the *Espedicion delos catalanes y aragoneses contra tvrcos y griegos* by Francisco de Moncada [2] (1586-1635), Conde de Osona. Gibbon (1737-1794) says with an air of resigned melancholy that Moncada seldom quotes his authority for a given

[1] Ed. E. de Ochoa, 1850, in Bib. de Autores Esp., XIII.—See: E. Gessner, *Zur Cibdareal-Frage.* Berlin, 1885; R. J. Cuervo, in *Diccionario de construcción y régimen de la lengua castellana.* Paris, 1886. I, pp. 50-53; C. Michaëlis de Vasconcellos, *Zur Cibdáreal-Frage,* in *Romanische Forschungen,* VII (1893), pp. 123-137.

[2] *Expedicion de los catalanes y aragoneses contra turcos y griegos,* ed. C. Rosell, 1858, in Bib. de Autores Esp., XXI; *Empresas y victorias alcançadas por el valor de pocos catalanes*

statement. This is perhaps excessive. Moncada is rather more careful than most contemporaries in quoting his references. He borrows freely from Ramon Muntaner, the old Catalan historian, but he quotes also Greek chroniclers. This concerns his substance. As for his manner he follows Mendoza, whose *Guerra de Granada* he undoubtedly read in manuscript. The *Espedicion* is extremely readable : the fact that it is based on Muntaner does not tell against it, for Muntaner had a first-hand knowledge of the events which he records and wrote with uncommon dash and fire. These qualities are reproduced by Moncada with an additional touch of dignity which he borrows from Mendoza. Altogether Moncada has been underrated, perhaps because he was rather closely followed in point of time by a historian who, though he was a Portuguese by birth, wrote in Spanish and on a subject which stirred general interest. This was D. Francisco Manuel de Mello[1] (1608-1666), whose *Historia de los movimientos y separacion de Catalvña* . . appeared in 1645. It was partly written in jail and was issued under the pseudonym of Clemente Libertino. Since 1580 Portugal had been annexed to Spain. Mello entered the Spanish army. In 1640 a rising took place in Cataluña as well as in Portugal. Mello at once rallied to Portugal. There he was detained in

y aragoneses contra los imperios de turcos y griegos, ed. [first redaction from the MS. in the R. Academia de Buenas Letras, Barcelona] R. Foulché-Delbosc, in *Revue Hispanique*, XLV (1919), pp. 349-509.

[1] *Guerra de Cataluña*, ed. J. O. Picón, 1912 (Bib. selecta de Autores clásicos Esp., 13).—See: E. Prestage, *D. Francisco Manuel de Mello*. Oxford, 1922 (Hispanic Notes and Monographs. Portuguese Series, III.)

THE AGE OF CALDERON

prison from 1644 to 1653, because he was supposed to be the successful rival of John IV in some love-affair: on a charge of murder he was exiled to Brazil in 1655. The accusations against him were almost certainly unfounded. Mello had universal ambitions. He wanted to be a great poet, a great soldier, a great prose-writer: he attained his aim mostly as a historian. He had his defects: a tendency to both *culteranismo* and *conceptismo*. Nevertheless he has positive merits of a very high order: the faculty of dramatic narrative with an exceptional knowledge of the minor side of events and an almost uncanny gift of impartiality. Mello takes rank as a writer of supreme excellence both in Portuguese and in Spanish and is no doubt one of the leading personalities of his time. Other historians came after him, but their defects are more pronounced, or, at any rate, their qualities have a greater admixture of alloy.

Among minor prose-writers may be mentioned the Sevillan priest Juan de Robles [1] (1574-1649), whose book, *El culto sevillano*, licensed by Quevedo in 1631, but not printed until 1883, treats of stylistic problems; the Carmelite Fray Gerónimo de San Josef [2] (1587?-1654)—whose name in the world was Gerónimo Ezquerra de Rozas—author of *El Genio de la Historia* (1651); and Jusepe Antonio Gonzalez de Salas [3]

[1] *Primera parte del Culto Sevillano.* 1883 (Soc. de Bibliófilos Andaluces.)

[2] See: J. Godoy Alcántara, 1870 [*Discurso*. R. Academia de la Historia]; M. Gómez Uriel, in *Bibliotecas antigua y nueva de escritores aragoneses de Latassa, aumentadas y refundidas*, etc. Zaragoza, 1884. I, pp. 465-470.

[3] See: M. Menéndez y Pelayo, in *Historia de las ideas estéticas en España*. Madrid, 1884. II, vol. II, pp. 380-384 (Col. de Escritores Castellanos.)

(1586-1651), whose *Nueva Idea de la tragedia antigua* (1633), a commentary on Aristotle's *On Poetry*, teems with ingenious ideas disfigured by an involved style. The distinguished bibliographer, NICOLAS ANTONIO (1617-1684), holds a high place among scholars through his *Bibliotheca Hispana* (1672-1696), which has proved an indispensable work of reference in Spanish literary history. His *Censura de historias fabulosas* (1742) reveals sound critical ability.

The Jesuit Juan Eusebio de Nieremberg[1] (1595-1658) writes a relatively pure if artificial prose in his *De la hermosura de Dios y su amabilidad . . .* (1641), in which a breath of mysticism is apparent. Sor Maria de Jesus de Agreda[2] (1602-1665), known in the world as Maria Coronel Arana, was at one time included among the mystics on account of the misleading title of her posthumous *Mystica civdad de Dios, milagro de sv omnipotencia y abismo de la Gracia* (1670). This work, which is really an edifying novel, had a great contemporary success, but it is now forgotten. Of more living interest is the nun's correspondence with Philip IV, which, beginning in 1643 and continuing during twenty-two years, is informed by a rare quality of strength and a remarkable appreciation of public affairs. A true mystic is the founder of quietism, Miguel de Molinos[3] (1627-1697), who enjoys a greater reputation abroad than in his own

[1] *Obras espirituales.* Madrid, 1890-1892. 6 vols.; *Epistolario*, ed. N. Alonso Cortés, 1915 (Clásicos Cast., 30).

[2] *Cartas de la venerable Madre*, etc., ed. F. Silvela y de Le-Vielleuze, Madrid, 1885.—See: P. Fabo, *La autora de la 'Mística Ciudad de Dios.'* Madrid, 1917.

[3] *Guía espiritual*, etc., reprint of the 1675 ed. by R. Urbano, Barcelona [1906].—See: M. Menéndez y Pelayo, in *Historia*

THE AGE OF CALDERON

country. He was born at Muniesa near Saragossa, was educated by the Jesuits and later received a living at Valencia. In 1665 he went to Rome, where he rapidly became the fashionable confessor of the day. There he published in 1675 his *Guia Espiritual*. It is a significant fact that at the time when this work, as interpreted by Mme. Guyon, was dividing public opinion in France into two camps, it should have been hardly known in Spain.

Before Lope de Vega died, he recognized that his successor as the autocrat of the Spanish stage would be PEDRO CALDERON DE LA BARCA[1] (1600-1681), whose biography has only been written quite recently. Like his famous predecessor, Calderon in his turn overshadowed all contemporary dramatists for nearly fifty

de los heterodoxos españoles. Madrid, 1880. II, pp. 559-576; H. C. Lea, *Molinos and the Italian mystics*, in *The American Historical Review*, XI (1906), pp. 243-262.

[1] *Comedias*, ed. J. J. Keil, Leipzig, 1827-1830, 4 vols.; *El Mágico Prodigioso*, ed. A. Morel-Fatio, Heilbronn, 1877; *La Vida es sueño*, ed. M. A. Buchanan, Toronto, 1909; *La selva confusa*, ed. G. T. Northup [*Revue Hispanique*, XXI], 1909; *La Española de Florencia*, ed. S. L. M. Rosenberg, Philadelphia, 1911; *Troya abrasada* [in collaboration with J. de Zabaleta], ed. G. T. Northup [*Revue Hispanique*, XXIX], 1913.—*Autos sacramentales*, ed. J. Fernandez de Apontes, Madrid, 1759-1760. 6 vols; ed. E. Gonzalez Pedroso [13], 1865, in Bib. de Autores Esp., LVIII; *Las ordenes militares*, ed. E. Walberg, in *Bulletin hispanique*, V (1903), pp. 383-408; VI (1904), pp. 44-66, 93-113, 134-258.—See: R. C. Trench, *An Essay on the Life and Genius of Calderon with translations*, etc. 2nd ed. London, 1880; M. Menéndez y Pelayo, *Calderón y su teatro*, 3rd ed. 1884 (Col. de Escritores Cast., 21); N. MacColl, *Select Plays of Calderon*, London, 1888; L. Rouanet, *Drames religieux de Calderon*. Paris, 1898; C. Pérez Pastor, *Documentos para la biografía de D. Pedro Calderón de la Barca*. I. Madrid, 1905; A. Ludwig, *Zu Calderons dramatischer Technik*, in *Studien zu*

years. An amiable man by nature and punctiliously polite as a rule, he made few enemies, but with all his gentleness, he seems to have been cold in temperament and, though he did not lack friends, it may be doubted whether any of them were ever admitted to his intimate confidence. His life was an unusually long one; his brothers died thirty years before him, and he survived all those of his own generation. He lost his mother when he was ten years of age and his father (who was secretary to the Council of the Treasury) died five years later. Calderon studied under the Jesuits at Madrid, went on to Alcalá de Henares and thence to Salamanca, where he read theology with the intention of accepting the living that was in the gift of the family. He abandoned this plan, however, and took to literature. Competing in 1622 at the literary festivities held at Madrid in honour of St. Isidore, he was complimented by Lope de Vega for 'gaining in his youth the laurels which Time generally confers together with grey hair.' He is said to have gone soldiering at this point of his career, but the evidence is far from convincing. In 1622 he and his brothers were fined for killing a noble's servant, Nicolas de Velasco, and in January 1629 he was concerned in another scrape. His brother, Diego Calderon, was wounded in a quarrel by the actor Pedro de Villegas (d. 1644). Villegas fled for sanctuary to the Convent of the Trinitarian nuns, where he was followed by

vergleichenden Literaturgeschichte, v (1905), pp. 297-322, VI (1906), pp. 41-76; A. Farinelli, *La Vita è un sogno*. Turin, 1916. 2 vols; E. Cotarelo y Mori, *Ensayo sobre la vida y obras de D. Pedro Calderón de la Barca*, I, 1924 (R. Academia Esp.); A. Valbuena Prat, *Los autos sacramentales de Calderón*, in *Revue Hispanique*, LXI (1924), pp. 1-302; J. B. Trend, *Calderon* [in the press].

THE AGE OF CALDERON

Calderon and his friends: the police interfered, and in the scene that followed, the nuns, so it was alleged, were rather roughly handled. This tale came to the ears of Hortensio de Paravicino who fulminated against Calderon and his companions in a sermon preached before Philip IV. The matter would probably have blown over, had not Calderon replied by inserting in *El Principe Constante* a passage ridiculing Paravicino's extravagant and unintelligible style. Not content with branding Paravicino's jargon as 'un sermón de Berbería,' he went on to identify the fashionable preacher by mentioning his name, ' y en emponomio Horténsico me quejo.' All Madrid giggled: Paravicino complained bitterly to the king and Calderon was imprisoned. He was soon released; his fame grew quickly and the little episode did him no sort of harm. He became a great personal favourite with Philip IV, who in 1637 made him a Knight of the Order of Santiago. In 1640 Calderon seems to have lost patience with a dull actor who retorted by wounding him during a rehearsal. In that year (1640), the rising in Cataluña took place, Calderon joined the dragoons and acquitted himself well. . His health broke down after he had seen two years' active service. He was invalided out of the service and was given a pension later. This pension was granted tardily and was paid unpunctually. In 1646, Calderon appears to have entered the household of the sixth Duke of Alba and to have remained with him some four years. In 1647, perhaps, his natural son Pedro José was born: of the child's mother nothing definite is known, except that she died about 1648: about this time too Calderon himself fell seriously ill. He took to religion, was ordained in 1651 and proved to be an edifying priest. He had meant to stop writing for the stage after his ordination, but gave way to the entreaty of Luis de Haro, the Prime Minister, who begged him for the King's sake to continue. However, when a piece of preferment which was about to be bestowed on Calderon was cancelled through the interference of some censorious busy-body, Calderon wrote a letter of protest to the Primate and made it clear that he would write no more *autos* till justice was done. The Primate perfectly understood. Calderon was made Chaplain of the Reyes Nuevos at Toledo in 1653, and for the rest of his life went on writing lay-pieces for the court and *autos* in profusion for the general public. His remaining years were comparatively peaceful, though he received in 1656 and 1662 attentions from anonymous heresy-hunters with which he could have dispensed. He became chaplain to Philip IV in 1663, and in 1666 was elected Senior Chaplain of San Pedro. He was no less a favourite at court in the reign of that pitiful person Charles II. Nevertheless when he died on Whit-Monday, May 25, 1681, he is said to have been very poor, perhaps because in 1679 an order in Council was issued granting him free rations on account of his eminent services, advanced age and great poverty. This is a perplexing incident, since there exists Calderon's will made less than two years afterwards, a will which shews him to have been very well off.

Calderon, like Lope de Vega, did not regard his plays as literature. He took no interest at all in his secular pieces. Two volumes of his theatre were brought out in 1636-1637, nominally by his brother Joseph, a third was published (1664) by his friend Sebastian Ventura de Vergara Salcedo and a fourth

THE AGE OF CALDERON

to which he wrote a prologue appeared in 1672. All these received Calderon's sanction. The same does not seem to have been the case with the fifth part (1677). In 1680, Calderon drew up for the seventh Duke of Veragua (1651-1710) a list of his secular plays: on this list was based the posthumous edition of his works (1682-1691) which was published by Juan de Vera Tassis y Villarroel (d. after 1701). With his *autos* it was otherwise. These he collected himself and issued in 1677 under the title *Autos sacramentales, alegóricos y historiales*: in these he took a justifiable pride. There is no doubt that out of Spain, Calderon is commonly thought to be a greater dramatist than Lope de Vega, and it is quite certain that he held his position in Spain itself far longer than Lope de Vega. Lope suffered because of his combined copiousness and indifference. His plays filled a huge array of volumes. They were issued by different publishers and were very hard to find. Calderon's plays were edited by Vera Tassis and could be obtained easily at any bookseller's. Lope could not be found complete anywhere. Tirso de Molina was still more inaccessible. Thus everything combined to concentrate attention on Calderon. Being accessible and being still acted in Spain, even during the latter part of the eighteenth century, when French influence was at its height, he came to be considered abroad as the leading representative of the Spanish drama. The chiefs of the Romantic movement in Germany, Tieck (1773-1853) and Schlegel (1767-1845), were exceedingly dogmatic and excessively loud in their praises; two great poets, Goethe and Shelley, were invoked as holding the same view. The exaggerated laudation spread to England and infected Trench (1807-1886), Fitzgerald

(1809-1883), and Alfred Tennyson (1809–1892). Calderon loses his miraculous halo now that we can compare him with his own most eminent contemporaries.

To an exceptional degree for so great a man, Calderon is given to borrowing ; for instance, the second act of *Los Cabellos de Absalon* is taken entirely from the third act of Tirso de Molina's sinister and terrible play *La venganza de Tamar*. From Tirso de Molina also Calderon borrowed in such plays as *A secreto agravio, secreta venganza* ; *El encanto sin encanto* ; *El secreto a voces* ; and possibly, as Stiefel suggests, in *La dama duende* and in *Casa con dos puertas mala es de guardar*. It took Lope de Vega more time to copy than to invent. His genius impelled him to creation, not always careful creation, but prodigal. Calderon's is more thrifty : he prefers to remodel something already in existence and his recasts are often most brilliant. Thus in *El Alcalde de Zalamea* he has converted one of Lope's headlong improvisations into an imposing work of art. That is true. It is also true that the central idea is Lope's and not Calderon's. Calderon perfects the details, burnishes the ornamentation, suffuses what he finds with an inimitable, imaginative grace ; but he does not attempt to meddle with the characters : these he leaves as he finds them in Lope's rapid sketch. He elaborated still further the conventions which Lope had imposed on the Spanish stage : the sentiment of passionate loyalty to the King, of uncompromising fidelity to the church, of feverish sensibility as to the point of honour. Moreover Calderon has an enviable gift of something which it would be unfair to call resplendent rhetoric : it is rather a glorious gift of enthralling diction. Archbishop Trench was not far wrong in comparing the speech of the Demon in *El Mágico prodigioso* with Milton. Manifestly the same comparison had suggested itself to Shelley, as his translation shows.

In tragedy, Calderon sometimes has magnificent moments as in *Amar después de la muerte* and *El mayor monstruo los zelos*. But in most of his tragedies, even in one so famous as *A secreto agravio, secreta venganza*, the basis of the play is a mere conventional code of honour, not a genuine passion. This makes it difficult to enter into the spirit of his tragic compositions. Calderon's verisimilitude is purely local. Hence it is now a limitation. He deals not with the abiding and the eternal aspects of human nature; but with the temporary and local aspects. Hence his appeal though strong is not universal, is not permanent. It is a world of blood-stained idealism. This glorification of punctilio makes Calderon very representative of his own age. He is also brilliantly represented in his cloak and sword plays, where the materials being always the same, the piquancy is in the presentation. It is for the playwright to subdue his public, or to transport them as the case may be by the adroitness of his manipulation, the novelty of his plot, the sparkle of his dialogue, the brilliant diversity of his episodes, the prolongation of a tense situation and so forth. Calderon is a master of all devices that go to make a thrilling play of this type. There is no need for character-drawing and as characterization is a weak point in Calderon's armour, one of his chief difficulties is got rid of. He is free to devote all his patient craftsmanship to contriving flashing dialogue, witty points, picturesque situations, startling episodes, amusing or poignant surprises. This type of play is based on an idealistic convention, and Calderon conforms to all the complicated rules of the game with a skill that is almost uncanny. He has only one serious defect in this *genre*. He has a superfluity of urbane wit. There is a grain of truth in the observation that Calderon is only interested in fine gentlemen or in *précieuses*. Calderon moved in the best society and passed much of his time in palaces and at court. He could not appreciate the rough and ready humour of the populace, and hence his *graciosos* have no vitality: their fun is so ingenious that it ceases to convey the passing illusion of reality. There is another point of weakness in Calderon's theatre. Few of his women are attractive, though they are clearly meant to be *simpáticas*. They are apt to be mannish, like Doña Mencia in *El médico de su honra*, and even in the cloak and sword plays there is something masculine in the *discreteo* of his heroines. One gradually perceives that Calderon knew very little about feminine character, that he simulates an interest in it solely for theatrical purposes and that his chief concern is to make personal beauty the theme of magnificent tirades and great poetic flights. No doubt he soars to great altitudes, but his flights are usually too long. Like most Spaniards, Calderon is far too copious. But in lyrical splendour he is unsurpassed by any Spanish poet and is surpassed by few poets in any language spoken elsewhere. Had he condescended to add more frequent realistic touches to his etherealized presentations, he would rank with the greatest dramatists in the world.

In one dramatic form peculiar to Spain Calderon ranks above everybody. As a writer of *autos* he is unapproached. The *auto* is a one-act play performed on the Feast of Corpus Christi and dealing exclusively with the mystery of the Eucharist. Its range is,

THE AGE OF CALDERON 383

therefore, extremely limited. Some authors tried to avoid the convention by introducing saints who were famous for their devotion to the Eucharist. This is a pious fraud. Such plays are not *autos* at all: they are *comedias devotas*. Calderon observes all the rules and conditions with great strictness and treats his solemn theme in a high spirit of devout art. He does not repeat himself unduly; his weakest *auto* is a success. And surely this is one of the greatest feats in literature: to impart a new artistic and poetic treatment seventy times over to a most abstruse theme. The *auto* was peculiarly suited to Calderon's temper and genius. He was much more interested in the mysteries of faith than in the passions of mankind; he was much more at his ease in inventing devout symbolism than in the presentation of human character. In the *autos* his figures are no doubt abstractions. But in abstractions he excels. He imposes them on us by virtue of his subtle and imaginative force, his sublime allegory, his ' vision splendid ' of the world invisible, his loveliness of versification, his outbursts of celestial raptures. It is most unfortunate for Calderon that the *autos* are little read in Spain and still less read out of Spain. It means that his greatest achievement is practically neglected.

Nevertheless Calderon has left his trace upon foreign literatures. In France and in England he was lavishly exploited. Thomas Corneille (1625-1709) was particularly active in this respect. *La Dame invisible ou l'Esprit follet* (1684) which he wrote in collaboration with Hauteroche (1617-1707 ?) is taken from *La Dama duende*, which also inspired d'Ouville's *L'Esprit follet ou la Dame invisble* (1642) and—through the French—Killigrew's (1612-1683) *The Parson's wed-*

ding. Thomas Corneille utilizes *El Astrologo fingido* in *Le Feint Astrologue* (1648) whence, by the way, Dryden's (1631-1700) *Evening's Love* derives; again he converts *El Alcaide de si mismo* into *Le Geôlier de soi-même*, and *Hombre pobre todo es trazas* into *Le Galant doublé*, which gave Colley Cibber (1671-1757) *The Double Gallant*; in the same way he uses *Amar despues de la muerte* in *Les illustres ennemis* and combines two plays, *Los empeños de un acaso* and *Casa con dos puertas mala es de guardar*, in *Les engagements du hasard*. Quinault and Scarron both laid Calderon under contribution. From *El Galan fantasma* Quinault derived *Le Fantôme amoureux*, just as he derived *L'Amant indiscret* from *El escondido y la tapada*. Scarron drew upon Calderon in *Le Gardien de soi-même* and in *La fausse apparence*, the originals of which are respectively *El Alcaide de si mismo* and *No siempre lo peor es cierto*; in collaboration with Tristan (1601-1655) he based on *Lances de amor y fortuna* the comedy *Les coups de l'amour* which Quinault shamelessly published under his own name. These are borrowings by second-rate men. Some more eminent names might be added to the list. Possibly—though this is disputed—Pierre Corneille in *Héraclius*: and there are points of resemblance between his *Théodore* and *Los dos amantes del cielo*, as there are analogies between Armande in Molière's *Les Femmes Savantes* and Beatriz in *No ay burlas con el amor*. Lesage's *Dom César Ursin* is an adaptation of *Peor está que estaba*, which was used by the Earl of Bristol (1612-1677) who drew his *Elvira* from *Mejor está que estaba* and from *No siempre lo peor es cierto*. There is no doubt that *The Gentleman Dancing Master* of Wycherley (1640 ?-1715) is an offshoot of *El maestro de danzar*. Robert

THE AGE OF CALDERON 385

Bridges has two plays which are indebted to Calderon: *The Humours of the Court* is contrived from *El Secreto a vozes* in combination with Lope de Vega's *El perro del hortelano*, and in *The Christian Captives* a hint has been borrowed from *El Príncipe Constante*, which with *El monstruo de los Jardines* was also used in *Achilles in Scyros*. In Italy Gozzi (1722?-1806) owes *Il pubblico secreto*, and *Le due notti affannose ossia Gl'inganni dell' imaginazione* to *El Secreto a vozes* and to *Gustos y disgustos son no más que imaginacion*, which in its turn was suggested to Calderon by Lope de Vega's *Comedia de la Reina Maria*. In Denmark, Heiberg's (1791-1860) *Isabella eller tre Aftener ved Hoffet* which is based on Lope's *El perro del hortelano* is inspired in one scene by *El Secreto a vozes*.

Enough has been said to prove how great and enduring was Calderon's vogue. He has been overrated: very possibly. He may be too easily underrated also. He has not Lope's creative genius and shimmering humour; he has not Tirso de Molina's sombre force nor his gift of realistic transcription; he has not Ruiz de Alarcon's sense of measure and Terentian fineness. But, when all deductions are made, Calderon is still a very splendid figure in the retrospect of Spanish literature. Of one great preeminence he can never be deprived. He must always be regarded as the most stately and typical representative of the devout patrician and picturesque society in which it was his lot to move. Though Calderon does not incarnate the whole Spanish genius, he does present a temporary aspect of it with unparalleled splendour, with a barbaric intensity of romantic colour, with a most sumptuous scheme of decoration. In these qualities he is resplendent. Again and again he waves his magic wand, and before our delighted eyes there passes a gorgeous pageant—noble and debonair—in which a passionate nationalism, set forth with all the dignity of idealistic art, combines with 'the fair humanities of old religion.' It is his laurel and his garland to have imposed his personal impression, his transfiguring vision on a dull generation in a drab, prosaic world.

Though *autos sacramentales* continued to be performed for another seventy or eighty years, the secret of producing these symbolical plays may be said to have perished with Calderon. It was not the same with the *comedia nueva* which Calderon had inherited from Lope de Vega, and which he maintained unchanged in all essentials, though he accentuated some of its characteristic features. Lope de Vega exercized a general influence over the Spanish stage; but, autocrat as he was, he did not form a school of dramatists. His contemporaries—men like Tirso de Molina and Ruiz de Alarcon—were a stout breed, not at all docile, not at all overwhelmed by Lope's greatness, and not at all prepared to be humble imitators. They took from Lope what suited them, and each went on his way independently. Calderon was very differently situated. He had not, as Lope had, to spend the best years of his life in creating a national theatre in the teeth of vigorous opposition. He found it already created: he had Olivares and the King to back him; and there was no serious competitor in the field. Clever playwrights were numerous but they were not of the same stature as Tirso de Molina and Ruiz de Alarcon. Calderon's contemporaries were men of ductile talent, but of no great originality; in whatever age they had lived, they

THE AGE OF CALDERON

would have imitated any man of commanding genius, and living when they did, they naturally imitated Calderon. In this sense, Calderon may be said to have founded a dramatic school.

No doubt some of the followers of Calderon were a good deal more than mechanical copyists. FRANCISCO DE ROJAS ZORRILLA[1] (1607-1648), for instance, is deservedly remembered as the author of *Del rey abajo, ninguno* which appeared posthumously in 1650 and has often been reprinted under the titles of *El labrador mas honrado*, of *Garcia del Castañar* and of *El Conde de Orgaz*. In it the Spanish view of loyalty to the throne is glorified with uncompromising vigour. Rojas Zorrilla certainly handles the theme with poignant force, and in the whole range of modern drama it would be difficult to find a situation more dramatically effective than the scene in the last act—the scene where Garcia kills Don Mendo, almost in the presence of the King whom he had hitherto wrongly supposed to be Blanca's paramour and whom he had spared simply because he was the Lord's Anointed. There is

[1] *Comedias escogidas* (27), ed. R. de Mesonero Romanos, 1861 (Bib. de Autores Esp., LIV) ; *Teatro* [*Del rey abajo, ninguno* and *Entre bobos anda el juego*], ed. F. Ruiz Morcuende, 1917 (Clásicos Cast., 35) ; *Cada cual lo que le toca* and *La Viña de Nabot*, ed. A. Castro, Madrid, 1917 (Teatro antiguo español, 2) ; *Vejamen de Don Francisco de Rojas*, ed. A. Paz y Mélia, in *Sales españolas*. 1902. II, pp. 311-322 (Col. de Escritores Cast., 121). —See: A. Morel-Fatio, in *L'Espagne au xvie et au xviie siècle*. Heilbronn, 1878. pp. 603-676 ; E. Cotarelo y Mori, *Don Francisco de Rojas Zorrilla : noticias biográficas y bibliográficas*. Madrid, 1911 ; A. Castro, *Obras mal atribuídas a Rojas Zorrilla*, in *Revista de Filología Esp.*, III (1916), pp. 66-68 ; H. C. Lancaster, *The Ultimate Source of Rotrou's 'Venceslas' and of Rojas Zorrilla's 'No hay ser padre siendo rey,'* in *Modern Philology*, XV (1917), pp. 115-120.

nothing specially new in the *donnée* of the play ; it is little more than a variant of the *donnée* in *La Estrella de Sevilla*, but it carries much further the current theories as to the point of honour and the king's inviolability. Rojas Zorrilla follows Calderon's example in other ways less praiseworthy. Gorgeous as Calderon's diction is, it tends to slip into gongorism. Naturally Rojas Zorrilla's style is energetic and direct ; his dialogue is easy and natural in *Don Diego de Noche* and *Lo que son mugeres*. He could have cultivated this vein easily enough : in *Sin honra no ay amistad* he pauses to satirize Góngora and the *cultos*. But Góngora was the prevailing model and hence in *Los encantos de Medea* and in *Los trabajos de Tobias*, Rojas Zorrilla outdoes the extravagances of the gongorists. Like Calderon too, Rojas Zorrilla did not hesitate to use material found in the works of his forerunners. In *Del rey abajo, ninguno* there are traces of Lope de Vega's *Peribañez y el Comendador de Ocaña* and *El Villano en su rincon*, of Velez de Guevara's *La luna de la Sierra* and of Tirso de Molina's *El Celoso prudente*. He has thus all Calderon's defects : his power of selection shews that he has some of his master's high qualities.

With the exception of *No ay amigo para amigo* (the source of Lesage's *Le Point d'Honneur*), most of the foreign adaptations of Rojas Zorrilla's plays deal with the lighter comedies. His *Entre bobos anda el juego* was used by Thomas Corneille in *Don Bertrand de Cigarral* and by Scarron in *Dom Japhet d'Arménie*. From his *Obligados y ofendidos* derive Thomas Corneille's *Les Illustres Ennemis* and Boisrobert's *Les Généreux Ennemis* as well as *L'Ecolier de Salamanque* by Scarron, who based his *Jodelet ou le Maistre Valet* on *Donde ay agravios no ay zelos* and his *Jodelet duelliste* on *La traycion busca el castigo* and *No ay amigo para amigo*. *La Traycion busca el castigo* was used by Lesage in *Le traître puni* and by Sir John Vanbrugh (1664-1726) in *The False Friend* (1702). It is alleged that Rotrou drew upon *No ay ser padre siendo rey* for his *Venceslas*, but it is possible that both plays had a common source in the *Historia Bohemica* (1552) of the Bishop of Olmütz, Jan Skálaz Doubravky (1486-1553). The glorification of monarchical sentiment was a trifle too exaggerated for the court of Louis XIV and hence Rojas Zorrilla's most prominent play remained unknown in Northern Europe. As against the theory that he chose an impossible theme void of reality, it must be kept in mind that even in Philip IV's closing years the monarchical feeling lingered latent in the people. Some additional verisimilitude is lent to the play by the scene's being laid in the first half of the fourteenth century. It has an air of local exactitude, a dignity of conception, and an energetic eloquence which distinguish it above the other plays of Rojas Zorrilla, though among these are included some excellent pieces.

One of the best, and, perhaps, the most readable and entertaining of Calderon's disciples was AGUSTIN MORETO Y CAVAÑA[1] (1618-1669), who carried borrowing to the point of a fine art. Inferior to his senior Rojas Zorrilla in energy, originality of talent and

[1] *Comedias escogidas* (33), ed. L. Fernandez-Guerra y Orbe, 1856 (Bib. de Autores Esp., XXXIX); *Teatro* [*El lindo don Diego* and *El desdén con el desdén*], ed. N. Alonso Cortés, 1916 (Clásicos Cast., 32); *Auto sacramental* [*La gran casa de Austria y divina Margarita*], ed. E. Gonzalez Pedroso, 1865, in Bib. de Autores Esp., LVIII.—See: E. Carrara, in *Studio sul teatro ispano-veneto di Carlo Gozzi*. Cagliari, 1901; J. Mariscal de Gante, in *Los*

force of execution, Moreto had little power of invention; he required a hint to build on; once he received a primary impulse, he set to work with amazing skill, developed an extraordinary verbal brilliancy in the handling of his themes and shewed himself to be a most gifted artist. Moreto was evidently inclined at an early stage to an ecclesiastical career. It is on record that he received minor orders at some date before 1642. He brought out a volume of plays in 1654. By 1657 he was ordained priest and rose to be Chaplain to Cardinal Baltasar de Moscoso y Sandoval (1589-1665), Archbishop of Toledo; in this city he settled and apparently went on writing for the theatre. He died while he was busy on *Sancta Rosa del Peru*, a *comedia devota* which was finished later by Pedro Francisco de Lanini (d. after 1713). It is difficult to say why Moreto confined his talent to adapting existing plays. In *Trampa adelante* he proved himself to possess no small endowment of native force and wit. But Moreto's recasts are not to be spoken of disdainfully. In *El Parecido* Moreto would seem to have drawn pretty freely on Tirso de Molina's *El castigo del penseque*. Again *La ocasion hace el ladron* is written under the influence of Tirso de Molina's *La villana de Vallecas*. Moreto borrows *Hasta el fin nadie es dichoso* from Guillen de Castro's *Los hermanos enemigos* and from Castro's *Las maravillas de Babilonia* he takes *El Bruto de Babilonia*. Moreto naturally found it safe to plunder Lope de Vega. Sometimes the resemblance

autos sacramentales. Madrid, 1911. pp. 329-354; S. G. Morley, *Studies in Spanish Dramatic Versification of the Siglo de Oro. Alarcón and Moreto*, in *University of California Publications in Modern Philology*, VII (1918), pp. 131-173.

is partial as in *El Eneas de Dios y Caballero del Sacramento*, where only the first act seems to be taken from Lope's *El Caballero del Sacramento*. In other cases the plagiary is more marked. Moreto takes *La Adultera penitente* from Lope's *El prodigio de Etiopia*; his *El Príncipe perseguido* comes from *El Gran Duque de Moscovia*; *Como se vengan los nobles* from *El testimonio vengado*; *De fuera vendrá quien de casa nos echará* from *De quando acá nos vino* ... and finally *El valiente justiciero* is an offshoot of *El rey don Pedro en Madrid o El Infanzon de Illescas* (a play which used to be ascribed to Tirso de Molina, but is now attributed to Lope de Vega.) Sometimes Moreto utilizes two or three of Lope de Vega's plays at once. The most celebrated of Moreto's pieces is *El desden con el desden*. It contains touches from three—possibly from four plays by Lope: *La vengadora de las mugeres*, *La hermosa fea*, *De Cosario a Cosario* and, perhaps, *Los milagros del desprecio*. It might be imagined that a play derived from so many different sources would hang heavily. Nothing of the sort: the intrigue is developed with convincing skill, the passages stand out in bold relief and the dialogue, which is Moreto's own, shines with a sparkling wit characteristic of both the author and the situation. This is a feat of no ordinary dexterity. Molière afterwards tried to treat Moreto as Moreto had treated others. The result is *La Princesse d'Elide*, one of Molière's fiascos. Gozzi failed later when he attempted the same feat in *La principessa filosofa*. Moreto shewed to no less advantage in *El lindo Don Diego*: in this play, which is based on Castro's *El Narciso en su opinion*, Moreto has fixed the type of the fatuous male who thinks himself irresistible: the writer displays a rare comic sense and a marvellous skill in adaptability, as well as a genuine dramatic insight. Just as Rojas Zorrilla is but little known out of Spain, Moreto's vogue is likewise circumscribed. Still, *No puede ser* (a recast of Lope's *El mayor impossible*), is the source of John Crowne's (1640 ?-1703) *Sir Courtly Nice*; Thomas Corneille derived *Le charme de la voix* from *Lo que puede la aprehension* and he took *Le Baron d'Albikrac* from *La Tia y la Sobrina*. There are reminiscences of *El lindo don Diego* in Ludwig Holberg's *Jean de France*. It is a compliment for a Spanish dramatist to be reproduced, even indirectly, in England, France and Denmark. This compliment has been paid to Moreto. *El desden con el desden* was done into Swedish not so long ago. The play is not undeserving of its distinction. It is a notable instance of tact, of the transformation of disparate elements into unified art. It consists of fragments from without; but each fragment is admirably assimilated, and as a whole this selection of fragments is far superior to any one of the plays from which the fragments are borrowed. This is highly characteristic of Calderon's method, and entitles Moreto to a place near the master.

Antonio Coello[1] (1611-1652) came into notice in

---

[1] *El Conde de Sex*, ed. R. de Mesonero Romanos, 1858, in Bib. de Autores Esp., XLV; *Comedias* [in collaboration] [*El privilegio de las mujeres, El pastor Fido*], ed. J. E. Hartzenbusch, 1850, in Bib. de Autores Esp., XIV; [*También la afrenta es veneno, El Catalan Serrallango* . . . and *Los tres blasones de España*] ed. R. de Mesonero Romanos, 1861, in Bib. de Autores Esp., LIV. —See: G. T. Northup, *Los yerros de naturaleza y aciertos de la fortuna* by Don Antonio Coello and Don Pedro Calderón de la Barca, in *The Romanic Review*, I (1910), pp. 411-425; E. Cotarelo y Mori, *Don Antonio Coello y Ochoa*, in *Boletín de la R. Academia Esp.*, V (1918), pp. 550-600.

THE AGE OF CALDERON

1629, and the following year was complimented as a poet by Lope de Vega in *El Laurel de Apolo*. Apart from *El Celoso extremeño*, known because it dramatized one of Cervantes's *Novelas Exemplares*, the most celebrated work of Coello is *El conde de Sex*. This seems to have been acted first of all at the Royal Palace on November 10, 1633, and was printed in 1638. It has often been reprinted and has been ascribed to various authors, even to Philip IV. The only other play by Coello which calls for special remark is *Los empeños de seis horas*. Under that title it is attributed to Calderon in the *Comedias Escogidas*. With the title of *Lo que pasa en una noche* it is ascribed to Coello. Its English adaptation, *The Adventures of Five Hours*, by Samuel Tuke (d. 1674) was highly popular in its day. Pepys (1633-1703) saw it and wrote in his diary that it made *Othello* seem 'a mean thing' beside it. Few will agree with Pepys's verdict; but *Los empeños de seis horas* is a good example of ingenuity; its complications are certainly amusing and its dialogue is brisk. Another dramatist of similar type is Alvaro Cubillo de Aragon[1] (1596 ?-1661). Though he is credited with the authorship of some hundred plays, they do not appear to have been collected separately. Probably the most famous and, perhaps, the best of his pieces is *Las muñecas de Marcela*. This the dramatist included in his oddly-named work, *El enano de las musas* (1654). He displays great skill in the conduct of an elaborate plot, and demonstrates that he is a master of versification in his *décimas* and *redondillas*.

[1] *Comedias* (7), ed. R. de Mesonero Romanos, 1858, in Bib. de Autores Esp., XLVII.—See: E. Cotarelo, *Alvaro Cubillo de Aragon*, in Boletín de la R. Academia Esp., v. (1918), pp. 3-23, 241-280.

A play which came close on the heels of this in the matter of popularity is one with a title suggested by Luis de Leon—*La perfecta casada prudente, sabia y honrada*. It has often been reprinted since it appeared in the twelfth volume of the collection of *Escogidas* in 1658. It contains excellent specimens of character-drawing and revolves on a solid plot. Cubillo clearly excelled in portraying women. He shews this in the personage of Estefanía as much as in the analysis of Marcela's character. *El Señor de Noches Buenas* suggested to Thomas Corneille *La Comtesse d'Orgueil*, and there are vague reminiscences of it traceable in *Cyrano de Bergerac*. Cubillo also tried his hand at the historical drama, and in *El Conde de Saldaña* (a recast of Lope's *Las mocedades de Bernardo del Carpio*) treats Bernardo del Carpio more handsomely than Fate has been pleased to treat Bernardo on the stage.

The Portuguese Juan de Matos Fragoso [1] (1608?-1689) borrows as freely as Moreto, but to nothing like such good purpose. If he introduces changes of his own, they are always, without any sort of exception, changes for the worse. He drew largely on Lope de Vega, but never so successfully as when he passed off as his own work *La venganza en el despeño y Tyrano de Navarra* upon which Gozzi based *La punizione nel precipizio*, unconscious doubtless of its original, Lope's *El principe despeñado*. Two playwrights who shewed a gift for burlesque parody are Jerónimo de Cancer y Velasco [2] (d. 1665) in *La Muerte de Baldovinos*

[1] *Comedias* (7), ed R. de Mesonero Romanos, 1858, in Bib. de Autores Esp., XLVII.

[2] *Vejámenes literarios*, ed. El Bachiller Mantuano [*i.e.* A. Bonilla y San Martín). Madrid, 1909 (Col. " Oro Viejo," 2).

and Francisco Antonio de Monteser[1] (d. 1668) in *El Cauallero de Olmedo*. With these may be mentioned Manuel de Leon Marchante (1631-1680),[2] a dexterous writer of humoristic verse and of *entremeses* such as *El Abad del Campillo* and *El gato y la montera*; Francisco de Leyba Ramirez (1630-1676), a native of Málaga and author of *La Dama presidente*; the brothers Diego (1619-1664?) and José (1629-1672) de Figueroa y Cordova whose *La Dama Capitan* was utilized and placed on the French stage by Montfleury in *La fille capitaine*. Both have a certain *vis comica* deserving of praise and both have their full share of Calderonian ingenuity. Montfleury based *La femme juge et parti* on another Spanish play *La Dama Corregidor* written in collaboration by Sebastian de Villaviciosa (c. 1663) and Juan de Zavaleta,[3] who is also author of *Dia de fiesta por la mañana* (1654) and *Dia de fiesta por la tarde* (1659), interesting sketches spoilt by affectations of style. There were dozens more like these. Schack draws up a list of some eighty dramatists of this time, all Calderonians to a man. Like Matos Fragoso, nearly all these playwrights are so many 'sedulous apes': they have not the compensating energy of Rojas Zorrilla nor the engaging wit of Moreto. If they are remembered now and then, it is because some foreigner of genius has taken, or is supposed to have taken, a hint from one of their plays. Who would

[1] See: E. Cotarelo y Mori, in *Colección de Entremeses*, etc. 1911. I, pp. cii-civ, cxciv-cxcv (Nueva Bib. de Autores Esp., 17).

[2] *Obras poeticas posthumas*. Madrid, 1722; *La Picaresca*, ed. R. Foulché-Delbosc, in *Revue Hispanique*, XXXVIII (1916), pp. 532-612.

[3] *Troya abrasada* [in collaboration with Calderon], ed. G. T. Northup, in *Revue Hispanique*, XXIX (1913), pp. 195-346.

read Fernando de Zárate y Castronovo's (c. 1660 ?) play *La presumida y la hermosa*, if Molière were not said to have utilized it in *Les Femmes Savantes* ?

Two women-writers figure among the dramatists of the period : the Portuguese nun, Sor Violante do Ceo (1601-1693), whose *Rimas varias* (1646) rather than her plays assure her a place in literature ; and Sor Juana Inés de la Cruz [1] (1651-1695) who is a disciple of Calderon in the *Avto sacramental del Divino Narciso* (1690) and in *Los empeños de una casa*. She reveals herself a gongorist in her poems (1689-1700), whose first volume bore the remarkable title, *Invndacion Castalida de la vnica Poetisa, Mvsa Dezima ... Que en varios metros, idiomas, y estilos, fertiliza varios assumptos : con elegantes, svtiles, claros, ingeniosos, vtiles versos : para enseñanza, recreo, y admiracion*. Her talent and reputation for learning caused her to be known in her native country as the 'Fenix de México.'

The last considerable dramatist of the classic age is no doubt Antonio de Solis [2] (1610-1686), whose imitation of Calderon is unmistakable in such spectacular plays as *Las Amazonas* and *Triunfos de amor y fortuna*. Solis is always neat and often elegant;

[1] See : M. Menéndez y Pelayo, in *Antología de poetas hispanoamericanos*. Madrid, 1893. 1, pp. lxvi-lxxiv; A. Nervo, *Juana de Asbaje*. Madrid, 1910; P. Henríquez Ureña, *Bibliografía de Sor Juana Inés de la Cruz*, in *Revue Hispanique*, XL (1917), pp. 161-214.

[2] *Comedias* (4), ed. R. de Mesonero Romanos, 1858, in Bib. de Autores Esp., XLVII ; *Historia de la con̦uista de Mejico*, ed. C. Rosell, 1853, en Bib. de Autores Esp., XXVIII ; *Cartas*, ed. E. de Ochoa, 1850, in Bib. de Autores Esp., XIII ; *Poesías*, ed. A. de Castro, in Bib. de Autores Esp., XLII.—See : D. E. Martell, *The Dramas of Don Antonio de Solis y Rivadeneyra*. Philadelphia, 1913.

THE AGE OF CALDERON

he rarely improvizes, and his versification is carefully finished; but he never rises into poetry, and though his knowledge of court life and the customs of good society lends a certain value to *El Amor al uso* (adapted by Thomas Corneille in *L'Amour à la mode*) he does not succeed in being interesting. He first became known in 1627 with the play *Amor y obligacion*, which is not among his collected *Comedias* (1681). In 1637, he became secretary to the Conde de Oropesa and wrote *Euridice y Orfeo* to celebrate the birth of his patron's son. He was later appointed chronicler of the Indies and in 1667 took orders. His present reputation depends almost wholly upon his *Historia de la conqvista de Mexico, poblacion y progressos de la America septentrional, conocida por el nombre de Nveva España* (1684). Solis is not a great historian, but he takes pains and writes good, clear prose, though it is often cloying in its sweetness. He has a picturesque theme: this and his very readable prose style keep his book alive.

All the copying and imitating and borrowing which began soon after Calderon succeeded Lope de Vega, and which increased rapidly after Calderon took orders and wrote as little as he need for the secular stage, all these practices and the growing taste for spectacular plays, were sure signs that the old formulae were exhausted. It may be taken as certain—the history of the drama all the world over proves it—that when the public can only be enticed into a theatre by lavish displays of scenery, costumes, stage-carpentry and the like, that theatre is dying, and is as good as dead. These devices were introduced early in Philip IV's time; they became more and more general under his rule, and they came into full possession of the stage during the reign of Charles II. It was the deathknell of the *comedia nueva*. Yet the theatres continued open and staged adaptations of the old plays. It was plain, however, that no real progress could be made in that direction, and that a new source must be tapped. The earliest sign of an effort at novelty was made by Juan Bautista Diamante [1] (1625-1687), a copious writer of *zarzuelas* and light pieces which are very heavy reading. In *La Judia de Toledo*, he merely drew on Mira de Amescua's *La desgraciada Raquel* and on *Alfonso Octavo* (1659) by Luis de Ulloa Pereira (1584-1674). But as far back as 1657, Diamante produced a play entitled *El honrador de su padre*, an imitation— often a tolerably literal rendering of Corneille's *Le Cid*, a line from which suggested to Diamante another play, *El valor no tiene edad, y Sanson de Extremadura*. There is nothing at all strange in the fact that the Spanish public should be curious to see Corneille's play in Spanish; but it is distinctly curious to note that neither Diamante nor the Spanish public of that day seem to have been aware that the French play had any relation to Guillen de Castro's *Las Mocedades del Cid*. And yet thirty or forty years earlier Castro's *Mocedades* had been one of the stock-pieces of the Spanish theatre. Nothing could shew more clearly that the national drama was going out of fashion. Still it survived in feeble and impoverished forms: in the work for instance

[1] *Comedias* (4), ed. R. de Mesonero Romanos, 1859, in Bib. de Autores Esp., XLIX.—See: A. Fée, *Études sur l'ancien théâtre espagnol: Les trois Cid* (G. de Castro, Corneille, Diamante). Paris, 1873; H. A. Rennert, *Mira de Mescua et 'La Judia de Toledo*,' in *Revue Hispanique*, VII (1900), pp. 119-140; E. Cotarelo y Mori, *Don Juan Bautista Diamante y sus comedias*, in *Boletín de la R. Academia Esp.*, III (1916), pp. 272-297, 454-497.

of Juan Claudio de la Hoz y Mota[1] (d. 1714), whose play *El Montañés Juan Pascual y primer asistente de Sevilla* is the source of *Una antigualla de Sevilla* by the Duque de Rivas as well as of *El Zapatero y el Rey* by José Zorrilla; and of Francisco Antonio de Bancés Candamo[2] (1662-1704), its more prominent representative. Bancés Candamo held much the same position at the court of Charles II as Calderon had held at the court of Philip IV. His best known play is *El esclavo en grillos de oro*, which appears to have procured him many vexations. At the time of Bancés Candamo's death in 1704, there was very little doing in the Spanish theatres. It was not till the War of Succession was over that dramatists could get a hearing, and they had then to work under new conditions. A Bourbon sat on the Spanish throne; French influence dominated Spanish policy; French fashions began to spread in all directions; and playwrights, like the rest of the world, trimmed their sails to catch the breeze.

[1] *El castigo de la miseria* and *El montañés Juan Pascual, primer asistente de Sevilla*, ed. R. de Mesonero Romanos, 1859, in Bib. de Autores Esp., XLIX.

[2] *Comedias* (4), ed. R. de Mesonero Romanos, 1859, in Bib. de Autores Esp., XLIX; *Las mesas de la fortuna*, ed. E. Gonzalez Pedroso, 1865, in Bib. de Autores Esp., LVIII—See: F. Cuervo-Arango y González Carvajal, *Don Francisco Antonio de Bances y Lopez-Candamo* ... Madrid, 1916.

XI

THE EIGHTEENTH CENTURY

THE first thirty years of the eighteenth century as the last thirty of the seventeenth are a period of dreary literary sterility as well as of political decline in Spain. And yet the century began well. It witnessed the foundation of three institutions : the *Biblioteca Nacional* (1711), the Spanish Academy (1714), and the Academy of History (1738). These are still to-day the chief centres of scholarship in Spain. The Spanish Academy owes its existence to Juan Fernandez Pacheco, Marqués de Villena and Duque de Escalona (1650-1725) of whom Saint-Simon (1675-1755) said : " Il savoit beaucoup, et il étoit de toute sa vie en commerce avec la plupart de tous les savants des divers pays de l'Europe ... C'étoit un homme bon, doux, honnête, sensé ... enfin, l'honneur, la probité, la valeur, la vertu même." Its meetings, held in his house, were probably more lively than the assemblies of the French Academy; to judge from his peremptory fashion of dealing with Alberoni (1664-1752), nothing is less likely than that Villena can ever have imitated ' le silence prudent ' ascribed in a famous phrase by Boileau to Conrart. In 1726 appeared the first volume of the Academy's *Diccionario de la lengua castellana*, whose six folios were finished by 1739.

THE EIGHTEENTH CENTURY

Viewed by modern standards, the work has obvious defects but at the time of publication it was the best compilation of the kind in Europe and far in advance of its day in Spain. In 1771, the Academy issued its *Gramática de la lengua castellana* and in 1780 an abridged edition of the *Diccionario* which has since been reprinted fifteen times.

Poetry in Spain was mediocre during this barren age. Among the more accomplished versifiers was Eugenio Gerardo Lobo[1] (1679-1750), a romantic soldier whose *Obras poeticas liricas* (1738) contain much that is of undeniable interest. A characteristic figure is Diego de Torres Villarroel[2] (1693 ?-1770). A picaresque priest, once a professor at Salamanca, Torres was a clever charlatan whose startling confidences are included in his *Vida, ascendencia, nacimiento, crianza y aventuras* (1743-1758), a work more interesting than the hundred and forty-two sonnets, the halting verses, and the *coplas de repente* which he brought together under the title of *Juguetes de Thalia* (1738). A good for nothing person, and a poor poetaster, Torres is saved from oblivion by his happy gift of caricature.

The eighteenth century cannot be said to have been anywhere a good period for the drama. Europe was becoming nationalized and that, if a political gain generally, is not an unmixed good in art. Perhaps this need not be so. But it has been so in Spain.

[1] *Poesías*, ed. L. A. de Cueto (Marqués de Valmar), 1869, in Bib. de Autores Esp., LXI.

[2] *Obras*. Madrid, 1794-1799. 15 vols.; *Vida*, etc., ed. F. de Onís, 1912 (Clásicos Cast., 7).—See: A. García Boiza, *Don Diego de Torres Villarroel*. Salamanca, 1911; A. García Boiza, *Nuevos Datos sobre Torres Villarroel*. Salamanca, 1918.

Little by little the national drama lost ground. Spaniards began to travel further afield, and it became the mode for travellers to return home with a great contempt for everything national. The theatre felt the effect of this new craze. The forces against it steadily increased in strength and in volume. It was only a question of time as to when the Spanish theatre should be pulled down by Spanish hands. The fatal blow was struck by one who had been trained—not in French schools, but—under Italian influence. Early in the thirties, a young man named Ignacio de Luzan, Claramunt de Suelves, y Gurrea[1] (1702-1754), returned to Spain from Naples with a critical treatise among his luggage, a treatise entitled *Ragionamenti sopra la poesia* which he had written for presentation to the Academy of Palermo in 1728. Luzan, who had been a pupil of Vico (1668-1744), soon attracted notice by the versatility of his accomplishments: he spoke Italian as if it were his native tongue; a Greek and Latin scholar, he rendered into Castilian prose passages from Milton's *Paradise Lost*; he published a compendium of Port-Royal's *Traité de Logique* while he was attached as secretary (1747-1750) to the Spanish Embassy at Paris and he is said to have known German. Luzan saw with dismay that his native land

[1] *La Poetica* . . . ed. E. Llaguno y Amirola, Madrid, 1789. 2 vols.; *Poesías*, ed. J. de Sancha, 1855, in Bib. de Autores Esp., xxxv, and ed. L. A. de Cueto (Marqués de Valmar), 1869, in Bib. de Autores Esp., LXI.—See: A. M. Alcalá-Galiano, in *Historia de la literatura española, francesa, inglesa e italiana en el siglo xviii*. Madrid, 1845; F. Fernandez y Gonzalez, in *Historia de la crítica literaria en España desde Luzan hasta nuestros dias*. 1867 [*Discurso*. R. Academia Esp.]; M. Menéndez y Pelayo, in *Historia de las ideas estéticas en España*. 1886. III, parte I, pp. 176-191 (Col. de Escritores Cast., 38).

was dead to all things of the spirit and he entered into an arduous campaign of enlightenment. In 1737 he published *La Poética o Reglas de la poesia en general, y de svs principales especies*, a recast of his Italian work, illustrated with copious references to Spanish literature. The *Poética* aimed at ' subjecting Spanish verse to the rules which obtain among cultured nations '; based on Aristotle, it embodied ideas drawn from Muratori (1672-1750), Gravina (1664-1718), Crescimbeni (1663-1728) and Jean Pierre de Crousaz (1663-1750) and inculcated the theories of Boileau, of Rapin (1621-1687) and of Le Bossu (1631-1680). A posthumous edition (1789), issued by Eugenio Llaguno y Amirola (d. 1799), who had translated Racine's *Athalie* in 1754, reveals an increased anti-national spirit ; but though it is probable that Luzan with time came to hold more pronounced French views, it would not be safe to infer it from this fact alone. Llaguno y Amirola is known to have suppressed passages in Diaz de Games's *Cronica de don Pero Niño* and was suspected by Menéndez y Pelayo of having dealt in similar fashion by Luzan's work.

Unoriginal as the *Poética* is, no one who reads it can think poorly of Luzan's ability. A little before his time the less dexterous Thomas Rymer (1641-1713) in his *Short View of Tragedy* (1693) dismissed *Othello* as ' a bloody farce without salt or savour.' Luzan had more polemical skill. He abounds with compliments to Lope de Vega—' the extent, variety and charm of his genius '—he recognizes the seductive grace of Calderon, the contagious gaiety of Moreto. These are only the ingratiating preliminaries to a fusillade of criticism, the point of which is that Lope and Calderon with all their splendid gifts were uncultured children of genius, full of artistic defects ; old barbarians whose day is over and who must make way for children of light. The destructive part of Luzan's criticism is extremely effective ; whatever flaws there are in Lope, Calderon, and their school are pointed out with remarkable acumen ; the attack on gongorism is delivered with great spirít. It is when Luzan tries to set up a counter-theory of dramaturgy or poetics that his weakness becomes manifest. Like other destructive critics he resembles the avenger in Macaulay's poem ' the priest that slew the slayer and shall himself be slain.' He maintains that Homer was a didactic poet, that the aims of poetry and moral philosophy are identical, that the epic exists to teach the ideal of the perfect military chief and finally that the period of a play's action must coincide with the number of hours taken to act it. Luzan's rigorous reasoning reduces to absurdity the theories of Scaliger (1540-1609), of Jean de la Taille and of d'Aubignac (1604-1676). His *poética* was a literary manifesto, a call to arms like Victor Hugo's Preface to *Cromwell*. Furious replies were of course forthcoming ; Francisco Manuel de Huerta y Vega, Juan Martinez Salafranca and Leopoldo Gerónimo Puig (d. 1763), editors of the celebrated *Diario de los Literatos de España* (1737), though friendly to the new theories and to Luzan personally, thought that he had put his case too strongly. But the *Diario's* judgements were premature and in 1742 the review was suspended. One of its contributors, José Gerardo de Hervas y Cobo de la Torre[1] (d. 1742), who wrote under the pseudonyms of Jorge Pitillas and Don Hugo Herrera

[1] *Carta* and *Poesías*, ed. L. A. de Cueto (Marqués de Valmar), 1869, in Bib. de Autores Esp., LXI.

THE EIGHTEENTH CENTURY

de Jaspedós, proved an unexpected ally to Luzan and published in the *Diario's* columns (VII, 1742) a *Satira contra los malos escritores de su tiempo*, an elegant composition conceived in the style of its unavowed model Boileau.

In the meantime the national theatre had grown more and more discredited. The destructive criticism which Luzan had directed against Lope de Vega and Calderon told with still more effect on their degenerate successors, of whom Tomas de Añorbe (d. 1741 ?) may be taken as the type. In 1740, three years after the publication of the *Poética*, Añorbe printed *Paulino*, a tragedy purporting to be constructed on the French model, but really combining all the defects of both the French and the Spanish theatre. The tempest broke and Añorbe with *Paulino* went down in a storm of ridicule. The *nueva comedia* as an organised institution broke up in the tempest; but masses of wreckage floated about for a long while. The younger generation of writers rallied to Luzan and leaders of society attended the *Academia del Buen Gusto* (1749-1751), which held its meetings twice a week at the palace of the Condesa de Lemos, and arranged a plan of campaign and methods of propaganda. Prominent among its members was Blas Antonio Nasarre[1] (1689-1751), who under the pseudonym of Isidro Perales y Torres reprinted (1732) Avellaneda's *Don Quixote*, contending that it was a far better book than the genuine Second Part. In 1749 with the title of *Comedias y entremeses de Miguel de Cervantes, el autor del Don Quixote*, he reissued Cervantes's *Ocho comedias y ocho entremeses*

[1] See: M. Menéndez y Pelayo, in *Historia de las ideas estéticas en España*. 1886. III, vol. II, pp. 372-381 (Col. de Escritores Cast., 38).

nvevos and maintained that they were the worst plays ever written and that they constituted a deliberate attempt on Cervantes's part to burlesque Lope de Vega's theatre. Nasarre had the support of Agustín Montiano y Luyando [1] (1697-1764), the President of the Academy of History, whose tragedies *Virginia* (1750) and *Ataulfo* (1753), models of cold academic correctness, failed to attract. Montiano was no more successful with his earlier work, *El Robo de Dina* (1727), a dull and heavy poem, of more merit, however, than his plays. Luis Josef Velazquez de Velasco [2] (1722-1772), who later became Marqués de Valdeflores, made the initial mistake of ascribing to Quevedo the poems of Francisco de la Torre. His *Orígenes de la poesía castellana* (1754), which discloses views even more emphatic than those of his contemporaries, exists in an excellent German rendering (1769) made by the hispanist Johann Andreas Dieze (1749-1785).

The premature death of Luzan in 1754 deprived the reformers of an astute leader; the *Academia del Buen Gusto* was already dissolved; and the Gallicists seemed to be checkmated. But the position was really a stale-mate. The *afrancesados* (as they were afterwards called) had not lost heart. Though unable to impose their own plays upon the public, they organized a steady opposition to the performance of old plays; and a company of authors assembled weekly at the principal restaurant in Madrid, the Fonda de San

[1] See: N. Alonso Cortés, in *Miscelánea Vallisoletana*. Valladolid, 1912. 1ª serie, pp. 12-23; N. Alonso Cortés, in *Viejo y Nuevo*. Valladolid, 1915. pp. 170-180.

[2] *Poesías*, ed. L. A. de Cueto (Marqués de Valmar), 1875, in Bib. de Autores Esp., LXVII; *Juicios críticos*, ed. A. de Castro, 1854-1857, in Bib. de Autores Esp., XXXII, XLII.

Sebastian, to carry on the work of the *Academia*. One of the chief figures at these meetings was Nicolas Fernandez de Moratin [1] (1737-1780), a young professor who was born in the very year that Luzan published his *Poética* and who was for war to the knife against the old drama. In practice Nicolas de Moratin was no more fortunate than Montiano. In vain did he announce that his play, *La Petimetra* (1762), was written ' according to the strictest rules of art.' The managers in Madrid refused to stage it; provincial managers were equally coy and the public shewed no burning anxiety to read the new masterpiece in print. His tragedy *Lucrecia* (1763) suffered the same fate ; no company could be induced to play it, and the illiterate public continued to patronize the theatres where the old drama was given in mutilated forms or where clumsy imitations were produced by inferior playwrights. But Moratin had secured an important ally in the editor of *El Pensador*, José Clavijo y Fajardo (1726-1806), whose subsequent adventures with Beaumarchais's sister, Louise Caron, form the subject of Goethe's play *Clavigo*. With some ability and with great persistence Clavijo opened fire on the *autos sacramentales*, arguing that the performance of these plays was a deplorable survival, leading too often to scandalous scenes. His argument was plausible, and on June 9, 1765, the performance of *autos* was prohibited by ministerial decree. The Gallicists had scored their first success and it was followed by others. Aranda was now in power, and resolved to make a clean sweep of everybody and everything connected

---

[1] *Comedias* and *Poesías*, ed. B. C. Aribau, 1846, in Bib. de Autores Esp., II ; *Poesías inéditas*, ed. R. Foulché-Delbosc, Madrid, 1892.

with the old order. In 1766 he drew up a list of plays that might be given ; all pieces bearing the names of Lope de Vega, Tirso de Molina and Calderon were excluded ; a company of actors was formed on the model of the *Comédie française* and they were supplied with a stock of plays translated from the French to be performed at the Royal Palaces of the Escorial, La Granja and Aranjuez. Moratin, owing to Aranda's strenuous backing, got a hearing for his *Hormesinda* in 1770. But it was of no avail, the public refused to be moved by the tragedy, which was taken off the boards after a six nights' run. Moratin was a charming poet as his justly celebrated poems, *Las naves de Cortés destruidas* (1777) and *Una fiesta de toros en Madrid*, shew; but he had no dramatic gifts. He was at heart a Romantic, quite out of place in the Academic Gallican atmosphere in which he chose to envelop himself.

Josef Cadalso[1] (1741-1782), a cultivated young officer who had been educated in France and had visited England, Germany and Italy, produced in 1771 *Don Sancho Garcia, Conde de Castilla*, a tragedy in rhymed distichs, embodying the principles of the French classical drama. This was given at the Teatro de la Cruz, and though the part of the Countess was acted by Maria Ignacia Ibañez (1746-1771), who had the strongest personal reasons for wishing the play to succeed, the piece was a failure, and after five performances to empty houses was taken off. Cadalso's other plays, *Las Circasianas* and *Numancia* are now lost. While Cadalso was stationed

---

[1] *Obras*. Madrid, 1821 ; *Poesías*, ed. L. A. de Cueto (Marqués de Valmar), 1869, in Bib. de Autores Esp., LX-I; *Obras inéditas*, ed. R. Foulché-Delbosc, in *Revue Hispanique*, I (1894), pp. 258-335.

THE EIGHTEENTH CENTURY 409

at Salamanca between 1771 and 1774, he fell in with Diego Tadeo Gonzalez[1] (1733-1794), author of the short poem *El Murciélago alevoso*; from their joint association probably arose the beginnings of the Salamanca School. In 1772 they were joined by Melendez Valdés, then a boy of eighteen with the stuff of a real poet in him, whereas Cadalso's *Ocios de mi juventud* (1773) and *Noches lúgubres*, written at the death of Maria Ignacia Ibañez and inspired by the *Night Thoughts* (1742-1744) of Young (1681-1765), prove him to have been rather an accomplished amateur. His prose is better than his verse; it is simple and straightforward in the *Cartas marruecas* (1793) derived from Montesquieu's *Lettres persanes* (1721) and perhaps also from Goldsmith's (1728-1774) *The Citizen of the World* (1762); while *Los eruditos a la violeta* (1772), an ingenious prose satire in which Cadalso holds up to ridicule pedantic scholars, is undoubtedly his best work. Cadalso, who died at the Siege of Gibraltar, had talent but little originality: his greatest quality was charm; a delightful and lovable personality, he looked upon literature as neutral ground in which racial and political enmities should not thrive. It should be, as Spenser says:

The port of rest from troublous toil,
The world's sweet inn from pain and wearysome turmoil.

A contrast to Cadalso is to be found in Vicente Garcia de la Huerta[2] (1734-1787), whose *Raquel*

[1] *Poesías*, ed. L. A. de Cueto (Marqués de Valmar), 1869, in Bib. de Autores Esp., LXI; *El murciélago alevoso*, ed. L. Verger, in *Revue Hispanique*, XXXIX (1917), pp. 294-301.

[2] *Poesías*, ed. L. A. de Cueto (Marqués de Valmar) 1869, in Bib. de Autores Esp. LXI.

(1778) observes the unities closely, but in everything else—subject-matter, versification, monarchical sentiment—indicates a return to the old classic models. Huerta did not fulfil the promise shewn in this play and in his early poems (collected in 1771). He brought out the *Theatro Hespañol* (1785-1786), a collection of plays in sixteen volumes in which Lope de Vega, Tirso de Molina and Ruiz de Alarcon are entirely unrepresented. This publication, remarkable neither for good taste nor completeness, involved Huerta in literary controversies with Forner, Samaniego, Iriarte and Jovellanos : these affected his brain and probably broke down his health.

Felix Maria Samaniego [1] (1745-1801), a writer of Basque origin educated in France, produced in 1781-1784 the *Fabulas en verso castellano* drawn mainly from Phaedrus, La Fontaine and Gay (1685-1732) and excelling in simplicity, clearness and good sense. A year previous to their appearance, the Jesuit Manuel Lasala (1738-1806), a refugee in Bologna, had published a Latin translation of Locman's Fables. It seems improbable that Samaniego knew of this work and he could afford to disregard the Castilian version of it made by Miguel Garcia Asensio in 1784. The case was otherwise when Tomas de Iriarte [2] (1750-1791) appeared upon the scene in 1782 with the *Fabulas*

[1] *Poesías*, ed. L. A. de Cueto (Marqués de Valmar), 1869, in Bib. de Autores Esp., LXI ; *Fábulas en verso*, ed. James Fitzmaurice-Kelly, Oxford, 1917 ; *Obras inéditas o poco conocidas* ed. [with a biography], E. Fernández de Navarrete, Vitoria, 1866.

[2] *Obras en verso y prosa*. Madrid, 1805. 8 vols. ; *Poesías*, ed. L. A. de Cueto (Marqués de Valmar), 1871, in Bib. de Autores Esp., LXIII ; *Poesías inéditas*, ed. R. Foulché-Delbosc, in *Revue Hispanique*, II (1895), pp. 70-76 ; *Fábulas literarias*, ed. James

literarias, which he made the medium for his literary theories. A more versatile talent than Samaniego, Iriarte had begun his career with a tedious didactic poem, *La Música* (1780), which was praised by Metastasio (1698-1782), and in 1788 and 1791 he brought out two plays—now more or less forgotten, *El Señorito mimado* and *La señorita mal criada*. These are not works of genius, but they are replenished with wit and denote uncommon powers of satirical observation. The *Fábulas literarias* were utilized by Florian (1755-1794); they have won for Iriarte a rather exaggerated reputation as a humorist and moralist, whereas it is in his mastery of verse technique that his distinction lies. Iriarte wasted much of his talent and time in polemics with Juan Pablo Forner [1] (1756-1797), who attacked him in *El Asno erudito* (1782), a most ferocious libel which exhibits its writer at his worst. Forner was a formidable controversialist and under various pseudonyms—Tomé Cecial, Pablo Segarra, Silvio Liberio, the Bachiller Regañadientes—became engaged in so many quarrels that by a royal decree in 1785 he was forbidden to publish anything

Fitzmaurice-Kelly, Oxford, 1917.—See: E. Cotarelo y Mori, *Iriarte y su época*. Madrid, 1897; *Proceso inquisitorial contra D. Tomás de Iriarte*, ed. E. Cotarelo y Mori, in *Revista de Archivos*, etc., IV (1900), pp. 682-683.

[1] *Obras*, ed. L. Villanueva, Madrid, 1844 [incompleto]; ed. L. A. de Cueto (Marqués de Valmar), 1871, in Bib. de Autores Esp., LXIII; *El Asno Erudito*, ed. E. Cotarelo y Mori, in *Iriarte y su época*. Madrid, 1897. pp. 540-544.—See: M. Menéndez y Pelayo, in *Historia de los Heterodoxos Españoles*. Madrid, 1882. III, pp. 330-337; M. Menéndez y Pelayo, in *Historia de las ideas estéticas en España*. 1886. III, vol. II, pp. 82-99 (Col. de Escritores Cast., 41); L. A. de Cueto (Marqués de Valmar), in *Historia crítica de la poesía castellana en el siglo xviii*. Madrid, 1893. III, pp. 91-127 (Col. de Escritores Cast., 102).

without express leave. His hand was against everyone; only the powerful escaped his lash; he could express himself in terms of ridiculous flattery to these; he addresses, for instance, Godoy as 'Benefactor of the human race.' Forner might have rendered valuable services to his country. A scholar of some eminence, he reveals critical insight and a wide range of learning in the *Exequias de la lengua castellana*, but he lacked taste and preferred to dissipate his gifts in rancorous attacks on his contemporaries.

BENITO GERÓNIMO FEYJOO Y MONTENEGRO [1] (1676-1764) gives evidence of markedly French sympathies in his *Theatro critico universal* (1726-1739) and *Cartas eruditas y curiosas* (1742-1760); these two works—written in a gallicized style—exposed many current errors and were deservedly successful in Spain. Shortly after the appearance of the first volumes, an *Anti-theatro critico* (1729-1731), now completely forgotten, was brought out by Salvador Joseph Mañer (d. 1751). Feyjoo had intelligence and intellectual curiosity; he was careful to observe an attitude of mental reserve amounting to scepticism on matters of which he was not sure: on others his insufferable airs of infallibility

---

[1] *Teatro crítico universal*. Madrid, 1765. 8 vols.; *Obras apologéticas*. Madrid, 1765; *Cartas eruditas y curiosas*. Madrid, 1765. 5 vols.; *Obras escogidas*, ed. V. de la Fuente, 1863 (Bib. de Autores Esp., LVI).—See: J. Sempere y Guarinos, in *Ensayo de una biblioteca española de los mejores escritores del reynado de Carlos III*. Madrid, 1786, III, pp. 19-46; E. Pardo Bazán, *Examen crítico de las obras del P. Maestro Feijóo*. Madrid, 1877; M. Menéndez y Pelayo, in *Historia de los heterodoxos españoles*. Madrid, 1881. III, pp. 67-82; M. Menéndez y Pelayo, in *Historia de las ideas estéticas en España*. 1886. III, vol. I, pp. 159-175 (Col. de Escritores Cast., 38); M. Morayta, *El Padre Feyjóo y sus obras*. Valencia, 1913.

THE EIGHTEENTH CENTURY 413

combined with his sharp tongue made him many enemies. These were not backward in bringing against him a charge of unorthodoxy. The Inquisition found the accusation baseless and Feyjoo was protected from further attacks by a royal order issued in 1780. His *Theatro critico universal* owed much to the careful revision of a friend and champion, the Benedictine Martin Sarmiento[1] (1695-1771), who issued in 1732 the *Demonstracion critico-apologetica del theatro critico universal*. Sarmiento, who had more varied interests than Feyjoo and whose botanical studies won admiration from Linné, was as modest as he was unselfish in helping others. He shrank from the publicity of the press and his reputation rests on the *Memorias para la historia de la poesia, y poetas españoles* (1775), a work which was printed posthumously and which marks a new point of departure in the study of Spanish literary history.

The eighteenth century is practically a blank in *belles lettres* as far as Spain is concerned. Only one novel survives from this disastrous age and it may be regarded as continuing in some sort the picaresque tradition. This is the *Historia del famoso Predicador Fray Gerundio de Campazas, alias Zotes* (1758), which the Jesuit JOSEF FRANCISCO DE ISLA[2] (1703-1781) issued under the name of Francisco Lobon de Salazar, beneficiary of Aguilar and *cura* of Villagarcía de

[1] See: A. López Peláez, *El gran Gallego*. La Coruña, 1895; A. López Peláez, *Los escritos de Sarmiento y el siglo de Feijoo*. La Coruña, 1901.

[2] *Obras escogidas*, ed. P. F. Monlau, 1850 (Bib. de Autores Esp., XV); *Fray Gerundio de Campazas*, ed. D. E. Lidforss, Leipzig, 1885. 2 vols. (Col. de Autores Esp., 42, 43).—See: A. Ferrer del Rio and J. E. Hartzenbusch, *La oratoria sagrada española en el siglo xviii*, 1853 [*Discursos*. R. Academia Esp.];

Campos. Isla, who was a native of Leon, shared in the banishment from Spain of his order (February 27, 1767) : he established himself in Bologna and remained there until his death. The *Cartas familiares* (1785-1790), written during his exile, shew him to be a master of the epistolary style and reveal an aspect of his character unsuspected in his other work. He began by publishing two letters in 1725 on the death of two nobles. These have no literary importance. His satirical gift is first displayed in the *Triunfo del amor y de la lealtad, Dia grande de Navarra* (1746), a burlesque description of the ceremonies held at Pamplona in honour of Ferdinand VI. Those who were responsible for the proceedings were immensely gratified : it only dawned upon them some weeks later that they had been the victims of Isla's sly humour and their protests were so vehement that the Jesuit had to leave Pamplona. The incident seems to have done Isla no sort of harm, and he soon became known as a preacher. The six posthumous volumes of the *Sermones morales* (1792-1793) are evidence that Isla was not at the outset free from the pulpit extravagances of the day, the fashion of which, inaugurated by Paravicino, had led to excesses such as those of the preacher who spoke of 'the divine Adonis, Christ, enamoured of that singular Psyche, Mary.' Isla had too keen a sense of the

L. Claretie, in *Lesage romancier*, etc. Paris, 1890; B. Gaudeau, *Les prêcheurs burlesques en Espagne au xviiie siècle. Étude sur le P. Isla.* Paris, 1891 ; V. Cian, in *L'immigrazione dei gesuiti spagnuoli letterati in Italia* [Memoria della R. Accademia d. Sc. di Torino], 1895 ; A. Baumgartner, *Der spanische Humorist P. Joseph Franz de Isla, S.J.*, in *Stimmen aus Maria Laach*, LXVIII (1905), pp. 82-92, 182-205, 299-315 ; N. Alonso Cortés, *El supuesto autor del 'Fray Gerundio,'* in *Miscelánea Vallisoletana.* Valladolid, 1912. 1[a] serie, pp. 39-47.

THE EIGHTEENTH CENTURY

ridiculous to follow this false path. Already two scholars, Feyjoo in his *Cartas eruditas y curiosas* and Mayáns, in *El Orador Christiano ideado en tres dialogos* (1733), had inveighed against the bombastic eloquence which was too apt to degenerate into profane buffoonery: Isla proceeded to satirize it.

Fray Gerundio is an attempt to do for bad preaching what *Don Quijote* did for foolish books of chivalry. Its hero belongs to the school of pedants who gongorized in the pulpit; he is a person of humble origin with a gift of cheap oratory, and his character may be considered as a piece of specialization in the picaresque field. A highly comical effect is obtained by the introduction of quotations from the Franciscan friar Soto y Marne's *Florilogio sacro. Que en el celestial ameno frondoso Parnasso de la Iglesia, riega (mysticas flores) la Aganipe sagrada fuente de gracia y gloria Christo: con cuya afluencia divina, incrementada la excelsa palma mariana (Triumphante à Privilegios de Gracia) se Corona de victoriosa Gloria: Dividido en discursos panegyricos, anagogicos, tropologicos y alegoricos: fundamentados en la Sagrada Escriptura: roborados con la authoridad de Santos Padres, y exegeticos, particularissimos discursos de los principales Expositores: y exornados con copiosa erudicion sacra, y prophana en ideas, Problemas, Hieroglificos, Philosophicas sentencias, selectissimas humanidades* (1738). Isla does not succeed in amalgamating rhetorical doctrine with satire: his diction is colourless: his narrative too lengthy—a defect particularly obvious in the Second Part (1770), which proved superfluous. The satire had done its work and though it raised a storm of controversy and was prohibited in 1760 by the Inquisition, it continued to circulate surreptitiously. Quite apart from its characterization of the clerical picaroon, *Fray Gerundio* is, as Macaulay justly says, 'a good book.' Like other picaresque tales, it gives a vivid picture of life among the masses and it was successful in its immediate aim of reforming pulpit abuses.

Under the anagram of Joaquin Federico Is-salps, which he had already used for his two panegyrical letters (1725), Isla translated *Gil Blas*, at the request, it is said, of Lorenzo Casaus, an old friend of his who was to benefit by its sale. In this version, published posthumously in 1783, the translator pretexted that he was 'restoring the book to its native land.' Isla spoke in jest, but he succeeded in hoaxing many of his countrymen. It was not unnatural perhaps that over-patriotic Spaniards should be deceived. Lesage had incorporated in *Gil Blas* about fifteen episodes from Espinel's *Marcos de Obregon* just as he had borrowed freely from other Spanish writers, both novelists and dramatists. But there is enough superiority of talent on Lesage's part to justify the proceeding and the treatment of the borrowed episodes is purely French. The charge of plagiarism was first brought against Lesage in a reprint (1775) of the *Siècle de Louis xiv* (1751). No hint of such an accusation is thrown out in the first edition and perhaps no such accusation would ever have been made if Lesage had not contrived to wound Voltaire's vanity in the interval which elapsed between the issue of the two editions.

Meanwhile the field of comedy was in possession of a writer who had begun as a common literary hack. This was RAMON DE LA CRUZ Y CANO [1] (1731-1794)

[1] *Teatro.* Madrid, 1786-1791. 10 vols.; *Coleccion de Sainetes tanto impresos como inéditos*, ed. A. Duran, Madrid, 1843. 2 vols. *Sainetes inéditos . . . existentes en la Biblioteca Municipal de*

whose *Hamleto, rey de Dinamarca* (1772) made from the French version (1769) by Ducis (1733-1816) was the first Spanish translation of Shakespeare. Beginning under French influence, Cruz had soon abandoned any idea of excelling in tragedy, and had declined upon the *sainete*, originally a sort of comic interlude which had gradually evolved into a species of one-act comedy, a rather farcical picture of popular manners. While Moratin and Cadalso were intent on placing Lope de Vega and Calderon in the background, Cruz was reviving the old Spanish tradition, rejuvenating and amplifying the *pasos* of Lope de Rueda. Cruz has no pretentions, but he had a facility scarcely less amazing than Lope's and he had amassed an inexhaustible store of material. Though not a man of good family, nor of position, he was familiar with every rank of society. He had apartments in the house of a duchess, but was always in want of half-a-crown and knew everybody worth knowing from grandees to bull-fighters. Till Cruz set to work the *zarzuela* (musical play) had been an aristocratic luxury. It ceased to be so after *Las Segadoras de Vallecas*. Cruz popularized it, broadened its framework and admitted on the boards every insignificant section of society: the irreligious *abbé*, the shopkeeper, the innocent-looking but crafty country-bumpkin, the vulgarian, sometimes even the rabble. Each piece is on a very small scale not lasting for more than twenty or twenty-five minutes. Cruz's

Madrid, ed. C. Cambronero, Madrid, 1900; *Sainetes de Don Ramón de la Cruz en su mayoría inéditos*, I, ed. E. Cotarelo y Mori, 1915 (Nueva Bib. de Autores Esp., 23).—See: B. Pérez Galdós, *Don Ramón de la Cruz y su época*, in *Revista de España*, XVII (1870), pp. 200-227; XVIII (1871), pp. 27-52; E. Cotarelo y Mori, *Don Ramón de la Cruz y sus obras. Ensayo biográfico y bibliográfico*. Madrid, 1899.

Teatro o Coleccion de los sainetes y demas obras dramaticas (1786-1791) is a huge whispering gallery where you hear all the political and social gossip of the day: all the middle and lower classes of Madrid flit past you, in a vivid and picturesque panorama, lighthearted, careless, full of impertinent grace and wit. It is the drama of the out-at-elbows, the romance of the hard-up, but nobody whines and everybody bubbles over with the sheer joy of life. A typical *sainete* by Cruz is as genuinely Spanish as Spain itself. Nothing makes better reading; nothing is more informing, more illuminating in a delightfully unpretentious way. Cruz's verisimilitude lends to his *sainetes* the value and interest of historical documents. For a picture of Madrid in the latter half of the eighteenth century, it is unnecessary to hunt up pedantic chronicles and musty memories. The material is supplied by Goya in his *Caprichos*, and what Goya does in colour Cruz does in words. Such pieces as *El Prado por la Noche*, *Las Tertulias de Madrid*, *Manolo*, *El muñuelo*, *Las castañeras picadas* and *La Petra y la Juana* are brimful of light humour and spontaneous gaiety.

A cognate spirit was JUAN IGNACIO GONZALEZ DEL CASTILLO[1] (1763-1800), prompter at the Cadiz theatre, who paints provincial manners as vividly as Cruz does those of Madrid. Gonzalez del Castillo attempted the serious drama in *Numa* (1779), a tragedy of some merit and impressive in certain scenes; but his true

---

[1] *Obras completas*, ed. L. Cano, Madrid, 1914. 3 vols. (Bib. selecta de Autores clásicos Esp., 14-16); *Sainetes*, ed. A. de Castro, Cádiz, 1845-1846. 4 vols.—See: E. Cotarelo y Mori, in *Don Ramón de la Cruz y sus obras*. Madrid, 1899; E. Cotarelo y Mori, in *Isidoro Máiquez y el teatro de su tiempo*. Madrid, 1902.

calling was towards comedy. Though his short life prevented him from rivalling Cruz in invention and fertility, he excels him in lyrical gift and in pieces like *Los majos envidiosos* and *El Cortejo sustituto*, equals him in qualities of fidelity to life, sympathetic observation, and contagious humour. Cruz and Gonzalez del Castillo kept alive the authentic Spanish tradition in the one-act farce and the few humorists of the French school could not compete with them in effects of comedy. As regards the serious drama, recasts of old *comedias* were prepared by such humble but useful personages as Trigueros and Dionisio Solis, who respectively took it upon themselves to re-write some of Lope de Vega's and Tirso de Molina's best plays. Despite the efforts of ambitious authors, backed by powerful ministers, the crowd had never taken kindly to Frenchified plays. The masses still hankered after the style of drama that had pleased their fathers. There was no one comparable with Cruz in the department of the serious drama and accordingly it fell into the hands of men who turned out a mass of extravagant episode without rhyme or reason or any pretence of art.

Perhaps the worst offender of the kind—and certainly the most notorious,—was Luciano Francisco Comella [1] (1751-1812), who, under the impression that he was in the direct line of descent from Lope, Tirso de Molina and Calderon, unconsciously caricatured their methods to the point of burlesque. Comella's plays were prodigiously popular in Spain, and though they were little more than parcels of exciting and

[1] See: C. Cambronero, *Comella: su vida y sus obras*, in *Revista contemporánea*, CII (1896), pp. 567-582; CIII (*id.*), pp. 41-58, 187-199, 308-319, 380-390, 479-491, 637-652; CIV (*id.*), pp. 49-60, 206-211, 288-296, 398-405, 497-509.

incredible incidents, they were reproduced before full houses in Italy to the annoyance of educated Spaniards in their travels. There is scarcely a spark of real talent in any one of them, but it would be unfair to deny that he had the mechanical knack of stringing breathless episodes together. In the safe obscurity of a footnote, the austere and learned Ticknor bashfully confesses that he has repeatedly read some of Comella's plays for the sake of their thrilling stories. Comella's extravagances and accumulated follies were too much for LEANDRO FERNANDEZ DE MORATIN [1] (1760-1828), a man of far higher dramatic gifts than his father, the author of *Hormesinda*. An idolater of Molière, he admits reminiscences of his model into his original work and made a decided hit in 1786, with *El viejo y la niña*, a brilliant Spanish variant of *L'École des Femmes*. Moratin (who adopted the pseudonym of *Inarco Celenio*) began life as a goldsmith's apprentice; in 1779 and 1782, he was awarded prizes by the Spanish Academy, and in 1787, through the influence of Jovellanos, was appointed secretary at the Spanish Embassy in Paris. In 1790 he was given a benefice as well as a pension: these were continued until 1816, when Moratin abandoned his ecclesiastical career.

[1] *Obras*, ed. B. C. Aribau, 1846, in Bib. de Autores Esp., II; *Obras póstumas*. Madrid, 1867-1868. 3 vols.; *Teatro*, ed. F. Ruiz Morcuende, 1924 (Clásicos Cast., 58.)—See: *Les Comédies de Don Leandro Fernandez de Moratin*. French trans. by E. Hollander, Paris, 1855; *Documentos referentes á D. Leandro Fernández Moratin* [transcribed by V. V.], in *Revista de Archivos*, etc., II (1898), pp. 221-222; V. Cian, *La Torino del tempo andato nelle relazioni d'alcuni viaggiatori italiani e stranieri*, in *Nuova Antologia*, CLXI (1898), pp. 293-310; J. Pérez de Guzmán, *El centenario de 'El sí de las niñas,'* in *La Ilustración española y americana*, LXXXI (1906), pp. 35, 42, 67-68, 75, 78, 98-99, 114-115, 130-131, 134, 146-147, 169, 174, 176, 183-184, 186.

THE EIGHTEENTH CENTURY

He later succeeded Samaniego as secretary to the *Interpretación de lenguas*, a post for which he seemed qualified by his sojourns in England, the Netherlands, Germany and Italy. In his Italian travels, Moratin had been irritated to find that Comella was regarded as a representative of the Spanish drama; he was more irritated on his return to find him in full possession of the stage and the idol of the masses. He fastened on Comella and introduced him as Don Eleuterio Crispin de Andorra in *La Comedia nueva* (1792), then called *El Café o la Comedia nueva*, a clever satire in which certain elements of *Le Misanthrope* and *Les Femmes Savantes* were utilized with a fine but cruel instinct. Moratin had grossly insulted Comella's wife and family, and when Comella proposed to retort by caricaturing his opponent in *El violeta universal*, Moratin, who had influence with the censors, contrived to get the performance prohibited.

Other circumstances give a poor idea of Moratin as a man. When the Napoleonic invasion occurred, Moratin dishonoured himself by going into hiding at Vitoria, coming out again to pass over to the enemy and became royal librarian in 1811 to Joseph Bonaparte (1768-1844). Finding himself on the losing side, he grew terrified, thought that he was being pursued by would-be murderers (who only existed in his scared imagination), fled to Italy and later to France. It is not pleasant to record the shame and degradation of a man of real talent verging on genius. As to Moratin's gifts, there is no question. He was a most accomplished man of letters, an admirable versifier, a spirited prose-writer and a master of brilliant dialogue. Nobody in his age matches him in this respect. His prose-plays, *El sí de las niñas* (1805) and *La Comedia nueva*, for instance, of which the eccentric Gérard de Nerval (1808-1855) began a verse-adaptation, are almost masterpieces of their kind.

Another writer of excellent but uneven prose was José Marchena y Ruiz de Cueto[1] (1768-1821), a declared Gallicist of unenviable tendencies who denied his country and his religion. He emigrated to France in his youth, was drawn into politics, imprisoned by Robespierre and became in 1808 secretary to Murat. Marchena never won the confidence of the French; they recognized his intellectual powers but despised his character. Chateaubriand in the *Mémoires d'Outre-Tombe* (1849-1850) describes him as an 'immonde savant et spirituel avorton.' It is significant of his character and scholarship alike that he could forge Latin texts in order to enjoy the sensation caused by his disclosures. A case in point is the *Fragmentum Petronii* (1802 ?). In spite of long absences from Spain, Marchena retained a complete mastery of his own idiom; in his translations of Montesquieu, Voltaire and Rousseau, his style at times rises to a high level of excellence but it is unequal and lacks the even grace and unvarying purity of Moratin's prose.

One of the few striking personalities of the age is the statesman GASPAR MELCHOR DE JOVELLANOS[2]

---

[1] *Obras literarias*, ed. [with introduction] M. Menéndez y Pelayo. Sevilla, 1892-1896. 2 vols.; *Une lettre de Marchena*, ed. A. Morel-Fatio, in *Bulletin hispanique*, IV (1902), pp. 256-257; *Documents sur Marchena*, ed. A. Morel-Fatio, in *Bulletin hispanique*, XXI (1919), pp. 231-242.

[2] *Obras publicadas é inéditas*, ed. C. Nocedal, 1858-1859. 2 vols. (Bib. de Autores Esp., XLVI, L); *Escritos inéditos de Jovellanos*, ed. J. Somoza García-Sala, Madrid, 1891; *La Satire de Jovellanos contre la mauvaise éducation de la noblesse*, 1787, ed. A. Morel-Fatio [Bibliothèque des Universités du Midi

THE EIGHTEENTH CENTURY 423

(1744-1811), who abandoned an ecclesiastical career to take up law at the wish of his uncle, the Duke of Losada. Appointed magistrate of Seville in 1768 and of Madrid in 1778, he was elected member of the Council of Military Orders in 1780. On the fall (1789) of the Count of Cabarrús (1752-1810), Jovellanos was exiled to the Asturias : in 1797 he was named Minister of Justice. Overthrown by intrigues in 1798, he was exiled to Gijón and from 1801 to 1808 was kept prisoner in the Fortress of Bellver in the Isle of Majorca ; when he returned to the Peninsula, Spain was under the yoke of France. The value of his prose-writings, political and economic, is admitted by good judges, and apart from their variety and didactic importance, they are highly interesting as examples of Ciceronian prose and as interpreting the intellectual

fasc. 3], Bordeaux, 1899 ; *Cartas de Jovellanos y Lord Vassall Holland sobre la guerra de la Independencia* (1808-1811), ed. J. Somoza García-Sala, Madrid, 1911. 2 vols.—See : J. Somoza de Montsoriu, *Catálogo de manuscritos é impresos notables del Instituto de Jove-Llanos en Gijon*, etc. Oviedo, 1883 ; J. Somoza de Montsoriu, *Jovellanos : nuevos datos para su biografía*. Habana-Madrid, 1885 ; J. Somoza de Montsoriu, *Las amarguras de Jovellanos : bosquejo biográfico*, etc. Gijon, 1889 ; E. Mérimée, *Jovellanos*, in *Revue Hispanique*, I (1894), pp. 34-68 ; J. Somoza de Montsoriu, *Inventario de un jovellanista*. Madrid, 1901 ; E. González Blanco, *Jovellanos. Su vida y su obra*. Madrid, 1911 ; J. Somoza García-Sala, *Documentos para escribir la biografía de Jovellanos*. Madrid, 1911. 2 vols. ; J. Gómez Centurión, *Jovellanos y las órdenes militares. Colección de documentos*. Madrid, 1912 ; G. de Artiñano y de Galdácano, *Jovellanos y su España*. Madrid, 1913 ; J. Juderias, *Don Gaspar Melchor de Jovellanos*. Madrid, 1913 ; J. Somoza García-Sala, *Jovellanos. Manuscritos inéditos, raros, ó dispersos*. Madrid, 1913 ; M. Artigas, *Los Manuscritos de Jovellanos de la Biblioteca*, in *Boletín de la Bib. Menéndez y Pelayo*, III (1921), pp. 118-152.

ideas of the eighteenth century to the Spanish public. The style of his academic speeches is decidedly gallicized, but later on, in the *Defensa de la Junta Central* (1810), where Jovellanos unites the classic elements with the modern ones reflecting modern thought, he gets rid of these gallicisms as regards vocabulary though not so completely as regards syntax. From a literary standpoint, Jovellanos's prestige rests less on his own productions than on the influence that he exercised on the Salamancan school. His dramatic attempts are not successful, whether they are judged by the early play *Pelayo* (1769), acted in a revised form with the title of *Munuza* in 1792 ; or by *El Delincuente honrado* (1774), an adaptation of *Le Fils Naturel* by Diderot (1713-1784). In verse Jovellanos is as a rule much less happy than in prose. But he has exceptions ; and the *Epístola de Fabio a Anfriso*, dedicated to the Duque de Veragua, while it reflects a serene nobility of character, is inspired by genuine poetic feeling.

The chief of the Salamancan group of poets was JUAN MELENDEZ VALDÉS[1] (1754-1817), known as *Batilo*, just as Jovellanos was *Jovino*. Melendez, who in his youth wrote erotic verses, thought of entering religion, but an unhappy marriage and trouble connected with his professorial chair threw him into politics. Through the influence of Jovellanos, he was

[1] *Poesías*, ed. L. A. de Cueto (Marqués de Valmar), 1871, in Bib. de Autores Esp., LXIII ; *Los besos de amor*, ed. R. Foulché-Delbosc, in *Revue Hispanique*, I (1894), pp. 73-83 ; *Poesías inéditas*, ed. R. Foulché-Delbosc, in *Revue Hispanique*, (1894), pp. 166-195 ; *Poesías y cartas inéditas*, ed. M. Serrano y Sanz, in *Revue Hispanique*, IV (1897), pp. 266-313.—See : E. Mérimée, *Meléndez Valdés*, in *Revue Hispanique*, I (1894), pp. 217-235.

THE EIGHTEENTH CENTURY

given a post under the government. Involved in his friend's fall, Melendez incited his countrymen against the French, veering round he accepted office under Joseph Bonaparte and finally ended by acclaiming the restoration of the Bourbons. The burden of dishonour proved too much for him. He fled to Montpellier, where he died. Melendez was a man open to every influence: his easily swayed impulses are in striking contrast to Jovellanos's stability of purpose, his remark to the latter—*Obra soy tuya*—was much nearer the truth than he perhaps guessed himself. But if his personal character inspires no respect, his poetical gifts are incontestable. He wrote everything from the *letrilla* to the philosophic ode and only once —in the play *Las bodas de Camacho* (1784)—did he court failure. The complete consonance between his thoughts, images, style and language produces a most happy effect. His qualities of facility and elegance reveal themselves in the ode *A las artes* and more particularly in *Los Besos de amor*, twenty-three odes written in imitation of the celebrated *Basia* of Juan Segundo (Jan Everaerts, 1511-1536). In these Melendez celebrates with delightful simplicity the passion of love and achieves what M. Foulché-Delbosc considers to be 'un des chefs d'œuvre de l'école anacréontique espagnole.' Among Melendez's followers may be mentioned Josef Iglesias de la Casa [1] (1748-1791); Nicasio Alvarez de Cienfuegos [2] (1764-

[1] *Poesías*, ed. L. A. de Cueto (Marqués de Valmar,) 1869, in Bib. de Autores Esp., LXI; *Poesías inéditas*, ed. R. Foulché-Delbosc, in *Revue Hispanique*, II (1895), pp. 77-96.

[2] *Poesías*, ed. L. A. de Cueto (Marqués de Valmar), 1875, in Bib. de Autores Esp., LXVII.—See: L. Batcave, *Acte de décès du poète Cienfuegos*, in *Bulletin hispanique*, XI (1909),

1809), a premature romantic, who fails in execution by affectation first of archaisms then of neologisms; and Gaspar Maria de Nava Alvarez, the future Count of Noroña[1] (1760-1815), whose *Poesías* were published in 1799 and his *Poesías asiáticas* not until 1833. Noroña was a sympathetic personality with wide intellectual interests but without great poetic gifts.

Though Spain's contribution to literature proper was not considerable during this century, she produced some works of scientific value. GREGORIO MAYANS Y SISCAR[2] (1699-1781), author of the first serious life (1737) of Cervantes, published in his *Origenes de la lengua castellana* (1737) Valdés's *Dialogo de la Lengua*. He also edited the works of Gaspar Ibañez de Segovia Peralta y Mendoza, Marqués de Mondéjar, in 1741; of Fray Luis de Leon in 1761, of Sanchez de las Brozas in 1766 and of Luis Vives in 1782. Previous to these publications, in 1733, Mayans had issued the collected letters of Nicolas Antonio and

p. 96; E. Piñeyro, *Cienfuegos*, in *Bulletin hispanique*, XI (1909), pp. 31-54.

[1] *Poesías* and *Poesías asiáticas*, ed. L. A. de Cueto (Marqués de Valmar), 1871, in Bib. de Autores Esp., LXIII.—See: James Fitzmaurice-Kelly, *Noroña's Poesías asiáticas*, in *Revue Hispanique*, XVIII (1908), pp. 439-467.

[2] *Elogio de Quevedo, juicios críticos*, etc., ed. A. Fernandez-Guerra y Orbe, 1852, in Bib. de Autores Esp., XXIII; *Vida y juicio crítico del maestro Fray Luis de Leon*, 1855, in Bib. de Autores Esp., XXXVII; *Juicios críticos*, etc., ed. A. de Castro, 1857-1873, in Bib. de Autores Esp., XLII, LXV; *Cartas*, ed. E. de Ochoa, 1870, in Bib. de Autores Esp., LXII; *Correspondencia literaria*, in *Revista de Archivos*, etc., XII (1905), pp. 271-280, 446-459; XIII (1905), pp. 51-56, 255-261, 421-439; XIV (1906), pp. 214-226, 373-378.—See: A. Morel-Fatio, *Un érudit espagnol au xviiie siècle*, in *Bulletin hispanique*, XVII (1915), pp. 157-226.

of Solis. His *Rhetorica* (1757), too bulky and voluminous for modern readers, remains the best anthology of Spanish prose-writers, and while a great part of his critical writings are now out of date, Mayans holds an honourable place as a pioneer. No less notable is the Jesuit ANDRÉS MARCOS BURRIEL [1] (1719-1762), who devoted his learning and unfailing industry to specialized research. With these may be mentioned Enrique Florez [2] (1702-1773), who in 1754 conceived the plan of the monumental *España Sagrada, Theatro geographico-historico de la Iglesia de España*, and was personally responsible for much of the material in the first twenty-six of its fifty-two volumes; the Jesuit Lorenzo Hervas y Panduro (1735-1809), the father of comparative philology, whose *Catalogo de las lenguas de las naciones conocidas* ... (1800-1805) marks an epoch in that science; and the minister and polygraph, Pedro Rodriguez Campomanes, Conde de Campomanes (1723-1803), author of *Cartas político-económicas*.[3] A writer whose interests centred rather in juridical history than in literature, Rafael de Floranes Velez de Robles y Encinas [4] (1743-1801), exhibited remark-

[1] See: Antonio Burriel, *Razon de la vida del jesuita Andrés Marcos Burriel*, ed. M. Salvá y P. Sainz de Baranda, in *Coleccion de documentos inéditos para la Historia de España*, VIII (1846), pp. 568-571; *Correspondencia*, ed. M. Salvá y P. Sainz de Baranda, in *Coleccion de documentos*, etc., XIII (1848), pp. 229-365; E. Gigas, *En spansk Manuskriptkommission i det 18de Aarhundrede og dens Leder*. Kjøbenhavn, 1911 (Bibliotekar foreningens smaaskrifter, 2).

[2] See: J. M. Salvador y Barrera, *El Padre Flórez y su España sagrada*. 1914 [Discurso. R. Academia de la Historia].

[3] Ed. A. Rodríguez Villa, Madrid, 1878.

[4] See: M. Menéndez y Pelayo, *Dos opúsculos inéditos de D. Rafael Floranes y D. Tomás Antonio Sánchez sobre los orígenes de la poesía castellana*, in *Revue Hispanique*, XVIII (1908), pp. 295-431.

able powers in discussing the thorny questions connected with the *Cronica general* and the *Cronica del Cid*. In the more special domain of history Juan Francisco de Masdeu (1744-1817) tells in his voluminous *Historia crítica de España y de la cultura española* (1783-1805) a complicated story in a clear cold way. Masdeu's work has the defect of not coming down any further than the eleventh century. This is not the highest or most interesting phase of development from the average reader's point of view. Consequently Masdeu is only consulted for a curious detail or some special reference. The value of his work is diminished also by the misplaced uncritical scepticism which distinguishes the end of the eighteenth century. A more scientific method was adopted by Juan Bautista Muñoz (1745-1799), a Valencian who in the face of great opposition brought out the *Historia del Nuevo Mundo* (1793), which reaches the year 1500 only. We are thus deprived of what no doubt would have been an excellent piece of critical examination of a most brilliant and interesting period packed with picturesque incident. Muñoz writes well; he knows what constitutes evidence and illustrates his work by careful documentation. In this respect he is a bold experimenter, if not absolutely an isolated initiator.

XII

THE REIGNS OF FERDINAND VII AND OF ISABEL II (1808-1868)

THE social character of French literature, its avoidance of local peculiarities, its cultivation of general ideas, carried it triumphantly over Europe; its influence on the Peninsula, where intellectual relations with France had always been favoured by geographical considerations, became more profoundly felt after 1700. And Spain, who from the discovery of America until the defeat of her once invincible infantry at Rocroi (1643) had set the fashion to her neighbour, henceforth shewed increasingly the impress of French taste and models. Evidence of French inclinations is clearly perceptible in the work of Manuel Josef Quintana[1] (1772-1857), the national poet of the War of Independence. His first volume of verse, published when

[1] *Obras completas.* Madrid, 1897-1898. 3 vols.; *Oda a la invencion de la imprenta*, [ed. R. Foulché-Delbosc and A. Bonilla y San Martín] Madrid, 1909 (Bib. Oropesa, 6); *Juicios críticos*, in Bib. de Autores Esp., VII, LXI, LXIII and LXVII; *Obras inéditas.* Madrid, 1892.—See: E. Piñeyro, *Manuel José Quintana.* Paris-Madrid, 1892; E. Mérimée, *Les poésies lyriques de Quintana*, in *Bulletin hispanique*, IV (1902), pp. 119-153; M. Menéndez y Pelayo, *Don Manuel José Quintana considerado como poeta lírico*, in *Estudios de crítica literaria.* 1908. V, pp. 297-352 (Col. de Escritores Cast., 137).

he was sixteen years old, reveals him as an offshoot of the School of Salamanca, where he studied law. In 1803 he became director of the review *Variedades de ciencias, literatura y artes* : he was appointed dramatic censor at Madrid in 1806 and later editor of *El Semanario patriótico*. When the French, under Napoleon in person, entered Madrid at the end of 1808, Quintana left the capital, drew up the manifestos of the *Junta Central* and in 1810 was given the post of Official Interpreter which Moratin the younger had received from Godoy. The proposal to set Quintana at the head of the *Secretaría de la Real Estampilla* stirred up the envious attacks of the polygraph Antonio de Capmany (1742-1813), author of *Filosofia de la Eloquencia* (1777), who accused Quintana of using in a proclamation to America concerning the convocation of the *Cortes* a phrase which stirred up the Colonies to declare their Independence. At the Restoration in 1814, Quintana was arrested and sentenced to six years' imprisonment in the fortress of Pamplona. On his release (1820) he obtained a subordinate position under the Government, remaining always more or less poor, so much more so that when he was publicly crowned in 1855, he had to borrow money to buy suitable clothes for the ceremony.

Quintana's period of poetic production is short : leaving out of view some juvenile essays and verses of occasion written in old age, he is a poet only from 1795 to 1808. And as he wrote much less copiously than is usual with his countrymen, scrupulously correcting and revising all his work, his total compositions amount to thirty-four. Among these, the most notable are the odes : *A la invencion de la imprenta* (1800), which celebrates in lines of impassioned eloquence man's escape from the tyranny of superstitious credulity; *A la expedicion española* (1803-1804) *para propagar la vacuna en América* (1806) and such patriotic poems as: *A Juan de Padilla* (1797); *Al armamento de las provincias españolas contra los franceses* (1808); *A España después de la revolucion de Marzo* (1808) and *Al Combate de Trafalgar* (1805) with its excellent description of the fighting. Quintana's verse breathes his love of liberty and love of country—things inseparable in his mind—and the *rencor inacabable* that, in spite of his leaning to France, he felt towards her for conspiring against Spain. Its main inspiration is patriotism, politics and philanthropy. It is unequal; its flights are of short duration, but its martial music and lofty rhetoric give faithful expression to one aspect of Spain's genius. As a general rule, Quintana's attitude is beyond reproach and his public life is marked by a high standard of unswerving rectitude. If he has occasional lapses, as when he condescends to flattery in the ode: *Con ocasion de la paz hecha entre España y Francia el año de* 1795, and in *Cristina* (1829), an epithalamic ode written in honour of Ferdinand VII's marriage to his fourth wife, these admit of excuse in view of the age in which he lived. A typical eighteenth-century philosopher, Quintana proved an inferior dramatist: *El Duque de Viseo* (1801) is a mediocre tragedy based on the even more mediocre play of Matthew Gregory Lewis (1775-1818), *The Castle Spectre* (1798), while *Pelayo* (1805) only succeeded at the time because of its patriotic spirit. He writes an excellent prose-style, elevated, resonant, forcible, in the *Vidas de españoles célebres* (1807-1833) and in the commentary to the *Poesías selectas castellanas* ... (1807, recast 1830-1833), an anthology in which an almost too rigorously classic choice prevails Quintana's stern independence of spirit had its counterpart intellectually in a certain rigidity of mind that opposed the acceptance of new ideas. He survived Espronceda by fifteen years, but the Romantic movement passed him by untouched.

Another poet of the Salamancan group, Juan Nicasio Gallego [1] (1777-1853) also outlived romanticism and, like Quintana, remained unaffected by it. Gallego became known by the *Oda a la defensa de Buenos Aires* (1807) and established his reputation the following year by the patriotic *Dos de Mayo* (1808) which celebrates the historic rising of the Spanish on May 2. It is a curious coincidence that Gallego's most representative pieces should be denunciations of the French whom he admired, and of the English who were to be instrumental in freeing Spain from the yoke of Napoleon. That he could sound other notes is evident from the elegy to the duchess of Frías, which is informed with genuine personal feeling. Gallego has left also one prose-work, a rendering (1836) of Manzoni's (1785-1873) *I Promessi Sposi* (1825-1827).

In opposition to the Salamancan School are the Sevillan poets; these were really survivors of the eighteenth century, elegant versifiers of cosmopolitan tastes who exercised little influence on their generation. Among them may be mentioned Félix José Reynoso [2]

[1] *Obras poéticas*, ed. R. Academia Esp. Madrid, 1854; *Poesías* ed. L. A. de Cueto (Marqués de Valmar), 1875, in Bib. de Autores Esp., LXVII.—See: E. González Negro, *Estudio biográfico de Don Juan Nicasio Gallego*. Zamora, 1901.

[2] *Obras*, ed. A. Martín Villa y F. de B. Palomo, 1872-1879. 2 vols. (Soc. de Bibliófilos Andaluces); ed. L. A. de Cueto (Marqués de Valmar), 1875, in Bib. de Autores Esp., LXVII.

FERDINAND VII AND ISABEL II 433

(1772-1841), dean of the Valencian Chapter; Manuel de Arjona [1] (1771-1820), canon of Cordova, and his disciples José Maria Blanco (1775-1841) and Alberto Lista [2] (1775-1848), canon of Seville. Lista, who was a professor at the College of San Mateo in Madrid, wrote the admirable ode *Á la muerte de Jesús* and the *romance*, *La Cabaña*, whose note of serene and gentle resignation is not uncharacteristic of its author's talent. Lista's gifts are critical rather than poetical, and in any case they are less noteworthy than his personal character. He is perhaps most widely remembered for the influence that he exercised over some of the best minds of his time, especially over his turbulent pupil Espronceda, who seems to have acknowledged his authority alone. Lista must have presented a striking contrast to his colleague Josef Gomez Hermosilla [3] (1771-1837), the formidable pedagogue, who composed the *Arte de hablar en prosa y verso* (1826), a model of pedantic correction and taste, and the less known but more useful *Juicio crítico de los principales poetas españoles de la última era*, which appeared posthumously in 1840. Lista's friend Blanco [4] —Blanco White—emigrated in 1810 to England,

[1] *La Tebaida, de Estacio*, ed. A. de Castro, 1855, in Bib. de Autores Esp., XXXVI.—See: B. J. Gallardo, in *Ensayo*, etc., Madrid, 1863. I, col. 300-302.

[2] *Poesías*, ed. L. A. de Cueto (Marqués de Valmar), 1875, in Bib. de Autores Esp., LXVII.—See: A Ferrer del Rio, in *Galeria de la literatura española*. Madrid, 1846, pp. 13-29.

[3] *Juicio crítico de los principales poetas españoles de la última era*, ed. V. Salvá, Valencia, 1840. 2 vols.; *Arte de hablar en prosa y verso*. Paris, 1893.

[4] *Poesías*, ed. L. A. de Cueto (Marqués de Valmar), 1875, en Bib de Autores Esp., LXVII.—See: M. Menéndez y Pelayo,

where he grew to know men as dissimilar in temperament as Southey (1774-1843), Lord Holland (1773-1840), John Stuart Mill (1806-1873) and the future Cardinal Newman (1801-1890), and became editor of two reviews: *El Español* (1810-1814), and *Variedades, o Mensagero de Londres* (1823-1825), founded in aid of the Spanish refugees. Like José Marchena, he was perhaps more learned than natural. His English sonnet, *Night and Death*, won him greater fame than any of his compositions, but as a result of his absence from Spain his fine and whimsical talent remains outside the sphere of Spanish thought and letters.

Romanticism, which is indigenous to Spain, had found in Lope de Vega a brilliant exponent. Calderon's followers were members of Lope's school and are consequently romantics of the purest water. They were not bound down by prosaic realities; they were indeed attached to the South, but to the South as a sort of East, where picturesqueness took the place of matter-of-fact and where every-day occurrences were of a poetic imaginative substance. A return to the old national drama was foreshadowed by the famous quarrel (1814-1819) between Juan Nicolas Böhl de Faber (1770-1836) and José Joaquin de Mora, in which the former protested strongly against the classical school. But the modern romantic movement of the nineteenth century was imported from abroad. In-

in *Historia de los heterodoxos españoles*. Madrid, 1881. III, pp. 547-583; E. Piñeyro, *Blanco White*, in *Bulletin hispanique*, XII (1910), pp. 71-100, 163-200; F. Rousseau, *Blanco White: Souvenirs d'un proscrit espagnol réfugié en Angleterre 1775-1815*, in *Revue Hispanique*, XXII (1910), pp. 613-647.

direct influences had been at work as early as 1803, when there appeared in Spain a version of Chateaubriand's *Atala* (1801), which was followed in 1816 by a translation of Bernardin de Saint-Pierre's (1737-1814) *Paul et Virginie* (1787). These two works were the forerunners of a whole series of romantic novels—chiefly translations from the French and rarely of much literary merit—issued from 1818 onwards, by a Valencian bookseller, Mariano Cabrerizo. In 1823 a romantic review, *El Europeo*, was founded at Barcelona, and Goethe's *Werther* (1774) was translated in 1835. Finally political oppression, which led to the banishment or flight of almost every Spaniard of literary taste or of liberal opinions, brought to an end the artificial rule of the dry and coldly-correct classical period. When the exiles returned to Spain, they brought with them new ideals in literature as in politics. To one of them, the ineffectual politician Francisco Martinez de la Rosa[1] (1787-1862), is due the importation of modern romanticism. Compelled to take refuge in Paris, he found the romantic movement in full course with Victor Hugo at its head. Martinez de la Rosa had no convictions; his early plays, *La*

[1] *Obras completas.* Paris, 1844-1845. 5 vols. (Col. de los mejores Autores Esp., 28-32).—See: A. Ferrer del Rio, in *Galeria de la literatura española.* Madrid, 1846. pp. 85-96; L. A. Rebello da Silva, *Memoria ácerca da vida e escriptos de D. Francisco Martines de la Rosa.* Lisboa, 1862; T. Rodríguez Rubí, *D. Francisco Martinez de la Rosa,* 1862 [Discurso. R. Academia Esp.]; F. M. Tubino, in *Introduccion del romanticismo en España,* in *Revista Contemporánea,* VII (1877), pp. 79-98; M. Menéndez y Pelayo, in *Estudios de crítica literaria.* 2ª ed. Madrid, 1893. Iª serie, pp. 237-288; C. de Castro, in *Antología de las Cortes de 1820.* Madrid, 1910; N. Alonso Cortés, *Retazo biográfico,* in *Viejo y Nuevo.* Valladolid, 1915. pp. 123-164.

Viuda de Padilla (1814) and *Moraima* (1818) are merely declamatory tragedies; his youthful poems shew the influence of Melendez Valdés and Quintana; and he reveals himself an imitator of Moratin the younger in his comedies. One of these, *La niña en casa y la madre en la máscara* (1821) was adapted by Théaulon de Lambert (1787-1841) in *La mère au bal et la fille à la maison* (1826) and had something of a success. This may have inspired Martinez de la Rosa, who was then in Paris, to write a French play. He readily took colour from those about him and he became a romantic as promptly as he had become a liberal. His *Aben Humeya ou La révolte des Maures sous Philippe II* was played at the Porte-Saint-Martin theatre on July 19th, 1830. The chances of politics, especially the amnesty following the death of the wretched Ferdinand VII, brought Martinez de la Rosa back to Spain. He tried romanticism in Madrid with *La Conjuracion de Venecia* (1834), a prose drama which had an astonishing success. *Aben Humeya*, which Martinez de la Rosa translated into Spanish, was not played until two years later (1836) and it proved a failure. But it has its importance in the history of literary evolution. With the exception of these two plays which he put together under French influence, Martinez de la Rosa's works represent him mainly at the time when he divided with the Mexican, Manuel Eduardo de Gorostiza [1] (1789-1851), author of the comedy *Indulgencia para todos* (1818), the right

---

[1] *Obras.* México, 1899-1902. 4 vols.; *Teatro escogido.* Bruselas, 1825. 2 vols.—See: J. M. Roa Bárcena, *Datos y apuntamientos para la biografía de Don Manuel Eduardo de Gorostiza*, in *Memorias de la Academia Mexicana*, I (1876), pp. 89-204.

of succession to the younger Moratin as followers of Molière. It is not, however, by any of these Moratinian pieces, nor by his historical novel *Doña Isabel de Solis, Reyna de Granada* (1837-1846), a colourless imitation of Walter Scott, that Martinez de la Rosa is remembered : he exists by virtue of his pioneer efforts in romanticism.

After the failure of *Aben Humeya*, it seemed as though the success of the new romantic movement was imperilled. But the standard was upraised by Angel de Saavedra Remirez de Baquedano, DUQUE DE RIVAS [1] (1791-1865), who in his early poems (1813) and in his dramas *Ataulfo* (1814) and *Lanuza* (1822) had shewn the influence of Melendez Valdés and Quintana. His change of poetic principles first became apparent during his exile (October 1, 1823—January 1, 1834) in *El Faro de Malta* (1828) and, more particularly, in *El Moro Expósito, o Córdoba y Burgos en el siglo x* (1834), whose anonymous prologue by Antonio Maria Alcalá Galiano (1789-1865) is something in the nature of a literary manifesto. This poem, which is in reality a rhymed novel like *Marmion* (1808), consists of a legend in twelve *romances* written in assonanted hendecasyllabics. It is preceded by a dedication to

[1] *Obras completas.* 1894-1904. 7 vols. (Col. de Escritores Cast.); *Romances*, ed. C. de Rivas Cherif, 1912. 2 vols. (Clásicos Cast., 9, 12).—See: A. Ferrer del Rio, in *Galeria de la literatura española.* Madrid, 1846. pp. 97-109; M. Cañete, in *Escritores españoles é hispano-americanos.* 1884. pp. 3-148 (Col. de Escritores Cast., 16); E. Piñeyro, in *El romanticismo en España.* Paris, 1904, pp. 51-93; " Azorín," in *Rivas y Larra : razón social del romanticismo en España.* Madrid, 1916; E. A. Peers, *Rivas and romanticism in Spain.* Liverpool, 1923; E. A. Peers, *Angel de Saavedra, Duque de Rivas : A critical study*, in *Revue Hispanique*, LVIII (1923), pp. 1-600.

John Hookham Frere, whom Rivas got to know in Malta and to whom the idea of exploiting the subject was probably due. Frere had made a speciality of old Spanish, was an excellent scholar and an admirable classic. He introduced Rivas to Shakespeare, Scott and Byron, and presented to him a copy of that extreme rarity—a complete edition of Lope de Vega's plays. Romanticism, which had triumphed in France with the staging of *Hernani* (1830), was destined to triumph in Spain some five years later with the staging of Rivas's *Don Alvaro o la fuerza del sino*, whose first performance took place on March 22, 1835, a date memorable in the history of the Spanish theatre. *Don Alvaro* does not move us now, but it caused a stupendous sensation that March night. Its strange admixture of prose and verse, of the sublime, the comic and the extravagant carried all before it. *Don Alvaro* is unquestionably the first and best of the Spanish romantic dramas: the freshness and absence of effort that characterize it set it far above Rivas's later and more artistically composed pieces. His *Romances históricos* (1841), like *El Moro Expósito*, contain vivid passages of poetic diction and picturesque national legends presented in semi-epical guise. But Rivas lacks feeling and often sinks into plain prose when the subject does not uplift him. He was born to tell stories, and he remained, as Cueto says, an epic poet of the decadence who included in his plays large contributions of legendary and traditional elements.

Verdi (1813-1901) who took the libretto *La forza del destino* (1862) from *Don Alvaro*, had borrowed his *Trovatore* (1853) from *El Trovador* (1836), another romantic drama, by a young medical student of Cadiz,

Antonio Garcia Gutierrez [1] (1813-1884). In this play Garcia Gutierrez scored a triumph which he failed to repeat in his later pieces, *Simon Bocanegra* (1843)—also used by Verdi in a libretto (1857)—*Venganza catalana* (1864) and *Juan Lorenzo* (1865). He has not the force of Rivas, nor the eloquence of Zorrilla, nor the art of Tamayo y Baus. And he is very unequal. But he can create charming woman-characters such as the Leonor of *El Trovador*. His strong point is his versification : it is easy, flowing, sweet and melodious. The romantic drama had, like romanticism generally, no very long career. The last genuine romantic play may be accounted *Los Amantes de Teruel* (1837) by Juan Eugenio Hartzenbusch [2] (1806-1880). The subject had already been chosen for treatment by Rey de Artieda, Tirso de Molina and Montalvan. Hartzenbusch, who had some pretensions to scholarship, had also a belief in painstaking effort. Hence he wrote and even re-wrote his play, not taking into account that each revision deprived his work of something of its original fire. Nevertheless, as it stands, it still

[1] *Obras escogidas.* Madrid, 1866; *El Trovador*, ed. A. Bonilla y San Martín, Madrid, 1916 (Clásicos de la Literatura esp., 4).—See : A. Ferrer del Rio, in *Galeria de la literatura española*. Madrid, 1846. pp. 253-270; E. Piñeyro, in *El romanticismo en España*. Paris, 1904. pp. 95-116; C. A. Regensburger, *Ueber den 'Trovador' des García Gutiérrez, die Quelle von Verdis Oper ' Il Trovatore.'* Berlin, 1911 ; N. B. Adams, *The Romantic Dramas of García Gutiérrez.* New York, 1922.

[2] *Obras*, 1887-1892. 5 vols. (Col. de Escritores Cast.).—See : A. Ferrer del Rio, in *Galeria de la literatura española*. Madrid, 1846. pp. 155-170; E. Hartzenbusch, *Bibliografía de Hartzenbusch. . . formada por su hijo*. Madrid, 1900; E. Piñeyro, in *El romanticismo en España*. Paris, 1904. pp. 117-137 ; E. Cotarelo y Mori, in *Sobre el origen y desarrollo de la leyenda de los ' Amantes de Teruel.'* Madrid, 1907.

eclipses its predecessors. Two other plays by the same author, *Doña Mencia o la boda en la Inquisicion* (1838) and *La Jura en Santa Gadea* (1844), were successful in their day, but they lack the qualities of his first attempt. A romantic play that scored a success of a noisy kind in which politics counted for much was *Carlos II el Hechizado* (1837) by Antonio Gil y Zárate (1793-1861), who exercised, however, no influence on the general current of literature.

The most potent lyrical poet of the nineteenth century was JOSÉ DE ESPRONCEDA[1] (1808-1842), once a pupil of Lista at the College of San Mateo. At the age of fourteen years, he joined a secret society, *Los Numantinos*, among whose members were his schoolfellows Ventura de la Vega, Patricio de la Escosura and Plazuela, the future Conde de Cheste, who became Director of the Spanish Academy. The papers of the young conspirators came by chance into the hands of the authorities and the offenders were

[1] *Obras poéticas y Escritos en prosa*, ed. P. de la Escosura, Madrid, 1884; *Obras poéticas*, ed. J. Cascales, Madrid, 1923; ed. J. Moreno Villa, 1923. 2 vols. (Clásicos Cast., 47, 50); *Canto a Teresa* [ed. R. Foulché-Delbosc and A. Bonilla y San Martín], 1909 (Bib. Oropesa, VII); *Blanca de Borbón*, ed. P. H. Churchman, in *Revue Hispanique*, XVII (1907); *More inedita*, ed. P. H. Churchman, in *Revue Hispanique*, XVII (1907), pp. 704-740; [P. H. Churchman] *Some Espronceda Miscellany*, II. *Some unpublished prose*, in *Revue Hispanique*, LVI (1922), pp. 511-521; *Sancho Saldaña, o El Castellano de Cuellar. Novela histórica original del siglo xiii* [reprint of the 1834 ed. 6 vols. in one], Madrid, 1914.—See: A. Cortón, *Espronceda*. Madrid, 1906; P. H. Churchman, *An Espronceda Bibliography*, in *Revue Hispanique*, XVII (1907), pp. 741-777; A. Bonilla y San Martín, *El pensamiento de Espronceda*, in *La España Moderna*, CCXXXIV (1908), pp. 69-101; J. Cascales y Muñoz, in *La España Moderna*, CCXXXIV (1908), pp. 27-48;

promptly punished : Espronceda was banished to the Franciscan convent at Guadalajara. In order to beguile the monotony of his exile, he was encouraged by Lista (who contributed a few stanzas) to write an epic poem. There is nothing distinctive about *El Pelayo* : nothing that marks Espronceda as the future chief of the romantic school. Soon after his return to Madrid, Espronceda probably conspired again ; at any rate he had to flee to Gibraltar and thence to Lisbon. Here he met Teresa Mancha, then a girl of fifteen years, who was to prove the source of his finest inspiration and a tragic influence in his life. In 1827, Espronceda, who was again in flight, met Teresa in London, where she had married : he eloped with her to Paris two years later, fought at the Barricades in 1830, made an unsuccessful attempt to sow the seeds of revolt in Navarre, and returning to Paris, was among those who volunteered to take part in the insurrection then in progress in Russian Poland. On the proclamation of the amnesty in 1833, Espronceda returned

P. H. Churchman, *Espronceda, Byron and Ossian*, in *Modern Language Notes*, XXIII (1908) ; James Fitzmaurice-Kelly, *Espronceda*, in *The Modern Language Review*, IV (1908), pp. 20-39 ; P. H. Churchman, *Byron and Espronceda*, in *Revue Hispanique*, XX (1909) ; R. Foulché-Delbosc, *Quelques réminiscences dans Espronceda*, in *Revue Hispanique*, XXI (1909), pp. 667-669 ; J. Cascales y Muñoz, *Apuntes y materiales para la biografía de Don José de Espronceda*, in *Revue Hispanique*, XXIII (1910), pp. 5-108 ; J. Cascales Muñoz, *Don José de Espronceda. Su época, su vida y sus obras*. Madrid, 1914 ; L. Banal, *Il pessimismo di Espronceda e alcuni rapporti col pensiero di Leopardi*, in *Revista crítica hispano-americana*, IV (1918), pp. 89-134 ; Ch. Tisserand, *Pour une édition d'Espronceda*, in *Revue Hispanique*, XLVI (1919), pp. 269-280 ; Angela Hämel, *Der Humor bei José de Espronceda*. Halle a. S., 1922 ; A. Lenz, *Contribution à l'étude d'Espronceda*, in *Revue Hispanique*, LVI (1922), pp. 522-529.

to Spain. His father was a brigadier and he easily obtained a commission in the 'Cuerpo de Guardias de Corps.' But he was not to hold it for long. He was cashiered and banished to Cuéllar for reading at a military banquet a poem which held the Government up to ridicule. Espronceda was in constant revolt and aggression. On his return to Madrid, he joined the National Militia and took part in the armed demonstrations of 1835 and 1836; he carried on an active political campaign in the columns of *El Español*. Shortly after the death of Teresa in 1839, Espronceda, who had definitely broken with her three years previously, published his *Poesías* (1840), which include some of his best lyrical pieces, and in 1841 appeared the unfinished *El Diablo Mundo* with its magnificent *Canto a Teresa*. Twelve years later a continuation was attempted by Miguel de los Santos Alvarez (1818-1892), a courtly poet who survives by the charming tale *La proteccion de un sastre* (1840). Meanwhile on the triumph of the Liberal Party in 1840, Espronceda's friends had come into power and Espronceda was appointed Secretary of Legation at The Hague. He returned to Madrid, was elected deputy for Almería, and died in his thirty-fourth year, on May 23, 1842, after an illness of four days.

Espronceda's attempt at the historical novel, *Sancho Saldaña o El Castellano de Cuellar* (1834), written during his banishment at Cuéllar, reveals him as a mediocre novelist: the book contains some picaresque passages but is not otherwise characteristic. His essays in the drama were not much more successful. *Doña Blanca de Borbón*, which appeared in abridged form in 1870, was only given in a complete edition in 1907. Espronceda wrote two plays in collaboration, the verse comedy *Ni el tío ni el sobrino* (1834) with Antonio Ros de Olano, later Marqués de Guad-el-Jelú (1802-1887) and author of the mysterious novel *El Doctor Lañuela* (1863); and the prose drama *Amor venga sus agravios* (1838) (which appeared under the pseudonym of Don Luis Senra y Palomares), with Eugenio Moreno Lopez.

Espronceda was naturally more susceptible to emotion than to reason : and he reacted strongly to the influence of Byron. His attitude towards life was a reflexion of the Byronic pose : his works are at times redolent with Byronic reminiscences. The *Cancion del Pirata* recalls *The Corsair* and Elvira's letter in *El Estudiante de Salamanca* is an inspired adaptation of Julia's letter in *Don Juan*. Espronceda, like Byron, became the hero of a legend. He was not averse from this presentation of himself. The protagonist of all his works, he figures in *El Estudiante de Salamanca* under the name of Don Félix de Montemar as a second Don Juan Tenorio—' fierce, insolent, irreligious, gallant, haughty, quarrelsome, insult in his glance, irony on his lips, fearing naught, trusting solely to his sword and courage.' ; disdainful, pessimistic, rebellious under his burden of disillusion, he is Fabio in *El Diablo Mundo* ; his artistic blending of aspiration and melancholy finds full expression in the declamatory *A Jarifa en una orgía*. Espronceda's spirit of revolt and his passion, almost elemental in its unrestraint, are characteristic of an epoch rather than of a race : in this respect he is more cosmopolitan than national. But his gift of cruel observation in *El Verdugo* is as representative of Quevedo as his conception of Elvira in *El Estudiante de Salamanca* is of Calderon, while his flights of superb rhetoric, the resonant melody of his diction, his picturesque imagery, his emphasis, all reflect the strength and the weakness of Spain. These qualities ensure Espronceda an eminent position among Spanish poets of any age.

A contemporary of Espronceda, the Catalan Manuel de Cabanyes [1] (1808-1833) draws his inspiration chiefly from Luis de Leon. The admirable hendecasyllabic poem, *A Cintio*, would seem to shew that this impeccable artist of form, who was essentially a poet's poet, might easily have become a disciple of the romantic school. Cabanyes died before his talent was fully developed, and his verse is measured rather by its promise than by its achievement. Though highly praised by critics, the *Preludios de mi lira* (1833) are less appreciated in Spain than they perhaps deserve. Juan Arolas [2] (1805-1849), a priest whose irregular life was in opposition to his calling and who died insane, displays a morbid sensuality in his *Poesías caballerescas y orientales* (1840) and *Poesías religiosas, orientales, caballerescas y amatorias* (1842). His orientalism is the conventional orientalism of Byron, Moore and Victor Hugo, but it contains a personal note lacking in Noroña's *Poesías asiáticas* (1833), which are only frigid versions of the Latin and English translations by Sir William Jones (1746-1794), Joseph Dacre Carlyle (1759-1804) and other orientalists. Nicomedes Pastor Diaz [3] (1811-1863), who was a gifted writer and a

[1] *The Poems of Manuel de Cabanyes*, ed. E. A. Peers, Manchester, 1923.—See: C. Oyuela, *Estudio sobre la vida y escritos del eminente poeta catalán Manuel de Cabanyes*. Barcelona, 1881.

[2] See: J. R. Lomba y Pedraja, *El P. Arolas, su vida y sus versos*. Madrid, 1898.

[3] *Obras*, ed. A. Ferrer del Rio, Madrid, 1867. 6 vols.—See: J. del Valle Moré, *Pastor Díaz, su vida y su obra*. Habana, 1911.

FERDINAND VII AND ISABEL II 445

clever versifier, adopted in his *Poesías* (1840) a pose of melancholy. His private life was untinged by the gloom which pervades all his work and which is visible in the autobiographical novel *De Villahermosa a la China, Coloquios íntimos* (1858). The failure of this book discouraged him profoundly and after writing a preface to Zorrilla's works, he was drawn into politics and became lost to literature. A link between two divergent types of romanticism was the Andalusian Salvador Bermudez de Castro (1814-1883) Duque de Ripalda and Marqués de Lema, whose reputation is based on the *Ensayos poéticos* (1841). In Latin-America his arrangement of stresses in the octave was known by the name of *bermudinas*. Though his popularity has declined, his energy and strain of resonant music ensure his revival if romanticism has a future before it. The same may be said of Gabriel Garcia Tassara[1] (1817-1875), a political satirist whose poems (1872) fell into partial disrepute because the predictions which they contained were contradicted by the events that followed them. But if he failed as a prophet, Garcia Tassara had a gift of authentic inspiration, and he expresses it in such pieces as the characteristic *Un diablo más*, whose sonorous harmony is in striking contrast to the sober melody of the *Himno al Mesías*.

The poet José Zorrilla[2] (1817-1893), whose *Recuerdos del tiempo viejo* (1880-1883) contain an

[1] *Poesías*, Madrid, 1872.

[2] *Obras dramáticas y líricas*, ed. M. P. Delgado, Madrid, 1895. 4 vols. ; *Galería dramática* : *Obras completas.* Madrid, 1905. 4 vols. ; *Obras* [with biography by I. de Ovejas], Paris, 1864. 3 vols. ; *Sancho Garcia*, ed. A. Bonilla y San Martín, 1917 (Clásicos de la Literatura española, 8) ; *Ultimos versos*

account of his life more fantastic than exact, first attracted notice in Spain when, as a young man of twenty years of age, he recited verses at Larra's open grave; on the Continent he had won a reputation as a dramatist and lyric some time before he went to France. Zorrilla was always extremely poor and his stay in Mexico (1855-1866) seems not to have benefited him materially in spite of the favour shewn him by the Emperor Maximilian (1832-1867). Help came to him towards his old age in the shape of a pension granted him in 1884 by the Spanish Government: in 1889 he received the empty honour of being publicly crowned at Granada. A born improviser, Zorrilla probably suffered less than others from being forced by poverty to rapid production. He had an amazing gift of fluency, but he lacked ideas, and his verse, as in the *Cantos del Trovador* (1840-1841) and *La Leyenda de Muhamad Al-Hamar el Nazarita, rey de Granada* (1847), attracts almost entirely through its verbal music. Zorrilla says that he composed *El Puñal del Godo* (1842) in twenty-four hours and that he wrote verses for the engravings by Gustave Doré (1832-1883) of Tennyson's poems. His worst enemy could not have fastened upon a more telling trait. On the stage Zorrilla's memory is kept green by such plays as: *El Zapatero y el Rey* (1840), whose inspiration derives from Hoz y Mota; *El Puñal del Godo*, drawn from Southey's *Roderick* (1814) and *Don Juan Tenorio* (1844), whose sources are *Les âmes*

inéditos y no coleccionados. Madrid, 1908.—See: N. Alonso Cortés, *Zorrilla, su vida y sus obras.* Valladolid, 1917-1920. 3 vols.; E. Cotarelo, *Centenario del nacimiento de Zorrilla*, in *Boletín de la R. Academia Esp.*, IV (1917), pp. 1-22; C. Eguía Ruiz, in *Crítica Patriótica.* Madrid, 1921. pp. 5-65.

FERDINAND VII AND ISABEL II 447

du Purgatoire (1825) by Prosper Mérimée, *Don Juan de Marana ou La chute d'un ange* (1836) by Alexandre Dumas and Zamora's well-known comedy, *No hay deuda que no se pague, y Convidado de piedra*, recast by Dionisio Solís. Though Zorrilla was not a finished artist, his qualities of lyrical spontaneity and dramatic insight, his essentially national spirit, won him deserved popularity. He had a faculty almost as miraculous as Lope de Vega's own, but he had not Lope de Vega's amplitude of dramatic conception. His negligences are in some measure redeemed by his flowing versification and his knack of devising effective combinations. Before Zorrilla left for Mexico he had collaborated in *Pentápolis*, *María* and *Un cuento de amores* (1852) with José Heriberto Garcia de Quevedo [1] (1819-?-1871), a Venezuelan who was killed during the Commune in Paris.

Manuel Breton de los Herreros [2] (1796-1873) continued the tradition of Moratin the younger; if he occasionally shews romantic tendencies—as in *Elena* (1834)—these do not form his happiest inspiration. He began his dramatic career with *A la vejez viruelas* (which was composed in 1817 but not produced until 1824) and he continued writing until 1867, the date of publication of *Los sentidos corporales*. *La Escuela de Matrimonio* (1852) is the most ambitious and perhaps the best of his numerous plays. In these faithful

[1] *Obras poéticas y literarias.* 2 vols. (Col. de los mejores Autores Esp., 57, 58).

[2] *Obras.* Madrid, 1883-1884. 5 vols.—See: A. Ferrer del Rio, in *Galeria de la literatura española.* Madrid, 1846. pp.127-140; Marqués de Molins, *Bretón de los Herreros, Recuerdos de su vida y de sus obras.* Madrid, 1883; G. le Gentil, *Le poète Manuel Breton de los Herreros et la société espagnole de 1830 à 1860.* Paris, 1909.

representations of middle-class life, the moral intention, at times too obvious, is relieved by touches of ironical humour. Breton was too prodigal a writer : but the ease of his versification is always very remarkable and the happy ingenuity of his expression, the felicitous oddity of his phrase are undeniable in such pieces as *Marcela o ¿ cuál de los tres ?* (1831), *¡ Muérete y verás!* (1837), *Ella es él* (1838), *El pelo de la dehesa* (1840) and *El cuarto de hora* (1840). Among minor playwrights Eulogio Florentino Sanz[1] (1825-1881) won success with *Don Francisco de Quevedo* (1848), though he is better known for his charming *Epístola*, dedicated from Berlin in 1856 to his friend Pedro Calvo Asensio (1821-1863), director of *La Iberia*; Narciso Sáenz Diez Serra (1830-1877) had a knack of improvisation and produced an excellent comedy in *¡ Don Tomás!* (1859), while Tomas Rodriguez Rubí[2] (1817-1890) is now only remembered by *La Rueda de la Fortuna* (1843).

Ventura de la Vega[3] (1807-1865), a schoolfellow of Espronceda and a native of the Argentine, was driven by poverty to adapt some sixty French plays before he could devote himself to original production. In *El*

---

[1] See : E. Carrere, *De la vida de un poeta. Florentino Sanz*, in *La Ilustración española y americana*, LXXXV (1908), pp. 139, 142.

[2] See : A. Ferrer del Rio, in *Galeria de la literatura española*. Madrid, 1846, pp. 291-303.

[3] *Obras poéticas*. Paris, 1866.—See : Conde de Cheste, *Elogio fúnebre* (Feb. 23, 1866), in *Memorias de la Academia Esp.*, II (1870), pp. 432-467 [this number contains Vega's verse trans. of Aeneid I] ; M. Menéndez y Pelayo, in *Antología de poetas hispano-americanos*. Madrid, 1895. IV, pp. CXLVI-CLXI; E. Piñeyro, in *El romanticismo en España*. Paris, 1904. pp. 221-232.

FERDINAND VII AND ISABEL II 449

hombre de mundo (1845) Vega shews himself a follower of Moratin the younger and of Breton. The subtle irony which characterizes this work degenerates too quickly into caricature, as for instance in *La Crítica de el Sí de las Niñas* (1848). His tragedy, *La Muerte de César* (1865) is not the most typical of his works; the undeniable vigour of his talent is best seen in *El Hombre de Mundo* and in such elegant compositions as *La Agitacion* and *Orillas del Pusa*.

Another American, GERTRUDIS GOMEZ DE AVELLANEDA[1] (1814-1873), born at Puerto Príncipe in Cuba, settled in Spain towards 1836 and under the pseudonym of *La Peregrina* published some verse in the periodical *La Aureola* (1839). Her novels, among which may be mentioned *Sab* (1839), a protest against slavery, and *Guatimozin, último emperador de Méjico* (1845) once found readers but are now dead. In them la Avellaneda is apt to deal exclusively with a thesis: she is too passionate to be a dexterous advocate, too absorbed to make an impressive exponent. In her early plays she is frequently only a gifted imitator with a certain grace of execution and adaptability in selection. It is as a poet that la Avellaneda survives,

[1] *Obras literarias*. Madrid, 1869-1871. 5 vols. [incomplete]; *Obras* [Centenary edition] Habana, 1914-1918. 4 vols.; *La Avellaneda: Autobiografía y cartas*.. ed. L. Cruz de Fuentes, Huelva, 1907; *Gertrudis Gómez de Avellaneda: Cartas inéditas y documentos relativos a su vida en Cuba de 1859 a 1864*, ed. J. A. Escoto, Matanzas, 1911; *Memorias inéditas de la Avellaneda*, ed. D. Figarola Caneda, Habana, 1914.—See: E. Piñeyro, in *El romanticismo en España*. Paris, 1904. pp. 233-253; J. M. Chacón y Calvo, *Gertrudis Gómez de Avellaneda, las influencias castellanas: examen negativo*. Habana, 1914; J. A. Rodríguez García, *De la Avellaneda*. Havana, 1914; E. B. Williams, *The Life and Dramatic Works of Gertrudis Gómez de Avellaneda*. Philadelphia, 1924.

in the *Poesías líricas* (1841) and in the virile dramas—*Alfonso Munio* (1844), the biblical tragedy *Saul* (1849), and especially *Baltasar* (1858). She has a gift of gloomy imagination which has its scenic effect, and her versification is usually admirable. Her first inspiration is the happiest: her emendations are nearly always unfortunate. She had the true poetic temperament, and in depth of lyrical fervour perhaps only one other woman poet, Christina Rossetti (1830-1894), surpassed her in her time.

The playwright MANUEL TAMAYO Y BAUS[1] (1829-1898) began by undergoing Italian and German influence. In his earliest printed play *Juana de Arco* (1847) he draws upon Schiller: *Virginia* (1853) is a dramatic essay in Alfieri's manner. The piece that established his reputation was *Locura de amor* (1855), whose heroine is Juana la Loca. The son of actors, Tamayo probably drank in at the fount a mastery of simple stagecraft. This would increase his popularity: he was amazingly popular in his day. But perhaps he owed as much to his finished versification and to his choice of themes: *La bola de nieve* (1856) is a protest against the frequent passion in Spain of jealousy, and *Lances de honor* (1863) is a declamation against the criminal folly of duelling. He was unable to devote himself wholly to original work owing to straitened circumstances and to the vagaries of the Madrid public whom he sought to please by adapting plays from Émile Augier (1820-1889), Octave Feuillet (1821-1891),

[1] See: B. de Tannenberg, *Un dramaturge espagnol: M. Tamayo y Baus*. Paris, 1898; E. Cotarelo y Mori, in *Estudios de historia literaria de España*. Madrid, 1901. pp. 363-403; N. Sicars y Salvadó, *Don Manuel Tamayo y Baus. Estudio crítico-biográfico*. Madrid, 1906.

FERDINAND VII AND ISABEL II

and from minor French dramatists like Léon Laya (1811-1872) and Paul Féval (1817-1887). He continued writing for the stage till he became librarian at the Biblioteca Nacional, but his activity on the boards ends with *Un drama nuevo* (1867) in which he had the boldness to present Shakespeare on the scene. It is a good play, perhaps the best of all Tamayo's works.

The dexterous politician Adelardo Lopez de Ayala [1] (1829-1879) has a lyric quality which entitles him to rank as a follower of Calderon, though a very tardy one. His *Epístola* to Emilio Arrieta is excellent for finish and intense sincerity, and his versification, though it has not Calderon's charm, is always good. Lopez de Ayala's note of exaggeration, his substitution of types for characters, are also due to the influence of Calderon. In *El tanto por ciento* (1861) and *Consuelo* (1878), both eloquent pleas for a higher idealism in public and private life, he skilfully combines romantic inspiration with satiric intention. He never surpassed *Un hombre de estado* (1851) and *Rioja* (1854), which are among his earlier efforts. Lopez de Ayala was somewhat too argumentative, too given to proving a thesis or a theory, but he had considerable power and occupies an honourable place in the history of the modern drama. Luis de Eguilaz y Eguilaz (1830-1874) reveals a deft touch in *La Cruz del Matrimonio* (1861). His best work is probably the *zarzuela*, *El molinero de Subiza* (1870), which is still acted.

[1] *Obras*, ed. M. Tamayo y Baus, Madrid, 1881-1885. 7 vols.; *Gustavo. Novela inédita* . . . ed. A. Pérez Calamarte, in *Revue Hispanique*, XIX (1908), pp. 300-427; *Epistolario inédito*, ed. A. Pérez Calamarte, in *Revue Hispanique*, XXVII (1912), pp. 499-622.

Among minor poets may be reckoned José Joaquin de Mora[1] (1783-1864), a Liberal exile and an unsympathetic personage who appears to have quarrelled wherever he went. He is remembered for his share in the Calderonian controversy (1814-1819), as well as for the *Leyendas Españolas* (1840) in which he reproduces Byron's ironical note with happy skill. His long exile in America seems to separate him from Spain, though he is very Spanish. Francisco Zea (1827 ?-1857) shews genuine talent in his posthumous *Obras en verso y prosa* (1858), of which one poem, *La Bandera*, finds a place in most anthologies. Bernardo Lopez Garcia (1840-1870), author of *Poesías* (1867), is best known for the virile composition *El Dos de Mayo*. He was too much interested in politics to develop his poetic gifts and the effect of his authentic musical vein is spoilt by the predominance of a metallic note. Ventura Ruiz Aguilera (1819 ?-1881), a Liberal Catholic, achieved popularity with his *Ecos Nacionales* (1849), which were followed by *Elegías y Armonías* (1863) and *Estaciones del año* (1879). He has charm but is unequal: his generous aspirations, his evident sincerity, his faith in human nature, all find expression in his verse, in which it is possible to catch a faint far-off echo of Italian influence, some muffled note of Manzoni's gentle, placid inspiration. A similar gentle strain is visible in José Selgas y Carrasco[2] (1822-1882), who contributed to the fighting review *El Padre Cobos*

---

[1] See: M. L. Amunátegui, *Don José Joaquín de Mora: apuntes biográficos*. Santiago de Chile, 1888; C. Pitollet, in *La querelle caldéronienne*, etc. Paris, 1909, pp. 48-71.

[2] See: R. Monner Sans, *Don José Selgas. El prosista. El poeta*, in *Revista de la Universidad de Buenos Aires*, XXXIV (1916).

FERDINAND VII AND ISABEL II 453

(1854-1856). The conventional tone of his verse in *Primavera* (1850) ensured its popularity, but with the passing of fashion, the book lost favour. As a prose-writer, Selgas y Carrasco has a rapid journalistic style, but he is a good versifier with a delicate touch and taste. Juan Martínez Villergas [1] (1816-1894), another journalist, is known for his *Poesías jocosas y satíricas* (1842), *El Baile de las Brujas* (1843) and *El Baile de Piñata* (1843), which are full of roguish humour. Martínez Villergas was not lacking in critical judgement: he was among the first to expose the attempt of Adolfo de Castro (1823-1898) to pass off *El Buscapié* as an authentic work of Cervantes.

As early as 1838 Ramón de Campoamor [2] (1819-1901) had come into notice with a romantic play, *Una muger generosa*. An astute Asturian, he abandoned his original intention of entering the Jesuit order, and after studying medicine at Madrid, divided his time between politics, philosophy, the drama and poetry. He made a false start as a romantic poet with *Ternezas y flores* (1840) and *Ayes del alma* (1842): his plays—*Guerra a la guerra* (1870), *El Palacio de la Verdad* (1871), *Cuerdos y locos* (1873), *Dies irae* (1873), *El*

---

[1] See: J. Chastenay, *Une épigramme de Martínez Villergas*, in *Revue Hispanique*, XVIII (1908), p. 286; XXII (1910), pp. 453-456; N. Alonso Cortés, *Juan Martínez Villergas*. 2nd ed. Valladolid, 1913.

[2] *Obras completas*, ed. U. González Serrano, V. Colorado and M. Ordóñez, Madrid, 1901-1903. 8 vols.; *Poesías*, ed. C. Rivas Cherif, 1921 (Clásicos Cast., 40).—See: H. Peseux-Richard, *Humoradas, Doloras et Petits Poèmes de D. Ramon de Campoamor*, in *Revue Hispanique*, I (1894), pp. 236-257; E. Pardo Bazán, in *Retratos y apuntes literarios*. Madrid, n.d. pp. 5-62 (*Obras completas*, XXXII); A. González-Blanco, *Campoamor* (*Biografía y estudio crítico*). Madrid, 1912.

Honor (1874)—though interesting, and successful in their day, are lacking in dramatic spirit. He was said to have inaugurated a new poetic genre with *Doloras* (1846), *Pequeños Poemas* (1872-1874) and *Humoradas* (1886-1888). Campoamor's definition of these forms is vague and does not establish a distinction between them. A *humorada* is a brilliant apophthegm : a *dolora* the poet defines as a dramatic *humorada*, and a *pequeño poema* is a *dolora* on a larger scale. It is upon the *dolora* that he appears to set most value. In this miniature drama of four, eight, or twelve lines, whose motive is some commonplace theme, some humoristic, philosophic epigram, Campoamor's gifts of grace, irony, wit and pathos find admirable expression. He displays a combination of ironical philosophy and emotion, of concision and delicacy of thought that makes him a master in this *genre*. Yet, as M. Peseux-Richard sagaciously remarks, Campoamor's originality is confined to the invention of a name for a form which is as old as any other form of literature. Though he may affect to be careless of technique, indulges at times in platitudes and substitutes sentimentalism for sentiment or a paradox for an epigram, he remains, nevertheless, an admirable craftsman and an accomplished artist. His longer poems, *Colón* (1853) and *El drama universal* (1869) are less characteristic of his talent. Campoamor was deservedly popular in Spain : he was also well known out of Spain, but he is not in any sense a national poet and owes perhaps more to Victor Hugo than he consciously realized.

GUSTAVO ADOLFO BÉCQUER[1] (1836-1870) was left an orphan at the age of ten years. Brought up by his

[1] *Obras*. 8th ed. Madrid, 1915. 3 vols.—See: E. W. Olmsted, Introduction to *Legends, Tales and Poems by Gustavo Adolfo*

godmother at Seville, he refused to adopt a career and came to Madrid to make a living. In 1857 he was given some small official post : he soon lost this through his inaptitude for business, and until his death eked out a miserable existence by translations and journalistic work. The three volumes of his *Obras* (1871) consist of prose legends and poetry which he modestly calls *Rimas*. Bécquer is an authentic poet and, perhaps, most a poet in his prose : it is reminiscent of Hoffmann, but it has a personal element and his morbid fancies find play in such legends as *Los ojos verdes*, where Fernando loses his life for love of the green-eyed mermaiden ; *El rayo de luna*, which tells the tale of Manrique's madness ; *La Rosa de pasion* with its account of Daniel's sacrilege and the potent fragment, *La mujer de piedra*. In his verse Bécquer undergoes the influence of Heine : he has not the incomparable irony of the German poet but substitutes instead a note of elfin witchery. He is not always equal ; at his best his musical cadences and the apparent simplicity of his rhymes give high artistic expression to the poet's fevered visions.

Controversial matters were the central object of the book that made Juan Antonio Llorente[1] (1756-1823) famous, the *Histoire critique de l'Inquisition d'Espagne depuis l'époque de son établissement par Ferdinand V*

Bécquer. Boston, 1907; J. López Nuñez, *Bécquer* : *biografía anecdótica*. Madrid [1915].

[1] See : M. Menéndez y Pelayo, in *Historia de los heterodoxes españoles*. Madrid, 1882. III, pp. 418-427 ; A. Morel-Fatio, *D. Juan Antonio Llorente*, in *Bulletin hispanique*, XXIII (1921), pp. 117-128 ; J. Sarrailh, *D. Juan Antonio Llorente*, in *Bulletin hispanique*, XXV (1923), pp. 226-236.

jusqu'au règne de Ferdinand VII (1817-1818), whose Spanish version for political reasons only appeared in 1822. Llorente had once been Secretary to the Inquisition and should, therefore, have been well-informed as to the events of which he wrote. But he had no skill in arranging his materials and deals with great questions in the narrowest sectarian spirit. The book created an enormous sensation both in and out of Spain: but this success was ephemeral. Its clumsy arrangement and its party-spirit amounting almost to bad faith deprive it of all permanent value, and for purposes of consultation it has been superseded by the work of Henry Charles Lea (1825-1905). Llorente had no literary gift nor power of criticism: in his *Observaciones críticas sobre el Gil Blas de Santillana* (1822) he brings forward the theory that Lesage translated a Spanish original by Antonio de Solís. A return of some sort to classical models was practised by José Maria Queipo de Llano, Conde de Toreno[1] (1786-1843), in his *Historia del levantamiento, guerra y revolucion de España* (1835-1837). This is really a history of the War of Independence told with a tiresome abundance of detail and comprising personal reminiscences. It contains some valuable matter, but it is ill-arranged, and the style though careful is not distinguished. Another writer of this period, José Antonio Conde[2] (1766-1820), was widely recognized

---

[1] *Historia del levantamiento, guerra y revolucion de España*, ed. L. A. de Cueto (Marqués de Valmar), 1872 (Bib. de Autores Esp., LXIV).—See: A. Ferrer del Rio, in *Galeria de la literatura española*. Madrid, 1846. pp. 67-84.

[2] See: P. Roca, *Vida y escritos de José Antonio Conde*, in *Revista de Archivos*, etc. VIII (1903), pp. 378-394, 458-469; IX (1903), pp. 279-291, 338-354; X (1904), pp. 27-42; XII (1905), pp. 139-

FERDINAND VII AND ISABEL II

as an authority in his special domain; he had the field almost entirely to himself till the rise of the great Arabist Dozy (1820-1883). A great many of the statements in Conde's *Historia de la dominacion de los árabes en España* (1820-1821) are no longer in popular favour. They are rejected on the ground of their inherent improbability and—partly—because his successors have declared against them. Conde's writing is not brilliant, but he has persuasive skill and knows how to present an argument. With the foregoing should be mentioned Modesto Lafuente (1806-1866), author of the *Viajes de Fray Gerundio por Francia, Bélgica, Holanda y orillas del Rhin* (1842) and the *Historia general de España*[1] (1850-1867), a verbose but conscientious compilation, invaluable in its presentation of different epochs, which holds a place unfilled as yet by later and more accurate histories; and the historian Antonio Ferrer del Rio (1814-1872), whose *Galeria de la literatura española* (1846) contains interesting portraits of contemporary writers.

MARIANO JOSEF DE LARRA[2] (1809-1837) was the son of a Spanish doctor who joined the French army of Napoleon. His early years were spent at Bordeaux,

---

148; L. Barrau-Dihigo, *Contribution à la critique de Conde*, in *Homenaje à D. Francisco Codera*. Zaragoza, 1904. pp. 551-569.

[1] Ed. Barcelona, 1887-1890. 25 vols.

[2] *Obras completas de Fígaro* (Col. de los mejores Autores Esp., 47, 48); *Colección de artículos escogidos* [with preface by J. Yxart], Barcelona, 1885; *Cuatro artículos*, ed. R. Foulché-Delbosc, in *Revue Hispanique*, iv (1897), pp. 314-328; *Artículos de costumbres*, ed. J. R. Lomba y Pedraja, 1923. 2 vols. (Clásicos cast., 45, 52).—See: M. Chaves, *Don Mariano José de Larra (Fígaro). Su tiempo, su vida, sus obras.* Sevilla, 1898; J. D. M. Ford, *English Influence upon Spanish Literature in the early part*

whence he returned to Spain at the age of ten years, hardly able to speak the language which was destined to become so formidable a weapon in his hands. He began to study law, tired of it and came to Madrid, where he made an unhappy marriage and took up journalism. In consequence of a disastrous love-affair with Dolores Armijo de Cambronero, Larra blew out his brains when he was twenty-eight years old. Among his dramatic pieces are *No más mostrador* (1831), an adaptation of *Les Adieux aux comptoirs* (1824) by Eugène Scribe (1791-1861) and Mélesville, the pseudonym adopted by Aimé Honoré Joseph Duveyrier (1787-1865), and *Macías* (1834), whose subject Larra treats again in the historical novel, *El Doncel de don Enrique el Doliente* (1834), a clever but rather dry piece of work not rich enough in movement or in picturesqueness. A born journalist, Larra had an unrivalled gift of satirical observation. Under various pseudonyms 'El Duende satírico,' 'Andrés Niporesas,' 'Ramon Arriala,' he eluded the rigours of the censor-

of the nineteenth century, in *Publications of the Modern Language Association of America*, XVI (1901), pp. 453-459; E. Piñeyro, in *El romanticismo en España*. Paris, 1904. pp. 1-50; J. Nombela y Campos, *Larra (Fígaro)*. Madrid, 1906; N. Alonso Cortés, *Un dato para la biografía de Larra*, in *Viejo y Nuevo*. Valladolid, 1915, pp. 67-71; 'Azorín,' in *Rivas y Larra: razón social del romanticismo en España*. Madrid, 1916. pp. 139-287; J. R. Lomba y Pedraja, *Mariano José de Larra (Fígaro) como escritor político*. Madrid, 1918; E. M'Guire, *A Study of the Writings of D. Mariano José de Larra*, in *University of California Publications in Modern Philology*, VII (1918), pp. 87-130; C. de Burgos (Colombine), *Fígaro (Revelaciones, 'Ella' descubierta, Epistolario inédito*. Madrid, 1919; A. González Blanco, *Larra (Fígaro)*. Madrid, 1919; J. R. Lomba y Pedraja, *Mariano José de Larra (Fígaro) como crítico literario*. Madrid, 1920.

FERDINAND VII AND ISABEL II 459

ship and achieved celebrity as 'Juan Perez de Munguia' and 'Fígaro' in the columns of *El Pobrecito hablador* (1832-1833) and the *Revista española* (1834). He was a master of style, and his articles on Spanish politics and racial defects are written with a mordant incisiveness which gives force to his satire to-day—as for instance in *El Día de Difuntos*. While his presentation of life is gloomy and his pessimism increasingly marked, his shrewd penetration, his sombre humour, his political instinct and his power of incisive expression give him a foremost position among the prose-writers of the nineteenth century. A somewhat similar but far less potent talent was that of the Peruvian Felipe Pardo (1806-1868), one of Lista's pupils and author of *El espejo de mi tierra* (1840) and of the pleasant comedy, *Una huérfana en Chorrillos* (1833), which won him a reputation in Latin-America.

José Somoza[1] (1781-1852), a delightful prose-writer, whose verse and 'ensayos rítmicos' (1822-1834-1835) are negligible, is remembered for his *Obras . . . Artículos en prosa* (1842), an interesting collection in which are set down in a fine and delicate manner the author's memories of a bygone, romantic Spain that would have charmed Théophile Gautier. A contrast to Somoza's direct and engaging simplicity is afforded by Serafin Estébanez Calderon[2] (1799-1867), 'El Solitario,' whose biography has been written by his nephew, Antonio Cánovas del Castillo. With the

[1] *Obras en prosa y verso*, ed. J. R. Lomba y Pedraja. Madrid, n.d.
[2] *Escenas andaluzas*. 1883 (Col. de Escritores Cast., 6); *De la conquista y pérdida de Portugal*. 1885. 2 vols. (Col. de Escritores Cast., 29, 31); *Poesías*. 1888 (Col. de Escritores Cast., 72).—See: A. Cánovas del Castillo, '*El Solitario*' *y su tiempo*. 1883. 2 vols. (Col. de Escritores Cast., 8, 9).

exception of the sonnet (not included in the *Poesías*, 1831) on a book-thief directed at the celebrated book-collector and bibliographer, Bartolomé José Gallardo (1776-1852), Estébanez Calderon's verse, as well as his novel *Cristianos y Moriscos* (1838) and the unfinished *De la conquista y pérdida de Portugal* (1885) are now forgotten. The *Escenas andaluzas* (1847), a record of manners and customs in old Andalusia, is marred by affectations of style, local mannerisms of speech or deliberate archaisms which make very difficult reading. Consequently, it never was popular, but it offers peculiar interest as recording the impressions of a man of talent who set an exaggerated value on the picturesque detail and the telling phrase.

Ramon de Mesonero Romanos [1] (1803-1882) has been frequently described as a follower of Larra. In reality the earliest chapters of his *Panorama Matritense* (1835)—which was reprinted with the addition of a series of fresh scenes in 1842 under the title of *Escenas matritenses*—anticipated by six months any work of a similar description by Larra. Mesonero avers having written at the age of seventeen years the anonymous *Mis ratos perdidos o ligero bosquejo de Madrid* (1822), which are the *Escenas* in embryo. If his memory is not at fault, then he conceived the idea of this *genre* (which he describes as a novelty in Spain) while Larra was a boy of eleven years. Mesonero lacks Larra's concise energy: he is inclined to be diffuse, but this prolixity is at times an attraction in his pictures of old Madrid. His vivid descriptions of the town before it lost its charm through modernization are so many

[1] See: R. Foulché-Delbosc, *Le modèle inavoué du 'Panorama matritense' de Mesonero Romanos*, in *Revue Hispanique*, XLVIII (1920), pp. 257-310.

documents for the reconstruction of the social life of a lost epoch. Mesonero writes simply and naturally; he preserves these qualities of style in his interesting *Memorias de un setenton, natural y vecino de Madrid* (1880).

Observation of customs and manners distinguished Cecilia Francisca Josefa Böhl de Faber, whose literary pseudonym, Fernan Caballero[1] (1796-1877) was taken from a village in La Mancha. The child of a German father and a Spanish mother, born and partly educated abroad, she possessed in a remarkable degree the gift of tongues. Her earliest novel *Sola, oder Wahrheit und Schein* (1840) and the first sketch of *La Familia de Albareda* (1856) were written in German: the original draft of *La Gaviota* (1849), with which she made her *début* in Spanish literature when she was over fifty years of age, was in French. This novel was translated into most European languages and with *La Familia de Albareda* remains, perhaps, the best of its author's works. Fernan Caballero, though not in any sense a literary artist, was a born teller of stories, and her transcriptions of provincial life in *Cuadros de costumbres* (1862) are set down with fidelity and a certain grace of style. A foreigner and yet essentially a native, she brought to her work a freshness of vision which, combined with a natural gift of observation, enabled her to produce excellent examples of picturesque narration. When the scene shifts to high life as

---

[1] *Obras completas*, 1893-1914. 17 vols. (Col. de Escritores Castellanos, 98, etc.); *Cartas*, ed. Fr. Diego de Valencia. Madrid, 1919.—See: A. Morel-Fatio, *Fernan Caballero d'après sa correspondance avec Antoine de Latour*, in *Études sur l'Espagne*. Paris, 1904. III, pp. 279-370; L. Coloma, *Recuerdos de Fernán Caballero*. Bilbao, n.d.

in *Clemencia* (1862) and *Magdalena*, there is a certain unreality visible which would seem to shew that Fernan Caballero invented traits without confirming them. The sentimentality in which she indulges belongs to her period; her didactic tendency is more marked in her later publications and by her insistence on the moral lesson, she loses much of her primitive charm and simplicity. A variant of pastoralism with an admixture of realism is found in the novels of Antonio de Trueba[1] (1819 ?-1889), author of *Cuentos de color de rosa* (1859) and *Cuentos campesinos* (1860), which even Fernan Caballero found too mild for every-day usage.

Under Sir Walter Scott's influence, a new direction had been given to the novel and it assumed the shape of historical fiction. It produced little that is memorable in this vein. The attempts of Espronceda and of Larra have already been mentioned; to these may be added a book by Enrique Gil y Carrasco[2] (1815-1846), *El Señor de Bembibre* (1844), which scored rather more than a *succès d'estime*. Gil was a poet too, but he was no contemptible prose-writer. The only thing, perhaps, that can be alleged against his novel is that its plot is too reminiscent of *The Bride of Lammermoor*; apart from this, the story has a dash and vigour which give it a distinctive place in the

[1] See: R. Becerro de Bengoa, *Trueba, estudio biográfico*. Madrid, n.d. (Personajes ilustres, 13); A. González-Blanco, *Antonio de Trueba. Su vida y sus obras*. Bilbao, 1914.

[2] *Obras* ... ed. G. Laverde, Madrid, n.d.; *Obras en prosa* ... ed. J. del Pino and F. de la Vera é Isla, Madrid, 1883. 2 vols.— See: N. Alonso Cortés, *Un centenario*, in *Viejo y Nuevo*. Valladolid, 1915. pp. 79-85; J. R. Lomba y Pedraja, *Enrique Gil y Carrasco: su vida y su obra literaria*, in *Revista de Filología Esp.*, II (1915), pp. 137-179.

history of the Spanish novel in the nineteenth century. The Navarrese Francisco Navarro Villoslada[1] (1818-1895), who began by writing an epic poem, *Luchana* (1840), wasted his talent in journalism. Some of his historical novels, such as *Doña Urraca de Castilla* (1849) and *Amaya o los vascos en el siglo viii* (1877) deserve to be remembered as reconstructions of a past epoch which Villoslada's vivid fantasy has sought magnificently to recall. Manuel Fernandez y Gonzalez[2] (1821-1888) had an untiring faculty of invention and a flowing pen; he produced in rapid succession a series of stirring episodes. He wrote too much—a fault for which his poverty was responsible—and of his numerous improvisations only *Men Rodriguez de Sanabria* (1853), *Martin Gil* (1854) and *El Cocinero de su Magestad* (1857) call for remembrance.

JUAN DONOSO CORTÉS[3] (1809-1853) is the author of the justly renowned *Ensayo sobre el catolicismo, el liberalismo y el socialismo, considerados en sus principios fundamentales* (1851). Intensely intolerant, as might be expected of one who modified his most intimate convictions from dawn to dusk, Donoso Cortés pours forth a flood of dogmatic statements but he gives no reasoned exposition. He is too emphatic: but he writes with eloquence and fire and with a belief in his own infallibility that has no parallel in literature.

[1] See: B. Q. Cornish, *Francisco Navarro Villoslada* [University of California Publications in Modern Philology, 7], Berkeley, 1918.

[2] See: A. Sánchez Moguel, *Discurso en honor de D. Manuel Fernández y González* [Ateneo de Madrid], 1888.

[3] *Obras*, ed. G. Tejado, Madrid, 1854-1855. 5 vols.—See: R. M. Baralt, in *Discursos leídos en las recepciones públicas que ha celebrado desde 1847 la R. Academia Esp.*, II (1861), pp. 5-53; M. Menéndez y Pelayo, in *Historia de los heterodoxos españoles*. Madrid, 1882. III, pp. 746-754.

This self-arrogance would be ridiculous in the majority of people : it is not so with Donoso Cortés. One feels behind it all the convictions and strength of the man. In reading him, one is reminded of Coleridge's words : ' The man who puts even Christianity before truth will go on to put the Church before Christianity, and will end by putting himself before the Church.'

If Donoso Cortés denounces man's reason as a faculty that leads naturally to error, JAIME BALMES[1] (1810-1848) makes no step without a direct appeal to it. His book, *El protestantismo comparado con el catolicismo en sus relaciones con la civilizacion europea* (1844), written in refutation of Guizot (1787-1874) is one of the most ingenious works of modern controversy. Balmes is not greatly concerned with questions of style—his journalistic work prevented his ever devoting himself entirely to literature—but his dexterity in argument and his subtle reasoning combined to create a striking specimen of destructive criticism. In the region of abstract philosophy he stands out less prominently, yet his *Filosofía fundamental* (1846), representing the scholastic system of thought and shewing Scotch and Cartesian influence, offers interest as indicating a tendency on the part of Spain to enter the modern philosophical movement.

A friend of Balmes, the eminent archaeologist José Maria Quadrado[2] (1819-1896) was a contributor to

[1] See: J. Elías de Molins, *Balmes y su tiempo*. Barcelona, 1906 ; M. Menéndez y Pelayo, *Dos palabras sobre el Centenario de Balmes*. Vich, 1910 ; N. Roure, *La vida y las obras de Balmes*, Madrid, 1910 ; N. Roure, *Las ideas de Balmes*, Madrid-Gerona, 1910 ; J. M. Ruano y Corbo, *Balmes apologista : estudio crítico*. Santiago, 1911.

[2] *Ensayos religiosos, políticos, y literarios*. 2nd ed. [preface by M. Menéndez y Pelayo, reprinted in *Estudios de Crítica*

the *Recuerdos y bellezas de España*, initiated by the efforts of the artist Francisco Javier Parcerisa (1803-1875) with Pablo Piferrer (1818-1848) and Francisco Pi y Margall (1824-1901) as collaborators. The first volume appeared in 1839. But Quadrado's energies were not limited to the field of archaeology. An amateur of verse, he recast three plays of Shakespeare : *Macbeth*, *King Lear* and *Measure for Measure* ; he also attempted a continuation to the *Discours sur l'Histoire Universelle* (1681) of Bossuet (1627-1704) and as archivist of the Balearic Isles wrote *Forenses y Ciudadanos* (1847), an interesting study in social history. Quadrado had a delicate artistic taste and an enviable gift of communicating his enthusiasms ; his rival Hübner (1834-1901) was moved to speak of him as 'vir optimus.'

literaria. 1895. II, pp. 3-71 (Col. de Escritores Cast., 106)], Palma de Mallorca, 1893-1894. 3 vols.

XIII

SPANISH LITERATURE SINCE 1868

The years following upon the fall of Isabel II in 1868 were years of political disturbance and anarchy culminating with the downfall of the Republic and the establishment on the throne of Alphonso XII (1874-1885). As regards literature the tendencies were perhaps more general, more cosmopolitan and less exclusively French. To Italy, the country to which she originally owed so much, Spain was in much the same relation as Roland to Sir Leoline in *Christabel*:

> 'They stood aloof, the scars remaining,
> Like cliffs that had been rent asunder ;
> A dreary sea now flows between.
> But neither heat, nor frost, nor thunder,
> Shall wholly do away, I ween,
> The marks of that which once hath been.'

Literature, after all, depends upon form, and the Italian form survived. Two of the most celebrated poets of this age, Campoamor and Núñez de Arce, both excelled and won their reputation as masters of the Italian metres introduced by Boscan and Garci Lasso de la Vega some four centuries ago. To this extent Italy still had an undisputed sway in the nineteenth century. With the advent of the South American poet, Rubén Darío, Spanish verse was profoundly revolutionized. A development almost as distinctive took place in the domain of the novel. In this an important part was played by the nephew of Alcalá Galiano, JUAN VALERA[1] (1824-1905), who was among the first to recognize the new talent of Rubén Darío. Valera began his diplomatic career in 1847 as unpaid attaché to the Spanish legation at Naples under the Duque de Rivas, and until within ten years of his death he took an active part in politics, representing Spain at the courts of St. Petersburg, Brussels, Vienna and at Washington. His earliest published work was a small volume of youthful poems called *Ensayos Poéticos* (1844), which was followed in 1858 by *Poesías*. Valera's verse is melodious and finished, but it lacks spontaneity and inspiration. It is the work—not of a poet, but—of a scholar of wide reading and delicate taste, with a mastery of technique. Valera could never reconcile himself to the hostile verdict pronounced against it; he turned to prose and to criticism in *Estudios críticos sobre la literatura* (1864), *Disertaciones y juicios literarios* (1878) and *Nuevos estudios críticos* (1888). He had ideal gifts for the task : varied interests, a vast knowledge and an entire absence of prejudice. But it was an almost indispensable condition of his art that he should deal with the past : his excessive urbanity towards living authors diminished the value of his appreciations and outweighs his very real qualities of taste, penetration and suggestiveness.

[1] See: E. Pardo Bazán, in *Retratos y apuntes literarios.* Madrid, n.d. pp. 217-280 (*Obras completas,* 32); Conde de Casa-Valencia, *Necrología del Excelentísimo Sr. D. Juan Valera.* Madrid, 1905; Conde de las Navas, *Don Juan Valera : apuntes del natural.* Madrid, 1905; *Noticia autobiográfica* [5 de enero de 1863], in *Boletín de la R. Academia Esp.*, 1 (1914), pp. 128-140.

His diplomatic cordiality had an unexpected result in the *Cartas americanas* (1889), whose exaggerated eulogy has all the effect of censure.

Valera was prominent neither as a poet nor as a critic : he was destined to triumph as a novelist. His first attempt at fiction, *Margarita y Antonio*, appeared in *El Contemporáneo* (February-June, 1861), which he had helped to found : it was premature and remained unfinished. It was not until his fiftieth year that he published the work which brought him fame—*Pepita Jiménez* (1874). Valera makes the humorous confession that this novel was the outcome of a course of mystical and pious reading. The hero, Lùis de Vargas, is a seminarist who thinks himself predestined to a life of sanctity and devotional fervour : his change of mind as he gradually succumbs to the attractions of Pepita is admirably drawn. The tale has blemishes, no doubt ; there are pauses in the action of the story and too many digressions. But it is essentially Spanish, the style is excellent, the love-story is told with subtlety and truth and with a touch of mischievous humour : the characters stand out as persons of flesh and blood. *Pepita Jiménez* sounds once more that characteristic note in Spanish literature which Coventry Patmore describes as ' that complete synthesis of gravity of matter and gaiety of manner which is the glittering crown of art, and which, out of Spanish literature, is to be found only in Shakespeare, and even in him in a far less obvious degree.' When all allowances are made for over-estimation, *Pepita Jiménez* remains a remarkable achievement. Valera's second novel, *Las ilusiones del doctor Faustino* (1875), superior in humour and analysis to its predecessor, was received with less favour, possibly because it suffers from over-refinement and cruelty of observation. More pathetic in inspiration and with a profounder significance is *El Comendador Mendoza* (1877), whose sincere emotion gives it the force of a piece of autobiography. Valera was not inventive: he could only relate from personal observation. *Doña Luz* (1879) has points of contact with *Pepita Jiménez* but it has a tragic element and reveals deeper psychological insight. Valera was no less successful in the dialogue and short story: a striking example of his art in this *genre* is afforded by *Asclepigenia* (1878). Towards the end of his life, he became blind and was forced to dictate his compositions; in spite of this disadvantage he produced *Genio y Figura* (1897), *De varios colores* (1898) and *Morsamor* (1899). These, though they have not, perhaps, the technical perfection of his earlier works, are full of a humour, sympathy and understanding eminently characteristic of their writer. Valera worked consistently until the end: death surprised him while he was engaged upon a speech in honour of Cervantes's tercentenary. Cosmopolitan in spirit, he was at the same time intensely Spanish in his flashing irony and his courtesy: he combined with these gifts a sense of measure uncommon in Spanish novelists. Valera broke entirely new ground in the history of the novel with *Pepita Jiménez*, and was admittedly one of the most eminent Spanish men of letters at the end of the nineteenth century.

Pedro Antonio de Alarcón [1] (1833-1891), who began life as a journalist and dramatist, published in 1855 *El final de Norma*, a novel of romantic tendencies written

[1] See: E. Pardo Bazán, in *Retratos y Apuntes literarios*. Madrid, s.f., pp. 117-216 (*Obras Completas*, 32); A. Bonilla y San Martín, *Los orígenes de ' El sombrero de tres picos,'* in

in an elegant prose. His drama, *El Hijo pródigo* (1857), was hissed off the stage, and Alarcón, piqued by this failure, enlisted as a volunteer for the Moroccan War. He embodied his experiences in the *Diario de un testigo de la guerra de África* (1859), a series of brilliant impressions told with a vigour and patriotic force that brought the author into immediate repute. But Alarcón's renown to-day rests almost entirely upon *El sombrero de tres picos* (1874), which appeared in the *Revista Europea* the very year of the publication of *Pepita Jiménez*. A prose version of the popular romance, *El Molinero de Arcos*, with elements from the sainete *El Corregidor y la Molinera* (1862), it gives in a picturesque setting a delightful record of Andalusian customs. Alarcón, who was a weathercock in politics and at the Restoration rated his former colleagues on *El Látigo* (to whose editorship he had been appointed in 1854), defended the neo-catholic reaction in the novel *El Escándalo* (1875), which created a sensation at the time but is now forgotten. The same fate befell *La Pródiga* (1882). Alarcón never repeated the triumph of *El sombrero de tres picos* and while some of the *Novelas cortas* (1881-1882) reveal a gift of minute observation and have its mischievous wit, none possess in the same degree its gaiety and charm. Flashes of its picaresque humour are caught in *El Capitán Veneno* (1881), which lacks, however, its ripeness and finish. Readers are still found for *El Niño de la Bola* (1880) on which Hugo Wolf (1860-1903) based his *Manuel Venegas* (1902) just as in *Der Corregidor* (1896) he had previously set to music *El sombrero de tres picos*.

Revue Hispanique, XIII (1905), pp. 5-17; R. Foulché-Delbosc, *D'où dérive 'El sombrero de tres picos,'* in *Revue Hispanique*, XVIII (1908), pp. 468-487.

José María de Pereda[1] (1833-1906), who has been accused by hostile critics of provincialism, was a born aristocrat who clung to the customs and manners of the past, disliked intensely the life of the capital and remained always devoted to his native place, Polanco, near Santander. He settled down there after he had completed his studies at Madrid and wrote (1858) for a local paper *La Abeja montañesa*. His sketches were reproduced in book form in 1864-1871 as the *Escenas montañesas* : they attracted little attention beyond a provincial circle. Pereda's realism was too strong for a public brought up on Trueba's rose-water sentimentalism. But he went on his way unheeding, and the complete success of *Bocetos al temple* (1876) proved that he had chosen the right path. In this collection of short stories, moulded on the same characteristic lines as the *Escenas montañesas*, the development of Pereda's talent is more clearly revealed. He is essentially a regional novelist : he loses his effect when he leaves the mountain air. Yet even in his more ambitious works such as *Don Gonzalo González de la Gonzalera* (1878), which is concerned with politics, the picaresque novel *Pedro Sánchez* (1883), which pictures a young man's experiences during the revolution of 1854, and *Sotileza* (1884), which treats of fisherfolk and the conditions of marine life, Pereda's characters keep all the local traits : they are universal types only in so far as they are types of humanity. The abuse of dialect and technical terms, particularly in *Sotileza* (for which the author prepared a vocabulary)

[1] See : B. de Tannenberg, *J. M. de Pereda*, in *Revue Hispanique*, v (1898), pp. 330-364 ; M. Menéndez y Pelayo, in *Estudios de crítica literaria*. 1908. 5ª serie, pp. 353-444 (Col. de Escritores Castellanos, 137) ; J. Montero, *Pereda*. Madrid 1919.

is an artistic blemish, less serious perhaps in Pereda owing to the regional savour with which his works are redolent. He has a gift of satirical observation most marked in *Tipos trashumantes* (1877), where his studies in portraiture are so many examples of mocking irony; but he is prone to carry to excess the caricature of an unsympathetic personage. His novels suffer at times from a didactic intention as well as from the campaigning spirit which drove him to refute innovations against long-established social customs. He is overemphatic and yields too readily to a polemical temptation, as when he replies to the *Petites misères de la vie conjugale* by Balzac (1799-1850) in *El buey suelto* (1877), and to Pérez Galdós's *Doña Perfecta* and *Gloria* in *De tal palo, tal astilla* (1879), where he endeavours to prove that tolerance in religion can only bring disaster. Pereda is assured that the sterner virtues do not easily survive the atmosphere of towns, and he recurs to this thesis in *Pedro Sánchez* as well as in his regional novels, *El sabor de la tierruca* (1882) and *Peñas arriba* (1895): here his powers of description are magnificently seen. On the whole, Pereda pictures life as a Christian naturalist, touched with the mystic and the picaresque spirit, sees it. His fidelity is unblenching: his characters are full of vitality; his style is supple, forcible, pure; and his eye for detail, his passionate sympathy with a Spain which is fast disappearing, make of his novels the chronicles of a picturesque and reactionary age—chronicles full of a singular charm since Pereda united to force and energetic realism a gift of generous sympathy, and genial understanding.

BENITO PÉREZ GALDÓS[1] (1843-1920), who published

[1] See: M. Menéndez y Pelayo, in *Estudios de crítica literaria*. 1908. 5ª serie, pp. 83-127 (Col. de Escritores Cast., 137);

SPANISH LITERATURE SINCE 1868

three novels, *La Fontana de oro* (1867-1868), *La Sombra* (1870) and *El Audaz* (1871), before either *Pepita Jiménez* or *El sombrero de tres picos* saw the light, had all his countrymen's copiousness of production. The fact that he was a Canary-Islander possibly gave him a slightly objective standpoint. He came to Madrid in 1864 in order to study law, became a journalist and drifted into literature. He did not confine himself to novels with a thesis such as *Doña Perfecta* (1876), *Gloria* (1877) and *La familia de León Roch* (1878), which tackled religious problems of the day and offered, consequently, only a transitory interest. Another aspect of his talent is visible in *Marianela* (1878), whose poetic qualities give beauty to a subject full of pathos. In 1873, Pérez Galdós began the first series of the *Episodios nacionales*, a kind of national epic in prose and a monument of patient and ingenious reconstruction. In the five series of these episodes, the author tells the most dramatic incidents of Spanish history during the nineteenth century. They are not all of equal merit, but some contain fine passages as for instance : *Bailén* (1873), *Cádiz* (1874), *Juan Martín el Empecinado* (1874), *Los Apostólicos* (1879), *Zumalacárregui* (1898), *La estafeta romántica* (1899), *Los duendes de la camarilla* (1903), *Carlos VI en la Rápita* (1905) and *España trágica* (1909). And all give evidence of marvellous powers of invention, adaptability and unflagging industry. A third phase of the author's talent is seen in *Fortunata y Jacinta*

Antón del Olmet y A. García Carraffa, *Los grandes españoles. Galdós.* Madrid, 1912; Andrenio, in *Novelas y Novelistas.* Madrid, 1918. pp. 9-112 ; S. de Madariaga, in *The Genius of Spain.* Oxford, 1923. pp. 46-63; A. F. G. Bell, in *Contemporary Spanish Literature.* New York, 1925, pp. 52-61.

(1886), a forcible picture of contemporary life. An inexhaustible inventor and an observer scarcely inferior to Dickens in *El Doctor Centeno* (1883), Pérez Galdós combines realism with fantasy and concision with poetic imagination: his study of the eccentric *Angel Guerra* (1891) is a notable achievement in psychological analysis. His attempts in the drama: *Realidad* (1892), *La de San Quintín* (1894) and *El Abuelo* (1904) are interesting; *La de San Quintín*, though it drags in parts has some striking scenes. The tragedies *Electra* (1900) and *Mariucha* (1903) are written in illustration of a thesis: we can pass them by as well as *Bárbara* (1903), *Casandra* (1910) and other tragi-comedies. Pérez Galdós's exuberant temperament accorded ill with the narrow limits of the stage: he needed the wider field afforded him by the novel. In spite of his abundant production, the charge of improvisation cannot with justice be brought against him: his observation is too careful, his rendering too scrupulous. His varied and powerful talent, his delicate psychological instinct and his picturesque conception of life are well illustrated in *La de Bringas* (1884), *Fortuna y Jacinta* and other notable works. Pérez Galdós's last years were saddened by poverty and loss of sight; a subscription was raised in his favour but it was not very successful.

One of the first Spanish novelists to respond to the wave of French naturalism which surged into Spain in 1880 was ARMANDO PALACIO VALDÉS[1] (b. 1853). Apart from some preliminary essays in criticism when he collaborated with Leopoldo Alas, Palacio Valdés's first published work was *El Señorito Octavio* (1881);

[1] See: H. Peseux-Richard, *Armando Palacio Valdés*, in *Revue Hispanique*, XLII (1918), pp. 305-480.

SPANISH LITERATURE SINCE 1868

this contains a germ of the promise fulfilled in *Marta y María* (1883) and *La Hermana San Sulpicio* (1889), two novels full of realism and sparkling humour with delightful woman-portraits. *Marta y María* was followed by *El idilio de un enfermo* (1883), an autobiographical fragment; the collection of short stories, *Aguas fuertes* (1884), of mediocre interest; *José* (1885), a pleasant, if slightly sentimental tale of life in a fishing village; *Riverita* (1886) with its sequel *Maximina* (1887), and *El cuarto Poder* (1888), which is concerned with journalistic life and contains the two charming feminine creations of Ventura and Cecilia. After *La Hermana San Sulpicio*, Palacio Valdés's art attempted a new direction in *La Espuma* (1890) and *La Fe* (1892). These two books were given an enthusiastic reception abroad: they are not national in character and could, with a few changes in nomenclature, be taken for admirable versions of French originals. Happily Palacio Valdés abandoned this false track. In *El Maestrante* (1893) he wavers still, but *Los Majos de Cádiz* (1896) and *La alegría del capitán Ribot* (1899) denote a welcome return to his earlier, more individual and better manner. A breath of idealism in *La aldea perdida* (1903) and *Tristán ó el Pesimismo* (1906) suggested that his impressionable talent might be taking a new turn. Palacio Valdés can execute well; he is a skilled portrayist, particularly of women, and a delicate, humorous observer with a gift of emotional imagination.

EMILIA PARDO BAZÁN,[1] later Condesa de Pardo Bazán (1851-1921), is undoubtedly the best woman

[1] See: Andrenio, in *Novelas y novelistas*. Madrid, 1918. pp. 293-330; A. A. Coello, *La Condesa Emilia Pardo Bazán*. Quito, 1922.

novelist that Spain has produced in the nineteenth century. Her literary career began with the *Examen crítico de las obras del P. Maestro Feijóo* (1877), which was awarded a prize at a literary contest held at Orense in 1876. Her first novel, *Pascual López* (1879), an uninteresting and entirely imaginary autobiography of a medical student, was succeeded by *Un viaje de novios* (1881), where a cautious attempt at realism is visible: this tendency becomes more pronounced in *La Tribuna* (1882), a book with fine qualities of style. After *La Cuestión palpitante* (1883), a kind of literary manifesto, Emilia Pardo Bazán openly threw in her lot with the naturalistic school in *Los Pazos de Ulloa* (1886) and *La Madre Naturaleza* (1887). These were her greatest triumph: their powerfully realistic scenes and the vindication of the primitive instinct in the latter novel gave Emilia Pardo Bazán a high place in the evolution of the new movement. With the passing of naturalism, the greater part of her productions went out of fashion. She is read with more pleasure in *La Quimera* (1905), an experiment in symbolism as well as a vivid presentation of Spanish aristocratic society, and in *Morriña* (1889), a picturesque study of customs and scenes whose rich colouring is the expression of the writer's exuberant temperament. In *Morriña* as in *De mi tierra* (1888) Emilia Pardo Bazán does in a minor degree for Galicia what Pereda did for Cantabria. A woman of versatile talent and of superabundant energy, her interest took many forms: the drama, lectures, politics, polemics, discussions and travel. She founded the *Nuevo Teatro crítico* (January 1891–December 1893) and made it a vehicle for her eclectic opinions on life and art. Her aspirations to enter the Academy were destined to be disappointed:

she would have figured there more fittingly than Isidra de Guzman y Lacerda, who as honorary fellow made her inaugural speech on December 28, 1784. But Emilia Pardo Bazán's spirit would ill have brooked any form of bureaucracy. It could suffer no limitations and for its full development needed air and unconfined liberty.

LEOPOLDO ALAS[1] (1852-1901), whose pungent criticism, presented under the pseudonym of 'Clarín,' made him a formidable power, attempted fiction in *La Regenta* (1884-1885), a novel in the manner of Paul Bourget. The relentless analysis of the false mysticism which proves the undoing of Ana Ozores, and the shrewd penetration which gives life to every character in the book, make it rank as one of the best novels of its time. In his short stories entitled *Cuentos morales* (1896) and *El gallo de Sócrates* (1901), Alas is not so successful: both books contain good passages but have less substance than the novel which made his reputation. Alas had a wide knowledge of other literatures beside his own: he is full of surprises, has disconcerting fancies and verges perilously on intolerance; nevertheless he was a sound critical force in his day.

There was no lack of talent in Eusebio Blasco (1844-1903), who since his death has fallen into somewhat unmerited oblivion. No doubt he produced too much and was over-prodigal of his lively caustic wit; yet some of his numerous dramatic works will survive, while the natural grace of his *Cuentos aragoneses* (1901) and the ease and charm of his articles and sketches will

[1] See: A. González-Blanco, in *Historia de la novela en España desde el romanticismo á nuestros días*. Madrid, 1909. pp. 495-511.

always find appreciation. The Jesuit Father Luis Coloma[1] (1851-1915) gave in *Pequeñeces* (1890) an unflatteringly satirical picture of the Madrid society whose spoilt child he had been. The novel made an immense sensation and attracted for a time the undivided attention of literary circles. Emilia Pardo Bazán went so far as to suggest that Balzac's fame would suffer by its publication. Balzac survived the shock, and Coloma, whose success was ephemeral, abandoned the novel for historical biography. In this *genre* he composed the not-uninteresting *Retratos de antaño* (1895) and *El Marqués de Mora* (1903). Coloma, who wrote fiction as though it were a painful duty, recognized that he was a missioner and not a romancer. There is nothing of the missionary spirit in Jacinto Octavio Picón[2] (1852-1923). A nephew of José Picón (1829-1873), the ingenious author of the *zarzuela*, *Pan y Toros* (1864), whose merrily infectious music was composed by Francisco Asenjo Barbieri (1823-1894), he shews in his novels—and particularly in *Dulce y Sabrosa* (1891)—a delicate talent and fine observation. For a time he seemed to incline to artistic criticism, and his biography of Velázquez (1899) obtained a well-deserved success. But he returned to the novel in *Juanita Tenorio* (1910), a work of subtle psychological analysis written in a pure and limpid style. Juan Ochoa (1864-1899), an Asturian who underwent the influence of Alas, gave evidence of promise as well as sympathy and insight in *Su amado discípulo* (1894), *Un alma de Dios* (1898) and *Los*

[1] See: C. Eguía Ruiz, in *Literaturas y literatos*. Barcelona, 1917. 2ª serie, pp. 71-197.

[2] See: H. Peseux-Richard, *Un romancier espagnol. Jacinto Octavio Picon*, in *Revue Hispanique*, xxx (1914), pp. 515-585.

señores de Hermida (1900). There is artistic realism in *La tierra de campos* (1897) by Ricardo Macías Picavea[1] (1847-1899), whose boldly drawn characters stand out clearly against the tawny background of the Castilian tableland.

Few prose-writers of this age shewed a more original talent than ANGEL GANIVET[2] (1865-1898). His qualities passed unnoticed by the majority owing to the fact that a great part of his work was published in the columns of a provincial paper, *El Defensor de Granada*. He entered the consular service, held appointments at Amsterdam, later at Helsingfors in Finland, where his first book, *Granada la bella* (1896), was printed, and finally at Riga. There in the month of November he tragically ended his life in the icy waters of the Dvina. By nature exceptionally impressionable, Ganivet easily assimilated the new intellectual ideas of his foreign environment, but he preserved at the same time a Spanish independence of spirit: the originality which shews at every turn in *Idearium español* (1896) no doubt contributed largely towards this happy result. In *La Conquista del reino de Maya por el último conquistador Pío Cid* (1897) and in *Los Trabajos del infatigable creador Pío Cid* (1898), his power of evocation is astonishingly vivid. Unconsciously, perhaps, he represents himself in Pío Cid, and as he narrates his experiences he intermingles

[1] See: N. Alonso Cortés, in *Viejo y Nuevo*. Valladolid, 1915. pp. 3-52.

[2] See: L. Rouanet, *Angel Ganivet*, in *Revue Hispanique*, v (1898), pp. 483-495; F. Navarro Ledesma, M. Unamuno, 'Azorín' y C. Román Salamero, *Angel Ganivet*. Valencia, 1905; A. Gallego y Burín, *Ganivet*. Granada, 1921; A. Bonilla y San Martín, *Angel Ganivet*, in *Revue Hispanique*, LVI (1922), pp. 530-540.

with them interesting and vivid sketches of Spanish life as it is seen in modest boarding-houses or in rural districts during electoral campaigns. But it was not in the novel that Ganivet's talent found its highest expression; the *Epistolario* (1904) reveals another aspect of his philosophic spirit. A shrewd and penetrating observer, he is no less successful in his pictures of exotic scenery, yet possibly his last work but one, *Cartas Finlandesas* (1898), owes something of its renown to the remote and unfamiliar subject.

VICENTE BLASCO IBÁÑEZ[1] (b. 1867), at one time secretary to the novelist Fernandez y Gonzalez, is not untinged with romanticism though he continues the naturalistic tradition of the novel. He reveals himself a disciple of Zola (1840-1903) in *Arroz y Tartana* (1894) and in *Flor de Mayo* (1895), striking studies of the middle-class and of the fisher-folk in his native country, Valencia. He touches a deeper note in *La Barraca* (1898), in which he presents in poignant fashion the tragedy of a life. Just as the best works of Pereda and Emilia Pardo Bazán deal with Cantabria and Galicia, so Blasco Ibáñez preferred to lay the scene of his first novels in the Valencian district, whose atmosphere he vividly reproduces in *Entre naranjos* (1900). But he soon went further afield In *Sónnica la Cortesana* (1901), an archaeological novel, he sought to revive a distant past and courted failure by his knack of hasty improvisation incompatible with the *genre*. He recovered himself in *Cañas y Barro* (1902), a work of acrid and penetrating realism. And in *La Catedral*

---

[1] See: E. Zamacois, *Mis contemporáneos*. I. *Vicente Blasco Ibáñez*. Madrid, 1910; C. Pitollet, *V. Blasco Ibáñez. Ses romans et le roman de sa vie*. Paris. n.d. [Spanish trans. by J. Moncada, Valencia, 1921.]

(1903), *El Intruso* (1904), *La Bodega* (1905) and *La Horda* (1905), he becomes the novelist of the social revolution. These are not exclusively fiction : they are more in the nature of a collectivist propaganda advanced under the guise of a literary form. There is little attempt at psychology : the shadow of the Cathedral at Toledo blots out Gabriel Luna, the hero of the plot; Sanabra and Aresti de Bilbao may be a little more clearly defined in *El Intruso*; but the remaining two novels of this series give only a vague and confused impression of an Andalusia in the throes of an agrarial crisis or of the proletariat in Madrid. Blasco Ibáñez returned to the portrayal of individuals in *La maja desnuda* (1906), a minutely detailed study of two unfortunates who once were lovers ; in *Sangre y Arena* (1908) with its types, the fatuous bullfighter and the great lady of society—both presented with forcible skill; and in *Mare Nostrum* (1917), his best work in the realistic vein. The hero, Ferragut, as well as Freya, are individually alive rather than merely subordinate to the central idea of the story, and the descriptions of Naples are as faithful in detail as they are vivid in general impression. Blasco Ibáñez has all the Spaniard's gift of copiousness : his distinguishing qualities are vitality and force. It may be objected that his style is colloquial, that his observation tends to be superficial as soon as he leaves the neighbourhood of Valencia and that, in such books as *Los Argonautas* (1914), *Los cuatro Jinetes del Apocalipsis* (1916) and *La Reina Calafia* (1922), he writes for a foreign public. His over-emphatic and blunt style, his occasional incorrections of language, his careless manner are well adapted to the intelligence of the masses, whose interpreter he has become. It is a fact that Blasco

Ibáñez knows the Valencian district as no one else knows it : it is equally a fact that he has received indelible impressions of the rest of Spain and that, a true apostle of combat, when he celebrates the epic of his revolutionary heroes against the forces of the established system, he describes his personal feelings with intensity and impressive eloquence.

There is a note more subtle and subdued in the work of Ramón del Valle-Inclán[1] (b. 1870) than in the more strident tones of Blasco Ibáñez. In his endowments nothing is left to accident. All is provident, stately, sculptural. Careful form, polished expression, refined qualities characterize the writer of *Femeninas* (1895) and of the curious memoirs (1902-1907) of the Marqués de Bradomín. These are entitled *Sonata de primavera*, *Sonata de estío*, *Sonata de otoño* and *Sonata de invierno* : as Sr. D. Julio Casares has shrewdly pointed out, they reveal in their author a certain susceptibility to external influence, the *Sonata de primavera* in particular betrays striking reminiscences from the *Mémoires* (1826-1838) of Giovanni Jacopo Casanova (1725-1798). Valle-Inclán's tendency to preciosity, evident in *Flor de santidad, Historia milenaria* (1904) and the fantastic collection, *Jardín novelesco* (1905) is much less pronounced in the happy transcription *La guerra carlista* (1908-1909), where the general atmosphere of the country during the Carlist disturbances is subtly and poignantly rendered. *Divinas Palabras* (1920) deals with the pilgrimage roads of Galicia and their picaresque procession of

[1] See : J. Casares, in *Crítica profana*. Madrid, 1916. pp. 17-130; S. de Madariaga, in *The Genius of Spain*... Oxford, 1923. pp. 128-147; A. F. G. Bell, in *Contemporary Spanish Literature*. New York, 1925. pp. 126-135, 185-187.

beggars and adventurers. A delicate artificer in his verse, *Aromas de leyenda* (1907), *Cuento de Abril* (1910) and *El pasajero* (1920), Valle-Inclán writes in prose a pure and polished style which should delight artists and amateurs of the rare and the exquisite.

There appears at first sight, to be less research in the restrained manner of 'Azorín,'[1] the pseudonym of José Martínez Ruiz (b. 1876). But his style is not the natural expression of unstudied art; there is premeditation and a distinct personal savour in the clipped phrases whose effect is leisurely rather than abrupt. *El Alma castellana* [1600-1800] (1900) is a skilful reconstruction of a bygone period and belongs as much to the domain of history as to that of literature. In the novels, *La Voluntad* (1902), *Antonio Azorín* (1903) and *Las Confesiones de un pequeño filósofo* (1904) the protagonist's reflexions and revelations are set down with an intentional air of candour through which peeps an elusive irony. Though he has returned to it in *Don Juan* (1922) and *Doña Inés* (1925), the novel is too artificial a form to appeal continuously to 'Azorín'; a stronger claim is made upon him by historic realities as in *Los Pueblos* (1904), a short and conclusive sketch of provincial life, or in *La ruta de Don Quijote* (1905), an attempt at evocation which he improved upon in *Castilla* (1912). In his later years Azorín devoted himself more exclusively to literary criticism. He is at times too much in love with his subject to be entirely impartial, but in *Los valores literarios* (1913), *Al margen de los clásicos* (1915) and *Rivas y Larra*

[1] See: G. Martínez Sierra, in *Motivos*. Paris, n.d. pp. 11-18; J. Casares, in *Crítica profana*. Madrid, 1916. pp. 133-242; S. de Madariaga, in *The Genius of Spain*. . . . Oxford, 1923. pp. 148-160.

(1916), he shews independence of thought and a fine perception of relative values. In *Los dos Luises* (1921) and *De Granada a Castelar* (1922) his tendency is to dwell more exclusively upon the personal and human aspect of the authors with whom he deals.

A prolific novelist is Pío Baroja[1] (b. 1872), whose philosophy of life seems to be a deep-rooted pessimism —an inheritance perhaps from his Basque ancestors— joined to a strain of intense energy. His trilogies are concerned with such subjects as the race, the cities and the sea: *Tierra vasca*, whose parts were published separately, includes *La casa de Aizgorri* (1900), a novel in dialogue on hereditary degeneration, *El mayorazgo de Labraz* (1902) and *Zalacaín el Aventurero* (1909); *La Lucha por la vida* (1904) is composed of *La busca*, *Mala hierba*, and *Aurora roja* which are not unlike the old-fashioned picaresque novels. Written in the twentieth century, they are more abundant in ideas: in solidity of invention they are defective. The flight of *La dame errante* (1908) through Spain has its sequel in *La ciudad de niebla* (1909), an interesting impression of London from a foreigner's point of view. The long series *Memorias de un hombre de acción*, which began in 1913 with *El aprendiz de conspirador*, relate the adventures of Eugenio de Aviraneta: the eleventh of these episodes, *El sabor de la venganza* (1921), is as astonishingly vivid and disconnected as its forerunners. The fantastic *El laberinto*

[1] See: H. Peseux-Richard, *Un romancier espagnol: Pío Baroja*, in *Revue Hispanique*, XXIII (1910), pp. 109-187; J. B. Trend, in *A Picture of Modern Spain*. London, 1921. pp. 56-79; S. de Madariaga, in *The Genius of Spain*. Oxford, 1923, pp. 111-127; A. F. G. Bell in *Contemporary Spanish Literature*. New York, 1925. pp. 107-120.

de las Sirenas (1923) has its scene in Calabria. In most of the writer's books, psychological elements are found side by side with autobiographical reminiscences. Baroja is an admirer of Dickens as a humorist: he has much of Dickens's power of observation and gift of visualizing. But he has all Dickens's blemishes: his use of neologisms, his tendency to stretch the meaning of words, his exaggerated vision. It is often alleged against Baroja that he is indifferent to graces of style, even to rules of grammar: however that may be, his prose, though arid, is never obscure.

Felipe Trigo[1] (1864-1916), who began life as an army doctor, created with his first novel, *Las Ingenuas* (1901), an impression in which aesthetic feeling did not, perhaps, count for much. A follower of D'Annunzio, he analyses the voluptuosity of passion with something akin to scientific precision and exalted lyrism in *La sed de amar* (1903), *Alma en los labios* (1905), *La Altísima* (1907), *Sor Demonio* (1908), *La Clave* (1910) and *Jarrapellejos* (1914). Though his insistence on sexual relations amounted to an obsession, Trigo was in a fair way to found a new school when his life was cut violently short. Among his disciples may be reckoned Alberto Insúa (b. 1883), who amply fulfilled the promise of *Don Quijote en los Alpes* (1907) in *Las flechas del Amor* (1914) and in *El Peligro* (1915): in both these volumes he shews artistic ability and psychological penetration, while he handles his subject skilfully in *La mujer que necesita*

---

[1] See: H. Peseux-Richard, *Un romancier espagnol: M. Felipe Trigo*, in *Revue Hispanique*, XXVIII (1913), pp. 317-389; A. Reyes, in *El Suicida*. Madrid, 1917. pp. 7-16; M. Abril, *Felipe Trigo. Exposición y glosa de su vida; su filosofía, su moral, su arte, su estilo.* Madrid, 1917.

amar (1923). Rafael López de Haro (b. 1887) became known by *En un lugar de la Mancha* ... (1906): he reveals narrative power and a wider outlook in *Dominadoras* (1907), a cruel study of feminine rapacity in various forms, in *El país de los medianos* (1913) and in other novels which betray Trigo's influence.

Ricardo León[1] (b. 1877), who published his verse in *La lira de bronce* (1901) and *Alivio de caminantes* (1911) first attracted attention as a novelist by *Casta de hidalgos* (1908). This was followed by *Comedia sentimental* (1909), *Alcalá de los Zegríes* (1910), *El Amor de los Amores* (1910), *Los Centauros* (1912) and *Amor de Caridad* (1922). *La escuela de los sofistas* (1910) and *Los caballeros de la Cruz* (1916) belong to the essay rather than to the novel. León has gifts of style and inventive skill: and his classic sobriety of diction, in accord with the subjects that he treats, has an old-fashioned savour of its own. Concha Espina (b. 1877), a woman novelist, produced in *La Esfinge maragata* (1913) a regional tale with realistic elements, whose charm she has not quite succeeded in recapturing in later novels such as: *La rosa de los vientos* (1915), *Ruecas de márfil* (1917) and *El metal de los muertos* (1920). Augusto Martínez Olmedilla (b. 1880) deals in orthodox spirit with educational and social problems, which he exposes with dramatic intensity in *Los hijos* (1912), *El derecho a ser feliz* (1912), *La ley de Malthus* (1913), *Todo por él* (1917) and *Resurgimiento* (1919).

[1] See: C. Eguía Ruiz, *El clasicismo español y Ricardo León*, in *Literaturas y literatos*. Madrid, 1914. 1ª serie, pp. 311-335; J. Casares, in *Crítica profana*. Madrid, 1916. pp. 245-348; C. Eguía Ruiz, *La vuelta a los clásicos*, in *Literaturas y literatos*. Madrid, 1917. 2ª serie, pp. 1-23.

Ramón Pérez de Ayala[1] (b. 1881) began as a poet in *La paz del sendero* (1904) : his verse tends to mysticism and symbolism in *El sendero inmemorable* (1916). He excels as a novelist in *La pata de la raposa* (1912), *Prometeo* (1916), and *Belarmino y Apolonio* (1919). A delicate instinct, tact and a fine sense of measure are the portion of this author : these qualities are prominent in *Luna de miel, luna de hiel* (1923) and its sequel *Los trabajos de Urbano y Simona* (1923), a modernized version of Daphnis and Chloë illustrated with humorous irony and grace. *El Ombligo del mundo* (1924) is a collection of sketches dealing with Asturian types. Pérez de Ayala has turned to the essay in *Las Máscaras* (1917), a series of suggestive studies on dramatic writers, and in *Política y toros* (1918). Gabriel Miró[2] (b. 1879), who ranges from passages of parenthetical humour in *El abuelo del rey* (1915) to flights of eloquent description in *Figuras de la Pasión del Señor* (1916-1917), handles the short story with dexterity and artistic feeling in the small volume of tales entitled, *El Angel, El Molino, El Caracol del Faro* (1921). Pedro de Répide (b. 1882) a good *madrileño* with a passionate attachment to all that concerns his birthplace, became generally known through the imaginative realism of *Del Rastro a Maravillas* (1907), with which may be mentioned *Costumbres y devociones madrileñas* (1914). Miró is probably the

[1] See : Andrenio, in *Novelas y Novelistas*. Madrid, 1918. pp. 281-292 ; S. de Madariaga, in *The Genius of Spain*. Oxford, 1923. pp. 71-86; A. F. G. Bell, in *Contemporary Spanish Literature*. New York, 1925. pp. 135-140.

[2] See : A. González Blanco, in *Los Contemporáneos*. Paris, s.f. 1ª serie, pp. 276-292 ; S. de Madariaga, in *The Genius of Spain*. Oxford, 1923. pp. 148-164 [Spanish ed., *Semblanzas literarias contemporáneas*. Barcelona, 1924. pp. 213-235].

more impressionable and therefore the more imitative of these two writers. Vague reminiscences of 'Azorín's' lambent humour or Baroja's acrid pessimism gleam from some of his best books. Julio Camba (b. 1884) shews shrewd observation and a sense of humour in *Alemania* (1916), *Londres* (1916) and *Playas, ciudades y montañas* (1916): he has recently published some of his essays under the title *La rana viajera* (1921). Ramón Gómez de la Serna[1] (b. 1890) aims at a new form of self-expression in literature. His theories, illustrated in *El Rastro* (1915), in which he displays a faculty about as keen as Dickens's for the interpretation of still life, and in *Greguerías* (1917), are set down in his preface to *Muestrario* (1918). His most interesting production from a contemporary point of view is, perhaps, the volume entitled *Pombo* (1918): this contains curious details—with original pen portraits of the members limned from life—of the odd literary circle in Madrid to which the author belongs.

José Echegaray[2] (1832-1916), who was a mathematician, a political economist, an orator and a minister before he inherited the popularity of Tamayo y Baus on the stage, began his dramatic career in 1874 with *El libro talonario*, which he produced under the anagram of Jorge Hayaseca. As a playwright he went through

[1] See: A. Reyes, *Ramón Gómez de la Serna*, in *Hispania* (Paris), I (1918). pp. 234-240.

[2] See: L. Antón del Olmet y A. García Carraffa, *Echegaray*. Madrid, 1912; H. de Curzon, *Le théâtre de José Echegaray: Étude analytique*. Paris, 1912; E. Mérimée, *José Echegaray et son œuvre dramatique*, in *Bulletin hispanique*, XVIII (1916), pp. 247-278; C. Eguía Ruiz, in *Crítica Patriótica*. Madrid, 1921. pp. 67-175.

three phases ; in the first of these he shewed himself a pure romantic with *La Esposa del Vengador* (1874), *En el puño de la espada* (1875) and *En el seno de la muerte* (1879). *El Gran Galeoto* (1881) might be by some earlier inheritor of Calderon : it could not be ascribed to Calderon himself, for Echegaray's versification has nothing of Calderon's verbal music and haunting charm : nor is there anything essentially Spanish in his work, which too frequently reflects foreign fashions. Echegaray began life as an engineer, and there is something suggestive in the solidity of construction of his dramas. He had a certain gift of imagination not inapt to impress in *El Gran Galeoto* and *Conflicto entre dos deberes* (1882) ; but he could not create characters, and he sought to win applause by indulging in cheap effects. In his second phase, Echegaray was much influenced by French dramatists of the school of the younger Dumas (1824-1895) : here he is least agreeable, for his prose is no less unpleasing than his verse and it can no longer be said that his failure is due to an unhappy choice of a vehicle. Finally, he tried to reproduce some of the symbolic effects of Ibsen (1828-1906). The imitation, as in *El hijo de don Juan* (1892), is very close : elsewhere, as in *El loco Dios* (1900), Echegaray moves with more freedom and independence. At this stage Echegaray produced his finest work, and following the later Ibsen he returned to romanticism of a kind : at heart he was always a romantic. As he felt the sceptre slipping from his hand, he generously translated and adapted for the stage some dramas of the Catalan Angel Guimerá (1847-1924), who seemed destined then to be his successor. In his last years he wrote and produced a few plays such as *La escalinata de un trono* (1903) and

A fuerza de arrastrarse (1905), but the feverish production of earlier days was no longer his. He became temporarily involved in politics in 1905 and ceased writing. A great part of his work is now forgotten and as much more is out of date. Echegaray had neither humour nor sympathy; he lacked the sense of verbal melody, a not unnatural defect considering his Basque origin; his prose is rigid and admits of no shades of meaning; his psychology is narrow. But he was always prompt to trim his sails and to catch the changing breeze of dramatic fashion; he constructed with remarkable skill, and his eloquence captured the fancy of playgoers of the sentimental type. There is nothing revolutionary in his attitude. He is essentially a Romantic middle-class man who, in spite of all his defects, enjoyed a vogue of some thirty years.

Apart from Leopoldo Cano (b. 1844), author of *La Mariposa* (1879) and *La Pasionaria* (1883), and Eugenio Sellés (b. 1844), Echegaray had no stage following. Sellés, who wrote *El nudo gordiano* (1878), was a master of versification much superior to Echegaray, but he had not Echegaray's literary fecundity, broke no new ground and can scarcely be said to have fulfilled his early promise. In originality he falls short of the Catalan José Felíu y Codina (1847-1897), who tried to create a regional theatre by laying the scene of his plays *La Dolores* (1892), *María del Carmen* (1896) and *La real moza* (1897) in Aragón, Murcia and Andalusia respectively. These attempts met with a fair measure of success, and the author's effort to do something more might have produced a permanent effect had not a premature death borne him away unexpectedly. A somewhat corresponding departure from the conventional was made by Joaquín Dicenta[1] (1863-1917) in *Juan José* (1895) and *El crimen de ayer* (1904), in which he glorifies the working-classes. His portraits of workmen do not strike one as being more exact than Echegaray's pictures of the Romantic middle-class. On the point of honour Dicenta seems to think that both classes are alike. Meanwhile he enlarged the scope of the theatre by introducing on the boards types of the new social order. Dicenta has not Echegaray's constructive knack, but he is more revolutionary in *Juan José* than Echegaray in all his sixty odd plays put together. And his varied interests are evident in his translation (1907) of *El Místich* by the Catalan Santiago Rusiñol (b. 1861).

A more Europeanized talent than any of the foregoing is that of Jacinto Benavente[2] (b. 1866), one of the chief living dramatists. He has no prejudices and by preference victimizes the well-to-do class. He exhibits these people and exposes their weaknesses in the process. He does not indict them by any procedure of direct attack or method of caricature : he manifests their worthlessness merely by allowing them to speak as in *Gente conocida* (1896) and *La comida de las fieras* (1898). It is often alleged that Benavente takes persons from real life and transfers them to the stage. It may be that *La comida de las fieras* would never have

[1] See : A. González Blanco, in *Los dramaturgos españoles contemporáneos*. Iª serie, Valencia, 1917. pp. 207-294 ; C. Eguía Ruiz, in *Crítica Patriótica*. Madrid, 1921. pp. 177-233.

[2] See : A. Bonilla y San Martín, *Jacinto Benavente*, in *Ateneo*, 1906, pp. 27-40 ; A. González-Blanco, in *Los dramaturgos españoles contemporáneos*. Valencia, 1917, Iª serie, pp. 27-168 ; R. Pérez de Ayala, in *Las Máscaras*. Madrid, 1919. I, pp. 105-213 ; W. Starkie, *Jacinto Benavente*. Oxford, 1924.

been written had not the ducal house of Osuna come to ruin ; similarly *El marido de la Téllez* (1897) might never have seen the light had not Fernando Díaz de Mendoza married María Guerrero, and the originals of *Más fuerte que el amor* (1906) may be sought in well-known contemporaries. These are not valid objections to Benavente's methods. The interest of his plays lies in their easy exposition and the subtle intelligence which gives life to his characters. This is particularly the case in the tragedy *La Malquerida* (1913). Agreeable and sarcastic in *Lo cursi* (1901), *El hombrecito* (1903) and *Los malhechores del bien* (1905), fatalistic and derisive in *La gata de Angora* (1900) and in *Alma triunfante* (1902), a profound critic in *Los intereses creados* (1909)—whose high level is not reached in its sequel *La ciudad alegre y confiada* (1916), in spite of the triumphant reception accorded to this play—Benavente presides impartially over the procession of his characters. He is capable at the same time of a generous and soaring fancy. But he deals too exclusively with a single social class, he is more cosmopolitan than Spanish and his productions are consequently lacking in national savour. Apart from this exotic taint, it is to be observed that in matters of taste Benavente is uncertain. He has not a delicate standard of values. He shewed this when he adapted for the Spanish stage the *Richelieu* of Edward Bulwer Lytton (1803-1873). On the other hand he has an unbounded admiration for Shakespeare (whose works as well as those of Molière he also arranged for the stage). It is as the admirer of Shakespeare that he appears in his *Teatro fantástico* (1892), in which is revealed a charming aspect of his talent.

Other present-day dramatists are Manuel Linares Rivas [1] (b. 1867), who began by cultivating what is conveniently called the *género chico* and gradually worked his way up from the compounding of unpretentious farces to the confection of higher comedy in such plays as *Aire de fuera* (1903), *María Victoria* (1904), *La Garra* (1914) and *El caballero lobo* (1919). He has not Benavente's gift of searching cynicism nor has he Benavente's gift of artistic indifference; but he is a shrewd observer of manners, which he satirizes in a kindly spirit with distinct effect. While Linares Rivas writes in prose, his younger competitor Eduardo Marquina [2] (b. 1879) writes in verse. Marquina's handling of Spanish blank verse is excellent. He had an initial success in *Las hijas del Cid* (1908), perhaps his greatest triumph. The Cid had two daughters, whose names are wrongly given in the *Poema del Cid*, where they take a legendary form. Yet it is to the *Poema* that Marquina goes for his inspiration. He writes—not historical plays, but—national dramatizations of popular legends as in *Doña María la Brava* (1909) and in *En Flandes se ha puesto el sol* (1910), where he deals with Spain's destiny in the Netherlands. Here Marquina is a poet before he is a playwright: it is perhaps otherwise with *Alondra* (1918), and *La extraña* (1921). His lyrism has free play in *Elegías* (1905), *Canciones del momento* (1910), and in *Vendimión* (1909), a work of sane and vigorous originality. Marquina writes a good prose-style in *Cuando florezcan*

---

[1] See: A. González-Blanco, in *Los dramaturgos españoles contemporáneos*. Valencia, 1917. Iª serie, pp. 169-204.

[2] See: A. González-Blanco, in *Los dramaturgos españoles contemporáneos*. Valencia, 1917. Iª serie, pp. 297-330.

los rosales (1912). Gregorio Martínez Sierra [1] (b. 1881) gained experience as a dramatist by translating Santiago Rusiñol as Dicenta had done. He tried his luck at novel-writing in *Sol de la tarde* (1904), *Tú eres la paz* (1907) and other books before attempting fortune on the boards. As a novelist he writes an extravagantly precious prose which one would have guessed would fail to produce any effect on the stage. One would apparently have been all wrong, for *Canción de cuna* (1911) carried all before it on its production. Nothing could be more Spanish than the theme of this play, in which the latent maternal instinct of the good nuns is skilfully shewn. The placidity of the conventual atmosphere is admirably rendered, and the story is allowed to develop on the most natural and engaging lines. The delicate quality which characterizes it is visible in other works such as *La sombra del padre* (1909), *Primavera en otoño* (1911), *Mamá* (1912) and *Don Juan de España* (1921). A different treatment of the latter subject is seen in *Don Juan de Carillana* (1913) by Jacinto Grau (b. 1877), author of *El Conde Alarcos* (1917) and *El hijo pródigo* (1918), an original conception of a biblical theme.

Some characteristic talents have developed in the *género chico*, a term applied to any play with songs and music whose representation does not exceed one hour, thus making it possible for theatrical managers to renew their audiences three or four times in a night. This may be a gain for acting companies, but not for art and literature. One feels tempted to say with Fígaro : ' Aujourd'hui, ce qui ne vaut pas la peine d'être dit, on le chante.' The abundance of these

[1] See : A. González Blanco, in *Los contemporáneos*, Paris, n.d. Iª serie, pp. 1-74.

compositions was an indication of their ephemeral nature; if any achieved a more than passing success, it was nearly always due to the music, some, at least, of whose composers were masters in their kind. Such are Manuel Fernández Caballero (1835-1906), Joaquín Valverde (1844-1910), Tomás Bretón (1850-1924), Ruperto Chapí (1851-1909), Federico Chueca (1846-1908) and Amadeo Vives (b. 1869). The plays generally consisted of three *tableaux* or sketches, the second of which was only introduced for conveniences of scene-shifting; they comprise every subject: popular scenes—the only ones destined to survive—melodrama, so compressed as to be cinematographic, fantasies, parodies and even reviews, as for instance *La gran vía* (1886) by Felipe Pérez y González (1846-1910), whose music, by Chueca and Valverde, made a great hit; the play was even adapted for the Greek stage.

Of more literary importance are the plays of Ricardo de la Vega (1839-1910), son of the author of *El hombre de mundo*. In *La Verbena de la Paloma, o El boticario y las chulapas, y celos mal reprimidos* (1894), probably the best and in any case the most typical of his pieces, he gives an admirable picture of low life. All Madrid rejoiced and still makes merry over this faithful and picturesque presentation of existence in its workmen's quarters. And its success was due to that rare occurrence—perfect harmony between Vega's words and Bretón's music. Other plays of Vega are *La canción de la Lola* (1880, music by Valverde and Chueca) and *Pepa la frescachona, o El colegial desenvuelto* (1886). In the same category may be quoted *Los valientes* (1886), *El mundo comedia es, o El baile de Luis Alonso* (1889, music by Gerónimo Giménez) and *La boda de Luis Alonso, o La noche del encierro* (1897, music by Gerónimo Giménez) by the genial *sainetero* Javier de Burgos (1842-1902); *La niña del estanquero* (1897, music by Chapí) by the no less gifted Tomás Luceño (b. 1844); *El padrino de ' El Nene,' o Todo por el arte* (1896, music by Fernández Caballero and Hermoso) by Julián Romea (1848-1903); *La marcha de Cádiz* (1896, music by Valverde and Estellés) by Celso Lucio (1865-1915) and Enrique García Alvarez; *La Revoltosa* (1897, music by Chapí), by José López Silva and Carlos Fernández Shaw; *El puñao de rosas* (1902, music by Chapí), an excellent work in its kind by Carlos Arniches (b. 1866) in collaboration with Ramón Asensio Más; and *La viejecita* and *Gigantes y Cabezudos* (both with music by Fernández Caballero) by Miguel Echegaray (b. 1848). A sparkling wit and contagious gaiety are displayed in some of their plays by José Jackson Veyán (b. 1852), Miguel de Palacios (b. 1860), Guillermo Perrín and Vital Aza (1851-1912).

Excellent work was done in the *género chico* by the brothers Serafín (b. 1871) and Joaquín (b. 1873) Alvarez Quintero before they advanced to the foremost rank of high comedy. It is no small compliment that the brethren should have been compared with Lope de Rueda, whose witty touches are repeated by his fellow-townsmen in *El ojito derecho* (1897). But the Quintero have a deeper vein of poetry and more sustained and various inspiration. This idea of their talent is revealed in *El patio* (1900) and *Las flores* (1901), which picture the south in all its splendour and all its radiance, painted with all the gorgeousness of a palette rich in colour. There is little character-drawing in the brothers' plays, the majority of which deal with scenes of Andalusian life. Analysis and depth are not their strong point: their appeal rests rather upon their dexterous handling of the dialogue, which is always gay, sparkling and vivacious and redeems their somewhat superficial presentation. This quality is marked in all their dramatic works, which include kinds as different as *Los Galeotes* (1900), *El genio alegre* (1906), *Malvaloca* (1912), *Cabrita que tira al monte* (1916) and *La calumniada* (1919). The brothers Quintero are poets who write in prose, unlike José López Silva (1861-1925), whose prosaic imagination hid its prosaic aspect under the form of verse. He has been mentioned in connexion with the *género chico*, but his talent found its more natural development in *Los Madriles* (1903), *Gente de tufos* (1905), *Chulaperías* (1906), *La gente del pueblo* (1908) and *Los hijos de Madrid* (1910), which deal mostly with scenes from popular life in Madrid.

Gaspar Núñez de Arce [1] (1832-1903), among whose plays *La cuenta del zapatero* (1859) can still be read with pleasure, conceived and executed in *El haz de leña* (1872) what is the best historical drama of the nineteenth century. There in dramatic guise beats the heart of a poet, and in fact Núñez de Arce soon afterwards gave himself up to pure lyric verse. But the times were not propitious to the development of his special conditions. Born to sing ordered liberty or to follow in the traces of his master, Quintana, Núñez de Arce was destined to live in an epoch of revolutionary excess and national disaster. And it was

[1] See: C. De Lollis, *Don Gaspar Núñez de Arce*, in *Nuova Antologia*, 1898, pp. 630-648; E. Pardo Bazán, in *Retratos y Apuntes literarios*, pp. 63-82 (*Obras completas*, 32); J. del Castillo y Soriano, *Núñez de Arce. Apuntes para su biografía*. Madrid, 1904; 2nd ed., Madrid, 1907; A. Symons, in *Cities and Sea-Coasts and Islands*. London, 1918. pp. 94-99.

as a political poet that he achieved renown in *Gritos del combate* (1875), a collection of poems calling upon Spaniards to set on one side their internal quarrels and to save Spain from anarchy. He was the singer of doubt. Is it doubt, pessimism, the anxiety of ill-health, or something of all three which is perceptible in the allegory of *Raimundo Lulio* (1875), the harmonious *Ultima lamentación de Lord Byron* (1879), and *La Visión de fray Martín* (1888), an echo of Leconte de Lisle? More charming in its impressionable realism and fine simplicity is *Un idilio y una elegía* (1879). The poet's sincerity, his austere perfection of style, his scrupulous observation, his love of nature are equally evident in *La Pesca* (1884). But Núñez de Arce's greatest title to glory is in the vibrating strophes of *Gritos del combate*, in which he shews himself a master of virile music and patriotic doctrine. He outlived his fame; his broken health and political isolation drove him to silence; he became immersed in his work as manager of the Banco Hipotecario and left unfinished *Luzbel* and *Hernán el Lobo*. His pessimism did not find its way into the *Poemas cortos* (1895) and his last piece bears the optimistic title ¡ *Sursum corda !* (1900). His force lies in his gracious vision, his sincerity of feeling and his power over his instrument; his weakness is in his rhetorical flow, his moods of sentimentalism and his divided sympathies.

The Valencian Vicente Wenceslao Querol[1] (1836-1889) was intended for a poet, but was fated to be a railway official. His first attempts such as the *Canto Épico o la guerra en África* reveal the influence of Quintana. Querol continued faithful all his life to

[1] *Rimas* [with a preface by T. Llorente], 1891 (Col. de Escritores Cast., 90).

SPANISH LITERATURE SINCE 1868

the classical tradition. His best work is to be found —not in his academic and patriotic compositions, but— in the *Cartas a María* and in the strophes *A la muerte de mi hermana Adela*, where he gives artistic expression to a sincere emotion. Querol was not an abundant writer, and his *Rimas* (1877) never became popular, but his sincerity and mastery of technique won him the praise of contemporaries and rivals. Teodoro Llorente [1] (1826-1911), also a Valencian, was a most successful and brilliant translator, and for his versions of Victor Hugo (1861), of Goethe (1882) and of Heine (1885) may be compared with Edward Fitzgerald. He has been accused of making Faust talk like a Spanish *caballero* : one might say that Fitzgerald makes the Persian talk like an English gentleman who has become an agnostic. As a poet Llorente must be judged by his collections of Catalan poems : *Llibret de versos* (1884-1885) and *Nou llibret de versos* (1902) ; his Castilian poems (1907) are frequently elegant in form. Under the pseudonym of 'Juan García,' Amós de Escalante y Prieto [2] (1831-1902) wrote charming studies on Santander and produced an interesting historical novel *Ave, Maris Stella* (1877). His volume of verse (published posthumously in 1907), records his impressions of the peaceful scenery and the stormy sea of his Northern home. In the posthumous collection of *Poesías* (1897) another Northern poet, Evaristo Silió y Gutiérrez [3] (1841-1874) strikes

[1] See : C. Eguía Ruiz, in *Literaturas y literatos*. Madrid, 1914. 1ª serie, pp. 270-280.

[2] *Poesías* [with a critical introduction by M. Menéndez y Pelayo], Madrid, 1907.

[3] *Poesías* [with a preface by M. Menéndez y Pelayo]. Valladolid, 1897.

a note of dreamy contemplation not unlike the tone of Escalante. Silió, however, died before he could fulfil the promise of *Una fiesta en mi aldea* (1867). In harsh contrast to his gentle melancholy is the pessimism of the Catalan Joaquín María Bartrina (1850-1880) whose philosophy of life is contained in Mirabeau's words, ' Cette tristesse et ce comique que d'être un homme.' Each page of the small collection *Algo* (1876) is illuminated with a sinister splendour, and a note of passionate sincerity rings out from the poet who, like Coventry Patmore, drank

> ' The moonless mere of sighs
> And paced the places infamous to tell
> Where God wipes not the tears from any eyes.'

Bartrina is not an artist: his Castilian is frequently defective, but he has an intensely personal accent that once heard is not easily forgotten.

It would take up too much space to dwell on all the versifiers of this period: a few representative names must suffice. Manuel del Palacio (1832-1907), a furious democrat and later an unyielding reactionist, had the qualities of a satirical poet. Unhappily, he was forced by circumstances to maintain an untiring production and his *Sonetos, canciones y coplas* (1884) give only a faint idea of the witty talent which was squandered on journalistic labours. Federico Balart (1831-1906), an art critic who enjoyed at one time a rather overrated reputation, was no longer young when he published *Dolores* (1895), in which is revealed the gradual transition from violent grief to resigned melancholy. Balart indulges in a false note of self-pity which is more noticeable in *Horizontes* (1897). During her lifetime the Galician verses of Rosalía de Castro

(1837-1885) won a local admiration; her poems in Castilian, collected under the title of *En las orillas del Sar* (1884) were unnoticed and forgotten until a later generation discovered the charm of these compositions, steeped in a vague and gentle melancholy, penetrated by a disquieting and morbid beauty. In these poems some critics would seek the germs of certain technical novelties which have been developed by the most recent school of Spanish poets. Be that as it may, *En las orillas del Sar* attracted no attention from contemporaries. Rosalía de Castro remains a solitary figure in her period. The current of taste took a different direction.

The two poets most in vogue in the nineteenth century each had their disciples. Among the countless followers of Campoamor, none reproduced his inflexion more exactly than Ricardo Gil (1854-1907), author of *La caja de música* (1898). Núñez de Arce was the model of José Velarde (1849-1892), of Emilio Ferrari (1850-1907); and—at first—of Manuel Reina[1] (1856-1905), author of *La Vida inquieta* (1894). In his later work Reina strikes a note entirely his own, and shews a delicate fancy and beauty of form in *El jardín de los poetas* (1899) and *Robles de la selva sagrada* published posthumously in 1906. Less happy was Carlos Fernández-Shaw (1865-1911) who had to be content with a renown which was limited to uncritical readers: his *Poesía de la Sierra* (1908) contains a strain of genuine inspiration rarely found in his vapid, declamatory verse. Two poets from Majorca, Miguel Costa y Llobera (1854-1922) and Juan Alcover (b. 1854)

[1] See: E. de Ory, *Manuel Reina: Estudio biográfico seguido de numerosas poesías de este autor no coleccionadas en sus libros.* Cádiz [1916].

have produced some Castilian verse of great beauty. Costa y Llobera is the author of *Líricas* (1899), whose potent and impetuous verse is dangerously suggestive of Carducci (1836-1907); Alcover's *Meteoros* (1901) combines religious unction with a knowledge of Baudelaire and a pagan joy in life. These two orthodox spirits, discouraged by the prejudices of Madrid's literary circles, confined themselves henceforward to their own tongue.

Ramón Domingo Perés (b. 1863), a Cuban by birth, brought up in Catalonia, where he lives, represents the Catalan element as well as the cosmopolitan in Castilian literature. A critic of refined taste, he is also a poet, and shews in *Cantos modernos* (1889-1893) a gift of imagination both lofty and contemplative. In *Musgo* (1902) he substitutes for the traditional sonority of Castilian verse an intentional note of simplicity. A place apart must be assigned to José María Gabriel y Galán[1] (1870-1905) who, in *Castellanas* (1902), evokes with serene artistry the impressions of scenery in Castilla and Extremadura: some subtle spark of Luis de Leon's genius seems to have illumined this solitary poet and sets him above other regional poets.

Among these may be mentioned Vicente Medina (b. 1866), who in *Aires murcianos* (1899) and *La canción de la Huerta* (1905) has described with singular skill the scenery and the half-Mussulman types of Murcia. A popular poet, Medina has written little since his voluntary exile to the Argentine Republic: in 1917 he published *Abonico (Nuevos aires murcianos)*, in which he

[1] See: E. Pardo Bazán, in *Retratos y apuntes literarios* (*Obras completas*, 32), Madrid, s.f. pp. 83-116; P. Henríquez Ureña, in *Horas de estudio*, Paris [1910], pp. 91-112.

SPANISH LITERATURE SINCE 1868

returns to the same theme. Salvador Rueda [1] (b. 1857) also draws his inspiration from Murcia in *Cuadros de Andalucía* (1883). His talent is unequal: he is too exuberant and lacks depth of thought and feeling. He is extreme in everything: his images, metaphors, colouring, invective, all are exaggerated. On every page over-emphasis and want of taste mar fine passages. A more moderate tone is visible in *En tropel* (1903).

Among South American authors only those names which have found a place in Spanish literature have hitherto been included in these pages. This precludes more than a passing reference to such writers as the Venezuelans, Rafael María Baralt (1810-1860), the historian who succeeded Donoso Cortés in the Spanish Academy, and Andrés Bello [2] (1781-1865), a prominent grammarian and jurisconsult as well as a cultured poet; the Ecuadorian José Joaquín de Olmedo [3] (1780-1847), who in his *Canto de Junín* emulates

---

[1] See: G. Ruiz de Almodóvar, *Salvador Rueda y sus obras*. Madrid, 1891; A. González-Blanco. *Los grandes maestros. Salvador Rueda y Rubén Darío* ... Madrid, s.f.

[2] *Obras completas*. Santiago de Chile, 1881-1893, 15 vols.; *Poesías*, ed. M. A. Caro, 1881 (Col. de Escritores Castellanos, 3, etc); *The Odes of Bello, Olmedo and Heredia*, ed. E. C. Hills, New York-London, 1920 (Hispanic Notes and Monographs. Peninsular Series, III).—See: M. L. Amunátegui, *Vida de don Andrés Bello*. Santiago de Chile, 1882; M. Menéndez y Pelayo, in *Antología de poetas hispano-americanos*. Madrid, 1893. II, pp. cxiv-clviii.

[3] *The Odes of Bello, Olmedo and Heredia*, ed. E. C. Hills, New York-London, 1920 (Hispanic Notes and Monographs. Peninsular Series, III).—See: M. Cañete, in *Escritores españoles é hispano-americanos*. 1884, pp. 151-380 (Col. de Escritores Castellanos, 16); M. Menéndez y Pelayo, in *Antología de poetas hispano-americanos*. Madrid, 1894. III, pp. cix-cxlii.

Quintana ; the Cubans José María Heredia[1] (1803-1839), whose poems reveal his classical traditions, and Juan Clemente Zenea (1831-1871), whose tragic death bore out the inspiration of his verse ; the Columbian poet Gregorio Gutiérrez González (1826-1872), author of the *Memoria sobre el cultivo del maíz* (1866) and the distinguished Peruvian Ricardo Palma[2] (1833-1919), author of *Tradiciones Peruanas* (1883). These all hold a high position in their own country, but they have left no imprint on Spanish literature. New conditions of life favoured the interchange of intellectual relations ; South American writers became in the habit of making prolonged sojourns in Madrid, and the exotic element and vital forces introduced by them were absorbed into the literature of Spain.

A poet from South America is the recognized initiator of a new poetic movement which began some years ago. RUBÉN DARÍO[3] (1867-1916), a Nicaraguan of exceptional genius, was in reality a Cosmopolitan who had studied in every school. He began with some youthful poems published about 1880 in a local

[1] *Poesías líricas*, Paris [1892] ; *The Odes of Bello, Olmedo and Heredia*, ed. E. C. Hills, New York-London, 1920 (Hispanic Notes and Monographs. Peninsular Series, III).—See : M. Menéndez y Pelayo, in *Antología de poetas hispano-americanos*. Madrid, 1893. II, pp. xv-xxvii ; J. M. Chacón y Calvo, *José María Heredia*, in *Cuba Contemporánea*, VIII (1915), pp. 154-163, 259-287.

[2] See : H. Petriconi, *Ricardo Palma, der Verfasser der 'Tradiciones peruanas,'* in *Revue Hispanique*, LVII (1923), pp. 207-285.

[3] *Obras completas*. Madrid, 1917-[1919]. 22 vols. (Editorial Mundo Latino) ; *Obras escogidas*, ed. [with a critical study which occupies vol. i], A González Blanco, Madrid, 1910. 3 vols. *Los primeros versos de Rubén Darío*, ed. V. García Calderón, in *Revue Hispanique*, XL (1917), pp. 47-55.—See : P. Henríquez

review. These were followed in 1885 by *Epístolas y Poemas*: in this volume as well as in *Abrojos* (1887) Darío shews himself a disciple of Zorrilla, Campoamor, Bécquer and Bartrina. The influence of Victor Hugo and of Núñez de Arce is perceptible in *Azul* (1888), but the note of originality in this work did not escape Valera, whose spirit, steeped in classical tradition, later took fright at the young poet's evolution. Darío's tendency to follow French models is more marked in *Prosas profanas* (1899), written after he had settled in Europe. His prose, flexible and vigorous in *Los Raros* (1893), *Parisiana* (1898), *Tierras solares* (1904), *El viaje a Nicaragua* (1909) and *Todo al vuelo* (1912) is slightly gallicized and has an exotic savour which does not awaken the same interest as his verse. Darío's intellectual spirit, open to all that was new or rare, eagerly received contributions from other languages. After throwing in his lot with the symbolists, he flung away all literary shackles and marked out an independent path in *Cantos de vida y esperanza* (1905), *El canto errante* (1907) and *El Canto a la Argentina y otros poemas* (1900), volumes redolent with beauty and emotion. A master of technique, the old measures

Ureña, in *Horas de estudio*. Paris [1910]. pp. 112-137; J. E. Rodó, in *Cinco Ensayos*. Madrid, [1915]. pp. 257-310 (Bib. Andrés Bello, 6); *La vida de Rubén Darío escrita por él mismo*. Barcelona [1916]; *Eleven Poems of Rubén Darío* [English trans. with text by T. Walsh and S. de la Selva, introdn. by P. Henríquez Ureña], New York-London, 1916 (The Hispanic Society of America); E. de Ory, *Rubén Darío: al margen de su vida y de su muerte*, etc. Cádiz [1917]; M. Henríquez Ureña, *Rodó y Rubén Darío*, La Habana, 1918. pp. 79-152; James Fitzmaurice-Kelly, *Rubén Darío*, in *The Year Book of Modern Languages*. Cambridge, 1920. pp. 166-168; P. Henríquez Ureña, *Rubén Darío y el siglo xv*, in *Revue Hispanique*, L (1920), pp. 324-327.

held no secrets for him : his *dezires* and *layes* have all the fragrance of bygone days, his *romances* and *silvas* are remarkable for perfection of form. He made an extensive use of alliteration, changed the position of the accent in the alexandrine and ventured on something very like the *vers libre*. Not all his innovations were good. But he effected what was practically a revolution in Spanish verse. Darío died comparatively young, yet not too young perhaps. His fame was established : his work in the domain of literature accomplished. A sensitive ear may even detect traces of fatigue in some of his latest productions. His power of metrical invention, the melody of his new cadences which gave suppleness to the old form of antique rhythm, his delicate sense of values, his ecstasy and daring genius give him a unique place among modern lyrical poets. The same quality of the rare and the exquisite is found in the verse of José Asunción Silva [1] (1865-1896), who might have proved a rival to Darío, had not an untimely death cut him short.

In America also the names of two women-poets from Uruguay have recently come into notice : Delmira Agustini (1890-1915) and Juana de Ibarbourou (b. 1895), both remarkable for their mastery of spontaneous verse. Delmira Agustini's works, *Libro blanco* (1907) and *Cantos de la montaña* (1910) have been reprinted with other poems under the title of *Los Cálices vacíos* (1913). Juana de Ibarbourou is first and last an authentic poet. Her verse, collected in *Las lenguas de diamante*, is the natural expression of her intense feeling for the beauty of love and life : it is the very essence of poetry—vital, passionate,

[1] *Poesías*, ed. B. Sanín Cano [with a preface by M. de Unamuno], Paris-Buenos Aires [1913].

SPANISH LITERATURE SINCE 1868 507

glowing, instinct with sincerity and fraught with primitive emotion.

There is no doubt as to Darío's influence on the admirable sonneteer Francisco Villaespesa (b. 1877), author of *Intimidades* (1898), *Tristitiae rerum* (1907), *El jardín de las quimeras* (1909) and other volumes of verse. He has not contrived to repeat in his plays the instant triumph which he attained in *Intimidades*. It does not seem that with all his gifts Villaespesa has the dramatic faculty. Juan Ramón Jiménez [1] (b.1881) is a poet of elegiac verse, simple in appearance but delicately wrought and full of lyrical ecstasy. A subdued and immitigable melancholy informs all his work, particularly *Arias tristes* (1903), *Jardines lejanos* (1904), *La soledad sonora* (1908), *Laberinto* (1910) and *Melancolía* (1912). In later volumes, such as *Sonetos espirituales* (1917), *Eternidades* (1918) and *Piedra y Cielo* (1919), his versification assumes greater variety and a richer tone. Jiménez writes with fine simplicity and a subtle touch of humour in the prose-fantasy, *Platero y yo* (1914). Antonio Machado (b. 1875) displays a certain power of evocation and original talent in the robust symbolism of *Soledades* (1903), *Campos de Castilla* (1912) and *Nuevas canciones* (1924). His elder brother, Manuel Machado (b. 1874), shews genuine inspiration in such poems as *Adelfos* in *Alma* (1901) and *Ars Moriendi* (1922). Enrique Díez Canedo (b. 1879), a poet of refined sensibility, reveals aesthetic emotion and an impressive simplicity in *Versos de las horas* (1906) and *La Visita*

[1] *Poesías escogidas* (1899-1917). New York, 1917 (The Hispanic Society of America).—See: P. Henríquez Ureña, *La obra de Juan Ramón Jiménez*, in *Cuba Contemporánea*, XIX (1919), pp. 251-263.

del sol (1907). His *Conversaciones literarias* (1922) is an interesting collection of critical sketches. Pedro García Morales (b. 1880) produced in *Gérmenes* (1910) a volume characterized by a dreamy melody and lightness of touch symbolical of its author's love for music. A return to the sonorous forms of ancient tradition is evident in Enrique de Mesa (b. 1878), whose *Tierra y alma* (1906), *Cancionero castellano* (1911) and *El silencio de la cartuja* (1916) have a note of the Archpriest of Hita's exuberance, and in Manuel de Sandoval (b. 1874). An imitator in the beginning of Núñez de Arce and Ferrari in *Prometeo* (1895) and *Aves de paso* (1904), Sandoval developed a personal talent in *Cancionero* (1909), *Musa castellana* (1911) and *De mi cercado* (1912), where he gives expression to his vigorous inspiration in a clear and limpid style. Enrique López Alarcón (b. 1881) became known by the patriotic sonnet, *Soy español*: he has an undoubted if somewhat harsh talent in *Constelaciones* (1906).

Politicians might perhaps be expected to have some measure of the wariness which commonly forms part of the critic's equipment. This has not happened in Spain. Antonio Cánovas del Castillo (1828-1897), who had talent but wielded a dull, colourless prose in *La campana de Huesca* (1852) and in more solid works such as *Estudios sobre Felipe IV* (1888), had no critical judgement. His lack of penetration in literary matters allowed him to believe in the authenticity of *El Buscapié*. His rival in politics, Emilio Castelar (1832-1899), exercised no literary influence either. Castelar's gifts lay wholly in oratory. As a speaker he has never been equalled in Spain: his inexhaustible resources of rhetoric, his fire, his inspired delivery in the tribune

SPANISH LITERATURE SINCE 1868

held every audience enthralled. But his marvellous eloquence and brilliancy of exposition fail him when he begins to write. The *Recuerdos de Italia* (1872) and the novel *Fra Filipo Lippi* (1877-1878) are packed with dithyrambical antitheses which the magic of his spoken word alone could carry off. The *Historia del movimiento republicano en Europa* (1873-1874) is a blind riot of phrases, a kind of caricature of Donoso Cortés's style.

Spain has produced her share of scholars who have made her name respected in the learned world. Among these may be mentioned the general José Gómez de Arteche (1821-1906), whose powers of research, skill and care are visible in the fourteen volumes of the *Guerra de la Independencia* (1868-1903); Cesáreo Fernández Duro (1830-1908), author of the *Memorias de la ciudad de Zamora, su provincia y su obispado* (1882-1883) and of the *Armada española desde la unión de los reinos de Castilla y Aragón* (1895-1903); Joaquín Costa (1844-1911), the prominent reformer and learned writer of *Poesía popular española y Mitología y literatura celto-hispanas* (1881), of *Estudios ibéricos* (1891) and of *Colectivismo agrario en España* (1898), and Rafael de Ureña y Smenjaud (b. 1852), director since 1918 of the *Revista de Ciencias jurídicas y sociales*, who in *La legislación gótico-hispana* (1905) and *Historia de la literatura jurídica española* (1906) has embodied the results of his scholarly investigation and added largely to the knowledge collected by Karl Zeumer. These writers have accumulated valuable materials for the Mariana of the future : many of their conclusions have been utilized by Rafael Altamira y Crevea (b. 1866) in his *Historia de España y de la civilización española* (1900-1911), a work superior in many respects to

Modesto Lafuente's lengthy and somewhat indigest compilation. Antonio Ballesteros y Beretta (b. 1880) has produced a striking piece of original research in *Sevilla en el siglo xiii* (1913) and a monumental *Historia de España y su influencia en la historia universal* (from 1919 onwards). This work is valuable from two points of view : its clear and careful exposition of every theory set forth with an entire impartiality of opinion, and its unequalled bibliographical documentation.

In the domain of literary history considerable progress has been made since Pascual de Gayangos (1809-1897) set on one side his Arabic studies in order to dedicate himself more exclusively to Spanish literature. His introductions to the *Libros de caballerías* (1857), *La Gran Conquista de Ultramar* (1858) and *Escritores en prosa anteriores al siglo xv* (1860), though in the nature of premature efforts, threw light on many literary monuments of the Middle Ages. Gayangos was in every way a much greater scholar than Pedro Felipe Monlau (1808-1871), Cayetano Rosell (1813-1883), José Amador de los Ríos (1818-1878), author of an ambitious *Historia crítica de la literatura española* (1861-1865) as well as of the useful *Historia social, política y religiosa de los judíos de España y Portugal* (1875-1876), and Florencio Janer (1831-1877). But the two greatest names in Spanish scholarship in the nineteenth century—and, in fact, the only two great names—are undoubtedly those of the Catalan Manuel Milá y Fontanals[1] (1814-1884) and

[1] See : J. Rubió y Ors, *Noticia de la vida y escritos de D. Manuel Milá y Fontanals.* 1887 (Discurso. R. Academia de Buenas Letras de Barcelona] ; M. Menéndez y Pelayo, in *Estudios de crítica literaria.* Madrid, 1908. 5ª serie, pp. 3-81 ; J. Roig i Roqué, *Bibliografía d'en Manuel Milà i Fontanals.* Barcelona, 1913.

of the Asturian Marcelino Menéndez y Pelayo[1] (1856-1912). The work of the former *De la poesía heróico-popular castellana* (1874) marks an epoch in Hispanic mediaeval studies. Subsequent studies and researches have only confirmed the intuitions, amounting almost to genius, of the author. Marcelino Menéndez y Pelayo won a reputation in the first instance through the wide learning and powers of reasoning which he shewed in *Ciencia española* (1876) and *Horacio en España* (1877). These qualities are present on a larger scale in the *Historia de los heterodoxos españoles* (1880-1881), whose polemical tone contributed in no small measure to its popularity. Whatever reserves may be made as regards its ultramontane views, it remains an almost incredible fact that this remarkable work on religious thought in Spain should have been written by a young man of twenty-four years of age. Menéndez y Pelayo's lectures (1881) on Caldcron, embodied in book-form under the title *Calderón y su teatro*, set up a reaction against the uncritical admiration lavished on this author. His verse attracted little attention when it was first collected in 1878 ; his *Odas, Epístolas y Tragedias* (1883), however, shew a depth of aesthetic emotion unexpected in an erudite critic. He was not a poet : but poets were his constant

[1] See : A. Bonilla y San Martín, *La filosofía de Menéndez y Pelayo (con un apéndice bibliográfico)*. Madrid, 1912 ; A. Bonilla y San Martín, *La representación de Menéndez y Pelayo en la vida histórica nacional.* Madrid, 1912 ; A. González Blanco, *Marcelino Menéndez Pelayo. Su vida y su obra.* Madrid, 1912 ; *Revista de Archivos*, etc. (julio-agosto), 1912) [Special number in memory of Don Marcelino Menéndez y Pelayo] ; A. Bonilla y San Martín, *Marcelino Menéndez y Pelayo* (1856-1912). Madrid. 1914.

preoccupation : he was well fitted to approach them by his delicate sense of beauty, his sure taste and his gift of sympathy. They figure in the *Historia de las ideas estéticas en España* (1883-1891): they occupy entirely the *Antología de poetas hispano-americanos* (1893-1895) and the *Antología de poetas líricos castellanos* (1890-1908), whose introductions are a treasure-house of information and an excellent history of Castilian poetry up to Boscan. For some twelve years Menéndez y Pelayo laboured at the stupendous task of preparing and commentating what was to have been a complete edition (1890-1902) of Lope de Vega's works. He collected some of his own scattered studies dealing with a variety of other subjects in the five series of *Estudios de crítica literaria* (1884-1908), and in *Ensayos de crítica filosófica* (1892). In the *Nueva Biblioteca de Autores Españoles* (whose director he was), he composed the long prologues to the first three volumes of the *Orígenes de la Novela* (1905-1915); prologues that are so many chapters of that history of Spanish literature which he was destined never to write. Death had been threatening for some time : it surprised him while he was compiling the definitive edition of his works, the first volume of which—the first also of the *Historia de los heterodoxos españoles*—was published in 1911. Some of his works, the *Historia de las ideas estéticas en España*, the edition of Lope, and the *Antología de poetas líricos castellanos* remain unfinished. Menéndez y Pelayo embraced too much, but his perseverance and his talent were remarkable. Time, while it deepened his influence, also matured his gifts : his vast intellectual sympathies, his sound scholarship, his clear and pleasant style.

Menéndez y Pelayo's efforts created an intellectual

movement which has produced excellent results in the works of his collaborators, disciples and contemporaries. As director of the Biblioteca Nacional, he had under him Antonio Paz y Mélia (b. 1842), a most distinguished palaeographer and a scholar indefatigable in research. Cristóbal Pérez Pastor (1842-1908), an eminent bibliographer and discoverer of *Documentos cervantinos* (1897-1902), has filled many blanks in Cervantes's biography. Francisco Navarro y Ledesma (1859 ?-1905), an amateur of literature and a conscientious stylist rather than a scholar, utilized Pérez Pastor's investigations somewhat fantastically in *El ingenioso Hidalgo Miguel de Cervantes Saavedra* (1905), a book which threw his didactic works into the shade. José Enrique Serrano y Morales (1852-1908) illumined many obscure points of literary history by his researches (1898-1899) on Valencian printers. Francisco Rodríguez Marín (b. 1855), a poet and a scholar who succeeded Menéndez y Pelayo at the Biblioteca Nacional, is the compiler of the anthology *Cantos populares españoles* (1882-1883). In *Luis Barahona de Soto* (1903) and *Pedro Espinosa* (1907) he envisages his authors from the point of view of their *milieu* and does not confine himself exclusively to their personal biographies; these books constitute two important pieces of documentation whose study is invaluable for a knowledge of literary circles. Rodríguez Marín ranks as an eminent cervantist by virtue of his *Nuevos documentos cervantinos* (1915), his editions (1911-1913 and 1916) of *Don Quixote* and of the *Novelas ejemplares* (1914-1917 and 1905-1918). In this context the name of Clemente Cortejón (1842-1911) should be mentioned for his annotated edition (1900-1913) of *Don Quixote*, whose last volume was finished by Juan Givanel Más and Juan Suñé Benajes. Antonio Rubió y Lluch (b. 1856), son of the Catalan poet Joaquín Rubió y Ors (1818-1899), and a fellow-student of Menéndez y Pelayo, is a recognized authority on the history of the Catalans in the East: he has published among other critical works on Spanish literature *El sentimiento del honor en el teatro de Calderón* (1882). Emilio Cotarelo y Mori (b. 1858), a prolific writer on the history of the drama, has published many rare comedies—particularly of Tirso de Molina and Lope de Vega. As an editor of texts he is neither consistently reliable nor scrupulously exact. He is the author of useful monographs which amplify and complete the information already collected by Cayetano Alberto de la Barrera (1815-1872). Juan Menéndez Pidal (1858-1915) published relatively little: this is a pity, for his collection of Asturian ballads (1885) and his critical examination of the legend of Don Rodrigo (1906) are works of singular merit. Julio Puyol y Alonso (b. 1865), author of an excellent study on the Archpriest of Hita (1906), has presented (1911) the problems connected with the formation of the *Crónica popular del Cid* with insight and perspicacity; has reconstituted (1911) as far as was possible the *Cantar de gesta de don Sancho II de Castilla* and has published an excellent annotated edition (1912) of *La Pícara Justina*. Ramón Menéndez Pidal (b. 1869), a disciple of Menéndez y Pelayo, is known principally by his fine work, *La leyenda de los Infantes de Lara* (1896), by an edition (1906) of the *Primera crónica general* and by his analysis (1907-1911) of the perplexed questions relating to the *Cantar de Mio Cid*. To him is due the foundation of the *Revista de Filología Española*, which is strictly modelled upon the *Zeitschrift für romanische Philologie*. Another disciple of Menéndez y Pelayo, Adolfo Bonilla y San Martín[1] (b. 1875), has won distinction in the triple domain of philosophy, literary history and law in such works as *Luis Vives y la Filosofía del Renacimiento* (1903), *Anales de la literatura española* (1904) and,in scholarly editions of *El diablo cojuelo* (1902 and 1910), *Libro de los engaños* (1904), *Libros de caballerías* (1907-1908) and *Tristan de Leonis* (1912). Had this writer concentrated his brilliant talents, powerful energies and untiring activities, he would probably have produced a really remarkable work. Narciso Alonso Cortés (b. 1875), an eminent critic whose research has led to some notable discoveries, has published many literary monographs, as well as collections of popular ballads. With these may be mentioned Joaquín Hazañas y La Rúa (b. 1862), editor (1895) of Gutierre de Cetina and author of *Los rufianes de Cervantes* (1906) and *Maese Rodrigo* [1444-1509] (1909); Julio Cejador y Frauca (b. 1864), a philologist and author of the *Tesoro de la Lengua Castellana* (1908-1915) and of a monumental *Historia de la lengua y literatura española* in fourteen volumes (1915-1922); Manuel Serrano y Sanz (b. 1866), editor of many texts and compiler of the excellent *Apuntes para una Biblioteca de escritoras españolas* (1903-1905); José Ramón Lomba y Pedraja (b. 1868), writer of important studies on Arolas (1898), Peter the Cruel in the drama (1899), José Somoza (1904) and Mariano Josef de Larra (1918-1919); and Victor Said Armesto (1874-1914), the learned investigator of the poetic origin of *La leyenda de don Juan* (1908).

[1] See: J. A. Galvarriato, *La obra de Adolfo Bonilla y San Martín*. Madrid, 1918.

RUFINO JOSÉ CUERVO [1] (1844-1911), a Columbian, achieved distinction as a philologist and scholar with his *Diccionario de construcción y régimen de la lengua castellana* (1886-1893), which is unfortunately unfinished. Eager in the pursuit of learning and undaunted by difficulties in early youth, Cuervo was able to consecrate his later life to his favourite studies. His alert intelligence and sure literary taste are manifest in the *Apuntaciones sobre el lenguaje bogotano* (1867; 6th edition 1914), which abounds in examples drawn from the best writers.

It remained for a Uruguayan, JOSÉ ENRIQUE RODÓ [2] (1872-1917), to win for South America a prominent place in aesthetic criticism in the literary citizenship of the world. His influence on Spanish literature was perhaps as paramount in its own sphere as Darío's was in the domain of poetry. Rodó's first works, *Rubén Darío* (1899) and *Ariel* (1900), in which are revealed his austere and subtle intelligence, his flights of paradoxical fancy, his vigorous yet exquisite sensibility, reflect all that is best and most typical in his exotic talent. They did not, however, create the same sensation as *Motivos de Proteo* (1909) and *El mirador de Próspero* (1913), where Rodó more nearly approaches Spanish models and to a certain degree compromises his innate originality of expression.

To the Cuban, José de Armas y Cárdenas (1866-

---

[1] See: *Homenajes a la memoria de Don Rufino José Cuervo*, in *Anuario de la Academia Colombiana*, II (1910-1911), pp. 287-349; Fr. P. Fabo, *Rufino José Cuervo y la lengua castellana*. Bogotá, 1912. 3 vols.

[2] See: M. Henríquez Ureña, in *Rodó y Rubén Darío*, La Habana, 1918. pp. 1-75; G. Zaldumbide, *José Enrique Rodó*, in *Revue Hispanique*, XLIII (1918), pp. 205-307.

1919), are due various critical essays and studies on questions relating to Lope de Vega and Cervantes. A more supple talent is that of the Guatemalan, Enrique Gómez Carrillo (b. 1873). A cosmopolitan settled in France, he displays a lively curiosity for everything new or uncommon: his delicate sensibility and ingenious spirit find characteristic expression in such subtly psychological works as *Sensaciones de París y de Madrid* (1899), *El alma japonesa* (1906), *Flores de penitencia* (1913) and *La sonrisa de la Esfinge* (1913). Rufino Blanco-Fombona (b. 1873) is a Venezuelan of more robust temperament, whose talents have found scope in such different branches as verse, journalism and politics. He gives evidence of considerable acumen in his annotated edition of the correspondence of Simón Bolívar (1783-1830), and has cultivated the novel in *El Hombre de oro* (1916). The Mexican author, Alfonso Reyes (b. 1889) is an ingenious and suggestive critic who combines concision and clarity with insight and a sense of measure. These qualities are represented in his essays, *Cuestiones estéticas* (1910), *El Suicida* (1911), *Cartones de Madrid* (1917), *Visión de Anáhuac* (1917), *El plano oblicuo* (1920) and *Simpatías y Diferencias* (1921-1923). Reyes's verse, which won him a reputation as a poet in México, was recently published in book form under the title of *Huellas* (1922).

Since the day of the clever and intransigent critic Antonio de Valbuena (b. 1840), whose disparagement of living authors in his series of *Ripios* (1883-1905) would justify the application to him of the phrase, ' He has no enemies, but he is intensely disliked by his friends,' a new note is visible in the field of Spanish criticism and belles-lettres. Among contemporary essayists the versatile talent of Miguel de Unamuno [1] (b. 1864) stands out. Of Basque descent, a scholar, versifier, critic and novelist he has written copiously on subjects as various as : *Vida de D. Quijote y Sancho Panza* (1905), *Del sentimiento trágico de la vida* (1913), *Andanzas y Visiones Españolas* (1922). His *Ensayos* (1916-1919), collected in seven volumes, shew an interesting aspect of his art. Apart from his lay sermons, his most attractive work is perhaps *De mi país* (1903), a series of studies on provincial customs written in a picturesque and vigorous style. Gabriel Alomar (b. 1873) reveals poetical imagination, a quick intelligence and a fine spirit of optimism in *Verba* (1908). More recent works of his are *La formación de sí mismo* (1920) and *Política idealista* (1923). Andrés González-Blanco (1866-1924), the standard-bearer of the new poetical school, has a note of personal conviction, though he lacks measure in his somewhat diffuse and uncompleted studies, *Los grandes maestros* (1908). Eduardo Gómez de Baquero (b. 1866), a critic of good taste and solid judgement, has published (under the pseudonym of ' Andrenio ') some of his work in *Novelas y Novelistas* (1918) and *El renacimiento de la novela en el siglo xix* (1924). Julio Casares (b. 1877) shews perspicacity and a power of subtle analysis in *Crítica profana* (1915), while he is more concerned with philological questions in *Crítica efímera* (1918). A more powerful intellect is that of José Ortega y

[1] See : Andrenio, in *Novelas y Novelistas*. Madrid, 1918. pp. 271-280 ; Q. Saldaña, *Los ' Ensayos' de M. de Unamuno*, in *Revista Crítica hispano-americana*, IV (1918), pp. 33-46, 60-88 ; S. de Madariaga, in *The Genius of Spain*, etc. Oxford, 1923. pp. 87-110; A. F. G. Bell, in *Contemporary Spanish Literature*. New York, 1925. pp. 233-244.

Gasset[1] (b. 1883), whose *Personas, Obras, Cosas* . . . (1916), *España Invertebrada* (1922) and *El Tema de nuestro tiempo* (1923) abound in philosophical reflexions, informed with a certain dignity of emotion. Ortega y Gasset divides with Unamuno the sphere of philosophic thought in the younger generation, but his production, unlike that of the Basque writer, is comparatively restricted. Some of his essays are included in *El Espectador*, a periodical publication reminiscent of its English forerunner. He was also the founder (1923) of a monthly review, *Revista de Occidente*.

[1] See: V. García Calderón, in *La Verbena de Madrid*. Paris, n.d. pp. 87-97; A. Reyes, in *Cuba Contemporánea*, XVI (1918), pp. 51-56; Andrenio, *El Renacimiento de la novela en el siglo xix*. Madrid, 1924. pp. 158-164.

GENERAL BIBLIOGRAPHY

I. BIBLIOGRAPHICAL WORKS

THE most minute details relative to bibliographical works and collections will be found in R. FOULCHÉ-DELBOSC and L. BARRAU DIHIGO, *Manuel de l'Hispanisant*. New York, 1920-1926. Tome I [*Répertoires*] contains the following divisions: I. Généralités.—II. Typo-bibliographies.—III. Biographies et bio-bibliographies.—IV. Bibliographies monographiques.—V. Archives, Bibliothéques et Musées.—VI. Collections dispersées. Tome II [Collections].

ANTONIO (Nicolas), *Bibliotheca Hispana vetus* and *Bibliotheca Hispana nova* (ed. F. Pérez Bayer, T. A. Sánchez, J. A. Pellizer and R. Casalbon). Matriti, 1788. 4 vols.

BARRERA Y LEIRADO (Cayetano Alberto de la). *Catálogo bibliográfico y biográfico del teatro antiguo español, desde sus orígenes hasta mediados del siglo xviii*. Madrid, 1860.

Bibliographie hispanique. New York, 1905-1917. 13 vols. [contains all the publications relating to Hispanic studies].

FOULCHÉ-DELBOSC (R.). *Bibliographie hispano-française*, 1477-1610, 1611-1660, 1661-1700. New York, 1912-1914. 3 vols.

GALLARDO (Bartolomé José). *Ensayo de una biblioteca española de libros raros y curiosos* (ed. M. R. Zarco del Valle and J. Sancho Rayon. Madrid, 1863-1889. 4 vols.

GARCÍA PERES (Domingo). *Catálogo razonado, biográfico y bibliográfico de los autores portugueses que escribieron en castellano*. Madrid, 1890.

LATASSA Y ORTIN (Felix de.) *Bibliotecas antigua y nueva de escritores aragoneses de Latassa* (1796-1802) *aumentadas y refundidas en forma de diccionario bibliográfico-biográfico por don Miguel Gómez Uriel*. Zaragoza, 1884-1886. 3 vols.

GENERAL BIBLIOGRAPHY

Pérez Pastor (Cristóbal). *Bibliografía madrileña ó descripción de las obras impresas en Madrid* (1566-1625]. Madrid, 1891-1907. 3 vols.

Salvá y Mallen (Pedro). *Catálogo de la biblioteca de Salvá.* Valencia, 1872. 2 vols.

Serrano y Sanz (Manuel). *Apuntes para una biblioteca de escritoras españolas desde el año 1401 al 1833.* Madrid, 1903-1905. 2 vols.

II. WORKS OF GENERAL REFERENCE

Barja (César). *Literatura española. Libros y Autores clásicos.* 3rd ed. Brattleboro, 1923.

Barja (César). *Literatura española. Libros y Autores modernos.* New York [1924].

Bell (Aubrey F. G.). *Portuguese Literature.* Oxford, 1922.

Bell (Aubrey F. G.). *Contemporary Spanish Literature.* New York, 1925.

Blanco García (El P. Francisco). *La literatura española en el siglo xix.* Madrid, 1891-1894. 3 vols.

Boletín de la Real Academia Española. Madrid, since 1914. 11 vols.

Bonilla y San Martín (Adolfo). *Anales de la literatura española* (Años 1900-1904). Madrid, 1904.

Cejador y Frauca (Julio). *Historia de la lengua y literatura castellana.* Madrid, 1915-1922. 14 vols.

Chandler (Frank Wadleigh). *Romances of Roguery.* I. *The Picaresque Novel in Spain.* New York, 1899.

Cotarelo y Mori (Emilio). *Estudios de historia literaria de España.* Madrid, 1901.

Croce (Benedetto). *La Spagna nella vita italiana durante la Rinascenza.* Bari, 1917.

Cultura Española. Madrid, 1906-1909. 4 vols.

Entwhistle (William J.). *The Arthurian Legend in the Literatures of the Spanish Peninsula.* London, 1925.

Farinelli (Artur). *Spanien und die spanische Litteratur im Lichte der deutschen Kritik und Poesie.* Berlin, 1892.

SPANISH LITERATURE

FITZMAURICE-KELLY (James). *Chapters on Spanish Literature.* London, 1908.

FITZMAURICE-KELLY (James). *The Relations between Spanish and English Literature.* Liverpool, 1910.

FITZMAURICE-KELLY (James). *Some Masters of Spanish Verse.* Oxford, 1924 (Hispanic Notes and Monographs. Spanish Series. VII).

FORD (J. D. M.) *Main Currents of Spanish Literature.* New York, 1919.

GONZÁLEZ-BLANCO (Andrés). *Historia de la novela en España desde el romanticismo á nuestros días.* Madrid, 1909.

HURTADO Y J. DE LA SERNA (Juan) and GONZÁLEZ PALENCIA (Angel). *Historia de la Literatura Española.* Madrid, 1921 ; 2nd ed. 1925.

MARTINENCHE (Ernest). *L'Espagne et le romantisme français.* Paris, 1922.

MENÉNDEZ Y PELAYO (Marcelino). *Historia de las ideas estéticas en España* [unfinished]. Madrid, 1883-1891 ; 2nd ed. I, 1890 (Col. de Escritores Castellanos).

MENÉNDEZ Y PELAYO (Marcelino). *Orígenes de la Novela.* Madrid, 1905-1915. 4 vols. (Nueva Bib. de Autores Esp., I, 7, 14, 21).

MENÉNDEZ Y PELAYO (Marcelino). *Historia de los Heterodoxos españoles.* Madrid, 1880-1882. 3 vols. ; 2nd ed. by A. Bonilla y San Martín, Madrid, 1911-1917. 3 vols. (*Obras Completas*, I, VII, VIII).

MENÉNDEZ PIDAL (Ramón). *L'épopée castillane à travers la littérature espagnole. Traduction de Henri Mérimée.* Paris, 1910.

MOREL-FATIO (Alfred). *L'Espagne au xvie et au xviie siècles.* Heilbronn, 1878.

MOREL-FATIO (Alfred). *Études sur l'Espagne.* Paris, 1888-1925. 4 vols. ; 2nd. ed. 1895-1906, I, II.

NORTHUP (George Tyler). *An Introduction to Spanish Literature.* Chicago, 1925.

PÉREZ PASTOR (Cristóbal). *Noticias y documentos relativos a la historia y literatura españolas (Memorias de la R. Academia Esp.*, X, XI). Madrid, 1910-1914. 2 vols.

GENERAL BIBLIOGRAPHY 523

PIÑEYRO (Enrique). *El romanticismo en España.* Paris, 1904.

POST (Chandler Rathfon). *Mediaeval Spanish Allegory.* Cambridge, U.S.A.—London, 1915 (Harvard Studies in Comparative Literature).

PUYMAIGRE (Th. de). *Les vieux auteurs castillans.* Metz, Paris, 1861-1862, 2 vols.; new ed. 2 vols. Paris, 1888-1890.

PUYMAIGRE (Le Comte de). *La cour littéraire de don Juan II, roi de Castille.* Paris, 1873. 2 vols.

Revista de Archivos, Bibliotecas y Museos, Tercera época. Madrid, since 1897. 44 vols.

Revista de Filología Española. Director, Ramón Menéndez Pidal. Madrid since 1914. 11 vols.

Revue Hispanique. Recueil consacré à l'étude des langues, des littératures et de l'histoire des pays castillans, catalans et portugais, dirigé par R. Foulché-Delbosc. Paris-New York since 1894. 64 vols.

Ríos (José Amador de los). *Historia crítica de la literatura española.* Madrid, 1861-1865. 7 vols.

RODRÍGUEZ MARÍN (Francisco). *Nuevos datos para las biografías de cien escritores de los siglos xvi y xvii.* Madrid, 1923.

ROUSSELOT (Paul). *Les mystiques espagnols.* Paris, 1867 [Spanish trans. with prologue by P. Umbert. Barcelona, 1907. 2 vols.].

SANVISENTI (Bernardo). *I primi influssi di Dante, del Petrarca e del Boccaccio sulla Letteratura Spagnuola.* Milano, 1902.

SCHEVILL (Rudolph). *Ovid and the Renascence in Spain.* Berkeley, U.S.A., 1913 (University of California Publications in Modern Philology).

SOUSA VITERBO (F. M. de). *A Litteratura Hespanhola em Portugal* (Historia e Memorias da Academia das Sciencias de Lisboa. Nova serie, 2ª classe. Sciencias moraes e politicas e bellas letras), XII, Pt. ii, No. 5, pp. 151-454. Lisboa, 1915.

THOMAS (Henry) *Spanish and Portuguese Romances of Chivalry.* Cambridge, 1920.

TICKNOR (George). *History of Spanish Literature.* Boston, 1849. 3 vols.; 6th ed. Boston, 1888. 3 vols. [Spanish trans. by P. de Gayangos and E. de Vedia, Madrid, 1851-1856. 4 vols.]

TREND (J. B.). *The Music of Spanish History.* Oxford, 1925 (Hispanic Notes and Monographs, Spanish Series, x).

TREND (J. B.). *Luis Milan and the Vihuelistas.* Oxford, 1925. (Hispanic Notes and Monographs, Spanish Series, xi).

UNDERHILL (John Garrett). *Spanish Literature in the England of the Tudors.* New York-London, 1899.

VAN VECHTEN (Carl). *The Music of Spain.* New York, 1918.

III. HISTORY OF THE DRAMA

BONILLA Y SAN MARTÍN (Adolfo). *Las Bacantes o del origen del teatro.* Madrid, 1921.

COTARELO Y MORI (Emilio). *Introducción general*, in *Colección de Entremeses, Loas, Bailes, Jácaras, y Mojigangas desde fines del siglo xvi á mediados del xviii.* 1911. I, pp. i-cccxv (Nueva Bib. de Autores Esp., 17).

CRAWFORD (J. P. W.). *The Spanish Pastoral Drama.* Philadelphia, 1915.

CRAWFORD (J. P. W.). *Spanish Drama before Lope de Vega.* Philadelphia, 1922 (Publications of the University of Pennsylvania, Extra Series in Romanic Languages and Literatures. 7).

CREIZENACH (Wilhelm). *Geschichte des neueren Dramas.* Halle a. S., 1893-1916, 5 vols.; 2nd ed. I, II, 1911-1918; III, 1923 (ed. Adalbert Hämel).

GONZÁLEZ-BLANCO (Andrés). *Los dramaturgos españoles contemporáneos.* I. Valencia, 1917.

MARISCAL DE GANTE (Jaime). *Los autos sacramentales desde sus orígenes hasta mediados del siglo xviii.* Madrid, 1911.

MÉRIMÉE (Henri). *L'Art dramatique à Valencia depuis les origines jusqu'au commencement du xviie siècle.* Toulouse, 1913 (Bibliothèque méridionale, 16).

MOREL-FATIO (Alfred). *La Comedia espagnole du xviie siècle.* Paris, 1885; 2nd ed. Paris, 1923.

GENERAL BIBLIOGRAPHY

PÉREZ PASTOR (Cristóbal). *Nuevos datos acerca del histrionismo español en los siglos xvi y xvii.* Madrid, 1901 ; 2nd series with index by G. Cirot. Bordeaux, 1914 (*Bulletin hispanique*).

RENNERT (Hugo Albert). *The Spanish stage in the time of Lope de Vega.* New York, 1909.

IV. COLLECTIONS OF TEXTS

Biblioteca de Autores Españoles, desde la formación del lenguaje hasta nuestros días. Madrid. Rivadeneyra, 1846-1880. 71 vols.

Bibliotheca Romanica. Biblioteca española. Strasburgo, s.f. 15 vols. (In course of publication.)

Bibliotheca hispanica. Director R. Foulché-Delbosc. Barcelona-Madrid-New York, 1900-1921. 22 vols. (In course of publication.)

Clásicos Castellanos. Madrid, 1910-1925. 63 vols. (In course of publication.)

Clásicos de la Literatura española. Ed. A. Bonilla y San Martín. Madrid, 1915-1917. 12 vols.

Colección de Autores Españoles. Leipzig, Brockhaus, 1863-1887. 48 vols.

Colección de Escritores Castellanos. Madrid, 1880-1915. 161 vols.

Coleccion de libros españoles raros ó curiosos. Madrid, 1871-1896. 24 vols.

Colección de los mejores Autores Españoles. Paris, Baudry, 1838-1872. 60 vols.

Colección de Poetas Españoles. Ed. Ramón Fernández [pseudonym of Pedro Estala]. Madrid, 1789-1820. 20 vols.

Libros de antaño. Madrid, 1872-1898. 15 vols.

Nueva Biblioteca de Autores Españoles. Director M. Menéndez y Pelayo. Madrid, Bailly-Baillière, 1905-19. 24 vols.

Obras dramáticas del siglo xvi. Ed. A. Bonilla y San Martín. Madrid, 1914.

Sociedad de Bibliófilos Andaluces (Texts published by), Sevilla, 1867-1907. 51 vols.

SPANISH LITERATURE

Sociedad de Bibliófilos Españoles (Texts published by), Madrid, since 1866. 48 vols.

Sociedad de Bibliófilos Madrileños (Texts published by), Madrid, 1909-1914. 11 vols.

V. ANTHOLOGIES

Biblioteca Oropesa. Ed. dos Hispanistas [R. Foulché-Delbosc and A. Bonilla y San Martín]. Madrid, 1905-1909. 7 vols.

BÖHL DE FABER (Juan Nicolas). *Floresta de rimas antiguas castellanas.* Hamburg, 1821-1825. 3 vols.

BONILLA Y SAN MARTÍN (Adolfo). *Antología de poetas de los siglos xiii al xv.* 1917 (Clásicos de la Literatura esp., 10).

BONILLA Y SAN MARTÍN (Adolfo). *Flores de poetas ilustres de los siglos xvi y xvii.* 1917 (Clásicos de la Literatura esp., 11).

BONILLA Y SAN MARTÍN (Adolfo). *Parnaso español de los siglos xviii y xix.* 1917 (Clásicos de la Literatura esp., 12).

CEJADOR Y FRAUCA (Julio). *La verdadera poesía castellana. Floresta de la antigua lírica popular.* Madrid, 1921-1924. 5 vols.

FARNELL (Ida). *Spanish Prose and Poetry Old and New.* Oxford, 1920.

FITZMAURICE-KELLY (James). *The Oxford Book of Spanish Verse xiiith Century–xxth Century.* Oxford, 1913.

FITZMAURICE-KELLY (James). *Cambridge Readings in Spanish Literature.* Cambridge, 1920.

FORD (J. D. M.) *A Spanish Anthology. A collection of lyrics from the thirteenth century, down to the present time.* New York, 1901.

FORD (J. D. M.). *Old Spanish Readings.* Boston [1911].

HILLS (Elijah Clarence), and MORLEY (S. Griswold). *Modern Spanish Lyrics.* New York, 1913.

LANG (Henry R.). *Cancioneiro gallego-castelhano. The extant Galician poems of the Gallego-Castilian lyric school (1350-1450).* New York-London, 1902.

LE STRANGE (Guy). *Spanish Ballads.* Cambridge, 1920.

LEMCKE (Ludwig). *Handbuch der spanischen Litteratur.* Leipzig, 1855-1856. 3 vols.

GENERAL BIBLIOGRAPHY 527

MENÉNDEZ Y PELAYO (Marcelino). *Antología de poetas líricos castellanos desde la formación del idioma hasta nuestros días* [unfinished]. Madrid, 1890-1908. 13 vols. [The critical introductions of this anthology have been reprinted separately in vols. IV., V, VI, of the *Obras Completas* of the author under the title *Historia de la Poesía Castellana en la edad media.* Madrid, 1911-1916. 3 vols.]

MENÉNDEZ Y PELAYO (Marcelino). *Antología de poetas hispano-americanos.* Madrid, 1893-1895. 4 vols. (R. Academia Esp). [The critical introductions of this anthology have been reprinted in vols. II, III of the *Obras completas* of the author under the title *Historia de la Poesía Hispano-Americana.* Madrid, 1911-1913. 2 vols.]

SEDANO (Juan Joseph Lopez de). *Parnaso español. Coleccion de poesías escogidas de los más célebres poetas castellanos.* Madrid, 1768-1778. 9 vols.

VALERA (Juan). *Florilegio de poesías castellanas del siglo xix.* Madrid, 1901-1904. 5 vols.

VI. WORKS OF REFERENCE FOR CHAPTERS I, II

BÉDIER (Joseph). *Les Fabliaux.* 2nd ed. Paris, 1895.

BÉDIER (Joseph). *Les légendes épiques.* Paris, 1908-1913. 4 vols. 2nd ed. Paris, 1914-1921. 4 vols.

BONILLA Y SAN MARTÍN (Adolfo). *Historia de la filosofía española.* Madrid, 1908-1911. 2 vols.

BOUCHIER (Edmund Spencer). *Spain under the Roman Empire.* Oxford, 1914.

COSTA (Joaquín). *Poesía popular española y mitología y literatura celto-hispanas.* Madrid, 1881.

DE WULF (Maurice). *Histoire de la philosophie médiévale.* 2nd ed. Louvain, 1905.

DOZY (R.). *Recherches sur l'histoire politique et littéraire de l'Espagne pendant le moyen âge.* Leyde, 1849. 3rd ed. Leyde-Paris, 1881. 2 vols.

GRÄTZ (Hirsch). *Geschichte der Juden von den ältesten Zeiten bis auf die Gegenwart.* Leipzig, 1865-1870. 11 vols.

SPANISH LITERATURE

Guillén Robles (F.). *Leyendas moriscas*. Madrid, 1885-1886. 3 vols. (Col. de Escritores Castellanos, 35, 42, 48.)

Homenaje á D. Francisco Codera en su jubilación del profesorado : Estudios de erudición oriental [with an introduction by E. Saavedra). Zaragoza, 1904.

Kayserling (M.). *Romanische Poesien der Juden in Spanien.* Leipzig, 1859.

Kayserling (M.). *Geschichte der Juden in Spanien und Portugal.* Berlin, 1861.

Menéndez Pidal (Ramón). *Poesía juglaresca y Juglares. Aspectos de la historia literaria y cultural de España.* Madrid, 1924.

Milá y Fontanals (Manuel). *De la poesía heróico-popular castellana.* Barcelona, 1874.

Milá y Fontanals (Manuel). *De los Trovadores en España. Estudio de poesía y lengua provenzal.* Barcelona, 1889 (*Obras completas*, II).

Nicholson (R. A.). *A Literary History of the Arabs.* London, 1907.

Pedro Alfonso. *Die Disciplina Clericalis des Petrus Alfonsi (das älteste Novellenbuch des Mittelalters)*, ed. A. Hilka u. W. Söderhjelm, Heidelberg, 1911 (Sammlung mittellateinischer Texte. 1).

Rashdall (Hastings). *Universities of Europe in the Middle Ages.* London, 1895. 2 vols. in 3.

Ríos (José Amador de los). *Historia social, política y religiosa de los judíos en España y Portugal.* Madrid, 1875-1876. 3 vols.

Saavedra (Eduardo). *La literatura aljamiada.* 1878 (Discurso R. Academia Esp.).

Schack (Adolf Friedrich von). *Poesie und Kunst der Araber in Spanien und Sicilien.* 2nd ed. Stuttgart, 1877. 2 vols. [Spanish trans. by Juan Valera. 3rd ed. Sevilla, 1881. 3 vols.]

INDEX

A.

'Abdallah ibn al-Muqaffa' ... 27.
Abencerraje y la hermosa Xarifa (Historia del) ... 183, 232, 325.
Abrabanel. *See* Leon Hebreo.
Abraham Aben-Chasdai ... 45.
Abril. *See* Simon Abril.
Abû Bakr Aḥmad ibn Muhammad al Râzî of Cordova ... 26, 99.
Abû'l Wafâ Mubashshir ibn Fâtik ... 22.
Academia del Buen Gusto ... 405, 406.
Academia Selvaje ... 281.
Academy (Spanish) ... **400-401**, 406.
Academy of History ... **400**.
Acosta (José de) ... **246**.
Acquaviva (Giulio) ... 270.
Acuña (Diego de) ... 113.
Acuña (Hernando de) ... **175-177**.
Adam de la Halle ... 154.
Agreda (Sor Maria de Jesus de) ... **374**.
Aguilar (Alonso de) ... 72.
Aguilar (Gaspar Honorat de) ... 294.
Agustini (Delmira) ... **506**.
Alanzuri ... 99.
Alarcon (Juan Ruiz de) ... 47, 90, 285, **317-320**, 385, 386, 410.
Alarcon (Pedro Antonio de) ... **469-470**.
Alas (Leopoldo) ... 474, **477**, 478.
Alba (Bartolomé de) ... 304.
Alba (2nd Duke of) ... 153.
Alba (5th Duke of) ... 295.
Alba (6th Duke of) ... 377.
Alberoni ... 400.
Albornoz (Gil Alvarez Carrillo de) ... 49.

Alburquerque (Duke of) ... 169.
Alcalá (Duke of) ... 221.
Alcalá Galiano (Antonio Maria) ... 437, 467.
Alcalá Yañez y Ribera (Gerónimo de) ... **367**.
Alcázar (Baltasar del) ... **221**.
Alcover (Juan) ... **501-502**.
Aldrete (Bernardo) ... **351**.
Aleman (Mateo) ... 194, **320-322**.
Alexander ... 21, 101.
Alexander VI ... 150, 153, 155.
Alexandre de Bernai ... 17.
Alexandre (Libro de) ... **16-17**, 18, 21, 50, 106.
Alfay (Josef) ... 317.
Alfieri ... 450.
Alfonso Onceno (Poema de) ... 37, **54**, 64, 96.
Al-Ghazālī ... 109.
Aliaga (Luis de) ... 285.
Aljamiada (Literatura) ... **39-40**.
Alomar (Gabriel) ... **518**.
Alonso de Córdoba (Fernando) ... 114.
Alonso Cortés (Narciso) ... 355, **515**.
Alphonso V [of Aragon] ... 69, 76, 111, 122.
Alphonso VI [of Castile] ... 2.
Alphonso X [*El Sabio*] ... 20, **23-33**, 41, 46, 47, 55, 56, 61, 75, 84, 105.
Alphonso XI [of Castile] ... 41, 43, **53-54**, 56, 62.
Alphonso XII ... 466.
Alphonso of Portugal ... 131.
Al-Râzî. *See* Abû Bakr Aḥmad ibn Muhammad.
Altamira y Crevea (Rafael) ... **509-510**.

INDEX

Alvarez (Miguel de los Santos) ... **442**.
Alvarez de Cienfuegos (Nicasio) ... **425-426**.
Alvarez Gato (Juan) ... **116**.
Alvarez Quintero (Joaquín) ... **496-497**.
Alvarez Quintero (Serafín) ... **496-497**.
Alvarez de Soria (Alonso) ... 323.
Alvarez de Toledo (Fernando) ... 226.
Alvarez de Villasandino. *See* Villasandino (Alfonso Alvarez de).
Amadis de Gaula ... 81, 87, 107, 111, **133-140**, 144, 145, 191.
Amalteo (Giambattista) ... 216.
Ampuero y Urbina (Diego de) ... 294.
Ampuero Urbina y Cortinas (Isabel de) ... 294.
Ana de Jesus (Sor) ... 235.
Anacreon ... 355.
Anales Toledanos ... **20-21**.
Andersen (Hans) ... 48.
Andrenio. *See* Gómez de Baquero (Eduardo).
Andújar (Johan de) ... **111-112**.
Angelo (Michael) ... 265.
Angulo y Pulgar (Martin de) ... 335.
Anticlaudianus ... 109.
Antiocha (*Cansó d'*) ... 39.
Antonio (Nicolas) ... 233, **374**, 426.
Añorbe (Tomas de) ... 405.
Apolonio (*Libro de*) ... 9, **11-12**, 282.
Aragon (Catherine of) ... 102, 150, 200.
Aragon (Fernando de) ... 103.
Aranda ... 407, 408.
Aranda (Condesa de) ... 147.
Arbolanche (Hierónimo) ... 231.
Arborea (Jacopo Serra, Archbishop of) ... 153.
Argensola (Bartolomé Leonardo de) ... 285, 317, **353-354**.
Argensola (Lupercio Leonardo de) ... **263-264**, 292, 347, 354.
Argote (Francisco de) ... 328.

Argote de Molina (Gonzalo) ... 42, 54, 259.
Arguijo (Juan de) ... **354-355**.
Arias Montano (Benito) ... 212, 240, 346, 348, 350.
Ariosto ... 160, 163, 175, 221, 222, 256, 257, 343.
Aristotle ... 178, 352, 374, 403.
Arjona (Juan de) ... **341**.
Arjona (Manuel de) ... 433.
Armas y Cárdenas (José de) ... **516-517**.
Armijo de Cambronero (Dolores) ... 458.
Arniches (Carlos) ... 496.
Arolas (Juan) ... **444**, 515.
Artemidoro. *See* Rey de Artieda (Andrés).
Arragel de Guadalajara (Rabbi Mosé) ... 117.
Arrieta (Emilio) ... 451.
Asenjo Barbieri (Francisco) ... 131, 153, 478.
Asensio Más (Ramón) ... 496.
Asumpció de madona Santa Maria (*Representació de la*) ... 118.
At de Mons ... 31.
Ate relegata et Minerva restituta ... 247.
Augier (Émile) ... 450.
Augustine (St.) ... 234.
Avalos (Alonso de), Marqués del Vasto ... 175.
Avellaneda (Alonso Fernandez de) ... **285-286**, 405.
Avellaneda (Gertrudis Gomez de) ... **449-450**.
Avendaño (Francisco de) ... **249**, 301.
Avila (Juan de) ... **198**, 237, 239.
Avila y Zúñiga (Luis de) ... **203-204**, 223.
¡*Ay panadera!* (*Coplas de*) ... **96**, 115.
Ayamonte (Marqués de) ... 221.
Aza (Vital) ... 496.
Azevedo (Alonso de) ... **342**.
'Azorín' ... **483-484**, 488.

B.

Badde (Josse) ... 157.
Bacon (Francis) ... 246, 265

INDEX

Baena (Juan Alfonso de) ... **84.**
Baladro del sabio Merlin con sus profecias (El) ... 139.
Balart (Federico) ... **500.**
Balbuena (Bernardo de) ... **343, 344.**
Balmes (Jaime) ... **464.**
Baltasar Carlos (Prince) ... 369.
Balzac (Honoré de) ... 472.
Ballesteros y Beretta (Antonio) ... **510.**
Bancés Candamo (Francisco Antonio de) ... **399.**
Bandello ... 229, 252, 255.
Barahona de Soto (Luis) ... **221-222.**
Baralt (Rafael María) ... 503.
Barbier d'Orléans (Messinier) ... 157.
Barceló (Francisco) ... 129.
Barlaam and Josaphat ... 45, 82, 83.
Baroja (Pío) ... **484-485,** 488.
Barrera (Cayetano Alberto de la) ... 514.
Barrientos (Lope de) ... 103.
Barrio Angulo. *See* Perez del Barrio Angulo (Gabriel).
Barros (Alonso de) ... 274.
Bartrina (Joaquín María) ... **500,** 505.
Barzûya ... 27.
Bassompierre (Marshal of) ... 367.
Bataille de Karesme et de Charnage (La) ... 50.
Baudelaire ... 502.
Baudouin (Nicolas) ... 278.
Beamonte (Juan de) ... 109.
Beaumarchais ... 316, 407.
Beaumont ... 322.
Bechada (Gregorio) ... 39.
Bécquer (Gustavo Adolfo) ... **454-455,** 505.
Béjar (7th Duque de) ... 221.
Belmonte (Brigida Lucia de) ... 259.
Belmonte Bermudez (Luis de) ... **316.**
Bella (Fr. Anton de la) ... 271.
Bello (Andrés) ... 503.
Bello (Francesco) ... 313.
Bembo ... 165, 167, 170.

Benavente (Conde de) ... 119.
Benavente (Jacinto) ... **491-492,** 493.
Benvenuto da Imola ... 93.
Berceo (Gonzalo de) ... **13-16,** 17, 18, 20, 30, 38, 48, 51.
Berçuire (Pierre) ... 57.
Bermudez (Gerónimo) ... **261.**
Bermudez de Castro (Duque de Ripalda and Marqués de Lema, Salvador) ... **445.**
Bernaldez (Andrés) ... **128-129.**
Bernard (St.) ... 14.
Berners (Lord) ... 141, 188.
Bertaut de la Grise (René) ... 188.
Berte ... 39.
Bessarion (Cardinal) ... 125, 178.
Béziers (Ramon de) ... 27.
Biblioteca Nacional ... 400.
Bickerstaffe ... 282.
Black Prince (The) ... 56, 59.
Blanco-Fombona (Rufino) ... **517**
Blanco de Paz (Juan) ... 286.
Blanco White (José Maria) ... **433-434.**
Blasco (Eusebio) ... **477-478.**
Blasco Ibáñez (Vicente) ... **480-482.**
Boabdil ... 142.
Bocados de Oro ... **22,** 29.
Boccaccio ... 37, 38, 62, 81, 87, 92, 93, 97, 107, 163, 257.
Bodel d'Arras (Jean) ... 77.
Bodin ... 351.
Boethius ... 62, 97, 356.
Böhl de Faber (Juan Nicolas) ... 434.
Boiardo ... 176.
Boileau ... 400, 403, 405.
Boisrobert ... 304, 364, 388.
Bolívar (Simón) ... 517.
Bonaparte (Joseph) ... 421, 425.
Bonilla (Alonso de) ... 357.
Bonilla y San Martín (Adolfo) ... **515.**
Bonium. See Bocados de Oro.
Borgia (St. Francis) ... 171, 237, 346.
Borrow (George) ... 296.
Boscan (Juan) ... **166-168,** 172, 173, 179, 183, 209, 216, 232, 239, 242, 466, 512.

INDEX

Bossuet ... 465.
Botero (Giovanni) ... 369.
Bourget (Paul) ... 477.
Boyl Vives de Canesmas (Carlos) ... **294-295.**
Brantôme ... 191.
Braulio (St.) ... 14.
Bretón (Tomás) ... 495.
Bretón de los Herreros (Manuel) ... **447-448,** 449.
Bridges (Robert) ... 385.
Brihuega (Bernardo de) ... 24.
Bristol (Count of) ... 384.
Brunetière ... 138.
Buddha ... 83.
Buelna (Conde de). See Niño (Pero).
Burgos (Javier de) ... 496.
Burriel (Andrés Marcos) ... **427.**
Butler ... 305.
Byron ... 314, 438, 443, 444, 452.
Bywater (Ingram) ... 164.

C.

Caballero (Fernan) ... **461-462.**
'Caballero Cesáreo (El)' ... 74, 202.
Cabanyes (Manuel de) ... **444.**
Cabarrús (Count of) ... 423.
Cabrera (Claudio Antonio de). See Saavedra Faxardo (Diego).
Cabrera de Córdoba (Luis) ... **349-350.**
Cabrerizo (Mariano) ... 435.
Cáceres (Francisco de) ... 109.
Cadalso (Josef) ... **408-409,** 417.
Calderon (Cristóbal) ... 293.
Calderon (Juan Antonio) ... 339.
Calderon de la Barca (Diego) ... 376.
Calderon de la Barca (José) ... 378.
Calderon de la Barca (Pedro) ... 45, 47, 78, 133, 159, 162, 163, 260, 265, 284, 298, 299, 309, 315, 317, 335, **375-387,** 388, 389, 392, 393, 396, 397, 399, 403, 404, 405, 408, 417, 419, 434, 443, 451, 489, 511.
Calderon de la Barca (Pedro José) ... 377.
Calisto y Melibea (Comedia de). See *Celestina (La).*

Camba (Julio) ... **488.**
Camões ... 78, 121, 165, 335, 338.
Campoamor (Ramón de) ... **453-454,** 466, 501, 505.
Campomanes (Pedro Rodriguez Campomanes, Conde de) ... **427.**
Camus (Bishop of Belley) ... 335.
'Cancer y Velasco (Jerónimo de) ... 394.
Cancion real a vna mudanza ... 317.
Cancioneiro da Ajuda ... 84.
Cancioneiro geral de Garcia de Resende ... 174.
Cancionero de Baena ... **84,** 86, 87, 100, 105, 134.
Cancionero General de Hernando del Castillo ... 79, 117, 140, 151.
Cancionero de Herberay ... 93.
Cancionero de obras de burlas provocantes a risa ... 114.
Cancionero de Stúñiga ... **111-112.**
Cano (Leopoldo) ... 490.
Cánovas del Castillo (Antonio) ... 459, **508.**
Canzoniere portoghese Colocci-Brancuti ... 31, 84, 135.
Canzoniere portoghese della Biblioteca Vaticana ... 54, 84.
Cañete ... 247, 248.
Capmany (Antonio de) ... 244, 430.
Caporali (Cesare) ... 283.
Carducci ... 502.
Carestas ... 99.
Carlyle (Joseph Dacre) ... 444.
Caro (Rodrigo) ... **356.**
Caron (Louise) ... 407.
Carpio (Bernardo de) ... 4, 70, 394; (*romances* on), 73.
Carpio y Lujan (Lope Felix del) ... 297, 298, 299.
Cartagena (Alfonso de) ... 62, 122.
Carranza (Bartolomé) ... 237.
Carrillo (Archbishop) ... 117, 127.
Carrillo de Albornoz (Pedro) ... 103.
Carrillo y Sotomayor (Luis) ... 327, 328.
Carvajal ... 69, 76, 96, **112,** 130.
Carvajal (Bernardo, Cardinal) ... 157.

INDEX 533

Carvajal (Micael de) ... 83, 159, **249.**
Carvajales. *See* Carvajal.
Casanova (Giovanni Jacopo) ... 482.
Casas (Bartolomé de las) ... **205-207.**
Casares (Julio) ... 482, **518.**
Casaus (Lorenzo) ... 416.
Cascales (Francisco) ... 335.
Castelar (Emilio) ... **508-509.**
Castellani ... 176.
Castellanos (Juan de) ... **227.**
Castellar (Conde del) ... 343.
Castellvi (Francisco de) ... 129.
Castiglione (Baldassare) ... 165, 166.
Castigos e Documentos (Libro de los) ... **33.**
Castillejo (Cristóbal de) ... 79, 159, **180-183,** 248.
Castillo (Hernando del). *See Cancionero General.*
Castillo (Juan del) ... 191.
Castillo Solórzano (Alonso de) ... **364.**
Castro (Adolfo de) ... 453.
Castro (Guiomar de) ... 113.
Castro (Leon de) ... 198, 210, 211, 212, 213, 240, 346.
Castro (Rosalía de) ... **500-501.**
Castro y Bellvis (Guillen de) ... 66, 295, 306, **308-309,** 390, 391, 398.
Catalina (of Portugal) ... 237.
Catullus ... 182.
Caxton ... 22.
Cecchi (Giovan Maria) ... 252, 256.
Cejador y Frauca (Julio) ... **515.**
Celenio (Inarco). *See* Moratin (Leandro Fernandez de).
Celestina (La) ... 50, 85, 108, 111, 115, **141-146,** 147, 149, 262, 298, 368.
Cellot (Louis) ... 304.
Centon Epistolario ... 299, **371.**
Cepeda (Rodrigo de) ... 234.
Cepeda y Ahumada (Teresa de). *See* Teresa de Jesus (Santa).
Cerdan (Beatriz) ... 239.
Cervantes (Juan de) ... 86.
Cervantes (Rodrigo de) ... 268.
Cervantes (Rodrigo de, brother of Miguel) ... 270, 272.

Cervantes Saavedra (Miguel de) ... 2, 11, 35, 72, 76, 77, 106, 111, 139, 148, 170, 192, 193, 195, 200, 201, 203, 218, 221, 222, 223, 227, 230, 231, 249, 252, 253, 261, 263, 265, **266-289,** 292, 293, 297, 300, 318, 323, 324, 329, 332, 353, 363, 393, 405, 426, 453, 469, 513, 517.
Cervantes de Salazar (Francisco) ... **186,** 206.
Céspedes y Meneses (Gonzalo de) ... **366.**
Cetina (Gutierre de) ... **174-175,** 515.
Chacon (Antonio) ... 331.
Chapelain ... 183.
Chapí (Ruperto) ... 495.
Chariteo. *See* Gareth (Benedetto).
Charlemagne ... 6, 70, 101.
Charles II ... 25, 378, 398, 399.
Charles V ... 150, 169, 170, 173, 176, 178, 181, 185, 187, 191, 194, 200, 203, 204, 242, 260.
Charles VI [of France] ... 56.
Charles le Téméraire ... 176.
Chartier (Alain) ... 92.
Chateaubriand ... 70, 422, 435.
Châtillon (Gautier de) ... 17.
Chaucer ... 38, 52.
Chevalier au Cygne ... 39.
Chrétien de Troyes ... 36.
Chueca (Federico) ... 495.
Churton (Archdeacon) ... 133.
Cibber (Colley) ... 384.
Cicero ... 190.
Cid Campeador (Ruy Diaz de Bivar, El) ... **2,** 18, 64, 65, 70, 308, 309, 493; (*romances* on), **74-75.**
Cid (Poema del) ... **1-4,** 5, 6, 63, 64, 74, 493.
Cid (Cronica particular del) ... 27, **104-105.**
Ciego de Ferrara (El). *See* Bello (Francesco).
Cifar (El Cauallero) ... **34-36.**
Circourt (Comte de) ... 105.
Civillar (Pedro de) ... 129.
Clarindo (Auto de) ... 249.
Claudian ... 292.
Clavijo y Fajardo (José) ... 407.
Clement VII ... 159, 199.

INDEX

Cobarruuias Orozco (Sebastian de) ... **351.**
Coello (Antonio) ... **392-393.**
Coleridge ... 464.
Coloma (Luis) ... **478.**
Colonna (Aegidius) ... 33.
Colonna (Ascanio) ... 270.
Colonna (Fabrizio) ... 151, 157.
Colonna (Giovanni) ... 101.
Colonna (Marco Antonio) ... 270.
Colonna (Vittoria) ... 199.
Colonne (Guido delle) ... 17, 62, 101.
Columbarius (Julius). *See* Lopez de Aguilar Coutiño (Francisco).
Columbus (Christopher) ... 128, 129, 205, 206, 219.
Comella (Luciano Francisco) ... **419-420,** 421.
Conde (José Antonio) ... **456-457.**
Conquista de la Nueva Castilla ... 225.
Conquista de Ultramar (Gran) ... **39.**
Conrart ... 400.
Conti (Niccolò) ... 98.
Contreras (Alonso de) ... 367.
Córdoba (Gonzalo de) ... 152, 205.
Cordova Sazedo (Sebastian de) ... 173, 232.
Corneille (Pierre) ... 66, 148, 304, 308, 309, 317, 319, 384, 398.
Corneille (Thomas) ... 383, 384, 388, 392, 394, 397.
Coronel Arana (Maria). *See* Agreda (Sor Maria de Jesús de).
Corral (Gabriel de) ... 232.
Corral (Pedro de) ... 73, **99-100,** 107.
Correas (Gonzalo) ... 198.
Cortejón (Clemente) ... 513.
Cortés (Hernando) ... 138, **204,** 207, 208.
Cortés (Juan Lucas) ... 25.
Cortinas (Leonor de) ... 269.
Costa (Joaquín) ... **509.**
Costa y Llobera (Miguel) ... **501-502.**
Coster (Adolphe) ... 210.
Cota (Rodrigo) ... 112, **115-116,** 142, 143, 155.
Cotarelo y Mori (Emilio) ... **514.**

Crashaw (Richard) ... 234.
Crescimbeni ... 403.
Croce (Benedetto) ... 151.
Cronan (Urban) ... 250.
Cronica de D. Alvaro de Luna. See Luna (Alvaro de).
Crónica de don Juan II de Castilla. See *Juan el segundo (Cronica de don).*
Cronica de Castilla ... **27,** 105.
Cronica de veinte Reyes ... **27.**
Cronica general (Primera) ... **23-27,** 34, 46, 55, 99, 202, 514.
Cronica general (Segunda) de 1344 ... **27,** 65, 66, 74, 99.
Cronica general (Tercera) ... **27.**
Cronica particular del Cid. See Cid (*Cronica particular del*).
Cronica Troyana ... 99.
Crousaz (Jean Pierre de) ... 403.
Crowne (John) ... 392.
Cruz y Cano (Ramon de la) ... 316, **416-418,** 419.
Cubillo de Aragon (Alvaro) ... **393-394.**
Cuervo (Rufino José) ... 371, **516.**
Cueto ... 438.
Cueva (Beltran de la) ... 113.
Cueva (Isabel de la) ... 169.
Cueva (Juan de la) ... **258-261,** 264, 292.
Cunninghame Graham (Gabriela) ... 234.
Cyrano de Bergerac ... 304.

D.

D'Alembert ... 334.
' Damasio ' ... 220.
D'Annunzio ... 485.
Danse Macabre ... 83.
Dante ... 87, 88, 90, 92, 93, 94, 95, 96, 112, 132, 163, 171.
Danza de la Muerte ... **83-84.**
Darío (Rubén) ... 467, **504-506,** 507, 516.
D'Aubignac ... 404.
D'Aubigné (Agrippa) ... 60.
Davalos ... 95.
Davdigvier ... 364.
Davidson (John) ... 30.
Débat du corps et de l'âme ... 9.
Delicado (Francisco) ... 196.

INDEX

Delphini (Domenico) ... 109.
Denuestos del Agua y el Vino ... 12.
Desportes ... 230.
Deza (Diego) ... 129.
Diamante (Juan Bautista) ... **398.**
Diario de los Literatos de España ... **404,** 405.
Diaz (Diego) ... 295.
Diaz (Francisco) ... 273.
Diaz (Juan) ... 192.
Diaz (Ximena) ... 2.
Diaz de Bivar (Ruy). See Cid Campeador (El).
Diaz Callecerrada (Marcelo) ... 311.
Diaz del Castillo (Bernal) ... **208.**
Diaz de Games (Gutierre) ... 99, **105-106,** 403.
Diaz de Mendoza (Fernando) ... 492.
Diaz de Mendoza (Ruy) ... 87.
Diaz Tanco de Frexenal (Vasco) ... 156.
Dicenta (Joaquín) ... **491,** 494.
Dickens ... 279, 474, 485, 488.
Dictes and Sayings of the Philosophers ... 22.
Diderot ... 424.
Díez Canedo (Enrique) ... **507-508.**
Diez Serra (Narciso Sáenz) ... **448.**
Dieze (Johann Andreas) ... 406.
Disputa del Alma y el Cuerpo ... **8-9.**
Disputoison du vin et de l'iaue ... 12.
Disraeli ... 204.
Dolce (Ludovico) ... 263.
Dolopathos ... 28.
Donoso Cortés (Juan) ... **463-464,** 503, 509.
Doré (Gustave) ... 446.
Dorimon ... 314.
Doze Sabios (Libro de los) ... 21.
Dozy ... 457.
Drake (Sir Francis) ... 295.
Dryden ... 384.
Du Bartas ... 342.
Du Bellay ... 139, 165.
Ducas (Demetrio) ... 164.
Ducis ... 417.
Dueñas (Johan de) ... **112.**
Dumas (Alexandre) *père* ... 148, 447.

Dumas (Alexandre) *fils* ... 489.
Du Moulin (Antoine) ... 188.
Duque de Estrada (Diego) ... **367.**
Duveyrier (Aimé Honoré Joseph) ... 458.

E.

Eannes (Rodrigo). See Yanez (Rodrigo).
Echegaray (José) ... **488-490,** 491.
Echegaray (Miguel) ... 496.
Eguilaz y Eguilaz (Luis de) ... **451.**
Elche (Misterio de) ... **118.**
Eleastras ... 99.
Elena y Maria ... **9-10,** 11.
Engaños e los asayamientos de las mugeres (Libro de los) ... **28,** 50.
Enriquez del Castillo (Diego) ... **126-127.**
Enriquez Gomez (Antonio) ... **366-367.**
Enriquez de Paz (Enrique). See Enriquez Gomez (Antonio).
Enzina (Juan del) ... 115, 116, 130, **152-156,** 158, 160, 161, 162, 250, 255, 291.
Epitoma Imperatorum ... 18.
Eracle (Roman d') ... 39.
Erasmus ... 164, 202.
Ercilla y Zúñiga (Alonso de) ... 215, **224-226,** 343.
Escalante y Prieto (Amós de) ... **499,** 500.
Escobar (Juan de) ... 75.
Escosura (Patricio de la) ... 440.
Escrivá (Joan) ... **133,** 234.
Español más amante y desgraciado Macias (El) ... 85.
Especulo (El) ... 33.
Espina (Concha) ... **486.**
Espinel (Vicente) ... **324-325,** 416.
Espinosa (Diego de) ... 270.
Espinosa (Pedro) ... 330, 332, **338-339.**
Espinosa Medrano (Juan de) ... 335.
Espronceda (José de) ... 432, 433, **440-444,** 462.
Esquilache (Francisco de Borja, Prince of) ... 357.
Estébanez Calderon (Serafin) ... **459-460.**

INDEX

Estebanillo Gonzalez, hombre de buen humor (*Vida y hechos de*) ... **367-368.**
Estella (Diego de) ... 240.
Estellés ... 496.
Estoria (*Grande et general*) ... **23-24.**
Estoria d'Espanna. See *Cronica general* (*Primera*).
Estrella de Sevilla (*La*) ... **306-307.**
Etienne de Besançon ... 82.
Euripides ... 247.
Everaerts (Jan). See Segundo (Juan).
Eximeniç (Francesch) ... 108.
Ezpeleta (Gaspar de) ... 281.
Ezquerra de Rozas (Gerónimo). See Gerónimo de San Josef.

F.

Fadrique (El Infante don) ... **28.**
Faret (Nicolas) ... 369.
Faria e Sousa (Manoel de) ... 216, 229, 335.
Farinelli (Arturo) ... 305, 314.
Fazio (Bartolommeo) ... 122.
Felíu y Codina (José) ... **490.**
Fénelon ... 237.
Ferdinand (of Castile, St.) ... 21, 22, 24.
Ferdinand (Emperor) ... 181.
Ferdinand IV (of Castile) ... 33, 43, 56, 75.
Ferdinand V ... 69, 150, 185, 194.
Ferdinand VI ... 414.
Ferdinand VII ... 431, 436.
Ferdinand (of Portugal, King) ... 84.
Fernan Gonçalez (*Poema de*) ... **17-18.**
Fernandez (Alonso) ... 285.
Fernandez (Lucas) ... **156,** 291.
Fernandez de Alarcon (Cristobalina) ... 339.
Fernandez de Andrada (Andrés) ... 356.
Fernandez de Avellaneda (Alonso). See Avellaneda (Alonso Fernandez de).
Fernández Caballero (Manuel) ... 495.
Fernández Duro (Cesáreo) ... **509.**

Fernandez Flores (Francisca) ... 292.
Fernandez y Gonzalez (Manuel) ... **463,** 480.
Fernandez-Guerra y Orbe (Aureliano) ... 217.
Fernandez de Moratin (Leandro). See Moratin (Leandro Fernandez de).
Fernandez de Moratin (Nicolas). See Moratin (Nicolas Fernandez de).
Fernández Shaw (Carlos) ... 496, **501.**
Fernandez de Toledo (Garci) ... 24.
Fernandez Vallejo (Felipe) ... 6.
Fernando (*Cantar del Rey*) ... 4.
Fernando de Aragon (Infante don) ... 56.
Ferrandes (Juan) ... 39.
Ferrandes (Pero). See Ferrus (Pero).
Ferrando ... 45.
Ferrari (Emilio) ... **501,** 508.
Ferreira (Antonio) ... 261.
Ferreira (Miguel Leite) ... 135.
Ferrer del Rio (Antonio) ... **457.**
Ferrus (Pero) ... **87,** 134.
Ferruz (Jaime) ... 256.
Feuillet (Octave) ... 450.
Féval (Paul) ... 451.
Feyjoo y Montenegro (Benito Gerónimo) ... **412-413,** 415.
Field (Nathaniel) ... 279.
Fielding ... 279.
Fígaro ... 494.
Figueroa (Francisco de) ... **217-218.**
Figueroa y Cordova (Diego de) ... 395.
Figueroa y Cordova (José de) ... 395.
Fitzgerald (Edward) ... 379, 499.
Flecker ... 79.
Fletcher ... 164, 279, 282, 309, 322, 366.
Floranes Velez de Robles y Encinas (Rafael de) ... **427-428.**
Flores (Juan de) ... 163.
Flores de Filosofia ... **21.**
Florez (Enrique) ... **427.**
Florian ... 411.

INDEX

Folengo (Teofilo) ... 341.
Fonseca (Cristóbal de) ... 165.
Forner (Juan Pablo) ... 410, **411-412.**
Foulché-Delbosc (R.) ... 33, 95, 115, 143, 218, 223, 269, 306, 331, 425.
Fox Morcillo (Sebastian) ... 245.
Franchi (Fabio) ... 299.
Francis I ... 139.
Francis of Assisi (St.) ... 131.
Francis Xavier (St.) ... 233.
Franco-Furt (Arnaldo) ... 311.
Francisco de Portugal (Don) ... 138.
François de Sales (St.) ... 237, 240.
Fray Gerundio. *See* Lafuente (Modesto).
Freire de Lima (Simon) ... 277.
Frere (John Hookham) ... 76, 230, 438.
Frías (Duchess of) ... 432.
Froude (Anthony) ... 207, 234.
Fuerb Juzgo ... **21,** 22.

G.

Gabriel y Galán (José María) ... **502.**
Gadio (Stazio) ... 152.
Galindez de Carvajal (Lorenzo) ... 104.
Galvez de Montalvo (Luis) ... **231,** 272.
Gallardo (Bartolomé José) ... 460.
Gallego (Juan Nicasio) ... **432.**
Ganivet (Angel) ... **479-480.**
Garay (Blasco de) ... **197.**
Garcia (Carlos) ... **363.**
García (Juan). *See* Escalante y Prieto (Amós de).
García Alvarez (Enrique) ... 496.
Garcia Arrieta (Agustin) ... 282.
Garcia Asensio (Miguel) ... 410.
Garcia de Castrogeriz (Juan) ... 33, 134.
Garcia Gutierrez (Antonio) ... **439.**
Garcia de la Huerta (Vicente) ... **409-410.**
García Morales (Pedro) ... **508.**
Garcia de Quevedo (José Heriberto) ... 447.

Garcia de Santa Maria (Alvar) ... 56, 104.
Garcia Tassara (Gabriel) ... **445.**
Garci Lasso de la Vega ... 166, **168-173,** **174,** **175,** 177, 179, 180, 183, 184, 209, 216, 218, 220, 230, 232, 239, 242, 466.
Garci Lasso de la Vega, *el Inca* ... **348-349.**
Gareth (Benedetto) ... **163.**
Garibay y Zamálloa (Esteban de) ... 326.
Garzoni (Tommaso) ... 318.
Gatos (Libro de los). See *Quentos (Libro de los).*
Gautier (Théophile) ... 75, 80, 459.
Gautier de Coincy ... 15.
Gay ... 410.
Gayangos (Pascual de) ... 45, **510.**
Gelves (Alvaro Colon de Portugal, 2nd Conde de) ... 219, 221.
Gelves (Leonor de Milá, Condesa de) ... 219.
Gentil (Berthomeu) ... **163.**
Geraldino (Alessandro) ... 150.
Geraldino (Antonio) ... 150.
Gerónimo de San Josef (Fray) ... **373.**
Gesta Romanorum ... 12.
Giancarli (Gigio Artemio) ... 253.
Gibbon ... 371.
Gibson ... 75.
Gil (Fray Juan) ... 271.
Gil (Ricardo) ... **501.**
Gil y Carrasco (Enrique) ... 462.
Gil Polo (Gaspar) ... **230,** 273.
Gil y Zárate (Antonio) ... **440.**
Giménez (Gerónimo) ... 495.
Giron (Diego) ... 218.
Giron (D. Pedro) ... 140.
Giron (Rodrigo) ... 72.
Givanel Más (Juan) ... 514.
Godefroi de Bouillon ... 101.
Godinez (Felipe) ... 315.
Godos (Estoria de los) ... **22.**
Godoy ... 412, 430.
Goethe ... 275, 286, 342, 379, 407, 435, 499.
Goldsmith ... 409.
Gomez (Pedro) ... **39.**
Gomez (Pero or Pascual) ... **34,** 39.
Gómez de Arteche (José) ... **509.**

INDEX

Gomez de Avellaneda (Gertrudis). See Avellaneda (Gertrudis Gomez de).
Gómez de Baquero (Eduardo) ... **518.**
Gómez Carrillo (Enrique) ... **517.**
Gomez de Cibdarreal (Fernan). See *Centon Epistolario*.
Gomez Hermosilla (Josef) ... **433.**
Gómez de la Serna (Ramón) ... **488.**
Góngora (Luis de) ... 77, 94, 317, **327-336,** 337, 338, 339, 342, 388.
Gonzaga (Ercole) ... 199.
Gonzaga (Giulia) ... 199.
Gonzalez (Diego) ... 211.
Gonzalez (Diego Tadeo) ... **409.**
Gonzalez (Fernan) ... 4, 18 ; (*romances* on), **73.**
González-Blanco (Andrés) ... **518.**
Gonzalez de Bovadilla (Bernardo) ... **231.**
Gonzalez del Castillo (Juan Ignacio) ... **418-419.**
Gonzalez de Clavijo (Ruy) ... **97-98.**
Gonzalez de Salas (Jusepe Antonio) ... **373-374.**
Gorostiza (Manuel Eduardo) ... **436-437.**
Gower ... 11.
Goya ... 418.
Gozzi ... 385, 391, 394.
Gracian Infanzon (Lorenzo). See Gracian y Morales (Baltasar).
Gracian y Morales (Baltasar) ... 317, 336, 345, **368-371.**
Grajar (Gaspar de) ... 211.
Granada (Luis de) ... **236-238,** 239, 286.
Granvela (Francisco Perrenot de) ... 293.
Grau (Jacinto) ... **494.**
Gravina ... 403.
Gray ... 341.
Gregory (St.) ... 61, 62.
Grimaldus ... 14.
Grosseteste (Robert) ... 10.
Groussac (P.) ... 30, 33.
Guardo (Juana de) ... 295, 296.
Guerrero (María) ... 492.
Güete (Jaime de) ... 159, 248.

Guevara (Antonio de) ... **187-191,** 369.
Guevara (Luis de). See Velez de Guevara (Luis).
Guevara (Miguel de) ... 233.
Guillen de Segovia (Pero) ... **117.**
Guillaume de Tyr ... 39.
Guimerá (Angel) ... 489.
Guizot ... 464.
Gustioz (Gonzalo) ... 5.
Gutierrez (Tomas) ... 276.
Gutiérrez González (Gregorio) ... 504.
Gutierrez de Montalvo. See Montalvo (Rodriguez de).
Guyon (Mme.) ... 375.
Guzman y Lacerda (Isidra de) ... 477.

H.

Hallam ... 286.
Hardy (Alexandre) ... 282, 291.
Haro (Juan Fernandez de Velasco, Conde de) ... 220-221.
Haro (Luis de, *Prime Minister*) ... 378.
Haro (Luis de) ... 183.
Hartzenbusch (Juan Eugenio) ... 90, 262, **439-440.**
Harvey (Gabriel) ... 196.
Hauréau ... 12.
Hauteroche ... 383.
Hazañas y La Rúa (Joaquín) ... **515.**
Hazlitt ... 272, 322.
Heiberg ... 385.
Heine (Heinrich) ... 30, 455, 499.
Henry of Trastamara ... 56, 57.
Henry III ... 56, 85, 89, 97, 102.
Henry IV ... 86, 112, 113, 118, 119, 125, 126, 127.
Henry IV of France ... 348.
Henry VIII of England ... 178, 200.
Herberay (Nicolas de) ... 135, 136, 140.
Herbert ... 28.
Heredia (José María de), *the Cuban poet* ... 504.
Heredia (José Maria de), *the French poet* ... 66, 208.
Hermoso ... 496.

INDEX

Hernandez (Alonso) ... 152.
Hernandez de Ayala (Roque) ... 297.
Hernandez de Oviedo y Valdés (Gonzalo). *See* Oviedo y Valdés (Gonzalo Hernandez de).
Hernault de Beaulande ... 18.
Herrera (Antonio de) ... 206.
Herrera (Fernando de) ... 94, 165, 168, **218-221**, 277, 331, 332, 355.
Herrera de Jaspedós (Don Hugo). *See* Hervas y Cobo de la Torre (José Gerardo de).
Herrick ... 340.
Hervas y Cobo de la Torre (José Gerardo de) ... **404-405**.
Hervas y Panduro (Lorenzo) ... 427.
Hoffmann ... 455.
Hojeda (Diego de) ... **342**.
Holberg (Ludwig) ... 284, 392.
Holland (Lord) ... 434.
Holland (Wilhelm) ... 26.
Homer ... 132, 193, 404.
Horace ... 171, 222, 325, 354.
Horozco (Sebastian de) ... 196, **198**, 255.
Hoz y Mota (Juan Claudio de la) ... **399,** 446.
Hozes y Córdoua (Gonzalo de) ... 331.
Huarte de Sant Juan (Juan) ... **245-246**.
Hübner ... 465.
Huet, *Bishop of Avranches* ... 68.
Huerta y Vega (Francisco Manuel de) ... 404.
Hugo (Victor) ... 11, 66, 72, 74, 282, 289, 404, 444, 454, 499, 505.
Humboldt ... 246.
Hunain ibn Ishâq al-'Ibâdî ... 21.
Hurtado (Luis) ... 83, **193,** 249.
Hurtado de Mendoza (Antonio) ... **316**.
Hurtado de Mendoza (Diego) ... 91.
Hurtado de Mendoza (Diego), *the historian. See* Mendoza (Diego Hurtado de).
Hurtado de Mendoza (Garcia) ... 224, 226.
Hurtado de Velarde (Alonso) ... 76.

I.

Ibañez (Maria Ignacia) ... 08, 409.
Ibarbourou (Juana de) ... **506-507**.
Ibsen ... 489.
Iglesias de la Casa (Josef) ... **425**.
Ignatius of Loyola (St.) ... 139, 198, 233, 234.
Ildefonso (Vida de San) ... **38**.
Imperial (Francisco) ... 81, **87-88**.
Innocent III ... 53.
Insúa (Alberto) ... **485**.
Iranzo (Relacion de fechos del condestable Miguel Lucas de) ... **127**.
Iriarte (Tomas de) ... 325, **410-411**.
Isabel the Catholic ... 69, 120, 121, 123, 124, 130, 131, 150.
Isabel de Valois ... 269, 270.
Isabel [of Bourbon] ... 336.
Isabel II ... 468.
Isidore of Seville (St.) ... 62, 82, 109.
Isidore of Madrid (St.) ... 376.
Isla (Josef Francisco de) ... **413-416**.
Is-salps (Joaquin Federico). *See* Isla (Josef Francisco de).

J.

Jackson Veyán (José) ... 496.
Jácome (Maestro) ... 32.
James I of England ... 31.
Janer (Florencio) ... 510.
Jauregui (Juan de) ... 311, 333, 335, **355**.
Jean de Meung ... 96.
Jean de la Haute-Seille ... 28.
Jerome (St.) ... 14.
Jérusalem (Chanson de) ... 39.
Jiménez (Juan Ramón) ... **507**.
Job (The Book of) ... 97.
John the Baptist (St.) ... 131.
John I ... 84.
John II ... 56, 84, 86, 92, 94, 95, 102, 103, 106, 107, 111, 118, 119.
John III [of Portugal] ... 184, 228.
John IV [of Portugal] ... 373.
John of Austria (Don) ... 214, 220, 223, 243, 270, 271.
John of Capua ... 28.
John of Gaunt ... 102.

INDEX

Jones (Sir William) ... 444.
Jonson (Ben) ... 279.
Jorge de Trebisonda ... 125.
José (Poema de) ... **40-41.**
Josephus ... 178.
Jovellanos (Gaspar Melchor de) ... 410, 420, **422-424,** 425.
Juan of Portugal (the Infante) ... 228, 229.
Juan el segundo deste nombre (Cronica del serenissimo rey don) ... 100, **103-104.**
Juan Alfonso ... 45.
Juan de los Angeles ... **239-240.**
Juan Clímaco (San) ... 225.
Juan de la Cruz (San) ... 172, 236, **238-239.**
Juan de la Magdalena ... 225.
Juan Manuel (El Infante Don) ... 26, 29, 33, 37, **41-48,** 53, 55, 78, 83.
Juan Poeta ... 114.
Juan de Valladolid. *See* Juan Poeta.
Juana (the Infanta) ... 228.
Juana Inés de la Cruz (Sor) ... **396.**
Jugement d'Amour (Le) ... 9.
Juromenha ... 121.

K.

Kalila et Digna ... **27-28,** 47.
Kant ... 280.
Keats (John) ... 227.
Killigrew ... 383.
Klopstock ... 342.

L.

Lafayette (Mme. de) ... 326.
La Fontaine ... 52, 188, 410.
Lafuente (Modesto) ... **457,** 510.
Lainez (Diego) ... 2, 65.
Lalita-Vistara ... 83.
Lamb (Charles) ... 286.
Lambert (Théaulon de) ... 436.
Lambert le Tors ... 17.
Lamberto (Alfonso) ... 286.
Lancelot ... 78.
Lancelot (Nicolas) ... 365.
Lando (Ferrant Manuel de) ... 88.
Landor ... 72.
Lanini (Pedro Francisco de) ... 390.

Lara (Cantar de Gesta de los Infantes de) ... **5,**, 25, 26.
Lara (*romances* on the Infantes de) ... **73-74.**
La Rochefoucauld ... 370.
Larra (Mariano Josef de) ... 85, 446, **457-459,** 460, 462, 515.
Lasala (Manuel) ... 410.
Lasso de la Vega (Gabriel Lobo). *See* Lobo Lasso de la Vega (Gabriel).
Lasso de la Vega (Pedro) ... 169.
Lastanosa (Vincencio Juan de) ... 369.
Latini (Brunetto) ... 34.
Latour (Antoine de) ... 219.
Laude Hispaniae (De) ... 18.
Lavater ... 246.
Law (William) ... 234.
Laya (Léon) ... 451.
Lazarillo de Tormes (La Vida de) ... **194-196,** 256, 320, 323.
Lea (Henry Charles) ... 456.
Le Bossu ... 403.
Lebrixa (Antonio de) ... 69, 125, 128, 151, 153, 154, **164,** 352.
Leconte de Lisle ... 66, 75, 76, 498.
Ledesma (Alonso) ... 357.
Leite Ferreira (Miguel). *See* Ferreira (Miguel Leite).
Leiva (Diego de) ... 243.
Lemos (Conde de) ... 281, 288, 296, 353.
Lemos (Condesa de) ... 405.
Leon X ... 159.
Leon (Luis de) ... 165, 172, **209-215,** 220, 235, 236, 240, 264, 335, 338, 346, 394, 426, 444, 502.
León (Ricardo) ... **486.**
Leon Hebreo ... **164-165,** 273, 349.
Leon Merchante (Manuel de) ... **395.**
Lerma (Duque de) ... 330.
Lesage ... 305, 308, 316, 325, 364, 384, 388, 389, 416, 456.
Lewis (Matthew Gregory) ... 431.
Leyba Ramirez (Francisco de) ... **395.**
Liberio (Silvio). *See* Forner (Juan Pablo).
Libertino (Clemente). *See* Mello (D. Francisco Manuel de).

INDEX

Linares Rivas (Manuel) ... 493.
Linné ... 413.
Liñan de Riaza (Pedro) ... 338, 339.
Liñan y Verdugo (Antonio) ... 365.
Lipsius (Justus) ... 358.
Lisandro y Roselia (Tragicomedia de) ... 148.
Lista (Alberto) ... **433**, 440, 441, 459.
Livy ... 57, 62, 243.
Loaysa (Jofré de) ... 24.
Lobeira (Joan de) ... 136.
Lobeira (Vasco de) ... 135.
Lobo (Eugenio Gerardo) ... **401**.
Lobo Lasso de la Vega (Gabriel) ... **339-340**.
Lobon de Salazar (Francisco) ... 413.
Locke ... 280.
Lockhart ... 72.
Locman ... 410.
Lo Frasso (Antonio de) ... **231**.
Lomba y Pedraja (José Ramón) ... **515**.
Longfellow ... 79, 121.
Lope de Vega. *See* Vega Carpio (Lope Felix de).
Lopez de Aguilar Coutiño (Francisco) ... 298.
López Alarcón (Enrique) ... **508**.
Lopez de Avalos (Ruy) ... 102.
Lopez de Ayala (Adelardo) ... **451**.
Lopez de Ayala (Pero) ... 37, 38, 39, 52, **55-62**, 81, 84, 87, 89, 92, 99, 100, 103, 104, 134, 243.
Lopez de Corella (Alonso) ... 185.
Lopez de Enciso (Bartolomé) ... 231.
Lopez Garcia (Bernardo) ... **452**.
Lopez de Gómara (Francisco) ... **207-208**.
López de Haro (Rafael) ... **486**.
Lopez de Hoyos (Juan) ... 270.
Lopez Maldonado (Gabriel) ... 339.
Lopez de Mendoza (Iñigo). *See* Santillana (Marqués de).
Lopez Pinciano (Alonso) ... **352**.
Lopez de Sedano ... 263, 325.
López Silva (José) ... 496, **497**.
Lopez de Ubeda (Francisco) ... 278, 285, **323-324**.

Lopez de Ubeda (Juan) ... 340.
Lopez de Velasco (Juan) ... 201.
Lopez de Velorado (Juan) ... 104.
Lopez de Vicuña (Juan) ... 331.
Lopez de Villalobos (Francisco). *See* Villalobos (Francisco Lopez de).
Lopez de Yanguas (Hernan) ... **250**.
Lorenzo (Juan) ... 17, 21.
Losada (Duke of) ... 423.
Louis XIV ... 389.
Lucan ... 94, 355.
Lucas (bishop of Tuy) ... 18, 24.
Lucena (Juan de) ... **122-123**.
Luceño (Tomás) ... 496.
Lucian ... 196, 200, 244.
Lucidario (El) ... 34.
Lucio (Celso) ... 496.
Lugo y Davila (Francisco de) ... **365**.
Luis of Portugal (Don) ... 178.
Lujan (Micaela de) ... 295, 297.
Lull (Raymond) ... 42, 43, 45.
Luna (Alvaro de) ... 93, 104, 117.
Luna (Coronica de don Alvaro) ... **104**.
Luxan (Pedro de) ... 192.
Luxan de Sayavedra (Matheo) ... **321**.
Luzan, Claramunt de Suelves, y Gurrea (Ignacio de) ... 216, 222, **402-405**, 406, 407.
Lyly ... 190.
Lytton (Edward Bulwer) ... 492.

Ll.

Llaguno y Amirola (Eugenio de) ... 105, 403.
Llorente (Juan Antonio) ... **455-456**.
Llorente (Teodoro) ... 499.

M.

Mabbe (James) ... 322.
Macaulay ... 404, 416.
Machado (Antonio) ... **507**.
Machado (Manuel) ... **507**.
Machiavelli ... 160, 351.
Macias (El Español mas amante y desgraciado) ... 85.

INDEX

Macias o Namorado ... **85,** 86, 92.
Macías Picavea (Ricardo) ... **479.**
Magos (Auto de los Reyes) ... **6-8,** 117.
Mainet ... 39.
Maldonado (Lopez). See Lopez Maldonado (Gabriel).
Maldonado (Juan) ... 247.
Male (Willem van). See Van Male (Willem).
Malipiero (Girolamo) ... 232.
Mal Lara (Juan de) ... **196-197,** 218, 256, 258.
Malon de Chaide (Pedro) ... 165, **239.**
Malpica (Marqués de) ... 296.
Mancha (Teresa) ... 441, 442.
Mandamientos (Diez) ... **20.**
Manrique (Gomez) ... 110, 116, **117-121.**
Manrique (Jorge) ... 87, 110, **121-122,** 132, 183, 228.
Manrique (Maria) ... 120.
Manrique de Lara (Jerónimo) ... 293.
Manto (Pleyto del) ... 114.
Mantuano (Pedro) ... 347.
Manuel (of Portugal) ... 159.
Manuel (Infante Don) ... 45.
Manuel de Lando (Ferrant). See Lando (Ferrant Manuel de).
Manuel de Mello (Francisco). See Mello (D. Francisco Manuel de).
Manzoni ... 432, 452.
Mañer (Salvador Joseph) ... 412.
Marcela de San Felix (Sor) ... 297, 299.
March (Ausias) ... 99, 175, 229.
March (Jaime) ... 117.
Marche (Olivier de la) ... 176.
Marchena y Ruiz de Cueto (José) ... 237, **422,** 434.
Maria (the Infanta) ... 228.
Maria Egipciaqua (Vida de Santa) ... 9, **10.**
Maria de Jesus de Agreda (Sor). See Agreda (Sor Maria de Jesus de).
Maria de la Visitacion (Sor) ... 237.
Mariana (Juan de) ... 31, 98, 201, 240, 297, **345-348.**

Marie l'Egyptienne (La Vie de Sainte) ... 10.
Marie de France ... 36.
Marineo Siculo (Lucio) ... 150, 166.
Marino ... 327, 328.
Marlowe ... 202.
Marot ... 50.
Marquez (Juan) ... 351, 369.
Marquina (Eduardo) ... **493.**
Martí (Juan) ... 286.
Martí (Juan José) ... 321.
Martial ... 171, 221.
Martin de Córdoba ... 24.
Martin de la Plaza (Luis) ... 339.
Martinez (Fernan) ... 32.
Martinez de Cantalapiedra (Martin) ... 211.
Martinez de Medina (Gonzalo) ... **88.**
Martínez Olmedilla (Augusto) ... **486.**
Martinez de la Rosa (Francisco) ... **435-437.**
Martínez Ruiz (José). See "Azorín."
Martinez Salafranca (Juan) ... 404.
Martínez Sierra (Gregorio) ... **494.**
Martinez de Toledo (Alfonso) ... **107-108,** 146.
Martinez Villergas (Juan) ... **453.**
Martir d'Anghiera (Pietro) ... 150.
Mary Stuart ... 298.
Mary Tudor ... 178, 191.
Masdeu (Juan Francisco de) ... **428.**
Massinger ... 284.
Masuccio ... 322.
Matos Fragoso ... 274, **394,** 395.
Maximilian [*Emperor of Mexico*] ... 446.
Maximilian II ... 352.
Maximus (Valerius) ... 124.
Mayans y Siscar (Gregorio) ... 195, 415, **426-427.**
Medina (Bartolomé de) ... 210.
Medina (Francisco de) ... 218, 221.
Medina (Vicente) ... **502.**
Medina Sidonia (Duque de) ... 277.
Medinaceli (Third Duque de) ... 252.
Medrano (Julian de) ... 278.

INDEX

Melendez Valdés (Juan) ... 409, **424-425,** 436, 437.
Mèlesville. *See* Duveyrier (Aimé Honoré Joseph).
Mello (D. Francisco Manuel de) ... **372-373.**
Mena (Gonzalo de) ... 61.
Mena (Juan de) ... 68, 71, 81, **94-96,** 97, 103, 104, 111, 112, 122, 125, 131, 132, 142, 143, 180.
Mendez (Simon) ... 281.
Mendoza (Diego Hurtado de) ... 54, 174, **177-179,** 181, 191, 195, 201, 222, 223, **242-244,** 281, 372.
Mendoza (Father Fernando de) ... 6.
Mendoza (Fray Iñigo de) ... **130, 131.**
Menéndez y Pelayo (Marcelino) ... 72, 77, 143, 155, 403, **511-512,** 513, 514, 515.
Menéndez Pidal (Ramón) ... 4, 26, 67, 218, **514-515.**
Meredith (George) ... 287.
Mérimée (Prosper) ... 30, 58, 447.
Merriman (Roger) ... 207.
Mesa (Cristóbal de) ... **343-344.**
Mesa (Enrique de) ... **508.**
Mesonero Romanos (Ramon de) ... **460-461.**
Metastasio ... 411.
Mexia (Hernan) ... **116.**
Mexia (Pero) ... **202-203.**
Michaëlis de Vasconcellos (Carolina) ... 174.
Middleton ... 282.
Milá (Leonor de). *See* Gelves (Leonor de Milá, Condesa de).
Milá y Fontanals (Manuel) ... 5, 76, **510-511.**
Milan (Duchess of) ... 178.
Mill (John Stuart) ... 434.
Milton ... 275, 381, 402.
Mingo Revulgo (Coplas de) ... 113.
Mira de Amescua (Antonio) ... **317,** 398.
Mirabeau ... 500.
Miranda (Luis de) ... **256.**
Miró (Gabriel) ... **487-488.**
Miseria de Homne (Libro de) ... 53.
Molière ... 283, 304, 314, 316, 365, 384, 391, 396, 420, 437, 492.

Molina (Tirso de) ... 260, 262, 285, **311-315,** 335, 379, 380, 385, 386, 388, 390, 391, 408, 410, 419, 439, 514.
Molinier (Guilhem) ... 154.
Molinos (Miguel de) ... **374-375.**
Moncada (Francisco de), Conde de Osona ... **371-372.**
Moncada (Miguel de) ... 270.
Mondéjar (Marqués de) ... 25, 426.
Monlau (Pedro Felipe) ... **510.**
Monroy y Silva (Cristóbal de) ... **310.**
Montaigne ... 165, 191, 207.
Montalvan (Alvaro de) ... 143.
Montalvan (Juan Perez de) ... 262, 291, 299, **310-311,** 319, 439.
Montalvo (Luis Galvez de). *See* Galvez de Montalvo (Luis).
Montalvo (Garci Rodriguez de) ... 81, **134,** 140, 191.
Montemayor (Jorge de) ... 79, 121, **227-230,** 231, 232, 233.
Montemôr (Jorge de). *See* Montemayor (Jorge de).
Monteser (Francisco Antonio de) ... 395.
Montesino (Fray Ambrosio) ... **130-131.**
Montesquieu ... 409, 422.
Montfleury ... 315, 395.
Montiano y Luyando (Agustin) ... 216, **406,** 407.
Montoro (Anton de) ... 112, **113-114,** 115, 116.
Moore ... 444.
Mora (José Joaquin de) ... 434, **452.**
Moraes Cabral (Francisco de) ... 193.
Morales (Ambrosio de) ... **241.**
Moratin (Leandro Fernandez de) ... 417, **420-422,** 430, 436, 437, 447, 449.
Moratin (Nicolas Fernandez de) ... **407-408.**
More (Sir Thomas) ... 148, 219.
Morel-Fatio (Alfred) ... 12, 82, 195.
Moreno Lopez (Eugenio) ... 443.
Moreto y Cavaña (Agustin) ... 317, **389-392,** 394, 395, 403.
Morillo (Gregorio) ... 341.

INDEX

Moros (Lope de) ... 12.
Moscoso y Sandoval (Cardinal Baltasar de) ... 390.
Mosé Arragel de Guadalajara (Rabbi). *See* Arragel de Guadalajara (Mosé).
Mosquera de Figueroa (Cristóbal) ... 276.
Mozart ... 314.
Mudarra (Alonso de) ... 121.
Muntaner (Ramon) ... 372.
Muñoz (Juan Bautista) ... **428.**
Muñoz y Romero (Tomas) ... 9.
Murat ... 422.
Muratori ... 403.
Musaeus ... 167.
Muzio ... 251.
Muzzarelli ... 176.

N.

Nágera (Esteban de) ... 80, 184.
Naharro (Pedro). *See* Navarro (Pedro).
Nájera (First Duke of) ... 157.
Napier (Sir William) ... 289.
Napoleon ... 430, 432, 457.
Nasarre (Blas Antonio) ... **405-406.**
Natas (Francisco de las) ... 250.
Navagero (Andrea) ... 167, 182.
Navarro (Pedro) ... **256.**
Navarro y Ledesma (Francisco) ... **513.**
Navarro Villoslada (Francisco) ... **463.**
Nazeri de Ganassa (Alberto) ... 254.
Nebrixa (Antonio de). *See* Lebrixa (Antonio de).
Negueruela (Diego de) ... **255.**
Nerval (Gérard de) ... 422.
Nevares Santoyo (Marta de) ... 297, 298, 299.
Newman (Cardinal) ... 434.
Nibelungenlied (Das) ... 64.
Nieremberg (Juan Eusebio de) ... 165, **374.**
Niño (Pero), conde de Buelna ... 84, **105,** 106.
Nobleza o Lealtat (Libro de la) ... **21.**
Noroña (Gaspar Maria de Nava Alvarez, Count of) ... **426,** 444.

North (Sir Thomas) ... 191.
Nucio (Martin) ... 80.
Núñez de Arce (Gaspar) ... 466, **497-498,** 501, 505, 508.
Nuñez de Toledo (Hernan) ... 164, 185, 186, 197, 198, 241, 247.

O.

Ocampo (Florian de) ... 25, 26, 27, **201-202,** 203.
Ocaña (Francisco de) ... **340.**
Ochino (Bernardino) ... 199.
Ochoa (Eugenio de) ... 112.
Ochoa (Juan) ... 478.
Odo of Cheriton ... 82.
Olid (Juan de) ... 127.
Olivares (Conde-Duque de) ... 274, 331, 359, 386.
Oliueros de Castilla y Artus dalgarve (Historia de los nobles caualleros) ... 139.
Olmedo (José Joaquín de) ... 503.
Oña (Pedro de) ... **226.**
Ordoñez de Montalvo (Garci) ... 134.
Oropesa (Conde de) ... 397.
Ortega y Gasset (José) ... **518-519.**
Ortiz (Agustin) ... **248.**
Ortiz Melgarejo (Antonio) ... 361.
Osorio (Elena) ... 293, 294.
Osorio (Isabel) ... 211.
Osorio (Rodrigo) ... 276.
Osuna (third Duke of) ... 359.
Oudin (César) ... 278.
Ouville (Antoine le Métel d') ... 383.
Ovid ... 50, 176, 177, 182, 222, 244.
Oviedo y Valdés (Gonzalo Hernandez de) ... 25, **204-205,** 206.

P.

Pacheco (Francisco) ... 218.
Pacheco de Narvaez (Luis) ... 358.
Padilla (Juan de) ... **131-132.**
Padilla (Pedro de) ... 272, 274.
Paez de Castro (Juan) ... 178.
Paez de Ribera [xvi c.] ... 192.
Paez de Ribera (Ruy) ... **88-89.**
Paez de Santa Maria (Alfonso) ... 97.
Palacio (Manuel del) ... **500.**

INDEX

Palacio Valdés (Armando) ... **474-475.**
Palacios (Miguel de) ... 496.
Palacios Salazar y Vozmediano (Catalina de) ... 273.
Palafox (Jerónimo) ... 271.
Palau (Bartolomé) ... 159, **248-249,** 253, 259.
Palencia (Alfonso de) ... **124-126.**
Palma (Ricardo) ... 504.
Palmart (Lamberto) ... 129.
Palmeirim de Inglaterra. See Moraes Cabral (Francisco de).
Palmerin de Oliva ... **192.**
Pamphilus ... 50.
Panchatantra ... 27.
Paravicino y Arteaga (Hortensio Felix) ... **337,** 377, 414.
Parcerisa (Francisco Javier) ... 465.
Pardo (Felipe) ... **459.**
Pardo Bazán (Emilia, Condesa de) ... **475-477,** 478, 480.
Paredes (Alonso de) ... 34, 39.
Paris (Gaston) ... 131.
Partidas (Las siete) ... **32-33.**
Pastor Díaz (Nicomedes) ... **444-445.**
Patmore (Coventry) ... 238, 468, 500.
Pauli (Johannes) ... 258.
Paz (Enrique de). See Enriquez Gomez (Antonio).
Paz (Felipa de la) ... 258.
Paz y Mélia (Antonio) ... 126, **513.**
Pedraza (Juan de) ... 250.
Pedro (Don), Constable of Portugal ... 68, 85, 92, **96-97.**
Pedro Alfonso ... 47, 50, 82.
Pellicer de Salas y Tovar (José) ... 29, 335.
Peñalosa (Francisco) ... 131.
Pepys ... 393.
Per Abbat ... 2, 17.
"Perales y Torres (Isidro)." See Nasarre (Blas **Antonio**).
Perálvarez de Ayllon ... 249.
Percy (Thomas) ... 72.
Pereda (José María de) ... **471-472,** 476, 480.
Pereira (Gomez) ... 245.

Pereira Marramaque (Antonio) ... 174.
Perés (Ramón Domingo) ... **502.**
Perez (Alonso), *novelist* ... 230, 231.
Perez (Alonso), *bookseller* ... 310.
Perez (Fray Andrés) ... 323.
Perez (Antonio) ... **344-345.**
Perez (Juan) ... 247.
Perez (Suero) ... 24.
Pérez de Ayala (Ramón) ... **487.**
Perez del Barrio Angulo (Gabriel) ... 284.
Pérez Galdós (Benito) ... **472-474.**
Pérez y González (Felipe) ... 495.
Perez de Guzman (Fernan) ... 90, 99, **100-103,** 128.
Perez de Hita (Ginés) ... 71, **325-326.**
Perez de Montalvan (Juan). See Montalvan (Juan Perez de).
Perez de Oliva (Hernan) ... **186,** 241, 247.
Pérez Pastor (Cristóbal) ... **513.**
Perez del Pulgar (Hernando) ... 127 *n.*
Perrín (Guillermo) ... 496.
Pescara ... 151.
Peseux-Richard (H.) ... 454.
Peter the Cruel ... 52, 56, 57, 515 ; (*romances* on), **75-76.**
Petrarch ... 92, 93, 94, 163, 168, 171, 175, 182, 298.
Petronius ... 52.
Phaedrus ... 50, 410.
Phillis et Flora ... 9.
Philip II ... 80, 178, 191, 228, 240, 242, 251, 269, 272, 277, 344.
Philip III ... 229, 285.
Philip IV ... 25, 374, 377, 378, 389, 393, 397, 399.
Philip the Fair of France ... 33, 150.
Philip-August ... 28.
Pi y Margall (Francisco) ... 465.
Piccolómini (Enea Silvio) ... 122.
Picón (Jacinto Octavio) ... **478.**
Picón (José) ... 478.
Pidal (Pedro José, first marqués de Pidal) ... 8.
Piferrer (Pablo) ... 465.
Pineda (Juan de) ... 224.

INDEX

Pineda (Juan de) [of the *Passo honroso*] ... 106.
Pineda (Pedro) ... 231.
Pius II. *See* Piccolómini (Enea Silvio).
Pitillas (Jorge). *See* Hervás y Cobo de la Torre (José Gerardo de).
Platir (*Cronica del muy valiente y esforçado caballero*) ... 192.
Plato ... 245.
Plautus ... 185, 247, 252, 257.
Plazuela, conde de Cheste ... 440.
Pliny ... 185, 247.
Plutarch ... 101.
Polo (Gaspar Gil). *See* Gil Polo (Gaspar).
Polo de Medina (Salvador Jacinto) ... 362.
Ponce (Bartolomé) ... 232.
Pontus de Thyard ... 165.
Pope ... 341.
Poridat de las Poridades ... **22.**
Portocarrero (Pedro) ... 214.
Prado (Andrés de) ... 255.
' Prete Jacopin, vecino de Burgos.' *See* Haro (Juan Fernandez de Velasco, Conde de).
Primaleon ... 192.
Proaza (Alonso de) ... 143.
Procter (Adelaide) ... 30.
Proverbios (*Libro de los buenos*) ... **21.**
Proverbios en rimo del sabio Salamon, rey de Isrrael ... **38-39.**
Proverbs (*Book of*) ... 213.
Provincial (*Coplas del*) ... **112-113,** 114, 125.
Prudentius ... 14.
Puig (Leopoldo Gerónimo) ... 404.
Pulgar (Hernando del) ... 112, **127-128.**
Puymaigre (Comte de) ... 105.
Puyol y Alonso (Julio) ... 5, **514.**

Q.

Quadrado (José Maria) ... **464-465.**
Quentos (*Libro de los*) ... **81-82.**
Querellas (*Libro de las*) ... 29.
Querol (Vicente Wenceslao) ... **498-499.**

Question de amor de dos enamorados ... **151-152.**
Quevedo y Villegas (Francisco de) ... 90, 197, 214, 215, 216, 265, 310, 316, 318, 335, 339, **357-363,** 373, 406, 443.
Quinault ... 283, 384.
Quintana (Manuel Josef) ... 244, **429-432,** 436, 437, 497, 498, 504.
Quiñones (Suero de) ... 106, 111.
Quiñones de Benavente (Luis) ... 284, **316.**

R.

Racine ... 403.
Raineri (Anton Francesco) ... 252.
Rapin ... 403.
Râzî (al). *See* Abû Bakr Aḥmad ibn Muhammad.
Rastell (John) ... 148.
Ravaillac ... 348.
Razon de amor, con los denuestos del agua y el vino ... **12-13.**
Rebolledo (Conde Bernardino de) ... 165, **357.**
Refranes que dizen las viejas tras el huego ... 197.
' Regañadientes (El Bachiller).' *See* Forner (Juan Pablo).
Regnier ... 50, 237.
Reina (Manuel) ... **501.**
Renan ... 40.
Rennert (H. A.) ... 228, 231, 264.
Répide (Pedro de) ... **487.**
Resende (Garcia de). *See* Cancioneiro geral de Garcia de Resende.
Revelacion de vn hermitanno ... **53.**
Rey de Artieda (Andrés) ... 249, **261-262,** 439.
Reyes (Alfonso) ... **517.**
Reyes (Pedro de los) ... 233.
Reyes dorient (*Libro dels tres*) ... 9, **10-11.**
Reyna (Casiodoro de) ... 350.
Reynoso (Félix José) ... **432-433.**
Rhua (Pedro) ... 189.
Ribeiro (Bernardim) ... 227.
Ribera (Diego de) ... 71.
Ribera (Luis de) ... **340-341.**
Rich (Barnabe) ... 252.
Riego (Miguel del) ... 132.

INDEX

Rioja (Francisco de) ... **356.**
Rios (José Amador de los) ... 510.
Rios (Nicolas de los) ... 292.
Riquier (Giraldo) ... 31.
Rivadeneyra (Pedro de) ... **350-351,** 369.
Rivas (Ángel de Saavedra Remirez de Baquedano, duque de) ... 399, **437-438,** 439, 467.
Rivers (Lord) ... 22.
Rixa animi et corporis ... 9, 53.
Roa (Martin de) ... 351.
Robespierre ... 237, 422.
Robles (Blas de) ... 273.
Robles (Francisco de) ... 278.
Robles (Juan de) ... 373.
Roca (Conde de la). *See* Vera y Figueroa (Juan Antonio de).
Roderick ... 4, 24, 70, 99; *romances* on, **72-73.**
Rodó (José Enrique)... **516.**
Rodrigo (Cantar de) ... **65-66,** 74, 75.
Rodrigo (Las mocedades de). See *Rodrigo (Cantar de).*
Rodrigues (João) ... 184.
Rodriguez (Gonzalo) ... 84.
Rodriguez de Almella (Diego) ... **124.**
Rodriguez de la Cámara (Juan) ... 68, 69, 85, **86-87,** 97, 130.
Rodriguez de Lena (Pero) ... 106.
Rodríguez Marín (Francisco) ... 222, **513.**
Rodriguez de Montalvo (Garci). *See* Montalvo (Garci Rodriguez de).
Rodriguez del Padron (Juan). *See* Rodriguez de la Cámara (Juan).
Rodriguez Rubí (Tomas) ... 448.
Rojas (Ana Franca de) ... 273.
Rojas (Fernando de) ... 143.
Rojas Zorrilla (Francisco de) ... 90, **387-389,** 392, 395.
Roland (Chanson de) ... 3, 6, 63, 77.
Roman de la Charette ... 78.
Romancero General ... 326, 330, 338.
Romances ... **63-80.**
Romea (Julián) ... 496.
Romero de Cepeda (Joaquin) ... 262

Roncesvalles ... **5-6.**
Ronsard ... 165.
Ros de Olano (Antonio), Marqués de Guad-el-Jelú ... 443.
Rosel y Fuenllana (Diego de) ... **283.**
Rosell (Cayetano) ... 510.
Rossetti (Christina) ... 450.
Rotrou ... 282, 304, 317, 389.
Rousseau (J. J.) ... 422.
Rowland (David) ... 196.
Rowley ... 282.
Rubió y Lluch (Antonio) ... **514.**
Rubió y Ors (Joaquín) ... 514.
Rueda (Lope de) ... **251-254,** 255, 256, 269, 291, 292, 417, 496.
Rueda (Salvador) ... **503.**
Ruffino (Bartolomeo) ... 272.
Rufo Gutierrez (Juan) ... **223-224,** 272.
Ruiz (Juan) ... 37, 46, 47, **48-52,** 60, 78, 84, 85, 108, 145, 146, 508, 514.
Ruiz Aguilera (Ventura) ... **452,**
Ruiz de Alarcon (Juan). *See* Alarcon (Juan Ruiz de).
Rusiñol (Santiago) ... 491, 494.
Ruskin ... 272.
Ruysbroeck ... 240.
Rymer (Thomas) ... 403.

S.

Sá de Miranda (Francisco de) ... **173-174.**
Saavedra (Gonzalo de) ... 232.
Saavedra (Isabel de) ... 273, 281.
Saavedra Faxardo (Diego) ... **368.**
Sabios (Libro de los doze). See *Doze Sabios (Libro de los).*
Sabuco (Oliva) ... **246-247.**
Sabuco y Alvarez (Miguel) ... **246.**
Said Armesto (Victor) ... **515.**
Sainte-Beuve ... 171, 304.
Sainte-More (Benoît de) ... 17, 62.
Saint-Pierre (Bernardin de) ... **435.**
Saint-Simon ... 101, 400.
Salamon, rey de Isrrael (Proverbios en rimo del sabio). See *Proverbios en rimo del sabio Salamon, rey de Isrrael.*
Salas Barbadillo (Alonso Gerónimo de) ... **363,** 364.

INDEX

Salazar (Eugenio de) ... 344.
Salazar (Gomez de) ... 97.
Salazar Mardones (Cristóbal de) ... 335.
Salazar y Torres (Agustin de) ... **337-338.**
Salazar y Vozmediano (Catalina de Palacios). *See* Palacios Salazar y Vozmediano (Catalina de).
Salcedo Coronel (Garcia de) ... 335.
Sallust ... 243, 244.
Samaniego (Felix Maria) ... **410,** 411, 421.
Sanchez (Francisco) ... 245.
Sanchez (Miguel) ... **264,** 292.
Sanchez (Tomas Antonio) ...1.
Sanchez de Badajoz (Diego) ... **250.**
Sanchez de Badajoz (Garci) ... **132.**
Sanchez de la Ballesta (Alonso) ... 298.
Sanchez de las Brozas (Francisco) ... 220, 426.
Sanchez Talavera (Ferrant) ... **87.**
Sanchez de Tovar (Fernand) ... 56.
Sanchez de Vercial (Clemente) ... **82-83.**
Sancho II [*of Castile*] ... 2.
Sancho II de Castilla (*Cantar de gesta de don*) ... 5.
Sancho IV [*of Castile*] ... 24, 33, 34, 39, 43, 46, 56.
Sandoval (Manuel de) ... 508.
Sandoval (Prudencio de) ... 204.
Sandoval y Rojas (Bernardo de), Archbishop of Toledo ... 324.
San Josef (Fray Gerónimo de). *See* Gerónimo de San Josef (Fray).
Sannazaro (Jacopo) ... 171, 227, 273, 343.
San Pedro (Diego de) ... **140-141.**
Santa Cruz (Marqués de) ... 221, 276, 293.
Santa Cruz de Dueñas (Melchior de) ... 258.
Santa Maria (*Cantigas de*) ... **29-31.**
Santa Maria (Pablo de) ... 103, 104.
Santillana (Marqués de) ... 68, 69, 70, 81, 85, **91-94,** 96, 122, 129, 130, 132, 166, 168.

Santistevan Osorio (Diego de) ... 226.
Santo. *See* Santob.
Santob (Rabbi) ... **52-53,** 83.
Santos (Francisco) ... 362, 366.
Santos Alvarez (Miguel de los). *See* Alvarez (Miguel de los Santos).
Sanz (Eulogio Florentino) ... 448.
Sarmiento (Diego de) ... 29.
Sarmiento (Martin) ... **413.**
Sarrasin ... 183, 230.
Scaliger ... 404.
Scarron ... 315, 322, 363, 364, 365, 384, 388.
Schack ... 395.
Schaumburg (Anna von) ... 182.
Schiller ... 450.
Schlegel ... 379.
Schneider ... 305.
Schopenhauer ... 245, 280, 370.
Schöppe (Gaspar) ... 285.
Sebastian [of Portugal] ... 214, 220.
Scott (Sir Walter) ... 283, 437, 438, 462.
Scribe (Eugène) ... 458.
Scudéry (Georges de) ... 164, 282.
Scudéry (Mlle. de) ... 326.
Secchi (Niccolò) ... 256.
Sedaine ... 365.
Segovia (Pero Guillen de). *See* Guillen de Segovia (Pero).
' Segundo (Juan) ' ... 425.
Selgas y Carrasco (José) ... **452-453.**
Sellés (Eugenio) ... 490.
Sempere (Hieronymo de) ... **193-194.**
Sem Tob (Rabbi). *See* Santob (Rabbi).
Seneca ... 21, 190.
' Senra y Palomares (Luis).' *See* Espronceda (José de).
Septenario ... 32.
Sepúlveda (*Comedia llamada de*) ... 256.
Sepúlveda (Juan Ginés de) ... 207.
Sepúlveda (Lorenzo de) ... 75, 256.
Serra (Jacopo). *See* Arborea (Jacopo Serra, Archbishop of).
Serrano y Morales (José Enrique) ... **513.**

INDEX

Serrano y Sanz (Manuel) ... **515.**
Sessa (Duke of), Viceroy of Naples ... 270.
Sessa (6th Duke of) ... 296.
Seven Sages (The Book of) ... 28.
Sforza (Bona) ... 151.
Shakespeare ... 11, 48, 145, 146, 149, 227, 230, 252, 265, 305, 417, 438, 451, 465, 468, 492.
Shelley ... 8, 275, 379, 381.
Shelton (Thomas) ... 278.
Shirley ... 305, 315.
Sidney (Sir Philip) ... 166, 171, 229, 230, 272.
Siete Partidas (Las). See *Partidas (Las siete)*.
Sigüenza (José de) ... 351.
Silió y Gutiérrez (Evaristo) ... **499-500.**
Silva (Feliciano de) ... 147, **148, 192,** 193.
Silva (Francisco de) ... 281.
Silva (José Asunción) ... 506.
Silveira (Simon de) ... 191.
Silvestre (Gregorio) ... 121, **184.**
Simon Abril (Pedro) ... **246.**
Sindibâd ... 28.
Skálaz Doubravky (Jan) ... 389.
Smollett ... 279.
Sofiano (Nicolas) ... 178.
Solis (Antonio de) ... 331, **396-397,** 427, 456.
Solis (Dionisio) ... 419, 447.
Soma (Duchess of) ... 167.
Somoza (José) ... **459, 515.**
Sophocles ... 247.
Soto (Hernando de) ... 349.
Soto y Marne (Francisco de) ... 415.
Southey... 77, 434, 446.
Speculum Naturale ... 34.
Spenser ... 196, 216, 409.
Statius ... 341.
Sterne ... 279.
Stiefel ... 309, 380.
Stúñiga (Elena de) ... 169.
Stúñiga (Lope de) ... 111.
Suarez de Figueroa (Cristóbal) ... **318-319.**
Suliman II ... 178.
Suñé Benajes (Juan) ... 514.
'Sylva (Antonio de).' See Bermudez (Gerónimo).

T.

Tacitus ... 101, 243, 244.
Tafur (Pero) ... **98-99.**
Taille (Jean de la) ... 191, 404.
Tamayo y Baus (Manuel) ... 439, **450-451,** 488.
Tamayo de Vargas ... 25.
Tansillo (Luigi) ... 163, 170, 171.
Tárrega (Francisco Agustin) ...294.
Tasso (Bernardo) ... 139, 167, 171, 172.
Tasso (Torquato) ... 216, 265, 296, 339, 343, 344, 355.
Taylor (Jeremy) ... 234.
Tebaldeo (Antonio) ... 155.
Tellez (Gabriel). See Molina (Tirso de).
Tendilla (Conde de) ... 237.
Tennyson (Alfred) ... 380, 446.
Teodor la donçella (El Capitulo que fabla de los ejemplos e castigos de) ... 29.
Terence ... 354.
Teresa de Jesus (Santa) ... 130, 132, 139, **233-236,** 238, 284, 359.
Tesoro ... 34.
Texeda (Hieronymo de) ... 231.
Thackeray ... 279.
Thomas (Henry) ... 192.
Thomas (Lucien-Paul) ... 328.
Thousand and One Nights (The) ... 28, 46.
Ticknor ... 52, 347, 365, 420.
Tieck ... 379.
Tignonville (Guillaume de) ... 22.
Timoneda (Juan) ... 73, 76, 252, **256-258.**
Timûr ... 97.
Tirant lo Blanch ... 139.
Tirso de Molina. See Molina (Tirso de).
Titian ... 174.
Todi (Jacopone da) ... 130.
Toreno (José Maria Queipo de Llano, Conde de) ... 456.
Toro (Archdeacon of). See Rodriguez (Gonzalo).
Torre (Alfonso de la) ... **108-109.**
Torre (Bachiller de la) ... 216.
Torre (Francisco de la) ... **215-216,** 217, 406.
Torrellas (Pedro) ... 116, 119.

INDEX

Torres Naharro (Bartolomé de) ... **157-160,** 162, 248, 257, 291.
Torres Rámila (Pedro de) ... 297.
Torres y Villarroel (Diego de) ... **401.**
Tourneur (Cyril) ... 279.
Trench (Archbishop) ... 379, 380.
Tribaldos de Toledo (Luis) ... 218, 243.
Trigo (Felipe) ... **485,** 486.
Trigueros ... 419.
Trilles (Rafaela Angela) ... 252.
Trillo de Armenta (Antonia) ... 295.
Tristan de Leonis ... 139.
Tristan ... 384.
Trueba (Antonio de) ... **462,** 471.
Tuke (Samuel) ... 393.
Turpin ... 18.

U.

Ulloa Pereira (Luis de) ... 398.
Unamuno (Miguel de) ... **518,** 519.
Urbanus VI ... 59.
Urbina (Diego de) ... 270.
Ureña y Smenjaud (Rafael de) ... **509.**
Urfé (Honoré d') ... 229.
Urrea (Pedro Manuel de) ... 110, **146-147.**

V.

Valbuena (Antonio de) ... 517.
Valdeflores (Marqués de). See Velazquez de Velasco (Luis Josef).
Valdegamas (Marqués de). See Donoso Cortés (Juan).
Valdés (Alfonso de) ... **200.**
Valdés (Juan de) ... **199-201,** 426.
Valdés (Luis de) ... 320.
Valdivia (Diego de) ... 276.
Valdivielso (José de) ... **340.**
Valencia (Pedro de) ... 333.
Valera (Cipriano de) ... **350.**
Valera (Diego de) ... 103, **123-124.**
Valera (Juan) ... **467-469,** 505.
Valverde (Joaquín) ... 495.
Valladares de Valdelomar (Juan) ... 367.
Valle-Inclán (Ramón del) ... **482-483.**

Vallés (Pedro) ... 197.
Vanbrugh (Sir John) ... 389.
Van der Hammen (Lorenzo) ... 361.
Van Male (Willem) ... 176, 204.
Varchi (Benedetto) ... 216.
Varela Osorio (Maria) ... 213.
Vatable ... 211.
Vaughan (Henry) ... 191.
Vazquez ... 151.
Vazquez (Mateo) ... 272.
Vazquez de Ciudad Rodrigo (Francisco) ... 192.
Vega (Alonso de la) ... 255.
Vega (Bernardo de la) ... 232, 278.
Vega (Carlos Felix de) ... 297.
Vega (Felices de) ... 292.
Vega (Ricardo de la) ... **495.**
Vega (Ventura de la) ... 440, **448-449.**
Vega Carpio (Lope Felix de) ... 5, 29, 43, 45, 74, 80, 85, 94, 109, 110, 120, 132, 133, 147, 158, 162, 163, 178, 202, 216, 222, 223, 229, 256, 260, 261, 262, 264, 265, 277, 278, 284, 285, **289-306,** 307, 309, 310, 311, 312, 313, 315, 316, 317, 332, 333, 334, 335, 336, 338, 339, 341, 352, 354, 361, 367, 375, 376, 378, 379, 380, 385, 386, 388, 390, 391, 392, 393, 394, 397, 403, 404, 405, 406, 408, 410, 417, 419, 434, 438, 447, 512, 514, 517.
Vega y Nevares (Antonia Clara de) ... 299.
Velarde (José) ... 501.
Velasco (Nicolas de) ... 376.
Velazquez (Diego) ... 478.
Velazquez (Jerónimo) ... 293.
Velazquez de Velasco (Luis Josef), marqués de Valdeflores ... 216, **406.**
Velazquez (Ruy) ... 5.
Velez de Guevara (Luis) ... **307-308,** 388.
Venegas del Busto (Alexo) ... **187.**
Venegas de Henestrosa ... 121.
Veneziano (Antonio) ... 272.
Veragua (7th Duke of) ... 379.
Veragua (Duke of) ... 424.
Veragüe (Pedro de) ... **53.**
Vera (Catalina de la) ... 268.

INDEX

Vera y Figueroa (Juan Antonio de), conde de la Roca ... 299, **371.**
Vera Tassis y Villarroel (Juan de) ... 379.
Verdi ... 438, 439.
Vergara (Juan de) ... 164.
Vergara Salcedo (Sebastian Ventura de) ... 378.
Verge Maria (Obres o Trobes dauall scrites les quals tracten de lahors de la sacratissima) ... 129.
Vergerio (Pier Paolo) ... 199.
Verlaine (Paul) ... 16.
Verzosa (Juan) ... 218.
Vezilla Castellanos (Pedro de la) ... **223.**
Viana (Carlos de) ... 109.
Vicencio (Valerio) ... 358.
Vicente (Gil) ... 79, **160-163,** 248, 250.
Vico ... 402.
Villaespesa (Francisco) ... **507.**
Villafranca (Pedro de Toledo, marqués de) ... 170.
Villalobos (Francisco Lopez de) ... **185-186,** 247, 257.
Villalon (Cristóbal de) ... **244-245.**
Villalpando (Johan de) ... **93,** 166.
Villalta (Andrés de) ... 276.
Villamediana (Juan de Tarsis, conde de) ... **336-337.**
Villasandino (Alfonso Alvarez de) ... 84, 88, 105.
Villaviciosa (José de) ...**341.**
Villaviciosa (Sebastian de) ... 395.
Villayzan (Gerónimo de) ... 310.
Villegas (Antonio de) ... **183,** 233.
Villegas (Esteban Manuel de) ... **355-356.**
Villegas (Pedro de) ... 376.
Villena (Enrique de) ... 81, 85, **89-91,** 93, 96.
Villena (Marqués de) [Juan Fernandez Pacheco, marqués de Villena and Duque de Escalona] ... 400.
Villiers ... 314.
Vincent de Beauvais ... 34, 83.
Violante do Ceo (Sor) ... 396.
Virgil ... 92, 155, 171, 172, 218, 344.

Virués (Cristóbal de) ... 249, 262, 292.
Vives (Amadeo) ... 495.
Vives (Juan Luis) ... 213, 245, 426.
Voiture ... 183, 326, 337.
Voltaire ... 225, 416, 422.

W.

Weber ... 282.
Wilkins (George) ... 279.
Wolf ... 72, 74.
Wolf (Hugo) ... 470.
Wolff ... 282.
Wordsworth ... 215, 300.
Wycherley ... 384.
Wynne (Ellis) ... 362.

X.

Ximenez de Cisneros (Cardinal Francisco) ... 164.
Ximenez de Enciso (Diego) ... 315.
Ximenez de Rada (Rodrigo) ... **22-23,** 24.
Ximenez de Urrea (Gerónimo) ... 170, 177, **184.**

Y.

Yannes (Rodrigo). *See* Yanez (Rodrigo).
Yanez (Rodrigo) ... **54.**
Young ... 409.
Yuçuf (Historia de) ... **39-41.**

Z.

Zamora (Antonio de) ... 447.
Zamora (Cantar del cerco de) ... 4.
Zamora (Juan Alfonso de) ... 62.
Zamora (Juan Gil de) ... 24, 101.
Zapata (Luis) ... 177, **222.**
Zárate y Castronovo (Fernando de) ... 396.
Zavaleta (Juan de) ... 395.
Zayas y Sotomayor (Maria de) ... **364-365.**
Zea (Francisco) ... 452.
Zenea (Juan Clemente) ... 504.
Zeumer (Karl) ... 509.
Zola ... 480.
Zorrilla (José) ... 314, 439, **445-447,** 505.
Zurita (Gerónimo) ... 25, **241,** 354.